WOMEN'S FIRSTS

Highlights

Women's Firsts is a reference source designed for users seeking information on landmark achievements by women from ancient times to the present. Entries cover all fields of endeavor and are arranged in chapters as follows:

- Activism
- The Arts
- Business
- Community Service
- Education
- Government
- Health Care
  Professions
- Literature

- Media
- Military Service
- Organization and
  Group Firsts
- The Professions
- Religion
- Science
- Sports

Women's Firsts provides information on nearly 2,500 groundbreaking achievements by women. Special features include:
- Foreword by Christine Todd Whitman, first woman governor of New Jersey
- Timeline of events in women's history
- Index by day of the month
- Index by year
- Keyword index listing women, important events, issues, and locations
- Bibliography of sources consulted
- Over 160 illustrations

WOMEN'S FIRSTS

CAROLINE ZILBOORG, EDITOR

SUSAN B. GALL, MANAGING EDITOR

Foreword by
Christine Todd Whitman,
Governor of New Jersey

GALE

DETROIT · NEW YORK · TORONTO · LONDON

Women's Firsts was produced by
Eastword Publications Development, Inc., Cleveland, Ohio.

Gale Research Staff

Marie Ellavich, Rebecca Nelson, and Andrea Kovacs Henderson,
Project Editors
Jessica Proctor, Associate Editor
Karen Uchic, Assistant Editor
Leah Knight, Acquisitions Editor
Lawrence W. Baker, Managing Editor

Mary Beth Trimper, Production Director
Evi Seoud, Assistant Production Manager
Shanna P. Heilveil, Production Assistant

Cynthia Baldwin, Production Design Manager and Page Designer
Barbara J. Yarrow, Graphic Services Manager
Tracey Rowens, Cover Designer.

Library of Congress Cataloging-in-Publication Data
Women's firsts / Caroline Zilboorg, editor.
    p. cm.
  Includes bibliographical references and index.
  ISBN 0-7876-0151-9 (acid-free paper)
    1. Women—History—Miscellanea. 2. World records—Miscellanea.
  I. Zilboorg, Caroline Crawford.
  CT3203.W66 1996
   908' .2—dc20   96-9792
                                       CIP

ISBN 0-7876-0151-9
Printed in the United States of America
10 9 8 7 6 5 4 3 2 1

Foreword

Over the years, women have been recognized for many great "firsts." But for every woman who reached the summit in her chosen field, dozens—or even hundreds—have come before her, lighting the way. In each individual woman's "first" we celebrate the courage, commitment, and camaraderie of all women—and the men who have supported and encouraged them. Often in the face of incredible frustration and adversity, women have made great gains throughout the twentieth century. Having begun the century without the right to vote or to receive a university education, we end with most legal and institutional barriers removed.

Many women have only recently been acknowledged for their contributions to our society. Their biographies offer fascinating and inspiring glimpses at centuries of mostly unsung heroines.

The women whose achievements are recorded here are all groundbreakers. Some, like well-recognized suffragist Susan B. Anthony, were outspoken advocates of women's rights, taking strong and symbolic action to draw public attention to their cause. She was even arrested, along with twelve other women, for trying to vote in the 1872 presidential election. Others, like child health pioneer and physician Sara Josephine Baker, preferred less public actions. In the early 1900s, Baker refused to accept a lectureship at New York University because it did not admit women to its graduate program. The university changed its policy, and Baker joined the faculty.

For many, the goal was attaining the opportunity to pursue their personal passions, whether they were interested in astronomy or athletics, medicine or the military, entertainment or engineering. Denied access to education and employment, these women often relied on a father, brother, or other male mentor for the training and opportunity needed to pursue their work. Even with a male mentor cracking open the door to opportunity, others inside were far from welcoming. For example, when Mary Whiton Calkins, a promising student of philosophy and psychology, was denied permission to attend regular Harvard University seminars, faculty members William James and Josiah Royce, along with Calkins's father, intervened on her behalf. But when she began attending James's seminar sessions, four of her fellow students dropped out in protest. Calkins persevered, however, and in 1906 went on to become the first woman president of the American Psychological Association.

No matter what path she chooses, every time a woman succeeds, or even climbs into the ring, she becomes a role model. For the young women of my daughter's generation—and for the rest of us—role models are so important. They show what we can achieve and to what we can aspire.

Women's Firsts has many of the same qualities. It tells stories that we need to hear and serves as a valuable reference. For all people—men and women, young and old—*Women's Firsts* offers a tribute to women of achievement whose stories can inspire, enlighten, and motivate.

Christine Todd Whitman

Christine Todd Whitman was elected the first woman governor of New Jersey on November 2, 1993. In January 1995, she became the first governor and first woman ever to give the response to the U.S. President's State of the Union address. She lives in Oldwick, New Jersey, with her husband, financial consultant John R. Whitman, and their daughter and son, Kate and Taylor.

SUGGESTIONS ARE WELCOME

Women's Firsts presents a comprehensive account of historical and cultural landmarks events involving women from all cultures throughout history.

We express our deepest gratitude to all those who stepped forward to share their knowledge or to provide their support. The staff at Gale Research—beginning with Christine Nasso and Leah Knight; progressing with Larry Baker, Rebecca Nelson, Marie Ellavich, Andrea Kovacs Henderson; and culminating with Shanna Heilveil and Evi Seoud—managed the project with competence and diligence. The staff at Eastword Publications Development—notably Debby Baron, Christina Carpadis, Janet Fenn, Matthew Markovich, Dianne Daeg de Mott, Sue Prise, Brian Rajewski, and Ariana Ranson—pulled all the elements together to produce the final volume.

A work the size of *Women's Firsts* may contain oversights and errors, and we appreciate any suggestions for correction of factual material or additions that will enhance future editions. Please send comments to:

Editor
Women's Firsts
Gale Research
835 Penobscot Bldg.
Detroit, MI 48226
(313) 961-2242

Caroline Zilboorg
September 1996

Table of Contents

Illustration Credits

Courtesy of ABC: page 301; Courtesy of American Association of Retired Persons (AARP): page 327; Courtesy of the American Public Health Association: page 247; © American Heart Association, used by permission: page 248; Courtesy of the American Medical Women's Association: page 244; AP/Wide World:pages 14, 21, 23, 26, 35, 41, 46, 47, 48, 49, 56, 59, 68, 69, 78, 83, 89, 90, 94, 96, 99, 132, 158, 168, 170, 171, 174, 175, 183, 184, 192, 235 (top), 266, 280, 282, 283, 376, 395, 406, 456; Architect of the U.S. Capitol: pages 119, 126 (top), 199, 384, 424 (bottom); Archive of the History of American Psychology, University of Akron: pages 151, 157 (bottom), 226, 398; Courtesy of Benetton: page 106; Bettman Archive: pages 53, 77, 114, 178, 181, 205, 296, 353, 379, 407, 411, 440, 457; Courtesy of Camp Fire Inc.: page 324; Photo by Sammy Still, courtesy of the Cherokee Nation: page 329; Courtesy of Christine Choy:page 60; Cleveland Antiquarian Books: pages 4, 304; Photo by Trout Ware, courtesy of the Archives of The Musical Arts Association, The Cleveland Orchestra: page 81; Photograph Collection, Cleveland Public Library: page 33; Courtesy of Roberta Cooper Ramo: page 342 (bottom); Courtesy of *Cosmopolitan* magazine: page 142; Courtesy of the Dwight D. Eisenhower Library: pages 207, 313; EPD Photos: pages 1, 3, 7, 37, 65 (top and bottom), 66, 102, 103, 121 (top and bottom), 126 (bottom), 134, 144, 153, 157 (top), 222, 223, 235 (bottom), 240, 257 (top and bottom), 258, 259, 260, 275, 280, 285, 291, 309, 322, 327, 365, 370; Courtesy of the Gerald R. Ford Library: page 213, 381; Courtesy of Girls Scouts of America: page 325; Courtesy of the Harlem Globetrotters: page 417; Courtesy of the Embassy of Iceland: page 177; Courtesy of International Planned Parenthood Federation: page 245; International Swimming Hall of Fame: pages 424 (top), 444, 445 (top and bottom), 446, 447, 448 (top and bottom); International Tennis Hall of Fame: pages 450, 452, 453; Courtesy of the Embassy of Ireland: page 180; John Carroll University: page 300; Photo by Yoichi R. Okamota, courtesy of the LBJ Library: page 209; Courtesy of the John F. Kennedy Library: page 249; League of Women Voters: page 36; Library of Congress: pages 338, 371; Courtesy of Lukens Steel: page 111; Courtesy of the U.S. Military Institute at West Point: page 315 (top); Courtesy of Mills College: page 127; Courtesy of MIT Archives: page 133; Courtesy of the Embassy of Norway: page 186; Courtesy of the Embassy of Paki-

Timeline of Events in Women's History

40,000 B.C. Modern *Homo sapiens* well-established in Europe.

25,000 B.C. Earliest known oil lamps in France.

24,000 B.C. Earliest known sculptured clay figurines in Europe.

11,000 B.C. Small bands of hunters make their way across the Bering Sea Land Bridge from Siberia.

9000 B.C. Jericho established; among earliest known towns.

9000 B.C. Earliest fired pottery in Japan.

8350 B.C. Cold-hammered copper in use in Turkey.

7000 B.C. Copper-casting in Near East.

3000 B.C. Oldest pottery in New World, Colombia.

3000 B.C. First bronze artifacts in Middle East.

2570 B.C. Queen Nefertari rules in Egypt, calling herself "God's wife."

2500 B.C. Pyramid construction begins in Egypt.

2500 B.C. Beginnings of Indus River civilization in India.

1490 B.C. Queen Hatsheput rules in Egypt, claiming rights of pharaoh.

1360 B.C. Queen Nefertiti rules in Egypt.

1200 B.C. Fu Hao, woman warrior in China, leads military expeditions.

40,000 B.C. Modern *Homo sapiens* well established in Europe.

24,000 B.C. Sculptured clay figurines in Europe.

9000 B.C. Jericho established; among earliest known towns.

50,000 B.C.   30,000   10,000   5,000

1180 B.C. Spartan Queen Helen kidnapped by Paris.

1150 B.C. Deborah leads Israel in victory over the invading Canaanites.

C.1000 B.C. First extensive use of wool clothing (Scandinavia).

1000 B.C. Earliest rotary hand mills for grain in Middle East.

776 B.C. First recorded Olympiad in Greece.

750 B.C. Assyrian Empire establishes world's first highway system.

C.625 B.C. Spartan woman are the most independent of all in the ancient world; Sappho, Greek poetess, flourishes on the island of Lesbos.

563 B.C. Beginning of Buddhism in India.

C.400 B.C. Peak of classical Greece.

C.400 B.C. Democritus introduces concept of atom.

250 B.C. Cultivation of locally domesticated plants begins in present-day northeastern United States.

C.240 B.C. Initial phases of construction of Great Wall of China.

226 B.C. Colossus of Rhodes destroyed by earthquake.

51 B.C. Cleopatra VII is queen of Egypt.

C.30 A.D. Crucifixion of Jesus of Nazareth; Christian faith established.

64 A.D. Burning of Rome.

330 A.D. Constantinople founded at Byzantium.

C.570 A.D. Muhammad, founder of Islam, is born.

700 A.D. *Beowulf* written in northern Europe.

700 A.D. Polynesian Triangle (Hawaii, Easter Island, New Zealand) now settled.

C.800 A.D. First porcelain produced in China.

C.1000 A.D. Arabic numerals begin to replace Roman numerals in Europe.

C.1000 A.D. Japanese author Murasaki Shikibu writes *The Tale of Genji*, generally considered the world's first novel.

1138 Byzantine princess Anna Comnena, early woman historian, writes the *Alexiad*, a 15-volume historical work.

1157 Hojo Masako is influential woman in medieval Japan.

1174 Eleanor of Aquitaine is influential woman in twelfth century Europe.

1215 Magna Carta limits royal power in England.

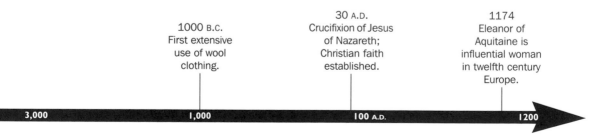

c.1250 Earliest development of cannons in Europe.

c.1300 Invention of spinning wheel.

c.1300 Beginning of Renaissance in Italy.

1342 Chinese Empress Ma is born.

c.1350 Cast-metal type developed in Korea.

1431 Joan of Arc burned at the stake.

1448 Margaret of Anjou, wife of Henry VI in England, founds Queens College of Cambridge University.

1470 Queen Isabella creates unified Spain with her husband Ferdinand.

1492 Queen Isabella approves the expedition to America led by Christopher Columbus; they touch ground in the Bahamas.

1494 Angela Merici founds the first women's teaching order in the Roman Catholic Church.

1497 Vasco da Gama rounds the Cape of Good Hope.

c.1503 Leonardo da Vinci paints the *Mona Lisa*.

1507 German mapmaker Martin Waldseemüller, after reading Amerigo Vespucci's descriptions of the New World, names it America after him.

1512 Michelangelo completes painting of the Sistine chapel ceiling.

1513 Juan Ponce de León discovers Florida. Vasco Nuñez de Balboa crosses Panama and sights the Pacific Ocean.

1517 Protestant Reformation begins when Martin Luther posts his "Ninety-Five Theses" on Nurenberg, Germany, church door.

1519 Hernán Cortéz lands in Mexico.

1520 First circumnavigation of globe by Ferdinand Magellan's crew.

1521 Maria von Habsburg becomes queen of Hungary and Bohemia.

1525 Martin Luther translates Bible into German; Luther marries former nun Katherine von Bora.

1542 Mary, Queen of Scots is the first known female golfer.

1542 Copernicus formulates theory of sun-centered solar system.

1553 Queen Mary I tries to reestablish Roman Catholicism in England.

1559 Sofinisba Anguissola is the first woman artist to become gain prominence as a painter.

1620 Pilgrims and others arrive in Plymouth, Massachusetts, aboard the *Mayflower.*

1630 Taj Mahal is constructed in Agra, India, as a memorial to emperor Shah Jahan's favorite wife, Mumataz Mahal.

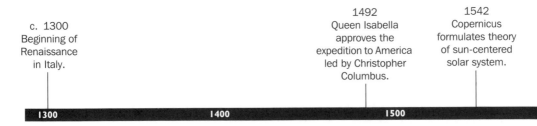

c. 1300
Beginning of
Renaissance
in Italy.

1492
Queen Isabella
approves the
expedition to America
led by Christopher
Columbus.

1542
Copernicus
formulates theory
of sun-centered
solar system.

1300   1400   1500   1600

1645 Deborah Moody is the first woman to receive a colonial land grant in America. Ten years later, Moody will be the first American woman to vote.

1665 Great plague in London kills 68,000 people.

1688 Aphra Behn's novel *Oroonoko* is published.

1695 Queen Anne (Totopotomoi) is the first female chief of a Native American tribe, the Pamunken trive in Virginia.

1717 Halley shows that solar system moves through space.

c.1738 Eliza Lucas Pinckney, first woman agriculturist in America, develops cultivation of indigo in South Carolina.

c.1750 Beginning of the Industrial Revolution.

1752 Benjamin Franklin proves lightning is electrical; develops lightning rod.

c.1760 Maria Theresa is the first and only woman to rule during the Habsburg era in Europe.

1762 Catherine the Great becomes empress of Russia.

1774 Marie Antoinette becomes queen of France.

1776 The American Revolution.

1782 England recognizes United States independence.

1787 Convention in Philadelphia writes United States Constitution.

1788 United States Constitution ratified and takes effect.

1789 French Revolution begins.

1789 First United States presidential election results in victory for George Washington. Martha Washington becomes first First Lady.

1792 Mary Wollstonecraft's *A Vindication of the Rights of Woman* is published.

1804 Sacajawea is the only woman guide on the Lewis and Clark Expedition.

1804 Napoleon crowns himself emperor.

1808 Beethoven's *Fifth* and *Sixth Symphonies* performed.

1809 Mary Kies becomes the first U.S. woman to receive a patent when she patents her method for weaving straw with silk or thread to make bonnets.

1813 Jane Austen's novel *Pride and Prejudice* is published.

1848 *Communist Manifesto* (Marx and Engels) published.

1848 Women's Rights Convention in Seneca Falls, New York. It produces the Declaration

1760
Maria Theresa is the first woman to rule during the Habsburg era in Europe.

1848
Women's Rights Convention in Seneca Falls, New York.

| 1700 | 1750 | 1800 | 1850 |

of Sentiments, patterned after the Declaration of Independence, calling for equal rights for women.

1849 Elizabeth Blackwell becomes first American woman to receive medical degree.

1850 World population reaches one billion.

1850 Elizabeth Barrett Browning's *Sonnets from the Portuguese* published.

1851 Taipei Revolution in China.

1852 Harriet Beecher Stowe's *Uncle Tom's Cabin* is published.

1853 Antoinette-Louisa Brown is ordained as a minister, becoming the first woman minister in the United States.

1854 Catherine Helen Spence becomes the first successful female novelist in Australia.

1854–1860 Susan B. Anthony crusades for women's rights in the United States and internationally.

1855 Lucy Stone is the first woman on record to keep her own name after marriage.

1859 *On the Origin of Species* published by Charles Darwin.

1860 Florence Nightingale publishes *Notes on Nursing*, the first textbook for nurses.

1861 First transcontinental telegraph line.

1861–1865 American Civil War.

1869 Transcontinental railroad completed in United States.

1869 National Woman Suffrage Association and American Woman Suffrage Association formed in the United States.

1869 John Stuart Mill publishes *The Subjection of Women.*

1871 Lucy Walker, an English mountaineer, is the first woman to successfully climb the Matterhorn in Switzerland.

1874 Sophia Jex-Blake establishes the London School of Medicine for Women.

1874 Women's Christian Temperance Union founded to fight alcohol abuse in the United States.

1876 Alexander Graham Bell invents the telephone.

1879 Belva Ann Lockwood becomes the first woman lawyer to practice before the U.S. Supreme Court.

1881 American Red Cross is founded by Clara Barton.

1890 Louise Blanchard Bethune becomes the first woman elected to full membership in the American Institute of Architects.

1893 New Zealand becomes the first nation to grant women the right to vote.

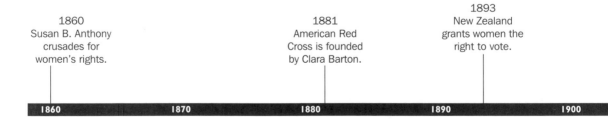

1860
Susan B. Anthony
crusades for
women's rights.

1881
American Red
Cross is founded
by Clara Barton.

1893
New Zealand
grants women the
right to vote.

1860   1870   1880   1890   1900

1896 The first women's intercollegiate basketball game in the United States is held, with Stanford University defeating the University of California at Berkeley.

1902 Australian women get the right to vote in all federal elections. Vida Goldstein runs for the senate there, becoming the first woman in the British Empire to run for a national office.

1903 Marie Curie is awarded Nobel Prize for Physics for discovery of radioactivity.

1909 Swedish writer Selma Lagerlöf is the first woman to receive the Nobel Prize for literature.

1911 Marie Curie is awarded second Nobel Prize for Chemistry for her discovery and isolation of pure radium.

1914 The Amateur Athletic Union in the United States allows women to register for swimming events for the first time.

1916 Margaret Sanger opens first birth control clinic.

1917 Russian Revolution; Soviet women get the vote.

1918 Canadian women get the vote.

1918 Hungarian feminist and pacifist Rosika Schwimmer becomes the world's first woman ambassador when she is appointed ambassador to Switzerland.

1920 With the passage of the Nineteenth Amendment to the U.S. Constitution, U.S. women get the vote.

1921 Lila Acheson Wallace is cofounder of the *Reader's Digest.* Edith Wharton wins the Pulitzer Prize for fiction.

1922 U.S.S.R. is established. Women's Amateur Athletic Association is founded.

1923 Maud Howe Elliott and Laura Howe Richards are the first women to win the Pulitzer Prize for biography. They share the award for their profile of their mother, entitled *Julia Ward Howe.*

1923 The first woman to receive the Pulitzer Prize for poetry is Edna St. Vincent Millay, for *The Ballad of the Harp-Weaver.*

1924 Nellie Tayloe Ross is elected first woman governor in U.S. (Wyoming).

1928 The first woman to swim the English Channel is U.S. swimmer Gertrude Ederle.

1928 Women compete for the first time in Olympic field events. U.S. anthropologist Margaret Mead publishes *Coming of Age in Samoa.*

1928 Age of suffrage is lowered from 30 to 21 in Great Britain.

1929 Collapse of stock market in the United States triggers world depression.

1930 World population reaches two billion.

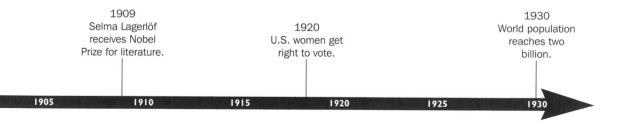

1909
Selma Lagerlöf
receives Nobel
Prize for literature.

1920
U.S. women get
right to vote.

1930
World population
reaches two
billion.

1905   1910   1915   1920   1925   1930

1931 Margaret Sanger publishes *My Fight for Birth Control.*

1932 Amelia Earhart becomes the first woman to fly across the Atlantic alone.

1933 Frances Perkins becomes Secretary of Labor, first woman cabinet member in U.S. history.

1939 World War II begins in Europe.

1945 World War II ends. Fashion magazine *Elle* is founded.

1949 Communists establish People's Republic of China; women get the vote.

1950 In India, women over 21 get to vote.

1958 Swedish diplomat Agda Rössel is the first woman to head a permanent delegation to the United Nations.

1963 Russian cosmonaut Valentina Tereshkova becomes first woman in space.

1966 National Organization for Women (NOW) is founded in the United States.

1966 Indira Gandhi becomes prime minister of India.

1967 World's first successful human heart transplant.

1968 Dr. Martin Luther King, Jr., is assassinated.

1969 Golda Meir becomes prime minister of Israel.

1976 World population reaches four billion.

1979 Margaret Thatcher elected first woman prime minister of Great Britain.

1981 Sandra Day O'Connor appointed first woman U.S. Supreme Court justice.

1983 Ellen Taafe Zwilich is the first woman to receive the Pulitzer Prize for music.

1984 Geraldine Ferraro becomes first woman vice-presidential nominee of a major U.S. political party.

1984 Kathryn Sullivan is first U.S. woman astronaut to walk in space.

1986 Major nuclear power plant accident at Chernobyl in the Soviet Union.

1986 Corazon Aquino elected president of Philippines.

1988 Benazir Bhutto sworn in as prime minister of Pakistan.

1993 Kim Campbell is elected the first woman prime minister of Canada; Tansu Cillar is elected the first woman prime minister of Turkey.

1994 United Nations Fourth World Conference on Women is held in Beijing, China.

1945
World War II
ends.

1963
Russian cosmonaut
Valentina Tereshkova
becomes first woman
in space.

1983
Ellen Taafe Zwilich
receives the
Pulitzer Prize for
music.

1940   1950   1960   1970   1980   1990

Activism

Abolition

1830s • Abolitionist Maria Stewart (1803–1879) was the first American-born woman to speak in public. In the 1830s, her lectures against slavery brought harsh criticism and she gave up public speaking for work in the fields of education and church-related community service.

Sources: Chicago, *The Dinner Party,* p. 182.

1832 • Maria Weston Chapman (1806–1885), an American abolitionist, was the cofounder of the Boston Female Anti-Slavery Society in 1832. She spoke and wrote on behalf of abolition of slavery in Massachusetts and continued to fight for black civil rights after the Civil War. She served as treasurer of the Massachusetts Anti-Slavery Society and published *The Liberty Bell,* an annual devoted to the anti-slavery cause.

Sources: Lutz, *Crusade for Freedom*; *National Cyclopedia of American Biography,* vol. II, p. 315; *Who Was Who in America, 1607–1896,* p. 102; Zophy, *Handbook of American Women's History,* p. 18.

Maria Weston Chapman

A group of black women in Salem, Massachusetts, formed the first black women's anti-slavery society on February 22, 1832. Free black women participated actively in societies open to both genders and to people of all colors, but this anonymous group was the first organized by black women.

Sources: Smith, *Black Firsts,* p. 67.

1836 • Angelina Emily Grimké (1805–1879) and Sarah Moore Grimké (1792–1873), both born in Charleston, South Carolina, were ardent campaigners against slavery. They were the first women to lecture for the American Anti-Slavery Society in New York. Their lectures, beginning in 1836, elicited violent criticism, partly because of their subject, but primarily because the speakers were female. The Grimké sisters soon added the issue of women's rights to their concerns.

Sources: Chicago, *The Dinner Party,* p. 183; James, *Notable American Women,* vol. 2, pp. 592–95; Lerner, *The Grimké Sisters of South Carolina*; Uglow, *The Continuum Dictionary of Women's Biography,* pp. 237–38; *Who Was Who in America, 1607–1896,* p. 221.

Anti-feminism and Anti-suffrage

1908 • Mary Augusta Ward (1851–1920), an English anti-suffrage leader and prolific writer who published fiction under the name of Mrs. Humphrey Ward, was the first person to serve as president of the Anti-Suffrage League, in London in 1908. While sympathetic to women's plight, Ward was wary of radical solutions and preferred to stress women's fulfillment in traditional roles and through higher education and voluntary social work. With these goals in mind, she founded the Local Government Advancement Committee, in London in 1911.

Sources: Magnusson, *Larousse Biographical Dictionary,* p. 1532; Uglow, *The Continuum Dictionary of Women's Biography,* pp. 568–69.

1972 • Phyllis Schlafly (b. 1924), a Republican who has supported increased military preparedness, was the first woman to lead "The Silent Majority" of conservative Americans in an anti-feminist backlash, beginning in speeches in 1972. She led the campaign against the Equal Rights Amendment in the 1970s and published her anti-feminist book, *The Power of the Positive Woman,* in 1977.

Sources: Uglow, *The Continuum Dictionary of Women's Biography,* pp. 483–84.

Feminism and Women's Rights

1789 • Théroigne de Méricourt (1762–1817), an ardent feminist and revolutionary, was the first woman at the head of the Women's March to Versailles, France, in October of 1789. She was also probably the first woman, dressed as an Amazon, to storm the Bastille on July 14 of that year.

Sources: Hamer, *Théroigne de Méricourt: A Woman of the Revolution*; Uglow, *The Continuum Dictionary of Women's Biography,* p. 158.

1790 • Olympe de Gouges (1748–1793) was the founder of the radical organization, the Club des Tricoteuses (the Knitters' Club) in France. In 1791 she wrote *Declaration of the Rights of Woman and Citizeness.* A feminist who was an ardent supporter of the French Revolution (1789–1799) and opponent of leader Maximilien Robespierre (1758–1794), de Gouges was guillotined in 1793.

Sources: Uglow, *The Continuum Dictionary of Women's Biography,* p. 232.

1791 • Etta Aelders Palm (1743–c. 1793) was the first Dutch woman to speak out for the rights of women during the French Revolution. She appeared before the legislative assembly in Paris, France, in 1791 to plead for women's rights.

Sources: Uglow, *The Continuum Dictionary of Women's Biography,* p. 416.

1793 • Claire Lacombe (b. 1765), a French actress, was the founder of the Republican Revolutionary Society, the first organization for working women in France, in Paris in April of 1793. Inspired by the spirit of the French Revolution, Lacombe worked for women's rights (including the right to vote and to participate in government) through this association. She was so ardent in her campaign that her club was suppressed by the Revolutionary government in November 1793, and in March 1794, Lacombe was arrested and imprisoned until 1795.

Sources: Uglow, *The Continuum Dictionary of Women's Biography,* p. 309.

19th century • Hasta Hansteen (b. 1824) was the founder of the women's rights movement in Norway. She advocated women's suffrage and the improvement of women's social position through her writing.

Sources: Chicago, *The Dinner Party,* p. 188.

1840 • Ernestine Rose (1810–1892) was the author of the first petition for a law granting married women the right to own property. The petition was reviewed by the New York State Legislature in Albany, New York, and led in 1848 to a law safeguarding the property of married women.

Sources: Read and Witlieb, *The Book of Women's Firsts,* p. 380; Whitman, *American Reformers,* p. 705.

1848 • Mary Upton Ferrin (1810–1881) was the first woman in Massachusetts to petition the legislature for "the redress of grievances of her sex." For six years between 1848 and 1853 she traveled from Salem to Springfield, Massachusetts, to petition the state to change its divorce laws and its laws regarding the property rights of married women. Changes in the laws, granting women equal rights to the custody of their children, occurred in 1855. These reveal a measure of her success and that of other women also seeking redress, but many problems involving divorce and property rights remained at issue for over a century.

Sources: Ferrin, *Woman's Defence*; James, *Notable American Women,* vol. 1, pp. 611–12; Stanton, *The History of Woman Suffrage,* vol. 1, pp. 208–15.

Elizabeth Smith Miller (1822–1911), an American feminist, was the first person to design "bloomers," the costume to which Amelia Jenks Bloomer gave her name when she wrote about it in her reform paper, *The Lily.* Miller originated the short skirt covering Turkish-style loose-fitting trousers as a gardening dress. She first wore the bloomers at her home in Geneva, New York, but the costume became well-known to other women when she wore it while visiting her friend Elizabeth Cady Stanton in Seneca Falls, New York. (*See also* **Business: Miscellaneous, 1848.**)

Sources: James, *Notable American Women,* vol. 2, pp. 540–41; Stanton and Blatch, *Elizabeth Cady Stanton as Revealed in Her Letters, Diary and Reminiscences,* vol. 1, pp. 171–72; Whitman, *American Reformers,* pp. 587–88.

Lucretia Coffin Mott (1793–1880) and Elizabeth Cady Stanton (1815–1902) organized the first Women's Rights Convention in Seneca Falls, New York. (*See also* **Activism: Feminism, 1869.**)

Lucretia Coffin was born on the island of Nantucket on January 3, 1793. Her Quaker family was among those who sought refuge on Nantucket from reli-

Lucretia Coffin Mott

An 1850s illustration of the Bloomer costume.

gious persecution by the government of Massachusetts Bay Colony. Lucretia was sent to boarding school in Duchess County, New York. Her future husband, James Mott, was a teacher there. In 1818, Lucretia was made assistant teacher, and three years later she and Mott married. The couple joined Lucretia's family in Philadelphia and established a profitable cotton business. Troubled by the dependence of their cotton plantations on slave labor, the Motts gave up their business. Lucretia Mott established a private school to supplement the family's resources until her husband's business prospects improved. Mott then devoted herself to Bible study and to the campaign against slavery. In June 1840, she was a delegate to the world anti-slavery convention in London, England. Upon her arrival there, she was denied access to the convention platform because no women were to be allowed to speak. This experience, in part, inspired her to add the cause of women's suffrage to her campaigns. In 1878, at the age of 86, Lucretia Mott gave her last public speech at the suffrage convention held in New York. She died November 11, 1880.

Sources: James, *Notable American Women,* vol. 2, pp. 592–95; Magnusson, *Larousse Biographical Dictionary,* p. 1047; *National Cyclopedia of American Biography,* vol. II, p. 310.

Second half of the 19th century • Baroness of Adlersparre, a Swedish feminist who advocated her ideas in her journal *For the Home,* was the founder

of the Frederika Bremer League, an organization named for the early Scandinavian women's rights leader.

Sources: Chicago, *The Dinner Party,* p. 187.

1850s • Jenny d'Hericourt, a nineteenth-century French feminist, was the first French woman to inspire the Russian feminist movement. During a visit to Russia in the 1850s, her energetic personality and career as one of the first female physicians in Europe encouraged the women she met with to start their own feminist groups.

Sources: Uglow, *The Continuum Dictionary of Women's Biography,* p. 166.

1850 • On October 23 and 24, the first national convention in the United States to advocate women's rights was the National Women's Rights Convention, called by a committee of seven chaired by Paulina W. Davis, and held in Worcester, Massachusetts. The convention resolved that "Women are clearly entitled to the right of suffrage, and to equality before the law, without distinction of sex or color."

Sources: Read and Witlieb, *The Book of Women's Firsts,* p. 491; Whitman, *American Reformers,* pp. 214–16.

1855 • Lucy Stone (1818–1893) was the first woman on record to keep her own name after marriage. A lifelong crusader for women's rights, Stone graduated from Oberlin College in Ohio in 1847. She married Henry Blackwell in Boston, Massachusetts, in 1855, but, with his agreement, did not take his name. The couple wanted to omit the word "obey" from the marriage vows and had to send for a minister from over 30 miles away who would agree to their wishes. Lucy was known thereafter as "Mrs. Stone," and "doing a Lucy Stone" became a common phrase used to refer to an independent woman's action.

Lucy Stone was born August 13, 1818, in West Brookfield, Massachusetts, one of nine children in her family. Her father, a prosperous farmer, sent her brothers to college, but refused to assist Lucy in her effort to acquire an education. He held the view, popular at the time, that it was a waste to educate females. Stone secured a position teaching school, earning enough money to enroll in Oberlin College in Ohio, the only institution of higher education to admit women. She continued to work to support herself, holding two jobs for most of her college years—teaching in the preparatory school and working as a housekeeper in the Ladies' Boarding Hall for three cents an hour. The Oberlin faculty nominated Stone to prepare an essay for graduation, but she declined when she learned that she would not be permitted to read it in public because she was a woman. After graduation, she embarked on her lifelong crusade for women's rights.

Sources: Chicago, *The Dinner Party,* p. 185; James, *Notable American Women,* vol. 3, pp. 387–90; *National Cyclopedia of American Biography,* vol. II, pp. 316–17; Read and Witlieb, *The Book of Women's Firsts,* pp. 427–28.

1857 • Barbara Leigh Smith Bodichon (1827–1891), a leading feminist in the early stages of the women's movement in England, was the founder of the first women's employment bureau in England, in 1857. Also that year, she published *Women at Work*.

Sources: Chicago, *The Dinner Party,* p. 186; Magnusson, *Larousse Biographical Dictionary,* p. 169.

c.1860 • Caroline Dexter (1819–1894), an Australian feminist, was the founder of the Institute of Hygiene in Melbourne in about 1860. She was also the cofounder, with Harriet Clisby, of the radical journal *The Interpreter,* in 1861.

Sources: Uglow, *The Continuum Dictionary of Women's Biography,* p. 166.

1860 • Jessie Boucherett (1825–1905), an English feminist and writer, was the cofounder, with Barbara Bodichon and Adelaide Ann Procter, of the Society for Promoting the Education of Women. This organization advocated jobs for women such as farming, nursing, clerical work, engraving, teaching, and bookkeeping.

Sources: Uglow, *The Continuum Dictionary of Women's Biography,* pp. 80–81; *Who Was Who,* vol. I, pp. 76–77.

1861 • Maria Susan Rye (1829–1903) was the first woman in England to help other women emigrate to Australia, New Zealand, and Canada. In order to help women find work and gain economic independence, Rye founded, with Jane Lewin, the Female Middle Class Emigration Society in London, England. For the next eight years she helped large numbers of women leave England and settle in Australia, New Zealand, and Canada.

Sources: Uglow, *The Continuum Dictionary of Women's Biography,* pp. 470–71.

1866 • Anna Nikitichna Shabanova (1848–1932), a Russian pediatrician and feminist activist, was the founder of the Ivanova Workshop, a dressmaking collective, in Moscow. In 1867, she became one of the first women to enroll at the new Women's Medical Academy. She later practiced medicine, wrote, taught, and continued to work for feminist causes.

Sources: Uglow, *The Continuum Dictionary of Women's Biography,* pp. 492–93.

1868 • Marie Goegg (1826–1899), a Swiss feminist and pacifist, was the founder and first director of the Association International des Femmes (International Association of Women), begun in Geneva, Switzerland. In 1872, she was also one of the leaders in the successful campaign to open the University of Geneva to women.

Sources: Uglow, *The Continuum Dictionary of Women's Biography,* p. 228.

1869 • Mary Ashton Rice Livermore (1821–1905) was the founder and first editor of *The Agitator,* a feminist publication that later merged into the *Woman's Journal.* (*See also* **Activism: Feminism and Women's Rights, 1873.**)

Sources: James, *Notable American Women,* vol. 2, pp. 426–28; Magnusson, *Larousse Biographical Dictionary,* p. 903; *National Cyclopedia of American Biography,* vol. III, p. 82; Read and Witlieb, *The Book of Women's Firsts,* pp. 256–57.

**ELIZABETH CADY
STANTON**

Elizabeth Cady Stanton (1815–1902) was the cofounder, with Susan B. Anthony (1820–1906), of the National Women's Suffrage Association (NWSA), dedicated to winning the right to vote for women through an amendment to the U.S. Constitution. A life-long feminist activist, Stanton worked for women's right to vote and for equality for women and blacks. Stanton and Anthony also collaborated on the multivolume *History of American Suffrage*. (*See also* **Activism: Suffrage, 1848.**)

Sources: Banner, *Elizabeth Cady Stanton*; Magnusson, *Larousse Biographical Dictionary*, p. 1387; Read and Witlieb, *The Book of Women's Firsts*, pp. 417–18; Stanton, *Eighty Years and More*.

1870 • Maria Desraismes (1828–1894), a French feminist, was the founder in 1870 of the Association pour le Droit des Femmes (the Association for Women's Rights), one of the main moderate feminist organizations in France until the twentieth century. She was a cofounder of the Société pour la Revendication des Droits de la Femme in 1866, and in 1881 she founded the paper *Le Républicain de Seine et Oise*.

Sources: Uglow, *The Continuum Dictionary of Women's Biography*, p. 162.

The first Married Women's Property Act in England was authored in 1870 by English barrister Richard Marsden Pankhurst (d. 1898), husband of English suffragist Emmeline Goulden Pankhurst (1857–1928).

Sources: Magnusson, *Larousse Biographical Dictionary*, p. 1122.

1871 • Marilla Marks Young Ricker (1840–1920), an American lawyer and lifelong feminist and freethinker, was the first woman in America to insist on casting a ballot. She based her position on the 14th Amendment to the U.S. Constitution and claimed that, as a taxpayer, she was thus qualified as an "elector" under the terms of the amendment. She voted in New Durham, New Hampshire, but her ballot was refused.

Sources: James, *Notable American Women*, vol. 3, pp. 154–56; Ricker, *I Am Not Afraid, Are You?*; Ricker, *I Don't Know, Do You?*; Willard and Livermore, *A Woman of the Century*.

1873 • Mary Ashton Rice Livermore (1820–1905) was the first president of the Association for the Advancement of Women. She devoted her life to feminist causes and worked for both the temperance and suffragist movements. (*See also* **Activism: Feminism and Women's Rights, 1869.**)

Sources: James, *Notable American Women*, vol. 2, pp. 426–28; Read and Witlieb, *The Book of Women's Firsts*, pp. 256–57.

Late 19th century • Anna Maria Mozzoni (1837–1920), an Italian feminist who used her wealth to argue for women's rights, was the founder of a league in defense of women's interests, La Lega Promotrice Degli Interessi

Femminili, in Milan, Italy. She fought for women's right to vote and argued for social equality throughout her life.

Sources: Uglow, *The Continuum Dictionary of Women's Biography,* pp. 390–91.

Josephine Elizabeth Grey Butler (1828–1906), an English feminist who worked against the exploitation of prostitutes, was the founder of two activist periodicals, *The Dawn* and *The Storm Bell,* both of which she edited until her death. Butler was an activist for women's education and campaigned against the licensing of brothels in England. She led the campaign against the Contagious Diseases Act in England that required women in port cities to submit to compulsory examination for venereal disease. Her autobiography, published in 1896, is entitled *Personal Reminiscences of a Great Crusade.*

Sources: Magnusson, *Larousse Biographical Dictionary,* p. 238; Uglow, *The Continuum Dictionary of Women's Biography,* pp. 98–99; *Who Was Who,* vol. I, p. 107.

Augusta Fickert (1855–1910) was the organizer of the General Women's Club of Austria, a group that sought to improve the social and economic position of Austrian women in a variety of ways.

Sources: Chicago, *The Dinner Party,* p. 188; Schmidt, *400 Outstanding Women of the World,* p. 52.

1882 • Pandita Ramabai (1858–1920), a pioneer in the Women's Rights Movement in India, was the founder of Sharada Sadan, an institutional home for Indian widows, many of whom were between the ages of nine and twelve.

Sources: Uglow, *The Continuum Dictionary of Women's Biography,* p. 446.

1884 • Australian feminist Henrietta Dugdale (1826–1918) became the first president of the first Women's Suffrage Society in Victoria, Australia, in 1884. A freethinker and a forceful writer, Dugdale campaigned for women's rights, including social and economic equality and educational opportunity.

Sources: Uglow, *The Continuum Dictionary of Women's Biography,* p. 176.

1886 • Danish feminist Matilde Bajer (1840–1934) founded the Danish Women's Progress Association, a precursor of later suffrage groups, in 1886. With the active support of her husband, Bajer worked for women's rights and founded a number of organizations that advocated women's education and suffrage.

Sources: Uglow, *The Continuum Dictionary of Women's Biography,* pp. 42–43.

1888 • Australian feminist Louisa Lawson (1848–1902) founded the Dawn Club, in Sydney, Australia, in 1888. The Dawn Club was a discussion group that focused on feminist issues and published a journal, *The Dawn,* with an entirely female staff. Lawson served as editor for seventeen years. She also founded the Darlinghurst Hostel for Working Girls.

Sources: Uglow, *The Continuum Dictionary of Women's Biography,* pp. 315–16.

1889 • German Clara Eissner Zetkin (1857–1933) was the first person to formulate a socialist theory of women's emancipation. In 1889, Zetkin presented her theories in two pamphlets: *The Question of Women Workers* and *Women* *at the Present Time.* In 1915 she organized the International Women's Conference Against the War. In 1917, Zetkin was one of the founders of the radical Independent Socialist Democratic Party (known as the Spartacus League) and in 1919 was one of the founders of the German Communist Party. She was a strong supporter of Vladimir Lenin, the Russian revolutionary, and of the Russian Revolution in 1917. She died in Moscow.

Sources: Chicago, *The Dinner Party,* p. 203; Magnusson, *Larousse Biographical Dictionary,* p. 1599; Uglow, *The Continuum Dictionary of Women's Biography,* p. 600.

1891 • Mary Elizabeth Windeyer (1836–1912), an Australian feminist, became in 1891 the first president of the Womanhood Suffrage League, founded by Rose Scott in Sydney, Australia. Committed throughout her life to the struggle for women's rights, she was also a founder and the first president of the Women's Hospital, also in Sydney, in 1895.

Sources: Uglow, *The Continuum Dictionary of Women's Biography,* pp. 584–85.

1892 • French feminist Eugénie Potonie-Pierre (1844–1898) founded the Federation Française des Societées Feministes, an amalgam of eight Parisian feminist groups, in 1892. Among them was the Union des Femmes (cofounded by Potonie-Pierre with Léonie Rouzade and Marguerite Tinyre in 1880), La Ligue Socialiste des Femmes (founded by Potonie Pierre in 1889), and Le Groupe de la Solidarité des Femmes (cofounded by Potonie-Pierre and Maria Martin in 1891). By 1896 she was the undisputed leader of the Socialist Feminist movement and became the first woman to lead a French delegation to a feminist congress in Brussels, in 1897.

Sources: Uglow, *The Continuum Dictionary of Women's Biography,* pp. 438–39.

1894 • Auguste Schmidt (1833–1902), a conservative German feminist who inspired more radical followers of the next generation, was the first president of the Federation of German Women's Associations. She assumed the post in Leipzig in 1894 and held it until 1899.

Sources: Uglow, *The Continuum Dictionary of Women's Biography,* p. 484.

1895 • Minna Cauer (1841–1922) founded the German feminist journal, *The Women's Movement* in 1895. Influenced by the American suffragist Susan B. Anthony (1820–1906), she challenged the Prussian law forbidding women from holding or attending political meetings.

Sources: Chicago, *The Dinner Party,* p. 187; Schmidt, *400 Outstanding Women of the World,* p. 207; Uglow, *The Continuum Dictionary of Women's Biography,* p. 114.

1896 • Kallirhoe Parren (1861–1940) was the organizer of the Federation of Greek Women, a group formed in 1896 to work for the social and political equality of women in Greece. The group belonged to the International Council of Women.

Sources: Chicago, *The Dinner Party,* p. 189; Uglow, *The Continuum Dictionary of Women's Biography,* pp. 420–21.

1899 • Marianne Hainisch (1839–1936), an Austrian feminist and pacifist, was the first president of the General Austrian Women's Association, which she founded in Vienna in 1899. The organization fought for the reform of marriage laws, the rights of illegitimate children, and the abolition of legalized prostitution.

Sources: Uglow, *The Continuum Dictionary of Women's Biography,* p. 243.

c.1900 • Gunda Beeg was the founder of Germany's dress reform movement, in the early years of the twentieth century. She designed a loose-fitting outfit for women to replace restrictive Victorian garments.

Sources: Chicago, *The Dinner Party,* p. 187.

1901 • Franciska Plamnikova (1875–1942) was the first Czech woman to organize a substantial feminist group, the Women's Club of Prague. She went on to found the Committee for Women's Suffrage in 1905 and to work politically for the rights of women. She was also concerned about labor conditions and nationalist issues. Arrested for her activism, she died in a concentration camp.

Sources: Uglow, *The Continuum Dictionary of Women's Biography,* p. 434.

1902 • Anita Augspurg (1857–1943), an ardent German feminist, was one of the founders and the first president of the Deutscher Verband für Frauenstimmrecht (German Union for Women's Suffrage) in 1902. After women gained the vote in Germany, Augspurg continued to campaign for women's civil rights and for peace.

Sources: Uglow, *The Continuum Dictionary of Women's Biography,* p. 35.

1904 • Helene Stöcker (1869–1943), a German feminist and advocate of free love, was the founder of the Bund für Mutterschutz und Sexualreform (the League for the Protection of Motherhood and Sexual Reform), in 1904. This organization, perceived as strikingly radical by more numerous conservative feminists, later became known as the Mutterschutz League.

Sources: Uglow, *The Continuum Dictionary of Women's Biography,* pp. 518–19.

1907 • Rachel G. Foster Avery (1858–1919), a feminist and a close friend and protégé of Susan B. Anthony (1820–1906), was the first woman to serve as vice-president of the National American Woman Suffrage Association. She was elected in Washington, D.C., in 1907, and served as vice-president until 1910 when she and others resigned in protest of what they saw as the weak leadership of Anna Howard Shaw (1847–1919). Throughout her life, Avery worked tirelessly for women's rights both in America and in Europe.

Sources: Flexner, *Century of Struggle*; James, *Notable American Women,* vol. 1, pp. 71–72; Whitman, *American Reformers,* pp. 35–36.

Teresa Billington-Greig (1877–1964) was cofounder (with suffragettes Charlotte Despard and Edith How) of the Women's Freedom League, a women's rights group, in 1907. Billington-Greig, an English suffragette particularly active between 1902 and 1913, married in 1907, and both she and her husband took the same combined surname.

Sources: Uglow, *The Continuum Dictionary of Women's Biography,* p. 66.

Harriet Eaton Stanton Blatch (1856–1940), daughter of activist and suffragist Elizabeth Cady Stanton (1815–1902) founded the Equality League of Self-Supporting Women in 1907 and campaigned tirelessly for women's rights. In 1908, Blatch founded the Women's Political Union.

Sources: Magnusson, *Larousse Biographical Dictionary,* p. 164; Whitman, *American Reformers,* pp. 87–88.

1908 • Anna Pavlovna Filosova (1837–1912), a Russian feminist concerned particularly with the education of women, was the first chair of the first All-Russian Women's Congress, in 1908.

Sources: Uglow, *The Continuum Dictionary of Women's Biography,* p. 203.

1909 • Elizabeth Ahern (1877–1969), a political activist throughout her life, was the founder of the Women's Socialist League, in Melbourne, Australia, in 1909. A dedicated feminist, she advocated both socialism and pacifism.

Sources: Uglow, *The Continuum Dictionary of Women's Biography,* p. 9.

1914 • Raicho Hiratsuka (1886–1971) was the founder of the Japanese feminist group Seitosha and the founder and first editor of its journal *Seito,* in Tokyo in 1914. With other Japanese feminists, Hiratsuka subsequently founded the New Women's Association. This group achieved the first political success of her country's women's movement, the amendment of the Public Order and Police Law, making possible women's limited participation in politics.

Sources: Uglow, *The Continuum Dictionary of Women's Biography,* pp. 260–61.

c.1920 • Hsiang-ning Ho (1879–1972), a Chinese feminist raised in Hong Kong, was one of the first women in China to bob her hair as a sign of independence. This was one of many feminist acts Ho engaged in while living in Kuomintang in the early 1920s. From 1949 to 1960, she was head of the Overseas Chinese Affairs Commission in Peking, and in 1960 she was made Honorary Chairwoman of the China Women's Federation.

Sources: Uglow, *The Continuum Dictionary of Women's Biography,* p. 262.

1920 • Huda Sh'arawi (1882–1947), an Egyptian feminist and pacifist, was the founder and first head of her country's first women's rights association, in Cairo in 1920. She established the Women's Union, which advocated education for girls and women and other feminist goals, in 1924. In the same year she also founded the Union's journal, *Egyptian Woman,* which was published in both Arabic and French in order to reach a wide audience. She was instrumental in founding her country's first secondary school for girls (in 1927) and in establishing the first coeducational university classes (in 1929). In 1944, she helped to set up the All Arab Federation of Women.

Sources: Uglow, *The Continuum Dictionary of Women's Biography,* p. 494.

Avra Theodoropoulou (1880–1963) was the founder of the League for Women's Rights, in Athens, Greece, in 1920. Trained as a musician, Theodoropoulou was a committed feminist who did much in her country to further equal rights for women. In 1911, she founded the School for Working Women in Athens, and in 1918, she started an organization called The Soldier's Sister. She served ably as the first president of the League for Women's Rights for 37 years.

Sources: Uglow, *The Continuum Dictionary of Women's Biography,* p. 539.

1922 • Bertha Lutz (1899–1976) was the organizer of the Brazilian Association for the Advancement of Women, a group dedicated to child welfare and to women's suffrage and education, and served as its first president, beginning in 1922. A graduate of the Sorbonne in biology, she joined the staff of the National Museum in Rio de Janeiro in the 1920s, thus becoming the first woman in Brazilian government service. A delegate in 1923 to the Pan-American Association for the Advancement of Women, Lutz also organized and led the fight for women's suffrage in her country and went on to serve in Brazil's Parliament in 1936. While remaining active on behalf of women, she taught biology for many years at the University of Rio de Janiero.

Sources: Chicago, *The Dinner Party,* p. 188; Uglow, *The Continuum Dictionary of Women's Biography,* p. 338.

Margaret Llewelyn Davies (1861–1944), an English feminist who worked for women's suffrage and workers' rights, was the first female president of the Co-operative Congress, in 1922. She supported the Russian Revolution and was one of the founders of the Women's International Co-operative Guild in 1921.

Sources: Uglow, *The Continuum Dictionary of Women's Biography,* pp. 149–50.

1923 • Alice Paul (1885–1977) organized a celebration in July 1923 in honor of the 75th anniversary of the First Women's Rights Convention at Seneca Falls, New York. At the celebration, she introduced the original draft of the Equal Rights Amendment to the U.S. Constitution that she authored. The Equal Rights Amendment was first introduced in the U.S. Congress in November the same year. (*See also* **Activism: Feminism and Women's Rights, 1928; Activism: Suffrage, 1912.**)

Sources: Magnusson, *Larousse Biographical Dictionary,* p. 1134; Read and Witlieb, *The Book of Women's Firsts,* pp. 332–34; Whitman, *American Reformers,* pp. 640–42.

1924 • Dora Russell (1894–1986), an English feminist, was the founder of the Workers' Birth Control Group, in London in 1924. A lifelong advocate of birth control, women's rights, and international peace, Russell demonstrated for her beliefs and publicized her activism through speeches and books.

Sources: Russell, *The Tamarisk Tree;* Uglow, *The Continuum Dictionary of Women's Biography,* p. 469.

1928 • Alice Paul (1885–1977) founded the World Party for Equal Rights for Women. (*See also* **Activism: Feminism and Women's Rights, 1923; Activism: Suffrage, 1912.**)

Sources: Magnusson, *Larousse Biographical Dictionary,* p. 1134; Read and Witlieb, *The Book of Women's Firsts,* pp. 332–34; Uglow, *The Continuum Dictionary of Women's Biography,* p. 425.

1929 • Ona Masiotene (1883–1949), a Lithuanian feminist, was the founder and first president of the Council of Lithuanian Women, in Vilnius, Lithuania, in 1929. Masiotene was active on behalf of women throughout her life. Educated as a teacher, she founded the Alliance of Lithuanian Women in 1905 in Vilnius, and in Moscow in 1917 she organized the Lithuanian Women's Freedom Association, through which she campaigned for Lithuanian independence.

Sources: Uglow, *The Continuum Dictionary of Women's Biography,* pp. 364–65.

1940s • Dori'a Shafiq (1910–1975), an Egyptian feminist educated at the Sorbonne, was the founder of Bint-E-Nil, the Daughters of the Nile, a women's rights organization, in Cairo, Egypt, in the 1940s. She was instrumental through this group in gaining the vote for women in her country in 1956.

Sources: Uglow, *The Continuum Dictionary of Women's Biography,* p. 494.

1960 • Vilma Espin (b. 1930) was the first head of the Federation of Cuban Women, an organization she helped to found in Havana in 1960. The group was designed to fight illiteracy and to increase women's political involvement. Espin later became a member of the Central Committee of the Cuban Communist Party and worked in Fidel Castro's government in the Ministry of Food.

Sources: Uglow, *The Continuum Dictionary of Women's Biography,* p. 192.

1961 • The first U.S. Presidential Commission of the Status of Women was created by President John F. Kennedy in 1961. It was chaired by Eleanor Roosevelt (1884–1962) assisted by Esther Peterson. As a result of the commission's investigations, President Kennedy announced that women were to be considered equally with men for promotion within the Civil Service and that all promotions within the executive department were to be based on merit.

Sources: Read and Witlieb, *The Book of Women's Firsts,* p. 419; Whitman, *American Reformers,* pp. 640–42.

Bella Savitzky Abzug (b. 1920), an American politician, lawyer, and feminist, was the founder of Woman Strike for Peace in the 1961 and cofounder of the National Women's Political Caucus in 1971. These organizations, each of which she directed for a period, reflect Abzug's dual concerns with peace and women's activism. Also in 1971, Abzug won a seat in U.S. Congress, where she earned the nickname, "Battling Belle."

Sources: Magnusson, *Larousse Biographical Dictionary,* p. 7.

1966 • Betty Goldstein Friedan (b. 1921) cofounded (with Dorothy Haener, Aileen Hernandez, and others) the National Organization of Women (NOW) in 1966 and served as its first president until 1970. Friedan has dedicated her life to working for and writing about feminist causes. She is perhaps best known

Betty Friedan is a dedicated feminist.

for her groundbreaking book about contemporary attitudes towards women, *The Feminine Mystique,* published in 1963. In 1970, Friedan led the National Women's Strike for Equality. Her later publications include *It Changed My Life* (1977) and *The Second Stage* (1981).

Sources: Magnusson, *Larousse Biographical Dictionary,* p. 550; Read and Witlieb, *The Book of Women's Firsts,* p. 168.

1969 • Shulamith Firestone (b. 1945), a Canadian feminist, was the co-founder and first editor of two radical journals: *Redstockings* in 1969 and *Notes from the Second Year* in 1970. She is best known for her book *The Dialectic of Sex: The Case for Feminist Revolution*, published in 1970.

Sources: Uglow, *The Continuum Dictionary of Women's Biography,* p. 204.

Early 1970s • Natalia Malakhovskaya (b. 1947), a Russian teacher, was the founder of the feminist group Club Maria, in St. Petersburg in the early 1970s. The illegal organization campaigned against domestic oppression and inadequate state provision for maternity and childcare. In 1980, Mala-khovskaya and other group leaders were exiled to Vienna.

Sources: Uglow, *The Continuum Dictionary of Women's Biography,* p. 350.

1970 • Monique Wittig (b. 1935), a radical French lesbian feminist who has made her career as a writer, became in 1970 the founder and was for a short period the first spokeswoman for Feministes Révolutionaires, in Paris, France. Now disillusioned with the organized protest for which she became notorious in the late 1960s, Wittig is known for her feminist utopian fiction (her first novel appeared in 1964) and for her lesbian and philosophical tracts. She was a frequent contributor to the French journal *Questions Feministes.*

Sources: Uglow, *The Continuum Dictionary of Women's Biography,* pp. 585–96.

1971 • Erin Pizzey (b. 1939), a leader in the feminist campaign against domestic violence, was the founder of the Chiswick Women's Aid Society in Chiswick, London, England, in 1971. She has attracted much publicity for her cause and in 1979 became Director of Chiswick Family Rescue. She has written both fiction and nonfiction on the subject of family violence.

Sources: Pizzey, *Infernal Child*; Pizzey, *Scream Quietly or the Neighbors Will Hear*; Uglow, *The Continuum Dictionary of Women's Biography,* p. 434.

1977 • Nan Waterman (b. 1920), a lifelong advocate of the rights of women, became the first woman to serve as chair of the board of Common Cause in April 1977. A board member since 1971, she has supported this organization's concern for social and feminist issues.

Sources: O'Neill, *The Women's Book of World Records and Achievements,* p. 731.

Labor Activism

1824 • The first women's labor organization was the United Tailoresses Society of New York, founded in New York City by Lavinia White and Louise Mitchell in 1824. Approximately 600 female members of the union struck for better working conditions in 1831.

Sources: Read and Witlieb, *The Book of Women's Firsts,* p. 436.

1843 • Flora Célestine Thérèse Tristan (1803–1844), a French socialist and writer also remembered as the grandmother of the artist Paul Gauguin, was the first person to propose a Socialist International in 1843, a combination of all artisan clubs into a single international union, in her *Union Ouvrière*, published in Paris. She died of typhoid in Bordeaux while traveling throughout France to publicize her ideas.

Sources: Gattey, *Gauguin's Astonishing Grandmother: A Biography of Flora Tristan*; Schneider, *Flora Tristan*; Uglow, *The Continuum Dictionary of Women's Biography,* pp. 543–44.

1844 • Sarah G. Bagley (1806–c.1847), an American mill worker and early labor organizer, was the founder and first president of the Lowell Female Reform Association, in Lowell, Massachusetts, in December 1844. She campaigned for a ten-hour working day. (*See also* **Media, 1846.**)

Sources: James, *Notable American Women,* vol. 1, pp. 81–82; Josephson, *The Golden Threads: New England's Mill Girls and Magnates*; Stern, *We the Women;* Whitman, *American Reformers,* pp. 37–39.

1860 • The Victoria Press, founded by Emily Faithfull (1835–1895), was the first printing house to employ only women compositors, in London in 1860. In 1862 Faithfull became the first woman to earn the title of Printer and Publisher in Ordinary to the Queen. She founded and published between 1863 and 1880 *The Victoria Magazine* and the *English Woman's Journal,* periodicals dedicated to matters of interest to the working woman. Their articles demanded equal pay for equal work. In 1876, she founded the Women's Printing Society.

Sources: Chicago, *The Dinner Party,* p. 192; Magnusson, *Larousse Biographical Dictionary,* p. 498; Shattock, *The Oxford Guide to British Women Writers,* p. 159.

1869 • The Daughters of St. Crispin (DOSC), the first national labor organization for women, was founded on July 28, 1869, in Lynn, Massachusetts. The DOSC elected Carrie Wilson as its first president. Thirty delegates from six states attended the first convention. The organization ceased to exist in 1876.

Sources: Read and Witlieb, *The Book of Women's Firsts,* p. 114.

1874 • The Women's League was founded in England in 1874, making women a force for the first time in the labor movement.

Sources: O'Neill, *The Women's Book of World Records and Achievements,* p. 284.

1875 • Emma Paterson (1848–1886), an English labor leader, was the first female delegate to the Trade Union Congress, at Glasgow, Scotland, in 1875. She was also the first female inspector of working conditions for women's trades and the founder of the Women's Trade Union League.

Sources: Chicago, *The Dinner Party,* p. 203; Goldman, *Emma Paterson*; Uglow, *The Continuum Dictionary of Women's Biography,* pp. 424–25.

1880 • Elizaveta Kolvalskaya (1850–1933), a Russian socialist and historian of the Russian Revolution, was the cofounder, with Saltykov Shchedrin, of the Union of Russian Workers of the South, in Kiev in 1880. Her protests against factory owners resulted in exile to Siberia, beginning in 1881. After her release in 1903, she went to Geneva and joined the Socialist Revolutionary Party, then returned to Russia in 1917 and worked in the state archives.

Sources: Uglow, *The Continuum Dictionary of Women's Biography,* p. 305.

1885 • The first department of women's work in an American labor union was the Women's Work Union of the Knights of Labor, organized by Leonora Barry, a hosiery worker, in Amsterdam, New York.

Sources: Read and Witlieb, *The Book of Women's Firsts,* pp. 491–92; Whitman, *American Reformers,* pp. 56–58.

1886 • Elizabeth Flynn Rodgers (1847–1939), an American labor leader, was the first woman to serve as a Master Workman (president of a district assembly) in the Knights of Labor. She assumed this position in August in District Assembly 24, a large organization that represented workers in all of Chicago and its suburbs except the stockyards.

Sources: Andrews and Bliss, *The History of Women in Trade Unions*; James, *Notable American Women,* vol. 3, pp. 187–88; Willard, *Glimpses of Fifty Years,* pp. 522–25.

1888 • Clementina Black (1853–1922) was the first woman to propose the Equal Pay resolution. She put forth her resolution at the Trade Union Congress of 1888 in England. A union organizer throughout her life, Black wrote three tracts about the needs of women workers (in 1907, 1909, and 1915) as well as five novels about the oppression of women.

Sources: Uglow, *The Continuum Dictionary of Women's Biography,* pp. 67–68.

1889 • Harriet Morison (1862–1925) was the founder of the first women's union in New Zealand, the Tailoresses' Union, in Dunedin in 1889. An ardent Unitarian as well as a leader in the labor movement, Morison was also one of the first women to preach in New Zealand.

Sources: Uglow, *The Continuum Dictionary of Women's Biography,* p. 389.

1892 • Mary Kenney O'Sullivan (1864–1943), a labor leader and tireless advocate of women's rights, was the first woman to serve as general organizer for the American Federation of Labor (AFL). She was appointed to this position by famed labor leader Samuel Gompers, in New York City in 1892, and served for five months in this capacity, organizing unions in New York and Massachusetts. A friend of Jane Addams (1860–1935), O'Sullivan was also active in settlement work in Chicago and Boston.

Sources: Davis, *Spearheads for Reform,* pp. 138–47; Gompers, *Seventy Years of Life and Labor,* vol. 1, pp. 483–86; Henry, *Women and the Labor Movement,* pp. 107–10; James, *Notable American Women,* vol. 2, pp. 655–56.

1893 • Adelheid Popp (1869–1939), an Austrian trade unionist who also worked for feminist causes, led the first women's strike in Austria in 1893. She led 600 female textile workers in a protest near Vienna. In the same year, Popp founded Libertas, a discussion group that offered women experience in political debate. She became increasingly interested in women's suffrage. After women gained the vote in Austria, she served briefly in Austria's government before the Nazi occupation.

Sources: Popp, *Autobiography of a Working Woman*; Uglow, *The Continuum Dictionary of Women's Biography,* p. 437.

1894 • Kate Richards O'Hare Cunningham (1877–1948) was the first woman to join the International Order of Machinists. Apprenticed to her father, she became a member in 1894. She went on to a career as an ardent socialist and reformer, publishing a socialist novel, *What Happened to Dan,* in 1904.

Sources: Read and Witlieb, *The Book of Women's Firsts,* pp. 109–10; Whitman, *American Reformers,* pp. 200–2.

1899 • The National Consumers League was founded in 1899, combining the leagues of the states of Massachusetts, New York, Pennsylvania, and Illinois. It was at the forefront of the struggle to aid working women and in the movement to establish a minimum wage. Members inspected workplaces, certifying manufacturers with a "consumers label." Florence Kelley (1850–1932) was the first general secretary. Eventually, the League would work on behalf of consumers of manufactured products and other goods.

Sources: Magnusson, *Larousse Biographical Dictionary,* p. 816; O'Neill, *The Women's Book of World Records and Achievements,* p. 285.

Helen Blackburn (1842–1903) cofounded with Jessi Boucherett, of the Freedom of Labour Defence League in England, a group that opposed protective legislation on the grounds that it diminished the earning capacity and personal liberty of women. A lifelong advocate of women's suffrage, Blackburn worked to improve the conditions of women workers in industry.

Sources: Magnusson, *Larousse Biographical Dictionary,* p. 160; Uglow, *The Continuum Dictionary of Women's Biography,* p. 68.

1901 • Margaret Angela Haley (1861–1939) was the first woman and the first elementary-school teacher to speak from the floor at the general convention of the National Education Association.

Sources: O'Neill, *The Women's Book of World Records and Achievements,* p. 297; Zophy, *Handbook of American Women's History,* pp. 246-47.

1903 • Agnes Nestor (1880–1948) became the first woman to be elected president of an international labor union, in 1903. She headed the Chicago branch of the International Glove Workers Union, a group she had founded the previous year.

Sources: James, *Notable American Women,* vol. 2, pp. 615–17; Read and Witlieb, *The Book of Women's Firsts,* p. 308.

Mary Kimball Kehew (1859–1918) became the first president of the National Women's Trade Union League in Boston, Massachusetts, in 1903. The League lobbied to improve living and working conditions for women. Kehew's commitment to the cause of labor is evidenced in a lifetime of public work. She joined the Women's Educational and Industrial Union in 1886, rising to the post of director in 1890 and president in 1892. With Mary Kenney, she founded the Union for Industrial Progress in 1896.

Sources: Read and Witlieb, *The Book of Women's Firsts,* pp. 237–38; Uglow, *The Continuum Dictionary of Women's Biography,* pp. 294–95.

1906 • Mary Reid MacArthur (1880–1921), a Scottish trade unionist, was the founder in 1906 of the National Federation of Women Workers, in London. In 1907, she started its magazine, the popular *Woman Worker.*

Sources: Uglow, *The Continuum Dictionary of Women's Biography,* p. 342.

c.1910 • Marie Juhacz (1880–1956), a German socialist and feminist, was the founder of the Workers' Welfare Organization in Berlin, Germany. She went on to become a member of the National Assembly in 1919 and a member of the Reichstag (1923–1933). While the Nazis were in power, Juhacz lived in France, but she returned to Germany in 1949 and resumed her work with the organization she founded.

Sources: Uglow, *The Continuum Dictionary of Women's Biography,* p. 288.

1910 • Adele Schreiber (c.1872–1957), an Austrian feminist who married a German physician, was the founder of the German Association for the Rights of Mothers and Children, in Berlin in 1910. In 1919, she became the first female member of the Social Democratic Party to hold a seat in the first Reichstag of the Weimar Republic.

Sources: Uglow, *The Continuum Dictionary of Women's Biography,* p. 485.

1911 • Elizabeth Maloney of Chicago became the first woman international vice-president of the Hotel & Restaurant Employees International Union in 1911 and served on its executive board until 1912.

Sources: O'Neill, *The Women's Book of World Records and Achievements,* p. 298.

1912 • Julia Clifford Lathrop (1858–1932) was appointed the first director of the U.S. Children's Bureau by President William Howard Taft in 1912, a post she held until 1921. Originally established in the Department of Commerce, the Children's Bureau was moved to the Department of Labor in 1913; its purpose was to monitor the welfare of children and the enforcement of child labor laws. Lathrop had joined Jane Addams's Hull House Settlement in Chicago and in 1903, with others, founded the Chicago Institute of Social Science. Lathrop served as a member of the child welfare committee of the League of Nations from 1925 to 1931.

Sources: Magnusson, *Larousse Biographical Dictionary,* p. 863; O'Neill, *The Women's Book of World Records and Achievements,* p. 329.

Alexandra van Grippenberg (1857–1911), a leading Finnish feminist and member of the temperance movement, was the founder and first president of the Finnish National Council of Women, in Helsinki, Finland, in 1912. She had earlier served as the first vice president of the International Council of Women, in 1889. She campaigned for women's suffrage in her country and throughout the world, and when Finnish women were granted the franchise in 1909, she was one of the first women elected to the Finnish Diet, where she directed her energies to increasing women's opportunities.

Sources: Schmidt, *400 Outstanding Women of the World,* p. 167.

c.1914 • Gertrude Baumer (1873–1954), a German feminist, was the founder of the Nationaler Fraudienst (National Women's Service) during World War I in Germany. She worked for women's rights and peace throughout her life, but advocated a national liberalism as opposed to the individual pacifism of other feminists. From 1910 to 1919, she was president of the League of

German Women's Associations. In 1917, she founded a socialist school for women in Germany.

Sources: Magnusson, *Larousse Biographical Dictionary,* p. 117; Uglow, *The Continuum Dictionary of Women's Biography,* p. 53.

1917 • Anusyabehn Sarabhai (1885–1972), an Indian woman educated at the London School of Economics, was the first woman to chair a meeting in India at which a labor strike was called. She chaired a meeting of mill workers at which there was a call for the first labor strike in her country. She supported Indian leader Mahatma Gandhi in his strike at Ahmedabad the following year and continued to work throughout her life for workers' rights.

Sources: Uglow, *The Continuum Dictionary of Women's Biography,* p. 479.

Dorothy Jacobs Bellanca (1894–1946), a U.S. union organizer born in Latvia, was the first woman to serve full time as an organizer for the Amalgamated Clothing Workers of America, a position to which she was appointed in New York City in 1917. A tireless worker for the cause of unionism and for the Labor Party in New York politics, Bellanca was one of the few immigrant women who rose to prominence in the U.S. trade union movement.

Sources: James, *Notable American Women,* vol. 1, pp. 124–26; Josephson, *Sidney Hillman.*

1918 • Mabel Edna Gillespie (1877–1923), an American trade unionist, was the first woman to serve on the executive board of the Massachusetts State Federation of Labor, in Boston in 1918. She was also the organizer and first president of the Boston Stenographers' Union, in 1917.

Sources: James, *Notable American Women,* vol. 2, pp. 35–36; Whitman, *American Reformers,* pp. 349–50.

Frances Perkins (1880–1965) was appointed by New York governor Alfred E. Smith as the first woman member of the New York State Industrial Commission; in 1926, she became chair of the commission, and in 1929, commissioner. Her annual salary, $8,000, was the highest paid to any woman in state government at that time. She was appointed U.S. Secretary of Labor (1933–1945), where she supervised New Deal labor regulations such as the Social Security Act (1935) and the Wages and Hours Act (1938). (*See also* **Activism: Labor Activism, 1933; Government: United States, 1933.**)

Sources: Magnusson, *Larousse Biographical Dictionary,* pp. 1145–46; O'Neill, *The Women's Book of World Records and Achievements,* p. 331.

c.1920 • Rachel Katznelson (b. 1888) was the cofounder of the Women Workers Council in Israel. Instrumental in the formation of Israel's governmental policies towards women, Katznelson also established and edited the weekly paper, *Savor Hapocht.*

Sources: Chicago, *The Dinner Party,* p. 201.

1920 • The U.S. Congress established the Women's Bureau, the only federal agency concerned solely with women's issues, on June 5. It succeeded the Women's Section of the Industrial Service Section of the Ordnance Department, which had been established in 1918 to oversee the wartime industrial activities of women during World War I.

Sources: O'Neill, *The Women's Book of World Records and Achievements,* p. 285.

Mary Anderson (1872–1964) became the first woman to head the Women's Bureau, the only federal agency concerned solely with women's issues, on June 5, 1920. Anderson, who immigrated to the United States from Sweden at the age of 16, joined her first labor union, the International Boot and Shoe Workers' union, at age 22. She served as president of Local 94 of her union for 15 years and as the only woman on the union's executive board for 11 years. She headed the Women's Bureau until her retirement in 1944.

Sources: O'Neill, *The Women's Book of World Records and Achievements,* p. 330.

Gertrude Tuckwell (1861–1951), an English trade unionist and social reformer, was the first woman to serve as Justice of the Peace for the County of London, in 1920. She was also the organizer of the Sweated Goods Exhibition, in London in 1906, an event which led to legal reform of sweated work, and the founder of the Maternal Mortality Committee, also in London, in 1927.

Sources: Tuckwell, *Women in Industry*; Uglow, *The Continuum Dictionary of Women's Biography,* p. 546.

1921 • Rose Schneiderman (1882–1972), a feminist who united working women and middle-class reformers, was the first woman to organize a summer school program for working women at a women's college. She organized the Bryn Mawr Summer School for women workers, a course of study at Bryn Mawr College in Pennsylvania. Schneiderman was also the first woman to run for the senate as a candidate of the New York Labor Party, in 1920. During Franklin Roosevelt's presidency, she was the first and only woman to serve in the National Recovery Administration, between 1933 and 1935.

Sources: Schneiderman, *All for One*; Uglow, *The Continuum Dictionary of Women's Biography,* p. 484; Whitman, *American Reformers,* pp. 723–25.

1922 • Anna Weinstock was appointed to the U.S. Conciliation Service in 1922, becoming the first woman to be qualified to serve as a federal mediator in labor disputes. In 1947, she was appointed commission for New England under the then-new independent federal agency, the Federal Mediation and Conciliation Service (FMCS). In 1957, Weinstock received the FMCS Distinguished Service Award.

Sources: O'Neill, *The Women's Book of World Records and Achievements,* p. 331.

1923 • Margaret Grace Bondfield (1873–1953) became the first woman elected chair of the British Trade Union Congress (TUC) in England in 1923. (*See also* **Government: England, 1929.**)

Margaret Bondfield

Sources: Magnusson, *Larousse Biographical Dictionary,* p. 176; O'Neill, *The Women's Book of World Records and Achievements,* p. 284.

Mary MacArthur Anderson (1872–1964) was the delegate from Britain to the first International Labor Organization (ILO) conference. In 1945, ILO became an agency of the United Nations.

Sources: O'Neill, *The Women's Book of World Records and Achievements,* p. 286.

1924 • After years of debate, the Journeymen Barbers International Union voted to admit women. Women had sought membership since 1909.

*Sources:*Read and Witlieb, *The Book of Women's Firsts,* p. 36.

1926 • Marion Phillips (1881–1932), an English socialist with a particular concern for women's rights, was the first person to organize relief for miners' families during the General Strike of 1926. In London she organized the Women's Committee for the Relief of Miners' Wives and Children.

Sources: Uglow, *The Continuum Dictionary of Women's Biography,* pp. 431–32; *Who Was Who,* vol. III, p. 650.

1931 • Louie Bennett (1870–1956) was the first woman to serve as president of the Irish Trades Union Congress, in 1931–1932. Bennett worked throughout her life for women's suffrage and for the rights of women workers.

Sources: Uglow, *The Continuum Dictionary of Women's Biography,* p. 61.

1933 • Dorothy Day (1897–1980) was in 1933 the cofounder, with Peter Maurin, of the Catholic Worker movement to establish shelters and farm communities where people struggling during the Great Depression could seek refuge. She wrote about the movement in *House of Hospitality,* published in 1939. Using her life savings, she launched the newspaper the *Catholic Worker,* publishing the first issue on May 1, 1933. A lifelong activist, Day was arrested in 1973 for challenging limits on United Farm Workers Union pickets in California.

Sources: Day, *The Long Loneliness*; Magnusson, *Larousse Biographical Dictionary,* p. 395; Miller, *Dorothy Day: A Biography*; Whitman, *American Reformers,* pp. 216–18.

Frances Perkins (1880–1965) was appointed by President Franklin D. Roosevelt to become Secretary of Labor. She was sworn in on March 4, 1933, becoming the first woman ever named to a U.S. president's cabinet. (*See also* **Activism: Labor Activism, 1918; Government: United States, 1933.**)

Sources: Magnusson, *Larousse Biographical Dictionary,* pp. 1145–46; O'Neill, *The Women's Book of World Records and Achievements,* p. 331; Whitman, *American Reformers,* pp. 646–49.

1934 • Opera singer Elizabeth Hoeppel (b. 1900) organized and became the first president of the Grand Opera Artists Association in 1934. In 1936, she helped found the American Guild of Musical Artists.

Sources: O'Neill, *The Women's Book of World Records and Achievements,* p. 298.

1942 • As a result of the pressing need for shipbuilders in the United States in 1942, the International Brotherhood of Boilermakers, Iron Shipbuilders and Helpers opened the union to women for the first time.

Sources: Read and Witlieb, *The Book of Women's Firsts,* p. 59.

Dorothy Day (left in photo) was arrested for challenging picket restrictions in 1973.

1943 • Anne Loughlin (1894–1979), an English union organizer who went to work in a clothing factory at the age of 12, was the first woman to serve as president of the General Council of the Trades Union Congress, in 1943, the same year she was made a Dame of the British Empire. In 1948, she was elected General Secretary of the Tailors and Garment Workers Union, the first woman in England to become head of a mixed union.

Sources: Uglow, *The Continuum Dictionary of Women's Biography*, p. 334; *Who Was Who*, vol. VII, p. 478.

1944 • Ruth Weyand (1912–1989) was the first woman attorney to argue before the U.S. Supreme Court for the National Labor Relations Board

(NLRB). The case would prevent an employer from offering a pay increase to an employee if he or she quit the union. Weyand won the case.

Sources: O'Neill, *The Women's Book of World Records and Achievements,* p. 334.

1948 • Shirley Vivien Teresa Brittain Williams (b. 1930), the daughter of the English writer Vera Brittain, became in 1948 the first woman to serve as Chair of the Labour Club, an organization concerned about issues of interest to British workers, in Oxford, England. Educated, like her mother, at Somerville College, Oxford, Williams worked as a journalist before becoming a politician.

Sources: Magnusson, *Larousse Biographical Dictionary,* p. 1565; Uglow, *The Continuum Dictionary of Women's Biography,* pp. 583–84; Williams, *A Job to Live*; Williams, *Politics Is for People*.

1957 • The Equal Pay and Opportunity Council was formed in New Zealand, comprised of twenty-two trade unions and nine women's organizations, to work for equal treatment for all employees in the workplace.

Sources: O'Neill, *The Women's Book of World Records and Achievements,* p. 297.

1960 • Ana Figueroa (1908–1970) of Chile became the first woman to hold the position of Assistant Director-General of the International Labor Organization (ILO).

Sources: O'Neill, *The Women's Book of World Records and Achievements,* p. 346.

1962 • Margaret L. Plunkett was appointed a U.S. labor attaché, the first woman appointed to such a post. She served in The Hague, The Netherlands (1962–1967), and in Israel (1967–1971).

Sources: O'Neill, *The Women's Book of World Records and Achievements,* p. 285.

1963 • As chair of the Tobacco Worker Union, Ella Jensen (b. 1907) was the first woman to chair a union with both men and women members in Denmark, a post she held until 1975.

Sources: O'Neill, *The Women's Book of World Records and Achievements,* p. 320.

Jane O'Grady became the first woman lobbyist for the AFL-CIO in 1963.

Sources: O'Neill, *The Women's Book of World Records and Achievements,* p. 299.

1970 • Olga Madar (1915–1996), a union organizer once called "the first lady of labor," was the first woman named international vice president of the United Auto Workers (UAW) union, in Detroit, Michigan. She had been hired at the Chrysler Corporation's Kercheval plant at the height of the Depression, when others were being laid off, simply because she could play softball. She was incensed, and thus began her life-long work for unions. She joined the staff of the union in 1944 and was later elected the first national president of the Coalition of Labor Union Women, in 1974.

Sources: Detroit Free Press, (17 May 1996), B6; Read and Witlieb, *The Book of Women's Firsts,* p. 265.

Native American Della Lowe originated a union in 1970, the Realistic Professional Indian Performers of America, an affiliate of the AFL-CIO, to represent ceremonial dance performers at the Wisconsin Dells resort.

Sources: O'Neill, *The Women's Book of World Records and Achievements,* p. 297.

1972 • Margo St. James (b. 1937) was the first woman founder of COYOTE (Call Off Your Old Tired Ethics), a prostitutes' union. A former prostitute, St. James started the union to help protect prostitutes and to work for the legalization of the profession.

Sources: McCullough, *First of All: Significant "Firsts" by American Women,* pp. 66–67.

1974 • Clara Belle Taylor Day (b. 1923) was the first woman elected to the executive board of the largest local unit of the International Brotherhood of Teamsters in Chicago, Illinois.

Sources: O'Neill, *The Women's Book of World Records and Achievements,* p. 314.

1975 • Betty Southard Murphy (b. 1929) became the first woman member of the five-member executive committee of the National Labor Relations Board (NLRB) when she was appointed by President Gerald R. Ford in 1975. She was also the first woman to chair the committee.

Sources: O'Neill, *The Women's Book of World Records and Achievements,* p. 285.

AFL-CIO labor leader George Meaney appointed Cynthia McCaughan (b.1928) as the organization's first coordinator of women's activities in 1975.

Sources: O'Neill, *The Women's Book of World Records and Achievements,* p. 309.

Kathleen Nolan (b. 1933) became the first woman elected president of the Screen Actors Guild of the AFL-CIO in 1975. An actor, she appeared as Wendy in *Peter Pan* and has made more than 800 guest appearances on television programs.

Sources: O'Neill, *The Women's Book of World Records and Achievements,* p. 297.

Grace Hartman (b. c.1919) became the first woman to head a major union in North America when she was elected president of Canada's largest union, the Canadian Union of Public Employees in 1975.

Sources: O'Neill, *The Women's Book of World Records and Achievements,* p. 319.

1977 • Carin A. Clauss became the first woman to held the post of solicitor in the U.S. Department of Labor, the agency's top legal post, when she was appointed by President Jimmy Carter in February.

Sources: O'Neill, *The Women's Book of World Records and Achievements,* p. 340.

Eula Bingham (b. 1929) became the first woman to head the Occupational Safety and Health Administration (OSHA) in the U.S. Department of Labor, when she was appointed by President Jimmy Carter in March 1977.

Sources: O'Neill, *The Women's Book of World Records and Achievements,* p. 340.

Coal miner Mary Maynard was elected president of her local United Mine Workers union.

Mary Maynard (b. 1938) became the first woman to serve as president of a local union of the United Mine Workers of America in 1977 when she was elected to head local 1971, a 98-member union in Run Creek, West Virginia.

Sources: Read and Witlieb, *The Book of Women's Firsts,* p. 274.

1980 • Joyce D. Miller (b. 1928) was the first woman to be elected to the AFL-CIO executive council in February. A lifelong union leader, Miller has devoted her attention particularly to social services and to women's concerns.

Source: Read and Witlieb, *The Book of Women's Firsts,* pp. 292–93.

1984 • Brenda Dean (b. 1943) was the first woman to become head of a large trade union. In 1984 she was elected general secretary of the Society of Graphical and Allied Trades, a union for which she had worked since 1959.

Source: Uglow, *The Continuum Dictionary of Women's Biography,* pp. 152–53.

Miscellaneous

1440s • Agnes Sorel (1422–1450), the mistress of Charles VII, was the first woman to make wearing diamonds fashionable at the French court, in Paris in the 1440s. Manipulative and shrewd, she earned the title "Dame de Beauté" from the estates of Beauté-sur-Marne given her by the king. Her early death was attributed to poisoning.

Sources: Hamel, *The Lady of Beauty*; Magnusson, *Larousse Biographical Dictionary,* p. 1372; Uglow, *The Continuum Dictionary of Women's Biography,* pp. 508–9.

1591 • Veronica Franco (1546–1591), an Italian Renaissance poet, was the first person to open a refuge for women of the streets, in Venice. Her poetry was neglected for centuries, but she is now known as an able writer with a concern for social issues of particular interest to women.

Sources: Masson, *Courtesans of the Italian Renaissance*; Uglow, *The Continuum Dictionary of Women's Biography,* p. 211.

c.1920 • Te Puea (1884–1952), a Maori princess, was the first woman to inspire the revival of traditional ways of life among her people. Working in New Zealand in the 1920s, she encouraged the Maori to return to traditional agriculture and to revive native crafts and long-forgotten arts.

Sources: Uglow, *The Continuum Dictionary of Women's Biography,* p. 534.

1935 • Tracey Thurman became the first woman to win a civil suit as a battered wife when she won her case against the police department in Torrington, Connecticut, in June 1985. The judge in the case decided that the police had violated Thurman's civil rights in ignoring her repeated complaints against her husband.

Sources: Read and Witlieb, *The Book of Women's Firsts,* pp. 445–46.

1965 • Joan Baez (b. 1941), American folksinger and political activist, was the founder of the Institute for the Study of Non-Violence in Carmel, California, in 1965. Baez was also the cofounder of Humanitas, the International Human Rights Commission, in 1979.

Sources: Who's Who of American Women, p. 39.

1973 • Amalia Fleming (1909–1986), a Greek physician and political activist who was married to the English scientist Sir Alexander Fleming, was the first woman to head the Greek Committee of Amnesty International, on her return to Athens from political exile in 1973. While practicing as a research physician earlier in her life, she was the first woman to serve as chief bacteriologist at the Evangelismos Hospital in Athens, in 1951.

Sources: Uglow, *The Continuum Dictionary of Women's Biography,* p. 206.

1991 • In Minneapolis, Minnesota, a federal judge issued a ruling that allowed the first-ever class-action sexual harassment lawsuit. A group of approximately 100 women miners alleged that the Eveleth Taconite Company engaged in hiring, compensation, and promotion practices that discriminated against women, and that male employees verbally abused them.

Sources: Read and Witlieb, *The Book of Women's Firsts,* p. 403.

Pacifism

c.1060 B.C. • Abigail, the wife of Nabal in the Hebrew Bible, has been called the first female pacifist because she persuaded David not to kill her husband. She later married David after Nabal died.

Sources: Chicago, *The Dinner Party,* p. 118.

c.800 B.C. • Hersilia was the first Sabine woman to plead for peace. The Sabines were members of an ancient tribe living outside of Rome. According to legend, no women lived in Rome when Romulus founded the city. When neighboring cities refused to allow Roman men to choose wives from among their women, Romulus staged a great festival to which all citizens from the surrounding areas were invited, and Roman men took Sabine women by force to be their wives. This became known as the "Rape of the Sabine Women," an important legendary event. By the time the Sabine men came to Rome to retrieve them, the abducted women had established families with their Roman husbands, and Hersilia became a hero when she argued for peace. The Roman festival of the Matronalia commemorates her success.

Sources: Chicago, *The Dinner Party,* p. 114.

1878 • Sarah Winnemucca (1844–1891), the daughter of a Piute (sometimes spelled Paiute) chief and a leader of Native Americans in the United States, was the first woman to persuade her people to make peace with the United States government, during the Bannock Wars in Oregon in 1878. She went on to lecture throughout the country about the ill-treatment of the Piutes and other Native Americans and was an ardent campaigner in Washington for their rights. Called Thos-me-tony, or Shell Flower, by the Piutes, she met in 1880 with U.S. President Rutherford B. Hayes. She established two schools for Native American children: one in Washington Territory and the other near Lovelock, Nevada.

Sources: Malinowski, *Notable Native Americans,* pp. 460–62; *Who Was Who in America, 1607–1896,* p. 590; Winnemucca, *Life Among the Piutes.*

1900 • Maud Gonne (1866–1953), an Irish actress and revolutionary, was the founder of the radical women's group Inghinidhe Na Eireann (the Daughters of Ireland), in Dublin in 1900. Devoted throughout her life to the Irish Republican cause, Gonne supported the Easter Rebellion of 1916 (her husband, John MacBride, was executed for his part in the uprising) and was an active relief worker during the troubles that followed. She is also remembered because of her friendship with the poet W.B. Yeats.

Sources: Leverson, *Maud Gonne*; Magnusson, *Larousse Biographical Dictionary,* p. 933; Uglow, *The Continuum Dictionary of Women's Biography,* p. 343.

1908 • Fannie Fern Phillips Andrews (1867–1950), a U.S. pacifist born in Canada, was the founder of the American School Peace League, in Boston, Massachusetts, in 1908. In 1918, it was renamed the American School Citizenship League. This organization promoted international justice and understanding. Andrews devoted her life to the cause of peace throughout the world.

Sources: Andrews, *Memory Pages of My Life*; James, *Notable American Women,* pp. 46–48; Whitman, *American Reformers,* pp. 22–23.

1915 • Kathleen D'Olier Courtney (1878–1974), English feminist and pacifist, was the cofounder of the Women's International League for Peace and the first chair of its British section from 1915 until 1925.

Sources: Who Was Who, vol. VII, p. 176.

Emily Greene Balch (1867–1961), an American feminist, was a cofounder of the Women's International Commission for Permanent Peace, later the Women's International Committee for Peace and Freedom, in the Hague in 1915. Born in Jamaica Plain, Massachusetts, Balch attended Bryn Mawr College from 1886 to 1889. In 1906, she became a socialist, openly opposing World War I. Although Balch had been a member of the Wellesley College faculty since 1896, her appointment was not renewed in 1919. That year, she helped found the Women's International League for Peace and Freedom and served as its secretary from 1919 to 1922. For her lifelong work on behalf of peace and justice, Balch received the Nobel Peace Prize, which she shared with John R. Mott, in 1946.

Sources: Magnusson, *Larousse Biographical Dictionary,* p. 95; Whitman, *American Reformers,* pp. 43–45.

1970s • Franca Rame (b. 1929), an Italian actress, director and writer, was the founder of Soccorso Rosso, an movement for the rights of political prisoners, in the 1970s. Rame is known for her work in theatre, which has become increasingly politicized and concerned with radical feminist issues. Collaborating with her husband, the writer Dario Fo, she has been a leading force in political avant-garde drama since 1956.

Sources: Uglow, *The Continuum Dictionary of Women's Biography,* p. 447.

1976 • Betty Williams (b. 1943), an Irish housewife, was the founder of the Northern Ireland Peace Movement, in Belfast in 1976. In response to the violent death of three children in her neighborhood, Williams began a grass-roots organization to work for peace. Soon joined by Mairead Corrigan, Williams remained a leader in this organization until 1980. In 1976, she and Corrigan were recognized for their work and were awarded the Nobel Peace Prize, the first Irish women to receive such acclaim.

Sources: Magnusson, *Larousse Biographical Dictionary,* p. 348; Uglow, *The Continuum Dictionary of Women's Biography,* p. 582.

1983 • Helen Broinowski Caldicott (b. 1938), an Australian-born physician, was the leading founder of Women's Action for Nuclear Disarmament in 1983. Caldicott has devoted her life to working against nuclear power and weapons.

Sources: Uglow, *The Continuum Dictionary of Women's Biography,* pp. 102–3.

Prison Reform

1821 • Elizabeth Gurney Fry (1780–1845), a Quaker, was the first woman in England to suggest that prisons should be a place for rehabilitation. Appearing before the British House of Commons in 1821, she influenced the passage of an important prison reform bill later that year.

Sources: Chicago, *The Dinner Party,* p. 201; Magnusson, *Larousse Biographical Dictionary,* p. 553; Rose, *Elizabeth Fry*; Uglow, *The Continuum Dictionary of Women's Biography,* pp. 215–16.

1920s • Jessie Donaldson Hodder (1867–1931), who made her career as a prison reformer within the Massachusetts state prison system, was the first U.S. woman to serve as a delegate to the International Prison Congress, in London in the early 1920s.

Sources: Glueck, *Five Hundred Delinquent Women*; James, *Notable American Women,* vol. 2, pp. 197–99; Whitman, *American Reformers,* pp. 439–40.

1921 • Margery Fry (1874–1958), an English woman who devoted her life to the cause of prison reform, was the first person to serve as education advisor at Holloway Prison in London, England, in 1921.

Sources: Jones, *Margery Fry*; Who Was Who, vol. V, p. 237.

Suffrage

1648 • Margaret Brent (1601–1671) was the first woman in America to demand suffrage. A landowner and businesswoman, she petitioned the Maryland Assembly in 1647 for the right to vote, but her request was denied.

Sources: Chicago, *The Dinner Party,* p. 167; Whitman, *American Reformers,* pp. 115–17; *Women's History,* p. 18.

1655 • Deborah Moody (c.1580–c.1659) was the first woman in America to vote. As a landowner in Kings County, New York, she was thus entitled to cast a vote. (*See also* **Business: Real Estate, 1645.**)

Sources: James, *Notable American Women,* vol. 1, pp. 569–70; Read and Witlieb, *The Book of Women's Firsts,* pp. 297–98.

1866 • Lucretia Coffin Mott (1793–1880) was the first president of the American Equal Rights Association, founded in Seneca Falls, New York, in

1866. It was the first organization in the United States to advocate national women's suffrage, adopting its constitution on May 10, 1866, in New York City. Mott served as the association's first president and Susan B. Anthony was secretary. Mott, a lifelong advocate of women's rights, devoted her energies to the issues of women's suffrage, the abolition of slavery, and Negro suffrage. (*See also* **Activism: Feminism and Women's Rights, 1848.**)

Sources: James, *Notable American Women,* vol. 2, pp. 592–95; Read and Witlieb, *The Book of Women's Firsts,* pp. 144–45, 302; Whitman, *American Reformers,* pp. 597–98.

1867 • Virginia Louisa Minor (1824–1894) was the first woman in Missouri to take a public stand for women's suffrage. Early in 1867 she circulated a petition to the state legislature in Jefferson City asking that the state constitution be amended to allow women to vote. When the lawmakers rejected her request by a vote of 89 to 5, she worked with other women to organize the Women's Suffrage Association of Missouri. On May 8, 1867, Minor was elected its first president, a post she held until 1872.

Sources: Conard, *Encyclopedia of the History of St. Louis,* vol. 4; James, *Notable American Women,* vol. 2, pp. 550–51; Lutz, *Created Equal*; Minor, *The Minor Family of Virginia.*

1868 • Lydia Ernestine Becker (1827–1890) became the first English woman to speak publicly on women's suffrage when she addressed a meeting at the Free Trade Hall in Manchester, England, in April 1868.

Sources: Uglow, *The Continuum Dictionary of Women's Biography,* pp. 56–57.

1869 • The first two women's suffrage associations in the United States were both founded in 1869: the National Woman Suffrage Association and the American Woman Suffrage Association. The NWSA was the more activist organization. In 1890, the two groups merged to form the National American Woman Suffrage Association.

Sources: Read and Witlieb, *The Book of Women's Firsts,* pp. 487–89.

c.1875 • Mary Lee was the founder and leader of the women's suffrage movement in the state of South Australia. Due in large measure to her efforts, women won the right to vote in South Australia in 1895, seven years before Parliament granted them voting rights in federal elections.

Sources: Chicago, *The Dinner Party,* p. 188.

1878 • Hubertine Auclert (1848–1914), a French feminist, was the founder of the women's rights group Droit de la Femme in 1878. This organization was renamed the Societé de Suffrage des Femmes in 1883.

Sources: Uglow, *The Continuum Dictionary of Women's Biography,* p. 34.

1879 • Caroline Elizabeth Thomas Merrick (1825–1908), an American suffragist and leader in the temperance movement, was, with her friends Elizabeth Lyle Saxon and Dr. Henriette Keating, the first woman in Louisiana to speak publicly on behalf of women's rights. Upset about women's limited legal rights, especially concerning the ownership of property, the three women addressed the Louisiana constitutional convention in Baton Rouge on June 16, 1879.

Sources: James, *Notable American Women,* vol. 2, pp. 530–31; Merrick, *Old Times in Dixie Land: A Southern Matron's Memories;* Willard, *Woman and Temperance,* pp. 560–69.

1888 • Katherine Sheppard (1848–1934) was the author of the first petition for women's suffrage submitted to the New Zealand House of Representatives, in 1888. She also submitted petitions in 1891, 1892, and 1893, the year in which one-third of the country's adult women signed the petition and in which the House of Representative finally granted women the right to vote.

Sources: Chicago, *The Dinner Party,* p. 189.

1891 • Rose Scott (1847–1925), an Australian feminist and pacifist, was the founder and first secretary of the Womanhood Suffrage League, in Sydney, Australia, in 1891. She also organized the League for Political Education in Australia in 1910 and served as its first president.

Sources: Schmidt, *400 Outstanding Women of the World,* pp. 38–39; Uglow, *The Continuum Dictionary of Women's Biography,* p. 489.

1893 • New Zealand was the first country in the world to grant women the right to vote. This achievement was brought about in large measure by an active women's suffrage movement led by Mary Müller (1820–1902).

Sources: Chicago, *The Dinner Party,* p. 188.

1897 • Dame Millicent Garrett Fawcett (1847–1929) was the first president of the National Union of Women's Suffrage Societies in England. A lifelong advocate of women's rights, especially to education and the vote, Fawcett was also a founder of the first Women's Suffrage Committee, the group that first petitioned Parliament to grant women the vote.

Sources: Chicago, *The Dinner Party,* p. 186; Fawcett, *What I Remember;* Strachey, *Millicent Garrett Fawcett;* Schmidt, *400 Outstanding Women of the World,* p. 160.

1899 • Margarete Forchhammer was the founder of the Danish National Council of Women, an organization that fought for suffrage and women's rights.

Sources: Chicago, *The Dinner Party,* p. 188.

1903 • In October 1903, Emmeline Goulden Pankhurst (1858–1928) and her daughter Christabel Harriette Pankhurst (1880–1958) founded the National Women's Social and Political Union (WSPU) in England with the slogan, "Votes for Women." The Pankhursts were known for their extreme militancy. (*See also* **Activism: Suffrage, c. 1920.**)

Sources: Magnusson, *Larousse Biographical Dictionary,* p. 1122; *Who Was Who,* vol. II, p. 811.

1905 • Annie Kenney (1879–1953), a militant feminist and an active participant in the women's movement, and her friend, Christabel Harriette Pankhurst (1880–1958), were the first women arrested and imprisoned for suffrage protest. Kenney went to work in a mill at the age of ten and soon involved herself in labor union activity. She became the first woman in the textile unions

to be elected to the District Committee and used her salary to enroll as a correspondence student at Ruskin College, Oxford. She continued to campaign for women's rights until her marriage in 1921.

The slogan adopted by the Women's Social and Political Union in England was "Votes for Women."

Sources: Chicago, *The Dinner Party,* p. 186; Kenney, *Memories of a Militant*; Uglow, *The Continuum Dictionary of Women's Biography,* p. 297.

When suffragists Annie Kenney (1879–1953) and Christabel Harriette Pankhurst (1880–1958) were arrested and imprisoned for suffrage protest in 1905, newspapers used the label "suffragette" for the first time in print.

Sources: Chicago, *The Dinner Party,* p. 186; Kenney, *Memories of a Militant*; Uglow, *The Continuum Dictionary of Women's Biography,* p. 297.

1907 • Elsa Ueland, the second daughter of the Minnesota women's rights leader Clara Hampson Ueland, was the first president of the College Equal Suffrage League, founded at the University of Minnesota in Minneapolis in 1907. (*See also* **Activism: Suffrage, 1919.**)

Sources: James, *Notable American Women,* vol. 3, p. 499.

Harriet Eaton Stanton Blatch (1856–1940) led the first parade for women's suffrage in New York City in 1907.

Sources: Magnusson, *Larousse Biographical Dictionary,* p. 164; Olsen, *Chronology of Women's History,* p. 187.

1908 • Elizabeth Robins (1862–1952), an American actress and author who settled in England in 1889, was the cofounder and first president of the Women's Writers Suffrage League, in London, England. She is remembered for her influential play, *Votes for Women!,* performed in London in 1907, and for her struggle to bring drama with substantial and unusual roles for women to the London stage.

Sources: Uglow, *The Continuum Dictionary of Women's Biography,* p. 461; *Who Was Who,* vol. V, p. 937.

Chrystal Macmillan (1871–1937), a graduate in mathematics and natural sciences and a lifelong feminist and pacifist, became the first woman to address the House of Lords, in London, England in 1908. She appealed for her right as a graduate to vote for the parliamentary candidates for the Scottish Universities seat. Her case was defeated after seven days of heated argument. She went on to campaign for suffrage, and in 1923 she founded the Open Door International for Economic Emancipation of Women Workers, which fought for the removal of legal restraints on women.

Sources: Uglow, *The Continuum Dictionary of Women's Biography,* p. 346; *Who Was Who,* vol. III, p. 880.

c.1910 • Alva Erskine Belmont (1853–1933) was the founder and first president of the Political Equality League, a women's suffrage group based in New York City that flourished in the 1910s. Belmont, a woman of tremendous wealth, devoted her resources and later life to militant feminism after her husband's death in 1908.

Sources: Magnusson, *Larousse Biographical Dictionary,* p. 134; Whitman, *American Reformers,* pp. 72–73.

1911 • Constance Lytton (1869–1923), an ardent English suffragist, was the first woman to be severely injured by government action against suffrage workers. Imprisoned (for the fourth time) in Liverpool in 1911 for inciting a riot on behalf of women's right to vote, Lytton undertook a hunger strike. She was forcibly fed in May 1912 and became so ill as a result of the trauma that she suffered a stroke and permanent paralysis. Although an invalid for the rest of her life, she continued to work for the suffrage movement.

Sources: Balfour, *Letters of Constance Lytton*; Lytton, *Prisons and Prisoners: Some Personal Experiences*; *Who Was Who,* vol. II, pp. 655–56.

1912 • Alice Paul (1885–1977) broke away in April 1912 from the National American Women's Suffrage Association to found and serve as first chair of the Congressional Union for Woman Suffrage (later the National Woman's Party).

In November of the same year, Paul began publishing *The Suffragist.* (*See also* **Activism: Feminism, 1923** and **1928.**)

Alice Paul stitches a suffrage banner with stars representing the 36 states that had ratified the 19th Amendment by 1932.

Sources: Read and Witlieb, *The Book of Women's Firsts,* pp. 332–34; Uglow, *The Continuum Dictionary of Women's Biography,* p. 425.

Hannah Sheehy-Skeffington (1877–1946), an Irish feminist and patriot, was the first woman to be dismissed from the Rathmines School of Commerce for her militant suffrage activities, in Dublin in 1912. A founding member of the Irish Association of Women Graduates, in Dublin in 1901, Sheehy-Skeffington was also the cofounder, with Constance Markiewicz, of the Irish Women's Franchise League, in 1908.

Sources: Magnusson, *Larousse Biographical Dictionary,* p. 1338; Uglow, *The Continuum Dictionary of Women's Biography,* p. 494.

1913 • Emily Wilding Davidson (1872–1913), a militant English feminist, was the first woman to kill herself for the cause of women's suffrage, on June 4, 1913. She wrapped herself in the flag of the Women's Suffrage and Political Union and threw herself under the king's horse during the Derby at Epsom, England. She was trampled and died four days later.

Sources: Colmore, *The Life of Emily Davidson;* Uglow, *The Continuum Dictionary of Women's Biography,* p. 151.

c.1915 • Emilie Gourd (1879–1946), a Swiss feminist, was the founder and first editor of the suffragist periodical *Le Mouvement Féministe,* a periodical she continued to oversee from the 1910s until her death.

Sources: Uglow, *The Continuum Dictionary of Women's Biography,* p. 232.

Carrie Clinton Lane
Chapman Catt

1919 • Carrie Clinton Lane Chapman Catt (1859–1947) was the first woman to call for the establishment of the League of Women Voters in 1919, a year before women's suffrage was granted. Catt devoted her life to the cause of women's suffrage not only in the United States but throughout the world. She also became an activist in the cause of world peace. (*See also* **Education, 1921.**)

Sources: Chicago, *The Dinner Party,* p. 184; Peck, *Carrie Chapman Catt;* Read and Witlieb, *The Book of Women's Firsts,* pp. 86–87; Whitman, *American Reformers,* pp. 154–58.

Maud Wood Park (1871–1955), a lifelong advocate for women's suffrage and women's rights, became the first national president of the League of Women Voters in 1919, just before the Nineteenth Amendment to the U.S. Constitution became law, in 1920.

Sources: Read and Witlieb, *The Book of Women's Firsts,* pp. 330–31.

Clara Hampson Ueland (1860–1927), a women's rights advocate who organized her state in its struggle for women's suffrage, became the first president of the Minnesota League of Women Voters, in Minneapolis in September of 1919. She is also remembered for her encouragement of the arts in Minnesota. (*See also* **Activism: Suffrage, 1907.**)

Sources: James, *Notable American Women,* vol. 3, pp. 498–99; Ueland, *Recollections of an Immigrant.*

c.1920 • Christabel Harriette Pankhurst (1880–1958), one of the leaders of the women's suffrage movement in England, was the founder of the radical newspaper, *The Suffragette.* She supervised its publication from Paris where she had retreated for a period to escape imprisonment in England. (*See also* **Activism: Suffrage, 1903.**)

Sources: Chicago, *The Dinner Party,* p. 186; Magnusson, *Larousse Biographical Dictionary,* p. 1122; *Who Was Who,* vol. V, p. 846.

1920 • Jessie Annette Jack Hooper (1865–1935), an American suffragist and pacifist, was the first woman to serve as president of the Wisconsin League of Women Voters, in Oshkosh, Wisconsin, in 1920. She held this position until 1922 when she resigned to run (unsuccessfully) as Wisconsin's first female Democratic nominee for the United States senate.

Sources: James, *Notable American Women,* vol. 2, pp. 215–16.

Militant suffragist Estelle Sylvia Pankhurst (1882–1960) was the founder of the East London Federation for Women's Suffrage. She was expelled by her mother, Emmeline Goulden Pankhurst (1857–1928), and sister, Christabel Harriette Pankhurst (1880–1958), from the organization they founded, Women's Social and Political Union (*see* **Activism: Suffrage, 1903**). Known as Sylvia, she was expelled by her family because of her focus not only on women's suffrage but on socialist solutions to women's oppression and working class poverty. She was arrested thirteen times during her life while working for women's rights.

Sources: Chicago, *The Dinner Party,* p. 187; Magnusson, *Larousse Biographical Dictionary,* p. 1122; *Who Was Who,* vol. V, pp. 846–47.

Taxation

c.1060 • Lady Godiva (1040–1080), the wife of the cruel Leofric, Earl of Mercia, was the first woman to ride naked through the streets of Coventry, England. Legend has it that she took on this feat in order to persuade her husband to lift the heavy taxes imposed on the people of the city. Hidden by her long hair, Lady Godiva was respected by the local citizens, except for "Peeping Tom" who peeked at her from his window, and, according to legend, was struck blind.

Sources: Magnusson, *Larousse Biographical Dictionary,* p. 598; Uglow, *The Continuum Dictionary of Women's Biography,* p. 228.

1695 • The first women required to pay a poll tax were self-supporting women in Massachusetts Bay Colony in 1695. Women were taxed at half the prevailing rate for men, however.

Sources: Read and Witlieb, *The Book of Women's Firsts,* p. 438.

Temperance

1873 • Eliza Daniel Stewart (1816–1908) was the founder of the first American women's temperance league, in Osborn, Ohio, in 1873. Her organization was a precursor of the Women's Christian Temperance Union, organized by Stewart and others in Cleveland, Ohio, the following year.

Sources: Read and Witlieb, *The Book of Women's Firsts,* p. 424; Whitman, *American Reformers,* pp. 769–70.

1874 • The Women's Christian Temperance Union (WCTU) was founded on November 18, 1874, in Cleveland, Ohio.

Annie Turner Wittenmyer (1827–1900), an American activist who established her reputation as a relief worker during the Civil War, was the first president of the Woman's Christian Temperance Union, a position to which she was elected when this organization was founded in Cleveland, Ohio, in November of 1874. A conservative leader in the Methodist church, Wittenmyer soon won wide religious support for her organization and was instrumental in establishing the WCTU's first official journal, *Our Union,* in 1875. The first corresponding secretary of the WCTU was Frances E. Willard (1839–1898). Wittenmyer lost the presidency to the more liberal feminist Willard in 1879,

Frances E. Willard

but during her five-year tenure she had set up more than one thousand local unions with nearly 26,000 members.

Sources: James, *Notable American Women,* vol. 3, pp. 552–53, 636–38; Read and Witlieb, *The Book of Women's Firsts,* p. 201; Whitman, *American Reformers,* pp. 885–88.

c.1875 • Amanda M. Way (1828–1914), an American temperance leader and women's rights activist, was one of the founders and the first president of the Kansas chapter of the Women's Christian Temperance Union (WCTU). She was instrumental in securing the prohibition amendment to that state's constitution in 1880.

Sources: Austin, *The Temperance Leaders of America*; James, *Notable American Women,* vol. 3, pp. 552–53.

1891 • The first convention of the World's Women's Christian Temperance Union (WCTU) was held in Boston, Massachusetts, in 1891.

Sources: Uglow, *The Continuum Dictionary of Women's Biography,* pp. 584–85.

The Arts

Dance

The first half of the 18th century • Marie Sallé (1707–1756) was the first female choreographer, as well as a costume designer. She performed in both her native France and in England, where she was criticized in the 1730s for appearing in simple Greek drapery as a boy in Handel's *Alcina* and for having a female lover.

Sources: Chicago, *The Dinner Party,* p. 205; Migel, *The Ballerinas from the Court of Louis XIV to Pavlova;* Uglow, *The Continuum Dictionary of Women's Biography.*

c.1730 • Marie-Anne Cupis de Camargo (1710–1770) has the reputation of being the first ballerina allowed to dominate a production. She is also reputed to be the first to perform complicated steps such as the *entrechat quatre* and was admired by both famed adventurer Giovanni Giacomo Casanova and the writer Voltaire.

Sources: Migel, *The Ballerinas from the Court of Louis XIV to Pavlova;* Uglow, *The Continuum Dictionary of Women's Biography,* p. 142.

Early 19th century • Suzanne Theodore Vaillande Douvillier (1778–1846), an American dancer born in France and educated in Paris, was the first female choreographer in the United States. She was also the first ballerina to gain celebrity in America through performances in New York, Philadelphia, Charleston, and New Orleans. In 1808, she appeared on the stage in male attire, probably the first woman to dance in crossdress in the United States. She was well-known on the east coast of the United States and had few rivals during her long career.

Sources: James, *Notable American Women,* vol. 1, pp. 513–14; Moore, "When Ballet Came to Charleston," *Dancing Times,* December 1956; Odell, *Annals of the New York Stage;* Waldo, *The French Drama in America in the Eighteenth Century.*

1832 • Marie Taglioni (1804–1884), an Italian ballerina born in Stockholm, Sweden, and trained by her father, a dancer and choreographer, was the first woman to go up on point on stage. She impressed audiences in Paris when she went up on her toes in the Romantic ballet *La Sylphide,* written by her father in 1832. She toured throughout Europe and was known for her graceful and apparently effortless movements.

Sources: Thomas, *Ballet,* p. 39; *The World Book Encyclopedia,* vol. 19, p. 15.

1840 • Fanny Elssler (1810–1884) was the first notable ballerina to tour the United States. When this Austrian dancer performed in Washington, D.C., in 1840, the U.S. Congress was forced to adjourn because of the lack of a quorum, due to members attending the show. She was known for her flamboyant, daring, and dramatic style.

Sources: Guest, *Fanny Elssler: The Pagan Ballerina;* Uglow, *The Continuum Dictionary of Women's Biography,* p. 190.

1840s and 1850s • Augusta Maywood (1825–1878), a ballerina trained in Philadelphia and Paris, was the first American woman to form her own traveling ballet company and win international fame. She performed at the Paris Opera, beginning in 1838, and she toured Europe in the 1840s with her own managers, partners, decors, and costumes. Maywood was particularly popular in Italy where she performed to wide acclaim in the 1840s and 1850s. A colorful personality, she made a fortune before retiring to a villa near Lake Como in northern Italy.

Sources: Guest, *The Romantic Ballet in Paris,* pp. 196–200; James, *Notable American Women,* vol. 2, pp. 518–19; Stern, *We the Women,* pp. 2–12; Tierney, *Women's Studies Encyclopedia,* vol. 2, p. 80; Wemyss, *Twenty-six Years of the Life of an Actor and Manager,* pp. 292–93.

1846 • Mary Ann Lee (1824–1899), who trained in Philadelphia and Paris, became the first American ballerina to dance the Romantic role of Giselle in the ballet of the same name, in Boston, Massachusetts, on January 1, 1846. She gained a national reputation and performed in major cities of the eastern United States.

Sources: James, *Notable American Women,* vol. 2, pp. 387–88; Magriel, *Chronicles of the American Dance.*

1895 • Mathilde Maria-Felixovna Kschessinskaya (1872–1971) was the first Russian ballerina to dance the 32 *fouettés,* a series of difficult, whipping leg movements first introduced by the Italian ballerina Pierina Legnani. The performance took place in 1895 in St. Petersburg, where she was trained at the Imperial Ballet School. In the same year she also became the first Russian to dance Aurora in *Sleeping Beauty,* and she received the title of "prima ballerina assoluta." She fled her homeland during the Russian Revolution of 1917 and settled in Paris where she opened her own ballet school in 1929. She continued as an influential teacher until her retirement at the age of 91 in 1963.

Sources: Kschessinskaya, *Dancing in Petersburg: The Memoirs of Kschessinskaya;* Uglow, *The Continuum Dictionary of Women's Biography,* pp. 306–7.

Early 20th century • Isadora Duncan (1879–1927), known as much for her unconventional life as for her art, revolutionized interpretive dance and was considered the founder of modern dance. Trained in classical ballet, Duncan rejected the traditional forms and costumes for movement that emphasized the natural body and what she felt were innately human spiritual power and grace. She opened a dance school for children in Berlin, Germany, in 1905

Opposite page: Dancer Ruth St. Denis appeared in the role of Pallas Athena.

and a school for dance in Moscow at the invitation of the Soviet government in 1921.

Sources: Chicago, *The Dinner Party,* p. 215; Duncan, *My Life*; Steegmuller, *Your Isadora*; Uglow, *The Continuum Dictionary of Women's Biography,* pp. 177–78.

1903 • Loie Fuller (1862–1928), an influential American dancer, was the first person to use luminous phosphorescent materials on a darkened stage. She produced stunning lighting effects in this way for her "Fire Dance" in Paris, France, in 1903. She helped to launch the careers of both Isadora Duncan (who joined Fuller's troop in 1903) and Maud Allan, another pioneer of modern dance.

Sources: Fuller, *Fifteen Years of a Dancer's Life*; James, *Notable American Women,* vol. 1, pp. 675–77; Magriel, *Chronicles of the American Dance.*

1913 • Anna Pavlova (1882–1931), the famous Russian ballerina, was the first woman to introduce western dance to countries such as Egypt, Japan, China and India. She went on international tours, beginning in 1913, and performed in the provinces as well as in capital cities in order to encourage the reputation and appreciation of classical ballet.

Sources: Kerensky, *Anna Pavlova*; Money, *Pavlova*; Uglow, *The Continuum Dictionary of Women's Biography,* pp. 425–26.

1915 • Ruth St. Denis (1879–1968), with her husband Ted Shawn, was the founder of the first nationally acclaimed dance school in the United States, Denishawn, in Los Angeles, California, in 1915. Martha Graham was one of her pupils. Denishawn closed in 1932, but St. Denis continued to choreograph and perform until 1955.

Sources: Read and Witlieb, *The Book of Women's Firsts,* pp. 387–88; St. Denis, *Ruth St. Denis: An Unfinished Woman*; St. Denis, *An Unfinished Life*; Shelton, *Divine Dancer;* Uglow, *The Continuum Dictionary of Women's Biography,* p. 475 .

1916 • In 1916, Flora Elizabeth Burchenal (1876–1959) founded the American Folk Dance Society and served as its first president. When the society became a division of the National Committee of Folk Arts in 1929, Burchenal became head of the new National Committee, a position she held until 1959.

Sources: Read and Witlieb, *The Book of Women's Firsts,* pp. 75–76.

1920s • Bronislava Nijinska (1891–1972) was the first woman to choreograph for ballet producer Sergey Pavlovich Diagilev, in Paris at the Ballet Russes during the 1920s. Trained as a dancer, she performed in Russia and in France before turning to choreography, a profession in which she established an international reputation.

Sources: Nijinska, *Early Memoirs*; Uglow, *The Continuum Dictionary of Women's Biography,* p. 402.

1920 • Mary Wigman (1896–1973), a German dancer, choreographer, and teacher, founded her own school in Dresden, Germany, in 1920. With Wigman as its first director and principal teacher, the school became the center of Central European dance style, emphasizing angular movements and psychological truth. Wigman's work has been claimed as the most significant influence on European modern dance.

Sources: Uglow, *The Continuum Dictionary of Women's Biography,* p. 580; Wigman, *The Language of Dance.*

Adeline Genée (1878–1970), a Danish dancer and teacher who was the most popular and acclaimed ballerina at the turn of the century in London's Empire Theatre, became the first person to serve as president of the Association of Operatic Dancing, in London in 1920. This organization became the Royal Academy of Dancing in 1935.

Sources: Guest, *Adeline Genée: A Lifetime of Ballet Under Six Reigns*; Uglow, *The Continuum Dictionary of Women's Biography,* p. 222 .

1921 • Lydia Lopokova (1892–1981) was a Russian ballerina who had already established a reputation in Russia, Paris, and London before her marriage to the British economist John Maynard Keynes in 1921. Together they founded the Arts Theatre in Cambridge in the same year. This theatre fostered both touring drama and local productions featuring Cambridge students, among them actors Kenneth Branaugh and Emma Thompson in the 1980s and 1990s.

Sources: Keynes, *Lydia Lopokova;* Uglow, *The Continuum Dictionary of Women's Biography,* p. 333.

1924 • Anita Zahn (1903–1994), who began to dance at Elizabeth Duncan's dancing school in Baden-Baden, Germany, at the age of seven, was the first person to establish an American branch of this school, in New York City in 1924. Called the Elizabeth Duncan School of the Dance, the school flourished under Zahn's direction both in New York and, during the summers, first in Nantucket and then in East Hampton on Long Island. Among her students were Jacqueline Bouvier (later wife of John F. Kennedy), her daughter Caroline Kennedy, and the editor Caroline Zilboorg.

Sources: The East Hampton Star (1 December 1994), pp. 1–2.

1926 • Marie Rambert (1888–1982), an English choreographer, dancer, and teacher, was the founder and first director of the Ballet Rambert, in Hammersmith, London, in 1926. She continued to direct this innovative company until 1966. The Ballet Rambert was known for its classical training combined with the encouragement of new ideas and put on a regular London season as well as provincial and continental tours. The company reflected the personality of its founder, for Rambert was known for her inspirational ability and energy. Until her late seventies, she was remarkable for turning sudden cartwheels in unexpected places.

Sources: Rambert, *Quicksilver;* Uglow, *The Continuum Dictionary of Women's Biography,* p. 446.

Carlotta Zambelli (1875–1968), an Italian ballerina who became principal dancer at the Paris Opera in 1898, was the first person to enter the Légion d'Honneur for dance, in Paris, France, in 1926. She was recognized for her brilliant technique and interpretations. She retired as a dancer in 1930 and went on to serve as director of the Paris Opera ballet school, a position she held until 1950.

Sources: Guest, *Carlotta Zambelli;* Uglow, *The Continuum Dictionary of Women's Biography,* p. 598.

1927 • Encarnçion Lopez (1895–1945), known throughout her career in dance as "La Argentenita" because of her birth in Buenos Aires, was the cofounder, with Garcia Lorca, of the Ballet de Madrid in 1927.

Sources: Uglow, *The Continuum Dictionary of Women's Biography,* p. 27.

1930 • Hanya Holm (b. 1895), a German dancer and choreographer, was the first person to introduce the Dalcroze Central European style of dance in the United States. She performed in New York in 1930, then went on to found her own school in this city, where she taught from 1931 until 1967. She also lectured about her art and created dances for Broadway shows, among them *My Fair Lady* and *Camelot.*

Sources: Sands, *Hanya Holm;* Uglow, *The Continuum Dictionary of Women's Biography,* pp. 263–64.

1931 • Ninette de Valois (b. 1898) was the founder and first director of the Royal Ballet, which she started in 1931. She continued to head this company until her retirement in 1963. An Irish dancer of great energy and charm, de Valois was also the founder of the National School of Ballet in Turkey, in 1947, and the first woman to receive the Erasmus Prize Foundation Award, in 1974.

Sources: de Valois, *Come Dance with Me*; de Valois, *Invitation to the Ballet*; de Valois, *Step by Step*; Uglow, *The Continuum Dictionary of Women's Biography,* pp. 165–66.

1933 • Alicia Markova (b. 1910), a distinguished English dancer of international reputation, was the first "prima ballerina" of the Vic-Wells Ballet Company, in London in 1933. She held this position for two years, partnered by dancer and choreographer Sir Anton Dolin. With him she founded the Markova-Dolin Ballet, with which she toured between 1935 and 1938, becoming the first great ballerina to undertake large provincial tours. In 1950 she was a cofounder of the London Festival Ballet. She went on to become Director of the Metropolitan Opera Ballet (in 1963), Governor of the Royal Ballet (in 1973), and President of the London Festival Ballet (in 1986).

Sources: Markova, *Giselle and I*; Markova, *Markova Remembers;* Uglow, *The Continuum Dictionary of Women's Biography,* p. 359.

1941 • Pearl Primus (b. 1919) was the first woman to study and perform African dance as a scholarly subject. Brought up in Trinidad, Primus studied anthropology at Columbia University in New York before turning to dance as a serious career. Her first solo performance occurred in New York City in 1941. She took up racial issues in her choreography, studied in Africa as well as the Caribbean, and has established a reputation in Africa as well as in the United States.

Sources: Afro-American Encyclopedia, p. 2116; Uglow, *The Continuum Dictionary of Women's Biography,* p. 440.

1945 • Pilar Lopez (b. 1912), a dancer and famous teacher, was the founder of the Ballet Espagnol in Spain. She founded this company in 1945 after the death of her sister, dancer Encarnaçion Lopez.

Sources: Uglow, *The Continuum Dictionary of Women's Biography,* p. 27.

1946 • Natalya Mikhailovna Dudinskaya (b. 1912), a ballerina with the Kirov Ballet in Russia, was the first woman to dance the lead role in Prokofiev's famous *Cinderella,* in Moscow in 1946. She continued to perform until her retirement in 1961 and has since concentrated on teaching.

Sources: Uglow, *The Continuum Dictionary of Women's Biography,* p. 176.

Mid-20th century • Margot Fonteyn (1919–1991) was the first ballerina of international stature to be trained and developed in England. She joined the Vic-Wells Ballet School in London in 1934 and went on to a distinguished career in dance, working for a decade as Rudolf Nureyev's partner, beginning in 1962.

Sources: Magnusson, *Larousse Biographical Dictionary,* p. 527; Stetler, *Almanac of Famous People,* p. 696; Uglow, *The Continuum Dicitonary of Women's Biography,* p. 209.

1957 • Agrippina Vaganova (1879–1951), a Russian ballerina known particularly as a gifted teacher, was the first woman to have a ballet school in St. Petersburg renamed after her. In 1957, the Leningrad Choreographic School, where she taught from 1921 until her death, was renamed the Vaganova School in her honor. She was also the first woman to write a book that became the basis for ballet training not only in Russia but in many dance schools in the West.

Sources: Uglow, *The Continuum Dictionary of Women's Biography,* p. 553; Vaganova, *Basic Principles of Classical Ballet.*

1961 • Barbara Karinska (1886–1983), a Russian costume designer best known for her work with George Balanchine and the New York City Ballet, was the first designer to win the prestigious Capezio Dance Award, in 1961. She was honored for her imaginative and colorful costuming in Paris and Hollywood as well as in New York and for a long career in her field, beginning in 1928. She continued to work productively until 1977.

Sources: Uglow, *The Continuum Dictionary of Women's Biography,* p. 292.

1964 • Beryl Grey (b. 1927), an English ballerina, became the first westerner to dance with the Peking and Shanghai Ballets when she visited China in 1964. Earlier, in 1957, she was the first foreign ballerina to perform as a guest artist with the Bolshoi, Kiev and other Russian ballet companies.

Sources: Grey, *Red Curtain Up*; Grey, *Through the Bamboo Curtain;* Uglow, *The Continuum Dictionary of Women's Biography,* p. 237.

1965 • Twyla Tharp (b. 1941), an American choreographer who studied at Pomona College, the American Ballet Theatre School, and Barnard College, was the founder of the Twyla Tharp Dance Company, in New York City in

Ballerina Margot Fonteyn

1965. She has created dances not only for her own troupe but for other companies and is known as one of the most original contemporary choreographers.
Sources: Stetler, *Almanac of Famous People,* p. 1868; *The World Book Encyclopedia,* vol. 19, p. 181.

1967 • Brigit Ragnhild Cullberg (b. 1908) was the first director of the Cullberg Ballet, a company she founded in 1967. She was also a cofounder of the

Svenska Dansteater in 1946. Cullberg has worked as a dancer and choreographer throughout Europe and the United States.

Sources: Uglow, *The Continuum Dictionary of Women's Biography,* pp. 141–42.

1972 • Judith Jamison (b. 1943), an American dancer, was the first woman elected to the board of the National Endowment for the Arts, in 1972. She was also the first black woman and the first black artist to serve in this capacity. In being named to the post, she was recognized for her wide experience in dance in the United States, Europe, and Africa. She is especially admired for her statuesque performances characterized by passionate intensity.

Sources: Stetler, *Almanac of Famous People,* p. 1009; Uglow, *The Continuum Dictionary of Women's Biography,* p. 281.

1981 • Martha Graham (1894–1991) was the first woman to receive the Samuel H. Scripps American Dance Festival Award. She was honored in Durham, North Carolina, in 1981 for her lifelong dedication to modern American dance.

Graham is regarded as one of the most influential figures in modern dance. Born in Pittsburgh, Pennsylvania, she spent her childhood in California. After studying with Ted Shawn at the Denishawn School (which he cofounded with his wife Ruth St. Denis) in Los Angeles, Graham performed, choreographed, and taught through the 1920s. In 1932, she became the first dancer to receive a Guggenheim Fellowship.

Among Graham's best-known works are dances based on the lives of famous women, such as Joan of Arc, Mary–Queen of Scots, Emily Dickinson, and Charlotte and Emily Brontë. After 1938, she choreographed to music expressly composed for her work by Aaron Copeland (*Appalachian Spring*), Gian-Carlo Menotti, and Samuel Barber. Graham choreographed over 180 works before her retirement in 1969. Graham received numerous awards, including the Presidential Medal of Freedom in 1976.

Sources: Read and Witlieb, *The Book of Women's Firsts,* pp. 182–83; Rolka, *100 Women Who Shaped World History,* p. 874.

Fashion Design

1920 • Coco Chanel (1883–1971), the French couturier, was the first person to introduce the chemise dress, in 1920 in Paris. In 1924, Chanel created the famous perfume, Chanel No.5.

Sources: Stetler, *Almanac of Famous People,* p. 371; Uglow, *The Continuum Dictionary of Women's Biography,* pp. 117–18.

1931 • Elsa Schiaparelli (1890–1973), who was born in Rome but settled in Paris in the early 1920s, was the first woman to design clothing with padded shoulders, in Paris during the 1931–32 fashion season. In 1939, introduced her trademark color, shocking pink.

Sources: Stetler, *Almanac of Famous People,* p. 1695; Uglow, *The Continuum Dictionary of Women's Biography,* p. 483.

Fashion designer Coco Chanel

Modern dance
choreographer Martha
Graham

1938 • Edith Head (1907–1986), the American fashion designer responsible for the costumes in such films as *She Done Him Wrong* (1933) and *Roman Holiday* (1954), in 1938 became the first woman to hold the post of Chief Designer at Paramount Studio in Hollywood. Head was nominated for 35 Academy Awards, and won the award eight times.

Sources: Stetler, *Almanac of Famous People,* p. 896; Uglow, *The Continuum Dictionary of Women's Biography,* p. 252.

Mary Quant popularized the
miniskirt.

1960s • Mary Quant (b. 1934), a British designer who began her career in
textiles in 1955, was the first female designer to popularize the miniskirt,
through her work in London in the 1960s. She became internationally famous
and produced over twenty collections a year by the end of the decade. Since
1970, she has been a member of the fashion establishment and has diversified
her interests, moving from clothing to cosmetics.

Sources: Quant, *Quant by Quant;* Stetler, *Almanac of Famous People,* p. 1563; Uglow, *The Continuum Dictionary of Women's Biography,* p. 443.

1970s • Rei Kawakubo (b. 1942), one of the most influential fashion designers of the late twentieth century, is known as the founder of "raven fashion." Her work is untraditional and emphasizes such elements as holes, asymmetry, rug-like textures, and austerity. She established her own brand of clothing, "Comme des Garçons," in 1973.

Sources: Uglow, *The Continuum Dictionary of Women's Biography*, p. 294.

Late 1970s • Gloria Morgan Vanderbilt (b. 1924), an American heiress who has tried numerous public careers, was the first woman to design high-priced jeans, in the 1970s. She is also remembered for the famous custody suit in which she as a child was the pawn of her wealthy parents.

Sources: Stetler, *Almanac of Famous People*, p. 1930; Uglow, *The Continuum Dictionary of Women's Biography*, p. 554; Vanderbilt, *Once Upon a Time*; Vanderbilt, *Woman-to-Woman*.

Film

1896 • Alice Guy (1873–1968) was the world's first producer-director of films. She may also have been the first person to bring a fictional film to the screen. At the International Exhibition in Paris in 1896, Guy's movie *La Fée aux Choux* (*The Cabbage Fairy*) was shown for the first time by the Gaumont film company. Guy went on to make numerous one-reelers for Gaumont, even experimenting with sound as early as 1905. In 1910, she founded Solax, her own studio and production company, in Paris, and served as its first president and director-in-chief. The French government awarded her the Legion d'Honneur in 1953.

Sources: Acker, *Reel Women: Pioneers of the Cinema, 1896 to the Present*, pp. 7–12; Freligh, "Pioneer's Films Show at Two Sites," *Cleveland Plain Dealer* (28 June 1994), 4-E; Katz, *The Film Encyclopedia*, p. 519; Uglow, *The Continuum Dictionary of Women's Biography*, p. 240.

Early 20th century • Lois Weber (1881–1939) was the first consistently successful American woman to direct motion pictures. Working first in New York City and then in Hollywood, California, Weber made her career in silent films directing such stars as Mildred Harris, Billie Dove and Anna Pavlova. In 1917, she opened her own studio, Lois Weber Productions. Her work spans the period of early cinema, beginning in 1911. She made her last film, *White Heat*, in 1934.

Sources: Acker, *Reel Women: Pioneers of the Cinema, 1896 to the Present*, pp. 12–16; James, *Notable American Women*, vol. 3, pp. 553–55.

Elvira Notari (1875–1946) was the first female filmmaker in her native Italy. She began her prolific career early in the twentieth century and is remembered for her documentary-style work on street life in Naples. Her popular movies were forerunners of the later neorealism style, but were suppressed by Italy's Fascist regime in the late 1930s.

Sources: Bruno, *Streetwalking on a Ruined Map*.

c.1910 • Florence Lawrence, known as "The Biograph Girl" when she began her career at the American Mutoscope and Biograph Company (one of the earliest film studios), was the first woman film star to receive screen credit by her name (until then, silent film stars had been anonymous, other than a stage star reenacting a stage role).

Sources: James, *Notable American Women,* vol. 2. pp. 374–75; Sanders, *The First of Everything,* p. 266.

1910s • Anita Loos (1893–1981), an American screenwriter and novelist, was the first person to use only "talking titles" (titles that conveyed dialogue) in silent films. She wrote movie scripts for D. W. Griffith between 1912 and 1916 (including the subtitles for his famous *Intolerance* in 1916) and later screenplays for films starring Douglas Fairbanks. Loos is also remembered for her novel *Gentlemen Prefer Blondes,* published in 1925 and produced as a play in 1951 and as a musical and a film in 1953.

Sources: Acker, *Reel Women: Pioneers of the Cinema, 1896 to the Present,* pp. 175–180; Stetler, *Almanac of Famous People,* p. 1218.

1913 • Mabel Ethelreid Normand (1893–1930), the actress who starred in Mack Senett comedies and often appeared opposite Charlie Chaplin, became the first film star to throw a custard pie when she flung one at Ben Turpin in 1913 in an early Sennett movie made in Edendale, California.

Sources: Fowler, *Father Goose*; James, *Notable American Women,* vol. 2, pp. 635–37; Parsons, *The Gay Illiterate*; Sennett, *King of Comedy.*

1915 • Natalie Kalmus (1892–1965), an American filmmaker, was the co-inventor, with her husband Herbert T. Kalmus, of Technicolor, a process they first developed in 1915. As the leading consultant for Technicolor, Natalie Kalmus persuaded Hollywood to use her process and worked with filmmakers as an artistic advisor. Until 1948, her name appeared as "Color Consultant" on every motion picture using Technicolor.

Sources: Acker, *Reel Women: Pioneers of the Cinema, 1896 to the Present,* pp. 277–79; Halliwell, *The Filmgoier's Companion,* p. 532.

Musidora (1884–1957), the stage name of French filmmaker Jeanne Roques, was the first woman to portray a vampire in a motion picture. She starred in *Les Vampires,* a film made in Paris in 1915. Wearing a single-piece black leotard, she impressed audiences as an androgynous force. Musidora went on to a distinguished career in film, collaborating with French author Sidonie-Gabrielle Colette and founding her own company, La Société des Films Musidora, in Paris in 1918. She starred in, produced, and directed films until 1950, but also made her career as a fiction writer and a journalist.

Sources: Acker, *Reel Women: Pioneers of the Cinema, 1896 to the Present,* pp. 292–95; Katz, *The Film Encyclopedia,* p. 990.

1916 • Nell Shipman (1892–1970), an American film director and producer, was the first person to direct a feature-length wildlife adventure film. *God's Country and the Woman* was made in southern California in 1916. Shipman, with this film, also became the first person to use an enclosed dark stage for interior film shots.

Sources: Acker, *Reel Women: Pioneers of the Cinema, 1896 to the Present,* pp. 59–61; Fulbright, "Queen of the Dog Sleds," *Classic Film Collector,* Fall 1969, p. 31; Shipman, *The Talking Screen and My Silent Heart.*

Mary Pickford (1893–1979) was the first movie star to form and own a film company. In 1916 she created the Mary Pickford Film Corporation in Hollywood, California. In 1919 she helped to establish United Artists (which absorbed her company) with her friends D. W. Griffith, Charlie Chaplin, and Douglas Fairbanks.

Sources: Acker, *Reel Women: Pioneers of the Cinema, 1896 to the Present,* pp. 53–56; Read and Witlieb, *The Book of Women's Firsts,* pp. 346–47; Uglow, *The Continuum Dictionary of Women's Biography,* pp. 432–33.

1917 • Marion E. Wong, an American actress, was the first president of the Mandarin Film Company, in Oakland, California, in 1917. This organization, the first film production company to be staffed entirely by Chinese Americans, had its own studio and starred Wong and her sister in its first movie, *The Curse of Quon Qwan,* released in 1917.

Sources: Acker, *Reel Women: Pioneers of the Cinema, 1896 to the Present,* p. 111; Weiser, *Womanlist,* p. 185.

1920s • Esther Shub (1894–1959) was the first woman to become a creative editor of Soviet compilation films. In 1927 she wrote and edited a compilation film for the anniversary of the Russian Revolution, *The Fall of the Romanov Dynasty.* Filmmaker Sergei Eisenstein consulted her when he made his famous *October.* She is also remembered for her outstanding work on such films as *Spain* (1939), *Twenty Years of Soviet Cinema* (1940), and *Across the Araks* (1947).

Sources: Acker, *Reel Women: Pioneers of the Cinema, 1896 to the Present,* p. 322; Uglow, *The Continuum Dictionary of Women's Biography,* p. 497.

In Hollywood in the 1920s, Gloria Swanson (1899–1983) became the first silent movie star to earn $20,000 a week. She founded Swanson Productions in 1926, which supported director Erich von Stroheim's *Queen Kelly,* in which she played one of her most powerful roles. She is also remembered for her portrayal of the character Norma Desmond in Billy Wilder's *Sunset Boulevard.*

Sources: Macpherson, *Leading Ladies;* pp. 29-31; Uglow, *The Continuum Dictionary of Women's Biography,* p. 526.

Mae West (1892–1980) was the first stage and later screen comedienne to make the work of 20th-century sexologists (among them Sigmund Freud, Carl Jung, Alfred Adler, and Havelock Ellis) an integral part of her work. Sexuality was an element in her early vaudeville career, but in such notorious shows as *Sex,* which ran on Broadway in the 1920s, West revealed a sophisticated understanding of the complexities of her subject. After this show, her first play, was closed down by the police, she mounted a second in 1927, *The Drag,* about homosexuality, which ran for only two weeks, again closing because of public out-

cry. West went on to a distinguished film career in Hollywood between 1932 and 1943 in which she exerted an extraordinary measure of creative control over her work.

Sources: Acker, *Reel Women: Pioneers of the Cinema, 1896 to the Present,* pp. 181–86; Stetler, *Almanac of Famous People,* p. 1998; West, *Goodness Had Nothing to Do with It*; West, *Mae West on Sex, Health and ESP.*

Anne Bauchens (1882–1967), a pioneering American film editor, was the first film editor to be written into a director's contract. Cecil B. De Mille was so impressed with her work on his films, beginning in Hollywood in 1919, that he refused to work with any other editor. Every one of his films after this date until 1956 was cut by Bauchens.

Sources: Acker, *Reel Women: Pioneers of the Cinema, 1896 to the Present,* pp. 262–64; De Mille, *The Autobiography.*

1920 • Maria Nikolaijevna Yermolova (1853–1928), a Russian actress known for her portrayal of active and independent women, was the first woman to receive the title of People's Artist of the Republic, in Moscow in 1920. She supported the Russian Revolution of 1917, and in 1922, a studio of the famous Maly Theatre in Moscow was named after her, later becoming the well-known Yermalova Theatre.

Sources: Uglow, *The Continuum Dictionary of Women's Biography,* p. 596.

Lillian Gish (1896–1993), the famous American film actress, was the subject of the first movie close-up. The pioneering director D. W. Griffith had his cameraman move in to shoot the icicles on Gish's face in *Way Down East* in 1920.

Sources: Acker, *Reel Women: Pioneers of the Cinema, 1896 to the Present,* pp. 62–64; Stetler, *Almanac of Famous People,* p. 782.

1922 • Pola Negri (1894–1987), a Polish actress, was the first European film star to be invited to Hollywood, in 1922. She had a popular career in silent films, but her heavy accent prevented her from playing parts after the coming of sound. In 1934, she returned to Europe, but settled again in the United States during World War II.

Sources: Stetler, *Almanac of Famous People,* p. 1416; Uglow, *The Continuum Dictionary of Women's Biography,* p. 398.

Jane Murfin (1893–1955), an American playwright and screenwriter, was the first person to write a series of film scripts starring a dog. In Hollywood, California, in 1922, Murfin wrote screenplays that featured her own German shepherd. Rin Tin Tin, her canine protagonist, made his debut two years later, in 1924.

Sources: Acker, *Reel Women: Pioneers of the Cinema, 1896 to the Present,* p. 208; Slide, *Early Women Directors.*

1923 • Marguerite Clark (1883–1940), an American stage and screen actress best known for her roles in *Wildflowers* (1914) and *Uncle Tom's Cabin* (1919), was the first woman from outside the city of New Orleans to serve as Queen of the Alexis Carnival Ball during the New Orleans Mardi Gras, in 1923.

Sources: James, *Notable American Women,* vol. 1, pp. 340–41; Zukor and Kramer, *The Public Is Never Wrong.*

1926 • Lotte Reiniger (1899–1981) was the first woman to make a full-length animated film. Collaborating with her husband, Carl Koch, she developed animation techniques using silhouette figures made out of cardboard, tin, and paper and made the first feature-length animated movie, *The Adventures of Prince Achmed,* in Germany in 1926.

Sources:; Acker, *Reel Women: Pioneers of the Cinema, 1896 to the Present,* pp. 241–42; Uglow, *The Continuum Dictionary of Women's Biography,* p. 453.

1927 • Bryher (1894–1983), who legally changed her name from Annie Winifred Ellerman, was the founder, with the imaginative support of her husband Kenneth Macpherson, of *Close-Up,* the first serious film journal, in Vevey, Switzerland. A British writer who supported numerous causes with her great wealth, Bryher is perhaps best known for her lifelong friendship with the poet H. D.

Sources: Guest, *Herself Defined: The Poet H.D. and Her World,* pp. 189–91; Uglow, *The Continuum Dictionary of Women's Biography,* p. 94.

Germaine Dulac (1882–1942), a French journalist and filmmaker, was the first person to make a Surrealist film. *The Seashell and the Clergyman*, written by Antonin Artaud, was released in 1927.

Sources:; Acker, *Reel Women: Pioneers of the Cinema, 1896 to the Present,* pp. 289–92; Uglow, *The Continuum Dictionary of Women's Biography,* p. 176.

1928 • Janet Gaynor (1906–1984) became the first woman to win an Academy Award when in 1928 she was named best actress. The first Oscars were awarded for cumulative work for the year. Gaynor's award included three films: *Sunrise, Seventh Heaven* (both 1927), and *Street Angel* (1928). She received a second Academy Award for her best-known film, *A Star Is Born*, in 1937.

Sources: Katz, *The Film Encyclopedia,* p. 472; Read and Witlieb, *The Book of Women's Firsts,* pp. 174–175.

1929 • Dorothy Arzner (1900–1979) was the first woman to direct a sound film. An experienced editor and director, she was chosen by Paramount to direct their first sound film, *The Wild Party*, in 1929. Arzner was also the first woman to become a major Hollywood director. She began her film career as a typist at Paramount, but moved on to movie editing and in 1925 wrote, helped shoot, and edited *Old Ironsides*. She directed 17 feature films and worked with many female stars.

Sources: Acker, *Reel Women: Pioneers of the Cinema, 1896 to the Present,* pp. 21–29; Johnston, *The Work of Dorothy Arzner: Towards a Feminist Cinema*; Read and Witlieb, *The Book of Women's Firsts,* pp. 25–26.

Wanda Jakubowska (b. 1907), a Polish film producer and director, was the cofounder of the radical Society of the Devotees of the Artistic Film, in 1929. She is know for her documentary films, especially *The Last Stop,* a film she made in 1948 about her concentration camp experiences. In 1955 she became artistic director of the society, known by the acronymn START.

Sources: Uglow, *The Continuum Dictionary of Women's Biography,* p. 280.

1931 • Frances Marion (1888–1973) was the first woman to win an Academy Award for writing. She was honored in Hollywood, California, in 1931 for her work on *The Big House* (1930), one of the first "talkies."

Sources: Acker, *Reel Women: Pioneers of the Cinema, 1896 to the Present,* pp. 171–75; Marion, *How to Write and Sell Film Stories*; Read and Witlieb, *The Book of Women's Firsts,* pp. 268–69.

Leontine Sagan (1899–1974), an Austrian filmmaker, was the first person to make a German film produced cooperatively. Her first film, *Mädchen in Uniform,* was made in Germany in 1931. With an all-female cast, no one was paid a salary, but shares of the profits were distributed to the actors and crew. The film's lesbian content and anti-authoritarian values later caused Nazi official Joseph Goebbels to ban it as "unhealthy."

Sources: Acker, *Reel Women: Pioneers of the Cinema, 1896 to the Present,* pp. 320–22; Erens, *Sexual Stratagems*; Russo, *The Celluloid Closet*; Uglow, *The Continuum Dictionary of Women's Biography,* p. 475.

Kinuyo Tanaka (1910–1971), one of Japan's most famous film stars, whose career spanned over 50 years of her country's cinema, was the first Japanese film actress to star in a "talkie." She played the female protagonist in Japan's first talkie, *Madame and Wife,* in 1931.

Sources: Uglow, *The Continuum Dictionary of Women's Biography,* p. 530.

1932 • Claire Parker (1906–1981), a pioneering American film animator working with Russian filmmaker Alexander Alexeieff in Paris in 1932, was the co-inventor of the "pinboard" animation technique, a process analogous to using halftones in black-and-white photography. They first used this technique in their now classic film *Night on Bald Mountain,* released in 1933.

Sources: Acker, *Reel Women: Pioneers of the Cinema, 1896 to the Present,* p. 243.

Mid-1930s • Marlene Dietrich (1901–1992), the German film actress who moved to the United States in 1930, was the first woman to refuse to make films in her own country. In the 1930s she refused to return to act in the cinema in a Nazi-dominated industry.

Sources: Dietrich, *My Life Story;* Uglow, *The Continuum Dictionary of Women's Biography,* p. 168.

1937 • Gale Sondergaard (1899–1985) was the first woman to receive an Academy Award for best supporting actress. She was honored in 1937, the first year this award was given, for her performance in *Anthony Adverse.*

Sources: Read and Witlieb, *The Book of Women's Firsts,* pp. 413–14.

1940s • American Maya Deren (1922–1961) was the first woman to succeed as an independent filmmaker. Her major works include *Meshes of the Afternoon* (1943) and *Ritual in Transfigured Time* (1946). A measure of her achievement is that she was the first person to receive an award from the John Simon Guggenheim Memorial Foundation, in 1946.

Sources: Acker, *Reel Women: Pioneers of the Cinema, 1896 to the Present,* pp. 95–97; Chicago, *The Dinner Party,* p. 214; Stetler, *Almanac of Famous People,* p. 541.

1940 • English animator Joy Batchelor (b. 1914–1991) cofounded Halas and Batchelor Cartoon Films in England with her husband, the Hungarian animator John Halas, in 1940. This company, an innovator in the production of animated cinema, produced and directed cartoons for cinema, television, and commercials as well as for promotional, scientific, and instructional films.

Sources: Halliwell, *The Filmgoer's Companion,* p. 90; Smith, *The World Encyclopedia of Film,* p. 17.

Opposite page: Actress Janet Gaynor as she appeared in "The Young in Heart."

Anne Bauchens (1881–1967) began her career as a film editor in 1918. She became the first woman to receive an Academy Award for film editing in 1940 when she won an Oscar for her work on *North West Mounted Police*.

Sources: Read and Witlieb, *The Book of Women's Firsts*, p. 42.

1940s through 1960s

• Ida Lupino (1918–1995) was the first woman to make her career in four areas of American film: as an actoress, a director, a producer, and a writer. After working with Paramount and Warner Brothers, she founded her own production company, Film Makers, with Collier Young. She wrote the script for its first production, and when the director died while on the film, she took over. She directed, produced, and co-wrote each subsequent film. The company was innovative in choosing controversial subjects, such as unmarried mothers and career women, and in fostering new talent.

Sources: Acker, *Reel Women: Pioneers of the Cinema, 1896 to the Present*, pp. 74–78; Stetler, *Almanac of Famous People*, p. 1235; Uglow, *The Continuum Dictionary of Women's Biography*, p. 337.

1941

• Screen actress Bette Davis (1908–1989) became the first woman to serve as head of the Academy of Motion Picture Arts and Sciences when she assumed the role in 1941. She was also the first woman to receive the American Film Institute's highest honor, the Life Achievement Award, in 1977.

Sources: Read and Witlieb, *The Book of Women's Firsts*, p. 115; Stetler, *Almanac of Famous People*, p. 512; Uglow, *The Continuum Dictionary of Women's Biography*, pp. 150–51; Walker, *Bette Davis*.

Mid-20th century

• Dorothy Jean Dandridge (1923–1965) was the first black actress to be acclaimed as a star in American cinema. She was the first black woman to have her picture on the cover of *Life* magazine, appearing there in 1953 after she won attention for her role in the all-black film *Bright Road*. In 1955, Dandridge was nominated for an Oscar for her performance in *Carmen Jones*.

Sources: Smith, *Notable Black American Women*, pp. 248-9; Stetler, *Almanac of Famous People*, p. 498.

1952

• Nancy Littlefield (b. 1929) was the first woman to gain acceptance into the Directors Guild of America, in 1952. Admission is based on a series of rigorous exams. Littlefield has made her film career in New York, working for television and teaching.

Sources: Read and Witlieb, *The Book of Women's Firsts*, pp. 255–56.

1956

• Grace Kelly (1929–1982) was the first American film actress to become a princess. She attained this distinction when she gave up a successful career in film to marry Prince Rainier III of Monaco in 1956.

Sources: Spader, *Grace: The Secret Lives of a Princess;* Uglow, *The Continuum Dictionary of Women's Biography*, p. 232.

1959

• Nuria Espert (b. 1935), a Spanish actress and director, was the founder of the Nuria Espert Company in Barcelona, Spain, in 1959. Espert has

Singer and actress Dorothy
Dandridge

toured with this theatre company as both performer and director, establishing
an international reputation.

Sources: Uglow, *The Continuum Dictionary of Women's Biography,* p. 192.

1960s • Margaret Rutherford (1892–1972), an English actress, was the
first woman to create an international reputation by playing mystery writer Agatha Christie's Miss Marple in films and television broadcasts during the
1960s. Rutherford is remembered for her portrayal of the apparently innocent
and naive elderly lady who is, in fact, a clever and sophisticated sleuth. The ac-

tress was also known for her many London stage performances, beginning in 1925.

Sources: Rutherford, *Margaret Rutherford: An Autobiography;* Uglow, *The Continuum Dictionary of Women's Biography,* pp. 469–70.

1962 • Shirley Clarke (b. 1925), an American filmmaker, was the cofounder, with Jonas Mekas, of the New York Filmmakers' Cooperative in 1962. She began making films in 1962 and became the first person to shoot a film in Harlem with her second film, *The Cool World,* in 1963.

Sources: Acker, *Reel Women: Pioneers of the Cinema, 1896 to the Present,* pp. 97–99; Uglow, *The Continuum Dictionary of Women's Biography,* p. 127.

1963 • Brianne Murphy (b. 1937), an American camerawoman born in England, was the first female director of photography to be admitted into the Hollywood feature-film union, in 1963. Murphy has made her career both in Hollywood films and in television.

Sources: Acker, *Reel Women: Pioneers of the Cinema, 1896 to the Present,* pp. 280–82.

1967 • Dede Allen (b. 1923), an American film editor who began to work in Hollywood in 1943, was the first person in her field to receive a solo credit among the screen titles. She was recognized for her skill and creativity in editing *Bonnie and Clyde,* directed by Arthur Penn in 1967. She is also remembered for her imaginative work on such films as *The Hustler* (1961), *Serpico* (1974), and *The Milagro Beanfield War* (1988).

Sources: Acker, *Reel Women: Pioneers of the Cinema, 1896 to the Present,* pp. 224–27; McGilligan, "Dede Allen," *Women and the Cinema,* ed. Karyn and Peary, pp. 199–207.

1968 • Katharine Hepburn (b. 1909) was the first woman to win an Oscar for best actress three times: in 1933, for *Morning Glory*; in 1967, for *Guess Who's Coming to Dinner*; and in 1968, for *The Lion in Winter*. In 1981, she became the first actress to win the Oscar for best actress four times, when she won for *On Golden Pond*. Hepburn's acting career has spanned over half a century in memorable film portraits that range from comedy to tragedy.

Sources: Chicago, *The Dinner Party,* p. 215; Edwards, *Katharine Hepburn*; Uglow, *The Continuum Dictionary of Women's Biography,* p. 255.

1970s • Christine Choy (b. 1954), an American filmmaker born in China to a Korean father and a Chinese mother, was the first Asian American woman to achieve a successful career in documentary filmmaking. She has worked as an editor, director, and producer since 1971, completing nearly 40 films. Her works include *Who is Vincent Chin*, which was nominated for an Academy Award, and *Fortune Cookie* for the Public Broadcasting Service. Choy founded Third World Newsreel and has served as chair of the New York University School of Film.

Sources: Acker, *Reel Women: Pioneers of the Cinema, 1896 to the Present,* pp. 123–25; Gall and Natividad, *Asian American Almanac,* p. 633.

Filmmaker Christine Choy

Chantal Anne Akerman (b. 1950), a Belgian filmmaker who directs in both Europe and America, was the first to work with an all-female staff of technicians. She began her career in the early 1970s and focuses on relationships among women and on female sexuality.

Sources: Acker, *Reel Women: Pioneers of the Cinema, 1896 to the Present,* pp. 317–19; Uglow, *The Continuum Dictionary of Women's Biography,* p. 11.

1970 • Barbara Loden (1934–1980), a film actress and director who grew up in poverty in Asheville, North Carolina, was the first American feminist film director. She made her reputation by directing *Wanda*, a documentary study of a poor woman from the coalfields of her childhood. The film won the International Critic's Prize in Venice in 1970 and has come to be seen as a plea not only for more opportunities for women but for female directors as well.

Sources: Uglow, *The Continuum Dictionary of Women's Biography,* pp. 331–32.

1971 • Stephanie Rothman (c.1925), an American filmmaker who began her career in exploitation films with Roger Corman, was the first woman to win a fellowship for directing from the Director's Guild of America, in 1971.

Sources: Acker, *Reel Women: Pioneers of the Cinema, 1896 to the Present,* pp. 46–47; Kay and Peary, *Women and the Cinema.*

Hannah Weinstein (1911–1984), an American film producer and civil rights and peace activist, was the founder of Third World Cinema, in New York City in 1971. This association, with forty percent of its stock owned by the East Harlem Community Organization, encouraged films that involved blacks and women in all aspects of production. Among the motion pictures Weinstein made with this group were *Claudine* (1972), *Greased Lightning* (1977), and *Stir Crazy* (1980).

Sources: Acker, *Reel Women: Pioneers of the Cinema, 1896 to the Present,* pp. 150–51; Uglow, *The Continuum Dictionary of Women's Biography,* p. 573.

1972 • Jane Fonda (b. 1937), the American film star also known as a political activist, was the cofounder, with fellow actor Donald Sutherland, of the Anti-War Troupe in 1972. This group advocated opposition to the war between the United States and Viet Nam.

Sources: Freedland, *Jane Fonda;* Stetler, *Almanac of Famous People,* p. 695; Uglow, *The Continuum Dictionary of Women's Biography,* pp. 208-9.

1974 • Julia Miller Phillips (b. 1944) was the first woman to win an Academy Award as a producer. She was honored in 1974 for *The Sting*, which won an Oscar for best movie. She wrote a popular book on life in Hollywood in 1990, *You'll Never Eat Lunch in This Town Again.*

Sources: Phillips, *You'll Never Eat Lunch in This Town Again;* Read and Witlieb, *The Book of Women's Firsts,* p. 345.

1975 • Kathleen Nolan (b. 1933) became the first woman to serve as president of the Screen Actors' Guild in Hollywood, California, when she was elected to this position in 1975. While the nominating committee favored a man for the job, Nolan ran successfully by petitioning to be slated as an independent candidate.

Sources: O'Neill, *The Woman's Book of World Records and Achievements,* pp. 309-12; Read and Witlieb, *The Book of Women's Firsts,* p. 314.

1977 • Perry Miller Adato was the first woman to win an award from the Directors Guild of America. She was honored in 1977 for her television documentary *Georgia O'Keeffe.*

Sources: O'Neill, *The Woman's Book of World Records and Achievements,* p. 496; Read and Witlieb, *The Book of Women's Firsts,* p. 9; Weiser, *Womanlist,* p. 189.

Dyan Cannon (b. 1939) was the first woman to be nominated for Academy Awards as both director and actress. She was nominated in 1977 for the category of director of the best short film (*Number One,* 1976) and in 1979 for best supporting actress in *Heaven Can Wait* (1978).

Sources: Read and Witlieb, *The Book of Women's Firsts,* p. 82; Weiser, *Womanlist,* p. 189.

1982 • Julie Andrews (b. 1935) became the first actress to play the part of a woman playing a man playing a woman, in the film *Victor/Victoria,* directed by her husband, Blake Edwards, in 1982. Known for her roles as nice women, Andrews has also shown wit and versatility.

Sources: Stetler, *Almanac of Famous People,* p. 58; Uglow, *The Continuum Dictionary of Women's Biography,* p. 18.

Susan Seidelman (b. 1952), a filmmaker educated at New York University, was the first American to direct an independent film shown in competition at the Cannes Film Festival in France. While *Smithereens,* Seidelman's first film, won no awards when shown at Cannes in 1982, she went on to a promising career when she directed the successful *Desperately Seeking Susan* in 1984.

Sources: Acker, *Reel Women: Pioneers of the Cinema, 1896 to the Present,* pp. 40–42.

1983 • Barbra Streisand (b. 1942), an American singer and actress, was the first woman to produce, direct, co-author, star in, and sing in a major motion picture, performing multiple roles in her film *Yentl,* in 1983. She is known for her concert performances, Broadway musicals, numerous popular recordings, and a film career in which she is assertive about maintaining a degree of creative control.

Sources: Acker, *Reel Women: Pioneers of the Cinema, 1896 to the Present,* pp. 87–89; Spender, *Streisand: The Woman and the Legend;* Uglow, *The Continuum Dictionary of Women's Biography,* p. 522.

Cathérine Deneuve (b. 1943), a French actress known for her beauty and acting skills, was the founder of a film group, the Société Cardeva, in 1983. From 1971 until 1979 she was president and director of Films de la Citronille.

Sources: Gerber, *Cathérine Deneuve;* Uglow, *The Continuum Dictionary of Women's Biography,* p. 160.

1985 • Donna Deitch (c.1945) was the first female filmmaker to make a taboo sexual topic a box-office hit. Her *Desert Hearts* (1985), based on Jane Rule's

1964 novel *Desert of the Heart,* was the first lesbian love story to obtain mainstream distribution.

Sources: Acker, *Reel Women: Pioneers of the Cinema, 1896 to the Present,* pp. 42–44.

1989 • Euzhan Palcy (b. 1957), an American filmmaker born in Martinique, was the first black woman to direct a feature-length Hollywood film. *A Dry White Season,* based on a novel by André Brink, concerns apartheid in South Africa and was released, with Marlon Brando as its star, in 1989.

Sources: Acker, *Reel Women: Pioneers of the Cinema, 1896 to the Present,* pp. 118–21; Smith, *Black Firsts,* p. 9.

1990 • Margaret Booth (b. 1898), a pioneering American film editor, was the first woman to receive a Lifetime Achievement Award from the American Cinema Editors, in Hollywood, California, in 1990. She was honored for a career of creative work in the cutting room, beginning in 1916. She is remembered for such films as *The Barretts of Wimpole Street* (1934), *The Way We Were* (1973), and *Annie* (1982).

Sources: Acker, *Reel Women: Pioneers of the Cinema, 1896 to the Present,* pp. 221–22.

Ruby Oliver (b. 1942) was the first black American woman to direct, write, produce, and sing in a 35 millimeter film. She created the film *Love Your Mama* while earning a degree from Columbia College in Chicago, Illinois, in 1990. This autobiographical film focuses on a mother-daughter relationship.

Sources: Acker, *Reel Women: Pioneers of the Cinema, 1896 to the Present,* pp. 121–22.

Fine Arts

Legendary • The legendary Greek woman Arachne was the first weaver. According to Greek myth, she discovered the art of making nets and weaving cloth so beautiful that her work angered the goddess Athena, who destroyed it. When Arachne hanged herself in despair, Athena took pity on her and turned her into a spider.

Sources: Chicago, *The Dinner Party,* p. 112.

7th century B.C. • Kora is one of the earliest female artists on record and is credited with being the first artist to create a bas-relief, in the seventh century B.C. in ancient Greece.

Sources: Chicago, *The Dinner Party,* p. 121.

10th century • Ende, a Spanish artist and illuminator during the tenth century, was the first woman to paint an extensive cycle of miniatures. She was also instrumental in painting the *Gerona Apocalypse.*

Sources: Chicago, *The Dinner Party,* p. 138.

12th century • Guda, a twelfth-century German writer and artist, is the first woman in the West whose self-portrait has survived. She signed her discourse on morality with a picture of herself; her manuscript is now in Frankfurt, Germany.

Sources: Chicago, *The Dinner Party,* p. 136.

15th century • Honorata Rodiana (d. 1472) was the first female fresco painter. She worked for the ruler of Cremona in Italy until one of his courtiers attempted to rape her. She fled, disguised as a man.

Sources: Chicago, *The Dinner Party,* p. 161.

16th century • Caterina van Hemessen (1528–1587) was the first Flemish female artist. Born and brought up in Antwerp, Belgium, she worked in that city, and between 1556 and 1568, in Spain under the patronage of Queen Mary of Hungary, former Regent of the Netherlands.

Sources: Tufts, *Our Hidden Heritage;* Uglow, *The Continuum Dictionary of Women's Biography,* p. 254.

1559 • Sofonisba Anguissola (Sophonisba Anguisciola) (c.1535–1625) was the first woman artist to become an eminent professional painter. She studied with Bernardo Campi, then established her own studio. In 1559, Anguissola was invited to serve as court portrait painter to Phillip II of Italy. Her work focuses on domestic life and her example is thought to have inspired other female artists.

Sources: Chicago, *The Dinner Party,* p. 160; Uglow, *The Continuum Dictionary of Women's Biography,* pp. 19–20.

Early 17th century • Clara Peeters (1594–c.1657) was the first Dutch woman to paint still lifes. She specialized in scenes of food and tableware and was particularly skilled in depicting reflected light.

Sources: Uglow, *The Continuum Dictionary of Women's Biography,* p. 428.

17th century • Artemisia Gentileschi (1590–1652) was the first established female artist to paint from a woman's point of view. She is known for her portraits of seventeenth-century figures as well as for her religious and historical works, and was honored by admission to the Academy of Design in Florence.

Sources: Chicago, *The Dinner Party,* pp. 81–82; Uglow, *The Continuum Dictionary of Women's Biography,* p. 222.

1631 • Judith Leyster (1609–1660) was the first female Dutch artist to portray sexual harassment. Her best work focuses on everyday life and she is unusual in recording the lives of women and children in domestic settings. Her work depicting men offering their unwanted sexual attention to women is *The Proposition,* painted in 1631.

Sources: Tufts, *Our Hidden Heritage*; Uglow, *The Continuum Dictionary of Women's Biography,* pp. 325–26.

1769 • Angelica Kauffman (1741–1807), a Swiss painter who worked widely throughout Europe, was a cofounder of the Royal Academy, in London in 1769. Paintings by her were included in every exhibition there between 1769

and 1782. She was an original colorist, and her feminine and graceful compositions were much admired by her contemporaries. Her work became well-
known through engravings by Francesco Bartolozzi.

Sources: Magnusson, *Larousse Biographical Dictionary,* p. 811; Schmidt, 400 Outstanding Women
of the World, p. 380–81.

1795 • Adelaide Labille-Guiard (1749–1803), a French portrait painter renowned for her pastel masterpiece, "Portrait of the Sculptor Pajou," was the
first woman to obtain an apartment in the Louvre, a famous French palace that
was converted into an art museum in the eighteenth century. It had previously
been the territory of male artists and students. A distinguished professional in
her field, she worked continuously for greater opportunities for female artists.

Sources: Passez, *Adelaide Baille-Guiard;* Uglow, *The Continuum Dictionary of Women's Biography,*
p. 308.

1800 • Jeanne Françoise Julie Adelaide Récamier (1777–1849) was the first
French salon hostess to be painted by David, in 1800 in Paris. His famous picture of her now hangs in the Louvre. Madame Récamier, who was called Julie,
is remembered for her parties that included both writers and politicians,
among them Benjamin Constant and Châteaubriand.

Sources: Uglow, *The Continuum Dictionary of Women's Biography,* p. 452; Wharton, *Queens of Society,* p. 329–375.

1833 • Anne Hall (1792–1863) was the first woman elected to full membership in the National Academy of Design. She was honored for her work as a
miniaturist in New York City in 1833.

Sources: James, *Notable American Women,* vol. 2, pp. 117–18; Read and Witlieb, *The Book of Wom-
en's Firsts,* p. 193.

Madame Récamier

1840s • Frances Flora Bond Palmer (1812–1876) was the first female lithographer in the United States. Born and trained in England, she settled in New
York City in the 1840s and opened a lithographic printing and publishing business with her husband. By 1847 she had established herself as the foremost
lithographer in America. In 1849, she joined the staff of the firm of Nathaniel
Currier. A creative lithographer, she drew directly on stone, doing her best
work in the 1850s. She is remembered particularly for her landscapes.

Sources: James, *Notable American Women,* vol. 3, pp. 10–11; Peters, *Currier and Ives: Printmakers
to the American People.*

1852 • Rosa Marie Rosalie Bonheur (1822–1899), the French artist known
for her vivid depiction of animals in her paintings, was the first woman to be
granted official police permission to wear male attire, in Paris in 1852. Bonheur
initially dressed as a man in order to be allowed to observe anatomy at Paris
slaughter houses, but her male attire later became a trademark. Her work was
first exhibited in the Fine Arts Exhibition of 1841 in Paris. In 1853, her work
was judged to be of such quality that she would automatically be admitted to
juried exhibitions, without having to submit works to the examining commit-

Rosa Bonheur

tee first. According to French tradition, this entitled Bonheur to receive the Legion of Honor—but it was denied to her because she was a woman.

Sources: Schmidt, *400 Outstanding Women of the World,* p. 186–87; Uglow, The Continuum Dictionary of Women's Biography, p. 77; Williams, *Queenly Women, Crowned and Uncrowned,* pp. 417–424.

1853 • Elizabeth Ney (1833–1907) was the first woman to attend the Munich Art Academy in Germany. She married and emigrated to the United States, deferring her career in sculpture for 20 years after the birth of her son. In 1893, she resumed her art when she produced a commissioned statue for the Colombian Exhibition in Chicago.

Sources: Chicago, *The Dinner Party,* p. 213.

1873 • Louisine Waldron Elder Havemeyer (1855–1929) was the first American woman to encourage the French Impressionist painter Edgar Degas. While still in boarding school in Paris, Havemeyer was introduced to Degas by Mary Cassatt; she bought one of his pictures soon after, in 1873. She is remembered as an art collector who donated a large part of her holdings to the Metropolitan Museum of Art in New York City.

Sources: Havemeyer, *Sixteen to Sixty: Memoirs of a Collector*; James, *Notable American Women,* vol. 2, pp. 156–57.

Maria Longworth Nichols Storer (1849–1932), an American patron of the arts, was the founder of the Cincinnati May Music Festival in Cincinnati, Ohio, in 1873. She is also remembered as the first person to open an art pottery in Ohio, in Cincinnati in 1880. Active in political circles in Washington, D.C., where her husband served in Congress in the 1890s, Storer became friendly with the Roosevelt family, establishing close ties with this dynasty when her nephew, Nicholas Longworth, married Theodore Roosevelt's daughter Alice.

Sources: James, *Notable American Women,* vol. 3, pp. 391–93; Upton, *Theodore Thomas: A Musical Autobiography.*

1875 • Anne Whitney (1821–1915), an American artist educated in New York, Philadelphia, and Rome, was the first person to win a commission to sculpt a memorial to American statesman Charles Sumner, in Boston in 1875. When it was discovered that she was a woman, however, the commission was revoked. Whitney went on to complete the piece anyway, and it now stands outside the Harvard Law School in Cambridge, Massachusetts. Remembered for her often politically charged work, Whitney was a friend of the major women's rights leaders of her day and supported both abolition and women's suffrage.

Sources: Uglow, *The Continuum Dictionary of Women's Biography,* p. 579.

1876 • Mary Cassatt (1844–1929), an American artist who studied and worked in France, was the first person to exhibit Impressionist paintings in the United States. She began to exhibit in America in 1876. In 1879, a number of her paintings received wide exposure when they appeared through the auspices of the newly formed Society of American Artists. She is particularly well known for her sensitive portraits of women and children in domestic settings.

Sources: Breuning, *Mary Cassatt*; James, *Notable American Women,* vol. 1, pp. 303–5.

1898 • Florence Nightingale Levy (1870–1947), an American advocate of the arts, was the founder of the influential *American Art Annual*, in New York City in 1898. This periodical quickly became a standard and valued reference guide to schools, museums, galleries, and art societies. It also provided biographical listings of artists and a yearly record of exhibits.

Sources: Howes, *Leaders in Education*; James, *Notable American Women,* vol. 2, pp. 395–97.

20th century • Hannah Höch (1889–1971) and a male colleague were the inventors of photomontage. Throughout her life, Höch created collages from lace, buttons, and bits of fabric, often focusing on female experience.

Sources: Chicago, *The Dinner Party,* p. 212; Tierney, *Women's Studies Encyclopedia,* vol. 2, pp. 142–43.

1901 • Isabella Stewart Gardner (1840–1924), an American art collector, was the founder of the Gardner Museum in Boston, Massachusetts. The institution opened its doors to the public on January 1, 1901. Gardner, who took a personal interest in the varied collection of art displayed there, presided over the museum, living on the top floor, for the next twenty years.

Sources: Cater, *Isabella Stewart Gardner and Fenway Court*; James, *Notable American Women,* vol. 2, pp. 15–17.

   May Wilson Preston (1873–1949), an American artist, was the first female member of the Society of Illustrators, which she joined shortly after its establishment in New York City in 1901. Founded by the Ashcan School of artists, illustrators, and painters, who favored a documentary realism in their work, the society included Robert Henri, John Sloan, George B. Luks and Preston's husband, James Preston.

Sources: Glackens, *William Glackens and the Ashcan Group*; James, *Notable American Women,* vol. 3, pp. 98–100; Kuhn, *The Story of the Armory Show.*

1905 • Vanessa Stephen Bell (1879–1961), an English artist and the sister of writer Virginia Woolf, was the founder of the Friday Club in 1905. This discussion group, held at the home Bell shared with her sister and brothers in Bloomsbury, London, drew together the artists and writers later known as the Bloomsbury Group. Bell trained as an artist under Sir Arthur Cope from 1901 to 1904 at the Royal Academy Schools and exhibited in the Post-Impressionist Exhibition in 1912 in London.

Sources: Magnusson, *Larousse Biographical Dictionary,* p. 132; Uglow, *The Continuum Dictionary of Women's Biography,* pp. 59–60.

1909 • Natalia Sergeyevna Goncharova (1881–1962), a Russian painter of international reputation, was the first woman to participate in the modern art Rayonist movement, which she founded with her husband in Moscow in 1909.

Isabella Stewart Gardner

The Rayonists' style of painting was based on their idea of manipulating invisible "rays" emanating from all objects, giving their work a futurist look.

Sources: Chamot, *Natalia Goncharova*; Uglow, *The Continuum Dictionary of Women's Biography,* p. 230.

Gabriele Munter (1877–1962), a German Expressionist painter, was the co-founder, with her close friend, the Russian painter Wassily Kandinsky, of the New Artists Association of Munich, in 1909. She completed her most original paintings in her youth and is remembered for her brilliant work with color and for her studies of women.

Sources: Gowing, *A Biographical Dictionary of Artists,* p. 481; Uglow, *The Continuum Dictionary of Women's Biography,* pp. 391–92.

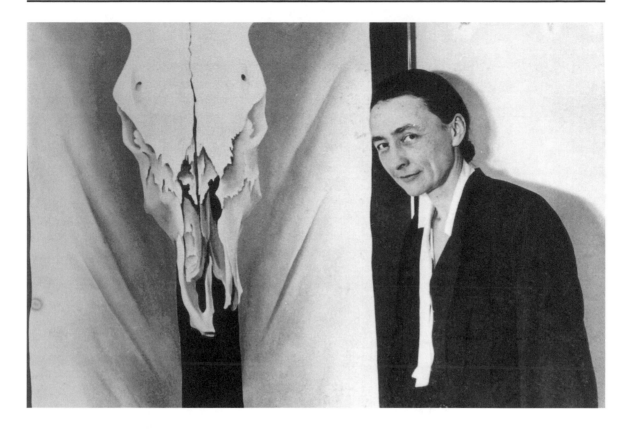

1910 • Cornelia B. Sage Quinton (1879–1936) became the first woman to   Artist Georgia O'Keeffe
head an art museum when she was selected as director of the Albright Art Mu-
seum and Gallery in Buffalo, New York, in 1910. She held this position until
1924.

Sources: Petteys, *Dictionary of Women Artists,* p. 618; Read and Witlieb, *The Book of Women's
Firsts,* p. 354–55.

1920s • Georgia O'Keeffe (1887–1986) was the first acclaimed female artist in America to paint sexually explicit subjects. She began to paint the large
erotic flower canvases in New York City in the 1920s for which she is well
known. She is also remembered for her symbolic still lifes set in the American
West, where she painted beginning in the 1940s, and as the subject of over 500
photographs taken by her life-long companion Alfred Stieglitz.

Sources: Magnusson, *Larousse Biographical Dictionary,* p. 1100; Uglow, *The Continuum Dictionary
of Women's Biography,* p. 411.

1921 • Angeliki Hatzimichali (1895–1956), a Greek writer and folklorist,
was the first person to put on a exhibit of folk art in Greece. Concerned that
traditional folkways and artistic cultural expression were being eclipsed by

modern life, she mounted a show in Athens in 1921. Hatzimichali has also written extensively about folk art and Greek crafts.

Sources: James, *Notable American Women,* vol. 1; Uglow, *The Continuum Dictionary of Women's Biography,* p. 250.

1927 • Anna Charlotte Rice Cooke (1853–1934), the daughter of American missionaries, was the founder of the Honolulu Academy of Arts in 1927. More than a traditional art museum of the time, the academy sought to establish links with the community through a variety of educational programs and constantly changing exhibits.

Sources: James, *Notable American Women,* vol. 1, pp. 377–78; *Koamalu: A Story of Pioneers on Kauai.*

1930 • Juliana Rieser Force (1876–1948) devoted her life to the visual arts. She assisted Gertrude Vanderbilt Whitney in managing the Whitney Studio, a New York City gallery that championed avant-garde American artists. When the gallery became the Whitney Museum in 1930, Force served as its first director, a position she held until her death.

Sources: James, *Notable American Women,* vol. 1, pp. 645–46; Read and Witlieb, *The Book of Women's Firsts.*

1934 • Peggy Guggenheim (1898–1980), an American art collector, was the founder, with the support of her friend Marcel Duchamp, of the Guggenheim-Jeune Art Gallery, in Paris in 1934. She went on to found another gallery in New York City, Art of This Century, in 1940. Guggenheim is remembered as a champion of modern art.

Sources: Guggenheim, *Confessions of an Art Addict;* Guggenheim, *Out of This Century;* Uglow, *The Continuum Dictionary of Women's Biography,* pp. 239–40.

1940 • Anna Mary Moses (1860–1961), known as "Grandma Moses" and remembered for her detailed primitive paintings of rural life, was the first female artist to have her first solo exhibition at the age of 80, in New York City. Her work was discovered by a collector in 1938 and included in an exhibition at the Museum of Modern Art in 1939. Moses is thus probably also the first female artist to exhibit her work at the age of 79.

Sources: Moses, *My Life's History;* Uglow, *The Continuum Dictionary of Women's Biography,* p. 390.

1959 • May Massee (1881–1966) became the first female member of the American Institute of Graphic Arts in 1959. In the same year she became the first woman to receive this organization's gold medal in honor of her work in the field of children's books.

Sources: Read and Witlieb, *The Book of Women's Firsts,* pp. 271–72.

1960s • Helen Kalvak (1901–1984), an artist who began drawing in her late sixties, was the first Inuit woman to chronicle the life of her people in her art. Traveling throughout Canada's Northwest Territories, Kalvak created over 3,000 pictures that vividly convey the traditional culture and activities of the

Copper Inuit, stressing their spiritual life, legends, and ceremonies. She was honored in 1975 with membership in the Royal Canadian Academy of Arts.

Sources: The Continuum Dictionary of Women's Biography, p. 291.

1964 • Sonia Delaunay (1885–1979), a pioneer abstractionist, was the first woman to have an exhibition at the Louvre during her own lifetime, in 1964. She was also the cofounder, with her husband Robert, of the art movement Orphism, which attempted to bring new energy to the decorative and applied arts.

Sources: Chicago, *The Dinner Party,* p. 212; Damase, *Sonia Delaunay: Rhythms and Colors;* Uglow, *The Continuum Dictionary of Women's Biography,* p. 156.

Sheila Hicks (b. 1934), an American weaver of international stature, was the first woman to found a weaving workshop in Germany, at the Wuppertal rug factory in 1964. Educated at Syracuse and Yale Universities, Hicks has traveled widely in South America, Europe, Africa, and India, working with and advising weavers. She also established her own studio in Paris, where she has lived since 1965.

Sources: O'Neil, *The Woman's Book of World Records and Achievements,* p. 606-7; Uglow, *The Continuum Dictionary of Women's Biography,* p. 259.

1965 • Judy Chicago (b. 1939), an American artist who took her surname from the name of the city where she grew up, was the cofounder of the Feminist Studio Workshop in Los Angeles, California, in the mid-1960s. The studio later became the Women's Building, an organization and place devoted to fostering women's art.

Sources: Chicago, *Through the Flower: My Life as a Woman Artist;* Uglow, *The Continuum Dictionary of Women's Biography,* p. 120.

1967 • Laura Knight (1877–1970), an English painter known for her depictions of circus life and the ballet and for her landscapes, was the first woman allowed to attend the annual members' banquet of the Royal Academy, in London in 1967. She had been a full member since 1936.

Sources: Dunbar, *Laura Knight;* Knight, *The Magic of a Line;* Knight, *A Proper Circus Drive;* Uglow, *The Continuum Dictionary of Women's Biography.*

1969 • Frances Hodgkins (1869–1947), a New Zealand artist of international reputation who finally settled in England, was the first woman to be the subject of a centenary exhibition at Auckland City Art Gallery, in 1969. She was honored in her own country, which had neglected her achievement during her lifetime, for her paintings in both watercolors and oils. Her early work is in a strong post-impressionist style, while her later painting is characterized by a freedom of forms and a rich use of color.

Sources: Uglow, *The Continuum Dictionary of Women's Biography,* pp. 261–62.

1974 • Magdelena Abakanowicz (b. 1930) was the first Polish woman to receive an honorary doctorate from the Royal College of Art in London. Known in her native Poland and internationally as a sculptor/weaver, she uses fibers (a traditional female medium) to express her view of the world and especially the human body.

Sources: Uglow, *The Continuum Dictionary of Women's Biography,* p. 1.

1981 • Wilhelmina Cole Holladay (b. 1922) was the founder and first president of the National Museum of Women in the Arts. Drawing on her own collection of art, Holladay founded the museum in 1981; in 1987 the museum opened in its own building in Washington, D.C.

Sources: Read and Witlieb, *The Book of Women's Firsts,* pp. 211–13; Tierney, *Women's Studies Encyclopedia,* vol. 2, p. 259.

1982 • Lucie Rie (b. 1902), a British potter born and educated in Austria, was the first female potter to have a retrospective exhibition of her work at the Victoria and Albert Museum in London, in 1982. She has worked in her own studios in Vienna and London and is known as an influential artist and teacher.

Sources: Birks, *Lucie Rie;* Uglow, *The Continuum Dictionary of Women's Biography,* p. 459.

1989 • Camille Claudel (1864–1943) was the first female sculptor to be the subject of a feature film. The story of her life is told in *Camille Claudel,* directed by Bruno Nuytten in 1989, with Gerard Depardieu playing the part of her lover, Auguste Rodin.

Sources: Paris, *Camille Claudel;* Uglow, *The Continuum Dictionary of Women's Biography,* pp. 127–28.

Miscellaneous

4th century B.C. • Phryne (365–410 B.C.), a Greek artist's model of acclaimed beauty, was the first woman granted permission to dedicate a golden statue of herself at Delphi. Praxiteles used her as a model for his Aphrodite of Cos and Aphrodite of Cnidos. This famous sculptor was also probably her lover.

Sources: Uglow, *The Continuum Dictionary of Women's Biography,* p. 432.

Late 8th century • Cynethryth, the Saxon queen consort of Offa II, King of Mercia from 757 until 796, was the first Englishwoman to have her portrait reproduced. She was the first queen consort allowed to issue coins in her own name, and her vivid pictures on them are the first extant portraits of an Englishwoman.

Sources: Uglow, *The Continuum Dictionary of Women's Biography,* p. 143.

1643 • Lady Anne Clifford, Countess of Dorset, Pembroke, and Montgomery (1590–1676), an English heiress, was the first woman to establish her name by restoring castles. She began her program when she inherited her family's wealth in 1643 and restored six castles: Skipton, Appleby, Brougham, Brough, Perdragon, and Bardon Tower.

Sources: Uglow, *The Continuum Dictionary of Women's Biography,* pp. 128–29; Williamson, *Lady Anne Clifford.*

The first half of the 18th century • Claudine de Tencin (1685–1749) was the first woman to hold a political salon that favored a constitutional government as opposed to a monarchy in France. She and her circle supported the idea of a French revolution.

Sources: Chicago, *The Dinner Party,* p. 207; Uglow, *The Continuum Dictionary of Women's Biography,* p. 165.

1761 • Hester Needham Bateman (1709–1794) was the first female silversmith to register her own hallmark, "H.B." She worked with her husband until his death in 1760, then carried on his business as her own. She is now regarded as one of the greatest eighteenth-century silversmiths.

Sources: Raven, *Women of Achievement: Thirty-Five Centuries of History,* p. 192; Uglow, *The Continuum Dictionary of Women's Biography,* p. 51.

1890s • Calamity Jane (1852–1903), the stage name of Martha Jane Cannary Burke, was the first woman to perform in the Buffalo Bill Wild West Show. She joined the group in the far western United States in the 1890s and traveled with it throughout America and to England, where she appeared in 1893.

Sources: Burke, *Life and Adventures of Calamity Jane;* Jennewein, *Calamity Jane of the Western Trails;* Uglow, *The Continuum Dictionary of Women's Biography,* p. 102.

1898 • Annie Oakley (1860–1926), an American markswoman who toured Europe with the Buffalo Bill Wild West Show, was the first person to shoot a cigarette out of the mouth of a reigning monarch. In Germany in 1889, she shot a cigarette out of the mouth of Kaiser William II.

Sources: James, *Notable American Women,* vol. 2, pp. 644–46; Swartout, *Missie: An Historical Biography of Annie Oakley;* Uglow, *The Continuum Dictionary of Women's Biography,* p. 409.

1921 • The first woman to win the Miss America Beauty Pageant was Margaret Gorman. At the age of 16, she won the first contest, held in Atlantic City, New Jersey, on September 7 and 8, 1921.

Sources: Kane, *Famous First Facts;* Read and Witlieb, *The Book of Women's Firsts,* pp. 181–82.

Music

16th century • Barbara Strozzi, a sixteenth-century singer and composer in Italy, was the first female musician to receive recognition for performing her own works in Venice, Italy.

Sources: Chicago, *The Dinner Party,* p. 155; Uglow, *The Continuum Dictionary of Women's Biography,* p. 523.

1620s • Francesca Caccini (1587–1640) was the first female opera composer. A talented musician in the court of the Medicis, she was commissioned to compose an opera during the 1620s.

Sources: Chicago, *The Dinner Party,* p. 155; Slonimsky, *Baker's Biographical Dictionary of Musicians, Sixth Edition,* p. 265; Uglow, *The Continuum Dictionary of Women's Biography,* p. 102.

1723 • Marguerite-Louise Couperin (1705–1778), member of a noted French family of musicians and organists and a musician at the court of the French king, was the first woman to receive the honor of being appointed a member of the Ordinaire de la Musique, in 1723.

Sources: Chicago, *The Dinner Party,* p. 198.

c.1750 • Susannah Maria Cibber (1714–1766) was the first woman to sing the contralto solo in Handel's *Messiah,* during its first performance in London in 1750. The part was written for her, as was the starring female part in Handel's *Acis and Galatea.*

Sources: Nash, *The Provok'd Wife: The Life and Times of Susannah Cibber;* Uglow, *The Continuum Dictionary of Women's Biography,* pp. 124–25.

1791 • Josepha Weber (1759–1819), a German soprano, was the first woman to sing the role of the Queen of the Night in Mozart's opera *The Magic Flute,* in Vienna in 1791. Mozart composed the part for Weber, whom he knew well, for he was married to her sister Constanze. He also composed music for a third Weber sister, Aloysia.

Sources: Uglow, *The Continuum Dictionary of Women's Biography,* p. 571.

1820s and 1830s • Giuditta Maria Costanza Pasta (1797–1865), an Italian soprano, was the first woman to inspire operas by three of the great composers of her day: Bellini, Donizetti, and Pacini. The title roles of Donizetti's *Norma* (1831) and *Anna Bolena* (1830) were written for her as was the part of Amina in Bellini's *La Sonnambula* (1831). She is also associated with the title role of Pacini's *Niobe* (1826).

Sources: Uglow, *The Continuum Dictionary of Women's Biography,* p. 423.

1824 • Karoline Unger (1803–1877), an Austrian contralto, was the first person to involve the deaf Beethoven in the late performances of his own work. During the première of his *Missa solemnis* and Ninth Symphony in Vienna in 1824, Unger turned the composer around to face the audience so that he could at least see the applause. She is also remembered because of the large number of operas written for her (and in which she was the first woman to sing the central female roles) by such composers as Donizetti, Bellini, Mercadante, and Pacini, at least six operas in all.

Sources: Uglow, *The Continuum Dictionary of Women's Biography,* p. 552.

1826–27 • Maria Malibran (1808–1836), a Spanish mezzo-soprano, starred in the first season of Italian opera in the United States, in New York in 1826–1827. Her father, the great tenor Manuel Garcia, brought her to America with his opera company, performing five operas by Rossini and one by Mozart.

Sources: Fitzlyon, *Maria Malibran: Diva of the Romantic Age;* Uglow, *The Continuum Dictionary of Women's Biography,* pp. 350–51.

1843 • Pauline Viardot (1821–1910), a mezzo-soprano whose mother was a French music teacher and whose father was the famous Spanish tenor Manuel Garcia, was the first woman to introduce Russian music to the West. After a visit to St. Petersburg in 1843, Viardot sang Russian songs in the original language in Paris. She is also remembered as the first woman to sing the central female parts in works composed for her, among them the role of Fidès in Meyerbeer's *Le Prophète* and of Dalila in Saint-Saëns's *Samson et Dalila.*

Sources: Fitzlyon, *The Price of Genius: A Life of Pauline Viardot;* Uglow, *The Continuum Dictionary of Women's Biography,* p. 558.

c.1850 • Marietta Alboni (1823–1894) was the star of the Royal Italian Opera Company's first performance during their first season at Covent Garden in the middle of the nineteenth century. She sang the part of Arsace in Rossini's *Semiramide.*

Sources: Larue, *International Dictionary of Opera,* pp. 18-20; Uglow, *The Continuum Dictionary of Women's Biography,* p. 12.

1864 • Annie Louise Cary (1841–1921) was the first American woman to sing in a work by German opera composer Richard Wagner in the United States. She sang the part of Ortrud in *Lohengrin* in New York City in 1864. Cary came to be known not only in the United States but also in Europe and Russia, where she toured in 1876 and 1877.

Sources: Edwards, *Music and Musicians of Maine,* pp. 204–19; James, *Notable American Women,* vol. 1, pp. 297–98.

1867 • Clara Louise Kellogg (1842–1916), a dramatic soprano from South Carolina, was the first American female singer to achieve a considerable reputation in Europe. She made her European debut in London in 1867, then toured regularly both in the United States and on the continent, even singing to acclaim in St. Petersburg, Russia, during the 1880–1881 season.

Sources: Hopkins, *The Kelloggs in the Old World and the New*; James, *Notable American Women,* vol. 2, pp. 319–21; Kellogg, *Memoirs of an American Prima Donna.*

1870s • Amy Fay (1844–1928), an American pianist who studied in Boston and in Germany, was the first pianist to play a full-length concerto at the Cambridge and Worcester, Massachusetts, music festivals, in the 1870s. For a dozen years before World War I, Fay also served as the first president of the Women's Philharmonic Society in New York City.

Sources: Fay, *Music-Study in Germany,* ed. Dillon; James, *Notable American Women,* vol. 1, pp. 602–3; Mathews, *A Hundred Years of Music in America,* pp. 137–41.

Vesta Tilley (1864–1952), an English music hall star, was the first woman to make her career on the English stage by wearing male attire consisting of a top hat and tails. This outfit, later popularized in the twentieth century by such famous film stars as Marlene Dietrich and Judy Garland, came to signify complex gender relations both from the point of view of the performer and the spectator. Tilley first dressed as a man at the age of five and went on to make her name as a male impersonator.

Sources: Maitland, *Vesta Tilley;* Uglow, *The Continuum Dictionary of Women's Biography,* p. 541.

1876 • Adelina Patti (1843–1919), the famous Italian soprano, was the first woman to sing the title role in Verdi's *Aida* when it was first performed in London in 1876. Her career spanned forty-five years and earned her a worldwide reputation as well as a financial fortune.

Sources: Klein, *The Reign of Patti;* Uglow, *The Continuum Dictionary of Women's Biography,* pp. 424–25.

1878 • Emma Abbott (1850–1891) was the first woman to form her own opera company. In 1878, she organized The Emma Abbott English Opera Company, which presented shortened versions of contemporary operas.

Sources: Read and Witlieb, *The Book of Women's Firsts,* p. 3; Slonimsky, *Baker's Biographical Dictionary of Musicians, Sixth Edition,* p. 2.

1879 • Maude Valérie White (1855–1937), an English composer and writer, was the first woman to win the Mendelssohn Scholarship, in London in 1879. She had to give up the prize in 1881 because of ill health, but went on to a distinguished career in music, writing over 200 songs and translating many of her texts, including poems by Victor-Marie Hugo and Heinrich Heine.

Sources: Uglow, *The Continuum Dictionary of Women's Biography,* p. 579; White, *Friends and Memories;* White, *My Indian Summer.*

1881 • Emma Cecilia Thursby (1845–1931), a concert singer and teacher trained in Pennsylvania and New York, was the first American to receive the commemorative medal of the Société des Concerts of the Paris Conservatory, in Paris, France, in February of 1881. Thursby was well-known because of her tours throughout both the United States and Europe.

Sources: Gipson, *The Life of Emma Thursby;* James, *Notable American Women,* vol. 3, pp. 459–61; Odell, *Annals of the New York Stage,* vols. 7–15.

1883 • Cosima Wagner (1837–1930), the daughter of Franz Liszt and the wife of Richard Wagner, was the first woman to serve as director of the Bayreuth Festival, in Bayreuth, Germany. She assumed this position after the death of her husband, to whom she had devoted her life, in 1883. Rigidly adhering to what she felt were Wagner's intentions, she controlled all aspects of the opera productions until she handed over direction to their son Siegfried in 1906.

Sources: Skelton, *Richard and Cosima Wagner: Biography of a Marriage;* Sokoloff, *Cosima Wagner: A Biography;* Uglow, *The Continuum Dictionary of Women's Biography,* p. 563.

1885 • Clara Wieck Schumann (1819–1896), a German composer and pianist, was the first person to edit the letters of her husband, Robert Schumann, the renowned composer. Her collection of correspondence between 1827 and 1840 appeared in 1885. Clara Schumann was also the first woman, with the help of German composer Johannes Brahms, to prepare a complete edition of Robert Schumann's works (1881–1893). She put aside her own promising career in music for the sake of her husband's career, and, after his death in 1856, turned increasingly to teaching. She was appointed principal piano teacher, the first woman to hold this post, at the Hoch Conservatory in Frankfurt in 1878.

Sources: Harding, *Concerto: The Story of Clara Schumann;* Stephenson, *Clara Schumann;* Uglow, *The Continuum Dictionary of Women's Biography,* p. 486.

Cosima Wagner

1886 • Lilli Lehmann (1848–1929), a German soprano known internationally for her performances in Wagnerian opera roles and for her early opera recordings, was the first woman to sing the part of Isolde in the United States. She starred in the première of Wagner's *Tristan* at the Metropolitan Opera House in New York City in 1886.

Sources: Lehmann, *My Path Through Life;* Uglow, *The Continuum Dictionary of Women's Biography,* pp. 319–20.

1888 • Matilda Sissieretta Joyner Jones (1869–1933) was the first black woman to sing opera and art songs in the United States. Trained in Boston and New York City, she made her debut in New York in 1888. A dramatic soprano, she toured in the United States and Europe, even performing at the White

House in 1892, and was hailed as the greatest singer her race had produced. By 1916, however, she ceased to perform.

Sources: James, *Notable American Women,* vol. 2, pp. 288–90; Sadie, *The New Grove Dictionary of Opera,* vol. 2, p. 916.

1891 • Julie Rivé-King (1854–1937), an American pianist trained in New York and Germany, was the first person to perform Paderewski's *Concerto in A Minor* in the United States. She played this piece to wide acclaim with the Boston Symphony Orchestra in Boston, Massachusetts, in 1891.

Sources: James, *Notable American Women,* vol., 3, pp. 168–69; Jones, *A Handbook of American Music and Musicians,* pp. 145–47; Loesser, *Men, Women and Pianos,* p. 534; Mathews, *A Hundred Years of Music in America.*

1893 • Ethel Mary Smyth (1858–1944) was England's first significant female composer. Her stature was first recognized with the performance of her *Mass in D* at Albert Hall in London in 1893. Educated in Leipzig and Berlin, she is remembered for her orchestral works and especially for her operas. She is also known for her active role in the women's suffrage movement, for which in 1911 she wrote the *March of the Women,* and for her nine largely autobiographical books.

Sources: Collis, *Impetuous Heart*; Smyth, *Impressions that Remained,* 2 vols.; Uglow, *The Continuum Dictionary of Women's Biography,* pp. 503–4.

Nellie Melba

1894 • Nellie Melba (1861–1931), an Australian coloratura soprano known throughout the world both for her operatic performances and for her many recordings, was the first female opera singer to have two dishes named after her. Both Peach Melba and Melba toast were created by French chef August Escoffier at the Savoy Hotel in London.

Sources: Radic, *Melba: The Voice of Australia*; Uglow, *The Continuum Dictionary of Women's Biography,* p. 372.

1897 • Olga Samaroff (1882–1948), a pianist and teacher, was the first American woman to win a scholarship at the Paris Conservatory, in 1897. Educated in Texas, Paris, and Berlin, she made her debut on January 18, 1905, at Carnegie Hall in New York City, and went on to an illustrious career as a performer, writer, and teacher. She is also remembered as the wife of conductor Leopold Stokowski, whom she married in 1911 and divorced in 1923.

Sources: James, *Notable American Women,* vol. 3, pp. 225–27; Samaroff, *An American Musician's Story.*

Late 19th century • Maggie Cline (1857–1934), a vaudeville performer, was the first female Irish comedy singer in America. She established her career in Boston, but by the end of the century was well known in Cincinnati and New York as well.

Sources: James, *Notable American Women,* vol. 1, pp. 352–53; Laurie, Jr., *Vaudeville.*

Jenny Lind (1820–1887), a Swedish operatic soprano of international fame, was the first woman to be represented in Westminster Abbey's Poets' Corner. She was honored after her death for her performances in works by Giacomo

Meyerbeer, Vincenzo Bellini, Gaetano Donizetti, and Guiseppe Verdi and for a career dedicated to singing and teaching. She was the cofounder, with her husband, the pianist Otto Goldschmidt, of London's Bach Choir, and became professor of singing at the Royal College of Music in London in 1883.

Sources: Bulman, *Jenny Lind;* Uglow, *The Continuum Dictionary of Women's Biography,* pp. 326–27.

Early 20th century • Wanda Landowska (1879–1959), a Polish musician, was the first person to revive the harpsichord, an instrument on which she continued to play and record throughout her life. She studied in Berlin, and beginning in 1903, she toured Europe and America. She founded the Ecole de Musique Ancienne at St-Leu-la-Fôret near Paris in 1925. After the German occupation of France in 1940, she moved to the United States. Harpsichord concertos were composed for her by Manuel de Falla and Francis Poulenc, but she is primarily associated with seventeenth- and eighteenth-century music, especially Johann Sebastian Bach.

Sources: Gavoty and Hauert, *Wanda Landowska;* Uglow, *The Continuum Dictionary of Women's Biography,* p. 311.

Teresa Carreño (1853–1917), a Venezuelan pianist who settled in Germany, was the first woman to manage the Giovanni Tagliapietra Opera Company. Known for her versatility, Carreño is also remembered as a singer and a conductor.

Sources: Peña, *Teresa Carreño;* Uglow, *The Continuum Dictionary of Women's Biography,* p. 107.

1901 • Clara Butt (1872–1936), an English contralto, was the first woman to sing Edward Elgar's "Land of Hope and Glory," in 1901. The song has become England's unofficial second national anthem.

Sources: Ponder, *Clara Butt;* Uglow, *The Continuum Dictionary of Women's Biography,* p. 99.

1906 • Maud Powell (1868–1928), an American violinist educated in Europe, was the first person to perform the Jean Sibelius violin concerto in D minor in the United States. She played this piece with the New York Philharmonic in New York City on November 30, 1906. Committed to the music of her time, Powell was a pioneering performer, and her career includes a number of such firsts. She was the first person to perform the following violin concerti in the United States: Saint-Saëns's in C major, Harry Rowe Shelley's in G minor, Dvorak's in A minor, Huss's in D minor, Arensky's in A minor, and Bruch's *Konzertstück.*

Sources: *Etude,* October 1911, p. 666; James, *Notable American Women,* vol. 3, pp. 90–92.

1908 • Corinne Rider-Kelsey (1877–1947), a concert and oratorio soprano, was the first singer trained in the United States to perform a major role with the Royal Opera at Covent Garden. She made her London debut in the part of Micaela in Bizet's *Carmen* on July 2, 1908.

Sources: James, *Notable American Women,* vol. 3, pp. 157–58; Reed, *Be Not Afraid: A Biography of Madame Rider-Kelsey.*

1910s • Lotte Lehmann (1888–1976), a German opera singer who settled in the United States towards the end of her career, was the first woman to appear successfully in all three soprano roles (Sophie, the Marschallin, and Octavian) in Richard Strauss's *Rosenkavalier*. She was also the first woman to sing the starring roles in the premières of Strauss's *Die Frau ohne Shatten* (in Vienna in 1919) and *Intermezzo* (in Dresden in 1924).

Sources: Larue, *International Dictionary of Opera,* pp. 730-32; Uglow, *The Continuum Dictionary of Women's Biography,* p. 320.

1912 • Margarethe Dessoff (1874–1944) was the first woman to conduct a women's chorus in public, in New York City in 1912. From 1925 through 1935, she directed the female Adesor Choir in New York City, a chorus that performed only music specifically composed for female voices.

Sources: Chicago, *The Dinner Party,* p. 198; Tierney, *Women's Studies Encyclopedia,* vol. 2, p. 208.

1913 • Lili Boulanger (1893–1918), a French composer, was the first woman to be awarded the Prix de Rome, in 1913. She was honored for her cantata *Faust et Hélène*. She composed prolifically and is known primarily for her choral work.

Sources: Rosenstiel, *The Life and Works of Lili Boulanger;* Uglow, *The Continuum Dictionary of Women's Biography,* p. 81.

1917 • Germaine Tailleferre (1892–1984), a French composer trained at the Paris Conservatory, was the first and only female member of Les Six, a group of innovative French musicians that included Arthur Honegger and Francis-Jean-Marcel Poulenc. Their first collective performance took place in Paris in 1917 and included Tailleferre's *String Quartet*. Known initially as Les Nouveaux Jeunes, they acquired the name Les Six Français or Les Six through reviews in 1920.

Sources: Tailleferre, *Mémoires à L'emporte Pièce*; Uglow, *The Continuum Dictionary of Women's Biography,* pp. 528–29.

Marguerite Canal (1890–1978) was the first woman to conduct orchestral concerts in France. She conducted a series of performances at the Palais de Glace in Paris in 1917 and 1918. She had a distinguished career as a conductor, composer and teacher at the Paris Conservatory.

Sources: Cohen, *International Encyclopedia of Women Composers,* vol. 1, pp. 130-31; Uglow, *The Continuum Dictionary of Women's Biography,* p. 105.

1918 • The Metropolitan Opera star Alma Gluck (1884–1938) was the first female recording artist to sell a million copies. In 1911–1912, she recorded James Bland's "Carry Me Back to Old Virginny," which was released as a single-sided disk. It was re-released as a double-faced disk (paired with "Old Black Joe") in 1915. This second version is reputed to have sold a million copies by 1918.

Sources: Larue, *International Dictionary of Opera,* vol. 1, pp. 518-20; Sanders, *The First of Everything,* p. 285.

Adella Prentiss Hughes (1869–1950) became the first woman to serve as manager of a major symphony orchestra when she assumed this position in the newly formed Cleveland Symphony Orchestra, conducted by Nikolai Sokoloff, in 1918.

Sources: James, *Notable American Women,* vol. 2, pp. 232–33; Read and Witlieb, *The Book of Women's Firsts,* pp. 220–21.

Rosa Ponselle (1897–1981), an American soprano, was the first person to sing the role of Leonora in *La Forza del Destino*, at the Metropolitan Opera House in New York City in 1918. At the suggestion of Italian tenor Enrico Caruso, this was her first operatic appearance. Ponselle went on to a distinguished career both as a performer and as a teacher.

Sources: Larue, *International Dictionary of Opera,* vol. 2, pp. 1033-35; Uglow, *The Continuum Dictionary of Women's Biography,* pp. 436–37.

Adella Prentiss Hughes

1919 • Marguerite Marie Charlotte Long (1874–1966), a French pianist and teacher at the Paris Conservatory from 1906 until 1940, was the first person to perform Maurice Ravel's *Tombeau de Couperin,* in Paris in 1919. She was also the first to play his Piano Concerto in G (with the composer conducting), also in Paris, in 1932. She was also the first pianist to record this concerto. She founded, with Jacques Thibaud in 1943, the international piano and violin competition that bears their names.

Sources: Slonimsky, *Baker's Biographical Dictionary of Musicians, Sixth Edition,* pp. 1079-80; Uglow, *The Continuum Dictionary of Women's Biography,* p. 332.

1920s • Ma (Gertrude Malissa) Rainey (1886–1939), an American singer known for her performances of the blues, was the founder and first director of the Georgia Jazz Band, a group with which she toured the eastern United States during the 1920s. She made 90 recordings between 1923 and 1928, but retired during the Depression in 1933.

Sources: Mother of the Blues: A Study of Ma Rainey; Uglow, *The Continuum Dictionary of Women's Biography,* p. 445.

1921 • Mary Garden (1874–1967) became the first woman to serve as director of a major opera company when she assumed this position at the Chicago Lyric Opera during the 1921–1922 season. She is known primarily, however, as a soprano particularly accomplished in French parts.

Sources: Garden and Biancolli, *Mary Garden's Story;* Read and Witlieb, *The Book of Women's Firsts*; Uglow, *The Continuum Dictionary of Women's Biography,* p. 220.

1925 • Ethel Leginska (1886–1970) became the first woman to conduct a major American orchestra when she conducted the New York Symphony Orchestra in New York City on January 9, 1925. Trained as a pianist, Leginska went on in 1926 to found the Boston Philharmonic and to compose for both orchestra and opera.

Sources: Read and Witlieb, *The Book of Women's Firsts,* pp. 250–51.

1926 • Amy Marcy Cheney Beach (1867–1944) was the first president of the Association of American Women Composers, a society she helped to found in 1926. Beach was a concert pianist and symphonic composer who played her own compositions in Europe and the United States. Her *Mass in E-flat Major* was the first work by a woman performed by the Boston Symphony Orchestra, in 1892. Her aria *Eilende Wolken* was the first work by a woman to be performed by the New York Symphony Orchestra, in 1892.

Sources: James, *Notable American Women,* pp. 117–19; Read and Witlieb, *The Book of Women's Firsts,* pp. 43–44; Uglow, *The Continuum Dictionary of Women's Biography,* p. 54.

1928 • Lotte Lenya (1898–1981), an Austrian singer of international reputation, was the first woman to play the part of Jenny, a major character in her husband Kurt Weill's *The Three-Penny Opera,* in Berlin at its première in 1928. She later starred in George Wilhelm Pabst's film version of this work. Lenya and Weill left Germany in 1933 and settled in New York City. Her voice, familiar through her many recordings, recalls the atmosphere of Berlin in the 1920s and 1930s.

Sources: Marx, *Weill-Lenya;* Uglow, *The Continuum Dictionary of Women's Biography,* p. 322.

1930 • Ruth Crawford Seeger (1901–1953) was the first American female composer to receive a Guggenheim Fellowship. Under the auspices of this award, she studied composition in Berlin and Paris in 1930. She is remembered for her interest in American folk music.

Sources: Gaume, *Ruth Crawford Seeger: Memoirs, Memories, Music;* Uglow, *The Continuum Dictionary of Women's Biography,* pp. 140–41.

1931 • Anne Catherine Macnaghten (b. 1908), an English musician, was the cofounder (with Iris Lemare and Elisabeth Lutyens) of the Macnaghten-Lemare Concerts, an ongoing series of performances of contemporary music, in London in 1931. The concerts have featured work by modern composers, mostly British, including Lutyens, Benjamin Britten, Davies, and, in 1981, Nicola Lefanu. Today the series is known as the New Macnaghten Concerts, and many musicians have dedicated their work to its founder.

Sources: Uglow, *The Continuum Dictionary of Women's Biography,* p. 347.

1935 • Grazyna Bacewicz (1909–1962), a Polish composer and violinist, was the first woman to win a prize at the Wieniawski Competition in Poland, in 1935. She taught in Lodz and in Warsaw, and in 1950 retired from performance to devote her musical skills to composition.

Sources: Cohen, *International Encyclopedia of Women Composers,* pp. 38-40; Uglow, *The Continuum Dictionary of Women's Biography,* p. 40.

1937 • Nadia Boulanger (1887–1979) was the first woman to conduct a symphony orchestra in London, in 1937. A French composer, teacher, and conductor, she was also the first woman to conduct regular subscription concerts with the Boston Symphony Orchestra (in 1938) and with the New York Philharmonic (in 1939) and the first woman to conduct the Hallé Orchestra (in 1963).

Sources: Rosenstiel, *Nadia Boulanger: A Life in Music;* Uglow, *The Continuum Dictionary of Women's Biography,* pp. 81–82.

Dorothy Fields (1905–1974) became the first woman to win an Oscar for songwriting when she was honored for her lyrics to Jerome Kern's tune "The Way You Look Tonight" in 1937. The song was featured in the 1936 movie *Swing Time* starring Ginger Rogers and Fred Astaire. In 1971 Fields became the first woman to be elected to the Songwriters' Hall of Fame.

Sources: Read and Witlieb, *The Book of Women's Firsts;* Tierney, *Women's Studies Encyclopedia,* vol. 2, p. 188.

1939 • Elisabeth Lutyens (1906–1983) was the first British woman to use serialism in her musical compositions. This technique appears in her *Chamber Concerto No. 1* in 1939. A prolific composer, Lutyens was also the cofounder of

Macnaughten-Lemare Concerts (in London in 1931), which fostered the work of young musicians such as Benjamin Britten.

Sources: Lutyens, *A Goldfish Bowl;* Uglow, *The Continuum Dictionary of Women's Biography,* pp. 337–38.

1940s • Myra Hess (1890–1965), a English pianist, was the first person to organize alternative music performances when the London concert halls were closed down during World War II. She organized a series of daily lunch-time concerts performed at the National Gallery. She herself performed at many of these, and in 1941 she was created Dame of the British Empire in recognition of her services as a public benefactor.

Sources: McKenna, *Myra Hess;* Uglow, *The Continuum Dictionary of Women's Biography,* p. 257.

Vera Lynn (b. 1917) was the first British singer to reach the top of the American hit parade (the most popular music of the day). She was so popular during World War II that she was the first woman to be named "Forces' Sweetheart." She sang in London revues and for the troops both in England and in Burma as well as on the radio. After the war, she appeared on television and in cabaret and variety shows throughout the world.

Sources: Lynn, *Vocal Refrain;* Uglow, *The Continuum Dictionary of Women's Biography,* pp. 339–40.

Kathy Florence Stobart (b. 1925), a British saxophonist, was the first female modern jazz musician to achieve international acclaim. Born in South Sheilds, she played in town bands before going to London in 1942. For the next 40 years she played with leading British and American jazz musicians, and in 1974 she formed her own group, the Kathy Stobart Quintet.

Sources: Uglow, *The Continuum Dictionary of Women's Biography,* p. 518.

1940 • Peggy Glanville-Hicks (1912–1990), an Australian composer, was the cofounder (with her husband Stanley Bate) of Les Trois Arts, a ballet company, in London in 1940. She was also the cofounder of the International Music Fund (in New York in the mid-1940s), and in New York in 1958, she founded The Artists' Company to promote American opera.

Sources: Uglow, *The Continuum Dictionary of Women's Biography,* p. 226.

1942 • Lena Horne (b. 1917), an American singer and actress, was the first black artist to be given a long-term contract with MGM, in Hollywood in 1942. Horne went on to a distinguished career in film, refusing to play stereotypical roles, but her color remained an issue for her work. In the 1960s, she was active in the civil rights movement and has continued to be outspoken about politics and discrimination.

Sources: Buckley, *The Hornes: An American Family;* Uglow, *The Continuum Dictionary of Women's Biography,* pp. 265–66.

1945 • Camilla Williams (b. 1925) was the first black woman to sing with the New York City Opera. In 1945, she sang the title role in Puccini's *Madame Butterfly.* She went on in 1954 to become the first black singer to appear on the stage of the Vienna State Opera. Camilla Williams was the first black woman to become a regular member of an opera company in the United States. A soprano, she sang the role of Cio-Cio-San in *Madame Butterfly* in 1946 and performed at the White House for President John F. Kennedy in 1960.

Sources: Smith, *Black Firsts,* p. 21; Smith, *Notable Black American Women,* pp. 712–14.

1946 • Kathleen Ferrier (1912–1953), an English contralto known primarily for her performance of lieder, was the first woman to sing the title role in Benjamin Britten's chamber opera *The Rape of Lucretia,* which premiered at Glyndebourne, England, in 1946.

Sources: Ferrier and Cardus, *Kathleen Ferrier: Her Life and a Memoir;* Uglow, *The Continuum Dictionary of Women's Biography,* p. 200.

Billie Holiday (1915–1959), an American performer known internationally both for her music and for her tempestuous life, was the first female jazz singer to give a solo performance at New York Town Hall, in 1946. She recorded with Benny Goodman, Count Basie and Lester Young, and died as a result of her addiction to heroin in a New York City hospital in 1959.

Sources: Holiday and Dufty, *Lady Sings the Blues;* James, *Billie Holiday;* Uglow, *The Continuum Dictionary of Women's Biography,* p. 263.

1948 • Joan Cross (b. 1900), English soprano and opera producer, was the founder (in 1948) and first director (until 1964) of the Opera School in London. The school was renamed the National School of Opera in 1955. She is also known as the first woman to sing the central female roles in a number of Benjamin Britten's works, including Ellen in *Peter Grimes* (1945), Mrs. Billows in *Albert Herring* (1947), Elizabeth in *Gloriana* (1953), and Mrs. Grose in *Turn of the Screw* (1954). She was a founding member of the English Opera Group.

Sources: Uglow, *The Continuum Dictionary of Women's Biography,* p. 141.

1949 • Edna White Chandler (1892–1992) was the first person to give a solo trumpet recital at Carnegie Hall in New York City, on February 19, 1949. During her pioneering career as a female trumpeter and composer for that instrument, Chandler achieved a number of firsts: she was the first female cornetist to play a solo at Carnegie Hall (on May 3, 1902, at the age of nine); she played for the first transcontinental telephone transmission (in March 1915); she was the first person to perform George Antheil's "Trumpet Sonata," at Columbia University in 1954; and she was the first woman to write a treatise on trumpet playing, *On Taming the Devil's Tongue,* published in 1982.

Sources: Chandler, *The Night the Camel Sang;* Fleet, "Edna White Chandler: A Brasswoman Pioneer," *Women of Note Quarterly: The Magazine of Historical and Contemporary Women Composers,* vol. 2, (November 1994), pp. 7–12.

Mid-20th century • Leontyne Price (b. 1927) was the first black American woman to achieve international acclaim in opera. Her rich soprano voice is primarily associated with Guiseppe Verdi's work, but she was also the first woman to sing the leading role in Samuel Barber's *Antony and Cleopatra,* which had its debut as the first opera performed at the new Metropolitan Opera

House at Lincoln Center in New York City in 1966. She retired from the stage in 1985.

Sources: Larue, *International Dictionary of Opera,* vol. 2, pp. 1047-49; Uglow, *The Continuum Dictionary of Women's Biography,* p. 440.

Mary Lou Williams (1910–1981), a jazz pianist and composer, was the founder of the Bel Canto Foundation, an organization to aid down-and-out musicians. Largely self-educated, Williams taught music at Duke University for many years.

Sources: Chicago, *The Dinner Party,* p. 199; Uglow, *The Continuum Dictionary of Women's Biography,* p. 583.

Evelyn Rothwell (b. 1911), an English oboist who married the distinguished conductor John Barbirolli in 1939, was the first person to perform oboe works written for her by such composers as Elizabeth Maconchy, Edmund Rubbra, and Gordon Jacob. She has written several books on oboe technique and repertoire, and in 1971 was appointed a Professor at the Royal Academy of Music in London.

Sources: Atkins and Cotes, *The Barbirollis: A Musical Marriage*; Uglow, *The Continuum Dictionary of Women's Biography,* p. 466.

1950s • Xiaoying Zeng (b. 1929) was the first woman to become a conductor in China. She first performed at the age of fourteen, then had further training both in China and in Moscow in the 1950s. On her return to China, she soon established a national reputation, and in 1977 she became principal conductor at the Central Opera Theatre in Beijing.

Sources: Uglow, *The Continuum Dictionary of Women's Biography,* pp. 599–600.

1952 • Doriot Anthony Dwyer (b. 1922), great grand-niece of Susan B. Anthony, was the first woman to be first chair in a major orchestra. She was hired as first-chair flutist by the Boston Symphony Orchestra in 1952.

Sources: O'Neil, *The Women's Book of World Records and Achievements,* pp. 633-34; Read and Witlieb, *The Book of Women's Firsts,* p. 129.

1955 • Joan Sutherland (b. 1926), the famous Australian coloratura soprano, was the first person to sing the part of Jenifer in Michael Tippett's opera *The Midsummer Marriage,* at Covent Garden in London in 1955. Trained in Australia and at the Royal College of Music and Opera School in London, Sutherland quickly established an international reputation. She is known particularly for her interpretations of Gaetano Donizetti's *Lucia* and Vincenzo Bellini's *Norma:* She was made a Dame of the British Empire in 1979.

Sources Adams, *La Stupenda: A Biography of Joan Sutherland*; Major, *Joan Sutherland: The Authorized Biography;* Uglow, *The Continuum Dictionary of Women's Biography,* p. 525.

In January 1955, Marian Anderson (1902–1993) became the first African-American woman soloist to sing on the stage of the Metropolitan Opera House in New York City. Her debut role at the Met was as Ulrica in *Un Ballo in Maschera (The Masked Ball).* Born in 1902 in Philadelphia, Pennsylvania, Anderson began singing at age six in her church choir. Her solo career was launched when she was selected over 300 singers in a contest, giving her the opportunity to sing with the New York Philharmonic Orchestra. Although praised by the famous conductor Arturo Toscanini as having a voice "heard once in a hundred years," Anderson was forced to perform in segregated concert halls. In 1939, the Daughters of the American Revolution (DAR) refused to allow Anderson to perform a concert in Philadelphia's Constitution Hall, claiming that the date had been previously booked. This action caused First Lady Eleanor Roosevelt to resign her membership in the DAR, and to assist Anderson in performing an open-air concert on Easter Sunday at the Lincoln Memorial in Washington, D.C. More than 75,000 people attended the concert, where Anderson performed the United States National Anthem and *Ave Maria,* among other works.

Her repertoire included both spirituals and opera. President Franklin Roosevelt later invited Anderson to perform for King George VI of England at the White House, making her the first African-American artist to sing there. In 1961, Anderson sang at the inauguration of President John F. Kennedy, and in 1963, she won the Presidential Medal of Freedom. In April 1993, she died after suffering a stroke.

Sources: Uglow, *The Continuum Dictionary of Women's Biography,* p. 16; Gaymon, *215 African American Women You Should Know*; Rolka, *100 Women Who Shaped World History,* p. 92.

1958 • Kirsten Malfrid Flagstad (1895–1962), a Norwegian soprano known primarily for her Wagnerian roles, was the first person to serve as director of the Norwegian State Opera in Oslo, from 1958 until 1960. She was also the first woman to sing the demanding roles of Sieglinde, Isolde, and Brunnhilde at the Metropolitan Opera in New York City in the year in which she made her debut there, 1935–1936.

Sources: McArthur, *Flagstad: A Personal Memoir;* Uglow, *The Continuum Dictionary of Women's Biography,* pp. 206–7.

Miriam Makeba (b. 1932) was the first black woman from South Africa to gain an international reputation as a singer. She performed in her native country as a girl, but gained international attention with her performance in the anti-apartheid film *Come Back Africa* in 1958. In the 1960s, encouraged by American singer Harry Belafonte, she had several record hits in the United States. She took an active role in the American Civil Rights Movement, then settled in African Guinea in the 1970s. She has continued to perform and to voice her political support of black causes.

Sources: Makeba, *Makeba: My Story;* Uglow, *The Continuum Dictionary of Women's Biography,* pp. 349–50.

1959 • Elizabeth Maconchy (b. 1907), an English composer, became the first woman to chair the Composers Guild of Great Britain, in London in 1959. She is remembered particularly for her chamber music and for her many stage works for children.

Sources: Uglow, *The Continuum Dictionary of Women's Biography,* p. 347.

1960 • Liza Redfield (b. 1930) became the first woman to conduct an orchestra on Broadway on July 4, 1960, when she took over the podium of the Broadway musical *The Music Man* after Herb Greene, the show's co-producer and conductor decided to step down. Redfield led the 24-piece orchestra at the Majestic Theater in New York.
Sources: McCullough, *First of All: Significant "Firsts" by American Women*, p. 27.

1961 • Ruth Gipps (b. 1921), an English composer and conductor, was the founder of the Chanticleer Orchestra, in London in 1961. Gipps has had a distinguished career in music, becoming musical director of the London Repertoire Orchestra in 1955 and a professor at the Royal College of Music in 1967.
Sources: Uglow, *The Continuum Dictionary of Women's Biography*, p. 225.

1964 • Dorothy (Dottie) March West (1932–1991) was the first female vocalist to win a country music Grammy award. She was honored in Nashville, Tennessee, in 1964 for her hit song "Here Comes My Baby."
Sources: Read and Witlieb, *The Book of Women's Firsts*, pp. 475–76.

Maria Callas (1923–1977), the American-born Greek opera diva, was the first woman to sing the title role in Peggy Glanville-Hicks's *Sappho,* in San Francisco, California, in 1965. Callas is ranked as one of the greatest dramatic sopranos of the twentieth century.
Sources: Ardoin, *The Callas Legacy*; Stassinopoulos, *Maria Callas: The Woman Behind the Legend;* Uglow, *The Continuum Dictionary of Women's Biography*, p. 103.

1967 • Jeanne Demessieux (1921–1968), a French organist and composer, was the first woman to play the organ in Westminster Cathedral and Westminster Abbey, in 1967. Trained at the Paris Conservatory, she gave concerts throughout Europe and America.
Sources: Uglow, *The Continuum Dictionary of Women's Biography*, p. 158.

1968 • Jacqueline du Pré (1945–1987), an English cellist of international reputation, was the first person to perform Alexander Goehr's *Romanze* for cello and orchestra, a work written for her, in London in 1968. Du Pré's career was cut short by multiple sclerosis.
Sources: Uglow, *The Continuum Dictionary of Women's Biography*, p. 178.

1971 • Dorothy Fields (1904–1974), daughter of well-known vaudevillian Lew Fields, was the first woman to be elected to the Songwriters' Hall of Fame, in March 1971. Fields was a lyricist, and was one of ten songwriters in the first group elected to the Songwriters' Hall of Fame. Among her hundreds of songs are such hits as "On the Sunny Side of the Street," "Exactly Like You," "I Won't Dance," and "Don't Blame Me."
Sources: McCullough, *First of All: Significant "Firsts" by American Women*, p. 28.

Eve Queler (b. 1936) was the first woman to conduct at Philharmonic Hall in New York City, in 1971. Her career includes a number of women's firsts: she was the first woman to conduct at a major European opera house (in Barcelona,

Songwriter Dorothy Fields

Spain, in 1974) and the first woman to serve as associate conductor of the U.S. Metropolitan Orchestra (in New York City in 1965). In 1967, she founded the Opera Orchestra of New York and served as its first director.

Sources: Read and Witlieb, *The Book of Women's Firsts,* pp. 352–53.

SARAH CALDWELL

1976 • Sarah Caldwell (b. 1928) was the first woman to conduct the Metropolitan Opera. In New York City in 1976, she conducted a performance of Verdi's *La Traviata* with soprano Beverly Sills. Known as an innovative and independent conductor, Caldwell founded the Opera Company of Boston in 1957. Caldwell was born in Maryville, Missouri, and attended the New England Conservatory of Music. She taught at the Berkshire Music Center from 1948 to 1952, headed the Opera Workshop Department at Boston University from 1952 to 1960, and in 1983, became artistic director of the New Opera Company of Israel.
Sources: McCullough, *First of All: Significant "Firsts" by American Women,* p. 27; Uglow, *The Continuum Dictionary of Women's Biography,* p. 103.

1979 • Beverly Sills (b. 1929), an American soprano, was the first female opera singer to be appointed Director of the New York City Opera, in 1979. She joined this company as a performer in 1955 and created an international reputation, although she did not make her debut at the rival Metropolitan Opera until 1975. She is particularly remembered for her performance as Manon in Jules Émile Frédéric Massenet's *Manon.*

Sources: Sills, *Bubbles: An Encore;* Uglow, *The Continuum Dictionary of Women's Biography,* p. 499.

1980 • Jane Alison Glover (b. 1949), an English pianist and conductor, was the first woman to serve as Director of the Glyndebourne Festival Opera, in 1980. She had joined the musical staff the previous year, and in 1984, became the first woman to serve as Festival Conductor.

Sources: Uglow, *The Continuum Dictionary of Women's Biography,* p. 227.

The San Francisco Women's Orchestra, founded in 1980, is the first women's orchestra to consist entirely of women and to perform only works composed by women. Its conductor is Joanne Flecta.

Sources: WCLV, November 2, 1994, evening program.

1983 • Ellen Taaffe Zwilich (b. 1939) was the first woman to win a Pulitzer Prize for music. She was honored in 1983 for her *Symphony No. 1, Three Movements for Orchestra,* a composition commissioned by the American Composers Orchestra.

Sources: Read and Witlieb, *The Book of Women's Firsts,* pp. 503–4.

1989 • Deborah Borda (b. 1949) became the first woman to serve as executive director of a major U.S. symphony orchestra when she was named executive director of the Detroit Symphony Orchestra in Detroit, Michigan, in 1989. Previously she had been with the San Francisco Symphony Orchestra for eight years, and in 1990 she was named president of the Minnesota Orchestra. In 1991 she became managing director of the New York Philharmonic.

Sources: Read and Witlieb, *The Book of Women's Firsts,* p. 62.

1991 • Shulamit Ran (b. 1949) was the first woman appointed composer-in-residence by a major U.S. orchestra. She took up this position at the Chicago Symphony Orchestra in 1991.

Sources: Read and Witlieb, *The Book of Women's Firsts,* pp. 357–58.

Photography

1863 • Julia Cameron (1815–1879), the aunt of writer Virginia Woolf, was the first major female photographer. She first took up a camera in 1863, and her sixteen-year career produced some of the most evocative pictures of the Victorian period.

Sources: Chicago, *The Dinner Party,* p. 214; Uglow, *The Continuum Dictionary of Women's Biography,* p. 104; Weiser, *Womanlist,* p. 259.

Early 20th century • Gertrude Stanton Käsebier (1852–1934) was the first American female photographer to gain international recognition as a professional artist. She established her first studio in New York City in 1897 and became one of the foremost portrait photographers in the city. She went on to become a significant force in the circle around Alfred Stieglitz. In international exhibitions she won numerous medals and citations, and her photographs were widely reproduced during the period of her greatest influence, 1898 until 1910.

Sources: James, *Notable American Women,* vol. 2, pp. 308–9.

c.1905 • Imogen Cunningham (1883–1976) was the first woman to photograph a male nude. She began her career in 1901 and shortly after photographed her husband naked on Mt. Ranier. The pictures were censored for many years. Cunningham is particularly well-known for her photographs of plants and flowers.

Sources: Chicago, *The Dinner Party,* p. 214; Dalch, *Imogen Cunningham: A Portrait;* Uglow, *The Continuum Dictionary of Women's Biography,* p. 142.

1965 • Dorothea Lange (1895–1965) was the first female photographer whose work was featured in a one-person show at the Museum of Modern Art in New York City, in 1965. Known for her documentary work during the Depression (1930s), Lange is particularly remembered for her famous picture "The Migrant Mother."

Sources: Meltzer, *Dorothea Lange: A Photographer's Life;* Uglow, *The Continuum Dictionary of Women's Biography,* p. 311.

1972 • Diane Nemerov Arbus (1923–1971) was the first American photographer to be included in the Venice Biennale, in 1972, the year after her suicide. Trained as a fashion photographer, Arbus is known for her independent work: disconcerting photographs of ordinary Americans as well as studies of "freaks."

Sources: Bosworth, *Diane Arbus: A Biography;* Uglow, *The Continuum Dictionary of Women's Biography,* p. 25.

Sculpture

1692 • Luisa Roldan (1656–1704), the daughter and wife of sculptors, was the first female sculptor to work at the court in Madrid. In 1692 she was appointed to serve under Charles II, then stayed on to work under Philip V. Though never adequately compensated, she was known for her professionalism and is remembered particularly for her sensitive sculpture of St. Catherine.

Sources: Tierney, *Women's Studies Encyclopedia,* vol. 2, p. 312; Uglow, *The Continuum Dictionary of Women's Biography,* p. 463.

19th century • Edmonia Lewis (1845–c.1909) was the first black female sculptor to exhibit in the United States. Educated at Oberlin College in Ohio, she also studied in Rome and exhibited with Harriet Hosmer's group of women sculptors. She settled in Rome in the 1880s and little is known of her later life.

Sources: Chicago, *The Dinner Party,* p. 182; Uglow, *The Continuum Dictionary of Women's Biography,* p. 325.

1866 • Vinnie Ream (1847–1914) became the first woman to receive a federal commission for sculpture when in 1866 she was asked to produce a full-scale marble statue of President Abraham Lincoln. It was unveiled on January 25, 1871, in the rotunda of the U.S. Capitol.

Sources: Hall, *Vinnie Ream*; Hoxie, *Vinnie Ream;* James, *Notable American Women,* vol. 3, pp. 122–23; Read and Witlieb, *The Book of Women's Firsts,* pp. 361–62.

1920 • Clare Frewen Sheridan (1885–1970) was the first Irish sculptor to be invited to work in Russia. She was asked to visit Moscow by the Soviet Trade Commission in 1920, and while there made busts of Zinoviev, Kamenev, Lenin, and Trotsky.

Sources: Sheridan, *Russian Diaries*; Sheridan, *To the Four Winds*; Uglow, *The Continuum Dictionary of Women's Biography,* p. 497.

1931 • Gertrude Vanderbilt Whitney (1875–1942), a sculptor in her own right as well as an art collector and patron, was the first woman to found a major museum devoted to American art, the Whitney Museum, in New York City in 1931.

Sources: James, *Notable American Women,* vol. 3, pp. 601–3; Read and Witlieb, *The Book of Women's Firsts,* pp. 479–80.

1932 • Käthe Kollwitz (1867–1945) is the first and only woman whose sculpture is featured at a German war memorial. At the cemetery of Eessen-Roggeveld containing World War I German soldiers who died while fighting near Dixmuiden in Belgium, Kollwitz's statues of a grieving mother and father

stand over the black slabs that mark the graves. Her work is in part a personal response to the death of her son Peter on the Western Front in 1914.

Gertrude Vanderbilt Whitney

Sources: Chicago, *The Dinner Party,* pp. 212; Keans, *Käthe Kollwitz: Woman and Artist;* Kollwitz, *Diaries and Letters of Käthe Kollwitz;* Uglow, *The Continuum Dictionary of Women's Biography,* p. 303.

Stunt Acting

1929 • Florence Lowe Barnes (1901–1975) was the first woman to be a stunt pilot in motion pictures. She flew her plane in Howard Hughes's 1929 movie *Hell's Angels.*

Sources: Read and Witlieb, *The Book of Women's Firsts,* p. 38.

1976 • Kitty O'Neill (b. 1947) was the first woman accepted into Stunts Unlimited, an organization of Hollywood's top stunt people, in 1976. As an athletic performer, O'Neill achieved numerous "firsts" in her field. Performing a stunt in 1979 for the television series *Wonder Woman,* O'Neill established a new world record for a high fall for a woman—127 feet.

Sources: Read and Witlieb, *The Book of Women's Firsts,* pp. 325–26.

Kitty O'Neill performs a
stunt for the television
series *Wonder Woman*.

Theatre

16th century • Isabella Andreini (1562–1604) was the first actress to establish a reputation throughout Europe. Born in Padua, Italy, she made her debut in Florence in 1578, then toured northern Italy and France for many years before dying in childbirth in Lyons. Andreini is also known for her verse.

Sources: Uglow, *The Continuum Dictionary of Women's Biography,* p. 18.

17th century • Marie Venier (1590–1619) was the first French actress whose achievements were recorded in her own name. She became famous for her portrayal of tragic heroines.

Sources: Chicago, *The Dinner Party,* p. 162.

1656 • The first woman to perform on the English stage was Mrs. Edward Coleman in 1656. She appeared in a work written by her husband, but after one appearance decided not to continue with an acting career.

Sources: Sanders, *The First of Everything,* p. 315.

1670 • Marie Desmares Champmeslé (1642–1698) was the first woman to play the title role of Bérénice in French playwright Jean Racine's famous play written for her in 1670. She is remembered as the actress responsible for initiating the traditional declamatory chant of French classical acting.

Sources: Uglow, *The Continuum Dictionary of Women's Biography,* p. 117.

Early 19th century • Rallou Karatza (1778–1830), a freedom fighter in the Greek War of Independence, was the first Greek woman to form a theatre group. Her production of sophisticated revolutionary plays and ethnic dramas transformed Greek theatre from entertainment to a didactic art that rallied the people to the cause of independence against the Turks. Karatza's work boosted national morale and contributed to the uprising of 1821. After the Greeks won their independence in 1829, she settled in Athens.

Sources: Uglow, *The Continuum Dictionary of Women's Biography,* p. 292.

1832 • Lucia Elisabetta Vestris (1797–1856), an English actress and theatre manager, was the first person to introduce the box set with ceiling, at the Olympic theatre, where she was the manager, in London in 1832. She went on after 1838 to manage Covent Garden and then the Lyceum Theatre.

Sources: Uglow, *The Continuum Dictionary of Women's Biography,* pp. 557–58; Williams, *Madame Vestris.*

1849 • Charlotte Saunders Cushman (1816–1876) was the first American actress to play the part of Hamlet in Shakespeare's play. She portrayed both male and female characters during her U.S. tour in 1849.

Sources: Leach, *Bright Particular Star: The Life and Times of Charlotte Cushman;* Uglow, *The Continuum Dictionary of Women's Biography,* p. 143.

1889 • Janet Achurch (1864–1916) was the first English actress to perform in a drama by Norwegian playwright Henrik Ibsen. In 1889, she played the part of Nora in Ibsen's famous play about female oppression, *A Doll's House.* She is known for portraying women who call into question traditional conventions.

Sources: Uglow, *The Continuum Dictionary of Women's Biography,* p. 3.

1899 • Augusta Gregory (1852–1932) was the cofounder, with William Butler Yeats and Edward Martyn, of the Irish Literary Theatre in Dublin in 1899. This important center for the literary and artistic movement known as the "Irish Renaissance" later attained international fame as the Abbey Theatre. Lady Gregory dedicated her energies to the restoring of Irish culture and to Irish political independence.

Sources: Adams, *Lady Gregory;* Smythe, *Seventy Years: Being the Autobiography of Lady Gregory;* Uglow, *The Continuum Dictionary of Women's Biography,* pp. 236–37.

Early 20th century • Sarah Bernhardt (1844–1923), the most celebrated actress in French history and known as "The Divine Sarah," was the first French woman to play the part of Hamlet in Shakespeare's play. She was known not only for her stage presence but for her daring and confidence.

Sources: Bernhardt, *Memoirs: My Double Life;* Chicago, *The Dinner Party,* p. 215; Uglow, *The Continuum Dictionary of Women's Biography,* pp. 63–64.

Sarah Bernhardt

Mistinguett (1873–1956), a French actress renowned for her beauty, was the first woman to have her legs insured for 1,000,000 francs. She came to fame through her performances at the Moulin Rouge and the Folies Bergère in Paris, beginning in 1910. She danced and sang at the latter theatre with Maurice Chevalier in 1917. She was also an outstanding comedienne and became known as the Queen of the Paris Revue.

Sources: Mistinguett, *Mistinguett: Queen of the Paris Night*; Uglow, *The Continuum Dictionary of Women's Biography,* pp. 377–78.

The first half of the 20th century • Ida Kaminska (1899–1980), an actoress and benefactor in Yiddish theatre, was the founder of the Warsaw Jewish Theatre and the Ida Kaminska Theatre in Warsaw. Forced to leave Europe because of anti-Semitism, Kaminska went to New York where she continued her work on behalf of Yiddish drama.

Sources: Chicago, *The Dinner Party,* p. 215.

1903 • Annie F. Horniman (1860–1937), an English actress and patron of the theatre in Britain, was the first person to finance the building and operating of the Abbey Theatre in Dublin, Ireland. She put up the initial funds in 1903, and the theatre constructed to foster the drama of the Irish Literary Renaissance opened the following year. Horniman continued her patronage until 1910. She went on to become a founder of the English Repertory Theatre.

Sources: Flannery, *Miss Annie F. Horniman and the Abbey Theatre;* Uglow, *The Continuum Dictionary of Women's Biography,* pp. 266–67.

1910 • Alla Nazimova (1879–1945), a Russian actress who settled in the United States in 1906, was the founder of the Nazimova Theatre in New York City in 1910. She specialized in drama by Ibsen, Chekhov, Turgenev, and O'Neill.

Sources: Uglow, *The Continuum Dictionary of Women's Biography,* p. 398.

1912 • Lilian Baylis (1874–1937) was the founder of both the Old Vic and Sadler's Wells theatre companies in London in 1912 and 1931 respectively. She made the Old Vic Theatre a principal center for the performance of Shakespeare's plays, while Sadler's Wells has specialized in opera and ballet.

Sources: Findlater, *Lilian Baylis: The Lady of the Old Vic;* Uglow, *The Continuum Dictionary of Women's Biography.*

1914 • Beatrice Stella Tanner Campbell (1865–1940), the English actress, was the first woman to play the part of Eliza Doolittle in George Bernard Shaw's famous drama *Pygmalion.* She debuted in this work, written for her, in London in 1914.

Sources: Campbell, *My Life and Some Letters;* Uglow, *The Continuum Dictionary of Women's Biography,* pp. 104–5.

1923 • Leni Riefenstahl (b. 1902), later an internationally known German filmmaker, was the first person to appear as a solo performer at the Deutsches Theater in Berlin, on December 20, 1923.

Sources: Hinton, *The Films of Leni Riefenstahl;* Riefenstahl, *A Memoir,* New York: St. Martin's Press; Uglow, *The Continuum Dictionary of Women's Biography,* p. 459.

1932 • Cheryl Crawford (1902–1986), an American theatre director, was the cofounder (with Harold Churman and Lee Strasberg) of the Group Theatre in 1932, which developed "method" acting. She was also the cofounder (with Eva Le Gallienne and Margaret Webster) of the American Repertory Theatre in 1945 and (with Elia Kazan and Robert Lewis) of the Actors' Studio in 1947.

Sources: Crawford, *My Fifty Years in the Theatre;* Uglow, *The Continuum Dictionary of Women's Biography,* p. 140.

1935 • In 1935, Hallie Flanagan (1890–1969) organized and became the first director of the Federal Theatre Project, a program of the Works Progress Administration (WPA) during the Depression. Her project became a national network of regional theatres throughout the United States and sponsored stage productions ranging from Shakespeare to vaudeville. Flanagan was also the founder in 1925 of the Vassar Experimental Theatre at Vassar College, where she was a professor from 1925 until 1942. She went on to serve as Dean and then Professor of Theatre at Smith College until 1955.

Sources: Flanagan, *Arena: The Story of the Federal Theatre;* Read and Witlieb, *The Book of Women's Firsts.*

1947 • Judith Malina (b. 1926), an American actress and director, was the co-founder, with her husband Julian Beck, of the Living Theatre, specializing in intellectual and avant-garde drama, in New York in 1947. Malina toured Europe with this group in 1961 and settled with the troupe in Bordeaux, France, in 1975.

Sources: Uglow, *The Continuum Dictionary of Women's Biography,* p. 351.

1953 • Joan Maud Littlewood (b. 1914), an English director, was the founder and first manager of the Theatre Workshop, in Stratford, England, in 1953. A graduate of the Royal Academy of Dramatic Art in London, Littlewood founded precursors of the Theatre Workshop in Manchester with her husband, the singer and writer Ewan McColl: the Theatre Union followed by the Theatre of Action. Littlewood has encouraged experimental drama and has been very influential on both British and continental directors. She became one of the most influential stage directors working in England after World War II.

Sources: Uglow, *The Continuum Dictionary of Women's Biography,* p. 328.

1955 • The first actress to win an Obie Award (award for off-Broadway theater) was Julie Bovasso (1930–1991), for her performance in *The Maids,* which opened on May 6, 1955. In 1973, Bovasso was the first woman to direct at the Lincoln Center playhouse in New York in 1973, when she directed *In the Boom Boom Room* at the Vivian Beaumont Theater.

Sources McCullough, *First of All: Significant "Firsts" by American Women,* p. 24.

1963 • Helen Bryant (1939–1983) was the founder and first president of the Afro-American Total Theater Arts Foundation and the Richard Allen Center of Culture and Art, both in New York City, in 1963 and 1968 respectively. Her life-long efforts on behalf of black American theatre were cut short by her early death.

Sources: Uglow, *The Continuum Dictionary of Women's Biography,* pp. 93–94.

1964 • Ariane Mnouchkine (b. 1939), a French theatre director, was the founder of the famous innovative collective Théâtre du Soleil, in Paris in 1964. The group has explored mime as well as the dramatic heritage of other theatrical traditions, including Chinese, Greek, and commedia dell'arte. The company continues to put on theatrical productions and remains organized on egalitarian principles.

Sources: Uglow, *The Continuum Dictionary of Women's Biography,* p. 382.

1973 • Mary Ann Goodbody (1946–1975) was the first person to serve as artistic director of The Other Place, an alternative theatre in Stratford, England. She assumed her position in 1973 and before her death two years later established the theatre as both a popular success and a site for artistic innovation.

Sources: Uglow, *The Continuum Dictionary of Women's Biography,* p. 231.

1983 • Glenda Jackson (b. 1936), a versatile and personable English actress known internationally for her film roles, is the first woman to serve as a director of United British Artists, a position she assumed in 1983. She is also one of the cofounders of the Women's Playhouse Trust. Jackson made her film debut in 1963 in *This Sporting Life,* and in the same year joined the Royal Shakespeare Company. She has won two Academy Awards for best actress: in 1969 for *Women in Love* and in 1973 for the comedy, *A Touch of Class.* In 1971, she won a British Academy Award for *Sunday Bloody Sunday,* and an Emmy Award for the title role in the telvision series *Elizabeth R.*

Sources: Briggs, *A Dictionary of 20th Century World Biography,* p. 290; Uglow, *The Continuum Dictionary of Women's Biography,* p. 277; Woodward, *A Study in Fire and Ice.*

GLENDA JACKSON

1984 • Dame Judith Anderson (1898–1992) was the first Australian-born woman to have a Broadway theatre in New York City named after her, in 1984. She was honored for her lifetime achievement in playing strong female roles on stage. Anderson is also known for her work in film.

Sources: Uglow, *The Continuum Dictionary of Women's Biography,* p. 16.

Business

Agriculture

1901 • Jessie Field Shambaugh (1881–1971) is one of those credited with founding 4-H. Shambaugh, while teaching at a one-room schoolhouse in Shenandoah, Iowa, organized corn clubs with the assistance of O.H. Benson in 1901. Born Celestia Josephine Field, she became a strong believer in the study of homemaking and agriculture. She publicized her club when she became superintendent of Page County, Iowa, schools in 1906 by advocating a focus on three "H's" for "head," "heart," and "hands;" she designed the three-leaf clover emblem for club awards. In 1913 she added a fourth focus on "home," which later became "health." The 4-H Club now has members in over 50 countries.

Other early 4-H pioneers include Marie Cromer of South Carolina, who founded the first canning clubs, and Ella Agnew of Virginia, who became the state agent for the U.S. Department of Agriculture's (USDA's) Girls' Tomato Clubs. Mary Cresswell of Georgia and, later, Gertrude L. Warren were both appointed by the USDA to provide leadership to girls' homemaking programs.

Sources: Read and Witlieb, *The Book of Women's Firsts,* pp. 154–55; Shambaugh, *A Real Country Teacher: The Story of Her Work.*

1927 • Edna Sewell (1881–1967) was the first director of the Associated Women of the American Farm Bureau Federation, a position she held from 1927 until her retirement in 1950. Sewell dedicated her career to communicating to farming women new and improved ways of caring for their farms, homes, and families.

Sources: Read and Witlieb, *The Book of Women's Firsts,* pp. 402–3.

1970s • Jane Smiley was the first girl to serve as a national officer of the Future Farmers of America. In the 1970s she became national vice-president of this organization that only began admitting girls in 1969.

Sources: O'Neill, *The Women's Book of World Records and Achievements,* p. 21.

1970 • Thelma Ballinger was the first woman to manage a farrowing house for the American Hog Company. Beginning in 1970, she ran the 840-sow feeder pig unit in Wiggins, Colorado.

Sources: O'Neill, *The Women's Book of World Records and Achievements,* p. 15.

1974 • Dee Van De Walle, a licensed artificial inseminator who serves as a midwife to hogs, was the first woman to receive the Iowa Master Pork Producers Award, in 1974. She and her husband raise hogs on their farm in Chelsea, Iowa.

Sources: O'Neill, *The Women's Book of World Records and Achievements,* p. 14.

Sharon Steffans, a farmer in Grand Rapids, Michigan, was the first coordinator of American Agri-Women, in 1974. Steffans edited the national organization's bi-monthly newsletter.

Sources: O'Neill, *The Women's Book of World Records and Achievements,* p. 8.

1975 • Ruth Kobell (b. 1918) became the first registered female lobbyist for the National Farmers Union in Washington, D.C. in 1975. She first joined the union in 1939, when she worked on a small wheat farm in Montana.

Sources: O'Neill, *The Women's Book of World Records and Achievements,* p. 9.

1977 • Lorena Croucher (b. 1959) was the first woman to be named "Star Farmer of Kansas," in 1977. She was honored for being the state's most enterprising farmer.

Sources: O'Neill, *The Women's Book of World Records and Achievements,* p. 21.

Banking

1861 • Lucy Holcombe Pickens (1832–1899) was the first woman to be pictured on Confederate currency, in 1861. Her picture was engraved on the Confederate one-hundred-dollar bill. For thirty years after her husband's death, she single-handedly managed their estate near Edgefield, South Carolina.

Sources: McCullough, *First of All: Significant "Firsts" by American Women,* pp. 63–64.

Martha Custis Washington

1886 • Martha Custis Washington (1732–1802) was the first woman pictured on U.S. currency; her picture was engraved on the one-dollar bill in 1886. She was also the first American woman pictured on a U.S. postage stamp, which was issued in 1902. Martha was married to George Washington in 1759.

Sources: McCullough, *First of All: Significant "Firsts" by American Women,* p. 64; *Who Was Who in American History, 1607–1896,* p. 565.

1903 • Maggie Lena Walker (1865–1934) was the first woman and also the first black woman to become a bank president when she founded the St. Luke Penny Savings Bank in 1903. Walker had the help of the Independent Order of St. Luke, a black insurance cooperative formed in 1867 by an ex-slave to support health care and funeral arrangements for its members. Highly successful, the St. Luke Penny Savings Bank absorbed other black Richmond, Virginia, banks and went on to become the Consolidated Bank and Trust Company in 1929.

Sources: James, *Notable American Women,* vol. 3, pp. 530–31; McCullough, *First of All: Significant "Firsts" by American Women,* p. 62; O'Neill, *The Women's Book of World Records and Achievements,* p. 526; Read and Witlieb, *The Book of Women's Firsts,* p. 467; Sanders, *The First of Everything,* p. 157; Smith, *Black Firsts,* p. 50.

1917 • Kate Gleason (1865–1933) became the first woman to serve as president of a national bank when she took over as head of the First National Bank of Rochester in Rochester, New York, in 1917. Its previous male president resigned to enter military service during the First World War.

Sources: Read and Witlieb, *The Book of Women's Firsts,* pp. 176–77; *Who Was Who in American History,* 1897–1942, pp. 460–61.

1919 • Brenda Vineyard Runyon was the first woman bank president to employ an all-female staff, including the janitor, in 1919. The bank was highly successful for seven years, until Runyon was forced to resign due to illness. With no one willing to assume her role, Runyon's staff liquidated their assets, and on June 8, 1926, merged with the First Trust and Savings Bank of Clarksville.

Sources: McCullough, *First of All: Significant "Firsts" by American Women,* p. 61.

1949 • Claire Giannini Hoffman (b. 1904) was the first female president of the world's largest bank, the Bank of America (later BankAmerica). She assumed this position in 1949 after the death of her father, the bank's founder and first president.

Sources: Read and Witlieb, *The Book of Women's Firsts,* pp. 210–11.

1975 • Madeleine McWhinney (b. 1922) was the first woman officer of the Federal Reserve System and the first woman president of the New York University School of Business Administration. In 1975, she became president of the Bank of New York, which was committed to providing banking services on a nondiscriminatory basis, particularly to women.

Sources: McCullough, *First of All: Significant "Firsts" by American Women*, pp. 61–62.

1979 • Susan B. Anthony (1820–1906) was the first woman to be pictured on a U.S. coin in 1979. A leader of the woman suffrage movement, Anthony founded the Daughters of Temperance Association, and with Elizabeth Cady Stanton, secured the first laws in New York guaranteeing women rights over their children and control of property and wages. Anthony was president of the National American Woman Suffrage Association from 1892 to 1900 and contributed to *The History of Woman Suffrage*.

Sources: McCullough, *First of All: Significant "Firsts" by American Women*, p. 63.

A Susan B. Anthony coin.

Business Management

1735 • Ann Smith Franklin (1696–1763) was the first female printer in New England. She took over her husband's printing business in Boston, Massachusetts, at the time of his death on February 4, 1735. She worked as a printer until her son took over the family establishment in 1748, although she continued to be active in the business until 1757.

Sources: Chapin, *Bibliographical Essays: A Tribute to Wilberforce Eames*; James, *Notable American Women,* vol. 1, pp. 662–63.

1852 • Charlotte Guest (1812–1895) was the first British woman to manage an ironworks. She inherited the Dowlais Iron Company in Glamorgan, Wales, from her husband in 1852 and was able to assume immediate control, since she and he had run the works together.

Sources: Chicago, *The Dinner Party,* p. 192; Uglow, *The Continuum Dictionary of Women's Biography,* p. 239.

Late nineteenth century • Harriet W. R. Strong (b. 1844) was the first president of the Business League of America. She was also the first woman elected to the Los Angeles Chamber of Commerce, having made a career as a water control engineer.

Source: Vare and Ptacek, *Mothers of Invention,* pp. 170–72.

1915 • Julia Crawford Ivers (d. 1930) was the first woman to serve as a general manager of a Hollywood film studio. In 1915 she took on this position at the Bosworth Company, where she was in charge of production and day-to-day business. She occasionally assumed the responsibilities of directing and screen writing.

Sources: Acker, *Reel Women: Pioneers of the Cinema, 1896 to the Present,* pp. 207–8; Slide, *Early Women Directors.*

1921 • Lila Acheson Wallace (1889–1984), an American entrepreneur and art patron, was the cofounder, with her husband De Witt Wallace, of the *Reader's Digest,* in New York City in 1921. The *Reader's Digest* is a magazine that excerpts articles and essays from other publications. The business was instantly successful. By the 1980s, subscriptions had reached thirty million and the publication was available in seventeen languages. Beginning in the 1930s, Wallace became a serious art collector, specializing in impressionist works. She was the first woman to donate a definitive and vast collection of impressionist art to a major museum, the Metropolitan Museum of Art in New York. She was also active in the restoration of Monet's house and gardens at Giverny.

Sources: Magnusson, *Larousse Biographical Dictionary,* p. 1525; Uglow, *The Continuum Dictionary of Women's Biography,* pp. 565–66.

1929 • Rose Markward Knox (1857–1950) was the first woman elected to the board of directors of the American Grocery Manufacturers' Association, in 1929. She was head of the Knox Company, still famous in the 1990s for its gelatin. Rose Markward Knox took over the business at the time of her husband's death in 1908 and built it into a major enterprise with plants in Johnstown, New York, and Camden, New Jersey.

Sources: Asbury, "Grand Old Lady of Johnstown," *Collier's,* Jan. 1, 1949; James, *Notable American Women,* vol. 2, pp. 343–44; Mullett, *American Magazine,* Oct. 1921; "Women in Business," *Fortune,* 1935.

Gertrude Battles Lane (1874–1941) was the first female vice-president of the Crowell Publishing Company, a position she assumed in New York City in

1929. Lane established her reputation as an editor of the *Woman's Home Companion,* on whose board she served from 1903 until 1937.

Sources: Ferber, *A Peculiar Treasure,* pp. 263–65; James, *Notable American Women,* vol. 2, pp. 363–65; Mott, *A History of American Magazines,* vol. 4, pp. 768–70.

1930 • Flora Solomon (1895–1984) was the first woman hired to improve working conditions at the British department store Marks and Spencer in London in 1930. Born in Russia and educated in Germany, Solomon moved to England with her family in 1914. An ardent socialist, she worked at Marks and Spencer until 1948, establishing an innovative "welfare committee," whose program included canteens, sickness and maternity benefits, health care, and paid holidays.

Sources: Solomon, *Baku to Baker Street: The Memoirs of Flora Solomon*; Uglow, *The Continuum Dictionary of Women's Biography,* pp. 505–6.

Gertrude Hickman Thompson (1877–1950) became the first woman to serve as head of the board of directors of a U.S. railroad. In October 1930, she was made chair of the board of Magma Arizona Railroad, a position her husband had held until his death three months earlier.

Sources: Read and Witlieb, *The Book of Women's Firsts,* p. 443.

1938 • Margaret Fogarty Rudkin (1897–1967) founded Pepperidge Farm, a nationwide bakery of premium bread and pastries, in Fairfield, Connecticut, in 1938. She began baking at the age of forty in order to produce a healthy bread without additives for her children with asthma. Under her leadership, the company expanded rapidly to become a multi-million-dollar operation.

Sources: Rudkin, *The Margaret Rudkin Pepperidge Farm Cookbook*; Uglow, *The Continuum Dictionary of Women's Biography,* p. 467.

1948 • Kamaldevi Chattopadhyay (b. 1903), an Indian reform leader and sponsor of the crafts movement, was the founder of the Indian Co-operative Union in 1948. This group was devoted to helping refugees participate in commercial enterprise after the partition of India in 1947. In 1952, Chattopadhyay helped to found the World Crafts Council.

Sources: Uglow, *The Continuum Dictionary of Women's Biography,* p. 119.

Margaret Rudkin founded Pepperidge Farm.

1949 • Mirabel Topham (d. 1980) was the first woman to own the Aintree Racecourse, home of the Grand National, the world's most famous steeplechase. She purchased the racecourse outright in 1949. The racecourse had been in her husband's family since 1843; she was the first woman to serve on its board (in 1935) and the first woman to manage the company (in 1936). She sold the course in 1973 for three million pounds.

Sources: Uglow, *The Continuum Dictionary of Women's Biography,* p. 542.

1951 • Armi Ratia (1912–1979), a Finnish designer, was cofounder with her husband of Marimekko, a textile design firm for which she became the first managing director in 1951. A very successful international business, Marimekko was exporting to over twenty countries by 1970. In 1968, Ratia became the

The founders of Benetton
are, left to right, Luciano,
Gilberto, Giuliana, and Carlo
Benetton.

first Finnish woman to be awarded the American Neiman Marcus Award in recognition for her art and business success.

Sources: Uglow, *The Continuum Dictionary of Women's Biography,* pp. 449–50.

1963 • Katharine Graham (b. 1917) took over as president of the Washington Post Company upon her husband's death in 1963. She was the first woman to head a Fortune 500 company. (*See also* **Media: Miscellaneous, 1973.**)

Sources: O'Neill, *The Woman's Book of World Records and Achievements*, p. 514.

1965 • Giuliana Benetton (b. 1937), with her three brothers Luciano, Gilberto, and Carlo, is the founder of the world's largest knitwear company, Benetton. She started Benetton in Treviso, Italy, the town near Venice where she grew up, in 1965. By 1996, the company had 7,000 outlets in 120 countries, making it the world's largest manufacturer of knitwear and greatest consumer of virgin wool.

Sources: Uglow, *The Continuum Dictionary of Women's Biography,* p. 61.

1966 • Mary Wells Lawrence (b. 1928), an American advertising executive, was the founder, first chairperson, and first chief executive of the prestigious Wells, Rich, Greene, Inc. She is said to have rejected a ten-year, million-dollar contract to found this company in New York City in 1966 ("Wells" was then her married name). By 1971, she was chair of the board and chief executive officer. In the 1980s she was reputed to have been the most powerful woman in the advertising industry as well as the highest paid advertising executive in the

United States. Lawrence started her advertising career in Youngstown, Ohio, where she worked from 1951 to 1952 at McKelvey's Department Store.

Sources: O'Neill, *The Women's Book of World Records and Achievements,* p. 516.

1974 • On May 16, 1974, Martha Peterson (b. 1916), president of Barnard College and a dean of Columbia University, became the first woman to serve on the board of directors of Exxon Corporation in Irving, Texas, the largest U.S. oil company.

Sources: The San Diego Tribune (17 May 1974).

1977 • Maria Pia Esmeralda Matarazzo inherited Brazil's tenth largest private company, Industrious Reunidas F. Matarazzo, from her father in 1977. She was 35 at the time and became the only woman chief executive officer at a major enterprise in Brazil. When she took over the company, it had 76 factories and employed 21,000 workers.

Sources: O'Neill, *The Women's Book of World Records and Achievements,* p. 525.

c.1979 • Margaret Shahenian (b. 1922) was the first woman to serve as a member of the board of directors of the Wine Institute of California, a position she assumed in the late 1970s.

Sources: O'Neill, *The Women's Book of World Records and Achievements,* p. 16.

c.1980 • Aduke Alakija (b. 1921), a Nigerian lawyer, was the first black African woman to hold the position of Director of Mobil Oil, in the 1980s. Educated in England, Alakija has worked throughout her life for social issues and particularly for women's rights.

Sources: Uglow, *The Continuum Dictionary of Women's Biography,* p. 12.

Cecilia Danieli (b. 1943) is the first woman to head Danieli of Buttrio, the steel conglomerate founded by her grandfather in 1914. She began work at the company as assistant to her father in 1965 and is known as "Italy's first lady of steel."

Sources: Uglow, *The Continuum Dictionary of Women's Biography,* p. 147.

Entertainment

1980 • Sherry Lee Lansing (b. 1944) was the first woman to be put in charge of production at a major film studio. In January of 1980, Lansing was appointed president of the feature-film division of Twentieth Century Fox, a position she held until 1983, when she left to form her own company, Jaffe-Lansing Productions.

Sources: Acker, *Reel Women: Pioneers of the Cinema, 1896 to the Present,* pp. 140–42; Uglow, *The Continuum Dictionary of Women's Biography,* pp. 312–13.

1987 • Dawn Steel (b. 1946) became the first woman to head a motion picture corporation in 1987 when she took over Columbia Pictures. In addition to overseeing production, marketing, and distribution for Columbia itself, she was also responsible for Tri-Star and other Columbia subsidiaries.

Sources: Acker, *Reel Women: Pioneers of the Cinema, 1896 to the Present,* pp. 143–45.

Entrepreneurs

1790s • Marie Grossholtz Tussaud (1761–1850) was the first woman to make her name as a wax-modeler and operator of wax museums. She and her brother learned wax-modelling in Bern, Switzerland, where they grew up. They moved to Paris in 1770, where her brother opened two museums, which Tussaud inherited at his death in 1794. By that time she had established her reputation as a modeler, even making death masks from guillotined people of prominence. Emigrating to England in 1802, she travelled throughout Britain, making models and exhibiting her work for thirty-three years. She founded her famous London waxworks in Baker Street in 1834.

Sources: Magnusson, *Larousse Biographical Dictionary,* p. 1482; Uglow, *The Continuum Dictionary of Women's Biography,* p. 548.

1817 • Elizabeth Veale Macarthur (1767–1850) left England for Australia with her husband John Macarthur in 1789. She is regarded as the first cultured, or educated, woman to settle in Botany Bay. When her husband fled the country after the rebellion against Governor Bligh in 1809, she took over the management of their property for eight years and became the first person to establish New South Wales as a wool producing area. She introduced merino sheep to her New South Wales farm, known as Elizabeth Farm, and developed an English market for Australian wool. After her husband's death in 1834, she passed on to her sons the wool empire she had started.

Sources: Ellis, *John Macarthur*; Magnusson, *Larousse Biographical Dictionary,* p. 932; Uglow, *The Continuum Dictionary of Women's Biography,* pp. 340–41.

1858 • Margaret Gaffney Haughery (1814–1882) was the first woman to establish a steam bakery in the American South. In June of 1858, Haughery opened the D'Aquin Bakery in New Orleans. One of her innovations was packaged crackers, and her bakery soon became the city's largest export business. She is remembered not only as a successful entrepreneur but as a generous philanthropist in this city, where she established a number of orphanages. New Orleans celebrates February 9 as "Margaret Day" each year.

Sources: Bolton, *Successful Women;* Gaffney, *Margaret's Work of Love;* Martinez, *The Immortal Margaret Haughery*; *Women's History: 100 American Women Who Made a Difference,* p. 30.

1860 • Ellen Louise Curtis Demorest (1824–1898) was the first person to put into practice the idea of accurate tissue-paper dress patterns. In New York City in 1860, with the support of her husband, a dry goods merchant, she launched a quarterly magazine, *Mme. Demorest's Mirror of Fashions*; a paper pattern was stapled into each issue. The success of this and later fashion ventures made both Demorest and her husband wealthy entrepreneurs.

Sources: Croly, *The History of the Woman's Club Movement in America*; James, *Notable American Women*, vol. 1, pp. 459–60; Ross, *Crusades and Crinolines: The Life and Times of Ellen Curtis Demorest and William Jennings Demorest.*

1875 • Lydia Estes Pinkham (1819–1883) was the first American woman to establish her reputation by selling medicine. In Boston in 1875 she decided to combat her family's poverty by selling an herbal mixture she called "Lydia E. Pinkham's Vegetable Compound." Although the mixture had no evident curative powers, it became the most widely advertised merchandise in the United States by 1898 and earned its maker fame and prosperity.

Sources: Burton, *Lydia Pinkham Is Her Name*; James, *Notable American Women* vol. 3, pp. 71–73; *Who Was Who in American History, 1607–1896,* p. 413.

1906 • Sarah Breedlove Walker (1867–1919), known as Madam C. J. Walker, was the first person to make a career by developing and selling hair straightener. Walker worked on hair products for black Americans, especially women, beginning in St. Louis, Missouri, in 1905, then opened her business in Denver, Colorado, in 1906. She built up a huge mail-order business, establishing an office in Pittsburgh in 1908 and founding laboratories in Indianapolis in 1910.

Sources: Ploski, *African American Almanac,* pp. 1393–94.

1914 • Madeleine Vionnet (1877–1975), a French fashion designer, was the founder and first head of the House of Vionnet, in Paris in 1914. She opened her first shop just before World War I, closing it during the war and reopening it in 1919. She remained head of her firm until closing her shop and retiring in 1939 at the beginning of World War II. She had a dominant influence on French fashion design for women, emphasizing clothes cut on the bias, "handkerchief point" skirts, and soft flowing materials such as silk and crepe. Her shop also included revolutionary social services for her workers, including health care and a gymnasium, both of which were uncommon at the time.

Sources: O'Neill, *The Women's Book of Records and Achievements,* p. 240; Uglow, *The Continuum Dictionary of Women's Biography,* pp. 559–60.

Inventors

1715 • Sybilla Masters (d. 1720) invented a device for cleaning and curing American corn. In London on November 25, 1715, her husband, Thomas Masters, applied for and was granted a patent for her invention.

Sources: Cobblestone: The History Magazine for Young People, (June 1994), p. 6; James, *Notable American Women,* vol. 2, pp. 508–9; Read and Witlieb, *The Book of Women's Firsts,* p. 272; Vare and Ptacek, *Mothers of Invention,* pp. 31–34.

1794 • Catherine Greene (1753–1814) was the actual inventor of the cotton gin, although her friend, Eli Whitney, is generally given credit for this invention, which he patented in 1794. This machine performed the important service of separating cotton seeds from fibers.

Sources: Chicago, *The Dinner Party,* p. 168; *Cobblestone: The History Magazine for Young People,* pp. 10–12; Haber, *Women Pioneers of Science,* p. 5; James, *Notable American Women,* vol. 2, pp. 85–86.

1809 • Mary Kies (b. 1752) was the first woman to receive a patent in the United States. In 1809, she patented a new method for weaving straw with silk or thread to make bonnets.

Sources: Cobblestone: The History Magazine for Young People, p. 3; Haber, *Women Pioneers of Science,* p. 5; Vare and Ptacek, *Mothers of Invention,* pp. 30–31.

1879 • Margaret Knight (1838–1914) was the first person to find a way to fold and seal the bottoms of paper bags in one operation. Her process, which she sold to the Eastern Paper Bag Company, was patented in 1879.

Sources: Cobblestone: The History Magazine for Young People, p. 15; Uglow, *The Continuum Dictionary of Women's Biography,* p. 300.

1893 • Nancy Green (1831–1898) was the first "Aunt Jemima" and the world's first living trademark. She made her debut serving pancakes for the Aunt Jemima Mills Company at the Columbian Exposition in Chicago, Illinois, in 1893.

Sources: Smith, *Black Firsts,* p. 49.

1908 • E. L. Todd was the first woman to invent an airplane. On July 30, 1908, she filed a patent in Washington, D.C., for her new invention: a collapsible airplane that folded up to a third of its full size.

Sources: Read and Witlieb, *The Book of Women's Firsts,* pp. 446–47.

1913 • Rose O'Neill (1874–1944) was the inventor of the Kewpie doll, which she patented in 1913. The name, derived from "Cupid," was an appropriate diminutive for the popular toy, which earned its creator more than a million dollars.

Sources: Cobblestone: The History Magazine for Young People, pp. 21–23; Horine, *Memories of Rose O'Neill;* James, *Notable American Women,* vol. 2, pp. 650–51; Ruggles, *The One Rose.*

Investments

1935 • Gretchen Schoenleber (1890–1953) was the first woman to become a member of a commodity exchange. As president of the Ambrosia Chocolate Company, she was elected to the New York Cocoa Exchange in 1935.

Sources: Read and Witlieb, *The Book of Women's Firsts,* pp. 394–95.

1958 • Mary Gindhart Roebling (c.1905–1994) was the first woman stock exchange director. She had been president of the Trenton Trust Company of New Jersey since 1937.

Sources: McCullough, *First of All: Significant "Firsts" by American Women,* p. 68.

1967 • Muriel Siebert (b. 1932) was the first woman to own a seat on the New York Stock Exchange, in 1967. A lifelong advocate for women's issues, Siebert's company, Muriel Siebert and Company, works exclusively for corporate and institutional clients.

Sources: Read and Witlieb, *The Book of Women's Firsts,* pp. 407–8.

1968 • Venita Walker VanCaspel (b. 1922) was the first female member of the Pacific Stock Exchange in San Francisco, California. She earned her seat in 1968 when she became president of her own stock brokerage firm.

Sources: Read and Witlieb, *The Book of Women's Firsts,* pp. 461–62.

1980s • Aisha Wayle (b. 1944), an Indian woman with a family heritage of feminist achievement, was the first woman to own a London investment company, in the 1980s. She is the granddaughter of Dhanvanthi Rama Rau, a social worker and one of the first Indian women to attend college, and the daughter of Santha Rama Rau, an Indian writer.

Sources: Rau, *An Inheritance*; Uglow, *The Continuum Dictionary of Women's Biography,* p. 450.

Manufacturing

1770s • Elizabeth Chudleigh (1720–1788) was the first Englishwoman to establish a brandy distillery, in the 1770s. Her distillery was located in St. Petersburg, Russia. Having created a scandal at the English court because of her licentious behavior, Chudleigh lived most of her life in Europe, and during the late 1770s she became a favorite in the court of Catherine II in Russia.

Sources: Browne, *Elizabeth Chudleigh*; Uglow, *The Continuum Dictionary of Women's Biography,* p. 124.

1825 • Rebecca Webb Lukens (1794–1854), the daughter of the founder of the Brandywine Rolling Mill, became the first female manager in the American iron industry when she took over this mill after the death of her husband in 1825. Lukens managed the business in Coatesville, Pennsylvania, until her death, creating a wide market for her high-quality boilerplate. In 1890, the mill was renamed Lukens Mills, and she became the first woman to have a steel mill named after her.

Sources: Uglow, *The Continuum Dictionary of Women's Biography,* p. 337; Wolcott, *A Woman in Steel: Rebecca Lukens*.

Rebecca Webb Lukens

Miscellaneous

1611 • Mary Frith (1590–1659), also known as Moll Cutpurse, was an English thief and transvestite who was also the first woman to be arrested for wearing men's clothes. She was detained in St. Paul's Cathedral in London on Christmas Day, 1611.

Sources: Uglow, *The Continuum Dictionary of Women's Biography,* p. 215.

1650s • Tofana (d. 1720) was the first person to invent and sell the "medicine" called "Manna of St. Nicholas of Bari," in Palermo, Sicily, in the 1650s. In fact, this popular potion was a poison, probably involving arsenic, sold by a society of women whom Tofana supplied. The mixture was used by women eager to get rid of their husbands.

Sources: Uglow, *The Continuum Dictionary of Women's Biography,* p. 542.

1848 • Amelia Jenks Bloomer (1818–1894) became the first woman to wear bloomers. She sponsored these pantaloons on July 19, 1848, at the first Women's Rights Convention in Seneca Falls, New York. The costume's design is attributed to Elizabeth Smith Miller. (*See also* **Activism: Feminism and Women's Rights, 1848.**)

Sources: Bloomer, *Life and Writings of Amelia Bloomer;* Kane, *Famous First Facts,* p. 126; Read and Witlieb, *The Book of Women's Firsts,* pp. 55–57.

1886 • Catherine Webb (1859–1947), a leader in the English co-operative movement, was the founder of the Battersea branch of the Women's Co-operative Guild in London, in 1886. Webb is also remembered for her histories of the co-operative movement throughout England.

Sources: Uglow, *The Continuum Dictionary of Women's Biography*, p. 571; Webb, *Industrial Co-operation*; Webb, *Woman with a Basket.*

1919 • Lena Madeson Phillips (1881–1955) was the founder of the National Federation of Business and Professional Women's Clubs, Inc., in 1919. She served as president of this organization from 1926 to 1929.

Sources: Read and Witlieb, *The Book of Women's Firsts,* pp. 345–46.

1976 • Susan R. Estrich (b. 1952) became the first female president of the *Harvard Law Review* in 1976. She went on to become the first woman to manage a major presidential campaign when she headed Michael Dukakis's Democratic campaign for the presidency in 1987.

Sources: Read and Witlieb, *The Book of Women's Firsts,* pp. 145–46.

Real Estate

1645 • Deborah Moody (c.1580–c.1659) was the first woman to receive a land grant in colonial America. She was given title to land in Kings County, New York, in 1645. As a landowner, she was entitled to vote, and when she exercised her right in 1655, Moody became the first woman in America to vote. (*See also* **Activism: Suffrage, 1655.**)

Sources: James, *Notable American Women.* vol. 2, pp. 569–70; Read and Witlieb, *The Book of Women's Firsts,* pp. 297–98; Rodgers, *Cleveland Rodgers, Brooklyn's First City Planner.*

1721 • Elizabeth Haddon Estaugh (1680–1762) was the founder of Haddonfield, New Jersey, in 1701. Armed with her father's power of attorney, she set out from London in that year to claim and develop 500 acres of land in Gloucester County, Western New Jersey, which he had bought in 1698. Then in better health, he had initially hoped to emigrate with his family. When this proved impossible, his twenty-one-year-old daughter set out in his stead and, as one of the youngest female landowners in the New World, founded a plantation she called "Old Haddonfield." In 1702, she married the Quaker minister John Estaugh. Together they developed their land, and after his death in 1724 she continued to manage the estate on her own.

Sources: James, *Notable American Women*, vol. 1, pp. 584–85; Nicholson, *Contributions of the Biography of Elizabeth Estaugh*; *Who Was Who in America*, 1607–1896, p. 172.

1880 • Emma Cons (1838–1912), a British artist and reformer, was the founder of the Old Vic Theatre, in 1880. During the course of a career that included the management of buildings and schools for the poor, Cons was also the first female designer of stained-glass windows for Powell's factory (a position that lead to restoration work at Merton College, Oxford) and a founder of the Women's Horticultural College at Swanley.

Sources: Uglow, *The Continuum Dictionary of Women's Biography,* pp. 136–37.

1930 • Elizabeth Thomas Werlein (1883–1946), a leader in preserving the French quarter of New Orleans, was the founder and first president of the Vieux Carré Property Owners Association in New Orleans, Louisiana, in 1930. Campaigning to enact and enforce zoning laws and building codes, Werlein devoted her life to preserving and restoring the architectural character and atmosphere of this historic city.

Sources: James, *Notable American Women,* vol. 3, pp. 568–69; Tallant, *The Romantic New Orleans.*

Services

1910s • Helena Rubinstein (1870–1965), the Polish-born entrepreneur who settled in the United States just before World War I (1914–19), was the first person to open a beauty salon in England, in London in about 1910.

Sources: Rubinstein, *My Life for Beauty*; Uglow, *The Continuum Dictionary of Women's Biography,* p. 467; Vare and Ptacek, *Mothers of Invention,* pp. 63–65.

1945 • Margery Berney Hurst (1914–1989) was the founder and first head of the Brook Street Bureau of Mayfair Ltd., an extremely successful employment agency for secretarial staff, in London in 1945. The company went public in 1965, and by the mid-1990s, it had over 200 offices throughout the world. In 1960 Hurst founded the Society for International Secretaries, and in 1970 she became one of the first female members of Lloyds Underwriters. She was awarded the Order of the British Empire in 1976, and in 1981 she became the first female member of the Worshipful Company of Marketers.

Sources: Hurst, *No Glass Slipper*; Uglow, *The Continuum Dictionary of Women's Biography,* p. 270.

c.1950 • Julia Child (b. 1912), the famous American cook, cookbook writer, and television personality, was the cofounder, with her friends Simone Beck

Helena Rubinstein

and Louise Bertholle, of L'Ecole des Trois Gourmandes, a cooking school in Paris, where Child lived from 1948 until 1954.

Sources: Uglow, *The Continuum Dictionary of Women's Biography,* p. 121.

Community Service

Children's Welfare

1908 • The first charity dedicated to the welfare of children established by Muslim women in Egypt was Jam'iyyat al-Safaqa bi'l-Atfal (the Society of Compassion for Children), founded in 1908 by Zaynab Anis. The group, made up of women from middle- and upper-class families, founded an orphanage with the support of other wealthy women.

Sources: Baron, *The Women's Awakening in Egypt: Culture, Society, and the Press,* p. 172.

1919 • Eglantyne Jebb (1876–1928) devoted her life to the cause of children in need throughout the world. Her efforts to help destitute children in Europe after World War I resulted in her establishment of the Fight the Famine Council, which led in 1919 to her founding of the Save the Children Fund. This organization provided direct aid as well as the provision of hospitals, homes, and schools. Jebb was also the sponsor of the Children's Charter, adopted by the League of Nations in Geneva, Switzerland, in 1924. She joined the League's Council for the Protection of Children in 1925 and continued her work throughout her life.

Sources: Uglow, *The Continuum Dictionary of Women's Biography,* p. 281; Wilson, *Eglantyne Jebb: Rebel Daughter of a Country House*.

1924 • Sophie Irene Loeb (1876–1929) was a cofounder and the first president of the Child Welfare Committee of America, in New York City in 1924. A lifelong advocate of children's rights, Loeb campaigned in the United States and abroad (through the League of Nations) for children's care within their communities rather than in institutions. She was also active in the Zionist movement.

Sources: James, *Notable American Women,* pp. 416–17; Uglow, *The Continuum Dictionary of Women's Biography,* p. 332.

1973 • An advocate for children's rights, Marian Wright Edelman (b. 1939) was the founder and first president of the Children's Defense Fund, in 1973. This organization specializes in such issues as teenage pregnancy, early death among infants, and child abuse.

Sources: Read and Witlieb, *The Book of Women's Firsts,* pp. 136–37.

Heroines

1337 • Agnes Dunbar (1312–1369), granddaughter of the Scottish king Robert Bruce, was the first woman to defend Dunbar Castle against English attack, in 1337. She sucessfully protected her territory and became a Scottish hero.

Sources: Uglow, *The Continuum Dictionary of Women's Biography,* p. 177.

1607 • Pocahontas (1596–1617), a Powhatan princess, was the first Native American woman to save the life of an Englishman. In Virginia in 1607 she saved the life of John Smith when he was attacked by her tribe. She then helped to establish a tenuous peace.

Sources: Fritz, *Pocahontas;* Uglow, *The Continuum Dictionary of Women's Biography,* p. 436.

1803 • Sacajawea (1787–1812), a Native American Shoshone brought up by the Minnataree, was the only woman on the Lewis and Clark Expedition to explore the territories west of the United States. Although her husband was actually hired as a guide in 1803, Sacajawea ultimately became the expedition's guide and interpreter.

Sources: Chicago, *The Dinner Party,* pp. 84–85; Frazier, *Sacajawea: The Girl Nobody Knows; Who Was Who in America, 1607–1896,* p. 460.

1793 • Charlotte Corday (1768–1793) was the first Frenchwoman to become a political assassin. In 1793, she stabbed Jean Paul Marat in his bathtub. She was guillotined for this act four days later.

Sources: Uglow, *The Continuum Dictionary of Women's Biography,* p. 137.

1856 • Ann Pamela Cunningham (1816–1875), a pioneering Southern club woman, was the founder of the first women's patriotic society in the United States. In Virginia in March of 1856, she started the Mount Vernon Ladies' Association of the Union, a club designed to preserve and restore George Washington's home at Mount Vernon.

Sources: James, *Notable American Women,* vol. 1, pp. 416–17; *Who Was Who in America, 1607–1896,* p. 130.

1878 • Vera Zasulich (1849–1919) was the first Russian revolutionary in the conspiratorial movement to perform an act of political violence. In St. Petersburg in 1878, she shot the city's governor, General Trepov, because of his brutality to a political prisoner. A jury refused to condemn her and she was acquitted.

Sources: Uglow, *The Continuum Dictionary of Women's Biography,* p. 599.

1881 • Sofya Lvovna Perovskaya (1853–1881), a Russian revolutionary, was the first woman to organize and direct a conspiracy that successfully assassinated a Russian czar, in Moscow in February of 1881. She was caught in March, sentenced to death, and hanged in April of the same year.

Sources: Uglow, *The Continuum Dictionary of Women's Biography,* p. 430.

This statue of Sacajawea, guide on the Lewis and Clark Expedition, stands on the grounds of the South Dakota capitol.

1915 • Edith Louisa Cavell (1865–1915) was the first Englishwoman to be shot by the Germans for resistance work during World War I. Stationed in Brussels during the war, in 1907 she became Berkendael Medical Institute's first matron; the institute later became a Red Cross hospital. While serving as a nurse in Brussels, Belgium, Cavell cared for the wounded regardless of their nationality and helped British and French soldiers escape from German captivity. She was executed on October 12, 1915.

Sources: Judson, *Edith Cavell;* Magnusson, *Larousse Biographical Dictionary*, p. 278; Ryder, *Edith Cavell: A Biography*.

1940s • Electra Apostoloy (1912–1944), an active Greek communist and feminist, was the first woman to play a leading role in the Greek resistance movement during World War II. She was tortured to death by the German-backed Greek secret police in 1944, but revealed no information about her communist comrades.

Sources: Uglow, *The Continuum Dictionary of Women's Biography,* pp. 23–24.

1953 • Ethel Greenglass Rosenberg (1915–1953) was the first and only American woman to be executed for treason during peacetime. With her husband, Julius Rosenberg, she was sentenced to die for conspiracy to commit wartime espionage. Ethel Rosenberg was also the first woman to be incarcerated in the maximum security prison, Sing Sing in Ossining, New York. The Rosenbergs were electrocuted there on June 19, 1953.

Sources: Read and Witlieb, *The Book of Women's Firsts,* pp. 380–81; Uglow, *The Continuum Dictionary of Women's Biography,* pp. 464–65.

1956 • Dorothy Nyembe (b. 1930) was the first woman to lead Natal women in protest against the South African government's policy of apartheid, in 1956. Repeatedly imprisoned and punished for her political activism, Nyembe has devoted her life to the cause of equality for blacks in her country.

Sources: Uglow, *The Continuum Dictionary of Women's Biography,* pp. 407–8.

1970 • Ulrike Meinhof (1934–1976), a German terrorist, was the first woman to lead the radical group called the Red Army Faction. After her daring efforts to free an arrested colleague, Andreas Baader, in 1970, her terrorist organization became known in the media as the Baader-Meinhof Gang. Arrested in June 1972, Meinhof was sentenced in 1974 to eight years in prison and committed suicide after the failure of terrorist attempts to gain her release.

Sources: Magnusson, *Larousse Biographical Dictionary,* p. 999; Uglow, *The Continuum Dictionary of Women's Biography,* pp. 370–71.

1986 • Christa McAuliffe (1948–1986) was the first citizen passenger to fly with astronauts on a space mission. She was selected from 11,000 teachers who applied for the opportunity in a program sponsored by President Ronald Reagan. She went up with six astronauts on the space shuttle "Challenger," launched from Cape Canaveral, Florida, on January 28, 1986. The ship exploded shortly after take off, killing all seven on board.

Sources: Read and Witlieb, *The Book of Women's Firsts,* p. 276; Uglow, *The Continuum Dictionary of Women's Biography,* p. 458.

Miscellaneous

First century B.C. • Clodia was the first woman to establish and lead a large influential salon in ancient Rome, in the first century B.C. Her salon was attended by many important thinkers and politicians, and she established a position of power through influence.

Sources: Chicago, *The Dinner Party,* p. 126.

A painting in the U.S. Capitol depicts the astronauts, including Christa McAuliffe, who perished in the 1986 "Challenger" explosion.

Missionaries and Adventurers

See also **Health Care: Missionaries**

1836 • Narcissa Prentiss Whitman (1808–1847) and Eliza Hart Spalding (1807–1851), American pioneer women and medical missionaries who travelled west with a caravan of the American Fur Company, were the first white women to cross the Continental Divide, at South Pass, Wyoming, on July 4,

1836. Whitman died in a Cayuse massacre; Spalding died of tuberculosis four years later.

Sources: Allen, *Narcissa Whitman;* Eaton, *Narcissa Whitman;* James, *Notable American Women,* vol. 3, pp. 330–31, 595–97; *Who Was Who in America, 1607–1896,* p. 577.

1837 • Margaret Barrett Allen Prior (1773–1842), an American woman devoted to charitable work, was the first female missionary commissioned by the New York Female Moral Reform Society, in New York City in 1837. The society, which she served in this capacity until her death, was dedicated to reclaiming "depraved and abandoned females" but worked primarily for "the preservation of the virtuous." Her reports to the society, which appeared regularly in its journal, the *Advocate of Moral Reform,* are particularly interesting as early social case studies of slum conditions.

Sources: Ingraham, *Walks of Usefulness, or Reminiscences of Mrs. Margaret Prior;* James, *Notable American Women,* vol. 3, pp. 101–3.

1869 • Isabel Arundell Burton (1831–1896) was the first woman to host interracial receptions in Damascus, Syria. Lady Burton travelled extensively with her husband, the explorer Sir Richard Burton, and supported him emotionally in his diplomatic work. While he was serving as British Consul in Damascus in 1869, Lady Burton enjoyed an influential position as an official hostess and inaugurated interracial gatherings.

Sources: Magnusson, *Larousse Biographical Dictionary,* pp. 235–36; Uglow, *Continuum Dictionary of Women's Biography,* pp. 97–98.

Notable by Birth

1587 • Virginia Dare (b. 1587) was the first child of English parents born in America on August 18, 1587, in Roanoke Island, North Carolina. She was the daughter of Ananian Dare and Elenor White Dare. Only the first nine days of her life are known.

Sources: James, *Notable American Women,* vol. 1, pp. 431–32; *Who Was Who in America, 1607–1896,* p. 633.

1893 • Esther Cleveland (1893–1980), the second child and second daughter of Frances Folsom and President Grover Cleveland, was the first child to be born in the White House, in 1893 during her father's second term.

Sources: The World Book Encyclopedia, vol. 4, p. 522.

Notable by Marriage

1774 • Abigail Stoneman, a colonial publican, was the first woman from Newport, Rhode Island, to marry a titled Englishman. In Hampton, Connecticut, on August 28, 1774, she married the Hon. Sir John Treville. The couple soon after settled in New York.

Sources: James, *Notable American Women,* vol. 3, pp. 390–91.

1789 • Martha Dandridge Custis Washington (1731–1802) became the nation's first "First Lady" when her husband, George Washington, was inaugurated as the first president of the United States in New York City on April 30, 1789. She did not enjoy her official position and said she felt like a "state prisoner." She dressed plainly and managed the home she shared with the President with dignity and grace. (*See also:* **Business: Banking, 1886.**)

Sources: James, *Notable American Women,* vol. 3, pp. 548–50; *Who Was Who in America, 1607–1896,* p. 565; *The World Book Encyclopedia,* pp. 85–86.

1800 • Abigail Adams (1744–1818) was the first "First Lady" to live in the White House after its completion in 1800. Known as a supporter and advisor of her husband, John Adams, who became president of the United States in 1797, she was an advocate of women's education and rights.

Sources: Williams, *Queenly Women: Crowned and Uncrowned,* pp. 481–86; *Who Was Who in America, 1607–1896,* p. 14.

Abigail Adams

1886 • Frances Folsom Cleveland (1864–1947) was the first woman to be married to a president in the White House. In a large formal ceremony in the Blue Room on June 2, 1886, she married Grover Cleveland.

Frances Folsom was born July 21, 1864, in Buffalo, New York. She was given a good education and met Grover Cleveland while she was a student at Wells College. When she graduated from that institution in 1885, she reportedly received extravagant floral arrangements from the White House greenhouses, sent by President Grover Cleveland. After a tour of Europe, Frances returned to the United States and was met in New York by President Cleveland's sister and personal secretary. The three travelled to Washington for the first-ever presidential wedding in the White House. As First Lady, Mrs. Cleveland was popular because of her youth and graceful demeanor. The Clevelands left the White House in 1889, and their daughter, Ruth, was born in New York City in 1891.

Sources: James, *Notable American Women,* vol. 2, pp. 350–52; *National Cyclopedia of American Biography,* vol. 2, p. 402; *Who Was Who in America, 1607–1896,* p. 657.

Frances Folsom Cleveland

1933 • Eleanor Roosevelt (1884–1962) was the first First Lady to hold a press conference. She spoke to reporters in the White House on March 6, 1933. This event attested to her significant and visible role as an activist for human rights issues beginning during this first year of her husband's first term as president of the United States.

Sources: Read and Witlieb, *The Book of Women's Firsts,* pp. 378–79; Whitman, *American Reformers,* pp. 697–701.

Philanthropy

First century • Dorcas, a wealthy woman of first-century Jerusalem, was the originator of the Dorcas Sewing Societies. This organization took her name because she was known for her charity and specifically for making clothes for the poor.

Sources: Chicago, *The Dinner Party,* p. 129.

1776 • Suzanne Necker (1739–1817), a Swiss author and philanthropist, was the founder of the Necker Hospital in Paris in 1776. She converted a local convent into a 120-bed institution and maintained it as a particularly clean and efficiently run establishment. The hospital took her name in 1820 and remained a significant center of pediatric medicine and research.

Sources: Uglow, *The Continuum Dictionary of Women's Biography,* p. 398.

1780 • Esther De Berdt Reed (1746–1780) and Sarah Franklin Bache, daughter of Benjamin Franklin, founded the first relief organization of the American Revolutionary War. In 1780, they formed a committee of 35 women, The Ladies Association of Philadelphia, which became known as "George Washington's Sewing Circle." Their purpose was to raise money to purchase clothing and supplies for soldiers serving in the Continental Army.

Sources: Read and Witlieb, *The Book of Women's Firsts,* p. 363.

1835 • Mary Carpenter (1807–1877), an English philanthropist, founded the Working and Visiting Society in England. This group devoted itself to the needs of poor children. Carpenter was a lifelong activist on behalf of a variety of causes, among them penal reform and the education of women. In 1829, she opened a girl's school in Bristol, England, and later opened several reformatories for girls.

Sources: Magnusson, *Larousse Biographical Dictionary,* p. 265; Uglow, *The Continuum Dictionary of Women's Biography,* pp. 106–7.

1849 • Caroline Jones Chisholm (1808–1877), an English philanthropist, was the founder of the Family Colonization Loan Society in Australia, in 1849. Chisholm established a government office in Australia to help immigrant women. Over 11,000 women and children were helped through this office. Concerned throughout her life with the plight of immigrants to the Far East, Chisholm was also the founder of the Female School of Industry for the Daughters of European Soldiers in Madras, India, in 1832, and of the Female Immigrants' Home in Sydney, Australia, in 1841.

Sources: Magnusson, *Larousse Biographical Dictionary,* pp. 304–5; Uglow, *The Continuum Dictionary of Women's Biography,* pp. 121–22.

1875 • Josephine Shaw Lowell (1843–1905) became the first female member of the New York State Board of Charities in 1875 in New York City, amid much publicity and opposition because of her gender. Heartbroken by the death of her husband in the Civil War followed by the death of her young daughter, Lowell directed her energies into philanthropy but soon became an active social reformer. She became the first president of the first Consumer Council in 1890, a position she held until 1896, then set up the Women's Municipal

League as a political lobby group. Her book, *Public Relief and Private Charity,* provided guidelines for state-administered charity.

Sources: Uglow, *The Continuum Dictionary of Women's Biography,* p. 336; *Who Was Who in America, 1607–1896,* pp. 543–44.

1907 • Grace Hoadley Dodge (1856–1914), an ardent American welfare worker, founded the New York Travellers Aid Society in New York City in 1907. After a career of unpaid work with needy people, she left over $1.5 million to charity at the time of her death.

Sources: Stein and Baxter, *Grace H. Dodge: Her Life and Work;* Uglow, *The Continuum Dictionary of Women's Biography,* p. 171.

American Margaret Olivia Slocum Sage (1828–1918) established the Russell Sage Foundation in 1907. The foundation provides funding for research devoted to the improvement of social and economic conditions in the United States, with an endowment of $10 million.

Sources: The World Book Encyclopedia, vol. 17, p. 18.

1953 • English philanthropist Sue Ryder (b. 1923), Baroness of Warsaw and Cavendish, founded the Mission for the Relief of Suffering. Under its auspices, she opened a home for concentration camp victims in Suffolk, England, in 1953. Her organization soon extended its purpose to helping the physically and mentally ill and eventually became the Sue Ryder Foundation for the Sick and Disabled of All Age Groups. Ryder homes operate in Britain, Poland, Bosnia, and Italy.

Sources: Magnusson, *Larousse Biographical Dictionary,* p. 1281; Ryder, *And the Morrow is Theirs;* Ryder, *Child of My Love;* Uglow, *The Continuum Dictionary of Women's Biography,* p. 470.

Volunteer Service

1701 • The first sexually integrated jury, comprised of six women and six men, was formed in Albany, New York, in 1701. Although women were routinely excluded or exempted from jury duty in the United States until the last half of the twentieth century, the American colonies set an early precedent for women's participation.

Sources: Read and Witlieb, *The Book of Women's Firsts,* pp. 234–35.

Education

College Deans and Presidents

1866 • Ann Preston (1813–1872) was the first dean of the first women's medical college in the United States. In 1866 she was promoted from Professor of Physiology and Hygiene to the new position of dean at the Female Medical College in Philadelphia, Pennsylvania.

Sources: James, *Notable American Women,* vol. 3, pp. 96–97; Read and Witlieb, *The Book of Women's Firsts,* pp. 349–50; *Who Was Who in America, 1607–1896,* p. 424.

1871 • Frances Elizabeth Willard (1839–1898) was the first female college president. In 1871, she was chosen president of Evanston College for Ladies in Evanston, Illinois. Two years later, the college became the Woman's College of Northwestern University. Willard became dean of women there, a position she held for a year. The state of Illinois has placed a statue of Frances Willard in Statuary Hall in the U. S. Capitol building. (*See also* **Activism: Temperance, 1874.**)

Sources: James, *Notable American Women,* vol. 3, pp. 613–18; Read and Witlieb, *The Book of Women's Firsts,* pp. 483–84; Whitman, *American Reformers,* pp. 885–88; *Who Was Who in America, 1607–1896,* p. 581.

1882 • Alice Elvira Freeman Palmer (1855–1902) was the first active president of Wellesley College in Wellesley, Massachusetts. Preceded by Ada L. Howard, who served for less than a year and in name only while affairs were managed by the college's founder Henry F. Durant, Palmer took over as acting president in 1881 and formally assumed the post in 1882. She served in this capacity until her marriage in 1887. In 1892 she became the first dean of women at the University of Chicago, a position she held until 1895.

Sources: Freeman and Palmer, *The Teacher: Essays and Addresses on Education;* Hazard, *An Academic Courtship;* James, *Notable American Women,* vol. 3, pp. 4–8.

1885 • Martha Carey Thomas (1857–1935) was the first female college faculty member to become a dean. She was appointed a professor and a dean of Bryn Mawr College in Bryn Mawr, Pennsylvania, when it opened in 1885. She was also the first female president of Bryn Mawr College, from 1894 until 1922. In addition, Thomas was the first woman to earn a doctoral degree from the University of Zurich, in November 1882.

Sources: James, *Notable American Women,* vol. 3, pp. 446–50; Read and Witlieb, *The Book of Women's Firsts,* p. 442; Whitman, *American Reformers,* pp. 797–98.

A statue of Frances Willard represents Illinois in Statuary Hall in the U.S. Capitol rotunda.

Elizabeth Mead

1889 • Elizabeth Storrs Billings Mead (b. 1890) was the first president of Mount Holyoke College, founded as Mount Holyoke Seminary in 1837 and headed by women with the title of principal until 1889. Mary Ann Brigham (1824–1889) was actually the first woman appointed to serve as president of Mount Holyoke, but she was killed in a railroad accident a few days before she was to assume the position. On January 23, 1893, Mount Holyoke was authorized by the state of Massachusetts to adopt the name Mount Holyoke College. *Sources: National Cyclopedia of American Biography,* vol. 4, pp. 462–63.

1890 • Susan Lincoln Tolman Mills (1825–1912), an American educator, was the first president of the oldest women's college on the Pacific coast. She was elected president of Mills College in Oakland, California, in 1890. This

school, which she and her husband, Cyrus, had established as a seminary in 1871, followed the model of Mount Holyoke in Massachusetts, from which Mills had graduated in 1845. Beginning in 1865, she served as lady principal of the Ladies Seminary, which her husband directed until his death in 1884. She held the position of the college's first president until her retirement at the age of 84 in 1909.

Sources: James, *Notable American Women,* vol. 2, pp. 546–47; James, *The Story of Cyrus and Susan Mills;* Keep, *Fourscore Years: A History of Mills College.*

Susan Lincoln Tolman Mills

Mary Mills Patrick (1850–1940), a missionary educator, was the first president of the American College for Girls in Istanbul, Turkey. She assumed her position when the American High School for Girls in that city, where she had taught since 1875, was chartered as a college in March of 1890 by the Commonwealth of Massachusetts. She served the college in this capacity until her retirement in 1924.

Sources: James, *Notable American Women,* vol. 3, pp. 25–26; Jenkins, *An Educational Ambassador to the Near East;* Patrick, *A Bosporus Adventure;* Patrick, *Under Five Sultans.*

1893 • Elizabeth Cabot Cary Agassiz (1822–1907) served as the first president of Radcliffe College in Cambridge, Massachusetts, from 1893 through 1903. Instrumental in founding this female counterpart of Harvard University, Agassiz believed that women should have the same educational opportunities as men.

Sources: James, *Notable American Women,* pp. 22–25; Ogilvie, *Women in Science,* pp. 23–25; Paton, *Elizabeth Cary Agassiz: A Biography;* Whitman, *American Reformers,* pp. 7–9.

1894 • Emily James Smith Putnam (1865–1944), an American scholar of Greek literature and history, was the first person to serve as dean of Barnard College in New York City in 1894. She held this position, even after her marriage in 1899 to the well-known publisher George Putnam, until she became pregnant with her only child, born the following year. She returned to Barnard to teach history in 1914 and then Greek in 1920. She is remembered for her pioneering work at Barnard and particularly for two of her books, *The Lady: Studies of Certain Significant Phases of Her History* (1910) and *Candaules' Wife and Other Old Stories* (1926).

Sources: Gildersleeve, *Many a Good Crusade;* James, *Notable American Women,* vol. 3, pp. 106–8; Miller and Myers, *Barnard College: The First Fifty Years;* White, *A History of Barnard College.*

Agnes Irwin (1841–1914), an American educator, was the first dean of Radcliffe College in Cambridge, Massachusetts. She assumed this position in May of 1894 at the request of the college's first president, Elizabeth Cary Agassiz, who needed someone to assist her in her duties. Irwin was especially astute in developing the delicate relationship between Radcliffe College and Harvard University.

Sources: James, *Notable American Women,* vol. 2, pp. 253–55; Whitman, *American Reformers,* pp. 387–88.

1898 • Ellen Spencer Mussey (1850–1936), an American lawyer and feminist, was the first dean of the Washington College of Law, a school she helped to found with her friend and colleague, Emma M. Gillett, in Washington, D.C. The cocducational school was incorporated in April of 1898. While maintaining an active private law practice, Mussey continued in the position of dean until August of 1913. The Washington College of Law, while keeping its name, merged with American University in 1949.

Sources: Croly, *A History of the Women's Club Movement in America,* pp. 347–50; James, *Notable American Women,* vol. 2, pp. 606–7; Whitman, *American Reformers,* pp. 597–99.

1974 • Pauline Jewett (b. 1922), who received her doctorate from Harvard University, was the first woman to serve as a college president in Canada. She was named president of Simon Frazer University in 1974.

Sources: O'Neill, *The Women's Book of World Records and Achievements,* p. 407.

1975 • Rosemary Murray, a professor of chemistry who had previously been president of New Hall, Cambridge, was the first woman to serve as vice-chancellor of Cambridge University. She assumed this position, first established in 1412, in 1975.

Sources: O'Neill, *The Women's Book of World Records and Achievements,* p. 407.

Jill Ker Conway (b. 1934) became the first female president of Smith College in Northampton, Massachusetts, in 1975, the year in which the college, founded and endowed by Sophia Smith, celebrated its hundredth anniversary. Conway, a native of Australia, later wrote about her experiences growing up in Australia and the challenges faced by women scholars in her two autobiographical works, *The Road From Coorain* (1990) and *True North: A Memoir* (1994).

Sources: O'Neill, *The Women's Book of World Records and Achievements,* p. 407; Read and Witlieb, *The Book of Women's Firsts,* p. 412.

1976 • Hélène Ahrweiler (b. 1916), a French historian, was the first woman to become president of the Sorbonne in Paris. She was elected in 1976 and held the post until her retirement in 1981.

Sources: Uglow, *The Continuum Dictionary of Women's Biography,* pp. 9–10.

1977 • Hanna Hollborn Gray (b. 1930) became the first woman to serve as acting president of Yale University in New Haven, Connecticut, when in 1977 she replaced her predecessor, Kingman Brewster, when he was named ambassador to Great Britain. Gray went on to become president of the University of Chicago in 1978, the first woman to serve in this capacity at a major university.

Sources: Read and Witlieb, *The Book of Women's Firsts,* pp. 184–85.

1986 • Niara Sudarkasa (b. 1939) was named Lincoln University's first female president in 1986. Sudarkasa (an adopted African name—her given name was Gloria Marshall) earned her Ph.D. in anthropology from Columbia University in New York City. Before taking the position of president at Lincoln Uni-

versity, in Jefferson City, Missouri, she was a tenured professor and associate vice-president of academic affairs at the University of Michigan in Ann Arbor.
Sources: Jet (27 October 1986), vol. 71, p. 22.

1990 • Donna Shalala (b. 1942) was appointed president of the University of Wisconsin at Madison in 1990, the first woman in this post and the first woman ever to head a Big Ten university. Shalala, an energetic and assertive leader, once worked in Iran for the Peace Corps, spent time as the president of Hunter College in New York City and was appointed assistant secretary of housing and urban development under President Jimmy Carter. In 1993, she left the University of Wisconsin-Madison to become secretary of health and human services in President Bill Clinton's administration.
Sources: Time (23 April 1990), vol. 135, p. 11.

1993 • Dr. Joann Horton (b. 1932) was named the first female president of Texas Southern University in Houston, Texas, in 1993. Horton earned her B.S. and M.A. degrees in French from Appalachian State University in Boone, North Carolina, and her Ph.D. in higher education administration from Ohio State University. Before being named president of Texas Southern University, Horton worked as the administrator of community colleges for the Iowa Department of Education in Des Moines.
Sources: Jet (23 August 1993), vol. 84, p. 16.

Judith Rodin (b. 1945) was appointed president of the University of Pennsylvania on July 1, 1993, becoming the first woman to head an Ivy League school. (Others had held the position of acting president, but Rodin was the first to receive the full appointment.) A University of Pennsylvania alumna, she was the president of the Women's Student Government there during her undergraduate years. Rodin felt that it was archaic to have separate men's and women's student governments, so before she left, she merged the two. After earning her Ph.D. in behavioral psychology from Columbia University in New York City, Rodin taught for two years at New York University, then joined Yale University's psychology department in 1972. She became chair of the department in 1989, then dean of the graduate school of arts and sciences at Yale in 1991, and provost of Yale University less than a year later. Passed over for the presidency of Yale after Benno Schmidt left, she accepted the position at University of Pennsylvania after turning down other offers. An expert on eating disorders and obesity, Rodin wrote the successful book *Body Traps,* published in 1992.
Sources: The Chronicle of Higher Education (15 December 1993), vol. 40, p. A20.

Judith Rodin

1994 • Dorothy Yancy (b. 1944) was elected the 12th president of Johnson C. Smith University in Charlotte, North Carolina, the first woman to be named to the post. Yancy earned her bachelor's degree in history from Johnson C. Smith University in 1964, a master of arts from the University of Massachusetts at Amherst, and a doctorate in political science from Atlanta University.
Sources: Jet (21 November 1994), vol. 87, p. 22.

Gillian Beer (b. 1935) is the first woman to serve as president of a Cambridge College that educates both men and women. She was inducted in October of 1994, becoming at the same time the first female president of Clare Hall. She is also the first woman of a wife and husband team who have both held chairs at Cambridge University. Educated at Oxford and Girton College, Cambridge, she became a professor of English at Cambridge in 1989 and is currently King Edward VII Professor of English Literature. She has published books on Meredith, George Eliot, and Charles Darwin and is particularly interested in the connections between literature and science.

Sources: Apter, "Gillian Beer, President Elect, Clare Hall, Cambridge," *Clare Hall Newsletter* (1993–1994).

Degrees and Graduates

1678 • Helena Cornaro (1646–1684) was the first woman to receive the degree of Doctor of Philosophy. On June 25, 1678, she presented her dissertation at the University of Padua, Italy, and was awarded her degree.

Sources: Chicago, *The Dinner Party,* pp. 163–64.

1850 • Lucy Ann Stanton of Cleveland, Ohio, was the first African American woman to graduate from college. She graduated from Oberlin College receiving a bachelor of literature degree.

Sources: Kane, *Famous First Facts,* p. 186.

1860 • Julie-Victoire Daubie (1824–1874) was the first woman to take and pass the French *baccalaureat* exam in 1860 before a jury from the Faculté des Lettres of Lyon. She went on to become the first woman to pass the advanced exam, the *licence,* in 1871.

Sources: Uglow, *The Continuum Dictionary of Women's Biography,* p. 148.

1861 • Lottie Digges Moon (1840–1912) was, with four other women, the first woman to receive a graduate degree in the American South. They received M.A. degrees from Albemarle Institute in Charlottesville, Virginia, in 1867. Moon went on to a distinguished career as a Baptist missionary to China.

Sources: James, *Notable American Women,* vol. 2, pp. 570–71; Lawrence, *Lottie Moon;* Moon, *Sketches of the Moon and Barclay Families.*

1877 • Kate Edger was the first woman to graduate from the University of New Zealand. In 1877, she earned a degree in mathematics. By 1893, over half the students at New Zealand universities were women.

Sources: Uglow, *The Continuum Dictionary of Women's Biography,* p. 145.

Helen Magill White (1853–1944) became the first woman to earn a doctoral degree from an American university when she received her Ph.D. in classics from Boston University in Boston, Massachusetts, in 1877.

Sources: James, *Notable American Women,* vol. 3, pp. 588–89; Read and Witlieb, *The Book of Women's Firsts,* p. 265.

1880 • Alice Bennett (1851–1925), an American physician, was the first woman to earn a doctorate from the University of Pennsylvania in Philadelphia in 1880. With a degree in anatomy, she was immediately appointed superintendent of the women's section of the State Hospital for the Insane in Norristown, Pennsylvania, the first woman to hold this position. When she was elected president of the Montgomery County Medical Society in 1890, she was also the first woman to hold this office. A specialist in mental illness, Bennett had a distinguished career in medicine.

Sources: Hall, *One Hundred Years of American Psychiatry*; James, *Notable American Women,* vol. 1, pp. 131–32.

1888 • Gertrude Margaret Lawthian Bell (1868–1926) was the first woman to obtain a first-class honors degree in history at a British university. She achieved this distinction at Lady Margaret Hall, Oxford University, in 1888. Bell went on to a flamboyant career as a travel writer and governmental advisor on the Arab world.

Sources: Uglow, *The Continuum Dictionary of Women's Biography,* pp. 58–59; Winstone, *Gertrude Bell.*

c.1891 • Maria Montessori (1870–1952) was the first woman to graduate from the University of Rome. In 1896, she became the first woman in Italy to receive a medical degree. She is famous for her innovative methods in the education of young children, and there are now Montessori schools throughout the world.

Sources: Briggs, *A Dictionary of 20th Century World Biography,* pp. 398–99; Chicago, *The Dinner Party,* p. 201.

1894 • Sarah Elizabeth Doyle (1830–1922), an American educator and club woman, was the first woman to receive an honorary degree from Brown University in Providence, Rhode Island, in 1894. An advocate of higher education for women, Doyle was also the first president of the Rhode Island Society for the Collegiate Education of Women. She served from 1896 until 1919.

Sources: Hawk, *Pembroke College in Brown University: The First Seventy-five Years, 1891–1966;* James, *Notable American Women,* vol. 1, pp. 515–17.

1898 • Milicent Washburn Shinn (1858–1940), an American psychologist who made her career as a writer, was the first woman to earn a doctoral degree from the University of California at Berkeley in 1898. She is particularly remembered for her meticulous study of her niece, published as *Notes on the Development of a Child,* between 1893 and 1907 and popularized as *The Biography of a Baby* in 1900.

Sources: Hinkel and McCann, *Biographies of California Authors and Indexes of California Literature,* vol. 1, pp. 195–96; James, *Notable American Women,* vol. 3, pp. 285–86.

1911 • Caroline Maria Hewins (1846–1926) was the first woman to receive an honorary master's degree from Trinity College in Hartford, Connecticut, in 1911. She was honored for her pioneering work as a librarian in the field of chil-

Maria Montessori

dren's literature. She is also remembered for her autobiographical volume, *A Mid-Century Child and Her Books.*

Sources: Hewins, *Caroline M. Hewins: Her Book;* James, *Notable American Women,* vol. 2, pp. 189–91; Root, "Caroline Maria Hewins," in *Pioneering Leaders in Librarianship.*

1925 • Annie Jump Cannon (1863–1941), an astronomer at the Harvard College Observatory from 1896 until 1940, became the first woman to receive an honorary doctorate from Oxford University. She was granted this honor in 1925, shortly after Oxford allowed women to receive degrees. Cannon was also the first woman awarded a Gold Medal by the National Academy of Sciences.

Sources: Noble, *Contemporary Women Scientists of America,* pp. 9–10; Read and Witlieb, *The Book of Women's Firsts,* pp. 81–82; Uglow, *The Continuum Dictionary of Women's Biography,* p. 105.

1930 • Dorothy Weeks (1893–1990) became the first woman to earn her doctorate in mathematics from the Massachusetts Institute of Technology in Cambridge, Massachusetts, in 1930. Weeks made her career in industry and university teaching, in which her specialty was physics.

Sources: Read and Witlieb, *The Book of Women's Firsts,* p. 474.

Dorothy Weeks

1974 • Noor Al-Hussein (b. 1951), the fourth wife of King Hussein of Jordan, is the first Jordanian queen to graduate from Princeton University. Born Elizabeth Halaby in America, she was admitted to Princeton in 1969, the first year women were accepted. With a degree in architecture and urban planning, she is also the founder of the Noor Al-Hussein Foundation, which specializes in educational and environmental projects.

Sources: Briggs, *A Dictionary of 20th Century World Biography,* p 281; Uglow, *The Continuum Dictionary of Women's Biography,* p. 405.

Founders

Fifth century • Eudocia (401–460) was the founder of the University at Constantinople. A scholar, writer, and patron of education, she encouraged the study of Greek literature. She traveled to Jerusalem in 443, where she built a number of churches including St. Stephen, where she is buried.

Sources: Schmidt, *400 Outstanding Women of the World,* pp. 213–14.

1448 • Margaret of Anjou (1430–1482), the wife of Henry VI and a powerful ruler in her own right (particularly after her husband went insane in the 1450s), founded Queen's College, Cambridge, in 1448.

Sources: The Concise Dictionary of National Biography: From Earliest Times to 1985, vol. 2, pp. 1945–46.

1501 • Lady Margaret Beaufort (1441–1509), the mother of Henry VII, was the first woman to found professorships of divinity at both Oxford and Cambridge Universities, in 1501. She was the founder of St. John's College of Cambridge University. One of the first female writers in England, Beaufort lectured on divinity at both Oxford and Cambridge Universities. She had completed the endowment of Christ's College, Cambridge, a college begun by Henry VII in 1505, and left most of her fortune for the endowment of St. John's College, Cambridge, at the time of her death.

Sources: Chicago, *The Dinner Party,* p. 151; *The Concise Dictionary of National Biography: From Earliest Times to 1985,* vol. 1, p. 186; Schmidt, *400 Outstanding Women of the World,* pp. 131–32.

1639 • Marie Guyard (1599–1672), a French missionary and Ursuline nun, was the first person to form an Ursuline convent and school in Quebec, Canada, in 1639. She taught both settlers and Indians, and her writings are an important source of information for early French Canadian history. She was pronounced Venerable by Pope Pius X in 1911.

Sources: Guyard, *Letters;* Guyard, *Retraits;* Repplier, *Mère Marie of the Ursulines;* Uglow, *The Continuum Dictionary of Women's Biography,* p. 240.

1686 • Madame Françoise de Maintenon (1635–1719), a Frenchwoman influential at the court of Louis XIV, was the founder of the Maison Royale de St. Louis in St. Cyr, France, a progressive school for impoverished aristocratic girls, in 1686.

Sources: Haldane, *Madame de Maintenon;* Uglow, *The Continuum Dictionary of Women's Biography,* p. 157.

Eighteenth century • Jeanne Campan (1753–1822) was the founder of the first secular school in France to offer a liberal education to girls. She also published several books on the subject of education.

Sources: Chicago, *The Dinner Party,* p. 178.

1768 • Selina Huntingdon, the Countess of Huntingdon (1707–1791), an ardent Calvinist-Methodist who supported the preacher George Whitefield in America, was the founder of Trevecca College in Brecknockshire, England, in 1768. Intended for the training of evangelical clergy, the college moved after her death first to Hertfordshire and finally to Cambridge.

Sources: Tytler, *The Countess of Huntingdon and Her Circle;* Uglow, *The Continuum Dictionary of Women's Biography,* p. 269.

1814 • Emma Hart Willard (1787–1870) was the organizer of the first institution for the higher education of women. In 1814, she opened the Middlebury Female Seminary in Middlebury, Vermont. She went on to found the Troy Female Seminary in 1821, which was renamed the Emma Willard School in 1895 and still operates today as a prestigious boarding school for girls in Troy, New York.

Sources: Chicago, *The Dinner Party,* p. 196; James, *Notable American Women,* vol. 3, pp. 610–13; Lutz, *Emma Willard: Daughter of Democracy;* Read and Witlieb, *The Book of Women's Firsts,* p. 482.

Mary Lyon

1837 • Mary Lyon (1797–1849), a pioneer in women's education in the United States, was the founder of the first women's college, Mt. Holyoke Seminary for Women, in 1837. She spent four years soliciting funds for the founding of the college, despite public criticism, and then became the school's first director. Because Lyon was technically the principal, not president, Frances Willard of the Evanston College for Ladies in Illinois became known as the first female college president in 1871.

Sources: Chicago, *The Dinner Party,* p. 196; James, *Notable American Women,* vol. 2, pp. 443–47; McCullough, *First of All: Significant "Firsts" by American Women,* p. 73.

1842 • Sarah Porter (1813–1900), an American educator, was the founder and first head of Miss Porter's School in Farmington, Connecticut, in 1842. One of the oldest and best known girls' boarding schools in the country, Miss Porter's, often known simply as "Farmington," continues today to have a reputation for academic excellence and social grace. Porter directed the life of the school through teaching and personal example until her death.

Sources: James, *Notable American Women,* vol. 3, pp. 88–89; *Who Was Who in America, 1607–1896,* p. 420.

1848 • Sarah Anne Worthington King Peter (1800–1877), an American civic leader and churchwoman, was the founder of the Philadelphia School of Design for Women, in 1848. A pioneering school for industrial art in the United States, the institution began with one teacher in Peter's home and continued until 1932, when it merged with the Moore Institute of Art, Science, and Industry. Peter also founded the Protestant Orphan Asylum, Cincinnati, the Women's Museum Association, and hospitals in Cincinnati and Covington, Kentucky.

Sources: James, *Notable American Women*, vol. 3, pp. 54–56; *Who Was Who in America, 1607–1896*, p. 407.

1851 • Myrtilla Miner (1815–1864), an American educator, was the first head of the Colored Girls School, which she founded in Washington, D.C., on December 3, 1851. Supported by funds from such illustrious feminists and abolitionists as Harriet Beecher Stowe, Henry Ward Beecher, and Johns Hopkins, the school emphasized teacher training. After the Civil War, the school was renamed the Miner Normal School and, merging with another institution in 1954, finally became the District of Columbia Teachers College.

Sources: James, *Notable American Women*, vol. 2, pp. 547–48; *Who Was Who in America, 1607–1896*, p. 359.

1852 • Barbara Leigh-Smith Bodichon (1827–1891), an English feminist, was the founder of Portman Hall School in London in 1852. Dedicated to rights for women, Bodichon was a pioneer in woman's education and instrumental in founding and endowing Girton College, Cambridge, in 1873.

Sources: The Concise Dictionary of National Biography: From Earliest Times to 1985, p. 276; Uglow, *The Continuum Dictionary of Women's Biography*, pp. 74–75.

Anna Peck Sill (1816–1889), an American educator, was the founder of Rockford Seminary, in Rockford, Illinois, in June of 1852. An outgrowth of a private school for girls founded by Sill in July of 1849, Rockford College was modeled on Mary Lyon's Mount Holyoke Seminary in Massachusetts and became Rockford College in 1892. Sill served as Rockford Seminary's first principal until her retirement in 1884, two years after the institution began to grant bachelor degrees.

Sources: James, *Notable American Women*, vol. 3, pp. 290–91; *Who Was Who in America, 1607–1896*, p. 483.

1853 • Mary Easton Sibley (1800–1878), an American educator, was the founder of Lindenwood College in St. Charles, Missouri, in 1853. An outgrowth of Linden Wood school for girls, which Sibley founded with her husband in 1828 and which she served as its first principal, Lindenwood College became formally associated with the Presbyterian Church in 1856.

Sources: James, *Notable American Women*, vol. 3, pp. 287–88; Templin, *Two Illustrious Pioneers in the Education of Women in Missouri.*

1862 • Laura Matilda Towne (1825–1901), an American teacher committed to the education of black people, was the founder of the Penn School on the island of St. Helena off the coast of South Carolina in September of 1862. This institution was one of the earliest and one of the longest-lasting of the freedman schools. Towne served as the institution's first director and stressed the traditional academic subjects of the New England school model.

Sources: Holland, *Letters and Diary of Laura M. Towne;* James, *Notable American Women,* vol. 3, pp. 472–74; Towne, *Southern Workman.*

1874 • Sarah Emily Davies (1830–1921), an English feminist and lifelong advocate of higher education for women, was the founder of Girton College, Cambridge, in 1874. Earlier, in 1859, she had founded the Northumberland and Durham Branch of the Society for Promoting the Employment of Women. In 1863, she was the first woman to persuade Cambridge University to hold an experimental examination for girls, a test that was later made permanent. In 1866, Davies founded the London Schoolmistresses' Association and became its first secretary. After the passage of the Education Act of 1870, she was the first woman elected to the School Board for Greenwich. In 1869, she founded her own college at Benslow House, Hitchin, to prepare women to take the Cambridge examinations by private arrangement with the examiners. The college moved to Cambridge in 1873, becoming Girton College the following year. Davies served as its first headmistress.

Sources: The Concise Dictionary of National Biography, vol. I, p. 750; *Who Was Who,* vol. II, p. 260.

Abbie Park Ferguson (1837–1919) and Anna Elvira Bliss (1843–1925) were the founders and first directors of the Huguenot Seminary (later Huguenot College) in Wellington, South Africa. Graduates of Mount Holyoke Seminary, both women strongly felt the call to establish similar schools elsewhere and in January, 1874, opened the school for women in Wellington. In 1916, Huguenot College was incorporated as a constituent college of the new University of South Africa. Ferguson served as the college's president until 1910, when Bliss took over, serving until 1920.

Sources: Du Plessis, *The Life of Andrew Murray of South Africa;* Ferguson, *The Builders of Huguenot;* James, *Notable American Women,* vol. 1, pp. 607–10.

1875 • Emily Huntington (1841–1909), an innovator in early childhood education, was the founder of the "kitchen garden" movement in New York City in 1875. She introduced the teaching of domestic skills at the Wilson Industrial School for Girls in order to train poor girls to be good housekeepers and servants. She later indicated that "domestic kindergarten" might more accurately describe her method and purposes.

Sources: Huntington, *Children's Kitchen-Garden Book;* Huntington, *How to Teach Kitchen Garden;* James, *Notable American Women,* vol. 2, pp. 239–40.

Sophia Smith (1796–1870) was the first woman to found and endow a women's college. She left money in her will to set up a women's college in Northampton, Massachusetts. Smith College was chartered in 1871 and opened in 1875.

Sources: Who Was Who in America, 1607–1896, p. 493.

1876 • Juliet Corson (1842–1897) was the founder of the first cooking school in the United States. She started the New York Cooking School in 1876. Corson published *Fifteen Cent Dinners for Working Men's Families* (1877), and *Family Living on $500 a Year* (1887), establishing a national reputation as an authority on cooking and domestic economy.

Sources: Read and Witlieb, *The Book of Women's Firsts,* pp. 103–4; *Who Was Who in America, 1607–1896,* p. 123.

1877 • Alice Winfield Gordon Gulick (1847–1903), who graduated from Mount Holyoke Seminary, was the founder and first head of the International Institute for Girls in Santander, Spain. She began this school, called the Colegio Norte Americano, as part of a missionary project in 1877. In 1892, it was chartered by the Commonwealth of Massachusetts and renamed the International Institute for Girls.

Sources: Gordon, *Alice Gordon Gulick: Her Life and Work in Spain;* James, *Notable American Women,* vol. 2, pp. 102–4.

1879 • Mary Foot Seymour (1846–1893) was the founder of the first secretarial school for women in America. She opened the Union School of Stenography in New York City in 1879.

Sources: Read and Witlieb, *The Book of Women's Firsts,* pp. 403–4.

1880 • Anne Clough (1820–1892) was the founder of Newnham College of Cambridge University, the first college to offer women university-level education, in 1880. Clough served the college as its first president until her death.

Sources: Chicago, *The Dinner Party,* p. 196; Clough, *A Memoir of Anne Jemima Clough;* Uglow, *The Continuum Dictionary of Women's Biography,* p. 130.

1881 • Sophia B. Packard (1824–1891), an American teacher, was the founder of Spelman College. Started as a school for black women in Atlanta, Georgia, on April 11, 1881, it gradually grew into Spelman Seminary in 1888, with Packard as its first president, and finally into Spelman College in 1924. Endowed by John D. Rockefeller, the school served an important need in educating young black women.

In February 1880, Sophia Packard traveled to the American South as a representative of the Woman's American Baptists Mission Society. She became committed to the cause of improving educational opportunities for young black girls. When Packard became ill, she called on her friend Harriet E. Giles (1891–1909) to assist her in her efforts.

Sources: Guy-Sheftall, *Spelman: A Centennial Celebration, 1881–1991,* p. 10; James, *Notable American Women,* vol. 3, pp. 2–4.

1889 • Helene Lange (1848–1930) was the founder of the German Women's Teachers' Association, in Berlin in 1889. A conservative feminist from a religious background, Lange argued that education for women would make them better wives and mothers. She herself decided against marriage, opting for a career in teaching and a life devoted to feminist causes. She was a leader

Sophia B. Packard and
Harriet E. Giles

of the moderate wing of the German feminist movement and founded the Berlin Women's Association in 1894.

Sources: Schmidt, *400 Outstanding Women of the World,* p. 204.

Annie Nathan Mayer (1867–1951), an American writer and sister of Maud Nathan, was the founder of Barnard College of Columbia University in New York City in 1889. She is remembered for her committment to women's education and to the women's suffrage movement.

Sources: James, *Notable American Women,* vol. 2, p. 608.

1890s • Lida Gustava Heymann (1867–1943), an ardent German feminist, was the first person to found a progessive kindergarten in Germany, in Hamburg in the 1890s. During this decade, she also started a day nursery, a lunch club for single women, an actresses' society, a women's home, and a society for female office workers. She also established a school to train women as apprentices and clerks. In 1902, she was one of the thirteen founders of the German Union for Women's Suffrage, along with her friends Minna Cauer and Anita Augsburg. In 1918, Heymann and Augsburg started the feminist periodical *Die Frau im Staat.* She continued to be active on behalf of pacifism and women's rights throughout her life.

Sources: Uglow, *The Continuum Dictionary of Women's Biography,* p. 258.

1892 • Dorothea Beale (1831–1906) was the founder of St. Hilda's Hall at Oxford University in 1892. Established to train teachers, it later became one of the Oxford colleges. Beale devoted her life to the education of women and was an active advocate of women's suffrage.

Sources: The Concise Dictionary of National Biography, vol. I, p. 180; *Who Was Who,* vol. I, pp. 48–49.

1896 • Alice Chipman Dewey (1858–1927) was the cofounder, with her husband, the philosopher John Dewey, of the Laboratory School at the University of Chicago in 1896. Insisting that her husband's ideas be put into practice, she oversaw the work at this famous school where "learning by doing" was emphasized.

Sources: James, *Notable American Women,* vol. 1, pp. 466–67; Mayhew and Edwards, *The Dewey School*; Schilpp, *The Philosophy of John Dewey.*

Lucy Wheelock (1857–1946), a leader in the American kindergarten movement, was the founder of Wheelock College in Boston in 1896. The institution began as Wheelock Kindergarten Training School with Wheelock as its first head, a position she maintained as the school expanded until her retirement in 1939. In 1941, it became formally Wheelock College.

Sources: Bain, *Leadership in Childhood Education;* James, *Notable American Women,* vol. 3, pp. 577–78; *Committee of Nineteen,* 1924; Willard and Livermore, *A Woman of the Century.*

1897 • Adelaide Hunter Hoodless (1857–1910), a tireless campaigner for women's education in domestic science, was the founder of the first women's institute for farm women, in Stoney Creek, Ontario, in 1897. She established classes in home economics at the YMCA at Hamilton in the 1890s and at the Ontario Agricultural Institute at Guelph in 1904. The organization is now incorporated in the Associated Country Women of the World, which has over eight million members. She died on a lecture platform, seeking more funds for her work.

Sources: O'Neill, *The Women's Book of World Records and Achievements,* p. 5; Uglow, *The Continuum Dictionary of Women's Biography,* p. 264.

1898 • Annie Besant (1847–1933) was the founder of the Hindu College in Benares, India, in 1898. An ardent English socialist and religious enthusiast, Besant worked and wrote on behalf of socialism in the nineteenth century, then travelled to India where she became involved in Indian politics. She devoted much energy in her later years to theosophy and learned Sanskrit so that she could translate the *Bhavagad Gita.*

Sources: The Concise Dictionary of National Biography, vol. I, p. 229; *Who Was Who,* vol. III, p. 104.

1899 • Ellen Swallow Richards (1842–1911) had a distinguished career in the field of chemistry and achieved many firsts throughout her life. Most notably, she was the founder of the science of home economics, a term she coined during a summer educational conference at Lake Placid, New York, in 1899. She founded the American Home Economics Association in 1908 and served as its first president until 1910.

Sources: Chicago, *The Dinner Party,* p. 201; Ogilvie, *Women in Science,* pp. 149–52; Read and Witlieb, *The Book of Women's Firsts,* pp. 366–67.

1905 • Sarah Luella Miner (1861–1935), an American Congregational missionary and educator, was the organizer and first president of the first college for women in China, the North China Union Women's College, founded in Tungchow, 13 miles east of Beijing, in 1905. Miner served as head of the college until it merged with Yenching University in Beijing in 1920. She was also the first person to write a geology text in Chinese in the 1880s, a book she and other teachers would use for 25 years.

Sources: Gates, *Life and Light* (December 1921), pp. 474–75; James, *Notable American Women,* vol. 2, pp. 548–50; Matthews, *Seventy-Five Years of the North China Mission.*

1908 • Marie Joseph Butler (1860–1940), an Irish nun, was the founder of the Marymount schools and colleges in America and Europe. She started her first school in 1908 in Tarrytown, New York. In 1926, a year before she became an American citizen, she was elected Mother General of the Congregation of the Sacred Heart of Mary, the first superior to head an American Catholic congregation whose motherhouse was in the old world.

Sources: Burton, *Mother Butler of Marymount*; James, *Notable American Women,* vol. 1, pp. 272–73.

1916 • Emily Griffith (1880–1947), an American teacher committed to the education of the working poor, was the founder and first principal of the Denver Opportunity School, in Denver, Colorado, on September 7, 1916. She served in this post until 1933, when the enrollment was 8,670 students, including both children and adults. In 1934, the school was renamed the Emily Griffith Opportunity School.

Sources: James, *Notable American Women,* vol. 2, pp. 94–95.

Clara Damrosch Mannes (1869–1948), a pianist and teacher who was the daughter of the famous musician Frank Damrosch, was the cofounder and codirector, with her husband, an illustrious violinist, of the David Mannes Music School in New York City in 1916. In 1953, the prestigious school became the Mannes College of Music, offering a five-year course leading to a B.S. degree.

Sources: James, *Notable American Women,* vol. 2, pp. 490–91.

1918 • Mabel Smith Douglass (1877–1933) was the founder and first dean of the New Jersey College for Women in New Brunswick, New Jersey, in 1918. In 1955 the college was renamed Douglass College of Rutgers University in her honor. She served as dean until her retirement in 1933. Shortly thereafter, severely depressed by the suicide of her 16-year-old son, she probably took her own life in what initially appeared a drowning accident on Lake Placid, New York. Her body was not recovered until 30 years later.

Sources: James, *Notable American Women,* vol. 1, pp. 510–11; Schmidt, *Douglass College: A History.*

Ida Sophia Scudder (1870–1960), an American physician and medical missionary, was the founder of the Vellore Christian Medical College in Vellore, India, in 1918. Her purpose was to train Indian women as doctors to serve medical needs where purdah, the Hindu practice of secluding women from public observation, was practiced.

Sources: Uglow, *The Continuum Dictionary of Women's Biography,* pp. 489–90; Wilson, *Dr. Ida: The Story of Dr. Ida Scudder of Vellore.*

1922 • Lizzie Pitts Merrill Palmer (1838–1916), an American philanthropist, was the founder of the Merrill-Palmer Institute of Human Development and Family Life, which opened its doors in Detroit, Michigan, in 1922. Made possible by her bequest of over $3 million, the school stressed home economics and teacher training.

Sources: James, *Notable American Women,* vol. 3, pp. 11–12; Palmer, *Early Days in Detroit; The Merrill-Palmer School: An Account of Its First Twenty Years, 1920–1940.*

1927 • Ellen Browning Scripps (1836–1932), an American journalist and philanthropist, was the founder of Scripps College for Women in Claremont, California, in 1927. The driving force in her family's newspaper empire from its earliest days in Detroit in the 1860s, Scripps settled in La Jolla, California, in 1897. She and her half-brother E.W. Scripps established the Marine Biological Association of San Diego in 1903, a society that became part of the University of California in 1912. Scripps is remembered for her generosity and for her lively mind and wide range of interests.

Sources: Britt, *Ellen Browning Scripps: Journalist and Idealist;* Harper, *Ellen Browning Scripps;* James, Notable American Women, vol. 3, pp. 250–52.

1967 • Iffat (b. 1910), wife of King Faisal of Saudi Arabia, was the founder of the College of Education, an institution designed to train girls as teachers, in 1967. A lifelong advocate of education, she also founded a government boys' school, Dar al Hanam, in 1942.

Sources: Uglow, *The Continuum Dictionary of Women's Biography,* p. 273.

Early 1970s • Mildred Dresselhaus (b. 1930) was the founder of the Women's Forum in the early 1970s at Massachusetts Institute of Technology. An electrical engineer specializing in solid state physics, Dresselhaus was instrumental in opening M.I.T.'s doors to female students and formed her organization to deal with women's issues in the university community.

Sources: Noble, *Contemporary Women Scientists of America,* pp. 138–51.

1985 • Helen Gurley Brown (b. 1927), an American journalist, was the founder of the Helen Gurley Brown Research Professorship at Northwestern University in Evanston, Illinois, in 1985. She has devoted her life to writing for and about women and is perhaps best known for her first book, *Sex and the Single Girl* (1962) and as the editor-in-chief of *Cosmopolitan* magazine.

Sources: Uglow, *The Continuum Dictionary of Women's Biography,* p. 91.

Helen Gurley Brown

Institutions

1840s • The first medical institution in the United States to admit women was Central Medical College in Syracuse, New York. It opened its doors to female students in the 1840s. Lydia Folger Fowler, the second American woman to receive a medical degree, graduated from this school and taught there briefly before the college closed in 1852.

Sources: Ogilvie, *Women in Science,* p. 88.

1870 • The University of Michigan in Ann Arbor was the first state university to open its medical school to female students, in 1870. It awarded its first diploma to Amanda Sanford, who had trained extensively in Philadelphia and Boston, in 1871.

Sources: Read and Witlieb, *The Book of Women's Firsts,* p. 459.

1884 • The Mississippi Industrial Institute and College for the Education of White Girls of the State of Mississippi was the first state college for women. Founded in 1884, the institution soon became Mississippi State College for Women. It was the last state women's college to admit men, in 1982, and changed its name again in that year to Mississippi University for Women.

Sources: Read and Witlieb, *The Book of Women's Firsts,* p. 294.

1886 • Spelman College, then called Spelman Seminary, in Atlanta, Georgia, organized the first nursing school for black women in 1886. The nursing school flourished until 1921.

Dr. Sophia Jones, a graduate of University of Michigan Medical College, was the first black female to join the faculty. She taught nurses training until 1888.

Sources: Smith, *Black Firsts,* p. 358.

1904 • The first public vocational high school for girls in America was established in Boston, Massachusetts, in 1904. The Trade School for Girls was designed to prepare young women for industrial jobs. Its first principal was Florence M. Marshall.

Sources: Read and Witlieb, *The Book of Women's Firsts,* p. 447.

Dr. Sophia Jones was a faculty member in the Spelman Seminary nursing school.

Leaders and Teachers

1694 • Mary Astell (1668–1731) was the first English woman publicly to demand higher education for women. In 1694 she published "Serious Proposal to the Ladies for the Advancement of Their Time and Greatest Interest," in which she advocated the foundation of an academic community for women. In 1697, she published Part II of her proposal, in which she detailed a plan of study.

Sources: The Concise Dictionary of National Biography, vol. I, p. 87.

Late eighteenth century • Sarah Trimmer (1741–1810), a leader in the English Sunday school movement, was the first person to introduce picture books for preschool children. In 1786, she was asked to advise Queen Charlotte on the founding of Sunday schools and wrote extensively on this subject. Trimmer also founded a school of industry in Brentford.

Sources: The Concise Dictionary of National Biography, vol. III, p. 3015.

1816 • Joanna Graham Bethune (1770–1860), an American educator and philanthropist, was the first woman to lead the Sunday School Movement in the United States. In New York City in 1816, she organized the Female Union

Phrenologists believed that personality could be determined by mapping irregularities in the shape of one's skull.

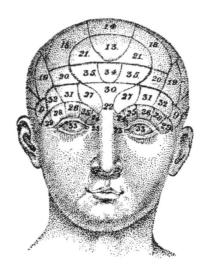

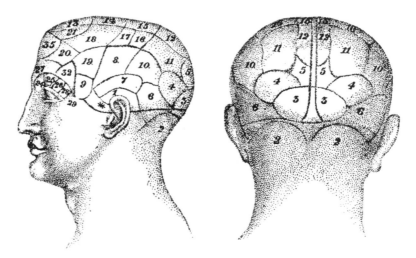

Society for the Promotion of Sabbath Schools. Drawing on her knowledge of the movement in Scotland, Bethune worked to set up Sunday schools that would teach basic reading and writing skills to poor children and adults. Her society later merged with the American Sunday-School Union, founded in 1824.

Sources: Bethune, *Memoirs of Mrs. Joanna Bethune;* James, *Notable American Women,* vol. 1, pp. 138–40.

Late 1830s • Charlotte Fowler Wells (1814–1901), an American phrenologist and publisher, was the first person in the United States to teach a regular class in phrenology, which assumes that the shape of the skull indicates personality traits. Working with her brothers at their phrenology center in New

York City beginning in 1837, Wells taught classes in this pseudo-scientific subject throughout the rest of her life.

Sources: James, *Notable American Women,* vol. 3, pp. 560–61.

Second half of the nineteenth century • Baba Petkova (1826–1894) was the first woman to establish a system for the education of women in Eastern Europe. She began teaching in her native Bulgaria in 1859 and campaigned throughout her life, despite government objections, for access to education for women.

Sources: Chicago, *The Dinner Party,* p. 196; Schmidt, *400 Outstanding Women of the World,* pp. 62–63.

1850s • Kalliopi Kehajia (1839–1905), a Greek teacher, was the first person to use open lectures as a means of education. Trained in London, she served as head of the Hill School for girls in Athens in the 1850s and delivered a series of 80 open lectures over two years on classical literature and social problems, focusing on the needs of women. In 1872, she founded the Society for Promoting Women's Education, and in 1875 she traveled to Turkey where she organized the Zappeion School for girls. She served as this school's first headmistress from 1875 until 1890. In 1888, she traveled to the United States and, on her return to Greece, wrote articles in praise of the opportunities available to American women.

Sources: Uglow, *The Continuum Dictionary of Women's Biography,* p. 294.

1856 • Charlotte L. Forten Grimké (1837–1914), a black civil rights leader and educator, was the first black woman to teach white children in Salem, Massachusetts. She was hired as a teacher in the Epes Grammar School in July of 1856. She held this position until March of 1858.

Sources: James, *Notable American Women,* vol. 2, pp. 95–97.

1857 • Margarethe Meyer Schurz (1833–1876) was the first person to operate a private kindergarten in America. Following European models, she opened her school in Watertown, Wisconsin, in 1857.

Sources: Read and Witlieb, *The Book of Women's Firsts,* p. 395.

1860 • Elizabeth Palmer Peabody (1804–1894), the first female publisher in Boston, beginning in the early 1840s, is remembered as the first person to organize a publicly funded kindergarten in the United States, in Boston in 1860. Influenced by the Froebels schools in Germany, Peabody crusaded for early childhood education and was the founder and first editor of the *Kindergarten Messenger,* a position she held from 1873 through 1875.

Sources: Who Was Who in America, 1607–1896, p. 400.

1865 • Rachel Littler Bodley (1831–1888) was the first female chemist to serve as a staff member of the Woman's Medical College in Philadelphia, Penn-

sylvania. She was named professor of chemistry in 1865. Bodley went on to earn a medical degree from the college in 1879.

Sources: James, *Notable American Women,* vol. 1, pp. 186–87; Uglow, *The Continuum Dictionary of Women's Biography,* p. 75.

1870s • Nadezhda Stasova (1822–1895), a Russian feminist, was the first director of the Bestuzehv Advanced Courses, the first advanced-level university courses open to women in Russia, in St. Petersburg in the early 1870s. Women were first formally admitted to the University of St. Petersburg in 1869, in large measure because of the efforts of Stasova and her two colleagues, Anna Filosova and Mariya Trubnikova. The three friends were known as "the female triumverate" and together were responsible for the founding of Russia's first feminist organizations, in the 1860s.

Sources: Uglow, *The Continuum Dictionary of Women's Biography,* p. 515.

1871 • Learmonth White Dalrymple (1827–1906), a New Zealand feminist, was the first woman to petition for the admission of women to the University of New Zealand, in 1871. She was an ardent feminist and campaigned for women's education throughout her life.

Sources: Uglow, *The Continuum Dictionary of Women's Biography,* p. 145.

1873 • Susan E. Blow (1843–1916) became the first woman to open and teach in a United States public kindergarten when, in 1873, she started a kindergarten in St. Louis, Missouri. The following year she opened the first training school for kindergarten teachers, also in St. Louis.

Sources: Fisher, *Pioneers of the Kindergarten in America,* pp. 184–203; Read and Witlieb, *The Book of Women's Firsts,* p. 57.

Late nineteenth century • Aikaterini Laskaridou (1842–1916) was the first person to open nursery schools in Greece. Concerned about the advancement of women in her country, Laskaridou toured schools in western Europe, then returned to Greece where she strove to implement advances in education. She spent her entire personal fortune on this project.

Sources: Uglow, *The Continuum Dictionary of Women's Biography,* p. 313.

1895 • Cecilia Beaux (1855–1942), an American portrait painter, was the first female instructor at the Pennsylvania Academy of the Fine Arts, in Philadelphia in 1895. She is remembered for her elegant portraits in the style of her contemporary John Singer Sargent, with whom she was often compared.

Sources: James, *Notable American Women,* vol. 1, pp. 119–21; Oakley, *Cecilia Beaux.*

1896 • Eliza Maria Mosher (1846–1928), an American physician and educator, was the first female faculty member at the University of Michigan in Ann Arbor. She served as Dean of Women and Professor of Hygiene from 1896 until 1902, when she returned to private practice and teaching in New York.

Sources: James, *Notable American Women,* vol. 2, pp. 587–88.

First half of the twentieth century • Sylvia Ashton Warner (1908–1984) was the first person to devise special teaching methods for use with aboriginal populations. She invented her "Creative Teaching Scheme" while working with Maori children in New Zealand. She emphasized primers written by the children themselves rather than conventional textbooks.

Sources: Ashton-Warner, *Teacher;* Chicago, *The Dinner Party,* p. 200; Uglow, *The Continuum Dictionary of Women's Biography,* p. 31.

1900 • Sarah Whiting (1847–1927), an American physicist and astronomer educated at Massachusetts Institute of Technology, was the first director of the Whitin Observatory at Wellesley College in Massachusetts. She served in this capacity from 1900, when the building was completed, until 1916. Whiting, a teacher at Wellesley from 1876 until 1912, was also the first person to introduce "applied physics" at the college (in 1880) and was instrumental in persuading a friend, Mrs. John Whitin, to donate funds for the observatory.

Sources: Uglow, *The Continuum Dictionary of Women's Biography,* p. 579.

1903 • Maria Kraus-Boelté (1836–1918), a kindergarten pioneer, was the first person to teach a university course in kindergarten education, at New York University in New York City in 1903. Born in Germany, Kraus-Boelté and her American husband, John Kraus, worked to bring the Froebel tradition of early childhood education to the United States. In New York City in 1873, they founded the New York Seminary for Kindergarteners, a teacher-training institute that they directed together until Kraus's death in 1896, after which time Kraus-Boelté served as sole principal until her retirement in 1913.

Sources: James, *Notable American Women,* vol. 2, pp. 346–48; Kraus and Kraus-Boelté, *The Kindergarten Guide,* 2 vols.

1904 • Fanny Bullock Workman (1859–1925) was the first American woman to lecture at the Sorbonne in Paris. In 1904 she lectured on the topic of her own scientific explorations, including accounts of mountain climbing expeditions with her family.

Sources: Read and Witlieb, *The Book of Women's Firsts,* p. 496; Uglow, *The Continuum Dictionary of Women's Biography,* pp. 590–91.

1908 • Isabel Bevier (1860–1942) became the first woman to establish a home economics laboratory on a college campus when, in 1908, she headed the Department of Household Science at the University of Illinois, Urbana-Champaign.

Sources: James, *Notable American Women,* vol. 1, pp. 141–42; Read and Witlieb, *The Book of Women's Firsts,* pp. 51–52.

1915 • Lillien Jane Martin (1851–1943) became the first woman to head a department at Stanford University in 1915. She served for a year as chair of the psychology department in which she had taught since 1899. She was also the first woman to receive an honorary Ph.D. from the University of Bonn in Germany, in 1913.

Sources: James, *Notable American Women,* vol. 2, pp. 504–5; Ogilvie, *Women in Science,* pp. 127–28.

Emmy Noether (1882–1935), a German mathematician, was the first woman to attempt to lecture at Göttingen University. On November 9, 1915, she presented her lecture for approval. She was denied status as a teacher on the basis of her sex, and for the next seven years she could only instruct as an "assistant" to a professor. In 1922, she was finally permitted to teach as a lecturer on her own but at a special salary below that of male professors.

Sources: Levin, *Women and Medicine,* p. 47; McGrayne, *Nobel Prize Women in Science,* pp. 64–89.

1916 • Margaret Gillespie Cousins (1878–1954) was the first non-Indian member of the Indian Women's University at Poona, in 1916. A feminist educator born in Ireland, Cousins was also a founder of the Indian Women's Association (in 1917) and the first Head of the National Girls' School at Mangalore (1919–1920). She later became the first female magistrate in India.

Sources: Uglow, *The Continuum Dictionary of Women's Biography,* p. 139.

1917 • Caroline Clark Myers (1888–1980) was the first woman employed by the U.S. Army, in 1917, as a teacher. She and her husband, Gary C. Myers, developed materials and methods to teach illiterate soldiers to read during World War I.

Sources: Read and Witlieb, *The Book of Women's Firsts,* p. 304.

c.1920 • Abala Das Bose (1865–1951) was the first person to introduce the Montessori system of education in India, in the 1920s. Bose worked throughout her life on behalf of the education of women in her country, founding several service organizations and advocating school reform and innovative teaching.

Sources: Uglow, *The Continuum Dictionary of Women's Biography,* p. 80.

1921 • Ruth Wheeler (1877–1948), an American home economist and dietician, was the first person to inaugurate professional training for dietitians at the College of Medicine at the State University of Iowa at Ames in 1921. In the same year she became the first female professor and the first head of the department of nutrition at the College of Medicine. She also established the first one-year dietetic internship course leading to a master's degree at Iowa State University.

Sources: James, *Notable American Women,* vol. 3, pp. 576–77.

1922 • Patty Smith Hill (1868–1946), an American educator, was the first person to introduce the area of nursery school education at Columbia University's Teachers College in New York City, in 1922. She taught at Columbia from 1906 until 1935. Hill is also remembered, with her sister Mildred J. Hill, as the composer of "Happy Birthday to You." Patty wrote the lyrics (originally

"Good Morning to All") and Mildred wrote the music. The song was first published in their *Song Stories for the Kindergarten* (1893).

Sources: James, *Notable American Women,* vol. 2, pp. 194–95.

1939 • Dorothy Garrod (1892–1968) became the first female professor at Cambridge University in 1939. She was elected professor of archeology even before women students were allowed to receive degrees. Her explorations from 1929 to 1934 in Gibraltar, Mount Carmel (Israel), Kurdistan, and Beirut, Lebanon, revolutionized the understanding of early Stone Age chronology and culture.

Sources: Magnusson, *Larousse Biographical Dictionary,* p. 568; *Times Literary Supplement* (21 October 1994), pp. 7–8; *Who Was Who,* vol. VI, pp. 414–15.

1941 • Adelaide Case (1887–1948) was the first woman to become a full professor at an Episcopal or Anglican seminary. In 1941, Case was named professor of Christian education at the Episcopal Theological School in Cambridge, Massachusetts.

Sources: James, *Notable American Women,* vol. 1, pp. 301–2; Read and Witlieb, *The Book of Women's Firsts,* p. 86.

1944 • Ludmilla B. Turkevich, an expert in Russian language and literature, was the first woman to become a teacher at Princeton University. She remained on the faculty for 17 years as a lecturer in Russian and Spanish literature until Rutgers University offered her a full professorship at Douglass College, its women's division, in 1961. She spent 18 years as chair of the Russian department there.

Sources: *The New York Times* (16 April 1995), p. 24Y.

1956 • Cecelia Payne Gaposhkin (1900–1979) was the first woman to become a tenured professor at Harvard University in Cambridge, Massachusetts, in 1956. During the same year, she was named chair of the department of astronomy, a position she held until 1960.

Sources: Read and Witlieb, *The Book of Women's Firsts,* p. 334.

1960s • Aisha Rateb (b. 1928), an Egyptian lawyer, teacher, and politician, became the first professor of international law at the University of Cairo, a post she held in the 1960s. In 1971, she left teaching for government, becoming minister of social affairs. She has since held a variety of government positions.

Sources: Uglow, *The Continuum Dictionary of Women's Biography,* p. 449.

Late twentieth century • Wangari Maathai (b. 1940), a Kenyan ecologist, was the first Kenyan woman earn a doctorate (in biology), to be appointed to a professorship, and to chair a department at the University of Nairobi (Department of Anatomy). She is known as the founder and coordinator of Kenya's Green Belt Movement, through which 80,000 women have planted over 15 million trees, thus earning her the nickname "Forest Queen."

Sources: Brockman, *An African Biographical Dictionary,* p. 199; *Utne Reader* 67 (January-February 1995), p. 69.

1970s • Fatima Meer (b. 1929) was the first black person to attain the rank of professor at a South African university. She began teaching sociology at the University of Natal in 1959, rising by the 1970s to the rank of full professor. Her outspoken objections to her country's policy of apartheid earned her severe censure before separatism was officially abolished in the early 1990s.
Sources: Uglow, *The Continuum Dictionary of Women's Biography,* p. 370.

1971 • Olga Taussky Todd (b. 1906) was the first female professor to be hired at the California Institute of Technology, in 1971. A mathematician, Todd was a protégé of Nobel Prize winner Emmy Noether.
Sources: McGrayne, *Nobel Prize Women in Science,* p. 159.

Organizations and Associations

1851 • On May 15, 1851, 16 women at Wesleyan College in Macon, Georgia, formed the first sorority. They were a secret society with the motto, "We live for one another." Originally calling themselves the Adelphian Society, members voted in 1904 to change their name to Alpha Delta Phi, then to Alpha Delta Pi in 1913.
Sources: McCullough, *First of All: Significant "Firsts" by American Women,* p. 77.

1865 • Luise Otto-Peters (1819–1895) was the first president of the Association for Women's Education, in Germany in 1865. Otto-Peters was the founder and first leader of the German Women's movement, advocating the emancipation of women as early as the Revolution of 1848.
Sources: Chicago, *The Dinner Party,* p. 188; Uglow, *The Continuum Dictionary of Women's Biography,* 414–15.

1880s • Mary Frances Buss (1827–1894), an English educator, was the first president of the Association of Headmistresses. An advocate of education for women, Buss founded the North London Collegiate School in 1845 and soon after the Camden School, also in London, which offered education at lower rates. In addition, she was one of the founders of the Training College for Women Teachers, which opened in Cambridge in 1886.
Sources: Kamm, *How Different From Us: A Biography of Miss Buss and Miss Beale;* Uglow, *The Continuum Dictionary of Women's Biography,* p. 98.

1897 • Alice McLellan Birney (1858–1907) founded the Parent-Teacher Association in Washington, D.C., in 1897. She served as the first president of this organization whose goal was to unite the forces of home, school, and community in behalf of children and young people.
Sources: James, *Notable American Women,* vol. 1, pp. 147–48; Read and Witlieb, *The Book of Women's Firsts,* p. 52.

1903 • Celestia Savannah Parrish (1853–1918), an American educator who dedicated her life to making university-level education available to southern women, was the founder and first president of the Southern Association of College Women, in Lynchburg, Virginia, in 1903. This organization sought to raise the standards of women's education.

Sources: Gibbs, *Some Georgia Historical Sketches;* James, *Notable American Women,* vol. 3, pp. 18–20; Parrish, *My Experience in Self-Culture.*

1907 • Mary Emma Woolley (1863–1947) was the first female senator of Phi Beta Kappa, an honor society for university students. She was elected to serve in this capacity in 1907 while she was president of Mount Holyoke College in South Hadley, Massachusetts, a position she held from 1901 until her retirement in 1937.

Sources: James, *Notable American Women,* vol. 3, pp. 660–63; Marks, *The Life and Letters of Mary Emma Woolley;* Read and Witlieb, *The Book of Women's Firsts,* p. 495.

1910 • Ella Flagg Young (1845–1918) was the first female president of the National Education Association. In 1910, while she was superintendent of the Chicago public schools, Flagg Young was elected to the presidency after considerable debate.

Sources: James, *Notable American Women,* vol. 3, pp. 697–99; McManis, *Ella Flagg Young and a Half Century of the Chicago Schools;* Read and Witlieb, *The Book of Women's Firsts,* pp. 499–500.

1918 • Mary Whiton Calkins (1863–1930) was elected as the first president of the American Philosophical Association in 1918. Having trained with William James at Harvard, she became a professor of psychology and philosophy at Wellesley College. She established a psychology laboratory there in 1891, the first in any women's college. (*See also* **Science: Psychologists, 1905.**)

Sources: James, *Notable American Women,* vol. 1, pp. 278–80; Ogilvie, *Women in Science,* p. 51; Read and Witlieb, *The Book of Women's Firsts,* p. 80.

Mary Whiton Calkins

1921 • Ada Comstock (Notestein) (1876–1973) became the first president of the American Association of University Women in 1921. She devoted her life to teaching and educational administration, serving from 1923 to 1943 as the first full-time president of Radcliffe College in Cambridge, Massachusetts.

Sources: James, *Notable American Women,* vol. 1, pp. 367–69; Read and Witlieb, *The Book of Women's Firsts,* pp. 98–99.

1924 • Florence Rood became the first female president of the American Federation of Teachers in 1924, the year in which it was founded in Chicago, Illinois. She was the organization's second president and served until 1926.

Sources: Read and Witlieb, *The Book of Women's Firsts,* p. 378.

1972 • Margery Ann Tabankin (b. 1948), an anti-war activist during the Viet Nam era, became the first female president of the National Student Association in 1972, the year after she graduated from the University of Wisconsin at Madison.

Sources: O'Neill, *The Women's Book of World Records and Achievements,* p. 726; Read and Witlieb, *The Book of Women's Firsts,* p. 434.

Early 1980s • Soia Mentschikoff (1915–1984), an American lawyer born in Russia, had a distinguished career in law and education that contained a number of firsts. She was the first female president of the Association of American Law Schools, a position she held in the early 1980s. Much earlier, in 1944, she set a pattern of innovation when, as a partner in the law firm of Spence, Windells, Waller, Hotchkiss and Angel, she became the first female partner on Wall Street. In 1946, Mentschikoff became the first woman to teach at Harvard Law School, and, in 1950, she became the first woman to teach at Chicago Law School. Finally in 1974 she was appointed dean of the University of Miami Law School, retaining that post until her retirement in 1982.

Sources: Uglow, *The Continuum Dictionary of Women's Biography,* p. 374.

Principals and Superintendents

1853 • Mary Mortimer (1816–1877), an American educator, was the first principal of Milwaukee Female College in Milwaukee, Wisconsin, in 1853. She remained in this position until 1857, when she left to serve as principal of a seminary in Baraboo, Wisconsin. She returned as head of Milwaukee Female College in 1866 and served for another eight years; the College merged with Downer College in 1885. Mortimer formed, with Catherine Beecher, the American Women's Educational Association.

Sources: James, *Notable American Women,* vol. 2, pp. 585–86; *Who Was Who in America, 1607–1896,* p. 370.

1863 • Anna Callender Brackett (1836–1911) was the first woman to serve as principal of a normal school. From 1863 until 1872 she was principal of the St. Louis Normal School in St. Louis, Missouri. Brackett went on to found a private school for girls and to serve as editor of *Women and the Higher Education* from 1893 through 1895.

Sources: Read and Witlieb, *The Book of Women's Firsts,* p. 63.

Sarah J. Smith Thompson Garnet (1831–1911) was the first black woman to attain the rank of principal in the New York City public school system. She was appointed head of P.S. 80 on April 30, 1863, and served continuously in this position until her retirement on September 10, 1900.

Sources: Black Firsts, pp. 106–7; Brown, *Homespun Heroines and Other Women of Distinction;* James, *Notable American Women,* vol. 2, pp. 18–19.

1865 • Hannah Lyman (1816–1871), an American educator, was the first woman to serve as "Lady Principal" of Vassar College, at the time of its opening in Poughkeepsie, New York, in 1865. Founded by Matthew Vassar, the first and second presidents were Milo P. Jewett (1862–64) and John H. Raymond (1865–78) respectively. Vassar hired Lyman, who was recommended for the position by her former teacher Zilpah Polly Grant, for the highest position to be filled at his new college by a woman.

Sources: James, *Notable American Women,* vol. 2, p. 75.

The Main Building at Vassar College.

1869 • Amy Bradley (1823–1904) became the first woman to supervise a public school system when in 1869 she was named superintendent of the Wilmington, North Carolina, school system.

Sources: Read and Witlieb, *The Book of Women's Firsts,* pp. 63–64.

Fanny Marion Jackson Coppin (1837–1913), a graduate of Oberlin College, was the first black woman to hold a position of independent trust in an educational institution. In 1869 she became head principal at the Institute for Colored Youth in Philadelphia. During her thirty-seven year career as a teacher and administrator at this school, she helped to shape the lives of many black leaders and influenced the development of education for blacks in nineteenth-century America.

Sources: Black Firsts, p. 107; Jackson-Coppin, *Reminiscences of School Life and Hints on Teaching;* James, *Notable American Women,* vol. 1, pp. 383–85.

Sarah Fuller (1836–1927) was the first principal of a day school for the deaf. She served as head of the Boston School for Deaf-Mutes for 41 years from the time of its opening in Boston, Massachusetts, on November 10, 1869. In 1877, its name was changed to the Horace Mann School for the Deaf. Fuller was innovative in advocating the use of oral speech and early, as well as nonresidential, education for deaf children.

Sources: James, *Notable American Women,* vol. 1, pp. 683–85; Keller, *The Story of My Life.*

1874 • Ellen Clara Sabin (1850–1949) was the first woman to serve as a school principal in Portland, Oregon. In 1874 she accepted this post at Old North School. She left in 1891 to take up the presidency of Downer College, a secondary school for girls in Wisconsin. When, in 1895, this insitution moved to Milwaukee and merged with Milwaukee College for Women, becoming Milwaukee-Downer College, Sabin became its first president, a position she held until her retirement in 1921.

Sources: Adams, *Ellen Clara Sabin: A Life Sketch;* James, *Notable American Women,* vol. 3, pp. 217–18.

1889 • Maria Louise Baldwin (1865–1922), an American educator, was the first black woman to serve as a school principal in Massachusetts. In 1889, she was appointed to head the Agassiz Grammar School near Harvard University in Cambridge. A dedicated teacher, Baldwin was also a noted speaker, and in 1897 she became the first woman invited to deliver the annual Washington's Birthday memorial address before the Brooklyn Institute in New York City.

Sources: Brown, *Homespun Heroines and Other Women of Distinction,* pp. 182–93; James, *Notable American Women,* vol. 1, pp. 86–88.

Fannie Pearson Hardy Ekstorm (1865–1946) became the first woman to serve as a superintendent of schools in Maine when she was appointed superintendent of the Brewer Schools in 1889. She held this position until 1891. Ekstrom is remembered as a writer, an ornithologist, and an authority on the history, Native Americans, and folksongs of Maine.

Sources: James, *Notable American Women,* vol. 1, pp. 549–51; *New England Quarterly* (March 1953).

1913 • Susan Almira Miller Dorsey (1857–1946), a California educator, was the first woman to serve as assistant superintendent of the Los Angeles city schools, a position to which she was appointed in 1913. She was also the first woman to be made an honorary life president of the National Education Association, in 1935, and in 1937 she became the first living person to have a Los Angeles school named after her.

Sources: James, *Notable American Women,* vol. 1, pp. 506–8.

1919 • Lucy Diggs Slowe (1885–1937), an American educator particularly dedicated to the advancement of black women, was the first principal of Shaw Junior High School in Washington, D.C., in 1919. At Howard University, which she entered in 1904, she was one of the founders and the first vice-president of Alpha Kappa Alpha, the first sorority among black college women. She received an M.A. in English from Columbia University in 1915 and went on to become dean of women at Howard University in 1922. She served as the first secretary of the National Council of Negro Women, in 1935, and as the first president of the National Association of College Women, from 1923 through 1929.

Sources: James, *Notable American Women,* vol. 3, pp. 299–300; *Journal of the College Alumnae Clubs of Washington* (January 1939).

School Boards and Unions

1875 • Lucretia Peabody Hale (1820–1900), an American writer of fiction for adults and children, was one of the first six women to serve as a member of the Boston School Committee. She was elected in 1875 and again the following year. Among the other five female members were Lucretia Crocker and Abby W. May.

Sources: Hale, *Memories of a Hundred Years*; James, *Notable American Women,* vol. 2, pp. 109–14.

1878 • Aline Valette (1850–1899), a French socialist and women's rights advocate, was the first secretary of the Paris Teachers' Union, in 1878. She also became one of the first voluntary labor inspectors, in Paris in the 1880s. She is further remembered as the cofounder, with Eugenie Potonie-Pierre, of the Federation Française des Sociétés Feministes, in Paris in 1882.

Sources: Uglow, *The Continuum Dictionary of Women's Biography,* pp. 553–54.

1887 • Anna Hallowell (1831–1905), an American welfare worker and a leader in the kindergarten movement, was the first female member of the Board of Public Education in Philadelphia, Pennsylvania. She was elected in 1887 and served for fourteen years.

Sources: Custis, *The Public Schools of Philadelphia;* James, *Notable American Women,* vol. 2, pp. 122–23.

1889 • Matilda Bradley Carse (1835–1917), a temperance leader and welfare worker, was the first woman to serve on the Board of Education of Cook County, Illinois, in 1889. A resident of Chicago, Carse served until 1890. She is remembered for her work on behalf of the Women's Christian Temperance Union and for her establishment in 1878 of the Bethesda Day Nursery for working mothers, the first of its kind in Chicago.

Sources: Chapin, *Thumb-Nail Sketches of White Ribbon Women;* James, *Notable American Women,* vol. 1, pp. 292–94.

1892 • Sarah Brown Ingersoll Cooper (1835–1896), an active volunteer for a variety of religious and social causes, was the first president of the Golden Gate Kindergarten Association, later the International Kindergarten Union, a post to which she was elected in San Francisco, California, in 1892. Over 8,000 children, ages 2-6, have been trained since then.

Sources: The International Kindergarten Union, *Pioneers of the Kindergarten in America,* pp. 270–79; James, *Notable American Women,* vol. 1, pp. 380–82.

1899 • Helen Barrett Montgomery (1861–1934), an American civic leader, was the first female member of the Rochester, New York, school board, a post to which she was elected in 1899. Also an active church member, Montgomery became the first woman to serve as head of any large Christian organizational body when in 1921 she was elected president of the Northern Baptist Convention. Montgomery was the author of many books, including her own translation of the New Testament of the Christian Bible into "Modern English."

Sources: James, *Notable American Women,* vol. 2, pp. 566–68; McKelvey, *Rochester: The Quest for Quality: 1890–1925.*

1912 • Annie Laws (1855–1927), a civic leader and committed clubwoman, was the first woman to serve on the Cincinnati Board of Education, to which she was elected in 1912. She held this position until 1916.

Sources: James, *Notable American Women,* vol. 2, pp. 375–76; Laws, *The History of the Ohio Federation of Women's Club.*

1920 • Mary Cooke Branch Munford (1865–1938) was the first woman to serve as a member of the Richmond, Virginia, school board. She held this position from 1920 until 1931. Committed to educational reform, she was also the first female member of the Board of Visitors of the College of William and Mary, in 1920.

Sources: Bowie, *Sunrise in the South;* James, *Notable American Women,* vol. 2, pp. 600–1; Munford, *Random Recollections;* Munford, Jr., *Richmond Homes and Memories.*

1930s • Martha McChesney Berry (1866–1942), an American educator, was the first female member of the University of Georgia's board of regents and planning board. Elected in Atlanta, Georgia, in the 1930s, Berry was honored for a lifelong career in education. She is remembered especially for her role as founder and first head of the Mount Berry School for Boys, begun in the Blue Ridge Mountains north of Rome, Georgia, in 1902, to which she added the Martha Berry School for Girls in 1909.

Sources: Byers, *The Sunday Lady of Possum Trot;* James, *Notable American Women,* vol. 1, pp. 137–38; Kane and Henry, *Miracle in the Mountains.*

Students

1630s • Anna Maria van Shurman (1607–1678), a Dutch philologist, was the first woman to attend the University of Utrecht, in the Netherlands in the 1630s. She was allowed to attend lectures on theology and oriental languages by arrangement with the university's rector, who required that she sit in a specially constructed cubicle so that she would not be seen.

Sources: Schmidt, *400 Outstanding Women of the World,* pp. 298–99; Uglow, *The Continuum Dictionary of Women's Biography,* p. 555.

1837 • Laura Dewey Bridgman (1829–1889), who lost her sight and hearing at age eighteen months from scarlet fever, became the first blind, deaf, and mute person to receive a formal education when in 1837 she entered the Perkins Institution, a school for the blind in Boston, Massachusetts. There she learned to read and to communicate with others.

Sources: James, *Notable American Women,* vol. 1, pp. 240–42; Read and Witlieb, *The Book of Women's Firsts,* pp. 67–68; *Who Was Who in America, 1670–1896,* p. 74.

Late 1840s • Lucy Ware Webb Hayes (1831–1889), wife of Rutherford B. Hayes, the nineteenth president of the United States, was the first female student to enroll at Ohio Wesleyan University in Delaware, Ohio, in the late 1840s. When she graduated in June of 1850, she gave the commencement oration, "The Influence of Christianity on National Prosperity." She is remembered for banning liquor from the White House during her husband's administration and as the first president of the Woman's Home Missionary Society of the Methodist Episcopal Church, a position she assumed in Freemont, Ohio, in 1880.

Sources: Holloway, *The Ladies of the White House;* James, *Notable American Women,* vol. 2, pp. 166–67; *Who Was Who in America, 1670–1896,* p. 242.

Lucy Ware Webb Hayes

1875 • Clara Marshall (1847–1931), an American physician, was the first woman admitted to graduate study at the Philadelphia College of Pharmacy, in 1875, the same year she earned her degree from the Woman's Medical College. She went on in 1882 to become the first woman appointed to the staff of the Philadelphia Hospital.

Sources: James, *Notable American Women,* vol. 2, pp. 501–2; Marshall, *The Woman's Medical College of Pennsylvania.*

1878 • Christine Ladd-Franklin (1847–1930), an American psychologist, was the first female graduate student at Johns Hopkins University. An 1869 graduate of Vassar College in her chosen field, Ladd-Franklin was unofficially admitted to graduate study at Johns Hopkins in 1878 and awarded an unofficial fellowship in 1879. She completed all the requirements for the Ph.D. in 1882, although she was not awarded a degree because of her gender. She went on to study in Germany and had a distinguished career in psychological research.

Sources: Hawkins, *Pioneer: A History of Johns Hopkins University;* James, *Notable American Women,* vol. 2, pp. 354–56; Scarborough and Furumoto, *Untold Lives: The First Generation of American Women Psychologists,* pp. 109–29.

Christine Ladd-Franklin

c.1880 • Henrietta Szold (1860–1945) was the first woman to attend the Jewish Theological Society, although she was only admitted on the condition that she promise not to attempt to become a rabbi. A Zionist throughout her life, Szold was also active in the women's rights movement. She became the first Secretary for Health, Education and Welfare for Jewish Palestine. Szold is remembered as the founder of the first night school at which immigrants could learn English and American history, opened in New York City in November of 1889. She was also the founder and first president of Hadassah, a women's Zionist organization, in New York on February 24, 1912. In May of 1930 she became the first woman to receive the honorary degree of Doctor of Hebrew Letters from the Jewish Institute of Religion.

Sources: Chicago, *The Dinner Party,* p. 202; Fineman,*Woman of Valor: The Life of Henrietta Szold;* James, *Notable American Women,* vol. 3, pp. 417–20; Levin, *Women and Medicine,* p. 55.

1887 • Jane Marie Bancroft Robinson (1847–1932), an American scholar and a leader in the deaconess movement, was the first woman to be admitted to the Ecole Pratiques des Hautes Etudes of the University of Paris, in 1887.

With a doctorate in history from the University of Syracuse, she became a professor of French language and literature at Northwestern University and was the founder of the Western Association of Collegiate Alumnae in 1883 in Evanston, Illinois. This organization was a forerunner of the American Association of University Women.

Sources: James, *Notable American Women,* vol. 3, pp. 183–84; Robinson, *A Historical Sketch of the Robinson Family of the Line of Ebenezer Robinson;* Willard and Livermore, *A Woman of the Century.*

1963 • Princess Anne (b. 1950), the only daughter of Queen Elizabeth and Prince Philip, was the first English princess to attend school. Like her brother Prince Charles before her, Anne was initially educated at home but then, breaking as he did with royal tradition, was sent to boarding school at the age of 13 in 1963.

Sources: Magnusson, *Larousse Biographical Dictionary,* p. 49; Uglow, *The Continuum Dictionary of Women's Biography,* pp. 20–21.

1977 • In 1977, 24 women from several one-time British colonies were selected as Rhodes Scholars. This was the first time that women had been permitted to receive this honor, which offers students scholarships for graduate study at Oxford University.

Sources: Read and Witlieb, *The Book of Women's Firsts,* pp. 365–66.

Shannon Faulkner

1994 • Shannon Faulkner (b. 1975) was the first female cadet at the Citadel, a conservative military college in Charleston, South Carolina. After a yearlong legal battle, a federal judge ordered the college to accept women on July 22, 1994. Faulkner brought the successful suit, using her own experience as a test case, so that she could attend the college beginning in the 1994–1995 academic year.

Sources: The New York Times (23 July 1994), pp. 1,7.

Government

Africa

1622 • Mbande Nzinga (1582–1663), founded the kingdom of Matamba in Africa in reaction to Portuguese colonial repression. Nzinga was a royal princess in Ndongo, a kingdom adjoining Portuguese West Africa (present-day Angola). She attempted to declare her kingdom independent of the Portuguese and free her people from the horrors of the slave trade. In 1622, she was sent to negotiate with the invading Portuguese by her brother, the King of Ndongo. While there, Nzinga converted to Christianity and was baptized Dona Aña de Souza. She ruled as Queen of Ndongo from 1624, but was driven out of Ndongo by Portuguese troops around 1630. Nzinga then established the new kingdom, which she called Matamba. She ruled with with iron brutality as Queen of Matamba (1630–1663). Her kingdom thrived and enjoyed relative stability, ironically, according to some historical accounts, by acting as brokers for the Portuguese in their slave trade.

Sources: Brockman, *An African Biographical Dictionary,* p. 271; Magnusson, *Larousse Biographical Dictionary,* p. 1092.

1840 • Mawa, a Zulu princess, was the first woman to lead her people into Natal, a province in present-day South Africa, where she settled permanently with several thousand Zulus. Mawa, like many other Zulu princesses, was a strong woman highly regarded as a leader.

Sources: Brockman, *An African Biographical Dictionary,* p. 219; Uglow, *The Continuum Dictionary of Women's Biography,* p. 396.

Argentina

1974 • Isabel Perón (b. 1931) of Buenos Aires, Argentina, known as Isabelita, became the world's first female president when she took over the office on the death of her husband, Juan Perón, on July 1, 1974. She held this position until she was ousted during a political coup on March 24, 1976.

Sources: Magnusson, *Larousse Biographical Dictionary,* p. 1146; Matthews, *The Guinness Book of World Records,* p. 178; Uglow, *The Continuum Dictionary of Women's Biography,* p. 430.

Australia

1903 • Vida Goldstein (1869–1949) became the first woman in the British Empire (an historical term for the British Commonwealth of Nations) to be nominated for Parliament. In the same year she founded the Women's Federal Political Association and, in 1908, she launched a new paper, *The Woman Voter.* A major leader of the Australian women's movement, Goldstein devoted her energies to the cause of women's suffrage, voicing her position in a feminist journal, *Australian Women's Sphere.*

Sources: Arnold, *Monash Biographical Dictionary of 20th Century Australia,* p. 212; Chicago, *The Dinner Party,* p. 188; Uglow, *The Continuum Dictionary of Women's Biography,* p. 230.

1920 • Edith Dirksey Brown Cowan (1861–1932) became the first woman member of the Australian Parliament. Her political career began in 1915 when she became a magistrate of the state children's court. There was a legislative ban on women serving in the Australian Parliament until 1920, when Cowan and five other women ran for office. Cowan used her term in office to fight for women's and children's rights. She sponsored the Women's Legal Status Act, which passed in 1923 and opened the legal profession to women. She was not reelected in 1924 or 1927, even though she ran in both years for a seat in Parliament.

Sources: Arnold, *Monash Biographical Dictionary of 20th Century Australia,* p. 129; Bolton, *Australian Dictionary of Biography,* vol. 8.

1943 • Enid Muriel Lyons (1897–1981) was the first female member of the House of Representatives for Darwin, Tasmania. She was elected in 1943 and served in this capacity until 1951. When she became vice president of the Executive Council in 1949, she also became the first female member of a Federal Cabinet in Australia.

Sources: Arnold, *Monash Biographical Dictionary of 20th Century Australia,* p. 331; Uglow, *The Continuum Dictionary of Women's Biography,* p. 340.

1954 • Minnie Mary "Ma" Fimmel Dalley (1880–1965) was the first female mayor of Kew, Melbourne, Australia. She held this post until 1963. Dalley was an Australian entrepreneur, achieving great success in the scrap metal business during World War I, who later became a justice of the peace, a magistrate, and finally, a mayor.

Sources: Arnold, *Monash Biographical Dictionary of 20th Century Australia,* p. 139; Bolton, *Australian Dictionary of Biography,* vol. 13.

1966 • Dame Annabelle Jane Mary Rankin (1908–1986), a member of the Australian Parliament since 1946, achieved a number of firsts in her political career. She became the first woman whip in the British Commonwealth, serving as opposition whip from 1947 to 1949, and government whip from 1951 to 1966. She became the first woman to control a federal department in Australia when she was made minister of housing on January 26, 1966, a position she held until 1971 when she became Australia's first female ambassador. In this capacity she took on the title of High Commissioner to New Zealand, a post she held until 1975. She was named a Dame of the British Empire (DBE) in 1957.

Sources: Arnold, *Monash Biographical Dictionary of 20th Century Australia,* p. 445; Magnusson, *Larousse Biographical Dictionary,* p. 1216; O'Neill, *The Women's Book of World Records and Achievements,* pp. 59, 61, 62.

1974 • Ruth Dobson (b. 1918), Australia's first female career diplomat, was the first woman to serve her country as ambassador to Denmark. She was appointed to this position in 1974.

Sources: O'Neill, *The Women's Book of World Records and Achievements,* p. 62.

Austria

1760s • Maria Theresa (1717–1780) was the only woman to rule during the Habsburg (also spelled Hapsburg) era. The Habsburgs were a royal family that ruled in Europe from the 1200s through the early 1900s. After Charles V's son, Charles VI, died, Charles V (d. 1740), the last male heir of the Austria Habsburgs, passed the Pragmatic Sanction allowing the female line to succeed to the throne. His daughter, Maria Theresa, and her husband, Francis I, ruled Austria. During her reign, she achieved a remarkable unification of the diverse parts of the Austro-Hungarian Empire and devoted her energies to making Vienna a great European capital. In the 1760s her policy of centralization encouraged important architectural, social, and cultural development in her native city.

Sources: Magnusson, *Larousse Biographical Dictionary,* p. 971; Schmidt, *400 Outstanding Women of the World,* p. 43.

Late nineteenth century • Adelheid Popp (1869–1939) was the founder of the Socialist Women's Movement in Austria. She dedicated her life to women's issues and socialism and served as an elected official in the Austrian government.

Sources: Chicago, *The Dinner Party,* p. 189.

1966 • Grete Rehor (1910–1972), an Austrian politician, was the first woman to serve in her country's government. In 1966, she was appointed minister of social administration, a post she held until 1970. In the same year she was honored for her lifetime of service with the Grand Medal of Honor of the Republic of Austria.

Sources: O'Neill, *The Women's Book of World Records and Achievements,* p. 56.

Barbados

1990 • Dame Ruth Nita Barrow (1916–1995) became the first woman governor general of Barbados. As such, she is the representative of Queen Elizabeth II of England. Barrow, the older sister of Prime Minister Errol Barrow who led Barbados to independence from Britain in 1966, represented Barbados at the United Nations before her appointment. She also served as president of the World Y.W.C.A. and the World Council of Churches.

Sources: New York Times (22 December 1995), p. C18.

Belgium

1965 • Marguerite De Reimacker-Legot, a Belgian politician, was the first person to serve as a minister in her country's government. In 1965, she was appointed minister of family and housing.

Sources: O'Neill, *The Women's Book of World Records and Achievements,* p. 61.

1973 • E. Dever was the first woman to serve as Belgium's ambassador to Sweden, a position to which she was appointed in 1973.

Sources: O'Neill, *The Women's Book of World Records and Achievements,* p. 62.

Brazil

1959 • Beata Vettori was the first female ambassador from Brazil to the European Economic Community headquartered in Strasbourg, France. She held this position until 1960.

Sources: O'Neill, *The Women's Book of World Records and Achievements,* p. 62.

Canada

1917 • Louise McKinney (1868–1933) was a leading member of the Non-partisan League and was elected as its candidate to the Alberta legislature in 1917, thus becoming the first female member of any legislative body in the British Empire. (The British Empire is an historical term referring to the British Commonwealth of Nations. The Commonwealth, a voluntary association of nations, includes 30 republics; 16 monarchies under British Queen Elizabeth II; and five national monarchies.) She dedicated her energies to temperance and feminist causes throughout her life.

Sources: Uglow, *The Continuum Dictionary of Women's Biography,* p. 345.

1921 • Agnes Campbell McPhail (1890–1954), a Canadian suffragist and politician, became the first female minister of parliament (MP) in Canada when she was elected to represent the United Farmers of Ontario for Southeast Grey County. She retained her seat until 1940, and from 1943 until 1951 she served in the Ontario, Canada, legislature. McPhail also represented Canada in the Assembly of the League of Nations.

Sources: Magnusson, *Larousse Biographical Dictionary,* p. 949; Stewart and French, *Ask No Quarter: A Biography of Agnes McPhail*; Uglow, *The Continuum Dictionary of Women's Biography,* p. 348.

Mary Ellen Smith (1862–1933), an English woman who emigrated to Canada, was the first woman in the British Empire to achieve cabinet rank. She was appointed minister without portfolio in British Columbia in 1921, a post she held until 1922. She served as a member of the legislature from 1917 until 1928.

Sources: O'Neill, *The Women's Book of World Records and Achievements,* p. 50.

1974 • Renaude Lapointe (b. 1912), a journalist from Quebec, Canada, was apppointed speaker of the Canadian Senate, becoming the first woman to hold the post, on September 16, 1974. She became the first female member of the editorial board of the Montreal newspaper *La Presse* in 1965. She was appointed to the Senate in 1971.

Sources: O'Neill, *The Women's Book of World Records and Achievements,* p. 50.

1983 • Jeanne Benoit Sauvé (1922–1993), a Canadian politician who began her career as a journalist, was the first woman to serve as governor general of Canada, a position to which she was appointed in December of 1983. She had a national reputation as an outspoken advocate of women's rights.

Sources: Uglow, *The Continuum Dictionary of Women's Biography,* p. 480.

1993 • Kim Campbell (b. 1947) was elected the first woman prime minister of Canada on June 25, 1993. She held this position only until October 1993, when she was defeated by Jean Chretien.. Earlier in 1993, Campbell became Canada's first woman defence minister.

Source: Canadian Who's Who, p. 172.

Central African Republic

1975 • Elizabeth Domitien, a politician in the Central African Republic, became her country's first prime minister in 1975. Appointed by the ruler Jean Bedel Bokassa (1921–) who had himself crowned emperor in an elaborate ceremony in 1977, she was essentially without power in this newly created post.

Sources: Magnusson, *Larousse Biographical Dictionary,* p. 1733; Uglow, *The Continuum Dictionary of Women's Biography,* pp. 171–72.

China

1920 • Jingyu Xiang (1895–1928), a Chinese feminist revolutionary, was the cofounder of the Chinese Communist Party, in Hunan province. She went on to become the first director of the Communist Party Women's Department, which she established in 1922. A friend of Mao Zedong, leader of the Communist revolution in China, and other important Chinese Communist leaders, she was arrested and executed in May of 1928 during Xiang Kai Shek's anti-Communist campaign.

Sources: Uglow, *The Continuum Dictionary of Women's Biography,* p. 594; Xiang, *A Thesis on the Emancipation and Transformation of Women.*

1975 • Zhengying Qian (b. 1923), one of China's first female engineers, was the first woman to become minister of water conservation, in Beijing. In 1982, her authority was broadened and she became the first woman in her country to serve as minister of water conservation and power.

Sources: Uglow, *The Continuum Dictionary of Women's Biography,* p. 443.

1978 • Yingchao Deng (b. 1904), the wife of Zhou Enlai, premier of China from 1949 until 1976, was the first woman to become a member of the Chinese Central Committee in Beijing, the nation's highest political office, a position she held from 1978 until 1985.

Sources: Uglow, *The Continuum Dictionary of Women's Biography,* p. 160.

1983 • Wu Wenying (b. 1932), a Chinese textile worker and politician, was the first woman to head the largest textile industry in the world. She became her government's minister of the textile industry in Beijing, China. She led textile delegations to Germany, Belgium, New Zealand, and Burma (present-day Myanmar) in 1985 and to Britain and Bulgaria in 1986.

Sources: Uglow, *The Continuum Dictionary of Women's Biography,* p. 576.

Colombia

1960 • Esmeralda Arboleda de Cuevas Cancino, a Colombian politician, was appointed minister of transport, becoming the first woman in Colombia to hold a cabinet-level position. She held this post until 1962. She was also the first Colombian woman to be elected to the Senate, and in 1966, she became her country's first female ambassador to Austria and Yugoslavia, a position she held until 1968.

Sources: O'Neill, *The Women's Book of World Records and Achievements,* p. 61.

Cuba

c.1970 • Haydee Santamaria (b. 1931), a Cuban revolutionary leader, was the first female president of the Latin American Organization of Solidarity. A friend of revolutionaries Che Guevara and Fidel Castro, Santamaria was instrumental in the 1959 overthrow of the government of Cuban dictator, Fulgencio Batista (1901–1973). Santamaria was involved in setting up the new communist regime in Cuba.

Sources: Uglow, *The Continuum Dictionary of Women's Biography,* pp. 478–79.

Denmark

1918 • Nina Bang (1866–1928) was the first woman to serve as a member of the Landsting (the upper house) in Denmark's Parliament. She was elected after the passage of women's suffrage in 1918 and served in Denmark's first

Social Democratic government. In 1924, she became minister of education. She was an economist and worked on behalf of the League of Nations.

Sources: Uglow, *The Continuum Dictionary of Women's Biography,* p. 46.

1972 • Margrethe II (b. 1940) became Denmark's first queen since 1000 A.D., when she succeeded her father Frederik IX to the throne in January 1972. The right of female succession was established only in 1953. Margrethe's role as queen is merely ceremonial and she spends most of her time with her family and working on her profession, archeology. She is also an artist and illustrator of children's books.

Sources: Magnusson, *Larousse Biographical Dictionary,* p. 970.

Dominica

1980 • Mary Eugenia Charles (b. 1919) became the first woman elected prime minister of Dominica in July 1980. She was active in politics throughout her life, cofounding the Dominica Freedom Party in 1968. She served twice as her country's prime minister; when she first took office in July 1980, she was the first woman to hold the post of prime minister in the Caribbean region.

Sources: Gall, *Worldmark Encyclopedia of the Nations,* vol. 3, p. 142.

Egypt

1960s • Hikmat Abu Zaid, an Egyptian physician, was the first woman to serve as minister of social affairs in the Egyptian government, in the 1960s.

Sources: Uglow, *The Continuum Dictionary of Women's Biography,* p. 449.

1965 • Karimah Al-Said was the first woman to serve as minister of education in the Egyptian government. She came from a remarkable family of a progressive physicians who believed in women's education.

Sources: Uglow, *The Continuum Dictionary of Women's Biography,* p. 14.

England

c.900 • Æthelflæd (d. 918) was the first woman to attempt to unify England under one ruler. The daughter of King Alfred, she is known as the Lady of the Mercians. She ruled jointly with her husband, Æthelred, ruler of West Mercia. She ruled in her own name after his death in 911, supporting her brother, Edward, King of Wessex, in his efforts to oust the Viking forces from eastern and northern England. She is known for her military power and political skill.

Sources: The Concise Dictionary of National Biography, vol. I, p. 944; Uglow, *The Continuum Dictionary of Women's Biography,* p. 7.

1509 • Catherine of Aragon (1485–1536), a Spanish princess, was the first woman to marry Henry VIII, king of England. Henry struggled to have his marriage to Catherine declared invalid, and in 1533 married Anne Boleyn. Catherine was the mother of Mary, who eventually became queen herself.

Sources: The Concise Dictionary of National Biography, vol. I, pp. 495–96; Magnusson, *Larousse Biographical Dictionary,* p. 276.

1536 • Anne Boleyn (1507–1536), the second wife of Henry VIII and the mother of Elizabeth I, was the first English queen to be beheaded for adultery. Despite her conviction for having allegedly had five lovers (including her own brother), she was executed for political reasons, a victim of her husband's desire for a male heir.

Sources: The Concise Dictionary of National Biography, vol. I, p. 58; Magnusson, *Larousse Biographical Dictionary,* p. 173.

1553 • Mary Tudor (1516–1558), Queen Mary I, also known as Bloody Mary, was the first woman to rule England in her own right. The daughter of Henry VIII and Catherine of Aragon, she ascended to the throne after the early death of her half brother Edward VI. During her five-year rule she struggled unsuccessfully to restore the pope in Rome as head of the church in England.

Sources: The Concise Dictionary of National Biography, vol. II, pp. 1969–70; Magnusson, *Larousse Biographical Dictionary,* p. 276.

1559 • Queen Elizabeth I (1533–1603) became the first woman to govern England successfully when she ascended the throne in 1558. Her 45-year rule as an unmarried woman of unprecedented power brought her country prosperity and growth.

Sources: Chicago, *The Dinner Party,* pp. 80–81; *The Concise Dictionary of National Biography,* vol. I, pp. 912–13; Schmidt, *400 Outstanding Women of the World,* pp. 134–35.

1689 • Mary II (1662–1694) became the first woman to rule England in legal equality with her husband. The daughter of James II, Mary married William of Orange in 1677 and settled in The Netherlands. In 1688, she and her husband returned to England and deposed her father in what has come to be known as "The Glorious Revolution," a peaceful restoration of Protestant rule to England. She and William were crowned as joint sovereigns and ruled together.

Sources: The Concise Dictionary of National Biography, vol. II, pp. 1970–71; Magnusson, *Larousse Biographical Dictionary,* p. 984.

1891 • May Mary Edith Tennant (1869–1946), an Irish reformer and feminist, was the first female factory inspector for the Royal Commission on Labour, in London, England. She concentrated on correcting such problems in the workplace as illegal overtime, bad sanitation, and safety.

Sources: The Concise Dictionary of National Biography, vol. III, p. 2944; *Who Was Who,* vol. IV, pp. 1139–40.

1909 • Eleanor Florence Rathbone (1872–1946), an English politician from a distinguished Liverpool family, was the first woman to serve on the Liverpool (England) City Council. She went on to a remarkable career in national government, taking as her particular interests the rights of women and social problems, both in Britain and throughout the Commonwealth of Nations, the political network of 51 countries that includes the United Kingdom, Canada, Australia, India, New Zealand, and South Africa.

Sources: The Concise Dictionary of National Biography, vol. III, p. 2487; *Who Was Who,* vol. IV, p. 955.

1915 • Edith Cavell (1865–1915) was the first English woman to be executed by the Germans for resistance work during World War I. While serving as a nurse in Brussels, Belgium, Cavell cared for the wounded regardless of their nationality and helped British and French soldiers escape from German captivity.

Sources: The Concise Dictionary of National Biography, vol. III, p. 499; Uglow, *The Continuum Dictionary of Women's Biography,* pp. 114–15.

1918 • Countess Constance Georgine Gore-Booth Markiewicz (1868–1927), an Irish political activist, was the first woman to be elected a minister of Parliament in the United Kingdom in Dublin, where she was serving a life-term in prison for her part in the Easter Rebellion of 1916. Markiewicz had been sentenced to death, but she received a reprieve in a general amnesty in 1917. She was elected to represent Sinn Fein in Parliament, but Markiewicz refused to serve as a Nationalist protest. She was active in Irish politics throughout her life. In 1909, she founded in Dublin the radical youth group Na Finanna. She went on to become the first female minister for labour in the illegal Irish parliament, Dail Eireann, in 1919.

Sources: Magnusson, *Larousse Biographical Dictionary,* p. 974; *Who Was Who,* vol. II, p. 702.

Emmeline Pethick-Lawrence (1867–1954) was the first woman to run for office as a Labour candidate. She was a candidate in Rusholme, Manchester, England, during the first election open to women. An ardent worker for labor and feminist issues, Pethick-Lawrence was the cofounder, with her husband, Frederick Lawrence, of the important periodical *Votes for Women* in London in 1907.

Sources: The Concise Dictionary of National Biography, vol. III, p. 2364; Uglow, *The Continuum Dictionary of Women's Biography,* p. 431.

1919 • Viscountess Nancy Witcher Langhorne Astor (1879–1964) took the oath of office as the first woman to serve as a minister of Parliament (MP) in England. Born in the United States, Astor became a British subject when she married William Waldorf Astor, the 2nd Viscount Astor. Her husband was Conservative MP for Plymouth; Nancy was elected in 1919 to succeed him as representative from Plymouth, and until 1921 she was the only female MP.

Sources: The Concise Dictionary of National Biography, vol. I, p. 89; Kane, *Famous First Facts,* p. 704; Magnusson, *Larousse Biographical Dictionary,* p. 73.

Viscountess Nancy Astor
pauses to speak to
reporters during a visit with
U.S. President Franklin
Roosevelt.

Charlotte Despard (1844–1939), an English feminist and Irish patriot, was the first woman to run for election to Parliament from the district of Battersea, London, in 1919. Her campaign was unsuccessful.

Sources: Linklater, *An Unhusbanded Life: Charlotte Despard, Suffragette, Socialist and Sinn Feiner;* Uglow, *The Continuum Dictionary of Women's Biography,* pp. 163–64.

Edith How-Martyn (1880–1954), an English feminist who fought for a woman's right to vote, was the first female member of the Middlesex County Council, in 1919. Concerned about women's rights and the welfare of children, she was cofounder (with Charlotte Despard) of the Women's Freedom League in

1907 and in the 1930s founded England's first child-care centre, in Hampstead Garden Suburb.

Sources: Uglow, *The Continuum Dictionary of Women's Biography,* p. 267.

1923 • Sarah Grand (1854–1943), a novelist whose actual name was Frances Elizabeth Clarke McFall, was the first woman to be elected mayor of Bath, England, where she was referred to as mayoress. She served as mayor both in 1923 and from 1925 to 1929. As Sarah Grand, she wrote feminist books, including *The Heavenly Twins* in 1893, *The Beth Book* in 1898, and *The Winged Victory* in 1916. Her works earned her a national reputation and popularity for her positions on emancipation of women.

Sources: Magnusson, *Larousse Biographical Dictionary,* p. 617; *Who Was Who,* vol. IV, p. 458.

1929 • Margaret Grace Bondfield (1873–1953) became the first female cabinet minister in England when she became minister of labour in 1929, a post she held until 1931. A lifelong trade union leader, Bondfield was the first female delegate to a Trade Union Congress (TUC) Conference (in 1889) and became the first woman to serve as chair of the Trade Union Congress in 1923. (*See also* **Activism: Labor Activism, 1923.**)

Sources: *The Concise Dictionary of National Biography,* vol. I, pp. 282–83; Magnusson, *Larousse Biographical Dictionary,* p. 176; *Who Was Who,* vol. V, p. 116.

1936 • Edward VIII, king of England, abdicated his throne to marry Wallis Warfield Simpson (1896–1986), making her the first woman for whom a British king gave up his crown. Later becoming the Duchess of Windsor, Simpson was a twice-divorced American. Edward VIII's family and the British Parliament disapproved of his marriage to Mrs. Simpson, who the king referred to as "the woman I love." The two were married in June of 1937 and lived for the rest of their lives primarily in France, except for a period in the Caribbean where Edward, now Duke of Windsor, served as governor of the Bahamas during World War II.

Sources: Uglow, *The Continuum Dictionary of Women's Biography,* p. 585; *The Concise Dictionary of National Biography,* vol. I, p. 899.

1945 • Ellen Cicely Wilkinson (1891–1947) became the first woman to serve as minister of education. She was appointed to serve in the Labour government of British Prime Minister Clement Atlee. An English trade unionist and feminist, Wilkinson was elected minister of Parliament (MP) in 1924 to represent Middlesborough, England, and served until 1931. In 1935, she served as Labour MP for Jarrow, and in 1940 she became secretary to the ministry of home security. Wilkinson made workers' issues her primary focus.

Sources: *The Concise Dictionary of National Biography,* vol. III, p. 3221; Magnusson, *Larousse Biographical Dictionary,* p. 1560; *Who Was Who,* vol. IV, p. 1236.

1952 • Elizabeth II (b. 1926), queen of the United Kingdom of Great Britain and Northern Ireland, was the first queen to serve as head of the British Commonwealth of Nations. (The Commonwealth is a voluntary alliance of 51 nations, including Canada, Australia, India, South Africa, and New Zealand.) She was proclaimed queen February 6, 1952, on the death of her father, George VI, and her coronation ceremony followed June 2, 1953.

Sources: Magnusson, *Larousse Biographical Dictionary,* p. 474; Uglow, *The Continuum Dictionary of Women's Biography,* p. 187.

1953 • Salote (1900–1965), queen of Tonga, was the first Polynesian queen to travel to England for a coronation. As her country's representative, she went to London for the coronation of Queen Elizabeth II in 1953.

Sources: Magnusson, *Larousse Biographical Dictionary,* p. 1291; Uglow, *The Continuum Dictionary of Women's Biography,* p. 476.

EDITH SUMMERSKILL

1956 • Baroness Edith Clara Summerskill (1901–1980), activist and feminist, was the first English woman to campaign against professional boxing and smoking. She published her book against the violent sport of boxing in 1956. As a physician, Summerskill was well-qualified to speak about the disadvantages of smoking, having earned a medical degree in 1924 following training at Charing Cross Hospital. Summerskill practiced medicine privately until she entered politics in the 1930s. In 1945 she became undersecretary at the ministry of food and was responsible for the Clean Milk Act of 1949. She served as chair of the Labour Party in 1954 and 1955. She is remembered for her illustrious political career and for her writings.

Sources: The Concise Dictionary of National Biography, vol. III, p. 2899; Magnusson, *Larousse Biographical Dictionary,* p. 1417; *Who Was Who,* vol. VII, p. 770.

1962 • Barbara Salt (1904–1975) was the first English woman named to serve as ambassador by her country. After a distinguished career in diplomacy, beginning in 1942, she was appointed ambassador to Israel in 1962. Severe illness, however, resulted in the amputation of both legs, preventing her from taking up this post.

Sources: The Concise Dictionary of National Biography, vol. III, p. 2639; *Who Was Who,* vol. VII, pp. 699–700.

1972 • Janet Baker Young (b. 1926), an English politician, was the first Conservative woman to serve as a whip in the House of Lords, in London, England, in 1972. A good friend of Margaret Thatcher, Young has had a distinguished political career, serving as vice-chair of the Conservative Party when Thatcher became its leader in 1975. After Thatcher became prime minister in 1979, Young served in her cabinet in several prominent positions, among them minister of state for the Foreign and Commonwealth office in 1983.

Sources: Uglow, *The Continuum Dictionary of Women's Biography,* p. 597.

1974 • Irene Ward (1895–1980), an English politician, was the first woman to serve for 38 years in the English House of Commons. She was first elected in Wallsend in 1931 and served as an active member of Parliament until her defeat in 1945. She was elected again, from Tynemouth, and served from 1950 until her retirement in 1974.

Sources: Uglow, *The Continuum Dictionary of Women's Biography,* p. 569.

1978 • Elizabeth, the Queen Mother (b. 1900), the mother of Elizabeth II of England, was the first woman to become lord warden of the Cinque Ports, a now honorary position and a title dating back to the 11th century.

Sources: Magnusson, *Larousse Biographical Dictionary,* p. 474; Uglow, *The Continuum Dictionary of Women's Biography,* p. 186.

1979 • Margaret Hilda Thatcher (b. 1925) was the first woman to serve as prime minister of Britain, a post she assumed as head of the Conservative Party in 1979. In 1975 she was elected leader of the Conservative Party, the first woman to head a British political party. She served her country in its highest position until relinquishing her post to fellow Conservative John Major, in 1991.

Sources: Magnusson, *Larousse Biographical Dictionary,* p. 1445; *The World Book Encyclopedia,* vol. 19, p. 181.

Margaret Thatcher

Fiji

1970s • Adi Losalini Dovi, a Fijian politician who began her career as a civil service stenographer, was the first woman in her country to achieve ministerial rank.

Sources: O'Neill, *The Women's Book of World Records and Achievements,* p. 60.

Finland

1927 • Miina Sillanpää (1866–1952), a Finnish politician who was first elected to Parliament in 1907, became minister of the Department of Social Affairs. Sillanpää was the first woman to serve as a cabinet minister in her country's government. She was the first female speaker of the Finnish Parliament from 1936 until 1947. She is remembered particularly for her commitment to improving the social conditions of working-class women and single parents.

Sources: Uglow, *The Continuum Dictionary of Women's Biography,* pp. 498–99.

France

1491 • Duchess Anne of Brittany (1476–1514) succeeded her father as leader of Brittany and struggled to maintain Breton independence. In 1491 she was forced to marry Charles VIII of France, uniting Brittany with France and making Anne queen. Anne was the first queen to give women an important place at court. She took over the government of France while Charles VIII was at war with Italy. A year after his death in 1498, she married his successor, Louis XII.

Sources: Chicago, *The Dinner Party,* p. 155; Magnusson, *Larousse Biographical Dictionary,* p. 49.

1562 • Catherine de Medici (1519–1589) was the first person to bring about official recognition of Protestantism in France, through the January Edict of 1562. Queen of France by virtue of her marriage to Henri, Duke of Orléans who became king in 1547, she remained powerful after his death in 1559 as regent for two of her sons and advisor to the third. She tried to bring about religious conciliation and consolidation of political power, but she was ruthless in using religious and political factionalism for her own ends.

Sources: Uglow, *The Continuum Dictionary of Women's Biography,* pp. 369–70.

1793 • Charlotte Corday (1768–1793) was the first French woman to become a political assassin when she stabbed the French leader Jean Paul Marat in his bathtub. She was guillotined for this act four days later.

Sources: Uglow, *The Continuum Dictionary of Women's Biography,* p. 137.

1849 • Jeanne Deroin (1810–1894), was the first woman to run for election to the French National Assembly. One of the first French feminists to link the emancipation of women with the struggle of the working class, she founded the Club for Emancipation of Women in 1848.

Sources: Newnan, *Historical Dictionary of France from the 1815 Restoration to the Second Empire,* pp. 321–22; Uglow, *The Continuum Dictionary of Women's Biography,* pp. 162–63.

1881 • Léonie Rouzade (1839–1916), a French novelist who championed socialist causes, was the first woman to stand for municipal election in France, in Paris. Her bid for office was unsuccessful.

Sources: Uglow, *The Continuum Dictionary of Women's Biography,* p. 438.

1945 • Marthe Ricard (1889–1982), a French feminist who worked for the French secret service during World War I and for the Resistance during World War II, was the first woman to campaign successfully against prostitution in France. As a city councilor after the liberation of Paris, she worked to rid her nation of legalized prostitution, which she felt exploited women as slaves. Her efforts resulted in the closure of Paris brothels in 1945 and in 1946 in legislation against prostitution throughout France.

Sources: Uglow, *The Continuum Dictionary of Women's Biography,* p. 455.

1974 • Françoise Giroud (b. 1916), a French journalist and politician, was the first person to serve the French government as secretary of state for women's affairs, a position to which she was appointed in 1974. She was also one of the first coeditors (with Hélène Gordon-Lazareff) of *Elle,* from the time of its first issue in 1945, and a cofounder and first coeditor (with Jean-Jacques Servan-Schreiber) of the weekly *l'Express,* a position she held from 1953 until 1971.

Sources: O'Neill, *The Women's Book of World Records and Achievements,* pp. 53–54; Uglow, *The Continuum Dictionary of Women's Biography,* p. 225.

Simone Weill (b. 1927), a French lawyer and an ardent feminist, was the first woman to achieve the rank of minister in France. On May 28, 1974, Weill was appointed minister of health and social security. She fought for the liberalizing of the state's abortion laws and, six months after her appointment, won the right to abortion for all French women. She also achieved another first: as a result of her campaign, France became the first nation of Latin, Catholic background to legalize abortion.

Sources: O'Neill, *The Women's Book of World Records and Achievements,* p. 54; Uglow, *The Continuum Dictionary of Women's Biography,* p. 557.

Germany

Ninth century • Engelberga, a ninth-century queen who was the wife of Ludovico II of Italy, was the first German woman to rule equally with her husband.

Sources: Chicago, *The Dinner Party,* p. 133.

1918 • Rosa Luxemburg (1870–1919) was the founder of the Communist Party in Germany. With Leo Jogisches, she founded the Social Democratic Party of Poland in 1893. She gained German citizenship in 1896 through her marriage to the anarchist Gustav Lubecks. During World War I, working with friends in Berlin, she organized the radical Spartacus League, which after the war became the German Communist Party, in opposition to the new moderate socialist regime. Having fled her native Poland because of her political activities, she was considered no less a political threat in Germany and was shot to death in 1919.

Sources: Chicago, *The Dinner Party,* p. 203; Thompson, *Historical Dictionary of Germany,* p. 327–28.

1934 • Gertrud Scholtz-Klink (b. 1902), a Nazi German who became the spokesperson for Adolf Hitler's policies towards women, was the first woman to be given the title "Reichsfrauenführerin" ("National Women's Leader"). The title was given to her in Baden, Germany. She also served as head of Frauenwerk, the organization of German women. In 1939 she went to England where she was billed as "The Perfect Nazi Woman." Imprisoned as a war criminal in 1948, she was banned on her release from participation in the new German government and from professional life. She was also restricted to living in her district.

Sources: Uglow, *The Continuum Dictionary of Women's Biography,* pp. 484–85; Wistrich, *Who's Who in Nazi Germany,* p. 238.

1940s • Louise Schroder (1887–1957), a German political and committed socialist, was the first woman to be called "Mother of Berlin." She earned her nickname in the late 1940s when, as the first female acting lord mayor of this city, beginning in 1947, she led Berlin during the Russian blockade. In 1949, she became a member of the Bundestag.

Sources: Uglow, *The Continuum Dictionary of Women's Biography,* p. 486.

1957 • Marie-Elizabeth Luders (1888–1966), one of the first women in Germany to obtain a doctoral degree in political science and economics (in 1912), was the first woman to be made honorary president of the Federal Democratic Party, in Berlin. She was chosen because of her distinguished career in political life. In 1914 she helped to found the National Women's Service and in 1919 joined the Democratic Party, serving first in the National Assembly, then in the Reichstag. Opposed to the Nazis, she spent the war in exile but returned to Berlin to serve in the senate in 1947. By 1953, Luders had become the senior member of the Bundestag, the first woman to attain this status.

Sources: Uglow, *The Continuum Dictionary of Women's Biography,* pp. 336–37.

Margot Honecker

1963 • Margot Honecker (b. 1927), an East German Communist, was the first woman to hold a cabinet-level position in her country. She was appointed minister of education in Berlin, East Germany. She was the wife of the head of the East German state and Communist Party President Erich Honecker.

Sources: O'Neill, *The Women's Book of World Records and Achievements,* p. 61; Thompson, *Historical Dictionary of Germany,* p. 295.

1969 • Ellinor Puttkamer was appointed to represent Germany as ambassador to the Council of European States, the first woman to hold the post.

Sources: O'Neill, *The Women's Book of World Records and Achievements,* p. 62.

1970 • Ulrike Meinhof (1934–1976), a German terrorist, was the first woman to lead the radical group called the Red Army Faction. After her daring efforts to free an arrested colleague, Andreas Baader, in 1970, her terrorist organization became known in the media as the Baader-Meinhof Gang. Arrested in June 1972, Meinhof was sentenced to eight years in prison and committed suicide after the failure of terrorist attempts to gain her release.

Sources: Thompson, *Historical Dictionary of Germany,* p. 472; Uglow, *The Continuum Dictionary of Women's Biography,* pp. 370–71.

1979 • Petra Karin Kelly (1947–1992), a German politician educated in the United States, was a founding member of Germany's Green Party and the first woman to run as its national candidate. In 1983 she became one of seventeen Green Party members of the West German Parliament, where she took a moderate position on environmental issues.In 1984, she became disenchanted with the government, and increasingly isolated herself from the mainstream.

Sources: Thompson, *Historical Dictionary of Germany,* p. 302–3; Uglow, *The Continuum Dictionary of Women's Biography,* p. 296.

1995 • Jutta Limbach is the first woman president of Germany's highest court, located in Nuremberg, Germany. The court, located in the Palace of Justice, Nuremberg, is remembered for trying the highest-ranking survivors of Adolf Hitler's Third Reich during 218 days of hearings in 1945 and 1946 that

Ulrike Meinhof

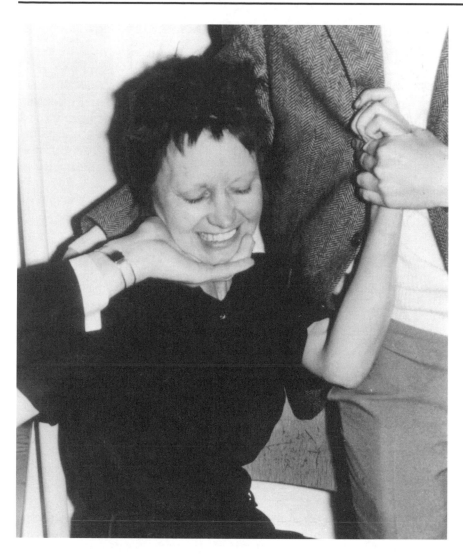

produced sentences ranging from death by hanging to acquittal. On the 50th anniversary of the Nuremberg trials, President Limbach and others held a panel discussion on war crimes. The 1945–1946 trial was based on the so-called Nuremberg principles that declared that government leaders were to be held accountable for breaches of international law and that no one could plead not guilty to war crimes by saying they were merely following orders.

Source: *The New York Times* (20 November 1995), p. A4.

Greece

527 • Theodora (508–548) was the first actress to become an empress. Theodora was the daughter of a bear trainer who performed with the circus. She supported herself as an actress and was known for her great beauty. Theodora was courted by Justinian I, and the two were married in 525. When Justinian became emperor of the East Roman Empire in 527, Theodora was crowned empress along with him in Constantinople (present-day Istanbul) in 527. As Empress of Byzantium, she served as an advisor to her husband.

Sources: Chicago, *The Dinner Party,* pp. 71–72; Magnusson, *Larousse Biographical Dictionary,* p. 1446.

797 • Irene of Athens (c.752–803) was the first woman to rule the Byzantine Empire alone, from 797 until 802. She had previously been co-ruler and regent for her feeble son Constantine VI. She imprisoned her son and may have be responsible for having him blinded. Ruling in her own right, in 787 Irene summoned the Seventh Ecumenical Council (known as the Council of Nicaea), which brought peace and stability to an empire divided by religious unrest. During her sole rule, she was addressed as "King." For her part in restoration of religion, she was made a saint by the Greek church.

Sources: Magnusson, *Larousse Biographical Dictionary,* p. 761; Uglow, *The Continuum Dictionary of Women's Biography,* p. 274.

Irene of Athens ruled the Byzantine Empire.

1920s • Maria Svolou (d. 1976) was the first person in Greece to reveal the appalling working and housing conditions of poor women. As an inspector of labour in the Ministry of Economics in Athens in the 1920s, she took great interest in working-class women and struggled to improve their situation. She is remembered for her anti-Fascist and pro-peace activities, especially between 1911 and 1936.

Sources: Uglow, *The Continuum Dictionary of Women's Biography,* pp. 525–26.

1940s • Electra Apostoloy (1912–1944), an active Greek Communist and feminist, was the first woman to play a leading role in the Greek resistance movement during World War II. She was tortured to death by the German-backed Greek secret police in 1944 but revealed no information about her Communist comrades.

Sources: Uglow, *The Continuum Dictionary of Women's Biography,* pp. 23–24.

1978 • Melina Mercouri (b. 1925), known internationally as a film actress, winning an Academy Award for *Never on Sunday,* is the first Greek actress to become a successful politician. She left her film career to work against the military junta that took power in her country in 1967. Living in Paris and America without a passport as an enemy of the Greek state, she returned to Athens in 1974 and in 1978 was elected to Parliament. She has since served as minister of culture and sciences (1981–1985), and in 1985 was made minister of culture, youth, and sports.

Sources: Briggs, *A Dictionary of 20th Century World Biography,* p. 386.

Guinea

1970s • Jeanne Martin Cissé (b. 1926), a Guinean diplomat, was the first woman to preside over the United Nations Security Council. She served as Guinea's first female delegate from 1972 until 1976.

Sources: O'Neill, *The Women's Book of World Records and Achievements,* p. 65; Uglow, *The Continuum Dictionary of Women's Biography,* p. 125.

Hungary

1918 • Rosika Schwimmer (1877–1948), a Hungarian feminist and pacifist, was the world's first female ambassador. She was appointed to serve her country as ambassador to Switzerland in October of 1918. She served in this post for a year. Due to political unrest in Hungary, she emigrated to the United States in the 1930s. In 1948 she was nominated for the Nobel Peace Prize.

Sources: Uglow, *The Continuum Dictionary of Women's Biography,* p. 488.

Iceland

1980 • Vigdís Finnbogadóttir (b. 1930) became the world's first female head of state to be elected democratically. She was declared president of Iceland after narrowly defeating three male opponents in the election. She was returned to office in 1984 when she ran unopposed and won reelection again in 1988. In 1972, nine years after she and her husband divorced, Finnbogadóttir adopted a daughter. This was one of the first adoptions by a single person in Iceland.

Sources: Magnusson, *Larousse Biographical Dictionary,* p. 516; Matthews, *The Guinness Book of World Records,* p. 178.

Vigdís Finnbogadóttir

India

c.1615 • Jahan Nur (1571–1634) was the first female ruler of India to issue coins in her own name. A flamboyant ruler of the Moghul court, she enjoyed almost 16 years of unchallenged power between 1611 and her retirement in 1627.

Sources: Uglow, *The Continuum Dictionary of Women's Biography,* p. 407.

1876 • Victoria (1819–1901), queen of England from 1837, was the first queen to hold the title of Empress of India, obtained for her by her favorite prime minister, Benjamin Disraeli. The most influential monarch of the modern era, Victoria's name and personality are associated with the last and greatest period of British Empire and with an entire system of values and attitudes.

Sources: Magnusson, *Larousse Biographical Dictionary,* pp. 1507–8; Schmidt, *400 Outstanding Women of the World,* pp. 151–152.

1925 • Sarojini Naidu (1879–1949), a feminist poet and politician, was the first Indian woman to serve as president of the Indian National Congress, in Delhi. Naidu is remembered for her verse and for her active involvement in the Indian independence movement. An associate of Mahatma Gandhi, she was imprisoned several times for civil disobedience. In 1947, she was appointed governor of the United Provinces, an area known in modern times as Uttar Pradesh.

Sources: Magnusson, *Larousse Biographical Dictionary,* p. 1062; Uglow, *The Continuum Dictionary of Women's Biography,* p. 396.

1946 • Vijaya Lakshmi Pandit (1900–1990), an Indian politician, was the first female minister of Parliament (MP) in India. She served her country as a distinguished diplomat, becoming president of the United Nations General Assembly in 1953–1954.

Sources: O'Neill, *The Women's Book of World Records and Achievements,* p. 63; Uglow, *The Continuum Dictionary of Women's Biography,* p. 417.

1947 • Rajkumari Amrit Kaur (1889–1964) was the first woman to hold a cabinet-level position in India when she was appointed minister of health in the year her country won its independence from Great Britain. She held this position until 1957. She is remembered as the founder and first president of the Indian Red Cross and as the founder of the All-India Women's Conference, in 1926.

Sources: O'Neill, *The Women's Book of World Records and Achievements,* p. 61.

1949 • Vijaya Lakshmi Pandit (1900–1990), an Indian politician, was the first woman ambassador to represent her country in the United States. She presented her credentials to President Harry S Truman.

Sources: Kane, *Famous First Facts,* p. 224; O'Neill, *The Women's Book of World Records and Achievements,* p. 63.

Indira Gandhi

1966 • Indira Gandhi (1917–1984) became India's first female prime minister, serving in this position until 1977. She governed during an especially turbulent period in her nation's history and often resorted to controlling unrest by declaring a "state of emergency," which restricted constitutional freedoms and imposed strict censorship on the citizens of India. After losing the election in 1977, she was arrested and acquitted on charges of corruption and left the Congress Parliamentary party to become leader of the newly formed Indian National Congress. She successfully ran again for prime minister in the 1980 general election. In October 1984, she was assassinated.

Sources: Magnusson, *Larousse Biographical Dictionary,* p. 564; O'Neill, *The Women's Book of World Records and Achievements,* p. 47.

Indonesia

1946 • Maria Ulfah Santoso, an Indonesian politician, was the first woman in her country to serve as a cabinet minister. In 1946, she was appointed minister of social affairs, a post she held until 1947.

Sources: O'Neill, *The Women's Book of World Records and Achievements,* p. 61.

1959 • Laili Rusad, an Indonesian diplomat, was the first woman to serve her country as ambassador to Belgium and Luxembourg. She was appointed to this position in 1959. In 1967, she went on to serve Indonesia as ambassador to Austria.

Sources: O'Neill, *The Women's Book of World Records and Achievements,* p. 62.

Ireland

1977 • Marie Geoghegan Quinn (b. 1951), a former schoolteacher from Carna in County Galway, was the first woman to serve as a parliamentary secretary in Ireland. A member of the Fianna Fail Party, she was appointed secretary to the minister of industry and commerce.

Sources: O'Neill, *The Women's Book of World Records and Achievements,* p. 59.

1990 • Mary Robinson (b. 1944), an international lawyer, activist, and Catholic, won election as the first woman president of Ireland in November 1990. This victory is notable in that it came in a period in Irish history of controversy over abortion and women's rights. Robinson promoted legislation that enabled women to serve on juries and gave 18-year-olds the right to vote. In 1974, while serving in the Irish legislature, she shocked her fellow countrypeople by calling for legal sale of contraceptives.

Sources: Almanac of Famous People, p. 1294; *National Geographic* (September 1994), vol. 186, no. 3, p. 13.

1995 • The first person to work for Sinn Fein in its new office in Washington, D.C., opened in 1995, was a woman. This organization represented the more dissident factions in the Republic of Ireland. Militant leader Gerry Adams declared that while the British had 600 employees working at their American embassy, Sinn Fein would have "one Irish woman. I think maybe the British are at a disadvantage."

Sources: Newsweek (27 March 1995), p. 19.

Israel

c.834 B.C. • Athaliah (d. 837 B.C.) was the first Queen of Judea (or Judah) and the only queen on record. She governed for six years after the death of her son, the king Ahaziah, who was murdered. Her brutal rule and overthrow is

Mary Robinson

told by French dramatist Jean Racine in his famous play *Athalie* (1691), for which composer Felix Mendelsohn added music.

Sources: Magnusson, *Larousse Biographical Dictionary,* p. 73; Uglow, *The Continuum Dictionary of Women's Biography,* p. 33.

1969 • Golda Meir (1898–1978), became the first woman to serve as prime minister of Israel. A lifelong Zionist, Meir immigrated to Palestine (present-day Israel) from the United States in 1921 and devoted her life to national politics. Prior to becoming prime minister, Meir served as Israeli ambassador to

the Soviet Union (1948–1949), minister of labor (1949–1956), and foreign minister (1956–1966). She resigned as prime minister in 1974.

Sources: Chicago, *The Dinner Party,* p. 201; Magnusson, *Larousse Biographical Dictionary,* p. 999; Meir, *My Life;* O'Neill, *The Women's Book of World Records and Achievements,* pp. 46–47.

1973 • Shulamit Aloni (b. 1931) founded the Civil Rights Party in Israel. A lawyer and feminist, Aloni has fought throughout her political career for the rights of children and women.

Sources: Uglow, *The Continuum Dictionary of Women's Biography,* p. 14.

Japan

1945 • Fusaye Ichikawa (1893–1981), a Japanese feminist and politician, was the first head of the New Japan Women's League, which successfully campaigned to win the vote for women in 1945. In 1920, she was a cofounder with Hiratsuko Raicho (1886–1971) of the New Women's Association, becoming an activist for women's rights. She traveled to the United States from 1921 to 1924, where she was influenced by the women's suffrage movement. Upon her return to Japan in 1924, she founded the Women's Suffrage League. In 1952 she was elected to the Upper House of Councillors in the Japanese Diet, where she had a distinguished career for over 20 years. She won reelection every time she sought it, except in 1971; after a defeat that year, she returned to win elections in 1975 and 1980.

Sources: Iwai, *Biographical Dictionary of Japanese History,* p. 343; Magnusson, *Larousse Biographical Dictionary,* p. 756.

1972 • Misako Enoki (b. 1939), a Japanese feminist, founded the Pink Panthers movement in Japan. The group, wearing white military uniforms and pink helmets, staged protests to focus on women's issues such as equal employment, equal property rights, contraception, and abortion. The group would be dissolved in 1977, when the New Japan Women's Party began to put forth candidates for political office.

Sources: Uglow, *The Continuum Dictionary of Women's Biography,* p. 190.

1976 • Sakado Ogata, a Japanese politician, became the first woman in her country to serve as a diplomat with ministerial rank.

Sources: O'Neill, *The Women's Book of World Records and Achievements,* p. 63.

1985 • Japan's Parliament reluctantly passed the country's first Equal Employment Opportunity Law as the United Nations Decade for Women (1975–1985) came to a close. The law prohibits employers from offering women fewer fringe benefits than men or forcing women to resign when they marry or become pregnant. It recommends "that employers give equal opportunities to men and women when recruiting and hiring workers" and "treat women workers on an equal footing" when deciding on assignments or promotions.

Source: New York Times (30 May 1993), pp. 6–18.

1986 • Takako Doi (b. 1928), a Japanese politician, one of whose chief concerns was international peace, was the first woman to become the leader of a major political party in Japan. In 1986, Doi was elected to lead the Japanese Socialist Party, the country's largest opposition party. In August 1993, Doi was the first woman to be elected speaker of Parliament.

Sources: Uglow, *The Continuum Dictionary of Women's Biography,* p. 171.

Jordan

1969 • Laurice Hlass, a Palestinian who lost her home in 1948 and settled in Amman, became the first woman to serve as ambassador for Jordan. A career diplomat, Hlass was appointed ambassador in 1969 and represented Jordan at three sessions of the United Nations General Assembly.

Sources: O'Neill, *The Women's Book of World Records and Achievements,* p. 63.

Malaysia

1973 • Tan Sri Fatimah, a Malaysian politician, became the first woman to hold a cabinet-level position in her country when she was appointed to serve as minister for social welfare.

Sources: O'Neill, *The Women's Book of World Records and Achievements,* p. 61.

Malta

1947 • Agatha Barbara (b. 1923) became the first female member of the Maltese Parliament in 1947. On February 16, 1982, after a distinguished career in Maltese politics, she was elected the first female president of the Republic of Malta. Barbara has demonstrated particular concern for social legislation and women's rights.

Sources: Uglow, *The Continuum Dictionary of Women's Biography,* p. 47.

Agatha Barbara

Mauritania

1975 • Toure Aissata Kane, a feminist politician in Islamic Mauritania, was the first woman to achieve cabinet rank in her country. On August 22, 1975, she was appointed minister for the protection of the family and for social affairs.

Sources: O'Neill, *The Women's Book of World Records and Achievements,* p. 60.

Netherlands

1948 • Wilhelmina (1880–1962) was the first Dutch queen to abdicate in favor of her daughter. In 1948, after valiantly serving as monarch of the Netherlands for 50 years, including a period of exile in England during World War II, Wilhelmina resigned in favor of her only child, Juliana. Wilhelmina is particularly remembered for her constant and morally uplifting broadcasts from London to the Netherlands between May of 1940 and her return to her country in July of 1945.

Sources: Uglow, *The Continuum Dictionary of Women's Biography,* p. 581.

Wilhelmina

New Zealand

1947 • Mabel Howard (1893–1972) was the first female cabinet minister both in New Zealand and in the British Commonwealth. Elected to Parliament in 1943, she was appointed minister of health and child welfare in 1947, a post she held for two years.

Sources: Uglow, *The Continuum Dictionary of Women's Biography,* p. 267.

Nicaragua

1950 • Olga Nuñez De Sassallow, the first woman to receive a law degree in Nicaragua, was the first woman to serve in a cabinet-level position in her country. She was appointed minister of public education in 1950, a post she held until 1956.

Sources: O'Neill, *The Women's Book of World Records and Achievements,* p. 61.

c.1980 • Nora Astorga (1949–1988) was the first Nicaraguan woman whose appointment as Nicaragua's ambassador to the United States was blocked by the Central Intelligence Agency. A revolutionary as well as a diplomat, she went on in 1986 to become the Nicaraguan ambassador to the United Nations in New York City.

Sources: Uglow, *The Continuum Dictionary of Women's Biography,* p. 33.

Nigeria

Late sixteenth century • Amina (1560–1610) a Nigerian queen who took over the throne after the death of her husband in 1576, was also known as a great military leader. She became the first woman to give her name to Nigerian fortifications because of her habit of building walled encampments wherever she traveled. As a result the ancient Hausa fortifications are called "Amina's walls."

Sources: Uglow, *The Continuum Dictionary of Women's Biography,* p. 15.

1876 • Mary Mitchell Slessor (1848–1919), a missionary sponsored by the United Presbyterian Church, was the first Scottish woman to be vested with the powers of a magistrate in Calabar, Nigeria. She was recognized by the government because of the authority she had earned through her work with the people of the Okoyong and Aros tribes.

Sources: Magnusson, *Larousse Biographical Dictionary,* p. 1359; Uglow, *The Continuum Dictionary of Women's Biography,* pp. 500–1.

Norway

c.1030 • Aelgifu (c.1010–1040) was the first Saxon woman to rule Norway. She was made regent for Sweyn, the son of her lover, Cnut of Denmark, when Sweyn was made King of Norway. Aelgifu was a cruel tyrant removed from power during an uprising in 1035.

Sources: Uglow, *The Continuum Dictionary of Women's Biography,* p. 6.

Twentieth century • Betsy Kjelsberg (c.1867–1950) was the first woman elected to the Norwegian legislature. She was a businesswoman who concerned herself particularly with women's rights and social legislation, especially for workers.

Sources: Chicago, *The Dinner Party,* p. 192.

1945 • Kirsten Moe Hansteen was the first woman in Norway to serve as minister without portfolio. She was appointed right after the end of World War II, in June 1945, and served until November of that year.

Sources: O'Neill, *The Women's Book of World Records and Achievements,* p. 61.

1958 • Inger Louise Andvig Valle (b. 1921), a Norwegian politician, was the first person to serve as head of the legal and economic section of the Consumer Council, in Oslo, Norway, in 1958. Valle went on to a distinguished career in her country's government as a member of the Labor Party.

Sources: Uglow, *The Continuum Dictionary of Women's Biography,* p. 554.

1981 • Gro Harlem Brundtland (b. 1939) became Norway's first female prime minister when Odvar Nordli resigned for health reasons. As leader of the Labor Party she became prime minister a second time in 1986. She heads a cabinet of eight women and nine men, the highest number of women in a cabinet in history. Because of her encouragement, female members comprise 34 percent of Norway's Parliament, the largest proportion of female governmental representation in the world. In 1988, she received the Third World Foundation prize for her international leadership on environmental issues.

Sources: Magnusson, *Larousse Biographical Dictionary,* p. 219.

Gro Harlem Brundtland

Pakistan

1954 • Liaquat Ali Khan (b. 1905), a Pakistani politician and an active feminist, was the first Muslim woman to serve as an ambassador when she was named ambassador to Belgium and the Netherlands. She later served as ambassador to Italy and Tunisia. Khan founded the All-Pakistan Women's Association in 1949. In 1973, she became the first woman to govern a Pakistani province, the province of Sind. In the 1970s, she was also selected as the Chancellor of the University of Karachi, and in 1978 the United Nations honored Khan with the Human Rights Award.

Sources: Uglow, *The Continuum Dictionary of Women's Biography,* p. 298.

1964 • Fatima Jinnah (1893–1967) was the first woman to run for president of Pakistan. She ran unsuccessfully as a candidate for the combined opposition parties. She was the sister of Mohammed Ali Jinnah, the first governor general of Pakistan, whom she assisted as hostess during his term (1947–1948). Jinnah was an activist who served Pakistan in a variety of ways. She was the first woman to lead the All-India Muslim Women's Committee at the time of its inception in 1938. An advocate of women's rights, she also founded the Fatima Jinnah Women's Medical College at Lahore, Pakistan.

Sources: Uglow, *The Continuum Dictionary of Women's Biography,* p. 284.

1988 • Benazir Bhutto (b. 1953) was the first woman to become prime minister of Pakistan, taking office on December 1, 1988. She is also the first Islamic woman prime minister. After her father, Prime Minister Zulfikar Ali Bhutto,

Benazir Bhutto

was deposed and put to death in 1979, she suffered imprisonment because of her family's and her own political beliefs. She rose to power as head of the Pakistan People's Party and became their charismatic leader in 1986.

Sources: Briggs, *A Dictionary of 20th Century World Biography,* pp. 61–62.

Paraguay

1945 • Isabel Arrua Vallejo was the first woman in Paraguay to attain diplomatic rank. She was made an attaché of the Embassy of Paraguay to Brazil in 1945 and served in this capacity until 1948.

Sources: O'Neill, *The Women's Book of World Records and Achievements,* p. 63.

Philippines

1890s • Melchora Aquino (1812–1919), known as "the mother of the Philippine Revolution," was the first female leader in the Philippines' struggle for independence from Spain. The country gained its freedom in 1898.

Sources: Uglow, *The Continuum Dictionary of Women's Biography,* p. 25.

1986 • Corazon Aquino (b. 1933) became the first female president of the Philippines in 1986. Supported by the United States and the Roman Catholic Church, Aquino's government faced innumerable obstacles; severe factionalism and social problems made success almost impossible.

Sources: Briggs, *A Dictionary of 20th Century World Biography,* p. 15; Magnusson, *Larousse Biogrpahical Dictionary,* p. 55.

Poland

Late fourteenth century • Jadwiga (1372–1399), queen of Poland from the time of her father's death in 1384, consolidated her power with her marriage at the age of 12 to the Grand Prince of Lithuania, Jagiello, who took the name Wladyslaw II, in 1386. She was the first woman to lend her support to the University of Krakow, the oldest university in her country, founded in 1364, reestablishing the institution as a center for learning and the arts, especially music.

Sources: Schmidt, *400 Outstanding Women of the World,* p. 316.

Portugal

1970 • Maria Teresa Carcomo Lobo, a Portuguese politician, was the first woman in her country to hold a cabinet-level post. On August 21, 1970, she was appointed undersecretary of state for welfare, a position she held until 1973.

Sources: O'Neill, *The Women's Book of World Records and Achievements,* p. 61.

1974 • Maria de Lourdes Pintassilgo (b. 1930) was the first woman to serve as secretary of state for social security and then minister for social affairs in the two provisional Portuguese governments set in place after the revolution in 1974. She has continued to be active in her country's political life and has taken a special interest in international affairs and women's issues.

Sources: Uglow, *The Continuum Dictionary of Women's Biography,* pp. 433–34.

1975 • Maria Manuela Morgado, a Portuguese politician with a number of firsts to her credit, was the first woman in her country to serve as undersecretary of state for public investments, a position she held from December 1975 until her appointment on July 29, 1976, as the first woman in Portugal to serve as secretary of state for finance. On March 25, 1977, she became her country's first female secretary of state for treasury.

Sources: O'Neill, *The Women's Book of World Records and Achievements,* p. 61.

Maria Isabel Carmelo Rosa was the first woman to serve as secretary of state for consumer protection in Portugal. She was appointed to this position in December 1975 and served until July 1976.

Sources: O'Neill, *The Women's Book of World Records and Achievements,* p. 61.

1977 • Maria Manuela Silva, a Portuguese politician, was the first woman to serve her country as secretary of state for planning. She was appointed to this ministerial position in July 1977.

Sources: O'Neill, *The Women's Book of World Records and Achievements,* p. 61.

Roman Empire

c.40 B.C. • Livia Drusilla (56 B.C.–29 A.D.) was the first Roman empress. She played a significant role in governing Rome for over 70 years as the wife of Augustus Caesar and mother of Tiberius. She struggled to assure that her son Tiberius would rule as her husband's heir.

Sources: Chicago, *The Dinner Party,* p. 129; Uglow, *The Continuum Dictionary of Women's Biography,* p. 330.

First century • Agrippina II (15–59) was the first woman permitted to ride in the Roman imperial chariot, previously reserved for priests. She had three husbands: her first husband was Domitius Ahenobarbus with whom she had a son, Nero, who would later rule the Roman Empire; her second husband was Crispus Passienus; her third was Claudius, whom she poisoned. She was ambitious and exercised influence over the rulers of the Roman Empire, including her son, Nero. In 59 A.D., Nero ordered her murdered.

Sources: Century Dictionary and Cyclopedia, vol. 9, p. 22; Chicago, *The Dinner Party,* p. 128.

Russia

1878 • Vera Zasulich (1849–1919) was the first Russian revolutionary to perform an act of political violence. In St. Petersburg, she shot the city's governor, General Trepov, because of his brutality to a political prisoner. A jury refused to condemn her and she was acquitted.

Sources: Uglow, *The Continuum Dictionary of Women's Biography,* p. 599.

1881 • Sofya Lvovna Perovskaya (1853–1881), a Russian revolutionary, was the first woman to organize and direct a successful conspiracy to assassinate a Russian czar. She was caught in March, sentenced to death, and hanged in April of the same year.

Sources: Uglow, *The Continuum Dictionary of Women's Biography,* p. 430.

c.1918 • Angelika Balabanoff (1878–1965) served after World War I as the first commissioner for foreign affairs in the new Soviet government. After a falling out with Nikolai Lenin, she left Russia in 1921 and lived the rest of her life abroad, where she continued to work for socialist causes.

Sources: Balabanoff, *My Life as a Rebel*; Uglow, *The Continuum Dictionary of Women's Biography*, p. 44.

1918 • Alexandra Kollontai (1872–1952), a Russian feminist and a leader in the Revolutionary movement, became the first commissar for public welfare in the first Bolshevik government; she was the first and only woman. She went on to found the Central Office for the Care of Mother and Child in the Soviet Union.

Sources: Chicago, *The Dinner Party*, pp. 202–3; Uglow, *The Continuum Dictionary of Women's Biography*, pp. 302–3.

1956 • Ekaterina Furtseva (1910–1974), a Russian politician, was the first woman to be elected as a member of the Communist Party Praesidium in the Soviet Union, in 1956. She was one of the few women to achieve such rank and power within the Communist establishment.

Sources: Uglow, *The Continuum Dictionary of Women's Biography*, pp. 216–17.

Scandinavia

1389 • Margaret (1353–1412) was the first woman to rule as queen in three different Scandinavian countries: her native Denmark, Norway, and Sweden. Her ascent to power was due to a variety of circumstances, including the early deaths of her husband and son, but she was an able queen who controlled both her nobles and the church. The tripartite union lasted until 1523.

Sources: Hill, *The Reign of Margaret of Denmark*; Uglow, *The Continuum Dictionary of Women's Biography*, p. 354.

Scotland

1587 • Mary Queen of Scots (1542–1587), mother of James VI of Scotland who was also James I of England, the first Stuart ruler, was the first Scottish queen to be executed in England, at Fotheringay on February 8, 1587. Mary's strong Catholic following, although a minority in England, was unsettling to Elizabeth I, who saw Mary as a rival and kept her under house arrest for 19 years. Parliament demanded Mary's execution, and Elizabeth signed the warrant on February 1; it was carried out seven days later. In 1612, Mary's body was moved to Henry VII's chapel at Westminster.

Sources: Magnusson, *Larousse Biographical Dictionary*, p. 983; Schmidt, *400 Outstanding Women of the World*, pp. 132–34.

1702 • Queen Anne (1665–1714), the last Stuart ruler, was the first English queen to speak in Parliament in favor of the union of England and Scotland, in the year of her ascension, 1702. She died without heirs, and succession passed to the Hanoverian line.

Sources: Gregg, *Queen Anne*; Uglow, *The Continuum Dictionary of Women's Biography,* p. 20.

South Africa

1953 • Margaret Livingstone Ballinger (1894–1980), one of the founding members of the Liberal Party in South Africa, became its first national chairperson in 1953. She served as a minister of Parliament from 1937 until 1959 and worked unstintingly for racial equality and against apartheid.

Sources: Uglow, *The Continuum Dictionary of Women's Biography,* p. 45.

1956 • Dorothy Nyembe (b. 1930) was the first woman to lead Natal women in protest against the South African government's policy of apartheid. Repeatedly imprisoned and punished for her political activism, Nyembe has devoted her life to the cause of equality for blacks in her country.

Sources: Uglow, *The Continuum Dictionary of Women's Biography,* pp. 407–8.

1959 • Helen Suzman (b. 1917) was the first minister of Parliament to represent South Africa's Progressive Party, which she cofounded in 1959. She served in the legislature in Cape Town where she struggled to sponsor and support anti-apartheid measures. She was recognized for her efforts with the United Nations Human Rights Award in 1979 and the Medallion of Heroism in 1980.

Sources: Uglow, *The Continuum Dictionary of Women's Biography,* p. 525.

1962 • Winnie Mandela (b. 1934), known internationally for her political activism in South Africa during the long imprisonment of her husband, Nelson Mandela, was the first woman to lead the African National Congress, in 1962 after his incarceration. Winnie Mandela has been a controversial figure in her own country both in her protest against black oppression and in her use of her authority; she is admired for her courage and feared because of her power.

Sources: Uglow, *The Continuum Dictionary of Women's Biography,* p. 351.

Spain

1492 • Isabella I of Castile (1451–1504), a Spanish queen who ruled independently of her husband Ferdinand II of Aragon, was the first person to support Christopher Columbus in his exploration of the New World, funding his expedition to America in 1492.

Sources: Schmidt, *400 Outstanding Women of the World,* p. 353–54.

1934 • Delores Gomez Ibarruri (1895–1989), a Spanish political activist who wrote for a workers' newspaper under the pen name La Pasionaria (The Passion Flower), was the founder of a women's group, the Agrupacion de Mujeres Antifacistas, in 1934. Through this feminist organization and in her capacity as a journalist and member of Parliament, to which she was elected in

1936, Ibarruri worked for the loyalist cause. She left Spain after dictator Francisco Franco came to power in 1939, not returning to Spain until May of 1977. In June of that year, at the age of 81, she was reelected to Parliament in the first election in 40 years.

Sources: O'Neill, *The Women's Book of World Records and Achievements,* p. 713; Uglow, *The Continuum Dictionary of Women's Biography,* p. 272.

1936 • Federica Montseny (b. 1905), a Spanish anarchist who was both antiroyalist and anticlerical in her politics, was the first woman to serve as minister of health in the Spanish Popular Front government that rose to power in Barcelona in February 1936. After dictator Francisco Franco's victory in 1939, Montseny settled in Toulouse, France, where she organized exiled anarchists.

Sources: Uglow, *The Continuum Dictionary of Women's Biography,* p. 386.

Sri Lanka

1960 • Sirimavo Bandaranaike (b. 1916) became the world's first female prime minister when her party, the Sri Lanka Freedom Party, won the general election in July 1960.

Sources: Matthews, *The Guinness Book of World Records,* p. 182; O'Neill, *The Women's Book of World Records and Achievements,* p. 46.

Sweden

1644 • Christina of Sweden (1626–1689), as sole heir to the throne of Sweden, was the first woman to be crowned king, at the age of 18 in 1644. She ruled for 10 years before abdicating because she refused to marry and wanted a more independent life than courtly criticism permitted.

Sources: Chicago, *The Dinner Party,* p. 158; Schmidt, *400 Outstanding Women of the World,* pp. 364–66.

Sirimavo Bandaranaike

1949 • Alva Myrdal (1902–1986), a politician and pacifist, was the first Swedish woman to serve as principal director of the Department of Social Sciences at UNESCO (United Nations Educational, Scientific and Cultural Organization), in New York City in 1949. She has written several books on the subjects of social responsibility and the need for world peace. In 1936, she founded and served as the first president of the Social Pedagogical Institute in Stockholm. She worked for this organization until 1948, promoting progressive educational theories and reforms in child care. She served as Sweden's first female ambassador to India from 1955 until 1961. In 1982, she shared the Nobel Peace Prize with her husband, the economist Gunnar Myrdal.

Sources: O'Neill, *The Women's Book of World Records and Achievements,* pp. 51–52; Uglow, *The Continuum Dictionary of Women's Biography,* p. 395.

1958 • Agda Rössel (b. 1910), a Swedish diplomat, became the first woman to head a permanent delegation to the United Nations on August 8, 1958. She represented her country in New York City for seven years. She is remembered for her work on behalf of refugee children after World War II and for her role as a champion of women's rights throughout the world.

Sources: O'Neill, *The Women's Book of World Records and Achievements,* p. 64.

1976 • Karin Söder (b. 1928), a Swedish politician, was the first woman to serve as minister for foreign affairs in her country. She was appointed by Prime Minister Thorbjörn Fälldin on October 8, 1976. She began service as a minister of Parliament in 1971.

Sources: O'Neill, *The Women's Book of World Records and Achievements,* p. 52.

Switzerland

1977 • Elisabeth Blunschy-Steiner (b. 1922), a Swiss lawyer and feminist, was the first woman to serve as president of the National Council of Switzerland. She was elected on May 2, 1977, having served on the council since 1971, the first year in which women were granted the right to vote in her country. She was the first woman elected a councilmember from her canton, Schwyz.

Sources: O'Neill, *The Women's Book of World Records and Achievements,* p. 50.

Turkey

1993 • Tansu Ciller (b. 1947), a former university professor, became the first woman prime minister of Turkey. Ciller won the leadership of the True Path Party in Turkey on June 14, 1993. On July 5, she won a vote of confidence, thus officially becoming Turkey's first woman prime minister. An economist educated in the United States, Ciller amassed a $60 million fortune in real estate speculation. Ciller's acheivements as prime minister include a loosening of restrictions on Turkish political life and running a successful campaign to bring at least some of Central Asia's oil through Turkey. She resigned in 1995, after her coalition government lost support.

Sources: Current Biography (September 1994), vol. 55, no. 9, pp. 7–11; *Facts on File* (8 July 1993), vol. 53, no. 2745, p. 507; *Facts on File* (19 October 1995), vol. 55, no. 2864, p. 786; *Facts on File* (16 November 1995), vol. 55, no. 2868, p. 859; *Maclean's* (12 July 1993), vol. 106, no. 28, pp. 26–28; *The New York Times* (21 September 1995), p. A15; *The New York Times* (19 October 1995), p. A8.

TANSU CILLER

Uganda

1975 • Bernadette Olowo, a Ugandan diplomat, became the first female ambassador to the Vatican in 1975. Her appointment broke a 900-year-old tradition that kept female envoys out of the Holy See.

Sources: O'Neill, *The Women's Book of World Records and Achievements,* p. 42.

United Nations

1951 • Ana Figuero (1908–1970), a Chilean feminist, was the first woman to head a United Nations Committee of the General Assembly. In 1951 she became head of the Social, Humanitarian, and Cultural Committee. In 1952, she became the first woman on the Security Committee of the United Nations, and in 1960, she became the first female assistant director general of the International Labour Organization.

Sources: Uglow, *The Continuum Dictionary of Women's Biography,* p. 202.

1964 • Marietta Peabody Tree (1917–1991) was the first woman to serve as a permanent ambassador to the United Nations. After three years as the U.S. representative to the Human Rights Commission and a chief U.S. delegate, Tree gained the rank of ambassador with her appointment as a U.S. representative on the Trusteeship Council in 1964.

Source: Read and Witlieb, *The Book of Women's Firsts,* pp. 448–49.

United States

1695 • The first woman to become a Native American chief was Queen Anne (Totopotomoi), who became Chief of the Pamunkey Tribe of Virginia. She ruled her people from about 1675 until 1715. She was the widow of Chief Totopotomoi, who died in 1654 while helping the English to repel an invasion of other tribes.

Sources: Champagne, *Chronology of Native North American History,* p. 65, 83; Kane, *Famous First Facts,* p. 17.

1775 • Mary Katherine Goddard (1738–1816), a printer who also ran a bookshop, became the first female postmaster when she took over this position in Baltimore, Maryland, in 1775. She served her community in this capacity until 1789.

Sources: James, *Notable American Women,* vol. 2, pp. 55–56; Read and Witlieb, *The Book of Women's Firsts,* pp. 177–78.

1776 • New Jersey was the first colony or state to allow women the right to vote. Its state constitution, passed on July 2, 1776, granted women full suffrage, but in 1807 the law was revoked in large part for local political reasons: women were not voting to support those legislators currently in power.

Sources: Read and Witlieb, *The Book of Women's Firsts,* p. 310.

1868 • Katharine Hayes Chapin Barrows (1845–1913) was the first woman to work for the U.S. State Department in Washington, D.C. During the summer of 1868, she took over her husband's position when he was ill and worked as stenographic secretary to Secretary of State William H. Seward. Periodically thereafter, she worked as a stenographer for Congressional committees, the first woman to do so. Trained as an ophthalmologist, Barrows gave up her medical career to support her husband's work in politics and on social issues, especially penal reform.

Sources: James, *Notable American Women,* vol. 1, pp. 99–101.

1869 • The first women's suffrage law in the United States was passed on December 10, 1869, in Wyoming. The liberal legislature that passed this law also passed laws granting married women control of their own property and requiring equal pay for female teachers.

Sources: Read and Witlieb, *The Book of Women's Firsts,* p. 489.

1870 • Mary Todd Lincoln (1818–1882), wife of President Abraham Lincoln, was the first widow of a U.S. president to receive a government pension. Five years after her husband's death, she was awarded a government pension, paid annually for the rest of her life.

Sources: Read and Witlieb, *The Book of Women's Firsts,* p. 253; Schmidt, 400 Outstanding Women of the World, pp. 13–14.

Esther McQuigg Slack Morris (1814–1902) was the first U.S. woman to serve as a justice of the peace. She was appointed on February 4, 1870, in South Pass City, Wyoming, and during her term (which was less than a year), she tried nearly 70 cases. Morris was also a key figure in the movement in Wyoming for women's suffrage. When she and her husband, John Morris, moved to the territory of Wyoming in 1869, the national movement for women's suffrage in the United States was in its infancy. Esther Morris argued successfully before the leaders of the Wyoming legislature that, by extending suffrage to women, more women would be encouraged to move to the territory. Wyoming not only gave women the vote, but passed other laws granting married women certain property rights and guaranteeing female teachers pay equal to male teachers. Esther Morris served as a delegate in 1895 to the national women's suffrage convention. She died in Cheyenne, Wyoming, in 1902.

Sources: Read and Witlieb, *The Book of Women's Firsts,* p. 300.

1872 • Victoria Claflin Woodhull (1838–1927) was born in Homer, Ohio, on September 28, 1838. She and her sister, Tennessee, opened a brokerage firm in New York City in 1868, with the financial support of Cornelius Vanderbilt. In 1872, Victoria Woodhull became the first woman to run for president of the United States. She was the candidate of the Equal Rights Party, who put forth as her running mate the noted African-American abolitionist, Frederick Douglass. Douglass did not participate in the campaign and, in fact, supported Ulysses S. Grant for president. Victoria Woodhull was a fervent supporter of women's rights and campaigned actively for women's right to vote. Because she was also an advocate of free love and extramarital affairs, eventually she found that all groups turned away from her, even the feminists.

Sources: Chicago, *The Dinner Party,* p. 186; James, *Notable American Women,* vol. 3, pp. 652–55; Read and Witlieb, *The Book of Women's Firsts,* pp. 493–95; Whitman, *American Reformers,* pp. 897–900.

1875 • Native American Rosana Chouteau was the first female chief of the Osage Beaver Band. She was elected in 1875 after the death of her uncle, the previous chief. Her situation was unusual because the Osage were a patrilineal tribe.

Sources: Chicago, *The Dinner Party,* p. 170.

1879 • Ida Zoradia Lewis (1842–1911) was the first U.S. woman to become a lighthouse keeper. She took over her father's job of tending the lighthouse at Limerock, Rhode Island, when he was incapacitated in 1857. In 1879, the federal government named her the official keeper, a post she held until her death.

Sources: Read and Witlieb, *The Book of Women's Firsts,* p. 252.

1881 • Sarah Elizabeth Van de Vort Emery (1838–1895), an effective speaker committed to Populist concerns, was the first female delegate to the Greenback Party's state convention in Lansing, Michigan, in 1881.

Sources: Arena (July 1892); James, *Notable American Women,* vol. 1, pp. 582–583.

Emma Millinda Gillett (1852–1927), a lawyer and a feminist active in the women's suffrage movement, was the first woman to serve as a notary public in Washington, D.C. She was appointed by President James A. Garfield in June 1881.

Sources: James, *Notable American Women,* vol. 2, pp. 36–37.

1883 • Mary F. Hoyt (1858–1958) was the first woman to serve in the U.S. Civil Service. She took the first civil service exam on July 12, 1883, and received the highest score. On September 5 of the same year she was appointed to a clerkship in the Treasury Department.

Sources: Read and Witlieb, *The Book of Women's Firsts,* p. 219.

1887 • Phoebe Couzins (1839–1913) of St. Louis, Missouri, was the first woman to serve as a U.S. marshal. When her father died in 1887, she took over his job for two years. Couzins was well qualified for this position: she had a law degree from Washington University and was active in the women's suffrage movement. Couzins was also the first woman to gain a law degree from Washington University in St. Louis, Missouri, in 1871.

Sources: James, *Notable American Women,* vol. 1, pp. 390–91; Read and Witlieb, *The Book of Women's Firsts,* p. 104.

Susanna Madora Salter (1860–1961) was the first female mayor. She was elected mayor of Argonia, Kansas, a town of five hundred people, in 1887, the first year women were allowed to vote in Kansas local elections.

Sources: Read and Witlieb, *The Book of Women's Firsts,* pp. 388–89; *Who Was Who in America,* 1607–1896, p. 657.

1890 • Alice B. Sanger was the first woman to be employed in the executive office of the United States government. She was White House stenographer for the 23rd president of the United States, Benjamin Harrison. Harrison's term was 1889 to 1893.

Sources: Read and Witlieb, *The Book of Women's Firsts,* pp. 390–91.

Emma Edwards Green (c.1890–1942) was the first woman to design a state seal, in 1890. After studying art in New York, Green moved back to her native Idaho to paint. When Idaho joined the Union in July 1890 Green was commissioned to design a picture for the state seal.

Sources: McCullough, *First of All: Significant "Firsts" by American Women,* p. 87.

1891 • Harriet Maxwell Converse (1836–1903) was the first white female to be made a Seneca sachem, or chief. An author, folklorist, and staunch defender of Native American rights, Converse was committed to preserving Native American culture. In 1891 she intervened against a bill in the New York legislature that would have broken up reservations. In 1902, she led a letter-writing campaign on behalf of the Senecas, seeking to cancel the $200,000 land liquidation fee they had been charged. As an honorary chief of the Six Nations, Converse was admitted to the secret Little Water Medicine Society.

Sources: McCullough, *First of All: Significant "Firsts" by American Women,* pp. 88–89; Whitman, *American Reformers,* pp. 189–90.

1894 • Lucy Louisa Coues Flower (1837–1921) was the first woman elected to a state office in Illinois. In 1894 she was elected to serve on the board of trustees of the University of Illinois. She struggled unsuccessfully to expand facilities for female students.

Sources: Farwell, *Lucy Louisa Flower*; James, *Notable American Women,* vol. 1, pp. 635–37.

1907 • Kate Barnard (1875–1930) was the first woman elected to a state-wide office. She was elected commissioner of charities and corrections for the state of Oklahoma in 1907.

Sources: James, *Notable American Women,* pp. 90–92; Sanders, *The First of Everything,* p. 152; Whitman, *American Reformers,* pp. 51–53.

1909 • Crystal Eastman (1881–1928), a U.S. lawyer committed to feminism, peace, and social reform, was the first female member of the New York State Employers' Liability Commission. She was appointed in Albany, New York, to serve as secretary from 1909 until 1911.

Sources: James, *Notable American Women,* vol. 1, pp. 543–45; Whitman, *American Reformers,* pp. 264–66.

1911 • Emma R. H. Jentzer (1883–1972) was the first woman to serve as a special agent for the Bureau of Investigation, precursor of the Federal Bureau of Investigation (FBI). Her husband was the bureau's first agent at the time of its founding in 1908; Jentzer became an agent in 1911 after her husband's death.

Sources: Read and Witlieb, *The Book of Women's Firsts,* pp. 229–30.

1912 • Caroline Bayard Stevens Wittpenn (1859–1932), a U.S. welfare worker, was the first Democratic National Committeewoman from the state of New Jersey, in 1912. A supporter of Woodrow Wilson, she advised him on welfare problems during his governorship of New Jersey before he went on to the presidency of the United States.

Sources: James, *Notable American Women,* vol. 3, pp. 638–39; Turnbull, *John Stevens*; Watkins, *Biographical Sketches of John Stevens, Robert L. Stevens, Edwin A. Stevens*.

Julia Clifford Lathrop (1858–1932) was the first woman to head an important U.S. government bureau. She was appointed to the Children's Bureau by President William Howard Taft in 1912. An advocate of women's suffrage, Lathrop headed the Children's Bureau, which was moved from the Department of Commerce to the Department of Labor in 1915, until her retirement in 1921.

Sources: Read and Witlieb, *The Book of Women's Firsts,* pp. 247–48; Whitman, *American Reformers,* pp. 511–13.

1914 • Katharine Bement Davis (1860–1935), a dedicated social worker whose special cause was penal reform, was the first woman to serve at the cabinet level in New York City government. In January of 1914 she was appointed commissioner of corrections of New York City by the reform mayor John Purroy Mitchel.

Sources: James, *Notable American Women,* vol. 1, pp. 439–41; Whitman, *American Reformers,* pp. 213–14.

1915 • Beatrice Winser (1869–1947) was the first woman to serve on a governing board of the city of Newark, New Jersey. She was appointed to the Newark Board of Education in 1915. In 1929, she became the first woman to serve as head of the Newark Public Library. In the same year, she became the first female secretary and the first female director of the Newark Museum.

Sources: James, *Notable American Women,* vol. 3, pp. 630–32; Newark Museum, *Beatrice Winser, 1869–1947*; Newark Public Library, *This Is to Be a People's Library*.

1916 • Jeanette Rankin (1880–1973) was the first woman elected to the U.S. House of Representatives. From Missoula, Montana, she was elected as a Republican to represent Montana. In Montana, women were given the right to vote in state elections prior to 1920 when national suffrage was won. She was the only member of Congress to vote against U.S. entry into World War I. When Rankin ran for reelection in 1919 as a Pacifist, she was defeated. In 1941, she was successful in her campaign for a second term in the House of Representatives. On December 8, 1941, she again was the only member of the congress to vote against entry into World War II. She continued her antiwar stance throughout her life—in 1968, she led the Jeanette Rankin Brigade to the capitol in Washington, D.C. to protest against the United States' involvement in the Vietnam War.

Sources: Chicago, *The Dinner Party,* p. 201; Read and Witlieb, *The Book of Women's Firsts,* pp. 360–61; Sanders, *The First of Everything,* p. 149; Whitman, *American Reformers,* pp. 676–78.

This full-length portrait of Jeanette Rankin was painted on the wall of the U.S. Capitol by Allyn Cox.

1917 • Three California suffragists—Mrs. W.C. Tyler, Mrs. Spinks, and Mrs. Wylie—were the first three women to sit in the U.S. Electoral College, in 1917. Mrs. Tyler was a delegate to the National Democratic Convention in 1916; she was also president of the Los Angeles Woman's County Democratic Committee.

Sources: Read and Witlieb, *The Book of Women's Firsts,* pp. 455–56.

1918 • Annette Abbott Adams (1877–1956) was the first female district attorney for the Northern California district. She was also one of California's first women school principals. In 1920, she was appointed an assistant to the U.S. attorney general by President Woodrow Wilson. At the time of her death, the

79-year-old Adams was presiding judge of the Third District Court of Appeals and California's ranking woman jurist.

Sources: McCullough, *First of All: Significant "Firsts" by American Women,* p. 87.

Anne Henrietta Martin (1875–1951) was the first woman to run for the U.S. Senate. She ran for a seat as an independent candidate in Nevada in 1918. Although she won 20 percent of the vote, she was defeated.

Sources: Read and Witlieb, *The Book of Women's Firsts,* pp. 269–70.

1919 • Mary Sherwood (1856–1935), an American physician, was the first woman to head a municipal bureau in Baltimore, Maryland. In 1919 she organized and became the first director of the Bureau of Child Welfare of the Baltimore City Health Department. She continued as head of this bureau until 1924. She later served as the first chair of the obstetrical section of the American Child Health Association. A committed suffragist and feminist, Sherwood was also active in encouraging higher education for women.

Sources: James, *Notable American Women,* vol. 3, pp. 283–84; Welsh, *Reminiscences of Thirty Years in Baltimore.*

Ruth Hanna McCormick Simms (1880–1944), an American politician and women's rights advocate, was the first person to serve as chair of the women's executive committee of the Republican National Committee, in Chicago, Illinois, in 1919. She went on to become the first female member of Congress from the state of Illinois, in 1928.

Sources: James, *Notable American Women,* vol. 3, pp. 293–95; Moley, *27 Masters of Politics.*

The Nineteenth Amendment to the U.S. Constitution, passed by Congress on June 4, 1919, was the first amendment that guaranteed women the right to vote. The resolution was first introduced, at the request of Susan B. Anthony, in 1878.

Sources: Read and Witlieb, *The Book of Women's Firsts,* p. 313.

Catherine Filene Shouse (1896–1994) became the first woman appointed to the Democratic National Committee. An active Democrat, she served under President Calvin Coolidge in the mid-1920s as chairwoman of the First Federal Prison for Women, where she instituted a job training and rehabilitation program. Shouse was a philanthropist and arts patron who was the founder and major benefactor of the Wolf Trap Farm Park for the Performing Arts in Virginia.

Catherine Filene Shouse was born in Boston. Her grandfather, William Filene, was the founder of the Filene's department store chain, and her father, Lincoln Filene, founded Federated Department Stores. She graduated from Wheaton College in Norton, Massachusetts, in 1918, and earned a master's degree in education at Harvard University in 1923. In 1977, President Gerald Ford gave her the Presidential Medal of Freedom. A year earlier, Queen Elizabeth II had made her Dame Commander of the British Empire. In October 1994, she was among 12 Americans to receive the National Medal of Arts.

Sources: New York Times (15 December 1994), p. 20.

1920 • Alice Dunbar Nelson (1875–1935), a writer of fiction and verse, was the first black woman to serve on Delaware's Republican State Committee, in Wilmington, Delaware, in 1920. She earned her living by teaching and is particularly remembered for her brief marriage to the poet Paul Lawrence Dunbar and for two books, *Violets and Other Tales* (1895) and *The Goodness of St. Rocque and Other Stories* (1899).

Sources: Brawley, *Paul Lawrence Dunbar*; Brown, *Homespun Heroines and Other Women of Distinction,* p. 212; James, *Notable American Women,* vol. 2, pp. 614–15; Loggins, *The Negro Author.*

Annette Abbott Adams (1877–1956) was the first woman to serve as assistant attorney general. She was appointed to this post in Washington, D.C. in 1920 by President Woodrow Wilson. Her job was to oversee prosecution of those who violated the recently enacted Eighteenth Amendment to the Constitution, the prohibition amendment.

Sources: Read and Witlieb, *The Book of Women's Firsts,* p. 5.

Mary Anderson (1872–1964) was the first director of the Women's Bureau of the U.S. Department of Labor. A Swedish immigrant to the United States, Anderson initially earned her living as a domestic, then as a factory worker. She then became involved in union organizing. Anderson was appointed to head the Women's Bureau by President Woodrow Wilson in 1920.

Sources: Read and Witlieb, *The Book of Women's Firsts,* p. 19; Uglow, *The Continuum Dictionary of Women's Biography,* pp. 16–17.

Helen Hamilton Gardener (1853–1925), a writer and freethinker who supported feminist causes, was the first woman to serve on the United States Civil Service Commission. She was appointed to this post by President Woodrow Wilson in Washington, D.C., on April 30, 1920, and served with distinction until 1925.

Sources: James, *Notable American Women,* vol. 2, pp. 11–13; Whitman, *American Reformers,* pp. 330–32.

1921 • Alice M. Robertson (1854–1931) became the first woman to preside over the U.S. House of Representatives in 1921 when she was given the position of president pro tem as a ceremonial gesture. She announced the vote on a minor appropriations bill.

Sources: Read and Witlieb, *The Book of Women's Firsts,* pp. 373–74.

1922 • Grace Abbott (1878–1939) was the first woman to serve as a U.S. delegate to the League of Nations. Her status was unofficial, since the United States was never an official member of the league. Abbott served on the organization's Advisory Committee on Traffic in Women and Children from 1922 until 1934.

Sources: Read and Witlieb, *The Book of Women's Firsts,* p. 3; Whitman, *American Reformers,* pp. 1–2.

Lucille Atcherson Curtis (b. 1894) was the first woman to serve in the U.S. Foreign Service. She was assigned to the State Department's Latin Affairs Division on December 5, 1922.

Sources: Sanders, *The First of Everything,* p. 153.

Rebecca Ann Latimer Felton (1835–1930), a journalist who spoke out and worked actively for various social and feminist causes, became the first woman to serve in the United States Senate. She was appointed at the age of 87 by the governor of Georgia on November 21, 1922, to fill the post of her predecessor's unexpired term. Congress was not in session, and therefore Felton served only one day. She gave an honorary speech in Washington, D.C., and then gave up her seat to Senator-elect Walter George. She returned to Georgia, but she received much national publicity for her one day as senator.

Sources: O'Neill, *The Women's Book of World Records and Achievements,* pp. 65–66; Read and Witlieb, *The Book of Women's Firsts,* pp. 150–51; Sanders, *The First of Everything,* p. 149; Whitman, *American Reformers,* pp. 284–86.

1923 • Mae Ella Nolan (1886–1973) was the first woman elected to the U.S. Congress to fill her husband's place. When John Nolan of California died in office, his wife Mae Ella was elected in 1923. She went on to become the first woman to chair a congressional committee—the House Committee on Expenditures in the Post Office Department, in 1924.

Sources: Read and Witlieb, *The Book of Women's Firsts,* p. 314.

Louise Stanley (1883–1954) was the first female director of the U.S. Bureau of Home Economics in Washington, D.C. She assumed this position in 1923 after several years of university teaching and research in the field of nutrition.

Sources: O'Neill, *The Women's Book of World Records and Achievements,* p. 22; Read and Witlieb, *The Book of Women's Firsts,* pp. 416–17.

Jessie Duckstein became the first woman to serve as a "special agent" in the Federal Bureau of Investigation (FBI) when she was appointed on November 6, 1923, by FBI director William Burns.

Sources: Parade, (1 June 1986).

1924 • Belle Kearney (1863–1939), a temperance reformer and suffragist, was the first woman in the American South to serve in a state senate. In 1924, she ran as a Democratic candidate and was elected to the Mississippi senate in Jackson, where she served two terms.

Sources: James, *Notable American Women,* vol. 2, pp. 309–10.

Nellie Tayloe Ross (1876–1977) of Wyoming was the first woman to be elected governor of a state. She technically shares this honor with Miriam Amanda "Ma" Ferguson (1875–1961) of Texas, since both women were elected in November 1924, but Ross was inaugurated three weeks before Ferguson. Both women followed their husbands into office.

Ferguson succeeded her husband after his impeachment for misuse of Texas state funds in 1924. A strong prohibitionist, Ferguson worked for prison reform and against the power and activities of the Ku Klux Klan. She was elected to a second term as governor in 1932.

Sources: Read and Witlieb, *The Book of Women's Firsts,* pp. 152–53; Sanders, *The First of Everything,* p. 151.

1925 • Pattie Field (b. 1902), of Denver, Colorado, was the first woman to serve in the United States consular service. She was appointed vice consul in Amsterdam, the Netherlands, on September 2, 1925, a position she held until July 1929.

Sources: Read and Witlieb, *The Book of Women's Firsts,* p. 155.

1926 • Bertha Ethel Knight Landes (1868–1943) was the first woman to serve as mayor of Seattle, Washington. She was elected in a nonpartisan election in March 1926, thus becoming also the first female mayor of a sizeable American city.

Sources: James, *Notable American Women,* vol. 2, pp. 362–63.

1928 • Mary Olszewski Kryszak (1875–1945) was the first woman of the Democratic Party to hold state office in Wisconsin. She was elected to congress from Milwaukee in 1928 and served in that capacity (as the first female legislator from her county), with only one interruption in 1938, until her death. She reflected the moderate to conservative views of her working-class constituents and was particularly interested in issues concerning social welfare, women, and Polish-Americans.

Sources: James, *Notable American Women,* vol. 2, pp. 350–31; Kryszak, *Poles of Chicago,* pp. 154–59.

Ruth Shipley (1885–1966) became the first woman to head a major division of the U.S. Department of State when in 1928 she was named chief of the Passport Division. She worked her way up to this position from being a clerk in the Records Department, a job she began in 1914.

Sources: Read and Witlieb, *The Book of Women's Firsts,* pp. 406–7.

1932 • Mary T. Hopkins Norton (1875–1959) was the first woman to head a U.S. state political party. She became head of the Democratic Party in New Jersey in 1932. She was elected to Congress by her state in 1925 and served in this capacity until her retirement in 1951.

Sources: Read and Witlieb, *The Book of Women's Firsts,* p. 317.

Hattie Wyatt Caraway (1878–1950) was the first woman elected to the U.S. Senate. Appointed by the governor of Louisiana to complete her dead husband's term in 1931, Caraway won election in 1932. She became the first woman to chain a Senate committee, to preside over Senate sessions, and to conduct Senate hearings. She served for three terms (1932–1944).

Sources: James, *Notable American Women*, vol. 1, pp. 284–86; O'Neill, *The Women's Book of World Records and Achievements*, p. 66; Read and Witlieb, *The Book of Women's Firsts*, pp. 83–84; Sanders, *The First of Everything*, p. 150.

1933 • Ruth Bryan Owen (1885–1977) was the first woman to serve as a U.S. foreign minister. The daughter of William Jennings Bryan, she was appointed minister to Denmark by Franklin Delano Roosevelt on April 13, 1933.

Sources: Read and Witlieb, *The Book of Women's Firsts*, pp. 327–28; Sanders, *The First of Everything*, p. 153.

Minnie Davenport Craig became the first woman to serve as speaker in a state house of representatives when she was elected speaker of the North Dakota House of Representatives on January 3, 1933. She served until March 31 of the same year.

Sources: Kane, *Famous First Facts*, p. 348; Read and Witlieb, *The Book of Women's Firsts*, p. 105.

Frances Perkins (1880–1965) was the first woman to serve in a presidential cabinet. She was appointed secretary of labor by Franklin Delano Roosevelt on March 4, 1933. She served until 1945, one of only two cabinet members to serve from 1933 until Roosevelt's death in 1945. Perkins sponsored legislation that included unemployment compensation; child labor, worker's compensation, and social security laws; and maximum hour and minimum wage controls.

Perkins was born in Boston, Massachusetts, attended Mount Holyoke College, and received her master's degree in economics from Columbia University in 1910. She became involved in issues of concern to working men and women, and in 1912 joined the staff of the New York State Committee on Safety. Perkins retained her own name when she married economist Paul Wilson in 1913, which was an unusual decision at the time. In 1918, when the governor of New York, Alfred E. Smith, appointed Perkins to a job at the New York State Industrial Commission with a salary of $8,000 per year, she became the highest paid state employee in the United States. After Roosevelt's death in 1945, his successor, Harry S Truman, appointed Perkins to the Civil Service Commission, where she served until 1953. In 1955, she joined the faculty of Cornell University's School of Industrial Relations where she taught until her death of a stroke in 1965.

Sources: Chicago, *The Dinner Party*, p. 201; McCullough, *First of All: Significant "Firsts" by American Women*, p. 81; Read and Witlieb, *The Book of Women's Firsts*, pp. 339–41; Rolka, *100 Women Who Shaped World History*, p. 78; Sanders, *The First of Everything*, p. 152.

1939 • Gene Cox (b. 1925) was 13 years old when she became the first woman to serve as a page in the U.S. House of Representatives on January 3, 1939. She was the daughter of U.S. Representative Edward Eugene Cox of Georgia. She worked for only one day and earned four dollars compensation for three hours' worth of errands. The House had to wait for 34 years before the next female page (Felda Looper) was hired—on a regular basis—in 1973.

Sources: Kane, *Famous First Facts*, p. 194; Read and Witlieb, *The Book of Women's Firsts*, p. 104.

Clare Boothe Luce

1943 • Clare Boothe Luce (1903–1987), a U.S. writer and politician, was the first woman elected to the U.S. Congress from Connecticut. She represented this state in Washington, D.C., from 1943 until 1947. She went on to a distinguished political career, serving as ambassador to Italy from 1953 through 1959. She is also known for her early career as a journalist and for novels and plays written between 1933 and 1952.

Sources: Magnusson, *Larousse Biographical Dictionary,* p. 923; Uglow, *The Continuum Dictionary of Women's Biography,* p. 79.

1944 • When Dorothy V. Bush (1916–1991) became secretary of the national Democratic Party in 1944, she was the first woman to serve as an officer for either major U.S. national political party. She held this post for over 40 years, until her resignation in 1989.

Sources: Read and Witlieb, *The Book of Women's Firsts,* pp. 77–78.

1948 • Margaret Chase Smith (1897–1995) was the first woman to be elected to both the U.S. House of Representatives and the U.S. Senate. When her husband, a congressman from Maine, died in 1940, she replaced him and served in the House for eight years—four full terms. In 1948, Chase Smith was elected to the U.S. Senate and was reelected three times, serving until 1973.

Sources: Read and Witlieb, *The Book of Women's Firsts,* pp. 411–12; Uglow, *The Continuum Dictionary of Women's Biography,* pp. 502–3; *World Book Encyclopedia,* vol. 17, p. 428.

1949 • Eugenie Moore Anderson (b. 1909) of Red Wing, Minnesota, was the first woman to serve as a U.S. ambassador. She was appointed ambassador to Denmark by President Harry S Truman on October 12, 1949. The swearing-in ceremony took place in the office of Secretary of State Dean Acheson on October 28, 1949. Anderson held the post until 1953. (*See also* **Government: United States, 1962.**)

Sources: Kane, *Famous First Facts,* p. 222; Read and Witlieb, *The Book of Women's Firsts,* pp. 18–19; Sanders, *The First of Everything,* p. 153.

Eugenie Moore Anderson

Georgia Neese Clark Gray (1900–1995) was the first woman to serve as treasurer of the United States. Her signature, then Georgia Neese Clark, appeared on $30 billion of the nation's currency during her term as the nation's 29th treasurer. She was appointed in 1949 by President Harry S Truman and was unanimously approved by the Senate.

Georgia Neese Clark was a highly visible figure in Democratic Party affairs, and was an associate of Eleanor Roosevelt, with whom she often shared the speakers' platform. Prior to her appointment, Clark had been a banker in Kansas, serving as president of the bank her father, Albert, had founded in 1892. She had also been an active national committeewoman in the Democratic Party beginning in 1936.

Georgia Clark served as treasurer until 1953, when Dwight D. Eisenhower was elected president. He appointed another woman, Utah Republican Ivy Baker Priest, to succeed her. Also in 1953, Georgia Neese Clark, divorced in the mid-1940s from her husband George Clark, married Andres J. Gray, a former newspaperman.

Sources: Coin World (22 May 1995); *New York Times* (28 October 1995), pp. A50, B33; Read and Witlieb, *The Book of Women's Firsts,* p. 91.

Georgia Neese Clark Gray

1950 • Lucy Maclay Alexander was the first woman to receive the U.S. Department of Agriculture (USDA) distinguished service gold medal, on May 25, 1950. The award citation read: " ... for outstanding achievement in applying fundamental scientific principles to meat and poultry cookery; for relating cooking shrinkage to chemical composition and to method of producing and

Oveta Culp Hobby is sworn in as secretary of health, education, and welfare.

processing for market; for formulating precise, practical directions for cooking meat and poultry; and for designing a practical meat thermometer."

Sources: Kane, *Famous First Facts,* p. 366.

Trained as a social worker, Loula Dunne became the first woman to serve as director of the American Public Welfare Association, in 1950. In 1959 she was appointed one of 12 members of a federal advisory panel on coordination of state and federal welfare benefits.

Sources: Read and Witlieb, *The Book of Women's Firsts,* p. 128.

1953 • Oveta Culp Hobby (1905–1995) was appointed by President Dwight D. Eisenhower to be the first woman secretary of health, education and welfare in a U.S. cabinet, a position she held until 1955. A Texas lawyer and newspaperwoman, Hobby worked for the War Department and helped in the education of a women's army corps. Appointed colonel of the Women's Army Auxiliary Corps (WAACS), Hobby retained her position in the corps when it changed to the Women's Army Corps (WACS) in 1943. (*See also* **Military: United States, 1942.**)

Sources: McCullough, *First of All: Significant "Firsts" by American Women,* pp. 82–83; *World Book Encyclopedia,* vol. 9, p. 243.

Ethel Greenglass Rosenberg (1915–1953) was the first and only U.S. woman to be executed for treason during peacetime, on June 19, 1953. With her husband, Julius Rosenberg, she was sentenced to die for conspiracy to commit wartime espionage. She was also the first woman to be incarcerated in the maximum security prison of Sing Sing in Ossining, New York, where both Rosenbergs were electrocuted.

Sources: Gardner, *The Rosenberg Story*; Read and Witlieb, *The Book of Women's Firsts,* pp. 380–81; Uglow, *The Continuum Dictionary of Women's Biography,* pp. 464–65 .

Clare Boothe Luce (1903–1987), the U.S. writer and politician, was the first woman to serve as U.S. ambassador to Italy. She was sworn in by Supreme Court Chief Justice Frederick Moore Vinson. She resigned on November 19, 1959.

Sources: Kane, *Famous First Facts,* p. 222; Magnusson, *Larousse Biographical Dictionary,* p. 923; Uglow, *The Continuum Dictionary of Women's Biography,* p. 79.

1960 • When Republican U.S. senator from Maine Margaret Chase Smith (1897–1995) ran for reelection in 1960, her opponent was Democrat Lucia Marie Cormier. The contest was the first time an election for a U.S. Senate seat involved two women candidates. Margaret Chase Smith won by a vote of 255,890 to 159,809.

Sources: Kane, *Famous First Facts,* p. 195.

1961 • Elizabeth Gurley Flynn (1890–1964), a lifelong political activist, joined the Communist Party in 1937 and became the first woman to chair the national committee of the American Communist Party in 1961. She was a founding member of the American Civil Liberties Union in 1920, but she was forced to resign in 1940 because of her Communist ties. She was the first person to be convicted of sedition under the Smith Act in 1952 and served three years in prison. When she died in Moscow, Russia, she was given a state funeral.

Sources: Chicago, *The Dinner Party,* p. 202; Read and Witlieb, *The Book of Women's Firsts,* pp. 160–61; Whitman, *American Reformers,* pp. 299–301.

1962 • Eugenie Moore Anderson (b. 1909) of Red Wing, Minnesota, was the first woman to serve as a U.S. ambassador to Bulgaria, becoming the first woman ambassador to represent the United States in a Communist nation, on August 3, 1962. (*See also* **Government: United States, 1949.**)

Sources: Kane, *Famous First Facts,* p. 222; Read and Witlieb, *The Book of Women's Firsts,* pp. 18–19; Sanders, *The First of Everything,* p. 153.

1964 • U.S. senator from Maine Margaret Chase Smith (1897–1995) was the first woman to campaign to become a major political party candidate for president. Smith was a Republican.

Sources: Kane, *Famous First Facts,* p. 195.

Dorothy H. Jacobson was the first woman to serve as an assistant secretary in the U.S. Department of Agriculture. From 1964 until 1968 she served as assistant secretary of agriculture for international affairs in Washington, D.C.

Sources: O'Neill, *The Women's Book of World Records and Achievements,* p. 22.

Bennetta Washington (1918–1991) was named by President Lyndon B. Johnson in 1964 to be the first person to head a national Job Corps program for

Constance Baker Motley chats with President Lyndon B. Johnson.

women. Washington had been director of the Cardozo Project in Urban Education, the President's Commission on Juvenile Delinquency, under Presidents John F. Kennedy and Lyndon B. Johnson from 1961 to 1964.

Sources: Read and Witlieb, *The Book of Women's Firsts,* pp. 471–72.

1965 • Patsy Mink (b. 1927), a Japanese-American, was the first woman of a racial or ethnic minority to sit in the U.S. House of Representatives. A Democrat from Hawaii, Mink began the first of three terms on January 4, 1965. She was a strong supporter of equal rights for women.

Sources: Sanders, *The First of Everything,* p. 150.

1966 • In 1966, President Lyndon B. Johnson in Washington, D.C., appointed Constance Baker Motley (b.1921) the first black female federal judge. Motley was appointed judge of the U.S. District Court for the Southern Division of New York. In 1964, she became the first African-American woman to be elected to the New York state senate. A civil rights lawyer who worked to eliminate state-enforced segregation in the South, prior to her judicial appointment Motley successfully argued nine civil rights cases before the U.S. Supreme Court. She was also the first African-American woman to serve as Manhattan borough president.

Sources: Gaymon, *215 African American Women You Should Know About,* p. 1; McCullough, *First of All: Significant "Firsts" by American Women,* pp. 90–91; Salem, *African American Women: A Biographical Dictionary,* pp. 369–70.

In 1966, Jane Cahill Pfeiffer (b. 1932) was appointed by President Lyndon B. Johnson in Washington, D.C.,to serve as the first woman White House fellow. Pfeiffer took a leave of absence from her position with IBM, where she was in charge of the company's space tracking system located on the island of Bermuda. During her White House fellowship, she worked with Robert Wood, undersecretary of the department of housing and urban development, to streamline the housing and home finance agency. (*See also* **The Professions: Miscellaneous, 1978.**)

Sources: Read and Witlieb, *The Book of Women's Firsts,* pp. 343–44.

1968 • Shirley Chisholm (b. 1924) was the first black congresswoman elected to the U.S. House of Representatives from New York in 1968. Born Shirley St. Hill on November 30, 1924, she grew up in New York City, the daughter of West Indian immigrants. Supported mainly by feminists, Chisholm was elected as a Democrat to the New York State legislature in 1964. Chisholm served as a member of the House of Representatives from 1969 to 1983. In 1969 Chisholm drew national attention by pushing through a bill that guaranteed minimum wages to domestic workers, many of whom are black or minority women. In 1972, she announced her intention to run for president; at the Democratic National Convention she drew 154 delegate votes. Chisholm then ran and was re-elected to her congressional seat for second and third terms.

Sources: Chisholm, *Unbought and Unbossed;* Gaymon, *215 African American Women You Should Know About,* p. 11; McCullough, *First of All: Significant "Firsts" by American Women,* pp. 84–85; Smith, *Black Firsts,* p. 180; Salem, *African American Women: A Biographical Dictionary,* pp. 105–7.

1969 • In 1969, Virginia Mae Brown (1923–1991) became the first woman to head an independent federal administrative agency when she was named director of the Interstate Commerce Commission. Brown has a host of other "firsts" to her credit: she was the first woman to serve on the Interstate Commerce Commission (1964), the first to be a state insurance commissioner (1961), the first to be executive secretary to the judicial council of West Virginia (1944), the first to be a West Virginia assistant attorney general (1952), and the first to serve on the West Virginia Public Service Commission (1962).

Sources: Read and Witlieb, *The Book of Women's Firsts,* p. 73.

1970s • Barbara Huddleston (b. 1939) was the first woman to become a division director in the U.S. Foreign Agricultural Service, in Washington, D.C., in the 1970s. She received this organization's Certificate of Merit for Special Achievement in 1975.

Sources: O'Neill, *The Women's Book of World Records and Achievements,* p. 25.

Jane Westenberger, after a distinguished career in the military and as a teacher, was the first woman to hold the position of staff director in the U.S. Forest Service, in California in the 1970s.

Sources: O'Neill, *The Women's Book of World Records and Achievements,* p. 26.

1970 • In 1970 the Secret Service chose seven women to join the Executive Protection Service. These seven women became the first to serve in the

White House Police Force. They were also periodically assigned to serve at diplomatic missions in Washington, D.C.

Sources: Read and Witlieb, *The Book of Women's Firsts,* p. 479.

1971 • In 1971 Jane W. Currie and Janene E. Gordon became the first two women appointed inspectors for the U.S. Postal Service since its inception 234 years earlier. They completed a rigorous course of study that included both academic and physical tests.

Sources: Read and Witlieb, *The Book of Women's Firsts,* p. 349.

The first female U.S. Secret Service agents were recruited at the request of President Richard M. Nixon, who wanted the appointment of more women to responsible government positions. Five women made up the first group sworn in in Washington, D.C., in 1971.

Sources: Read and Witlieb, *The Book of Women's Firsts,* pp. 398–99.

Carol Bellamy (b. 1942) was the first woman (also the youngest) council president in New York City, elected in 1971. After spending two years in the Peace Corps and returning to New York to become a lawyer, Bellamy ran for the New York State senate and was elected for three successive terms. Ignored by the press, Bellamy was mainly supported by feminists; she successfully beat Paul O'Dwyer in the primary and went on to win the election.

Sources: McCullough, *First of All: Significant "Firsts" by American Women,* pp. 85–86.

1972 • Anne L. Armstrong (b. 1927) was the first woman to deliver the keynote address at a major U.S. political party's national convention. She spoke on behalf of President Richard M. Nixon's reelection in 1972 in Miami, Florida. At the time she was also the first woman to serve as national cochair of the Republican Party.

Sources: Read and Witlieb, *The Book of Women's Firsts,* pp. 24–25; Uglow, *The Continuum Dictionary of Women's Biography,* p. 28.

Jean Westwood (b. 1923) was the first U.S. woman to chair a national political party. On July 14, 1972, she was elected chair of the Democratic National Committee. She brought over 30 years of experience in politics to this job. In her new position, she became the first woman to cochair a presidential campaign, that of George McGovern, who made an unsuccessful bid for the presidency in 1972.

Sources: O'Neill, *The Women's Book of World Records and Achievements,* p. 74.

1973 • Lelia Kasensia Smith Foley (b. 1942) became the first African-American woman to be elected mayor of an American city in April 1973, when she was elected mayor of Taft, Oklahoma, a predominantly black town of approximately 600 people.

Sources: Gaymon, *215 African American Women You Should Know About,* p. 46.

1974 • Kathy Kozachenko was the first avowed lesbian elected to a city council when she won election in Ann Arbor, Michigan, in April 1974. A senior at the University of Michigan, she ran and was elected to the city council from a ward primarily populated by students.

Sources: McCullough, *First of All: Significant "Firsts" by American Women,* p. 85.

Virginia Yapp Trotter (b. 1921) was the first woman to serve as head of the education division of the U.S. Department of Health, Education and Welfare. She assumed this position when she was appointed assistant secretary for education in 1974.

Sources: Read and Witlieb, *The Book of Women's Firsts,* pp. 449–50.

Janet Gray Hayes (b. 1926) became the first woman to head a large U.S. city when she was elected mayor of San Jose, California, in a race against six male opponents. She was inaugurated in January 1974.

Sources: Sanders, *The First of Everything,* p. 152.

Mary Louise Smith (b. 1914) was the first woman to chair the Republican National Committee. Elected on September 16, 1974, she held this leadership position until after the 1976 presidential election. An ardent Republican, Smith is also an avowed feminist and helped to organize Iowa's Women's Political Caucus.

Sources: O'Neill, *The Women's Book of World Records and Achievements,* p. 74.

1975 • Carla Anderson Hills (b. 1934) was the first woman appointed secretary of housing and urban development (HUD) in a U.S. cabinet, on March 10, 1975. Recognized as one of California's most prominent trial attorneys, Hills became assistant attorney general in the Justice Department's Civil Division, in 1974. After she was appointed secretary of HUD, she remained in office until she was succeeded by the first black woman in the cabinet, Patricia Roberts Harris.

Sources: McCullough, *First of All: Significant "Firsts" by American Women,* p. 83; O'Neill, *The Women's Book of World Records and Achievements,* pp. 365–66.

Elaine Brown (b. 1943), a black activist who devoted her career to furthering the cause of blacks and poor people of color in the United States, became the first woman to head the Black Panther Party, in 1975. This radical party, started by Huey Newton and Eldridge Cleaver in the late 1960s, was a powerful advocate of black civil rights in the 1970s.

Sources: O'Neill, *The Women's Book of World Records and Achievements,* p. 716; Williams, *The African American Encyclopedia,* pp. 222–23.

Shirley Temple Black (b. 1928) became the first woman to serve as chief of protocol when she was named to this position by President Gerald Ford in 1975. She was responsible for entertaining heads of state while they visited Washington.

Sources: Sanders, *The First of Everything,* p. 154.

Ella Tambussi Grasso (1919–1981) was the first woman to be elected governor of a state in which her husband had not previously held the same office.

Shirley Temple Black and
President Gerald Ford

She was inaugurated in Connecticut on January 8, 1975, and served until her resignation on December 31, 1980, because of illness. She died of cancer on February 5, 1981.

Sources: Read and Witlieb, *The Book of Women's Firsts,* pp. 183–84; Sanders, *The First of Everything,* pp. 151–52; Uglow, *The Continuum Dictionary of Women's Biography,* pp. 234–35.

1976 • Lindy Boggs, (b. 1916), a congressional representative from Louisiana, was the first woman to chair the national convention of a major U.S. political party. She chaired the Democratic National Convention in July 1976. Boggs has been a staunch supporter of increased opportunities for women throughout her long political career.

Sources: O'Neill, *The Women's Book of World Records and Achievements,* p. 75.

1977 • Bette B. Anderson (b. c.1929) was the first woman to serve as undersecretary of the Treasury. She was appointed in Washington, D.C., by President Jimmy Carter in 1977.

Sources: Read and Witlieb, *The Book of Women's Firsts,* pp. 18–19.

Patricia Roberts Harris (1924–1985) became the first black woman to serve officially in a president's cabinet when, in 1977, President Jimmy Carter appointed her secretary of housing and urban development and later secretary of health and human services.

Sources: Gaymon, *215 African American Women You Should Know About,* p. 12; Salem, *African American Women: A Biographical Dictionary,* pp. 235–38.

Joan Scott Wallace (b. 1930) was the first woman and the first black person to serve as assistant secretary for administration in the U.S. Department of Agriculture. She assumed this position in Washington, D.C., on December 2, 1977, after a distinguished career in business and university teaching.

Sources: O'Neill, *The Women's Book of World Records and Achievements,* pp. 22–23; Smith, *Black Firsts,* pp. 162–63.

Juanita Morris Kreps (b. 1921) was the first woman to serve as secretary of commerce in the U.S. government. She was appointed by President Jimmy Carter shortly after his inauguration in January 1977, in Washington, D.C., and served until 1979. She had previously served as the first female director of the New York Stock Exchange, in 1972, and the first female vice president of Duke University, in 1973. Working her way through school and escaping from the poverty of her coal mining town in eastern Kentucky, Kreps earned a Ph.D. in economics. Although she was recognized as a specialist in labor economics, Kreps is an acknowledged expert in income distribution, manpower, and problems of aging and has written a number of books on these subjects.

Sources: McCullough, *First of All: Significant "Firsts" by American Women,* p. 81; Read and Witlieb, *The Book of Women's Firsts,* pp. 244–45; Uglow, *The Continuum Dictionary of Women's Biography,* pp. 305–6.

Henrietta Duncan McArthur (b. 1945), born and educated in Georgia and a friend of President Jimmy Carter, was the first woman to serve as deputy assistant secretary of agriculture for rural development. She assumed this post in Washington, D.C., on June 17, 1977.

Sources: O'Neill, *The Women's Book of World Records and Achievements,* p. 24.

Eleanor Holmes Norton (b. 1937) became the first woman to chair the Equal Employment Opportunities Commission when she was appointed in Washington, D.C., by President Jimmy Carter in 1977. Norton was also the cofounder of the Black Feminist Organization in 1973.

Sources: Read and Witlieb, *The Book of Women's Firsts,* pp. 315–316; Salem, *African American Women: A Biographical Dictionary,* pp. 375–78.

1978 • Nancy Hays Teeters (b. 1930) was the first woman appointed to the board of governors of the Federal Reserve Bank. She was appointed by President Jimmy Carter and sworn in on September 18, 1978. Teeters retired from the Federal Reserve on January 31, 1984.

Sources: Kane, *Famous First Facts,* p. 259; Read and Witlieb, *The Book of Women's Firsts,* p. 439.

1979 • Jane Margaret Burke Byrne (b. 1933) became the first woman mayor of Chicago, Illinois. Byrne's campaign attracted national interest because she won an upset victory in the primary over the well-established Democratic Party structure in that city. In the mayoral election, Byrne won 82 percent of the vote, the highest percentage earned by a candidate in Chicago history. Throughout her career Byrne fought against corruption in politics. She served as mayor until 1983, when she was defeated in her reelection bid by Harold Washington.

Sources: Uglow, *The Continuum Dictionary of Women's Biography,* pp. 98–99; *World Book Encyclopedia,* vol. 2, p. 633.

Shirley Mount Hufstedler (b. 1925) became the first secretary of the U.S. Office of Education when she was appointed by President Jimmy Carter. She assumed this position after a distinguished career in law. In 1968, President Lyndon B. Johnson appointed Hufstedler to the United States Court of Appeals in San Francisco, making her, at the time, the highest ranking woman judge in the United States.

Sources: Read and Witlieb, *The Book of Women's Firsts,* p. 220; *World Book Encyclopedia,* vol. 9, p. 372.

Sandra Day O'Connor visits with President Ronald Reagan in the Oval Office.

1981 • Sandra Day O'Connor (b. 1930) was the first woman to become an associate justice of the U.S. Supreme Court. Born in El Paso, Texas, in 1930, O'Connor became the first woman to serve on the high court when President Ronald Reagan named her to fill the vacancy created by the retirement of Justice Potter Stewart. Nominated by President Reagan on July 7, 1981, she was sworn in three months later, on September 22, 1981. O'Connor received her law degree from Stanford University in 1952 and had a distinguished career in law and politics before her appointment to the Supreme Court. For over a decade, O'Connor was the only woman on the court; her appointment was a significant event for the judiciary, which early in its history had barred women from the practice of law.

Sources: Read and Witlieb, *The Book of Women's Firsts,* pp. 323–24.

1984 • Geraldine Anne Ferraro (b. 1935) became the first woman to be nominated by a major political party as a candidate for vice president of the United States. She was selected by Walter Mondale, the Democratic Party's presidential candidate, to be his running mate in 1984. Mondale and Ferraro lost the election (to Ronald Reagan and his running mate George Bush), and Ferraro retired from politics, although she continued to be involved in activist and feminist causes.

Sources: Ferraro, *Ferraro: My Story*; Magnusson, *Larousse Biographical Dictionary,* p. 510; Read and Witlieb, *The Book of Women's Firsts,* pp. 153–54; Uglow, *The Continuum Dictionary of Women's Biography,* p. 200.

1995 • Enid Waldholtz (b. 1958), U.S. representative from Utah, was the first woman in the U.S. Congress to give birth while still serving as a representative. Anticipating the experience, she said confidently, "There will be a playpen in my office."

Sources: Newsweek (27 March 1995), p. 19.

Venezuela

1969 • Aura Celina Casanova, a Venezuelan politician, was the first woman to serve her country as minister for development. She was appointed to this ministerial post in 1969.

Sources: O'Neill, *The Women's Book of World Records and Achievements,* p. 61.

Viet Nam

1950 • Thi Binh Nguyen (b. 1927), a teacher and political leader, organized the first anti-American demonstration in Viet Nam, in Saigon. Nguyen was a political leader in the Central Committee of the National Liberation Front (NLF), leading their delegation to the Paris Peace Conference in 1968. She was the first woman to sign the agreement to end the war in Viet Nam, in Paris in 1973. Later Nguyen became the first person to serve as minister of education in a unified Viet Nam. She was appointed just after the two parts of her country were united on July 2, 1976.

Sources: O'Neill, *The Women's Book of World Records and Achievements,* pp. 60–61; Uglow, *The Continuum Dictionary of Women's Biography,* p. 400.

Yemen

Early twelfth century • Arwa (1052–1137), a Yemeni queen who assumed the throne after the death of her husband in 1091, was the founder of

the city of Jiblah, which she had established as a new capital in the fertile plains of Yemen to replace the old fortress city of San'a.
Source: Uglow, *The Continuum Dictionary of Women's Biography,* p. 29.

Yugoslavia

1982 • Mila Planinc (b. 1925), a Yugoslav politician and a dedicated follower of Yugoslav leader Josip Broz Tito, became the first female prime minister of a Communist country when she was appointed to this post in Zagreb.
Source: Uglow, *The Continuum Dictionary of Women's Biography,* p. 434.

Zaire

1966 • Lusibu Z. N'Kanza (b. 1940) was the first woman to serve as minister of state for social affairs in Zaire, then called the Democratic Republic of the Congo. She was appointed in 1966 and served until 1971.
Sources: O'Neill, *The Women's Book of World Records and Achievements,* p. 61.

Zambia

1969 • Lombe Phyllis Chibesakunda (b. 1944), a Zambian lawyer and diplomat who studied in England, was the first woman to serve as state advocate in her country's ministry of legal affairs.
Source: Uglow, *The Continuum Dicitonary of Women's Biography,* p. 120.

Health

Australia

1880s • Constance Stone (1856–1902) was the first woman to practice as a doctor in Victoria, Australia, in the 1880s. Educated at the Presbyterian Ladies College in Melbourne, Stone went abroad to earn a medical degree. Determined to be a physician, she earned her credentials at the Women's Medical College in Philadelphia in the United States and then returned to Australia to set up private practice. She was later instrumental in the establishment of the Queen Victoria Hospital for the Melbourne poor.

Sources: Uglow, *The Continuum Dictionary of Women's Biography,* p. 519.

1933 • Elizabeth Kenny (1880–1952), an Australian nurse known as "Sister Kenney," founded a clinic in Australia where she was the first person to practice a new technique for the treatment of poliomyelitis. Her method involved muscle therapy rather than immobilizaton of the legs with casts and splints. Kenny went on to found clinics in Britain (1937) and Minneapolis, Minnesota (1920).

Sources: Arnold, *Monash Biographical Dictionary of 20th Century Australia,* pp. 290–91; Magnusson, *Larousse Biographical Dictionary,* p. 820.

Austria

1925 • Helene Deutsch (1884–1982), a pioneering psychoanalyst, was the first woman to serve as director of the Vienna Psychoanalytic Institute, a position she assumed in 1925 and held until she was obliged by the rise of Adolph Hitler and Nazism to leave Vienna for the United States in 1933.

Sources: Deutsch, *Confrontations with Myself: An Epilogue;* Uglow, *The Continuum Dictionary of Women's Biography,* p. 165.

Bolivia

1926 • Amelia Villa (d. 1942) was the first female physician in Bolivia. She earned her degree in 1926 and was honored by the government at the end of her career for her work in pediatrics. A children's ward in the hospital at Oruro bears her name.

Sources: Chicago, *The Dinner Party,* p. 191.

Brazil

1834 • Marie Durocher (1809–1893) was the first woman to receive a degree from the Medical School of Rio de Janeiro in Brazil, in 1834. One of the first female doctors in Latin America, Durocher practiced medicine in Brazil for sixty years.

Sources: Chicago, *The Dinner Party,* p. 190; Uglow, *The Continuum Dictionary of Women's Biography,* p. 179.

Canada

1875 • Jennie Kidd Trout (b. 1841) became the first licensed woman doctor in Canada after graduating from the Women's Medical College of Pennsylvania in 1875. She helped to establish two women's medical colleges, fought great opposition in regards to the admission of women to medical schools, and became a fervent promoter of women in medicine. Trout later helped to endow the Women's Medical College of Kingston in 1883. She was one of the most significant contributors to breaking down the barriers to the entry of women into medicine in Canada.

Sources: Dembski, "Jennie Kidd Trout and the Founding of the Women's Medical Colleges at Kingston and Toronto," in *Ontario History,* 77 (3) 1985; Hacker, *The Indomitable Lady Doctors;* Hacker, "Jennie Kidd Trout" in *The Canadian Encyclopedia.*

1880s • Emily Howard Stowe (1831–1903), a Canadian physician, was the first woman admitted to the College of Physicians and Surgeons in Ontario in 1880. She received her medical degree from the New York College of Medicine for Women in 1867. A leading feminist, she became the first president of the Dominion Woman Suffrage Association, an organization she was instrumental in founding, in 1893.

Sources: Uglow, *The Continuum Dictionary of Women's Biography,* p. 521.

1884 • Elizabeth Smith (b. 1859), a pioneering Canadian physician, was the first woman to receive a medical degree from Queen's University in Toronto, Canada, in 1884. She practiced medicine in Hamilton until her marriage in the late 1880s.

Sources: Levin, *Women and Medicine,* pp. 146–50; Smith, *The Diaries of Elizabeth Smith.*

1898 • Maude Elizabeth Seymour Abbott (1869–1940) was the first person to develop a medical catalogue of the circulatory system. A physician who worked as Curator of the medical museum at McGill University in Montreal, Canada, Abbott published her *Osler Catalogue of the Circulatory System* in 1898.

Sources: Uglow, *The Continuum Dictionary of Women's Biography,* p. 2.

China

1896 • Shih Mai-yu (1873–1954), known as Dr. Mary Stone, graduated from the Medical School of the University of Michigan in Ann Arbor on June 22, 1896, becoming the first Chinese woman physician with a doctor of medicine degree. She then returned to China, where she established the Women's Hospital at Kuikiang.

Sources: Kane, *Famous First Facts,* p. 467.

1920s • Ch'iao-chih Lin (b. 1901) was the first Chinese woman to receive a degree in gynecology from an English university. She had intended to become a pediatrician, but was distressed at tending to dying infants and switched to gynecology.

Sources: Levin, *Women and Medicine,* p. 33.

Egypt

Early twentieth century • Sheldon Amos Elgood was the first female physician to be appointed by the Egyptian government. Having received her medical degree from London University in 1900, she opened the first outpatient department for women and children in an Egyptian government hospital and founded the first free children's dispensaries in Egypt.

Sources: Levin, *Women and Medicine,* p. 67.

England

c.1100 • Queen Matilda (c.1100–1135), the wife of Henry I of England, was the first woman to enact a welfare program for pregnant women in need. She also founded two free hospitals.

Sources: Chicago, *The Dinner Party,* p. 143.

1671 • Jane Sharp was the first Englishwoman to write a textbook on midwifery, *The Midwife's Book,* published in 1671. She was influenced by the contemporary activist midwife Elizabeth Cellier, who campaigned for the rights of mothers and their infants.

Sources: Uglow, *The Continuum Dictionary of Women's Biography,* p. 116.

1718 • Mary Wortley Montagu (1689–1762) was the first person to introduce smallpox inoculation in England. She had observed the practice during her stay in Constantinople, where her husband was serving as ambassador from England.

Mary Pierrepont Wortley, the daughter of an English aristocrat, eloped at age 23 with Edward Wortley Montagu, against her father's wishes. From 1716 to 1718, the couple lived in Constantinople (now Istanbul, Turkey), where Edward served as English ambassador. While there, Mary learned about smallpox inoculation. Upon returning to England, she promoted the technique despite

Lady Mary Wortley Montagu poses for a portrait in Turkish costume.

heated opposition from the medical profession. The English government, skeptical of the procedure, appointed a four-physican panel to monitor the effects of the inoculation on the Montagu's own daughter. When the procedure appeared to be a success, they reluctantly approved its use. While in Turkey, Lady Montagu also published *Letters from the East,* the first account of that region by a woman. Her literary reputation rests on her entertaining and finely crafted letters, addressed chiefly to her sister, husband, and daughter. In them, she records much about contemporary events and customs, particularly about the daily lives of women.

Sources: Chicago, *The Dinner Party,* p. 180; Schmidt, *400 Outstanding Women of the World,* pp. 136–38; Wharton, *The Queens of Society,* pp. 135–36.

Early nineteenth century • Miranda Berry (d. 1865) was the first English woman to practice as a male physician. She worked her entire life as James Berry, becoming Inspector General of Hospitals for the British Army. Her sex was only discovered upon her death.

Sources: Levin, *Women and Medicine,* p. 90.

c.1815 • Miranda Stuart (1795–1865) was the first English-speaking woman to receive a degree from an established university. She wore men's clothes to attend classes at the University of Paris.

Sources: Chicago, *The Dinner Party,* p. 191; Rose, *The Perfect Gentleman;* Uglow, *The Continuum Dictionary of Women's Biography,* pp. 523–24.

c.1854 • Florence Nightingale (1820–1910) elevated the practice of nursing to a professional level by laying the foundations of the system of modern nursing during her work in the Crimean War. On her return from the front, she established the Nightingale School and Home for Nurses in England. In 1860, she published Notes on Nursing, the first textbook for nurses. Nightingale was also the first woman to receive the Order of Merit, in 1907.

Sources: Chicago, *The Dinner Party,* p. 191; McGrayne, *Nobel Prize Women in Science,* p. 252; Williams, *Queenly Women, Crowned and Uncrowned,* pp. 123–24.

Florence Nightingale

c.1865 • Elizabeth Garrett Anderson (1836–1917) was the first English female physician. She was the sister of Millicent Fawcett, English suffragist. Refused admission to various medical schools, she studied at the London Hospital and at St. Andrew's, becoming a pioneer for other women in the profession. Although there was much resistance to her receiving training to become a doctor, in 1865 she passed the Apothecaries' Hall examination to qualify as a medical practitioner. In 1866, she established the London School of Hospital for Women that was later renamed the Elizabeth Garrett Anderson Hospital in London. Anderson was the first—and from her appointment in 1873 through 1892, the only—female member of the British Medical Association. She was also active in the women's suffrage movement and was elected Mayor of Aldeburgh in 1908, becoming the first female mayor in England.

Sources: Anderson, *On the Progress of Medicine in the Victorian Era;* Chicago, *The Dinner Party,* p. 190; Levin, *Women and Medicine,* pp. 112–22; Magnusson, *Larousse Biographical Dictionary,* p. 44; Ogilvie, *Women in Science,* pp. 28–31; *Who Was Who,* vol. II, p. 21.

1890 • Kate Marsden (1859–1931), an English nurse, was the first English woman to receive a medal from the Russian Red Cross, in St. Petersburg in 1890. She was honored for her work in treating Russian soldiers during the Russo-Turkish War in 1877. From this time, when she first encountered lepers, she devoted her energy to their care. She founded a hospital to treat those afflicted with leprosy, in Viluisk, Russia, in 1897. Marsden is also remembered as a traveler: she was made a Free Life Member of the Royal Geographical Society in 1916.

Sources: Johnson, *The Life of Kate Marsden;* Uglow, *The Continuum Dictionary of Women's Biography,* p. 360.

1895 • Lilian Murphy (1871–1959) was the first British woman licensed to practice dentistry. After three years of apprenticeship, she began work at the National Dental Hospital in Edinburgh in 1895. She continued to practice after her marriage and became the first woman to be a branch president; she later was the first woman to serve as President of the British Dental Association.

Sources: Uglow, *The Continuum Dictionary of Women's Biography,* p. 393.

1899 • Ethel Gordon Fenwick (1857–1947) was the first president of the International Council of Nurses, a group she organized in London in 1899 and the first such organization among health care professionals, as well as the first for professional women. A decade earlier, Fenwick had helped to organize the British Nurses' Association and served as its first president. A tireless organizer working throughout her life for higher standards in the nursing profession, Fenwick started the Matrons' Council of Great Britain and Ireland in 1894 and went on to found the British College of Nurses in 1926.

Sources: Uglow, *The Continuum Dictionary of Women's Biography,* p. 200; *Who Was Who,* vol. IV, p. 379.

Margaret McMillan (1860–1931) was the first person to instigate a government-backed school medical inspection, in Bradford, England, in 1899. Working with her sister Rachel, Margaret opened the first school clinic in England in 1908 and the first open-air nursery school in 1914. The McMillan sisters devoted their lives to better health for school children. To carry out their ideas, she founded the Rachel McMillan Open Air Nursery School in London in 1917 following Rachel's death, as a memorial to her.

Sources: Magnusson, *Larousse Biographical Dictionary,* p. 946; *Who Was Who,* vol. III, p. 881.

Early twentieth century • Marie Charlotte Carmichael Stopes (c.1880–1958) was the founder of England's and the world's first family planning center, in London. In 1904, she became the first woman to receive a doctorate from the Botanical Institute in Munich, Germany, and was the first woman to lecture in science at Manchester University. Stopes devoted her life to the cause of birth control, and was the designer of a pessary (a device worn in the vagina), which she called the "pro-race" cap.

Sources: Chicago, *The Dinner Party,* p. 200; Levin, *Women and Medicine,* pp. 214–23; Magnusson, *Larousse Biographical Dictionary,* p. 1405; *Who Was Who,* vol. V, p. 1050.

1914 • Sylvia May Payne (1880–1976), an English physician who went on to specialize in psychiatry in the 1920s, was the first woman to serve as Commandant and Medical Officer in charge of the Red Cross Hospital at Torquay.

She assumed this position in 1914 and served in this capacity throughout World War I.

Sources: Uglow, *The Continuum Dictionary of Women's Biography,* p. 426; *Who Was Who,* vol. VII, p. 613.

Hilda Clark (1881–1955), an English Quaker, was the cofounder with Edmund Harvey of the Friends War Victims Relief Organization in 1914. Trained as a physician, Clark worked throughout her life for pacifist causes and war relief.

Sources: Uglow, *The Continuum Dictionary of Women's Biography,* pp. 126–27.

1925 • Cecily Williams (b. 1893), an English physician, was the first woman doctor to be assigned overseas by the Colonial Office. In 1925, she went to work in Koforidua, Ghana, where she was the first person to identify the childhood nutritional disease kwashiorkor, one of the most widespread pediatric diseases of the tropics. She later worked in Malaya, where she was the first woman to head the division of Maternity and Child Welfare, attaining the highest position held by a woman until that time in the Colonial Service.

Sources: Levin, *Women and Medicine,* pp. 207–13; Uglow, *The Continuum Dictionary of Women's Biography,* pp. 582–83.

1930 • Lady Gertrude Mary Denman (1884–1954), an English feminist, was the first woman to chair the National Birth Control Council. She was head of this organization, which later became the Family Planning Association, from its foundation in 1930 until her death.

Sources: Uglow, *The Continuum Dictionary of Women's Biography,* pp. 160–61; *Who Was Who,* vol. V, p. 297.

1933 • Christine Murrell (1874–1933) was the first woman to be elected a member of the General Medical Council of Great Britain, in London in 1933. She had a career as a physician in general practice, serving in the Women's Emergency Corps during World War I and publishing a book, *Women and Health,* in 1923.

Sources: St. John, *Christine Murrell, M.D.*; Uglow, *The Continuum Dictionary of Women's Biography,* pp. 393–94.

Early 1940s • Edith Pye (1876–1965), a British nurse who was also an ardent Quaker, was the first woman to successfully argue that the Allied Blockade be lifted to prevent starvation in Europe during World War II. She worked for Quaker relief organizations during both world wars as well as during the Spanish Civil War and is remembered for her energy and unstinting dedication to those in need throughout her life.

Sources: Uglow, *The Continuum Dictionary of Women's Biography,* pp. 441–42.

1940 • Dorothy Russell (1895–1983), a British physician trained at Cambridge University and the London Hospital, was the first woman to serve as Head of Pathology in the Neurological Department of the Nuffield Military Hospital in Oxford, during World War II. Working with Dr. Hugh Cairns, Russell collaborated to make Oxford the center for brain injuries and research during the war. Beginning in 1946, she became Professor of Morbid Anatomy at the London Medical College. She is remembered for her pioneering work in neuropathology and for her publications, now regarded as classics in her field.

Sources: Uglow, *The Continuum Dictionary of Women's Biography,* p. 469; *Who Was Who,* vol. VIII.

1945 • Janet Maria Vaughan (1899–1993) was the first British female doctor to work with cases of extreme starvation in Nazi concentration camps, in Europe in early 1945 before the end of World War II. Already a distinguished physician, Vaughan went on to become principal of Somerville College, Oxford, in late 1945, and served in this capacity until her retirement in 1967. Throughout her life, she published widely in her field.

Sources: Uglow, *The Continuum Dictionary of Women's Biography,* p. 556.

1952 • Anna Freud (1895–1982), daughter of Sigmund Freud and a psychoanalyst who left Vienna, Austria, for London with her father in 1938, was the first director of the Hampstead Child Therapy Clinic, in 1952.

Sources: Uglow, *The Continuum Dictionary of Women's Biography,* p. 214; *Who Was Who,* vol. VIII.

1979 • Josephine Mary Taylor Barnes (b. 1912), a British obstetrician and gynecologist, became the first female President of the British Medical Association in 1979. She worked on behalf of women and women's medicine throughout her life.

Sources: Uglow, *The Continuum Dictionary of Women's Biography,* p. 49.

Anna Freud

France

c.1600 • Louyse Bourgeois (1563–1636), a French midwife, was the first person to treat anemia with iron. In 1608, she published a famous treatise in which she discussed the anatomy and health of women and newborn babies. Among her other important observations was establishing undernourishment as the cause of anemia.

Sources: Alic, *Hypatia's Heritage;* Uglow, *The Continuum Dictionary of Women's Biography,* p. 82.

c.1750 • Angélique de Coudray (1712–1789), a French midwife who stressed the science of her work, was the first person to use a model of the female torso and an actual fetus when teaching obstetrics. She was given an annual salary by Louis XV to teach in all the provinces.

Sources: Uglow, *The Continuum Dictionary of Women's Biography,* p. 175.

c.1790 • Marie La Chapelle (1769–1821) was the organizer of the maternity and children's hospital at Port Royal in France. Trained in midwifery by her mother, La Chapelle wrote an important three-volume work on obstetrics that became a major text for many years.

Sources: Chicago, *The Dinner Party,* p. 191; Uglow, *The Continuum Dictionary of Women's Biography,* pp. 308–9.

c.1820 • Marie Anne Victoire Boivin (1773–1847), trained as an obstetrician, was the first French woman to invent a pelvimeter and a vaginal speculum. She was honored for her work in women's medicine in 1827 when she received an honorary medical degree from the University of Marburg in Germany.

Sources: Uglow, *The Continuum Dictionary of Women's Biography,* p. 75.

c.1890 • Lou Andreas Salomé (1861–1937), a writer as well as an analyst, was the first female psychotherapist in France. Known primarily as an inspiration for German philosopher Friedrich Nietzche, as the confidante of Austrian psychoanalyst Sigmund Freud, and as the lover of Austrian poet Rainer Maria Rilke, Salomé was well-known during her lifetime because of her fiction and essays.

Sources: Chicago, *The Dinner Party,* p. 205.

1898 • Agnes McLaren (1837–1913), a Scottish doctor, earned her degree from the Université de Montpellier in 1878 and set up a practice in Cannes, France. She was the first person to advocate the appointment of Catholic nuns as doctors; women in religious orders were forbidden to become physicians under canon law until 1936. McLaren converted to Catholicism in 1898 and began her life's work of providing female doctors for Catholic missions. Her work was continued after her death by Anna Dengel and Joanna Lyons, who founded the Society of Catholic Medical Missionaries in 1925.

Sources: Burton, *According to the Pattern: The Story of Doctor Agnes McLaren and the Society of Catholic Medical Missionaries;* Uglow, *The Continuum Dictionary of Women's Biography,* p. 346.

1899 • Madeleine Pelletier (1874–1939), a French physician who worked for feminist causes, was the first woman to be appointed to the staff of the Assistance Publique, in Paris in 1899. In 1906, she became the first woman in France to qualify to work in mental hospitals. She was also one of the first female freemasons.

Sources: Hutton, *Historical Dictionary of the Third French Republic, 1870–1940,* pp. 761–63.

Germany

c.1120 • Hildegard van Bingen (1098–1178) was the first German woman to practice medicine. As Abbess of Rupertsberg Abbey, van Bingen wrote a number of medical works based on her own experiences as a physician.

Sources: Levin, *Women and Medicine,* p. 37.

1754 • Dorothea Christianan Leporin Erxleben (1715–1762) on June 12, 1754, was the first woman to earn a medical degree from a German university. She was granted her M.D. from the University of Halle, Germany, but only practiced for eight years before her death from breast cancer.

Sources: Ogilvie, *Women in Science,* pp. 82–83; Uglow, *The Continuum Dictionary of Women's Biography,* pp. 191–92.

1815 • Regina Josepha von Siebold (1771–1849) was the first woman to receive a doctorate in obstetrics from a German university. A practicing midwife, she earned her degree from the University of Giessen in 1815. She also fostered the medical career of her daughter, Charlotte Heidenreich von Siebold, who received the same degree from the University of Giessen in 1817.

Sources: Uglow, *The Continuum Dictionary of Women's Biography,* p. 498.

1819 • Charlotte Heidenreich von Siebold (1788–1859), a German physician, was the first female doctor to assist at the birth of an English queen. Von Siebold attended the birth of Queen Victoria in London in 1819.

Sources: Uglow, *The Continuum Dictionary of Women's Biography,* p. 498.

1920s • Karen Horney (1885–1952), a German psychoanalyst who established her reputation at the Berlin Psychoanalytic Institute in the 1920s, was the first woman actively to challenge Freudian ideas about female psychology, calling into question his theories of the oedipal complex and penis envy. In 1932 she moved to the United States and settled in New York where she founded the Association for the Advancement of Psychoanalysis and the American Institute of Psychoanalysis, both in 1941. The Karen Horney Clinic in New York, named after this distinguished teacher, therapist, and writer, opened shortly after her death, in 1952.

Sources: Rolka, *100 Women Who Shaped World History,* p. 82; Sayers, *Mothers of Psychoanalysis.*

Greece

Fourth century B.C. • Agnodice, a Greek woman of the fourth century B.C., was the first female gynecologist. Dressed in men's clothing, she studied with another doctor, Herophilos, and practiced her profession disguised as a man. When her female identity was revealed, she had to contend with much criticism from jealous colleagues.

Sources: Ogilvie, *Women in Science,* p. 28; Uglow, *The Continuum Dictionary of Women's Biography,* p. 8.

Seventh century B.C. • Hygeia, the daughter of the seventh-century B.C. physician Aesculapius, was the first person to advocate preventive medicine. It is from her name that we have the word "hygiene."

Sources: Levin, *Women and Medicine,* p. 75.

1890s • Mary Kalopathakes, a Greek physician who earned her medical degree in Paris in the 1880s, is credited with being the first person to establish nursing as a profession in Greece.

Sources: Levin, *Women and Medicine,* p. 78.

1896 • Angelique G. Panayotatou was the first woman to graduate from the Medical School of the University of Athens, in 1896. She went on to practice medicine and to write a history of hygiene among the ancient Greeks.

Sources: Levin, *Women and Medicine,* p. 78; Uglow, *The Continuum Dictionary of Women's Biography,* p. 416.

India

1881 • Edith Pechey-Phipson (1845–1908), a pioneering English physician, was the first woman elected to the Senate of the University of Bombay, India. Her career contained a number of firsts. She was the first woman to be awarded the Chemistry Prize and the first to win the Hope Scholarship at the University of Edinburgh, Scotland, in 1870, but she was denied both because she was female. After earning her medical degree from the University of Bern, Germany, and working in private practice in Leeds, England, she went to India. There she became the first woman to direct the Cama Hospital in Bombay, in 1883. She was also the founder of the Pechey-Phipson Sanitarium near Nasik, India. She died of breast cancer.

Sources: Lutzker, *Edith Pechey-Phipson, M.D.: The Story of England's Foremost Pioneering Woman Doctor;* Uglow, *The Continuum Dictionary of Women's Biography,* p. 427.

1886 • Twenty-one year old Anandibai Joshee (1865–1887) graduated from the Women's Medical College of Pennsylvania in Philadelphia on March 11, 1886, becoming the first Hindu woman to earn the doctor of medicine degree. Because she died less than a year later in her native India, she was never able to realize her goal of a career in medicine.

Sources: Kane, *Famous First Facts,* p. 467.

c.1900 • Mary Ann Scharlieb (1845–1930), an English physician specializing in abdominal surgery, was the founder of the Victoria Hospital for Caste and Gosha Women, in Madras, India. Alternating her professional life between Britain and India, Scharlieb helped to form a Women's Medical Service for India during World War I. In 1920, she became one of the first female magistrates in England.

Sources: Scharlieb, *Reminiscences;* Uglow, *The Continuum Dictionary of Women's Biography,* p. 481.

1940s • Shushila Nayar (b. 1914) was the first woman to serve Mahatma Gandhi as a medical attendant, in the 1940s. A physician educated both in her native India and in the United States, Nayar was an active member of her country's Independence Movement and became increasingly interested in politics. After Independence, she gained the title of Senior Medical Officer and served as Minister of Health from 1962 through 1967.

Sources: Uglow, *The Continuum Dictionary of Women's Biography,* pp. 397–98.

Italy

c.200 A.D. • Metrodora, a physician in second century Rome, was the first female medical writer. She wrote a detailed treatise on the diseases of women, prescribing various methods of dealing with diseases of the uterus, stomach, and kidneys.

Sources: Chicago, *The Dinner Party,* p. 127.

390 A.D. • Fabiola (d. 399) founded the first public hospital in Rome, Italy. She worked there as a nurse, a physician, and a surgeon and taught Christianity. With Paula, Eustochium, and Jerome, Fabiola was important in advocating a specifically female order of Christianity.

Sources: Chicago, *The Dinner Party,* p. 130; Uglow, *The Continuum Dictionary of Women's Biography,* p. 195.

Eleventh century • Tortula of Salerno (d. 1097), an eleventh-century Italian physician and medical writer, was the first person to stitch a perineum after a difficult childbirth. She was the first person to introduce support for the perineum during labor to prevent tearing. And she was also the first physician to give written advice on the care of newborn children, in her important book on gynecology and obstetrics, *Diseases of Women.*

Sources: Chicago, *The Dinner Party,* pp. 73–74; Uglow, *The Continuum Dictionary of Women's Biography,* p. 545; Vare and Ptacek, *Mothers of Invention,* pp. 27–28.

c.1320 • Alessandra Giliani (1307–1326) was the first person to color veins and arteries for examination. Trained as a physician and working in her native Italy, she devised a method of drawing blood from cadavers and then filling the veins and arteries with different colored liquids to render them more visible during autopsy.

Sources: Chicago, *The Dinner Party,* p. 154.

Jamaica

1840s • Mary Jane Seacole (1805–1891) was the first Jamaican woman to work as a self-trained healthcare professional. She gained nursing experience in Kingston in the 1840s, where she nursed victims of yellow fever and cholera epidemics. She traveled as a healthcare worker in Colombia and Panama and finally in the 1850s to the Crimea, where she met Florence Nightingale. There she tended battlefield wounds under gunfire. Her later life was spent in Jamaica and London.

Sources: Uglow, *The Continuum Dictionary of Women's Biography,* p. 490.

Japan

1885 • Ogino Ginko (1851–1913) was the first Japanese woman licensed to practice Western medicine. Her medical career followed a divorce from her first husband, on the grounds of childlessness. Her inability to bear children, however, was caused by a venereal disease that she had contracted from him. In 1882, she graduated from Kojuin, a private medical school for men. Ultimately overcoming objections, she was allowed to take the medical qualifying examination and established a practice in 1885. Ogino served as the physician for Meiji Girls' School and contributed to the women's magazine *Jogaku zasshi*.

Source: Itasaka, *Kodansha Encyclopedia of Japan*.

The Netherlands

c.1875 • Aletta Jacobs (1849–1929) was the first female physician in the Netherlands. An active feminist, Jacobs joined American suffragists in an attempt to forge an international women's rights movement. In Amsterdam in 1882 she started the world's first birth control clinic. In 1894, also in Amsterdam, she founded the Association for Women's Suffrage.

Sources: Chicago, *The Dinner Party*, p. 188; Levin, *Women and Medicine*, pp. 43–45; Uglow, *The Continuum Dictionary of Women's Biography*, p. 279.

Norway

1924 • Katti Moeler was the the first woman to organize a family planning center in Norway, in Oslo in 1924. She wrote and spoke on behalf of liberal abortion laws and fought for the rights of single women and their children.

Sources: Chicago, *The Dinner Party*, p. 200.

The Philippines

c.1900 • Trinidad Tescon (1848–1928), a Filipino freedom fighter, was the first person to start Red Cross work in the Philippines, in the early twentieth century. After years of military service fighting for her country's independence, Tescon turned her attention to health care. She organized a nursing facility and founded a hospital in the fort of Baik-na-Bota. Her work was recognized by the International Red Cross.

Sources: Uglow, *The Continuum Dictionary of Women's Biography*, p. 536.

Poland

1877 • Anna Tomaszewicz-Dobrska (1854–1918), a Polish physician educated in Zurich, Vienna, Berlin, and St. Petersburg, was the second woman in her country to become a doctor and the first to return to Poland to practice medicine. She established herself in Warsaw in 1877. In 1882, she became the first woman to serve as Chief of Lying-In Hospital No. 2 in Warsaw. She remained in this position until the hospital closed in 1911.

Sources: Uglow, *The Continuum Dictionary of Women's Biography,* p. 542.

Russia

1860s • M.A. Brokova and Nadya Prokofievna Suslova were the first two Russian women to receive medical degrees, from the University of Zurich in Switzerland. An 1863 Russian charter prohibited the acceptance of women into universities to study medicine or science so Brokova and Suslova sought education outside of their own country.

Sources: Levin, *Women and Medicine,* p. 29.

1872 • Varvara Alexandra Kashevarova-Rudneva was the first woman to receive a degree under the auspices of the Women's Medical Courses. Russia passed a law in 1863 prohibiting women from studying science or medicine at Russian universities. The shortage of physicians prompted the institution of the Women's Medical Courses to be established in in St. Petersburg 1872.

Sources: Levin, *Women and Medicine,* p. 30.

1877 • Anna Schabanoff was the first woman to graduate from the Academy of Medicine in St. Petersburg, Russia, in 1877. She specialized in pediatrics and established a child welfare association.

Sources: Chicago, *The Dinner Party,* p. 191.

Scotland

1878 • Sophia Jex-Blake (1840–1912) became Scotland's first female physician when she settled there. In 1876, Jex-Blake had campaigned for and won a change in the English law that until then had prevented medical examiners from evaluating women students. Jex-Blake, a British physician, founded the London School of Medicine for Women in 1874. An assertive advocate of women's rights, Jex-Blake also founded the Women's Hospital in Edinburgh in 1885 and organized the Edinburgh School of Medicine for women in 1894. Although she fought successfully with five other women to be admitted to the University of Edinburgh in 1869, the university officials there reversed their decision in 1873. She eventually earned her medical degree from the University of Bern, Germany, in 1877. She had initially studied in New York under Elizabeth Blackwell, another female medical pioneer, working for a degree at the Women's Medical College of the New York Infirmary, where in 1866 she was the first woman to register for courses. When she settled in Edinburgh in 1878, she became Scotland's first female physician.

Sources: Levin, *Women and Medicine,* pp. 123–32; Ogilvie, *Women in Science,* pp. 105–7; Todd, *Sophia Jex-Blake;* Uglow, *The Continuum Dictionary of Women's Biography,* p. 283.

1914 • Elsie Inglis (1874–1917), a British doctor and feminist, was the founder and first head of the Scottish Women's Hospitals, a medical team she organized in 1914 to help in the war effort. Her group consisted of an entirely female staff and provided two medical units in France and one in Serbia, headed by Inglis herself. A lifelong advocate of women's rights, she was the cofounder, with Jessie MacGregor at the turn of the century, of the only maternity center run by women in Scotland, an institution that later became the Elsie Inglis Hospital. Weakened and ill as a result of her work in Serbia, Inglis returned to England in November of 1917; she died on November 26, the day after she arrived.

Sources: Balfour, *Dr. Elsie Inglis;* Lawrence, *Shadow of Swords: A Biography of Elsie Inglis;* Uglow, *The Continuum Dictionary of Women's Biography,* pp. 273–74.

South Africa

1975 • Mamphela Ramphele (b. 1948), a South African physician and political activist, was the founder of the Zanempilo Health Clinic at King William's Town in 1975. She also founded the Ithuseng Community Health Centre in 1978. Working as an itinerant doctor, Ramphele was a friend of Mapetla Mohapi and Steven Biko, both of whom died as a result of their protests against apartheid.

Sources: Uglow, *The Continuum Dictionary of Women's Biography,* p. 447.

Switzerland

Sixteenth century • Marie Colinet, a sixteenth-century Swiss physician who specialized in surgery and bone-setting, was the first woman to employ a magnet when extracting a piece of steel from the eye. Historians have often wrongly attributed this achievement to her husband and fellow physician.

Sources: Chicago, *The Dinner Party,* p. 176.

United States

1620 • Susanna White was the first woman aboard the *Mayflower* to give birth in North America. The Mayflower was one of the first ships to carry Pilgrims from England to settle in North America. Susanna White gave birth at Provincetown Harbor, Massachusetts, on November 20.

Sources: McCullough, *First of All: Significant Firsts by American Women,* p. 1115.

1804 • Elizabeth Marshall (1768–1836), daughter of Charles Marshall, the president of the Philadelphia College of Pharmacy from 1821 to 1824, was the first woman to work as a pharmacist. Marshall operated the apothecary opened by her grandfather in Philadelphia, Pennsylvania, from 1804 to 1825. She graduated in 1857 from the Women's Medical College of Pennsylvania—one of the only schools founded for women.

Sources: Kane, *Famous First Facts,* p. 459.

1835 • Harriot Kezia Hunt (1805–1875) was the first woman to practice medicine in the United States, opening her office with her sister in Boston, Massachusetts, in 1835. Hunt applied several times to Harvard Medical School but was refused admission until accepted by Dean Oliver Wendall Holmes in 1850. She was forced to withdraw when the male students rioted in protest. In 1843, Hunt organized the Ladies' Physiological Society in Boston, and in 1853 she was awarded an honorary medical degree from the Female Medical College of Pennsylvania.

Sources: Levin, *Women and Medicine,* p. 98; Read and Witlieb, *The Book of Women's Firsts,* pp. 221–22; *Who Was Who in America,* p. 267.

1838 • Mary Sargeant Neal Gove Nichols (1810–1884) was the first American woman to lecture on female anatomy, physiology, and hygiene. She began her career by speaking in public in Lynn and Boston, Massachusetts in 1838. She became a well-known novelist as well as a writer in the field of health care, supported in her interests and feminist views by her physician husband.

Sources: James, *Notable American Women,* vol. 2, pp. 627–29; *Who Was Who in America,* p. 276.

1849 • Elizabeth Blackwell (1821–1910) became the first American woman to receive a medical degree when she graduated from Geneva Medical College in Geneva, New York, in 1849. She devoted her life to the practice of medicine and founded the New York Infirmary for Women and Children, the only hospital in the U.S. with an all-female staff. She was also the first accredited physician to practice in Great Britain, where she was born and lived for a period of her adult life. Blackwell became the first woman enrolled as a recognized physician in the Medical Registered of the United Kingdom in 1859.

Sources: Read and Witlieb, *The Book of Women's Firsts,* pp. 54–55; Rolka, *100 Women Who Shaped the World,* p. 56; Sanders, *The First of Everything,* pp. 156–57.

c.1850 • Emily Blackwell (1826–1910) was the first female doctor to engage extensively in major surgery. Educated at Cleveland (Western Reserve) University, she was dean and professor of obstetrics and diseases of women at the Women's Medical Colelge attached to the NEw York Infirmary for Indigent Women and Children. Known primarily as the younger sister of Elizabeth Blackwell, she worked throughout her life with her sister and helped to manage the New York Infirmary for over forty years, beginning in 1846.

Sources: Haber, *Women Pioneers of Science,* p. 6; James, *Notable American Women,* vol. 1, pp. 165–67.

1851 • Lydia Folger Fowler (1822–1879) was the first woman to hold a chair at a legally authorized school. She was appointed Professor of Midwifery and Diseases of Women and Children at her alma mater, Rochester Eclectic Medical College, in 1851.

Sources: James, *Notable American Women,* vol. 1, pp. 654–55; Uglow, *The Continuum Dictionary of Women's Biography* p. 210.

Elizabeth Blackwell

Hannah E. Myers Longshore (1819–1901) became the first woman to serve as a faculty member in an American medical school when she worked as a demonstrator of anatomy at the Female Medical College in Philadelphia, Pennsylvania, in 1851. Longshore earned her medical degree from this college in the same year.

Hannah E. Myers Longshore married Thomas E. Longshore in 1841 and settled with him in Philadelphia. Her brother-in-law, Joseph S. Longshore, was interested in and committed to providing medical education to women. Under his guidance and with access to his library, Hannah began her studies, joining

Hannah Longshore

the first class of women to graduate from the Female Medical College and subsequently joining its faculty.

Sources: Read and Witlieb, *The Book of Women's Firsts,* p. 258.

Sarah Read Adamson Dolley (1829–1909), an American physician and feminist, was the first woman to serve as a hospital intern in the United States, beginning her internship on May 12, 1851, at Blockley Hospital in Philadelphia, Pennsylvania, and finishing a year later. She made her career in private practice in Rochester, New York.

Sources: Corson, *The Corson Family;* James, *Notable American Women,* vol. 1, pp. 497–99; Parker, *Rochester: A Story Historical,* pp. 264–66, 379.

1855 • The Woman's Hospital opened its doors on May 4, 1855, in New York City; it was the first hospital established for the treatment of women's diseases. The hospital is now part of St. Luke's Hospital complex.

Sources: Read and Witlieb, *The Book of Women's Firsts,* pp. 216–17.

1858 • Marie Zakrzewska (1829–1902), who supported Elizabeth and Emily Blackwell in launching the New York Infirmary for Women and Children in 1858, was the first person to introduce the idea of medical records. A pioneering physician like the Blackwells, Zakrzewska instituted medical record keeping at the new hospital.

Sources: James, *Notable American Women,* vol. 3, pp. 702–4; Levin, *Women and Medicine,* pp. 98–101; Victor, *A Woman's Quest: The Life of Marie Zakrzewska, M.D.;* Zakrzewska, *A Practical Illustration of "Woman's Right to Labor."*

c.1860 • Clemence Sophia Harned Lozier (1813–1888), an American physician trained at Syracuse Medical College, was the first woman to deliver a paper before the New York State Homeopathic Society. She was also instrumental in founding the New York Medical College and Hospital for Women, which opened its doors in New York City on November 1, 1863. This homeopathic institution was the first of its kind for women in the state, and Lozier served as its first president until the time of her death.

Sources: James, *Notable American Women,* vol. 2, pp. 440–42; Lovejoy, *Women Doctors of the World,* pp. 63–68; Parton, *Eminent Women of the Age,* pp. 517–22; *Who Was Who in America, 1607–1896,* p. 324.

1861 • Dorothea Lynde Dix (1802–1887) was appointed by Secretary of War Edwin Stanton to serve as the first head the Army Nursing Corps in 1861. She organized this group according to rigid standards: nurses had to be religious, of a high moral character, thirty years old or older, and plain. Dix served as head of the Corps until 1866.

Sources: Chicago, *The Dinner Party,* p. 200; Marshall, *Dorothea Dix: Forgotten Samaritan;* Read and Witlieb, *The Book of Women's Firsts,* pp. 122–23; *Who Was Who in America, 1607–1896,* p. 324.

Mary Edwards Walker (1832–1919), who received her medical degree from Syracuse Medical College in 1855, became the first woman to serve on the surgical staff of a modern army in wartime when she volunteered for service with the Union Army in 1861. When women were commissioned as doctors or nurses in 1864, Walker became acting Assistant Surgeon and a first lieutenant. An active supporter of women's rights, Walker dressed in male attire from the time of her Civil War service.

Sources: Levin, *Women and Medicine,* p. 102.

1862 • Phoebe Yeats Levy Pember (1823–1913) was the first female administrator at Chimborazo Hospital outside of Richmond, Virginia, during the Civil War. Appointed in 1862, Pember served as matron; before the end of the war Chimborazo Hospital would become the largest military institution of its kind in the world at that time. Approximately 15,200 patients passed through her care during the Civil War.

Sources: James, *Notable American Women,* vol. 3, pp. 44–45; Pember, *A Southern Woman's Story.*

1863 • Mary Harris Thompson (1829–1895), an American physician and surgeon educated at the New England Female Medical College in Boston, was the first woman to perform major surgery, in Chicago, Illinois. She was instrumental in the founding of the Woman's Hospital Medical College in Chicago in 1870, in which she served as the first professor of hygiene from 1870 until 1877. In 1891, the institution became the Northwestern University Woman's Medical School. Thompson became a specialist in abdominal and pelvic surgery, and in 1881 she was elected the first female vice-president of the Chicago Medical Society in recognition of her achievements in her field.

Sources: James, *Notable American Women,* vol. 3, pp. 454–55; Kane, *Famous First Facts,* p. 468; Kelly and Burrage, *The Dictionary of American Medical Biography,* pp. 1205–6.

1864 • Rebecca Lee (b. 1833) was the first black female physician in the United States. She earned her degree from the New England Female Medical College in Boston, Massachusetts, on March 1, 1864, and, after the Civil War, established a practice in Richmond, Virginia.

Sources: Chicago, *The Dinner Party,* p. 191; Haber, *Women Pioneers of Science,* pp. 8–9; Kane, *Famous First Facts,* p. 467; Levin, *Women and Medicine,* p. 96; Smith, *Black Firsts,* p. 352.

The first woman to practice dentistry independently was Emeline Roberts Jones, in 1864. She began practice in Danielsonville, Connecticut, in May 1855, as an assistant to her husband. After training with him for four years, Jones became his partner, and in 1864, she took over his practice following his death. A degree in dentistry was not a requirement at that time.

Sources: Kane, *Famous First Facts,* p. 219; McCullough, *First of All: Significant Firsts by American Women,* p. 116.

1866 • Lucy Beaman Hobbs (1833–1910) became the first woman to graduate from an U.S. dental school when she received her degree from the Ohio College of Dental Surgery in Cincinnati, Ohio, on February 21, 1866. Five years earlier, she had been rejected by that school on the basis of her sex. After opening her own practice and gaining the respect of her fellow dentists, Hobbs reapplied to the college; she was admitted into the senior class and was graduated after only four months of study.

Sources: Haber, *Women Pioneers of Science,* p. 9; McCullough, *First of All: Significant Firsts by American Women,* pp. 116–7; Read and Witlieb, *The Book of Women's Firsts,* p. 207.

1870 • Clara A. Swain (1834–1910), an American physician who earned her degree from Woman's Medical College of Pennsylvania in 1869, was the first woman to represent the United States as a trained medical missionary in Asia. Appointed by the Woman's Foreign Missionary Society of the Methodist Episcopal Church, she joined the mission of Bareilly, India, in January of 1870. On January 1, 1874, she opened a hospital there, the first for women in that country. Swain dedicated her life to her mission, greatly expanding its medical facilities. The Clara Swain Hospital still stands at Bareilly and serves a large number of women and men each year.

Sources: Balfour and Young, *The Work of Medical Women in India;* James, *Notable American Women,* vol. 3, pp. 411–13; Swain, *A Glimpse of India;* Wilson, *Palace of Healing: The Story of Dr. Clara Swain.*

1871 • Mercy Ruggles Bisbee Jackson (1802–1877), a homeopathic physician, was the first woman member of the American Institute of Homeopathy in Philadelphia, Pennsylvania.

Sources: Kane, *Famous First Facts,* p. 284; *Who Was Who in America, 1607–1896,* p. 274.

1872 • Mary Jane Safford (1834–1891), an American physician who served as a nurse during the Civil War, was the first person to perform an ovariotomy at Breslau in Germany, in 1872. Safford graduated from New York Medical College for Women in 1869, then studied for three years in Europe before going into private practice in Chicago.

Sources: Cleave, *A Biographical Cyclopedia of Homeopathic Physicians and Surgeons;* James, *Notable American Women,* vol. 3, pp. 220–22; Livermore, *My Story of the War;* Young, *The Women and the Crisis.*

Mary Putnam Jacobi (1842–1906), a physician with an interest in both women's education and health, was the founder of the Association for the Advancement of Medical Education of Women, in 1872. She was also the first woman to be admitted to the New York College of Pharmacy (from which she graduated in 1863) and to the Ecole de Médécine in Paris (in 1868), as well as the first to be elected to the New York Academy of Medicine (1880). She also organized the first consumers' organization in America, the National Consumers' League, which worked to abolish sweatshops.

Sources: Levin, *Women and Medicine,* pp. 137–45; Putnam, *Life and Letters of Mary Putnam Jacobi;* Read and Witlieb, *The Book of Women's Firsts,* p. 228; Uglow, *The Continuum Dictionary of Women's Biography,* pp. 278–79.

1873 • Linda A. J. Richards (1841–1930), a pioneering nurse and educator, was the first person to receive an American diploma in nursing. Richards was the first student in a class of five to register for the nursing program at the New England Hospital for Women and Children in Boston, Massachusetts, in September of 1872; a year later, she became the first person to receive her diploma. Her career included a number of firsts. She was the first person to set up a training school for nurses in Japan, in 1886 at the Doshisha Hospital in Kyoto; she went on to become the first president of the American Society of Superintendents of Training Schools, in 1894; and she was the first person to purchase a share of stock in the *American Journal of Nursing,* in 1900. In 1962, she was honored by the National League for Nursing, which created an award in her name that would be given periodically to a practicing nurse who made a pioneering contribution to the field.

Sources: James, *Notable American Women,* vol. 3, pp. 148–50; Richards, *Reminiscences of Linda Richards;* Sloane, *America's First Trained Nurse;* Worcester, "Linda A. J. Richards," *New England Journal of Medicine* (29 May 1930).

1875 • Emeline Horton Cleveland (1829–1878) devoted her life to the study, teaching, and practice of medicine. Her specialty was diseases of women, and in 1875 she became the first professional ovariotomist (one who performs surgery on ovaries), serving as chief resident at the Woman's Hospital of Philadelphia.

Sources: James, *Notable American Women,* vol. 1, pp. 349–50; Read and Witlieb, *The Book of Women's Firsts,* p. 93.

1876 • Mary Frame Myers Thomas (1816–1888), an American physician and lifelong advocate of women's suffrage, was the first woman regularly admitted to membership in the Indiana State Medical Society, in Richmond, Indiana, in 1876.

Sources: James, *Notable American Women,* vol. 3, pp. 450–51; Waite, "The Three Myers Sisters: Pioneer Women Physicians," *Medical Review of Reviews,* March 1933.

Sarah Hackett Stevenson (1841–1909) was the first female member of the American Medical Association (AMA). After graduating from the Women's Hospital Medical College of Chicago in 1874, she was chosen by the Illinois State Medical Society as its delegate to the American Medical Association's convention in Philadelphia, Pennsylvania, in 1876. She was admitted to membership at the convention. Stevenson was also the first woman to work on the staff of Cook County Hospital in Chicago, as well as the first woman appointed to the Illinois State Board of Health.

Sources: Kane, *Famous First Facts,* p. 384; McCullough, *First of All: Significant Firsts by American Women,* p. 113; Read and Witlieb, *The Book of Women's Firsts,* pp. 423–24.

1878 • Charlotte Amanda Blake Brown (1846–1904), an American physician, was the founder of the San Francisco Children's Hospital, in 1878. An innovative doctor, Brown was the first woman on the Pacific coast to perform an ovariotomy, also in 1878, the year she became the first female member of the San Francisco Medical Society.

Sources: James, *Notable American Women,* vol. 1, pp. 251–53.

1879 • Mary Elizabeth Mahoney (1845–1926) was the first black woman to earn a degree in nursing. In 1879 she graduated from the nursing program at the New England Hospital for Women and Children in Boston, Massachusetts.

Sources: Gaymon, *215 African American Women You Should Know;* James, *Notable American Women,* vol. 2, p. 486; Smith, *Black Firsts,* p. 358.

Clara Barton

1881 • Clara Barton (1821–1912) was the founder and first president of the American Red Cross, heading this organization from 1881 until 1904. She modeled her organization on the International Committee of the Red Cross, formed in Geneva, Switzerland, in 1863. Among the disasters the Red Cross responded to under Clara Barton's leadership were catastrophic fires in Michigan, an earthquake in Charleston, South Carolina, and floods on the Ohio and Mississippi Rivers and at Johnstown, Pennsylvania.

Sources: Barton, *Life of Clara Barton;* Boardman, *Under the Red Cross Flag;* Chicago, *The Dinner Party,* p. 190; Kane, *Famous First Facts;* Read and Witlieb, *The Book of Women's Firsts,* pp. 40–41.

1882 • Mary Frost Niles, an American physician, was the first Presbyterian woman to serve as a medical missionary in China. She arrived in Canton in 1882 and worked with an American colleague, Dr. Mary Hannah Fulton, to establish a dispensary at Fati in 1891.

Sources: Cadbury and Jones, *At the Point of a Lancet: One Hundred Years of the Canton Hospital, 1835–1935;* Fulton, *Twenty-Five Years of Medical Work in China;* James, *Notable American Women,* vol. 1, p. 685.

1883 • Susan Hayhurst was the first female pharmacist, receiving her degree from the Philadelphia College of Pharmacy on March 16, 1883. She graduated in 1857 from the Women's Medical College of Pennsylvania—one of the only schools founded for women.

Sources: McCullough, *First of All: Significant Firsts by American Women,* p. 119.

Elizabeth Fedde (1850–1921), a Norwegian Lutheran deaconess and a pioneer welfare worker, was the first person to organize effective nursing among Scandinavians in America. She came on a mission to the United States, arriving in New York City in April of 1883. Here she set up the Voluntary Relief Society for the Sick and Poor among the city's Norwegians. This organization developed into a hospital by 1892 and was eventually renamed the Lutheran Medical Center in Brooklyn.

Sources: Folkedahl, "Elizabeth Fedde's Diary, 1883-1888," *Norwegian-American Studies and Records,* XX, 1959, pp. 170–96; James, *Notable American Women,* vol. 1, pp. 605–6.

Sarah Pierce (1855–1938) and Frances M. Wetmore, both of whom received their medical degrees in the United States, were the first two female physicians to practice in Hawaii.

Sources: Levin, *Women and Medicine,* pp. 236–37.

1889 • Susan La Flesche Piccotte was the first Native American woman to study western medicine. The daughter of an Omaha chief, she received her degree from the Women's Medical College of Pennsylvania in 1889, then returned to practice medicine among her people, founding a hospital in 1913.

Sources: Chicago, *The Dinner Party,* p. 191; James, *Notable American Women,* vol. 3, pp. 65–66; *Who Was Who in America, 1607–1896,* p. 300–301.

1894 • On March 1, 1894, the American School of Osteopathy in Kirksville, Missouri, conferred degrees on its first women graduates: Jenette Hubbard Bolles, Mamie B. Carter, and Lou J. Kern.

Sources: Kane, *Famous First Facts,* p. 468.

1896 • Ada Stewart became the first industrial nurse when she was hired by the Vermont Marble Company of Proctor, Vermont.

Sources: Kane, *Famous First Facts,* p. 468.

1897 • Isabel Hampton Robb (1860–1910) was an organizer of the American Nurses Association and served as its first president from 1897 through 1901. She dedicated her life to nursing and to the teaching of nursing.

Sources: James, *Notable American Women,* vol. 3, pp. 171–72; Read and Witlieb, *The Book of Women's Firsts,* p. 373.

1898 • Elizabeth Hurdon (1868–1941), a Canadian-born gynecologist and pathologist, was the first woman to serve on the staff of the Johns Hopkins Hospital and to hold simultaneously a faculty appointment in the Johns Hopkins University Medical School, in Baltimore, Maryland, in 1898.

Sources: Chesney, *The Johns Hopkins Hospital and the Johns Hopkins University School of Medicine;* James, *Notable American Women,* vol. 2, pp. 242–44.

Dorothy Reed (1874–1964) and Margaret Long were the first two women to be employed by a U.S. Navy hospital. As medical students, Reed and Long worked in the operating room and the bacteriological laboratories at the Brooklyn Navy Yard Hospital, in New York City, in 1898.

Sources: Read and Witlieb, *The Book of Women's Firsts,* pp. 362–63.

1899 • Ella Phillips Crandall (1871–1938), a leader in public health nursing, became the first director of the School of Nursing at Miami Valley Hospital in Dayton, Ohio, in 1899. Crandall devoted her life to nursing administration and was influential in organizing nurses during World War I.

Sources: James, *Notable American Women,* vol. 1, pp. 398–99; Martin, *The Joy of Living.*

c.1900 • Elise L'Espérance (1878–1959), an American physician, was the first woman to serve as a professor at Cornell Medical College in New York City. A distinguished pathologist remembered as a pioneer in the detection of cancer, L'Espérance was a friend of Dr. Emily Blackwell.

Sources: James, *Notable American Women,* vol. 1, p. 167.

1900 • Sister Mary Alphonsa (1851–1926), the daughter of Nathanial and Sophia Peabody Hawthorne, converted to Roman Catholicism in 1891. After her husband's death, she joined the lay sisters of the Dominican third order and in 1900 founded, with her associate Alice Huber, the nation's first hospice, in New York City, to care for those suffering from incurable cancer.

Sources: Read and Witlieb, *The Book of Women's Firsts,* pp. 248–49.

Sophia Palmer (1853–1920) became the first editor in chief of the *American Journal of Nursing* in 1900. Palmer was active throughout her life in nursing and nursing administration.

Sources: James, *Notable American Women,* vol. 3, pp. 14–15; Read and Witlieb, *The Book of Women's Firsts,* pp. 329–30.

1901 • Anita Newcomb McGee (1864–1940), a physician, drafted the section of the Army Reorganization Act of 1901 that established the Army Nurse Corps in that year. Opposed by the American Red Cross who saw the recruitment and deployment of nurses as their function under the Geneva Treaty, McGee was prevented from serving as the Nurse Corps' first director. Her opponents forced through legislation that required that the director be a graduate nurse.

Sources: James, *Notable American Women,* vol. 2, pp. 464–66; Read and Witlieb, *The Book of Women's Firsts,* p. 281.

Love Rosa Hirschmann Gantt (1875–1935), an American physician and public health worker, was one of the first two women to receive a degree from the Medical College of South Carolina at Charleston, in 1901. She specialized in diseases of the eye, ear, nose, and throat, and practiced in Spartanburg, South Carolina.

Sources: James, *Notable American Women,* vol. 2, pp. 10–11.

1903 • Emily Dunning (1876–1961) devoted her life to the practice of medicine. She became an ambulance surgeon at Gouverneur Hospital in New York City and became the first woman to work in this capacity when she answered her first emergency call in a horse-drawn vehicle on June 29, 1903.

Sources: Read and Witlieb, *The Book of Women's Firsts,* pp. 128–29.

1906 • Mary Adelaide Nutting (1858–1948) was the first American nurse to become a university professor. When Teachers College at Columbia University in New York City established a nursing program in 1899, Nutting was named its first director; in 1906, she was made professor of household administration, a position she held until 1910, when she switched to professor of nursing education. In 1923, she became professor of nursing at the Helen Hartley Foundation, where she remained until her retirement in the summer of 1925.

Sources: James, *Notable American Women,* vol. 2, pp. 642–44; Kane, *Famous First Facts,* p. 435; Nutting and Dock, *History of Nursing, 1907–1912;* Read and Witlieb, *The Book of Women's Firsts,* p. 321.

1908 • Sara Josephine Baker (1873–1945), an American physician, was the founder of the Bureau of Child Hygiene, in New York City in 1908. She worked on behalf of public health issues throughout her life. When she refused a lectureship at New York University because it did not admit women to its graduate programs, the university changed its policy. She was the first woman to earn a doctorate of public health in 1917 from New York University Bellevue Hospital Medical School.

Sources: James, *Notable American Women,* vol. 1, pp. 85–86; Vare and Ptacek, *Mothers of Invention,* pp. 135–39.

c.1910 • Rosalie Slaughter Morton (1876–1968), an American physician, was the first woman to serve as an officer of the American Medical Association. She was also the first woman to become a professor at the Medical School of Columbia University, in 1917.

Sources: Levin, *Women and Medicine,* pp. 192–98; Morton, *A Doctor's Holiday in Iran;* Morton, *A Woman Surgeon.*

Alice Hamilton (1869–1970), an American physician who received her degree from the University of Michigan Medical School in 1893, was the founder of the discipline of industrial medicine. She identified the source of toxic substances in factories and mines. (*See also* **Health: United States, c.1936.**)

Sources: Rolka, *100 Women Who Shaped World History,* p. 72; Vare and Ptacek, *Mothers of Invention,* p. 117.

1910 • Louise Mathilde Powell (1871–1943), an American nurse trained at St. Luke's Hospital in Richmond, Virginia, and at Teachers College at Columbia University, was the first superintendent of nursing at the University of Minnesota School of Nursing, the first such school in any American college or university. The school was established in Minneapolis-St. Paul in 1909, and Powell took up her post when it opened in 1910. She held this position until 1924 when she moved on to Cleveland, Ohio, to become the first dean at Western Reserve University School of Nursing, a position she held until her retirement in 1927.

Sources: Densford, "Louise M. Powell," The University of Minnesota School of Nursing *Alumnae Quarterly,* January 1944; Gray, *Education for Nursing: A History of the University of Minnesota School;* James, *Notable American Women,* vol. 3, pp. 89–90; Wayland, *Louise M. Powell.*

Elinor McGrath was the first female veterinarian, graduating from the Chicago Veterinary College in 1910. McGrath practiced in Chicago for 37 years before moving to Hot Springs, Arkansas, in 1947 to treat alligators and ostriches.

Sources: McCullough, *First of All: Significant Firsts by American Women,* p. 112.

1911 • Mary Elizabeth Bass (1876–1956) was one of the first two women appointed to the faculty of Tulane University's School of Medicine, in 1911. After her retirement in 1941, she devoted her energies to chronicling the history of female physicians in America.

Sources: Bailey, *The Remarkable Lives of 100 Woman Healers and Scientists,* pp. 16–17.

Clara Dutton Noyes (1869–1936) founded the first U.S. school for midwives at Bellevue Hospital in New York City in 1911. Noyes devoted her life to the nursing profession and was active in nursing administration in a large number of organizations throughout her life.

Sources: Read and Witlieb, *The Book of Women's Firsts,* pp. 318–19.

1912 • Lillian Wald (1867–1940) became the first President of the National Organization for Public Health Nursing in 1912. Wald dedicated her life to nursing, to the education of nurses, and to the cause of better public health care.

Sources: Read and Witlieb, *The Book of Women's Firsts,* p. 466; Uglow, *The Continuum Dictionary of Women's Biography,* p. 564.

1913 • Carolyn C. Van Blarcom (1879–1960) was the first female nurse in America to become a licensed midwife. She earned her license in England in 1913 because the United States did not formally train or license midwives.

Sources: Read and Witlieb, *The Book of Women's Firsts,* p. 460.

1914 • Alice Gertrude Bryant (1862–1942) and Florence West Duckering (1869–1951) were the first two women admitted to the American College of Surgeons at the organization's second annual convention on June 22 in Philadelphia, Pennsylvania. They were among approximately 1,000 candidates accepted into the society in 1914.

Sources: Read and Witlieb, *The Book of Women's Firsts,* pp. 73–74, 126.

Bertha Van Hoosen

1915 • Bertha Van Hoosen (1863–1952) was the cofounder and first President of the American Medical Women's Association in 1915. Trained in gynecology, obstetrics, and surgery, Van Hoosen practiced medicine in Chicago, Illinois, and in 1918 was appointed professor and head of obstetrics at Loyola University Medical School.

Sources: Read and Witlieb, *The Book of Women's Firsts,* pp. 463–64; Van Hoosen, *Petticoat Surgeon.*

1916 • Margaret Sanger (1883–1966), with her sister Ethyl Byrne, opened the first birth-control clinic in the nation. The clinic was in Brownsville, a neighborhood of Brooklyn, New York.

Sanger's personal experience and work as a nurse convinced her that women needed to know about birth control so that they could choose the size of their families, especially where poverty was a factor. The education of women was a necessary step in social progress, according to Sanger, who in 1914 began a monthly newsletter, *The Woman Rebel,* which set forth her ideas about the necessity of contraception and birth control. The newsletter was later banned as obscene literature, and Sanger had to flee the country in order to escape imprisonment. Eventually the charges against Sanger were dropped, and in 1916 she returned to the United States, continuing the crusade that became her life's mission. After opening her birth-control clinic, Sanger quickly found herself deeper than ever in controversy. The police shut the facility down because "obscene materials" (contraceptives) were being dispensed, and Sanger spent a year in jail. Although her promotion of birth control brought indictments and arrests, public and court support gradually grew. In 1923, she organized the first American conference on birth control and formed a committee to lobby for birth-control laws, which helped establish clinics around the world. In 1925, she staged an international birth-control conference. By 1930, 55 clinics had been opened across the country. Sanger devoted her life to educating

Margaret Sanger

women about birth control, and in 1953 she was the founder and first president of the International Planned Parenthood Federation.

Sources: Levin, *Women and Medicine,* pp. 214–23; Read and Witlieb, *The Book of Women's Firsts,* pp. 391–93; Rolka, *100 Women Who Shaped the World,* p. 80.

1917 • Augusta Fox Bronner (1881–1966) was the cofounder, with her husband William Healy, of the Judge Baker Foundation in Boston, Massachusetts. This organization was dedicated to the psychological treatment of juvenile delinquents, a cause which Bronner made her life's work.

Sources: Bailey, *The Remarkable Lives of 100 Women Healers and Scientists,* pp. 30-31.

1920 • Louise Pearce (1885–1959), an American physician, was the discoverer of tryparsamide, a drug used to conquer African sleeping sickness in the Congo, a colony of Belgium at the time. She was honored for her research with the Order of the Crown of Belgium in 1920, the King Leopold II Prize in 1950, and the Royal Order of the Lion.

Sources: Levin, *Women and Medicine,* p. 158.

1923 • Gladys Rowena Henry Dick (1881–1963) discovered the bacteria that causes scarlet fever. Dick made her discovery while working with her husband, George Francis, at the University of Chicago. The two also developed the skin test, known as the Dick test, that indicates susceptibility to the disease.

Sources: Bailey, *The Remarkable Lives of 100 Woman Healers and Scientists,* pp. 52–53.

1928 • Mary Breckinridge (1881–1965), who dedicated her life to bringing medical services to isolated mountain families, founded the Frontier Nursing Service. The organization emphasized care for mothers and children and evolved into the American Association of Nurse-Midwives.

Sources: Read and Witlieb, *The Book of Women's Firsts,* p. 65.

1930s • Alice Isabel Bever Bryan (1902–1992) was the first person to develop the concept of bibliotherapy (the reading of books for the promotion of mental health) as a preventative measure for healthy people, as well as a therapy for the mentally ill. Bryan worked as a psychologist at Columbia University in New York City.

Sources: Bailey, *The Remarkable Lives of 100 Woman Healers and Scientists,* pp. 32–33.

1930 • Martha Wollstein (1868–1939) was the first female member of the American Pediatric Society. She was honored in 1930 for her extensive research on meningitis, mumps, pneumonia, and polio.

Sources: James, *Notable American Women,* vol. 3, pp. 642–44; Levin, *Women and Medicine,* p. 48; Read and Witlieb, *The Book of Women's Firsts,* p. 487.

c.1936 • Alice Hamilton (1869–1970), an American physician, was the first woman to win the Lasker Award, a United States Public Health Service award. She was recognized in the mid-1930s for her work in industrial medicine. In 1919, she became the first woman professor at Harvard University's Medical School. (*See also* **Health: United States, c.1910.**)

Sources: Haber, *Women Pioneers of Science,* pp. 12–29; Rolka, *100 Women Who Shaped the World,* p. 72.

1936 • Adah B. Samuels Thoms (1863–1943), a leader in the nursing profession, was the first person to receive the Mary Mahoney Medal from the National Association of Colored Graduate Nurses, in Washington, D.C. She was recognized for her distinguished contributions in her field, particularly for her pioneering book, *Pathfinders: A History of the Progress of Colored Graduate*

Nurses, written during her retirement from active nursing and first published in 1929.

Sources: James, *Notable American Women,* vol. 3, pp. 455–57; Staupers, *No Time for Prejudice: A Story of the Integration of Negroes in Nursing in the United States;* Thoms, *Pathfinders: A History of the Progress of Colored Graduate Nurses.*

1937 • Sara Elizabeth Branham (1888–1962) was the first person to demonstrate that sulfa drugs successfully inhibited the activity of meningococcal bacteria, after a decade of research at the National Institute of Health in Chicago, Illinois.

Sources: Bailey, *The Remarkable Lives of 100 Woman Healers and Scientists,* pp. 26–27.

1938 • Kate Campbell Hurd-Mead (1867–1941) published *A History of Women in Medicine from the Earliest Times to the Beginning of the Nineteenth Century,* becoming the first author to write a comprehensive chronicle of women in medicine.

Sources: Chicago, *The Dinner Party,* p. 191.

1939 • Gerty Theresa Radnitz Cori (1896–1957) was the first woman to synthesize glycogen in a test tube. This revealed how the human body converts sugar into glycogen. She worked with her husband, Carl Cori, at Washington University School of Medicine in St. Louis, Missouri. In 1947, Cori and her husband were awarded the Nobel Prize in medicine for their work. They were only the third husband and wife team to win a Nobel Prize (the first was in 1903, Marie and Pierre Curie, and the second in 1935, their daughter and her husband, Irene and Jean Frederic Joliot-Curie). (*See also* **Science: Biochemists, 1947.**)

Sources: Bailey, *The Remarkable Lives of 100 Woman Healers and Scientists,* pp. 50–51; Kane, *Famous First Facts,* p. 432; Magnusson, *Larousse Biographical Dictionary,* p. 346.

c.1940 • Hattie Elizabeth Alexander (1901–1968) was the first woman to discover an antiserum for influenza meningitis. Working with Michael Heidelberger at Columbia-Presbyterian Medical Center Babies' Hospital in New York City, she discovered the antiserum that has prevented many deaths from this rare disease. She was also the first female president of the American Pediatrics Society.

Sources: Bailey, *The Remarkable Lives of 100 Woman Healers and Scientists,* pp. 6–7; Vare and Ptacek, *Mothers of Invention,* pp. 121–22.

1947 • Martha May Eliot (1891–1978) was the first woman to serve as president of the American Public Health Association. Elected in 1947, Eliot held this office for one term before going on to serve as assistant director general of the World Health Organization from 1949 to 1951.

Sources: Read and Witlieb, *The Book of Women's Firsts,* pp. 142–43; Vare and Ptacek, *Mothers of Invention,* p. 118.

c.1950 • Virginia Apgar (1909–1974) was the first person to become a full professor of anesthesiology. She attained this rank at Columbia University in New York City because of her achievements in neonatal care. In 1952 Apgar

Martha May Eliot

invented the standard newborn scoring system, known as the "Apgar Score," for evaluating general health of infants in the first moments after birth.

Sources: Bailey, *The Remarkable Lives of 100 Woman Healers and Scientists,* pp. 10–11; Vare and Ptacek, *Mothers of Invention,* pp. 133–34.

Myra Adele Logan (1908–1977), an American physician and surgeon, was the first woman to operate on the heart. She was also the first African American woman to be elected a Fellow of the American College of Surgeons.

Sources: Haber, *Women Pioneers of Science,* pp. 97–104.

Dorothy Brown (b. 1919), an American surgeon, was the first black female surgeon to practice in the South. She made a career in private practice and in teaching at Meharry Medical College in Nashville, Tennessee.

Sources: Levin, *Women and Medicine,* p. 232.

Dorothy Hansine Anderson (1901–1963) was the first person to identify cystic fibrosis. She was also the first to devise an easy method for diagnosing the disease in its early stages.

Sources: Vare and Ptacek, *Mothers of Invention,* p. 118.

Helen Brooke Taussig

1950 • Helen Brooke Taussig (1898–1986) was the first woman elected to the Association of American Physicians at the organization's 63rd annual convention in Atlantic City, New Jersey, on May 3. (*See also* **Health: United States, 1965.**)

Sources: Kane, *Famous First Facts,* p. 384.

Lois E. Hinson (b. 1926) was the first female graduate of the University of Georgia College of Veterinary Medicine in Athens, Georgia. Her career contains a number of firsts: she was the first female supervisor in the U.S. Department of Agriculture Federal Meat Inspection Division; the first female inspector in charge of the USDA Federal Meat Inspection Division; the first female veterinary staff officer at the USDA Headquarters of Federal Meat and Poultry Inspection; the first female chief staff veterinarian in the USDA; the first woman to serve as national president of the National Association of Federal Veterinarians; and the first female delegate to the American Veterinary Medical Association House of Delegates.

Sources: O'Neill, *The Women's Book of World Records and Achievements,* p. 33.

1955 • Emma Sadler Moss (1898–1970) became the first woman to be elected president of a major medical society when she assumed the position of president of the American Society of Clinical Pathologists at the organization's 34th annual meeting on October 13. Moss practiced medicine at Charity Hospital in New Orleans, Louisiana.

Sources: Kane, *Famous First Facts,* p. 385; Read and Witlieb, *The Book of Women's Firsts,* p. 300.

1958 • Marion E. Kenworthy (1891–1980) became the first female president of the American Psychoanalytic Association. She had a distinguished career in psychiatry, having been the first director of the mental hygiene clinic of

Janet Graeme Travell

the YWCA (in 1919) and the first female professor of psychiatry at Columbia University (in 1930).

Sources: Read and Witlieb, *The Book of Women's Firsts,* pp. 240–41.

1961 • Janet Graeme Travell (b. 1901) was the first woman to serve as a U.S. president's personal physician. Travell served as the official doctor for President John F. Kennedy and remained in the position of White House Physician until 1965.

Sources: Read and Witlieb, *The Book of Women's Firsts,* pp. 447–48.

1965 • Helen Brooke Taussig (1898–1986) became the first female president of the American Heart Association. Trained as a physician, Taussig taught at Johns Hopkins Medical School in Baltimore, Maryland, specializing in heart surgery. In 1959, she had become the first woman full professor at Johns Hopkins. (*See also* **Health: United States, 1950.**)

Sources: Haber, *Women Pioneers of Science,* p. 10; Levin, *Women and Medicine,* pp. 159–63; Read and Witlieb, *The Book of Women's Firsts,* pp. 437–38; Vare and Ptacek, *Mothers of Invention,* pp. 139–41.

1966 • The first woman to receive a Medicare identification card was Elizabeth "Bess" Wallace Truman (1885–1982), wife of former President Harry S. Truman, on January 20. (Mrs. Truman's card was No. 2.) The cards were presented by President Lyndon Baines Johnson at the Truman Library in Independence, Missouri. Medicare, a national health insurance plan in the United States, was created by Public Law 89–97 on July 30, 1965.

Sources: Kane, *Famous First Facts,* p. 385.

1967 • Jane C. Wright (b. 1919), an American physician and pioneer in chemotherapy, was appointed associate dean and professor of surgery at the New York Medical College in New York City on July 1. Wright was the first African American woman to be appointed to a high post in medical administration.

Sources: Noble, *Contemporary Women Scientists of America,* pp. 117–27.

1971 • Roberta Fenlon (b. 1910), a specialist in internal medicine at the University of California, was the first woman to be elected president of a state medical society.

Sources: Levin, *Women and Medicine,* pp. 8–9.

1973 • Judith Senderowitz (b. 1942) was the first woman to be elected to serve as president of Zero Population Growth, in Washington, D.C. in April. She was well qualified to assume this position, having written a book on population control. At the time, she was working as a liaison office for the Population Institute.

Sources: O'Neill, *The Women's Book of World Records and Achievements,* p. 728.

1975 • May Edward Chinn (1896–1980) was the cofounder of the Susan Smith McKinney Stewart Society in New York City. This organization was designed to promote the role of African American women in medicine. Chinn was also the first African American woman to graduate from the University of Bellevue Medical Center and the first African American woman to intern at Harlem Hospital, both in 1926.

Sources: Bailey, *The Remarkable Lives of 100 Woman Healers and Scientists,* pp. 44–45; Haber, *Women Pioneers of Science,* p. 10.

Julie Roy (b. 1938) was the first woman to succeed in suing her psychiatrist for sexual abuse. Roy filed charges and won her suit against Renatus Hartogs in New York City. Hartogs had persuaded Roy to have sexual intercourse with him as a part of her therapy.

Sources: Read and Witlieb, *The Book of Women's Firsts,* pp. 383–84.

1976 • Rosalyn S. Yalow (b. 1921) became the first woman to receive an Albert Lasker Basic Medical Research Award. She was honored for her pioneering work in the field of radioimmunoassay. Yalow developed a new method for the precise measurement of substances in the blood. In 1977 she became the first American-born woman to receive a Nobel Prize in science. At the beginning of her career in 1945, she was the first female engineer at the Federal Telecommunications Laboratory in New York.

Sources: Levin, *Women and Medicine,* pp. 49–52; McGrayne, *Nobel Prize Women in Science,* pp. 333–55; Noble, *Contemporary Women Scientists of America,* pp. 128–40; Vare and Ptacek, *Mothers of Invention,* pp. 130–32.

1990 • Upon graduating from Stanford University Medical School in May, Lori Cupp became the first female Navaho Indian to become a surgeon. She believes that Navaho culture, which is matriarchal, gives women a sense of power and independence, an asset in a medical specialty in which only 6 percent of the practitioners are women.

Sources: Cohen, "Old Ways and New, in Harmony," *The New York Times* (17 February 1994), B1.

Antionia T. Novello (b. 1944) was the first woman appointed Surgeon General of the United States Public Health Service. She was sworn in by the first woman Supreme Court justice, Sandra Day O'Connor in Washington, D.C.

Sources: Read and Witlieb, *The Book of Women's Firsts,* pp. 317–18.

Literature

Argentina

1916 • Alfonsina Storni (1892–1938), an Argentine poet, is considered the first writer in her country to write from a woman's point of view. She published her first volume of verse (*La inquietud del rosal*) in 1916.

Sources: Chicago, *The Dinner Party,* p. 210; Phillips, *Alfonsina Storni: From Poetess to Poet*; Uglow, *The Continuum Dictionary of Women's Biography,* p. 521.

1931 • Victoria Ocampo (1890–1978), an Argentine writer, was the founder of the important literary periodical *Sur,* in Buenos Aires in 1931. Ocampo is remembered for her vigorous advocacy of modern writers in Argentina. Through her feminist and modernist interests and her friendships with authors such as Virginia Woolf, she introduced Argentine readers to new ideas in contemporary literature.

Sources: Meyer, *Victoria Ocampo: Against the Wind and the Tide*; Uglow, *The Continuum Dictionary of Women's Biography,* p. 410.

Australia

1854 • Charlotte Helen Spence (1825–1910), a feminist reformer, was the first successful female novelist in Australia. Her first book, *Clare Morrison: A Tale of South Australia During the Gold Fever,* appeared in 1854 and was soon followed by many others. Spence continued to write fiction for the next 30 years, while also writing journalism for papers in South Australia and Victoria. An active suffragist, she founded the Effective Voting League in 1895, and in 1897 she became the first woman to run for elected office in her country.

Sources: Schmidt, *400 Outstanding Women of the World,* p. 38; Women Uglow, *The Continuum Dictionary of Women's Biography,* pp. 509–10.

1861 • Australia's first journal to be produced by women was *The Interpreter.* Founded in Melbourne in 1861, this literary magazine was edited by, among others, Harriet Clisby and Caroline Dexter.

Sources: Uglow, *The Continuum Dictionary of Women's Biography,* p. 129.

(*See also* **Literature: England, 1908.**)

Austria

Twelfth century • Frau Ava (d. 1127) was the first woman to compose biblical and evangelical stories in German, and the first woman poet to write in German. Her work in the vernacular made Christian ideas available to the common people in the twelfth century. Among her works are *The Life of Christ,* and *The Anti-Christ and The Last Judgment.*

Sources: Chicago, *The Dinner Party,* p. 136; Schmidt, *400 Outstanding Women of the World,* p. 41.

1900 • Marie Ebner-Eschenbach (1830–1916) was the first woman to receive an honorary doctorate from the University of Vienna. She was honored in 1900 for her literary work, which included poetry and drama as well as the novels and stories for which she is best known.

Sources: Kunitz and Colby, *European Authors 1000–1900,* pp. 248–50; Uglow, *The Continuum Dictionary of Women's Biography,* p. 183.

1905 • Rosa Mayreder (1858–1938) was the first Austrian feminist theorist. Her books, *A Survey of the Woman Problem,* first published in German in 1905, and *Geschlecht und Kultur,* which appeared in 1923, contain a wide variety of theoretical and critical essays on feminism and ideas of her time. Mayreder was also an ardent pacifist and an artist as well as a writer of both fiction and non-fiction.

Sources: Uglow, *The Continuum Dictionary of Women's Biography,* p. 367.

Canada

1769 • Frances Brooke (1724–1789) was the first Canadian novelist. She published her novel, *The History of Emily Montague,* in 1769.

Sources: Chicago, *The Dinner Party,* p. 195.

Chile

Early twentieth century • Gabriela Mistral (1889–1957) is considered the founder of the modern poetry movement in Chile. She worked as a teacher and in her country's government, but she was also an important poet and was honored for her writing with the Nobel Prize for literature in 1945.

Sources: Chicago, *The Dinner Party,* p. 210; Weiser and Arbeiter, *Womanlist,* p. 449.

China

First century • Pan Chao (45–115) was China's first great female scholar. She is remembered as the writer who completed a work begun by her father and continued by her brother, the great *History of the Han Dynasty*. She is also known for her book of advice to women, *Nu Chien*.

Sources: Swann, *Pan Chao: Foremost Woman Scholar of China*; Uglow, *The Continuum Dictionary of Women's Biography*, pp. 416–17.

Early twentieth century • Bing Xin (b. 1902), the pen name of Xie Wanying, was the first Chinese woman to become a successful writer in the twentieth century. She began to publish in 1919 and is known both for her poetry and prose, for her work for children as well as for adults. Her subjects include the problems of being a woman and social oppression. Although her reputation suffered during the Cultural Revolution (1967–1972), except for this period, she has been honored in China throughout her life.

Sources: Uglow, *The Continuum Dictionary of Women's Biography*, p. 66.

1981 • Jie Zhang (b. 1937), a Chinese author, was the first woman to write a book officially declared the most popular novel in China. This designation was accorded to her *Leaden Winds* in 1981, the year in which it was published. In 1987, a collection of her short stories, *As Long as Nothing Happens, Nothing Will*, appeared in English translation.

Sources: Uglow, *The Continuum Dictionary of Women's Biography*, p. 601.

Colombia

1878 • Soledad Acosta de Samper (1833–1903) was the founder of the Colombian feminist journal *La Mujer* and served as its first editor from 1878 through 1881. She wrote historical fiction, biography, and history, and she dedicated her life to feminist causes.

Sources: Uglow, *The Continuum Dictionary of Women's Biography*, pp. 3–4.

Egypt

1959 • Aisha Abdel Rahman (b. 1920) was the first woman to research the women surrounding the prophet Mohammed. Between 1959 and 1966, she published, under the pseudonym Bint-al-Shah, three books about Mohammed's wives, daughters, and mother.

Sources: Uglow, *The Continuum Dictionary of Women's Biography*, p. 2.

1972 • Nawal El Saadawi (b. 1930) was the first woman in Egypt to call for revolutionary changes in the position of Egyptian women within the family and as wage-earners. Trained as a physician, El Saadawi published her controversial feminist study *Women and Sex* in 1972. She went on to a career as a journalist and novelist. In 1982 she founded the Pan-Arab Women's Organization.

Sources: Uglow, *The Continuum Dictionary of Women's Biography*, p. 189.

England

1393 • Julian of Norwich (1342–1413) was the first English woman to write a spiritual work. Her book, *XVI Revelations of Divine Love,* composed in 1393, some 20 years after the visions it recorded, reflected the spirit of the Middle Ages.

Sources: Chicago, *The Dinner Party,* p. 145; Echols and Williams, *An Annotated Index of Medieval Women,* p. 279; Schmidt, *400 Outstanding Women of the World,* p. 131.

1438 • Margery Kempe (b. c.1373) was the author of the first autobiography in English. An uneducated woman, she dictated the story of her life to scribes between 1431 and 1438. Her account, *The Boke of Margery Kempe,* was discovered in an English library in 1934.

Sources: Chicago, *The Dinner Party,* p. 152; Shattock, *The Oxford Guide to British Women Writers,* p. 245.

Katherine Philips was referred to as "The Matchless Orinda."

Mid-seventeenth century • Katherine Philips (1631–1664), who wrote poetry under the pseudonym "Orinda," was the founder of a London literary salon called the Society of Friendship, which included such luminaries as Jeremy Taylor and Henry Vaughn.

Sources: Garnett and Gosse, *Illustrated History of English Literature,* p. 153; Shattock, *The Oxford Guide to British Women Writers,* pp. 335–36.

Late seventeenth century • Aphra Behn (1640–1689) was the first English woman to earn her own living by writing. The author of several plays and 18 novels, Behn defended her own work and the rights of women writers against hostile criticism.

Sources: Chicago, *The Dinner Party,* p. 163; Magnusson, *Larousse Biographical Dictionary,* p. 129; Shattock, *The Oxford Guide to British Women Writers,* p. 245.

1708 • Elizabeth Elstob (1683–1756) was the first woman to become a scholar of Anglo-Saxon. In 1708 she began to publish her translations, and, in her prefaces she argued for women's right to study.

Sources: Brink, *Female Scholars*; Shattock, *The Oxford Guide to British Women Writers,* p. 152–53; Uglow, *The Continuum Dictionary of Women's Biography,* p. 190.

1711 • Mary de la Rivière Manley (1663–1724), one of the first English women to become a professional writer, became the first female editor of *The Examiner,* succeeding Jonathan Swift, in 1711. She is remembered for her novels and for her collaboration with Swift on Tory pamphlets.

Sources: Magnusson, *Larousse Biographical Dictionary,* p. 963; Shattock, *The Oxford Guide to British Women Writers,* pp. 278–79.

1740s • Hannah Allgood Glasse (1708–1770) was the first person to write a cookbook for the English housewife. Her guide, *The Art of Cooking Made Plain and Simple,* reached a fourth edition by 1751 and a tenth by 1784, remaining in print until 1824.

Sources: Todd, *A Dictionary of British and American Women Writers, 1660–1800,* pp. 136–37; Uglow, *The Continuum Dictionary of Women's Biography,* p. 227.

1763 • Catharine Macaulay (1731–1791) was the first woman to write an authoritative history of England. She published the first book of her eight-volume *History of England* in 1763; the last volume appeared 20 years later in 1783. Macaulay created controversy because of her republican sympathies (she supported the American Revolution, for example), but she was much admired by feminists of her time, among them Mary Wollstonecraft.

Sources: Shattock, *The Oxford Guide to British Women Writers,* pp. 273–74; Schmidt, *400 Outstanding Women of the World,* p. 244.

1770s • Hester Lynch Thrale (1741–1821) (or Piozzi), an English intellectual who established a small but elite literary salon in London, became in the late 1770s the first person to introduce the novelist Fanny Burney to literary society. Thrale is also remembered as a close friend of the writer Samuel Johnson, who lived for 16 years in her house and with whom she traveled to Wales and France in 1774 and 1775.

Sources: Magnusson, *Larousse Biographical Dictionary,* p. 1164; Shattock, *The Oxford Guide to British Women Writers,* pp. 338–39.

1792 • Mary Wollstonecraft (1759–1797) was the first Englishwoman to challenge Rousseau's notions of female inferiority. Her influential feminist book, *Vindication of the Rights of Women,* was first published in London in 1792. Here Wollstonecraft argues for the equality of women and men, women's right to education and employment, and their suitability as companions with men. This work continues to be regarded as germinal by modern feminists. Wollstonecraft died of puerperal fever (commonly called "childbed fever") after the birth of her only child, Mary Wollstonecraft Shelley, the author of *Frankenstein.*

Sources: Magnusson, *Larousse Biographical Dictionary,* p. 1577; Schlueter and Schlueter, *An Encyclopedia of British Women Writers,* pp. 482–83; Todd, *A Dictionary of British and American Women Writers 1660–1800,* pp. 330–33.

Mary Wollstonecraft

Late eighteenth century • Janc Austen (1775–1817), the first major female novelist, was also the first female novelist to be admitted to the "canon." Her finely crafted narratives focus on women's lives and the marriage plot, the only script available to women of her time.

Jane Austen was born in the parsonage where her father was a rector, in Hampshire, England. She and her sister Cassandra were educated at home and enjoyed a happy, cheerful childhood. Jane began writing at an early age and completed *Pride and Prejudice* in 1797, followed by *Sense and Sensibility* almost immediately, and *Northanger Abbey* in 1798. None of these works were accepted by a publisher, although many reviewed them. After the death of her father in 1804, Austen stopped writing until she and her sister moved to Chawton Cottage in a village near her birthplace. It was there that she began writing again after finding a publisher for both *Sense and Sensibility* and *Pride and Prejudice. Emma* appeared in 1815, and her works were favorably analyzed in

This drawing depicts Jane Austen's writing desk at Chawton Cottage.

Hannah More

Quarterly Review by Sir Walter Scott. Jane Austen is buried at Winchester Cathedral.

Sources: Chicago, *The Dinner Party,* p. 194; Garnett and Gosse, *Illustrated History of English Literature,* p. 153; Shattock, *The Oxford Guide to British Women Writers,* pp. 14–15.

1795 • The work of Hannah More (1745–1835) led to the founding of the Religious Tracts Society. She is remembered for her poetry and drama but particularly for her religious writing, especially her influential *Cheap Repository Tracts,* published in London between 1795 and 1798.

Sources: Shattock, *The Oxford Guide to British Women Writers,* pp. 302–4; Schmidt, *400 Outstanding Women of the World,* pp. 139–40; Williams, *Queenly Women, Crowned and Uncrowned,* pp. 39–56.

1837 • Harriet Martineau (1802–1876) was the first English woman to publicize in her own country the American abolitionist movement. Based on her travels in the United States in 1834 through 1836, *Society in America* was published in England in 1837. Martineau is remembered as a distinguished writer of both fiction and nonfiction and as an advocate of feminist causes.

Sources: Magnusson, *Larousse Biographical Dictionary,* p. 980; Nadel and Fredeman, *Dictionary of Literary Biography,* pp. 227–33.

1843 • Sara Coleridge (1802–1852), daughter of the poet Samuel Taylor Coleridge (1772–1834), was the first person to edit her father's works, a task she began after the death of her husband in 1843.

Sources: Magnusson, *Larousse Biographical Dictionary,* p. 330; Shattock, *The Oxford Guide to British Women Writers,* p. 111.

1848 • Cecil Frances Alexander (1818–1895) was the first English woman to become a hymn writer. She began to publish verse in 1842, but her 1848 collection *Hymns for Little Children,* which included "All Things Bright and Beautiful" (1848), established her reputation for many popular hymns still sung today.

Sources: Magnusson, *Larousse Biographical Dictionary,* p. 980; Shattock, *The Oxford Guide to British Women Writers,* pp. 5–6.

1850s • Elizabeth Barrett Browning (1806–1861), whose reputation as an English poet in her own time exceeded that of her famous husband Robert Browning, was the first woman to be seriously considered for the position of Poet Laureate. She reached the height of her career with the publication of *Sonnets from the Portuguese* in 1851 and *Aurora Leigh* in 1857.

Sources: Shattock, *The Oxford Guide to British Women Writers,* pp. 71–3; Schmidt, *400 Outstanding Women of the World,* p. 149–50.

1857 • Elizabeth Cleghorn Gaskell (1810–1865), an English novelist who developed a friendship with Charlotte Brontë, was the first person to write a biography of Charlotte Brontë, which she published in Manchester in 1857, after two years of research.

Sources: Shattock, *The Oxford Guide to British Women Writers,* pp. 176–78; Uglow, *The Continuum Dictionary of Women's Biography,* p. 221.

1859 • Isabella Mayson Beeton (1837–1865), famous as a writer of recipes, was the first editor of *Mrs. Beeton's Book of Household Management,* which appeared in 30 monthly parts beginning in 1859–60. Published in book form in 1861, it was extremely popular and went through many editions before the end of the century.

Sources: Magnusson, *Larousse Biographical Dictionary,* p. 128; Shattock, *The Oxford Guide to British Women Writers,* pp. 32–33.

Elizabeth Cleghorn Gaskell

1867 • Ellen Wood (1814–1887), a conservative Victorian author who wrote under the pen name of Mrs. Henry Wood, was the founder and first editor of *Argosy,* in Norwood, England, in 1867. This literary periodical featured Wood's popular, melodramatic, and conservative stories. Wood is particularly

Elizabeth Barrett Browning

remembered for her sentimental novels, among them *East Lynne,* which first appeared in 1870 and by 1900 had sold over 500,000 copies.

Sources: Shattock, *The Oxford Guide to British Women Writers,* pp. 472–73; Uglow, *The Continuum Dictionary of Women's Biography,* p. 588.

1877 • Lady Anne King Blunt (1837–1917) was the first English woman to travel in and describe the Arabian peninsula. She left England for Turkey, Algiers, and Egypt in 1877, and in 1878 published her book, *The Bedouin Tribes of the Euphrates.*

Sources: Uglow, *The Continuum Dictionary of Women's Biography,* p. 73.

1884 • Edith Nesbit (1858–1924), an English writer best known for her children's novels, among them *The Five Children and It* (1902) and *The Railway Children* (1906), was a cofounder (with her husband Hubert Bland and a circle of literary friends that included H. G. Wells and George Bernard Shaw) of the Fabian Society, a socialist organization, in London in 1884.

Sources: Shattock, *The Oxford Guide to British Women Writers,* pp. 311–12; Uglow, *The Continuum Dictionary of Women's Biography,* pp. 398–99.

1890 • Daisy Ashford (1881–1972) was the first woman to write a novel at the age of nine, in 1890. Her book, *The Young Visitors, or Mr. Salteena's Plan,* was first published in 1916 and has been a great success ever since.

Sources: Shattock, *The Oxford Guide to British Women Writers,* pp. 10–11; Uglow, *The Continuum Dictionary of Women's Biography,* pp. 30–31.

1892 • Alice Christiana Thompson Meynell (1847–1922), an English poet and essayist, was the first woman proposed as Poet Laureate, at Tennyson's death in 1892. She lost to Alfred Austin, appointed in 1896. She is remembered as a minor poet, whose published works include *Preludes* (1875) and collections of essays, *The Rhythm of Life* (1893), *The Colour of Life* (1896), and *Hearts of Controversy* (1917). Meynell maintained friendships with many important writers from those of the Rossetti circle to D.H. Lawrence.

Sources: Magnusson, *Larousse Biographical Dictionary,* p. 1008; Uglow, *The Continuum Dictionary of Women's Biography,* p. 376.

1894 • Constance Garnett (1861–1946), who taught herself Russian while recovering from a difficult childbirth in 1892, was the first person to translate major Russian writers into English. Her translations of Turgenev, Tolstoy, Dostoyevsky, Chekhov, and Gogol appeared between 1894 and 1928.

Sources: Schlueter and Schlueter, *An Encyclopedia of British Women Writers,* pp. 185–86; Shattock, *The Oxford Guide to British Women Writers,* pp. 175–76.

1908 • Ethel Florence Lindesay Robertson (1870–1946), an Australian author who wrote under the male pseudonym of Henry Handal Richardson, was the first person to publish a novel in England that treated homosexuality openly. In 1908, she published her first book, *Maurice Guest,* based on her own experiences, whose central character was modeled on Eleanor Duse. She is considered by some people to be Australia's finest novelist.

Sources: Uglow, *The Continuum Dictionary of Women's Biography,* p. 457.

Mabel Louise Atwell (1879–1964) became the first woman to illustrate *Mother Goose,* in 1908. Born and educated in London, Atwell also illustrated an edition of *Alice in Wonderland* in 1910 and editions of Andersen's and Grimm's fairy stories in 1913 and 1925.

Sources: Uglow, *The Continuum Dictionary of Women's Biography,* pp. 33–34.

1915 • Dorothy Richardson (1873–1957) was the first woman to write a modernist "stream-of-consciousness" novel. In 1915 she published *Pointed Roofs,* the first volume in the 11-volume spiritual autobiography of the character she called Miriam Henderson. Richardson published the whole saga as *Pilgrimage* in 1938.

Sources: Shattock, *The Oxford Guide to British Women Writers,* pp. 359–60; Uglow, *The Continuum Dictionary of Women's Biography,* pp. 456–57.

1917 • Katherine Mansfield (1888–1923), a New Zealander remembered for her short stories and her friendships with D.H. Lawrence and John Middleton Murray, was the first woman to have her work published by the Hogarth Press in London, run by Virginia and Leonard Woolf. Published in 1917, *Prelude* was her most famous work and included stories based on her childhood in New Zealand.

Sources: Schlueter and Schlueter, *An Encyclopedia of British Women Writers,* pp. 314–15; Uglow, *The Continuum Dictionary of Women's Biography,* pp. 352–53.

Virginia Woolf (1882–1941), one of the most important twentieth-century novelists, was the cofounder, with her husband, Leonard Woolf, of the Hogarth Press, in Bloomsbury in London in 1917. This press published nearly all of her work as well as that of friends, among them T.S. Eliot and Katherine Mansfield. Woolf is particularly remembered for her fiction, characterized by modernist stream-of-consciousness techniques, and for her two important feminist book-length essays, *A Room of One's Own* (1929) and *Three Guineas* (1938).

Sources: Shattock, *The Oxford Guide to British Women Writers,* pp. 473–75; Uglow, *The Continuum Dictionary of Women's Biography,* pp. 589–90.

1920s • Beatrix Potter (1861–1943), known to the world as the author of *Peter Rabbit* and other children's books, was the first female president of the Herdwick Sheep Breeders' Association. Brought up in London, Potter was a self-taught writer, artist, and naturalist. Beginning in 1913, when Potter married and moved to England's Lake District, she also devoted herself to farming and conservation, becoming an important influence in the founding of the National Trust.

Sources: Schlueter and Schlueter, *An Encyclopedia of British Women Writers,* pp. 370–71; Uglow, *The Continuum Dictionary of Women's Biography,* p. 439.

1928 • (Marguerite) Radclyffe Hall (1886–1943) was the author of the first book to be judged obscene because of its sympathetic depiction of lesbian love. In 1928, Hall's novel, *The Well of Loneliness,* was found obscene by an English judge in a famous London trial. Among Hall's defenders were Virginia Woolf and Richard Aldington.

Sources: Baker, *Our Three Selves: A Life of Radclyffe Hall*; Chicago, *The Dinner Party,* p. 205; Shattock, *The Oxford Guide to British Women Writers,* pp. 201–2; Uglow, *The Continuum Dictionary of Women's Biography,* pp. 244–45.

Vita Sackville-West (1892–1962) was the first woman whose life was chronicled in fiction as both male and female. Her friend Virginia Woolf published a novel, *Orlando: A Biography,* in 1928, and based the central character on Sackville-West. Orlando is born a man and lives as a man for half the book, then wakes up as a woman and continues his/her life.

Sources: Chicago, *The Dinner Party,* p. 210; Uglow, *The Continuum Dictionary of Women's Biography,* pp. 473–74.

1939 • Margaret Storm Jameson (1891–1983), a prolific English writer known for her journalism as well as her many novels, was the first woman to serve as president of the British section of PEN, an international society of authors. She was elected in 1939 and served through the war until 1945. During this period, in addition to supervising the club's regular activities, Jameson worked unstintingly on behalf of refugee writers.

Sources: Schlueter and Schlueter, *An Encyclopedia of British Women Writers,* pp. 249–51; Uglow, *The Continuum Dictionary of Women's Biography,* pp. 280–81.

1955 • Nancy Freeman Mitford (1904–1973), an English novelist, was the first person to popularize the social terms "U" and "non-U" (to refer snobbishly to those who are upper-class and those who are not), in her edition of A.S.C. Ross's *Encounter* in 1955.

Sources: Schlueter and Schlueter, *An Encyclopedia of British Women Writers,* pp. 330–31; Uglow, *The Continuum Dictionary of Women's Biography,* p. 382.

1968 • Anita Brookner (b. 1928) was the first woman to hold the Slade Professorship at Cambridge University, in 1968. Brookner is a novelist and an international authority on eighteenth-century painting. She is the author of *Watteau* (1968), *The Genius of the Future* (1971), and *Jacques-Louis David* (1981). She won the Booker Prize for literary achievement for her novel *Hotel du Lac* in 1986; Brookner's other works of fiction include *Family and Friends* (1985) and *Friends from England* (1987).

Sources: Magnusson, *Larousse Biographical Dictionary,* p. 211; Schlueter and Schlueter, *An Encyclopedia of British Women Writers,* pp. 62–64.

1972 • Carmen Therese Callil (b. 1938), an Australian who has made her career in English publishing, was the founder of Virago Press in London in 1972. This publishing company has been a powerful force in modern British feminism.

Sources: Uglow, *The Continuum Dictionary of Women's Biography,* pp. 103–4.

1974 • Jan Morris (b. 1926) was the first woman to earn her reputation as a male travel writer. She was born James Morris, served in the British Army, and worked as a foreign correspondent. As a man, she married and had children, but since a sex-change operation, completed in 1974, she has lived as a woman. She is known for her courageous autobiography (*Conundrum,* 1977) and for many books about history and travel.

Sources: Uglow, *The Continuum Dictionary of Women's Biography,* p. 389; Weiser and Arbeiter, *Womanlist,* p. 219.

Finland

1885 • Minna Canth (1848–1897), born Ulrika Vilhelmina Johnsson, was the first woman to write a book against the Church's attitude toward women in Finland. In 1885 she published *The Worker's Wife,* an ardent feminist critique, followed in 1888 by *Children of Misfortune.* As a playwright, her works were mainly psychological dramas about women.

Sources: Chicago, *The Dinner Party,* p. 187; Magnusson, *Larousse Biographical Dictionary,* p. 257; Schmidt, *400 Outstanding Women of the World,* p. 166.

France

Twelfth century • Marie de France (c.1150–c.1190) was the first woman to be a professional writer in France. She wrote poetry and short narratives and collected folktales, legends and songs. Throughout her work she presented a female perspective on the activities she recorded.

Sources: Chicago, *The Dinner Party,* p. 141; Uglow, *The Continuum Dictionary of Women's Biography,* pp. 357–58; Weiser and Arbeiter, *Womanlist,* p. 216.

Early seventeenth century • Madeleine de Sable (1598–1678) introduced and popularized the practice of the maxim, the written condensation of life's experiences in the form of an epigram, which has become a characteristically French form. De Sable also presided over a literary salon in Paris.

Sources: Chicago, *The Dinner Party,* p. 207.

1611 • Marie de Vivonne, Marquise de Rambouillet (1588–1665) was the first woman to organize and host a great salon in France. For over 50 years, beginning in 1611, she opened her Paris home to the important writers of her age. Those attending were encouraged to share ideas in a sophisticated and virtuous environment, and de Rambouillet insisted on the equality of the sexes in her home.

Sources: Chicago, *The Dinner Party,* p. 207; Magnusson, *Larousse Biographical Dictionary,* p. 1213; Schmidt, *400 Outstanding Women of the World,* pp. 173–74.

1804 • Madame de Staël (1766–1817), a French Romantic writer known for her revolutionary sympathies, in 1884 became the first woman to be exiled from France by Napoleon. He saw her influence, through her salon and her political writing, as dangerous to his rule. She lived in Switzerland until Napoleon's abdication in 1814.

Sources: Kunitz and Colby, *European Authors 1000–1900,* pp. 881–83; Uglow, *The Continuum Dictionary of Women's Biography,* p. 164.

1844 • Anne of Austria (1601–1666) was the first French queen to become a central character in a novel. Anne, a clever and passionate woman who was the wife of Louis XIII, is one of the protagonists in French novelist Alexandre Dumas's *The Three Musketeers* (1844).

Sources: Uglow, *The Continuum Dictionary of Women's Biography,* p. 21.

1933 • Gertrude Stein (1874–1946), an American expatriate who lived in Paris and patronized the arts, was the first person to write her own biography in the guise of an autobiography of her lover. Her famous book, *The Autobiography of Alice B. Toklas,* was published in 1933.

Sources: Chicago, *The Dinner Party,* pp. 205–6; Uglow, *The Continuum Dictionary of Women's Biography,* p. 516.

1938 • Nathalie Tcherniak Sarraute (b. 1920) was the first woman to write an "anti-novel." Educated as a lawyer in Paris, Oxford, and Berlin, she was influenced by Virginia Woolf and in 1938 published her "anti-novel," *Tropismes,* a fictional work that explored the dimensions of consciousness in a series of sketches about bourgeois life. Sarraute gave up a career in law in 1940 and devoted herself to her writing, developing her techniques of description that rejected traditional literary devices.

Sources: Magnusson, *Larousse Biographical Dictionary,* p. 1297.

1945 • Sidonie Gabrielle Claudine Colette (1873–1954) was the first woman to become a member of the Académie Goncourt. Known always by only her last name, Colette became famous not only for her literary work but also for her flamboyant personality. A woman who led a dramatic and original life, she experienced several marriages and affairs, as well as careers on the stage and in business.

Sources: Briggs, *A Dictionary of 20th Century Biography,* pp. 128–29; Uglow, *The Continuum Dictionary of Women's Biogrpahy,* p. 132.

1963 • Yvette Roudy (b. 1929), a French politician and feminist, was the first person to translate the work of the American feminist writer Betty Friedan into French. In 1963 she published her translation of Friedan's *The Feminine Mystique*. Roudy is also remembered for her role as a champion of women's rights in various posts in the Mitterand government during the 1980s.

Sources: Uglow, *The Continuum Dictionary of Women's Biography,* p. 466.

1965 • Christiane Rochefort (b. 1917), a French writer and feminist, many of whose works have been made into films, was the first person to translate the work of John Lennon into French. In 1965, she published his book *In His Own Write* as *En Flagrant Délire.*

Sources: Uglow, *The Continuum Dictionary of Women's Biography,* p. 462.

1969 • Hélène Cixous (b. 1937), one of the most influential of contemporary French intellectuals, was the cofounder of the literary periodical *Poétique* in 1969. A professor of literature, Cixous is particularly interested in the relationship between psychoanalysis and language.

Sources: Brosman, *Dictionary of Literary Biography,* vol. 83, pp. 52–61; Uglow, *The Continuum Dictionary of Women's Biography,* pp. 125–26.

Colette

1976 • Xavière Gauthier (b. 1942), a French feminist and university professor, was the founder of the feminist journal *Sorcières,* in Paris in 1976. She has written several books on the nature of female language and sexuality.

Sources: Uglow, *The Continuum Dictionary of Women's Biography,* p. 222.

1980 • Marguerite Yourcenar (1903–1987) was the first female member of the prestigious Académie Française. She was honored with election in 1980 for her career's work as a writer in French.

Sources: Read and Witlieb, *The Book of Women's Firsts,* p. 501; Savigneau, *Marguerite Yourcenar: Inventing a Life,* p. 386.

Germany

Late eighth century • Gisela (d. 807), Charlemagne's sister, was the director of the first major convent scriptorium. At a Benedictine abbey that she founded in Germany, Gisela supervised female scribes who created 13 manuscripts, including a three-volume commentary on the Psalms.

Sources: Chicago, *The Dinner Party,* p. 136.

Tenth century • Hrosvintha of Gandersheim (935–c.1000), Germany's earliest poet and dramatist, was the first playwright in medieval Europe. Educated in the convent of Gandersheim, she began to write as a young woman and is best known for her series of plays that deal with the conflict between spiritual aspiration and the temptation of sin. Her manuscripts were discovered around 1500 by Conrad Celtis.

Sources: Chicago, *The Dinner Party,* pp. 72–73; Echols and Williams, *An Annotated Index of Medieval Women,* p. 220.

c.1802 • Amelia Holst, an early nineteenth-century feminist, was the first German woman to write a book advocating the education of women. Her work offered a theoretical foundation for later German feminists' social and political activities.

Sources: Chicago, *The Dinner Party,* p. 188.

1931 • Ricarda Huchs (1864–1947), a distinguished German novelist and historian, was the first woman admitted to the Prussian Academy of Literature, in 1931. She resigned two years later in protest over the academy's expulsion of Jewish writers. In 1947, she served as the first president of the first congress of German writers in Berlin. Throughout her life, Huchs was an ardent feminist and an intellectual leader.

Sources: Uglow, *The Continuum Dictionary of Women's Biography,* p. 268.

1932 • Helen Diner (1874–1948) was the pseudonym of Bertha Eckstein-Diener, the first person to write a matriarchal history of culture. Her *Mothers and Amazons,* published in Germany in 1932, argued that primitive societies were matriarchal and investigated these cultures with the intention of providing women with an understanding of their tradition.

Sources: Chicago, *The Dinner Party,* p. 211.

1946 • Nelly Sachs (1891–1970) was the first German poet to focus her work on the concentration camp experience. In 1940, she and her mother fled Nazi Germany and settled in Sweden; the rest of the family perished as persecuted Jews in the camps. Sachs' first volume of verse, *In den Wohnungen des Todes,* appeared in 1946 and her second in 1949. Both explored the tragedy of European Jewry under Hitler. Her next two books, published in 1957 and 1959, linked this experience with broader Jewish themes. Although Sachs' work is not well known in the West, she received the Nobel Prize for literature (with Shmuel Agnon) in 1966.

Sources: Uglow, *The Continuum Dictionary of Women's Biography,* p. 473.

1959 • Ingeborg Bachmann (1926–1973), an Austrian writer, was appointed the first professor of poetics at the University of Frankfurt in Germany in 1959. Her work focuses on the plight of women who are often helpless in a world of successful, egotistic men.

Sources: Uglow, *The Continuum Dictionary of Women's Biography,* p. 40.

Ghana

1970s • (Christina) Ama Ata Aidoo (b. 1942) is the first female writer from Ghana to achieve an international reputation. Her fiction, poetry, and drama have established her achievement as an African author and an advocate for women's rights and self-expression.

Sources: Blamires, *A Guide to 20th Century Literature in English,* p. 4; Uglow, *The Continuum Dictionary of Women's Biography,* p. 10.

Greece

Seventh century B.C. • Sappho (b. c.650 B.C.), the famous Greek poet from the island of Lesbos, was the first female writer to create the personal, subjective lyric. Her poems, few of which survive today except in fragments, often focus on her relationships with other women—her beloved daughter, her circle of companions, and her intimate friends.

Sources: Goring, *Larousse Dictionary of Writers,* pp. 855–56; Magnusson, *Larousse Biographical Dictionary,* p. 1296; Schmidt, *400 Outstanding Women of the World,* pp. 211–12.

Twelfth century B.C. • Phantasia is reputed to have invented, along with another poet, the heroic meter, the hexameter. She is said to have gone from Greece to Egypt in pre-Homeric times, around the twelfth century B.C.

Sources: Chicago, *The Dinner Party,* p. 116.

Mid-seventeenth century • Alexandra Mavrokordatou (1605–1684), a Greek intellectual from Constantinople, was the first woman to introduce the idea of a literary salon in Greece. She turned her house into a meeting place for writers, artists, and diplomats from Greece and elsewhere.

Sources: Uglow, *The Continuum Dictionary of Women's Biography,* p. 367.

1880s • Soteria Aliberty (1847–1929), a Greek teacher and feminist, was the first person to compile biographies of Greek women. In the 1880s she published "Biographies of Greek Women" in the *Women's Newspaper* in Athens. In the 1890s she founded the first feminist association in Greece, called Ergani Athena.

Sources: Uglow, *The Continuum Dictionary of Women's Biography,* p. 13.

Late nineteenth century • Sappho Leontias (1832–1900), a Greek feminist and teacher, was the founder and first editor of the literary periodical *Euridice.* She encouraged female contributors and welcomed works written in vernacular Greek. For many years she served as head of girls' schools on the Greek islands of Samos and Smyrna and was one of many Greek feminists who emphasized the education of women as a means of improving their status in Greek society.

Sources: Uglow, *The Continuum Dictionary of Women's Biography,* p. 323.

Guatemala

1983 • Rigoberta Menchu (b. 1959), a Guatemalan political activist and Quichua Indian, was the first woman to draw international attention to the oppression of the people in Guatemala. Her autobiographical account of political struggle, *I, Rigoberta* was published in 1984. In recognition of her work, Menchu received the Nobel Peace Prize in 1992.

Sources: Dallas Morning News (17 October 1992), p. A1; Uglow, *The Continuum Dictionary of Women's Biography,* pp. 372–73.

Hungary

Early twentieth century • Margit Kaffka (1880–1918) was the first great Hungarian female writer. A feminist and a pacifist, she started writing fiction in 1912. Her pioneering work explored the inner psychology of her protagonists. Her female heroes often reject their traditional roles but are frustrated by the lack of alternatives for women. She died during the influenza epidemic which followed World War I.

Sources: Uglow, *The Continuum Dictionary of Women's Biography,* p. 291.

Ireland

c.1910 • Beatrice Grimshaw (1871–1853), an Irish travel writer who explored the South Pacific beginning in 1906, was the first woman to go up the Sepik and Fly rivers in Papua New Guinea. She wrote more than 40 books about her adventures among the islands of Southeast Asia and Papua New Guinea.

Sources: Uglow, *The Continuum Dictionary of Women's Biography,* p. 238.

1920s • Peig Sayers (1873–1958), an Irish storyteller and singer living in a small community on Great Blasket Island in Ireland, was the first person to record a large number (over four hundred) of Irish stories and folksongs. These were collected by the Irish Folklore Commission in the 1920s. Sayers's two volumes of autobiography, dictated in Gaelic in 1936 and 1970 respectively, vividly recount a harsh way of life and are now considered classics.

Sources: Uglow, *The Continuum Dictionary of Women's Biography,* p. 481.

Israel

1975 • Simone de Beauvoir (1908–1986), a French feminist, was the first woman to win the International Jerusalem Prize. The prize, which she received in April 1975, is given in recognition of an author whose work has made an outstanding contribution to the concept of the freedom of the individual in society.

Sources: Uglow, *The Continuum Dictionary of Women's Biography,* pp. 153–54; Wallechinsky and Wallace, *The People's Almanac,* p. 1129.

Italy

First century • The poet Sulpicia (63 B.C.–14 A.D.) was the first Roman woman to encourage other women to write poetry as accomplished as that of their Greek models. She is best known for a substantial poem on married love.

Sources: Chicago, *The Dinner Party,* p. 127.

Fifteenth century • Giovanna Dandolo, a Venetian aristocrat, was the first woman to encourage the printing of books. Many volumes printed in Venice in the late fifteenth century bear expressions of gratitude to her.

Sources: Uglow, *The Continuum Dictionary of Women's Biography,* p. 146.

1451 • Isotta Nogarola (1418–1466), an Italian scholar living in Venice, was the first woman to write a treatise in defense of Eve's part in the fall from grace. In 1451 she published *De Pari aut Impari Evae atque Adae Peccato.*

Sources: Echols and Williams, *An Annotated Index of Medieval Women,* p. 245; Uglow, *The Continuum Dictionary of Women's Biography,* pp. 404–5.

1843 • Cristina Trivulzio (1808–1871), an Italian revolutionary and writer in both Italian and especially French, was the founder of the *Gazetta Italiana,* in Paris in 1843, and the newspaper *Italia,* in Turin in 1850. She was an active supporter of a united Italy and campaigned for this cause in her own and other journals as well as in her books and in her participation in the uprisings of 1848.

Sources: Uglow, *The Continuum Dictionary of Women's Biography,* p. 544.

1899 • Sibilla Aleramo (1876–1960), a writer known for her feminism throughout her life, was the first editor of the Italian journal *L'Italia Femminile ("Female Italy"),* in 1899. Her most famous work is her autobiographical novel *Una Donna,* which caused a sensation when it was published in 1906.

Sources: Uglow, *The Continuum Dictionary of Women's Biography,* pp. 12–13.

Japan

Early eleventh century • Lady Shikibu Murasaki (978–1030), a woman of the Kyoto court, was the first known novelist. She merits this distinction for her narrative, *The Tale of Genji,* which recounts in 54 volumes the romantic and adventurous experiences of a royal family. Probably written over several years, *The Tale of Genji* has been called the finest work of Japanese literature and one of the greatest novels of the world.

Sources: Newsweek (14 November 1994), p. 59; Uglow, *The Continuum Dictionary of Women's Biography*, p. 392.

1050s • Sarashina (1008–1060), the daughter of a minor nobleman, was the first Japanese woman to write a diary now considered to be a classic. Just before her death, she wrote *Sarashina Nikki,* an account of her journey from Shimosa to Kyoto in 1021.

Sources: Uglow, *The Continuum Dictionary of Women's Biography,* pp. 479–80.

Twentieth century • Higuchi Ichiyo (1872–1896), a Japanese novelist known especially for her portrayal of the emotions of women and children, was the first and only woman to be represented in the Museum of Contemporary Literature in Yokohama, Japan. She grew up in poverty in Tokyo and died young of tuberculosis.

Sources: Uglow, *The Continuum Dictionary of Women's Biography,* p. 273.

1901 • Akiko Yosano (1878–1942), a Japanese poet, was the first modern female writer in her country to express her emotions in print. With her first collection of poems, *Midaregami,* published in 1901, she broke the centuries-old ban against women's written expression of their feelings.

Sources: Uglow, *The Continuum Dictionary of Women's Biography,* p. 596.

1972 • Sawako Ariyoshi (1921–1984) was the first Japanese author to write a bestseller. Her 1972 novel, *Kokotsuno Hito (The Twilight Years),* which sold over two million copies on publication, deals with the problems of old age and is now a modern classic in Japan.

Sources: Uglow, *The Continuum Dictionary of Women's Biography,* p. 27.

Middle East

2300 B.C. • Enheduanna, a Sumerian priestess, was the first known author. (Sumer, a region in ancient Babylonia, is part of modern-day Iraq.) Around 2300 B.C., she inscribed her hymns to the moon goddess on stone tablets in an ancient system of writing called "cuneiform."

Sources: Chicago, *The Dinner Party,* p. 107; Uglow, *The Continuum Dictionary of Women's Biography,* p. 191.

Nigeria

1972 • Buchi Emecheta (b. 1944) was the first person to write about women's problems in Nigeria. Her first novel, published in 1972, was based on her own experiences. She emphasizes women's issues in the context of history, social change, and civil war. In addition to fiction for adults, her work includes several books for children.

Sources: Uglow, *The Continuum Dictionary of Women's Biography,* p. 190.

1974 • Flora Nwapa (b. 1931), a Nigerian novelist educated as a teacher in Nigeria and Scotland, was the first woman in her country to be commissioned by her government to set up a publishing company and printing press. After this nation gained its independence in 1974, Nwapa was assigned this work in order to produce children's books, novels, and stories about local life.

Sources: Uglow, *The Continuum Dictionary of Women's Biography,* p. 407.

Norway

1855 • Jacobine Camilla Collett (1813–1895), a feminist novelist, was the first Norwegian woman to expose the injustices suffered by women both within and outside marriage. Her book, *Daughter of an Official,* was published in 1855 and is considered the first Norwegian social novel. Her later works, *Last Leaves* (1869–1873), *From Those Who Are Silent* (1877), and *In the Long Nights* (1862), she writes about women's emancipation.

Sources: Kunitz and Colby, *European Authors 1000–1900,* p. 184; Schmidt, *400 Outstanding Women of the World,* pp. 308–9.

Twentieth century • Sigrid Undset (1882–1949), Norway's foremost female novelist, was the first major Norwegian woman writer to have nearly all of her work translated into English. Her first novel, *Jenny* (1911), focused on problems confronting contemporary women, but Undset is best known for her historical novels, which explore women's issues within the context of faith. Her conversion to Roman Catholicism in 1924 marked an increase in the influence of religion on her writing. Her three-volume masterpiece, *Kristin Lavransdatter* (1920–1922) tells the story of medieval love and religion. She next published a four-volume work, (1925–1927), *Olav Audunssön, Gymadenia* (1929), and *Den trfaste hustru* (The Faithful Spouse, 1936). Undset was awarded the Nobel Prize for literature in 1928.

Sources: Magnusson, *Larousse Biographical Dictionary,* p. 1489; Uglow, *The Continuum Dictionary of Women's Biography,* p. 552.

Peru

1884 • Clorinda Matto de Turner (1854–1909) in 1884 wrote the first guide to literature for Peruvian women. A dedicated feminist, Matto de Turner also worked on behalf of the Andean Indians. She founded *El Recreo,* a periodical for women, in 1876 and the weekly *El Peru Illustrado* in 1887. Her novels, such as *Birds without a Nest* (1889), convey a vivid picture of Peruvian life and argue against the oppression of native Peruvians and women.

Sources: Uglow, *The Continuum Dictionary of Women's Biography,* pp. 365–66.

Russia

1783 • Ekaterina Romanovna Dashkova (1743–1810), a Russian princess favored by Catherine II, was in 1783 appointed the first president of the Russian Academy, founded to preserve and study the Russian language. In the same year, Dashkova also became the first woman to serve as Director of the Academy of Arts and Sciences in St. Petersburg.

Sources: Uglow, *The Continuum Dictionary of Women's Biography,* p. 148.

1910 • Anna Akhmatova (1889–1967), acclaimed as Russia's greatest female poet, was the first woman in the Acmeist movement, which she founded with her husband Gumilov in 1910. The movement emphasized Russian traditions in reaction to contemporary Symbolism.

Sources: Uglow, *The Continuum Dictionary of Women's Biography,* pp. 11–12.

1916 • Inesse Armand (1874–1920), a Russian revolutionary and feminist, in 1916 became the first person to translate Lenin's works into French. She was also the founder and first director of the Women's Bureau Zhenotdel. She went on to direct the first International Conference of Women Communists. She is buried in Red Square.

Sources: Uglow, *The Continuum Dictionary of Women's Biography,* pp. 27–28.

South Africa

1884 • Olive Schreiner (1855–1920) was the first South African novelist to write about the oppression of women in her country. Her first book, the autobiographical fiction *The Story of an African Farm,* was published in London in 1884. In it, she passionately denounced the treatment of women in South Africa and attacked traditional Christianity. Schreiner is remembered for this book, her significant study *Women and Labor* (1911), her pacifist activities, and her friendship with the English sexologist Havelock Ellis.

Sources: Uglow, *The Continuum Dictionary of Women's Biography,* pp. 485–86.

1970s • Bessie Head (1937–1986), one of modern Africa's most famous novelists, was the first "coloured" South African writer to establish an international reputation. The daughter of a white mother and a black father, Head was a victim of apartheid who fled South Africa for Botswana in her early 20s. She settled there and wrote the works for which she is now known, among them *When Rain Clouds Gather* (1969), *Maru* (1971), and *Question of Power* (1973).

Sources: Blamires, *A Guide to 20th Century Literature in English,* p. 117–18; Uglow, *The Continuum Dictionary of Women's Biography,* p. 252.

Spain

1906 • Emilia Pardo-Barzán (1852–1921), believed by some scholars to be the greatest Spanish novelist of the nineteenth century, was the first woman to chair the literature section of the Atheneum in Madrid, Spain. She was awarded this honor in 1906 for her achievements as a novelist. When she was later appointed professor of Romance literature at the Central University of Madrid, the university faculty protested her appointment and male students boycotted her classes.

Sources: Chicago, *The Dinner Party,* p. 210; Schmidt, *400 Outstanding Women of the World,* pp. 360–61.

Sweden

Early eighteenth century • Hedwig Nordenflycht (1718–1763) was the first female poet to achieve national importance in Sweden. She collected her poems in "yearbooks" under the title, *Womanly Thoughts of a Shepherdess of the North.*

Sources: Chicago, *The Dinner Party,* p. 195; Kunitz and Colby, *European Authors 1000–1900,* pp. 688–89.

1856 • Frederika Bremer (1801–1865) was the first feminist writer in Sweden. Her book, *Hertha,* published in 1856, became the textbook for the Swedish women's movement. Bremer was a lifelong advocate of peace and social legislation. In 1885, Bremer became the first woman in her country to have a national women's organization named after her.

Sources: Chicago, *The Dinner Party,* p. 187; Kunitz and Colby, *European Authors 1000–1900,* pp. 120; Schmidt, *400 Outstanding Women of the World,* pp. 368–370.

1909 • Selma Lagerlöf (1858–1940) was the first woman to receive the Nobel Prize for literature, in her native Stockholm, in 1909. Honored for her sagas and legendary narratives, she was also the first woman to become a member of the Swedish Academy.

Sources: Chicago, *The Dinner Party,* p. 209; Uglow, *The Continuum Dictionary of Women's Biography,* p. 310.

Selma Lagerlöf

Turkey

1912 • Halide Edib Adivar (1883–1964), a writer and Turkish nationalist, was the first woman elected to the Ojak, the Turkish nationalist club, in 1912. Adivar worked in Syria and Lebanon during World War I and after Turkish independence dedicated herself to writing. In 1938, Adivar became professor of English at the University of Istanbul.

Sources: Adivar, *Memoirs*; Uglow, *The Continuum Dictionary of Women's Biography,* p. 6.

United States

1650 • Anne Bradstreet (1612–1672) was the first U.S. woman to become a published poet. Her collection of verse was published in England in 1650, the first volume of original poetry to be written in New England.

Sources: Chicago, *The Dinner Party,* p. 167; James, *Notable American Women,* vol. 1, pp. 222–23; Mainiero, *American Women Writers,* vol. 1, pp. 214–16.

1682 • Mary White Rowlandson (c.1635–c.1678) was the first woman to write and publish a book in the American colonies. Anonymously published in Cambridge, Massachusetts in 1682, *The Narrative of the Captivity and Restoration of Mrs. Mary Rowlandson* relates the story of Rowlandson's capture by Narragansett Indians in 1676. She was ransomed after three months of marching through the wilderness.

Sources: Read and Witlieb, *The Book of Women's Firsts,* pp. 382–83; Todd, *A Dictionary of British and American Women Writers 1160–1800,* p. 274.

Eighteenth century • Phillis Wheatley (1753–1784) was the first black poet in America. Wheatley was bought directly off a slave ship when she was eight years old by Mrs. John Wheatley, who taught her to read and write.

Sources: Chicago, *The Dinner Party,* p. 168; James, *Notable American Women,* vol. 3, pp. 573–74; Todd, *A Dictionary of British and American Women Writers 1160–1800,* p. 321.

Late eighteenth century • Hannah Adams (1755–1831) was the first U.S. woman who sought to support herself by her writing. Well-regarded by her contemporaries in Medfield, Massachusetts, Adams compiled two books of historical data: *View of Religions: An Alphabetical Compendium of the Various Sects* (1784) and *A Summary History of New England* (1799). Adams received 50 copies of *View of Religions* that she sold herself. In 1791, the second edition, which was also printed in Great Britain, was successful enough to provide Adams with a comfortable income. By the fourth edition, the title had become *Dictionary of Religions.* She also wrote three religious works: *The Truth and Excellence of the Christian Religion Exhibited* (1804), *History of the Jews* (1812), and *Letters on the Gospels* (1824). Her autobiography was published posthumously in order to gain a small income for her sister.

Hannah Adams

Sources: James, *Notable American Women,* vol. 1, pp. 9–11; Todd, *A Dictionary of British and American Women Writers 1160–1800,* p. 28.

1808 • Jane Aiken (1764–1832), a Philadelphia printer, bookbinder, and bookseller, was the first U.S. woman to print an edition of the Bible. In 1808, she published the four-volume Thompson Bible, the first English translation of the Septuagint.

Sources: James, *Notable American Women,* p. 26; Thomas, *History of Printing in America,* pp. 77–78.

1826 • Lydia Maria Child (1802–1880) was the founder of the first American periodical for children. She began publishing the *Juvenile Miscellany* in

1826. Child is known not only for her own fiction but for her writing and political work on behalf of the cause of abolition.

Sources: Mainiero, *American Women Writers,* vol. 1, pp. 354–55; Read and Witlieb, *The Book of Women's Firsts,* pp. 88–89.

1833 • Lydia Maria Child (1802–1880) was the first woman to write an antislavery book in the United States. In 1833 Allen and Ticknor in Boston published *An Appeal in Favor of That Class of Americans Called Africans.* Child continued to be active on behalf of black Americans both during the time of slavery and after emancipation.

Sources: Kane, *Famous First Facts;* Mainiero, *American Women Writers,* vol. 1, pp. 354–55; Uglow, *The Continuum Dictionary of Women's Biography,* p. 121.

1839 • Caroline Matilda Stansbury Kirkland (1801–1864) was the first author to write sustained realistic fiction about the American frontier. She based her novels and stories on her experiences as a pioneer with her family in Livingston County, Michigan, between 1836 and 1843, when she returned to her native New York City. Her first novel, an autobiographical narrative, *A New Home—Who'll Follow? or, Glimpses of Western Life,* was published in 1839. Her second book, *Forest Life,* appeared in 1842. Throughout the 1850s her work continued to be printed in many eastern periodicals.

Sources: James, *Notable American Women,* vol. 2, pp. 337–39; Mainiero, *American Women Writers,* vol. 2, pp. 471–73.

1840s • Margaret Fuller (1810–1850), a feminist and a writer associated with the American Transcendentalists, was the first female foreign correspondent for *The Dial,* an important literary journal, in the 1840s. She is best known for her feminist tract, *Woman in the Nineteenth Century,* published in 1845.

Sources: Chicago, *The Dinner Party,* p. 195; Uglow, *The Continuum Dictionary of Women's Biography,* p. 414.

1848 • Elizabeth Fries Lummis Ellet (1812–1877), a historian, was the first U.S. writer to emphasize the role of women in the development of the United States. Her first book, *The Women of the American Revolution,* was published in two volumes in 1848. Ellet added a third volume in 1850. She went on to write *A Domestic History of the American Revolution* (1850), *Pioneer Women of the West* (1852), and *The Court Circles of the Republic* (1869).

Sources: James, *Notable American Women,* vol. 1, pp. 569–70; Mainiero, *American Women Writers,* vol. 1, pp. 581–83.

1852 • Harriet Beecher Stowe (1811–1896), a U.S. writer, was the first woman to advance the American abolitionist cause through a popular novel. Her *Uncle Tom's Cabin: or Life Among the Lowly* first appeared in 1852. It sold three million copies before the outbreak of the Civil War, and Lincoln is reputed to have been influenced by it in his Emancipation Proclamation.

Sources: Magnusson, *Larousse Biographical Dictionary,* p. 1406; Mainiero, *American Women Writers,* vol. 4, pp. 175–78.

1860 • Mary Elizabeth Farnsworth Mears (1830–1907), a U.S. writer born in Massachusetts, was the first poet in Wisconsin. Raising a family in Fond du Lac, she published her first volume of verse under the pen name "Nellie Wildwood" in 1860. She is also remembered as the mother of the sculptor Helen Mears (1872–1916).

Sources: James, *Notable American Women,* vol. 2, p. 522.

1867 • Lucy McKim Garrison (1842–1877) was the first person to collect American slave songs. She visited the South Carolina Sea Islands in 1862 and began the process of writing down the songs she heard. She annotated these with William Francis Allen and Charles Pickard Ware and in 1867 published *Slave Songs of the United States,* the first such collection.

Sources: Uglow, *The Continuum Dictionary of Women's Biography,* p. 220.

1869 • Alice Cary (1820–1871), a U.S. writer remembered for her regionalist story and poems about rural Ohio, became the first president of Sorosis, a pioneering women's club in New York City, in 1869. She and her sister Phoebe, with whom she lived throughout her life, were active abolitionists sympathetic to the women's movement.

Sources: Clemmer, *A Memorial of Alice and Phoebe Cary*; James, *Notable American Women,* vol. 1, pp. 295–97; Mainiero, *American Women Writers,* vol. 1, pp. 308–10.

1873 • Mary Elizabeth Mapes Dodge (1831–1905), an author of children's literature, was the first editor of the highly influential children's magazine, *St. Nicholas,* which began publication by Scribner's in New York City in November 1873. She published the work of leading American and British writers and artists and made the magazine an impressive literary and financial success.

Sources: James, *Notable American Women,* vol. 1, pp. 495–96; Mainiero, *American Women Writers,* vol. 1, pp. 518–19.

1876 • Julia Evelina Smith (1792–1886) was the first woman to translate the Bible. Aided in this task by her knowledge of Latin, Greek, and Hebrew, she published her translation in 1876 in Hartford, Connecticut.

Sources: Kane, *Famous First Facts,* p. 111.

1878 • Anna Katherine Green (1846–1935) was the first woman to write detective stories. She established her literary career with the publication of *The Leavenworth* in 1878 and went on to use her detective, Ebenezer Gryce, and his occasional assistant, Amelia Butterworth, in several subsequent novels. Green also invented the female detective Violet Strange.

Sources: Uglow, *The Continuum Dictionary of Women's Biography,* p. 235.

c.1884 • Sarah Orne Jewett (1849–1909), a U.S. writer best known for her work in literary regionalism, was the first person to write extensively about her native state of Maine. She wrote several novels and collections of stories, beginning with *A Country Doctor* in 1884. Her work detailed the flora and fauna of the New England region and the customs of its people, especially women, in the late nineteenth century. Jewett is remembered particularly for her autobiographical collection of interrelated stories, *The Country of the Pointed Firs,* first published in 1896.

Sources: James, *Notable American Women,* vol. 2. pp. 274–76; Mainiero, *American Women Writers,* vol. 2, pp. 401–4.

1886 • Isabel Florence Hapgood (1850–1928), who began her career with translations from the French, was the first U.S. woman to translate the works of great Russian writers into English. In Boston, Massachusetts, in 1886, she published her first book of Russian works, which included pieces by Tolstoy and Gogol. She traveled in Russia between 1887 and 1889 and met many Russian literary figures, Tolstoy among them. When she returned to the United States, she translated Kovalevsky and Gorky, and she is remembered particularly for her 16-volume translation *The Novels and Stories of Ivan Turgenev,* published in 1903 and 1904.

Sources: James, *Notable American Women,* vol. 2, pp. 129–30.

1891 • Mabel Loomis Todd, an Amherst neighbor and friend of Emily Dickinson, was the first person to edit and publish in book form the poetry of this important U.S. writer. Only seven poems of Dickinson's were published during her lifetime (1830–1886).

Sources: James, *Notable American Women,* vol. 3, pp. 468–69; Mainiero, *American Women Writers,* vol. 4, pp. 245–47.

1892 • Frances Ellen Watkins Harper (1825–1911) was the first black American to publish a book. Her novel about the post–Civil War South, *Iola Leroy, or Shadows Uplifted,* appeared in 1892. A free black, she worked for the abolition of slavery and, after the Civil War, for black civil rights, helping to found the National Association of Colored Women in 1896.

Sources: Chicago, *The Dinner Party,* p. 182; James, *Notable American Women,* vol. 2, pp. 137–39; Smith, *Black Firsts,* pp. 420–21.

1898 • Ida A. Harper (1851–1931), a close friend of Susan B. Anthony, was the first person to edit Anthony's work and write her biography, thus championing the feminist cause. Harper published the first two volumes of *The Life and Work of Susan B. Anthony* in 1898; the third volume appeared ten years later. After Anthony's death in 1906, Harper completed the final two volumes of the six-volume *History of Woman Suffrage.* Anthony had written the first three volumes, and the two women had worked on the fourth volume together.

Sources: Mainiero, *American Women Writers,* vol. 2, pp. 246–48; Uglow, *The Continuum Dictionary of Women's Biography,* pp. 248–49.

1899 • Kate O'Flaherty Chopin (1851–1904) was the first U.S. woman to write a novel about a woman's repressed sexuality. In 1899, Chopin published *The Awakening,* a book that angered the public by its frank portrayal of sexual desire and suicide.

Sources: Mainiero, *American Women Writers,* vol. 1, pp. 358–60; Uglow, *The Continuum Dictionary of Women's Biography,* p. 123.

Early twentieth century • Natalie Clifford Barney (1876–1972) was the first U.S. woman to have a salon in Paris. She and her comrades frequently met at her home, which served as a center for women and literary intellectuals of all sorts, including lesbians who were open about their sexuality. Among Barney's friends were author Djuna Barnes and artist Romaine Brooks.

Sources: Chicago, *The Dinner Party,* p. 204; Uglow, *The Continuum Dictionary of Women's Biography,* p. 49.

1908 • Julia Ward Howe (1819–1910), the author of "The Battle Hymn of the Republic," became the first woman to be elected to the American Academy of Arts and Letters on January 28, 1908.

Sources: Kane, *Famous First Facts,* p. 39; Mainiero, *American Women Writers,* vol. 2, pp. 340–42; Read and Witlieb, *The Book of Women's Firsts,* p. 218.

1909 • Charlotte Perkins Gilman (1860–1935), the American feminist author, founded her own journal, *The Forerunner,* for which she served as both editor and writer from 1909 until 1916. She is remembered particularly for her famous story of a woman undergoing a mental breakdown, "The Yellow Wallpaper," published in 1892.

Sources: Mainiero, *American Women Writers,* vol. 2, pp. 131–33; Uglow, *The Continuum Dictionary of Women's Biography,* p. 224.

1912 • Harriet Monroe (1860–1936) founded *Poetry: Magazine of Verse,* the first journal devoted solely to modern poetry, in Chicago, Illinois, in 1912. She championed modernist causes and is remembered as the first to publish the Imagist poets, among them H.D., Richard Aldington, F.S. Flint, and Ezra Pound, who served for a period as her "foreign correspondent."

Sources: James, *Notable American Women,* vol. 2. pp. 562–64; Mainiero, *American Women Writers,* vol. 3, pp. 205–7; Read and Witlieb, *The Book of Women's Firsts,* pp. 296–97.

1913 • Amy Lowell (1874–1925), a U.S. poet from an old New England family, was the first woman to lecture on modernist verse in the United States, in Boston in 1913. Excited by the "Imagist" poems by H.D., Richard Aldington, and Ezra Pound, she began to correspond with these young poets who were writing the first modernist work in England. She, with Harriet Monroe of *Poetry,* who published their work in Chicago, became the American champions of what became the modernist movement in literature.

Sources: James, *Notable American Women,* vol. 2, pp. 434–37; Mainiero, *American Women Writers,* vol. 3, pp. 43–45.

1916 • Maud Howe Elliot (1854–1948) and her sister Laura Howe Richards (1850–1943), daughters of the abolitionist and women's suffrage advocate Julia Ward Howe, were the first women to win the Pulitzer Prize for biography. In 1916, they were awarded this honor for their biography of their mother, *Julia Ward Howe,* (1819–1910) published in 1915.

Sources: Mainiero, *American Women Writers,* vol. 3, pp. 467–69; Read and Witlieb, *The Book of Women's Firsts,* p. 143.

Julia Ward Howe's "Battle Hymn of the Republic" became a rallying song for the Union troops during the Civil War.

Edith Newbold Jones Wharton

1921 • Zona Gale (1874–1938), a prolific writer of novels, biographies, essays and plays, became the first woman to win the Pulitzer Prize for drama when she was honored in 1921 for her play *Miss Lulu Bett,* which opened on Broadway the previous year.

Sources: Mainiero, *American Women Writers,* vol. 2, pp. 97–98; Read and Witlieb, *The Book of Women's Firsts,* p. 171.

Edith Newbold Jones Wharton (1862–1937) was the first woman to receive the Pulitzer Prize for fiction. She was honored in 1921 for her novel *The Age of Innocence* (1920). Wharton was also the first woman to be chosen as a grand

Pearl Sydenstricker Buck

officer in the Legion of Honor (in 1923) and the first woman to receive an honorary degree from Yale University (also in 1923).

Sources: Mainiero, *American Women Writers,* vol. 4, pp. 368–74; Read and Witlieb, *The Book of Women's Firsts,* pp. 477–78.

1923 • Edna St. Vincent Millay (1892–1950) was the first woman to receive the Pulitzer Prize in poetry. She was honored for her fourth book of verse, *The Ballad of the Harp-Weaver* (1923). She is remembered particularly for her intimate sonnets.

Sources: Mainiero, *American Women Writers,* vol. 3, pp. 173–76; Read and Witlieb, *The Book of Women's Firsts,* pp. 290–91.

1926 • Marianne Craig Moore (1887–1972), an important modernist poet, was the first woman to serve as editor of *The Dial,* in New York City from 1926 to 1929. Her generous personality and sharp eye for literary details shaped the poetry that was published in this significant periodical, giving the journal an international and lasting influence.

Sources: Magnusson, *Larousse Biographical Dictionary,* p. 1037; Mainiero, *American Women Writers,* vol. 3, pp. 216–18.

1935 • Pearl Sydenstricker Buck (1892–1973) was the first American woman to win a Nobel Prize for literature. She received this honor in 1935 in recognition for her novels that vividly depicted Chinese life, the most famous of which was *The Good Earth,* published in 1931.

Sources: Magnusson, *Larousse Biographical Dictionary,* p. 224; Mainiero, *American Women Writers,* vol. 1, pp. 267–71; Read and Witlieb, *The Book of Women's Firsts,* pp. 74–75; *The World Book Encyclopedia,* p. 551.

Margaret Petherbridge
Farrar

1942 • Margaret Petherbridge Farrar (1897–1984) became the first editor of the *New York Times* crossword puzzle on February 15, 1942. In 1924 she wrote, with F. G. Hartswick and Prosper Buranelli, the first book of crossword puzzles. A 1919 graduate of Smith College, in 1926 she married John Farrar, cofounder of the publishing house of Farrar, Strauss & Giroux.

Sources: Read and Witlieb, *The Book of Women's Firsts,* pp. 149–50.

1945 • Louise Bogan (1897–1970) in 1945 became the first woman to be appointed by the Library of Congress in Washington, D.C., as consultant in poetry in English. A distinguished poet, Bogan also wrote literary criticism and an autobiography, *Journey Around My Room,* published posthumously in 1981.

Sources: Mainiero, *American Women Writers,* vol. 1, pp. 183–86; Read and Witlieb, *The Book of Women's Firsts,* pp. 58–59.

1950 • A native of Topeka, Kansas, Gwendolyn Brooks (b. 1917) was the first African-American woman to win the Pulitzer Prize for poetry. She was awarded the prize in 1950 for her second volume of verse, *Annie Allen.*

Sources: Gaymon, *215 African American Women You Should Know About*; Mainiero, *American Women Writers,* vol. 1, pp. 241–43.

1959 • Lorraine Hansberry (1930–1965) was the first African-American woman to have a play she had written produced on Broadway in New York City. Her work, *A Raisin in the Sun,* appeared in 1959. It was also the first production by a black writer to receive the New York Drama Critics Circle Award.

Sources: Chicago, *The Dinner Party,* p. 209; Uglow, *The Continuum Dictionary of Women's Biography,* pp. 247–48.

1960 • Esther Forbes (1891–1967), novelist and historian, was honored for her life's work in 1960 when she became the first woman to be elected to the American Antiquarian Society. Forbes wrote many historical novels and is perhaps best known for her children's novel, *Johnny Tremain* (1943).

Sources: Read and Witlieb, *The Book of Women's Firsts,* pp. 161–62.

On May 25, 1960, the American-born poet Hilda Doolittle (1886–1961), who lived most of her life in Europe, was the first woman to receive an award from the American Academy of Arts and Letters. She was recognized for her contributions beginning with her Imagist poems in 1912. She is known not only for her verse (including her war poems in *Trilogy* in 1944–1946 and her epic poem *Helen in Egypt* in 1961) but for her autobiographical novel *Bid Me to Live* (1960).

Sources: Friedman and DuPlessis, *Signets,* p. 45; Magnusson, *Larousse Biographical Dictionary,* p. 431; Uglow, *The Continuum Dictionary of Women's Biography,* p. 172.

1963 • Jessica Lucy Mitford (b. 1917), an English author who settled in the United States and became known for her investigative journalism, was the first person to expose the American funeral business. Her book, *The American Way of Death,* published in 1963, is considered a masterpiece of its kind.

Sources: Uglow, *The Continuum Dictionary of Women's Biography,* pp. 381–82.

1974 • Adrienne Cecile Rich (b. 1929), a U.S. lesbian feminist writer known for her poetry and essays, was the first woman to reject the National Book Award, given to her in 1974 for her volume of verse *Diving into the Wreck.* She rejected it as an individual but accepted it with Alice Walker and Audrey Rich on behalf of all women. She has made her career as a radical and imaginative thinker, author, and teacher.

Sources: Uglow, *The Continuum Dictionary of Women's Biography,* p. 456.

1979 • Barbara Wertheim Tuchman (1912–1989) was the first female president of the American Academy and Institute of Arts and Letters. She was elected in 1979 in part as a tribute to her illustrious career in letters. In 1963, she was the first woman to receive the Pulitzer Prize for general nonfiction for *The Guns of August.*

Sources: Read and Witlieb, *The Book of Women's Firsts,* p. 452; Tuchman, *Practicing History*.

1983 • Novelist Alice Walker (b. 1944) was the first person to use the term *womanist,* which she claimed had wider implications and was stronger and more inclusive than the term *feminist.* Walker developed the implications of this term in her collection of autobiographical and reflective essays *In Search of Our Mothers' Gardens,* (1983). Walker's novel, *The Color Purple* (1982), was the first novel by a black woman to win the American Book Award and the Pulitzer Prize (both in 1983) and to be made into a major motion picture (by Steven Spielberg in 1985). Walker is also responsible for rediscovering the African-American writer and anthropologist Zora Neale Hurston.

Sources: Smith, *Black Firsts,* p. 416; Uglow, *The Continuum Dictionary of Women's Biography,* pp. 564–65.

1993 • Novelist Toni Morrison (b. 1931) became the first African-American woman to win the Nobel Prize in literature on December 7, 1993. Morrison, who taught at Princeton University, was also the recipient of a Pulitzer Prize in 1988 for her novel *Beloved* (1987).

Sources: New York Times (8 October 1993), p. A1.

Maya Angelou (b. 1928) was the first woman poet to read from her work at a presidential inauguration. Angelou is perhaps best known for her award-winning biography *I Know Why the Caged Bird Sings.* Just as Robert Frost read from his work at John F. Kennedy's inauguration in 1961, Bill Clinton asked Angelou to read from her verse at his inauguration on January 20, 1993. Angelou read with passion her poem "On the Pulse of Morning," composed especially for the occasion.

Sources: The Guardian (25 January 1993), p. F5.

Rita Dove

Rita Dove (b. 1952) was the first African-American to be named Poet Laureate of the United States on May 18, 1993. At age 40, Dove is also the youngest person ever chosen for the honor. A native of Akron, Ohio, Dove was earlier the recipient of a Pulitzer Prize (1987) for her volume of poetry, *Thomas and Beulah* (1986).

Sources: New York Times (19 May 1993).

Media

Magazines and Journals

c.1740 • Eliza Haywood (1693–1756), an English novelist and playwright, was also the publisher of *The Female Spectator,* in London in the 1740s and 1750s. She thus became the first woman to edit a periodical for women.

Sources: Uglow, *The Continuum Dictionary of Women's Biography,* p. 251; Whicher, *The Life and Romances of Haywood.*

1828 • Sarah Josepha Hale (1788–1879) became the first female editor of the first magazine for women in the United States. The magazine, first published in Boston, Massachusetts, in January 1828, was called "Ladies' Magazine." In 1837, the magazine headquarters moved to Philadelphia and became *Godey's Lady's Book,* and by 1860 it had the largest circulation for a magazine of its kind in America.

Sources: National Cyclopedia of American Biography, vol. 3, p. 357; Read and Witlieb, *The Book of Women's Firsts,* pp. 190–91; Uglow, *The Continuum Dictionary of Women's Biography,* pp. 243–44.

Sarah Josepha Hale was born in Newport, New Hampshire on October 24, 1788. When her husband, David Hale, died, she was left to support five children alone, which she did with her writing. She first published a volume of poetry, and followed with a novel, *Northwood.* In addition to her association with the women's magazine, *Godey's Lady's Book,* Sarah Josepha Hale also published *Dictionary of Poetical Quotations, The Ladies' Wreath* (a collection of works by English and American women writers), *Women's Record* (a collection of biographies of notable women), and many other works. She died in Philadelphia on April 30, 1879.

SARAH HALE

1833 • Abigail Goodrich Whittelsey (1788–1858) was the first editor of the first American magazine for mothers. She began to edit the newly formed *Mother's Magazine* in Utica, New York, in 1833. She served as editor until 1848.

Sources: Read and Witlieb, *The Book of Women's Firsts,* pp. 480–81.

1852 • Joana Paula Manso de Noronha (1819–1875) was the founder of the influential feminist periodical *O Jornal das Senhoras,* in Rio de Janeiro in 1852. She reported, among other topics, examples of women's progress she had experienced during a trip to the United States in 1846. The journal continued to appear until 1855.

Sources: Lavrin, *Latin American Women*; Uglow, *The Continuum Dictionary of Women's Biography,* p. 406.

1867 • Mary Louise Booth (1831–1889), a U.S. writer, was the first person to serve as editor of *Harper's Bazaar* in New York City. This magazine, initially a sixteen-page family weekly directed especially to women, featured fashion news and serial fiction by British and American authors. By 1877, it had a circulation of 80,000.

Sources: James, *Notable American Women,* vol. 1, pp. 207–8; Spofford, *Our Famous Women,* pp. 117–33.

1874 • Violante Atabalipa de Bivar e Vellasco, a Brazilian feminist, was the founder of the women's periodical *O Domingo,* in Rio de Janeiro. Journals such as this one were important voices for feminist causes in Brazil.

Sources: Lavrin, *Latin American Women*; Uglow, *The Continuum Dictionary of Women's Biography,* p. 406.

1888 • Josephina Alvares de Azevedo was the founder of the feminist journal *A Familia,* in Rio de Janeiro, Brazil. More radical than most of its predecessors, this periodical supported women's rights and worked to raise its readers' consciousness of their oppression.

Sources: Lavrin, *Latin American Women,* 1978; Uglow, *The Continuum Dictionary of Women's Biography,* p. 406 .

1890 • Anna Kulisciov (1854–1925), an Italian feminist who worked throughout her life for socialist causes, was the cofounder and the first coeditor, with her partner Filippo Turati, of the socialist journal *Critica Sociale,* in Milan, Italy. Interested in the problem of women's social and economic inferiority, Kulisciov earned a degree in medicine and practiced among the working classes. From the turn of the century on, she worked for women's right to vote, and in 1912 she helped to form the Unione Femminile Nazionale Socialista.

Sources: Uglow, *The Continuum Dictionary of Women's Biography,* p. 307.

1892 • The first women's magazine in Egypt, *al-Fatah (The Young Woman),* debuted in November 1892. As founding editor Hind Nawfal described it, it was the "first of its kind under the Eastern sky," and she promised to "adorn its pages with pearls from the pens of women." Nawfal's magazine was the first of many Arabic women's magazines in Egypt that came to be known as al-majallat al-nisa'iyya (women's journals).

Source: Baron, *The Women's Awakening in Egypt: Culture, Society, and the Press,* pp. 1, 14.

1899 • Esther Azhari Moyal (1873–1948) was the first Syrian Jewish woman to found a women's magazine in Cairo, Egypt. Most of the other early editors of the women's press in Egypt were Syrian Christians. Involved in women's associations and concerned with international women's affairs, Esther Moyal organized a small group of Syrian women to mount an exhibit at the World Columbian Exposition in Chicago in 1893, despite being told they would have no official government support. Moyal also translated many works from French into Arabic, including novels by Emile Zola, about whom she later wrote a biography.

Source: Baron, *The Women's Awakening in Egypt: Culture, Society, and the Press,* pp. 20–21.

1901 • Probably the first women's magazine founded by a Muslim Egyptian woman, *Shajarat al-Durr* (named after a famous medieval sultana) appeared in 1901. A bilingual Turkish-Arabic monthly edited by Sa'diyya Sa'd al-Din Zadeh, it included features on a variety of topics including women's rights, as well as correspondence. The only bilingual journal of that time, *Shajarat al-Durr* did not last long, most likely because the Turkish language had all but disappeared by then.

Source: Baron, *The Women's Awakening in Egypt: Culture, Society, and the Press,* pp. 22–24.

1913 • Beatrice Potter Webb (1858–1943), an English socialist leader, was the cofounder, with her husband, Sidney Webb, of the influential periodical the *New Statesman,* in London, England, in 1913. An active reformer, Webb and her husband worked in a successful partnership and are also remembered for their instrumental role in founding the London School of Economics (in 1895) and for their important books on British economic history.

Sources: Adam and Muggeridge, *Beatrice Webb: A Life, 1858–1943*; Uglow, *The Continuum Dictionary of Women's Biography,* pp. 570–71; Webb, *My Apprenticeship*; Webb, *Our Partnership.*

1915 • Mary Roberts Rinehart (1876–1958) was the first American correspondent to report from the front during World War I. She sent back news articles for the *Saturday Evening Post* from the Western Front in France and Belgium in 1915.

Sources: Read and Witlieb, *The Book of Women's Firsts,* pp. 372–73; Rinehart, *My Story.*

c.1920 • Missy Meloney was the first woman to have a seat in the press gallery of the U.S. Senate. At the time (about 1920), she was the editor of the *Delineator,* one of the largest women's magazines in the country.

Sources: McGrayne, *Nobel Prize Women in Science,* p. 33.

1920 • Margaret Haig Thomas Rhondda (1883–1958), a Welsh feminist, was the founder of the important British literary journal *Time and Tide,* in London in 1920. This publication moved from espousing left-wing feminism to conservative idealism and was the leading weekly in England for over 30 years.

Rhondda served as its editor, beginning in 1926, and published such writers as Rebecca West and Winifred Holtby.

Sources: Thomas, *This Was My World*; Uglow, *The Continuum Dictionary of Women's Biography,* p. 455.

1927 • Lotte Eisner (1896–1983) was the first female film critic in Germany. She began to work for the German periodical *Film Kurier* in Berlin, Germany, writing articles on German Expressionist filmmakers. She fled Nazi Germany in 1933 for Paris, and from 1945 until the early 1970s was the curator of the Cinémathèque Française.

Sources: Uglow, *The Continuum Dictionary of Women's Biography,* p. 184.

1945 • Hélène Gordon-Lazareff (1909–1988), a French journalist born in Russia, was the cofounder (with Françoise Giroud) and first director of the famous fashion magazine *Elle,* in Paris in 1945.

Sources: Read and Witlieb, *The Book of Women's Firsts,* p. 475; Uglow, *The Continuum Dictionary of Women's Biography,* p. 232.

1947 • Teresa Noce (b. 1900), a labor organizer and writer, was the founder of the periodical *La Voce dei Tessili* ("The Voice of the Textile Workers"), in Italy. From her youth as a factory worker in Turin, Italy, Noce worked for socialist, communist, and feminist causes, joining the French Resistance during the World War II and surviving incarceration at the Ravensbruck concentration camp.

Sources: Uglow, *The Continuum Dictionary of Women's Biography,* p. 404.

1950s • Pauline Kael (b. 1919) was the first U.S. woman to establish her reputation as a serious film critic. She began to write reviews during the 1950s, at a time in the United States when film was beginning for the first time to be taken seriously as an art. She contributed to such scholarly journals as *Sight and Sound, Partisan Review, Film Culture,* and *Film Quarterly.* She eventually became film critic for the *New Yorker,* the weekly magazine with which she is identified. She has published numerous collections of her reviews and is widely regarded as one of the outstanding critics in the history of cinema.

Sources: Magnusson, *Larousse Biographical Dictionary,* p. 804; Uglow, *The Continuum Dictionary of Women's Biography,* p. 290.

1964 • Shirley Pearce Conran (b. 1932), an English designer and writer, was the first women's editor of the *Observer Color Magazine.* She is known as designer for the home and as an author of both fiction and nonfiction.

Sources: Uglow, *The Continuum Dictionary of Women's Biography,* p. 136.

1970s • Cathy Machan became the first woman to serve as dairy editor of the *Farm Journal* in the 1970s. Machan, a graduate of the University of Wisconsin College of Agriculture and Life Sciences, has made a career in journalism.

Sources: O'Neill, *The Women's Book of World Records and Achievements,* pp. 11–12.

c.1970 • Aminah Al-Said (b. 1914) was the first woman to be elected to the Egyptian Press Syndicate Executive Board. A journalist concerned with feminist issues, Al-Said is the editor of *Hawa* ("Eve"), a woman's weekly magazine that has the largest foreign circulation of any Arabic paper.

Sources: Uglow, *The Continuum Dictionary of Women's Biography,* p. 14.

1971 • Gloria Steinem (b. 1934), a U.S. feminist and a leader in the women's movement beginning in the 1960s, was the cofounder, with Patricia Carbine, of *Ms.* magazine, in New York City in 1971. Also that year, Steinem helped found the National Women's Political Caucus and the Women's Action Alliance; both organizations were formed to promote women's rights and fight discrimination. Steinem has made her living as a writer, for *Ms.* and other journals. In 1983, she published a collection of articles, *Outrageous Acts and Everyday Rebellions.* In 1986, her book-length study of Marilyn Monroe, *Marilyn,* was published. She has also published accounts drawn from her own experiences: *Revolution from Within: A Book of Self-Esteem,* in 1992, and *Moving Beyond Words,* in 1994. Steinem is often seen as a spokesperson for contemporary liberal feminism.

Sources: Magnusson, *Larousse Biographical Dicitonary*, p. 1392; Uglow, *The Continuum Dictionary of Women's Biography,* pp. 516–17.

1982 • During her senior year at Harvard University in 1982–83, Lisa Henson became the first woman to serve as president of *The Harvard Lampoon,* the university's comic review. Henson, who majored in ancient Greek and folklore mythology, went on to become president of Columbia Pictures in 1994.

Sources: New York Times (4 April 1994), B1-2.

Miscellaneous

1846 • Sarah E. Bagley, an American mill worker and early labor organizer, became the first female telegraph operator when she assumed the post at the newly opened Lowell, Massachusetts, telegraph office. (*See also* **Activism: Labor Activism, 1844.**)

Sources: James, *Notable American Women,* vol. 1, pp. 81–82; Josephson, *The Golden Threads: New England's Mill Girls and Magnates*; Stern, *We the Women.*

1916 • Martha Bol Poel (1877–1956), a Belgian feminist, was the first woman to organize a secret news correspondence service during the German occupation of Belgium during World War I. She was imprisoned for her resistance activities in 1916. During the 1920s, Bol Poel became a leading figure in the women's movement in Belgium.

Sources: Uglow, *The Continuum Dictionary of Women's Biography,* p. 76.

1948 • Frieda B. Hennock (1904–1960) was the first woman appointed to serve on the U.S. Federal Communications Commission (FCC). Trained as a lawyer, she was active throughout her life in work for the Democratic Party.

Sources: Read and Witlieb, *The Book of Women's Firsts,* pp. 201–2.

1957 • Anne W. Wheaton (1893–1977) was the first woman to serve as a presidential spokesperson. During President Dwight D. Eisenhower's administration, she served in this capacity when she was appointed White House associate press secretary, a position she held from 1957 until 1961.

Sources: Read and Witlieb, *The Book of Women's Firsts,* p. 478.

1969 • The first female journalists were accepted into membership in Sigma Delta Chi, an American society dedicated to the promotion of excellence in journalism. In November 1969, 16 women were initiated after the vote to admit women for the first time in the organization's 60-year history. Among those admitted was Charlayne Hunter (later Gault), a reporter for the *New York Times.* She was the only African American woman among the first women admitted into membership in Sigma Delta Chi.

Sources: Read and Witlieb, *The Book of Women's Firsts,* p. 408.

1970 • Sally Aw Sian (b. 1931), a Chinese journalist, was the first woman to chair the International Press Institute, a position she held in Hong Kong from 1970 to 1971. She was also the founder and first chair of the Chinese Language Press Institute.

Sources: O'Neill, *The Women's Book of World Records and Achievements,* p. 465.

1973 • Katharine Meyer Graham (b. 1917) was the first woman to receive the John Peter Zenger Award for her distinguished service on behalf of freedom of the press. Graham became president of the Washington Post Company after her husband's suicide in 1963. When she took over the giant media company founded by her father, she became the first woman to head a *Fortune* 500 company. In 1974 she became the first female member of the board of the Associated Press.

Sources: O'Neill, *The Woman's Book of World Records and Achievements,* p. 514; Read and Witlieb, *The Book of Women's Firsts,* p. 182; Uglow, *The Continuum Dictionary of Women's Biography,* p. 233.

1992 • Dee Dee Myers (b. 1961) was the first woman to be White House press secretary. Myers served as President Bill Clinton's campaign spokeswoman and then as White House press secretary from 1992 to 1994.

Source: New York Times (24 December 1992), p. 7.

Newspapers

1738 • Elizabeth Timothy (c.1700–) was the first woman to publish a newspaper. After the death of her husband in 1738, she took over publication of their weekly paper, the *South Carolina Gazette.* She continued to publish this journal in Charleston, South Carolina, until she gave the job over to her son in 1746.

Sources: Cohen, *The South Carolina Gazette*; James, *Notable American Women,* vol. 3, pp. 465–66; Read and Witlieb, *The Book of Women's Firsts,* p. 446.

1831 • Anne Newport Royall (1769–1854) was the first U.S. newspaper-woman. A travel writer and novelist, Royall was independently wealthy when she began to publish her first newspaper, *Paul Pry,* a weekly gossip sheet, in Washington, D.C., on December 3, 1831. With an established reputation for sharp editorial comment, Royall published this journal until November 19, 1836. On December 2, 1836, she began a new paper with a broader range, *The Huntress,* which she continued to edit until July 2, 1854, a few months before her death.

Sources: Jackson, *Uncommon Scold: The Story of Anne Royall*; James, *Notable American Women,* vol. 3, pp. 204–5; Porter, *The Life and Tomes of Anne Royall*; Woodward, *The Bold Woman.*

1868 • Myra Colby Bradwell (1831–94) was the first editor of the *Chicago Legal News,* a paper she founded in 1868. A special charter was granted to free her from her dependent status as a married woman so that she could serve as both proprietor and manager of this publication, which included official court reports. Bradwell managed the *Chicago Legal News* until her death, and her daughter then continued her work until 1925.

Sources: Chicago History; Uglow, *The Continuum Dictionary of Women's Biography,* p. 85.

1869 • Paule Mink (1839–1900), a French feminist and ardent socialist, founded the radical Republican paper *Les Mouches et L'Araignée,* in Paris in 1869. A year earlier, she had founded a women's aid society. She later wrote for numerous socialist periodicals and campaigned for the rights of oppressed groups. She is remembered as one of the female leaders of the Communard Movement and was very popular in France during her lifetime.

Sources: Hutton, *Historical Dictionary of the Third French Republic, 1870–1940,* p. 646; Uglow, *The Continuum Dictionary of Women's Biography,* p. 379.

1876 • Eliza Jane Poitevent Holbrook Nicholson (1849–1896) was the first woman to become a publisher of a newspaper in the Deep South of the United States. Raised as a southern belle, Nicholson was nevertheless determined to be a writer. In 1870, she became literary editor of the New Orleans, Louisiana, paper, the *Picayune,* the first woman to hold this position. (Her father and brothers were strongly opposed to her taking the position, since women in journalism were rare in most places and unheard of in the American South.) After serving in her position on the *Picayune* staff for a few years, she married the the paper's owner, Colonel A. H. Holbrook. When he died in 1876, she took over as publisher, a position she held until her death from influenza. A gifted businesswoman, she had a distinguished career in her field, becoming in 1884 the first honorary member of the New York Woman's Press Club.

Eliza J. Nicholson

Sources: James, *Notable American Women,* vol. 2, pp. 630–31; *National Cyclopedia of American Biography,* vol. I, p. 126.

1880s • Sévèrine (1855–1929), the pseudonym for the French feminist journalist Caroline Guebhard, was the first female reporter to go down into a mine in France. She was also the first person to conduct investigative interviews designed to reveal the subject's personality and values. She was also the first person to write an editorial for the popular French evening newspaper *Paris-soir,* in Paris in 1923. She is further remembered for her outspoken articles on socialism, feminism, abortion, and sexual violence.

Sources: Hutton, *Historical Dictionary of the Third French Republic, 1870–1940,* p. 931–32; Uglow, *The Continuum Dictionary of Women's Biography,* p. 492.

c.1880 • Mary Ann Cary, publisher of Canada's first anti-slavery newspaper, *The Provincial Freeman,* was the first African American newspaperwoman in North America. She was also the second African American woman to earn a law degree in the United States in 1883.

Sources: Gaymon, *215 African American Women You Should Know;* James, *Notable American Women,* vol. 1, pp. 300–1.

1882 • Emily Edson Briggs (1830–1910), who wrote under the pen name "Olivia," became the first president of the Women's National Press Association, an organization formed in Washington, D.C. to support the purposes and careers of professional female reporters.

Sources: James, *Notable American Women,* vol. 1, pp. 242–43; Read and Witlieb, *The Book of Women's Firsts,* p. 68.

1890s • Winifred Sweet Black (1863–1936), a sensational journalist associated throughout her career with newspapers of U.S. publisher William Randolph Hearst, was the first woman to report a prize fight. Her feature articles include a number of firsts, among them the first female account of the tidal wave that killed over 7,000 people in Galveston, Texas, in September 1900. In order to cover this event, Black dressed as a boy and thus managed to get through police lines.

Sources: James, *Notable American Women,* vol. 1, pp. 154–56; Ross, *Ladies of the Press.*

1897 • Marguerite Durand (1864–1936) was the first person to found a daily paper for women, *La Fronde,* a socialist feminist newspaper that was run entirely by women from 1897 until 1903 in France. Between 1903 and 1905, this paper went from publishing daily to monthly. Durand then founded the journal *l'Action.* She was also the first female director of *Les Nouvelles,* a Parisian evening newspaper, from 1908 until 1914.

Sources: Hutton, *Historical Dictionary of the Third French Republic, 1870–1940,* p. 309–10; Uglow, *The Continuum Dictionary of Women's Biography,* pp. 178–79.

Motoko Hani (1873–1957), a Japanese journalist and feminist, was the first woman to work as a full-time reporter in Japan. She covered women, education, and religion for the newspaper *Hochi Shimbun.* With her husband, she founded *Woman's Friend* in 1901, a magazine that advocated female self-reliance. Also interested in education, she and her husband founded a liberal private school, Jiyu Gakuen, in 1921. She served as the school's first female principal.

Sources: Uglow, *The Continuum Dictionary of Women's Biography,* p. 247.

1902 • Katharine Margaret Brownlee Sherwood (1841–1914), a U.S. journalist and pioneering clubwoman, served as the first president of the Ohio Newspaper Women's Association, in 1902. She is also remembered for two volumes of verse inspired by the Civil War.

Sources: Croly, *The History of the Woman's Club Movement in America,* pp. 981-82; James, *Notable American Women,* vol. 3, pp. 281-83; Scribner, *Memoirs of Lucas County and the City of Toledo;* Willard and Livermore, *A Woman of the Century.*

1912 • Konkordiya Samoilova (1876–1921) was the first female editor of the revolutionary newspaper *Pravda,* in Russia. Samoilova assumed this position at the time of *Pravda's* founding in St. Petersburg. She was one of the great female leaders of the Bolshevik period in Russia. The Bolsheviks were members of the Communist Party formed in Russia in the early 1900s under the leadership of Vladimir Ilyich Lenin.

Sources: Uglow, *The Continuum Dictionary of Women's Biography,* p. 476.

1914 • Louella Oettinger Parsons (1893–1972) was the first woman to write a regular column on the movies for an American newspaper. From 1914 through 1918 she wrote a column featuring film gossip and information for the *Chicago Record-Herald.* Parsons continued to write about the movies and movie stars, and by the 1930s and 1940s her column was carried by over 400 newspapers.

Sources: Acker, *Reel Women: Pioneers of the Cinema, 1896 to the Present,* pp. 332–33; Parsons, *The Gay Illiterate;* Parsons, *Tell It to Louella;* Read and Witlieb, *The Book of Women's Firsts,* p. 331.

1918 • Eleanor Farnham (1896–1995) was the first female reporter to work on *The Plain Dealer* in Cleveland, Ohio. She began her job as secretary to the city editor shortly after graduation from Lake Erie College in 1918 and was writing stories for the paper by the end of World War I. She later left reporting to head her own public relations firm.

Sources: The Plain Dealer (28 January 1995).

Louise Weiss (1893–1983), a French feminist and journalist, was the founder of *L'Europe Nouvelle,* in Paris in 1918. This paper became one of the most influential weeklies in France during the 1920s. In the 1930s, Weiss formed the feminist suffragist group, La Femme Nouvelle, and in 1971 she founded the Institute for the Science of Peace, in Strasbourg. In 1974, she became the first woman to propose herself for membership in the French Academy. Her application was unsuccessful, despite her distinguished career.

Sources: Uglow, *The Continuum Dictionary of Women's Biography,* p. 574; Weiss, *Mémoires d'une Européenne;* Weiss, *Tempête sur L'Occident, 1945–1975.*

1920s • Anna Strong (1885–1970), a U.S. journalist, was the first woman to serve as editor of *Moscow News,* a newspaper for Americans working in the Soviet Union. She assumed this position in Moscow in the 1920s and continued until 1949, when she was accused of spying and deported. An ardent Communist, Strong is also remembered for her writings about China, including *China's Millions,* published in 1928. Friendly with Chinese leader Mao Zedong, she settled in Beijing, China in 1958.

Sources: Uglow, *The Continuum Dictionary of Women's Biography,* p. 522.

1921 • Milena Jesenska (1890–1944), a Czech journalist who initiated a friendship with the writer Franz Kafka in 1920, was the first person to recognize his stature as a major twentieth-century author. Her obituary of Kafka, which appeared in Czech papers in 1921, was the only one to acknowledge the greatness of his work.

Sources: Kafka, *Letters to Milena*; Uglow, *The Continuum Dictionary of Women's Biography,* p. 282.

1922 • Caroline Alice Lejeune (1897–1973) was the first female film critic in England. After earning a B.A. at Manchester University, she began to write a regular film column for the *Manchester Guardian.*

Sources: Lejeune, *Thank You for Having Me*; Uglow, *The Continuum Dictionary of Women's Biography,* p. 321.

1924 • Dorothy Thompson (1894–1961) was the first U.S. woman to head a news service in Berlin, Germany. Thompson was a journalist educated at Syracuse University in New York and the University of Vienna in Austria. As a foreign correspondent for newspapers in New York and Philadelphia, she assumed the post of chief of their Central European Service in Berlin. She served in this capacity until 1928. She remained in Germany as a freelance journalist until her differences with the Nazi government after 1933 led to her return to New York. She is also remembered because of her second marriage, to the American writer Sinclair Lewis.

Sources: Thompson, *The Courage to be Happy*; Uglow, *The Continuum Dictionary of Women's Biography,* p. 540.

1928 • Agnes Smedley (1890–1950) was the first U.S. woman to serve as a special correspondent to China for a German newspaper, in 1928. Smedley went to China as a reporter for the *Frankfurter Allgemeine Zeitung.* She continued in this capacity until 1932 and later served as a correspondent in China for the *Manchester Guardian,* from 1938 to 1941. Smedley is remembered for her vivid autobiographical novel, *Daughter of Earth* (1928), and for several books on China.

Sources: MacKinnon, *Agnes Smedley: The Life and Times of an American Radical*; Smedley, *Battle Hymn of China*; Smedley, *China's Red Army Marches*; Uglow, *The Continuum Dictionary of Women's Biography,* p. 501.

1934 • Eleanor Medill Patterson (1881–1948) became the first woman to publish a large metropolitan daily newspaper when she persuaded her friend

William Randolph Hearst to let her take over the *Washington Herald* in Washington, D.C. (*See also* **Sports: Adventure and Travel, 1921**)

Sources: Hoge, *Cissy Patterson*; James, *Notable American Women,* vol. 3, pp. 26–29; Read and Witlieb, *The Book of Women's Firsts,* p. 322.

1937 • Anne O'Hare McCormick (1880–1954) was the first woman to receive the Pulitzer Prize for distinguished correspondence. She was honored for work at the *New York Times.* McCormick also became in 1936 the first woman to sit on this newspaper's editorial board.

Sources: Read and Witlieb, *The Book of Women's Firsts,* pp. 278–79.

1940 • After four years of trying to sell her work, on June 19, 1940, Dale Messick (b. 1906) published her first "Brenda Starr" comic strip in the *Chicago Tribune,* becoming the first woman to create and publish a syndicated comic strip. While trying to find a publisher for her cartoons, she changed her name from Dalia to Dale to conceal the fact that she was a woman. "Brenda Starr" was also notable as the first comic strip to feature a woman.

Sources: McCullough, *First of All: Significant "Firsts" by American Women,* p. 25; *Modern Maturity* (June–July 1992), p. 14.

1947 • Agness Wilson Underwood (b. 1902) became the first female city editor of a major daily newspaper. She was made city editor of the *Los Angeles Herald* in 1947. She began her reporting career in 1926 and retired in 1968.

Sources: Read and Witlieb, *The Book of Women's Firsts,* pp. 457–58; Underwood, *Newspaper Woman.*

c.1950 • Helene Vlachou (b. 1911), a Greek journalist, was the first woman to publish two Athens newspapers inherited from her father: *Kathimerini,* an independent daily with a circulation of 70,000, and *Messinvrine.* Refusing to submit to censorship, she ceased publication in 1967 and went into exile in London, England, until the Greek government ousted the military junta in 1974. On her return to Athens, she resumed publication of both papers.

Sources: Uglow, *The Continuum Dictionary of Women's Biography,* p. 560; Vlachou, *House Arrest.*

1951 • Marguerite Higgins (1920–1966) was the first woman to win the Pulitzer Prize for international reporting, in 1951. She was honored with fellow reporter Homer Bigart for their coverage of the Korean War for the *New York Herald Tribune.* Higgins was the only woman reporting from the battlefront in Korea.

Sources: Read and Witlieb, *The Book of Women's Firsts,* pp. 202–3.

1964 • Hazel Brannon Smith (1914–1994) was the first woman to be awarded the Pulitzer Prize for editorial writing, in 1964. She was honored for her work in the *Lexington Advertiser* published in Lexington, Mississippi.

Sources: Read and Witlieb, *The Book of Women's Firsts,* pp. 410–11.

1966 • Charlotte Curtis (c.1928–1987) became the first woman to be listed on the masthead of the *New York Times* in 1966. She joined the paper as a re-

Marguerite Higgins
interviews General John S.
Bradley in Korea in 1951.

porter in 1961 and served as editor of the "Family/Style" section from 1966 until 1974, when she became associate editor of the paper and editor of its op-ed page. She focused on serious women's issues and refused to let trivial news dominate the "society" section for which she was responsible.

Sources: O'Neill, *The Women's Book of World Records and Achievements,* pp. 466–67.

1971 • Lucinda Franks (b. 1946) became the first woman to receive the Pulitzer Prize for national reporting. Franks, a U.S. journalist working with Thomas Powers for United Press International, won the prize for her five-article series on Diana Oughton, a New York society woman turned political radical, entitled "The Making of a Terrorist." Franks later became a professor of writing and journalism at Vassar College, her alma mater, and Princeton University.

Sources: O'Neill, *The Women's Book of World Records and Achievements,* p. 465; Read and Witlieb, *The Book of Women's Firsts,* pp. 165–66.

Esther Van Wagoner Tufty (1896–1986) became the first woman elected to the National Press Club in Washington, D.C., in 1971. She was honored for her lifelong reporting and for her establishment of the Tufty News Service, an organization in which she served as president, editor, and writer from 1935 to 1985.

Sources: Read and Witlieb, *The Book of Women's Firsts,* pp. 452–53.

1972 • Betsey Wade (b. 1929), a U.S. journalist, was the first woman to head a copy desk at the *New York Times* when she became head of the foreign copy desk. An ardent feminist, Wade has fought for women's causes throughout her career.

Sources: O'Neill, *The Women's Book of World Records and Achievements,* p. 465.

1974 • Carol Sutton (1933–1985) was named managing editor of the *Courier-Journal* in Louisville, Kentucky, in 1974, thus becoming the first woman to head the news staff of a major U.S. daily newspaper.

Sources: Read and Witlieb, *The Book of Women's Firsts,* p. 431.

Helen A. Thomas (b. 1920) was the first woman to head the White House bureau of a major news service. She became the White House bureau chief for United Press International in 1974.

Sources: Read and Witlieb, *The Book of Women's Firsts,* pp. 441–42; Thomas, *Dateline: White House.*

1975 • Robin Herman, a U.S. journalist, became the first woman to serve as a sportswriter on the *New York Times* when she joined the staff of 51 men. A graduate of Princeton University, Herman's particular interest is hockey.

Sources: O'Neill, *The Women's Book of World Records and Achievements,* p. 463.

Mary McGrory (b. 1918) was the first woman to receive a Pulitzer Prize for commentary. She was honored for her political journalism for the *Washington Star* in 1975. McGrory covered the hearings chaired by Senator Joseph McCarthy seeking to identify communist sympathizers in the United States in the 1950s and the Watergate scandal involving an illegal burglary of the Democratic Party headquarters under the administration of Republican President Richard M. Nixon in the early 1970s.

Sources: Read and Witlieb, *The Book of Women's Firsts,* p. 282.

Photojournalism

Early 1940s • Margaret Bourke-White (1904–1971), a U.S. photojournalist, was the first woman to serve as an U.S. Army Air Force photographer in

Helen A. Thomas became head of the UPI White House bureau in 1974.

combat in North Africa and Italy during World War II. Attached to U.S. General Patton's Third Army, she was one of the first photographers to enter the Nazi concentration camp at Buchenwald in 1945; her pictures of the camp provoked worldwide outrage.

Sources: Magnusson, *Larousse Biographical Dictionary,* p. 189; Uglow, *The Continuum Dictionary of Women's Biography,* pp. 82–83.

1954 • Virginia M. Schau (1915–1989), an amateur photographer, was the first woman to receive a Pulitzer Prize for spot news photography, in 1954. She was honored for the photographs she took of her husband, Walter, during his rescue of a truck driver from a crash near Redding, California.

Sources: Read and Witlieb, *The Book of Women's Firsts,* pp. 393–94.

Radio

1939 • Pauline Frederick (1906–1990) was the first woman to work as a network news analyst and diplomatic correspondent in American radio, beginning with her first broadcast from Washington, D.C., in 1939. She became the first woman to anchor network radio's coverage of a presidential convention, in 1960. (*See also* **Media: Television, 1970** and **1976.**)

Sources: Read and Witlieb, *The Book of Women's Firsts,* p. 167; Uglow, *The Continuum Dictionary of Women's Biography,* p. 214.

1941 • Rebecca West (1892–1983), a distinguished Englishwoman of letters known for her novels, journalism, and criticism, was the first woman to supervise British Broadcasting Corporation (BBC) broadcasts to Yugoslavia in London during World War II. She was born Cecily Isabel Fairfield in County Kerry, Ireland, and adopted the nom de plume Rebecca West in about 1912 She was honored for her life's work in 1959 when she was made a Dame of the British Empire.

Sources: Magnusson, *Larousse Biographical Dictionary,* p. 1547; Uglow, *The Continuum Dictionary of Women's Biography,* p. 577.

1960 • Pauline Frederick (1906–1990) was the first woman to anchor radio coverage of a political party's national convention. (*See also* **Media: Radio, 1939** and **1970.**)

Sources: Read and Witlieb, *The Book of Women's Firsts*; Uglow, *The Continuum Dictionary of Women's Biography,* p. 214.

1976 • Alison Steele (1938–95), professionally known as the "Night Bird," became the first woman to receive Billboard's FM (radio) Personality of the Year. Steele had developed a tremendous following doing a latenight show on WNEW-FM in New York City. Like the other disc jockeys (DJs) on WNEW-FM in the late 1960s and the 1970s, she helped an entire generation cope with the social upheaval and emerging counterculture through what was called a free-form or progressive format.

Source: New York Times (29 October 1995), p. C38.

Television

1947 • Dorothy Fuldheim (1893–1989) became the first female television news anchor at WEWS-TV in Cleveland, Ohio. At first, the sponsor was reluctant to back a newscast anchored by a woman, but the station, the largest between New York and Chicago, stood by her. Eventually, the beer company relented and sponsored the broadcast with Fuldheim at the anchor desk for 18 years. During her career she interviewed such notables as Nazi leader Adolf Hitler, U.S. President Jimmy Carter, and Queen Farida of Egypt. By 1979, at age 86, she was still anchoring the early newscast in Cleveland, earning the distinction of being on the job longer than any other television broadcaster.

Sources: McCullough, *First of All: Significant "Firsts" by American Women,* pp. 33–34.

Dorothy Fuldheim

1949 • Shirley Dinsdale (b. 1928) was the first woman to win an Emmy award for her work on television. She was recognized as "most outstanding television personality" for her work on her puppet show "Judy Splinters" in 1949.

Sources: Read and Witlieb, *The Book of Women's Firsts,* p. 122.

1970 • Pauline Frederick (1906–1990) was the first woman to moderate a presidential debate. (The televised encounter occurred between the Democratic Party candidate, Jimmy Carter, and the Republican party candidate, Gerald Ford. (*See also* **Media: Radio, 1939.**)

Sources: Read and Witlieb, *The Book of Women's Firsts,* p. 167; Uglow, *The Continuum Dictionary of Women's Biography,* p. 214.

1971 • Aline B. Saarinen (1914–1972), a U.S. art and architecture critic, became the first woman to head an overseas television news bureau when she was named chief of the Paris bureau of NBC television in 1971.

Sources: Read and Witlieb, *The Book of Women's Firsts,* p. 386; Uglow, *The Continuum Dictionary of Women's Biography,* p. 472.

1972 • Lin Bolen (b. 1941) became the first woman to direct daytime programming at a major television network. NBC in New York hired her for this job, making her at that time the highest-ranking woman at any network.

Sources: Read and Witlieb, *The Book of Women's Firsts,* pp. 59–60.

Rachel Flint Heyhoe (b. 1939), whose sports specialties are field hockey and cricket, was the first female sports reporter to work for Independent Television in Britain. From 1981 to 1986 she served as vice chair of the Women's Cricket Association.

Sources: Uglow, *The Continuum Dictionary of Women's Biography,* p. 258.

1976 • Marlene Sanders (b. 1931) was the first woman to anchor a network television evening newscast. She took over for Ron Cochran when he lost his voice during a broadcastof the ABC evening news in 1976. She went on to a successful career in writing and producing television documentaries.

Sources: Read and Witlieb, *The Book of Women's Firsts,* p. 390; Sanders and Rock, *Waiting for Prime Time.*

Barbara Walters (b. 1931) was the first female co-anchor of a daily evening news program. She was hired by ABC to work on television with Harry Reasoner on the "ABC Evening News" from 1976 to 1978.

Sources: Read and Witlieb, *The Book of Women's Firsts,* pp. 468–69; Uglow, *The Continuum Dictionary of Women's Biography,* pp. 566–67.

1986 • Karen Arthur, a U.S. film director, became the first woman to direct an American television mini-series, "Crossings." She worked as a dancer and an actor before turning to directing, and has made movies in Hollywood since 1975.

Sources: Acker, *Reel Women: Pioneers of the Cinema, 1896 to the Present,* pp. 35–37.

Barbara Walters

1987 • Gayle Sierens (b. 1954) was the first woman to do play-by-play coverage of a National Football League game, on December 27, 1987. She reported the game between the Kansas City Chiefs and the Seattle Seahawks for NBC.

Sources: Read and Witlieb, *The Book of Women's Firsts,* p. 408.

1993 • Lucie Salhany (b. 1946) became the first woman to head a national television network when she was named chair of Fox Broadcasting in Hollywood, California. After a dispute with Fox owner Rupert Murdoch, Salhany left Fox in July 1994 after 18 months on the job.

Sources: Newsweek (18 July 1994), p. 65.

Military

Bolivia

1809 • Juana Azurduy (1781–1862) was the first Bolivian woman to lead a revolt against Spanish rule in her country. She was a military leader of both women and men in the guerilla wars for independence in Bolivia between 1809 and 1825.

Sources: Uglow, *The Continuum Dictionary of Women's Biography,* p. 74.

Canada

c.1900 • Laura Ingersoll Secord (1775–1868) was the first Canadian woman to have a chocolate bar named after her. She was immortalized because of her heroic efforts as an unofficial Canadian spy during the War of 1812 against the United States. In June 1813, Secord overheard U.S. soldiers planning an attack on a British military post in southern Ontario. She walked across dangerous terrain the 20 miles (32 kilometers) to warn the British. Two days later, Native Americans, allies of the British, ambushed the U.S. soldiers in the Battle of Beaver Dam.

Sources: Uglow, *The Continuum Dictionary of Women's Biography,* p. 491.

Colombia

1780 • Manuela Beltran was the first woman to organize a revolt against the Spanish government in Colombia. In 1780, she led an uprising against undue taxation by the colonial government in her country.

Sources: Uglow, *The Continuum Dictionary of Women's Biography,* p. 74.

Ecuador

1778 • Chuiza Baltazara was the first woman to lead a revolt against the Spanish in her native Ecuador. Her leadership role in Ecuadorian independence is characteristic of a long tradition of female freedom fighters in Latin America.

Sources: Uglow, *The Continuum Dictionary of Women's Biography,* p. 74.

Queen Boadicea

England

60 A.D. • According to legend, Boadicea (c.25–62 A.D.) was the first woman in what came to be England to revolt against Roman rule. Her story was recorded by the Roman historian Tacitus in *Agricola,* published around 98 A.D. The legendary Queen Boadicea seems to be based upon the real-life Boudica, queen of the Iceni, an ancient British people that controlled territories including areas that make up modern Norfolk and North Suffolk in England. The Iceni, and their Queen Boudica, were confident and aristocratic and were recognized for the massive gold, bronze, and silver necklaces they wore, many weighing over one thousand grams (about two pounds). When her husband, King Prasutagus, died in 60 A.D., Queen Boudica was flogged and their two daughters were brutally raped by Romans, who were dissatisfied with the conditions of his will. (Prasutagus had left part of his estate to the Romans and part to his wife, Boudica, in trust for his daughters.) In response to this outrageous treatment, Queen Boudica led the Iceni (one account estimated the number of troops to be 120,000) in a series of successful attacks against the Romans in 60–61 A.D. When she was finally defeated in 62 A.D., the revolt and Iceni resistence collapsed. In the seventeenth century, her story was cast as the story of Queen Boadicea. A statue of her with her daughters in a chariot with scythe blades on its wheels was installed in London, England, in 1902.

Sources: Fraser, *The Warrior Queens,* pp. 43–106; Greenspan, *Timetables of Women's History,* p. 48; Schmidt, *400 Outstanding Women of the World,* pp. 129–30.

1750 • Hannah Snell (1723–1792) was the first Englishwoman to make her reputation disguised as a male soldier. Deserted by her husband in 1743, she donned male attire and sought him by joining an English foot regiment in Coventry. She served in this disguise during the Stuart rebellion in Scotland and then with troops in the Far East. When she returned to England in 1750, she revealed her female identity, left the army, and wrote a book about her experiences. She appeared in uniform on the London stage to advertise her exploits, and after receiving a military pension, she opened an inn, *The Female Warrior,* in Wapping, England.

Sources: Snell, *The Female Soldier: or The Surprising Adventures of Hannah Snell*; Uglow, *The Continuum Dictionary of Women's Biography,* pp. 504–5.

1926 • Flora Sandes (1876–1956) was the first English nurse to become an army captain. She went abroad with the Serbian Red Cross in 1914, then joined the 2nd Infantry Regiment in which she served as a soldier in battles with the Bulgarians. At the end of the war, she was decorated for bravery. In 1915, Sandes was awarded the Gara George Star, the highest medal awarded to noncommissioned officers; she was made captain in 1926.

Sources: Burgess, *The Lovely Sargeant;* Uglow, *The Continuum Dictionary of Women's Biography,* p. 478.

1946 • Odette Hallowes (1913–1995) was the first woman awarded the George Cross, Britain's second-highest honor. Hallowes, born Odette Marie Celine Brailly, was a British agent captured and tortured by the Gestapo, the German state police under the Nazi regime in World War II. During her capture, Hallowes' back was burned with a hot iron and her toenails wrenched out, but she refused to identify two agents sought by the Gestapo.

Sources: Facts on File, vol. 55, no. 2834, p. 220; *The New York Times* (21 March 1995), p. D21.

France

1429 • Joan of Arc (1412–1431) was the first woman to lead the French army into battle, at Orléans in 1429. As a young woman she had visions that her mission was to free France from the English and to assure the coronation of Charles VII. Dressed in male attire and armed as a soldier, she led Charles's army as a captain. Her success in battle resulted in his coronation in her presence at Rheims. She led French troops into battle once more at Compiègne in 1430, where she was captured by the British, convicted of wearing men's clothing, and finally burned in the square at Rouen in May of 1431. In the nineteenth century she came to be seen as a great French hero, and she was canonized as a Catholic saint in 1920.

Sources: Greenspan, *Timetables of Women's History,* pp. 125–27; Schmidt, *400 Outstanding Women of the World,* p. 173.

c.1980 • Valérie André (b. 1922) was the first French woman to become a general in the French army. Trained as a physician, André served in Vietnam as the Chief of Medicine of a women's infirmary in 1948. André went on to an illustrious career that included service in Algeria.

Sources: Uglow, *The Continuum Dictionary of Women's Biography,* p. 17.

Greece

Fifth century B.C. • Telessilla, a Greek poet who wrote during the fifth century B.C., was the first woman to lead a defense of Argos. During a siege by the Spartans, while the men were away fighting, Telessilla moved the women, through her powerful verse, to take up arms and defend their city. The women were successful in their attack, and later the people of Argos dedicated a statue to Telessilla in gratitude.

Sources: Greenspan, *Timetables of Women's History,* p. 33; Uglow, *The Continuum Dictionary of Women's Biography,* p. 534.

Late eighteenth century • Moscho Tzavella (1760–1803), a hero throughout Greece, was the first woman in her country to lead a band of resisters against Turkish soldiers. Defending her mountain town of Souli, Tzavella lead the village women, armed only with sticks and stones, against the invading Turks, driving them back and preserving the town's independence. In honor of her courage, Tzavella was given the title of "captain" and allowed to participate in the town's war councils, the first woman permitted to do so.

Sources: Uglow, *The Continuum Dictionary of Women's Biography,* p. 549.

1820s • Manto Mavrogenous (d. 1848) was the first woman to receive the title lieutenant-general in recognition for her military leadership of the Greeks in their struggle for independence against the Turks beginning in 1821. She devoted her entire personal fortune to this cause.

Sources: Uglow, *The Continuum Dictionary of Women's Biography,* pp. 366–67.

c.1821 • Laskarina Bouboulina (1771–1825), an ardent Greek freedom fighter, was the first person to enter the beseiged city of Tripoli during the Greek War of Independence against Turkish occupation in the 1820s. She rode on horseback at the head of the liberating army and protected the women of the harems against the Greek soldiers. Her life has inspired many folk songs and literary accounts.

Sources: Schmidt, *400 Outstanding Women of the World,* pp. 218–19; Uglow, *The Continuum Dictionary of Women's Biography,* p. 80.

Lithuania

Early nineteenth century • Emilija Plater (1806–1831) was the first woman to lead Lithuanian soldiers into battle. Using Joan of Arc as her model, Plater studied military tactics and led troops into battle against occupying Russian forces in Daugavpils, Latvia, and Vilnius, Lithuania. When her attempts to dislodge the Russians failed, she tried to escape to Poland but died of illness en route.

Sources: Uglow, *The Continuum Dictionary of Women's Biography,* pp. 434–35.

Mexico

1810 • Gertrudis Bocanegra (1765–1817) was the first Mexican woman to create an underground army of women. She was a militant leader who fought in support of Mexican freedom during the War of Independence.

Sources: Uglow, *The Continuum Dictionary of Women's Biography,* pp. 73–74.

NATO

1973 • Reba C. Tyler was the first woman to command a North Atlantic Treaty Organization (NATO) military unit. She was appointed to this position in Mannheim, Germany, where she was in charge of the Forty-eighth Adjutant General Postal Detachment.

Sources: Read and Witlieb, *The Book of Women's Firsts,* p. 455.

Peru

1780 • Micaela Bastidas was the first woman to lead a rebellion against the Spanish in Peru. She joined her husband, Tupac Amaru, in leading both women and men into battle. Bastidas also recruited freedom fighters and organized supplies.

Sources: Uglow, *The Continuum Dictionary of Women's Biography,* p. 74.

Russia

1917 • Mariya Bochkareva (c.1889) was the first woman to organize female fighting troops during the World War I. Using the pseudonymn "Yashka," she formed the "Women's Battalion of Death," a group of nearly two thousand women whom she led into battle in July 1917. After the Russian Revolution, Bochkareva fled to the United States.

Sources: Bochkareva and Levine, *My Life as Peasant Officer and Exile;* Uglow, *The Continuum Dictionary of Women's Biography,* p. 74.

1918 • Larissa Mikhailovna Reisner (1895–1926), a Russian revolutionary and journalist, was the first woman to serve as a political commissar in the Red Army. She was fighting as a soldier and intelligence officer on the Eastern Front of World War I. She went on in 1921 to become the first female Soviet ambassador to Afghanistan. Her journalism and autobiographical writing appeared in several books before her early death from typhus.

Sources: Porter, *Larissa Reisner;* Reisner, *Afghanistan;*Reisner, *The Front;* Uglow, *The Continuum Dictionary of Women's Biography,* p. 453.

Spain

c.1820 • Augustina Zaragoza (1786–1857), who became known as Agostina La Saragossa, was the first female hero to be painted by the famous Spanish painter, Goya. She helped to defend her city, Saragossa, Spain, against French invaders in 1808. Saragossa was near Goya's birthplace, Aragon. Goya, whose full name is Francisco Jose de Goya y Lucientes, was best known for his depictions of war. Agostina La Saragossa, the "Maid of Saragossa," was buried with military honors and has become a symbol of national pride and personal courage in defense of liberty.

Sources: Schmidt, *400 Outstanding Women of the World,* p. 355–56; Williams, *Queenly Women, Crowned and Uncrowned,* pp. 359–66.

United States

1942 • Ann Leah Fox (b. 1918) became the first woman to be awarded the order of the Purple Heart. She was wounded while serving as a military nurse at Pearl Harbor in Hawaii during the Japanese attack on December 7, 1941.

Sources: Kane, *Famous First Facts,* p. 379.

1978 • The first women to join the White House Honor Guard were five representatives, one from each branch of the U.S. armed services. They made their debut on May 17, 1978, in Washington, D.C. during a welcoming ceremony for President Kenneth Kaunda of Zambia. The first guards were air force Sergeant Elizabeth Foreman, army Specialist Fourth Class Christine L. Crews, coast guard Apprentice Edna Dunham, marine Private First Class Myrna Jepson, and navy Seaman Apprentice Catherine Behnke. Their assignment came about through the efforts of First Lady Rosalynn Carter, wife of President Jimmy Carter, who responded to a letter she had received from Elizabeth Foreman, protesting the exclusion of women.

Sources: Read and Witlieb, *The Book of Women's Firsts,* p. 479; correspondence with editor, White House Historical Association, 1995.

Agostina La Saragossa became known as the national hero, the Maid of Saragossa.

1994 • In July, Lieutenant Kara S. Hultgreen (1965–1994) was the first woman assigned to fly an F-14 fighter jet in combat for the U.S. Navy. Hultgreen ranked third in a class of seven pilots. She was killed on October 25, 1994, during a failed landing on an aircraft carrier.

Source: "Navy Pilot's Body Found," *The New York Times* (17 November 1994), p. B13; "Navy Highly Rates Female Pilots Who Crashed," *The New York Times* (21 November 1994), p. A10.

United States–Air Force

1948 • Geraldine Pratt May (b. 1895) became the first director of Women in the Air Force (WAF) on June 15, when the Women's Armed Services Integration Act declared the WAF to be a formal part of the U.S. Air Force. May was a graduate of the first WAF officer candidate class in 1942.

Sources: Holm, *Women in the Military: An Unfinished Revolution,* p. 128; Read and Witlieb, *The Book of Women's Firsts,* pp. 272–73.

1957 • Naomi M. McCracken became the first female Air Force Academy officer. On April 26, she assumed her duties as assistant director of cadet records at the Academy's temporary headquarters in Denver, Colorado.

Sources: Kane, *Famous First Facts,* p. 9.

Jeanne Marjorie Holm

1971 • Jeanne Marjorie Holm (b. 1921) became the first female Air Force general in Washington, D.C. on July 16. She served at the Pentagon in Washington as Director of Women in the Air Force from 1965 until 1972. In 1973, she became the first Major General, the highest rank achieved by any woman in the American armed forces. After her retirement in 1974, she founded Women in Government and served as this organization's first chairperson.

Sources: Holm, *Women in the Military: An Unfinished Revolution,* p. 203; Kane, *Famous First Facts,* p. 9; Read and Witlieb, *The Book of Women's Firsts,* p. 213.

On April 8, Susanne M. Ocobock became the first woman to serve as an industrial civil engineer in the Air Force at Kelley Air Force Base, Texas.

Sources: Kane, *Famous First Facts,* p. 10.

1972 • Karen Riale (b. 1949) became the first female member of the U. S. Air Force Band. She joined as a clarinetist. She refused to play at President Nixon's inauguration in 1973 because no proper uniform for female band members had been provided.

Sources: Read and Witlieb, *The Book of Women's Firsts,* p. 366.

1973 • On September 26, Captain Lorraine Potter became the first female Air Force chaplain at San Antonio, Texas. She served at the West Webster United Church of Christ in Webster, New York, and completed an orientation course at Maxwell Air Force Base in Montgomery, Alabama.

Sources: Kane, *Famous First Facts,* p. 9.

1976 • On June 28, the first 155 women were admitted to the Air Force Academy in Colorado Springs, Colorado. At the end of the first year, 138 remained.

Sources: Kane, *Famous First Facts,* p. 9; Read and Witlieb, *The Book of Women's Firsts,* p. 458.

1994 • The U.S. Air Force announced its first female fighter pilot on February 14. She was First Lieutenant Jeannie Flynn, whose appointment signaled a trend in the American armed forces to open new combat positions to women.

Sources: People Weekly (17 May 1993); Schmitt, "Navy Women Bringing New Era on Carriers," *The New York Times* (21 February 1994), A12.

"All our revolutionary historians are eloquent in their praises of the bold hero-ine of Monmouth, "Captain Molly." They tell us how she was carrying water to the men of Proctor's battery on that hot and bloody afternoon in July, when a ball crushed in the skull of her husband, just as he was ramming a charge into his field piece, and he fell at her feet a bloody corpse. "Lie there, my darling, till I avenge your death!" exclaimed Molly, and seizing the rammer, she went on with the work which death had cut short, while the men cheered her all along the line. All through that afternoon, till night covered the landscape and closed the battle, Molly stood by her gun, and made good her husband's place, swabbing the piece, and forcing home the successive charges with the vigor and coolness of the bravest soldier. The next morning she was presented to General Wayne, all soiled and bloody as she had fought; and Washington gave her a commission as sergeant, and by his recommen-dation her name was placed on the list of half-pay officers for life."

CAPTAIN MOLLY

—*Women of the War,* 1866

United States–Army

1779 • Margaret "Molly" (Cochran) Corbin (1751–1801) was the first woman to receive a U.S. army pension in July 1779. During the Revolutionary War, Corbin accompanied her husband, John, to the battlefield in Fort Washington, New York. On November 16, 1776, her husband was fatally wounded in the British attack on Fort Washington. Molly took his place and continued to reload his cannon and shoot until the battle was over. In July 1779, Molly Corbin was awarded a full military pension by the Supreme Council of Pennsylvania. The Continental Congress additionally decided that she was entitled to half of a soldier's disability pay for life.

Sources: James, *Notable American Women,* vol. 1, p. 386; McCullough, *First of All: Significant Firsts of American Women,* pp. 10–11; Read and Witlieb, *The Book of Women's Firsts,* p. 102.

1802 • Deborah Sampson (1760–1827) was the first woman on record to enlist in the U.S. Army. She enlisted as a man, adopting the name Robert Shurtleff when she signed on with the Fourth Massachusetts Regiment in May of 1782. Her sex was discovered only when she was hospitalized with a fever in 1783. She was discharged from the army as a result. In 1802, she lectured on her military experience, becoming the first woman to do so.

Sources: Chicago, *The Dinner Party,* p. 168; James, *Notable American Women,* vol. 3, pp. 227–28; Read and Witlieb, *The Book of Women's Firsts,* p. 389.

1822 • Mary McCauley (1754–1832), known as "Molly Pitcher" for her role as voluntary water bearer during the American Revolutionary War, was the first woman to be granted a military pension from a state government, in Phil-adelphia, Pennsylvania.

Sources: Read and Wittlieb, *The Book of Women's Firsts,* pp. 277–78.

1861 • Sally Louisa Tompkins (1833–1916), known as "Captain Sally," was the first woman to become a commissioned officer in the Confederate Army.

An artist's portrait of Deborah Sampson.

MARY EDWARDS WALKER

Dr. Mary Edwards Walker (1832–1919) was a Civil War medical worker, dress reformer, and the first woman to receive the Congressional Medal of Honor in 1865. Walker attended Syracuse Medical College and then went into practice in Columbus, Ohio, and Rome, New York, with her husband. Scorning conventional female attire, Walker appeared in trousers and became an ardent proposer of dress reform. When the Civil War broke out, Walker offered her services at the medical corps but was refused on the basis of her sex. She was given work as an unpaid volunteer and after two years finally began to receive a salary. In 1865 she was captured and imprisoned, after which she was exchanged for a confederate soldier. Recognized for her bravery and devotion, General Sherman recommended her for the Congressional Medal of Honor, which President Andrew Jackson presented to her on November 11, 1865. Her unconventional behavior, however, continued to alienate people, and she was forced to appear in sideshows to make a living. On June 3, 1917, the Federal Board of Medal Awards declared that her Civil War citation had been unwarranted and officially withdrew it. Walker never gave up her medal and continued to wear it until her death three years later, at the age of sixty-seven. On June 10, 1977, through the efforts of her family and members of congress, her medal was officially restored.

In 1861, Jefferson Davis, president of the Confederacy, appointed her a calvalry officer so that she could maintain her own infirmary, Robertson Hospital, in Richmond, Virginia.

Sources: McHenry, *Famous American Women,* p. 415; Read and Witlieb, *The Book of Women's Firsts,* p. 447.

1863 • Susan "Susie" Baker King Taylor (1848–1912) was the first black woman to serve as a nurse in the U.S. armed services. In 1863 she nursed with the First Regiment of the South Carolina Volunteers.

Sources: Smith, *Black Firsts,* p. 358; Smith, *Notable Black American Women,* pp. 1108–13.

1865 • Dr. Mary Edwards Walker (1832–1919) of the U.S. Army was the first woman to be awarded the Congressional Medal of Honor. She was honored in a presentation ceremony on November 11 for medical services she provided during the Civil War.

Sources: Kane, *Famous First Facts,* p. 372; Women in Military Service for America Memorial, *The Women's Memorial Special Edition Calendar, 1995,* cover.

1897 • Sarah Emma Edmonds (1841–1898) became the first and only female member of the Grand Army of the Republic (GAR), an organization of veterans. She had enlisted in the Union Army sometime between in 1859 and 1861 and became the only woman to serve as a soldier in the U.S. Civil War, although other women were involved on both sides of the conflict in supporting positions. According to one source, Edmonds deserted the Army in 1863. To achieve her goals of joining the military, she assumed a male identity under the

Oveta Culp Hobby

name of Franklin Thompson. In 1865 she published her memoirs, *Nurse and Spy in the Union Army.*

Sources: Greenspan, *The Timetables of Women's History,* p. 243; McHenry, *Famous American Women,* p. 117; Read and Witlieb, *The Book of Women's Firsts,* pp. 138–39.

1942 • Oveta Culp Hobby (1905–1995) was the first director of the Women's Army Auxiliary Corps, which later became The Women's Army Corps. She was sworn in by Secretary of War Lewis Stimson in Washington, D.C., on May 15, 1942, with the rank of major, later raised to colonel. (*See also* **Government: United States, 1953.**)

Sources: Graham, *Current Biography Yearbook,* p. 627; McHenry, *Famous American Women,* p. 191–92; Read and Witlieb, *The Book of Women's Firsts,* pp. 208–9.

1944 • In May, Cordelia E. Cook, a first lieutenant in the Army Nurse Corps, was the first woman to be awarded the Bronze Star. The Bronze Star was established in February 1944 by Executive Order of President Franklin D. Roosevelt. It could be awarded to anyone serving in the U.S. military who distinguished themselves on or after December 7, 1941, the day the Japanese attacked U.S. naval operations in Pearl Harbor, Hawaii. Cook received this honor in recognition for her work at an Italian field hospital during World War II between November 1943 and January 1944, when her area was repeatedly under attack. Despite being wounded during one attack, Cook continued to perform her duties. Cook was also awarded the Order of the Purple Heart, the first U.S. military decoration to be established. It was created by president George Washington in 1782. Cook was the first woman who served during World War II to receive two military decorations.

Sources: Kane, *Famous First Facts,* p. 366; Read and Witlieb, *The Book of Women's Firsts,* p. 101.

1947 • Florence Aby Blanchfield (1882–1971) was the first woman to receive a regular commission in the United States Army; she was appointed lieutenant colonel. She made her career in the Army Nurse Corps, joining in 1917 and achieving the rank of superintendent in 1943. With the passage of the Army-Navy Nurse Act in 1947, nurses were granted full status and Blanchfield finally received her commission.

Sources: Bailey, *The Remarkable Lives of 100 Women Healers and Scientists,* pp. 20–21; Kane, *Famous First Facts,* p. 36.

1948 • Colonel Mary Agnes Hallaren (b. 1907) became the first female army officer to serve in the regular army and not in the medical department. She served as the director of the Women's Army Corps, Regular Army, in Washington, D.C.

Sources: Kane, *Famous First Facts,* pp. 35–36; McHenry, *Famous American Women,* p. 174.

In a televised ceremony on July 8, Vietta M. Bates was sworn in as the first member of the Women's Army Corps, Regular Army, as technician third grade. The ceremony was conducted by General Omar Bradley, Army Chief of Staff.

Sources: Kane, *Famous First Facts,* p. 30; Read and Witlieb, *The Book of Women's Firsts,* p. 42.

1956 • On March 11, Fae Margaret Adams (b. 1918) became the first female doctor to receive a regular commission in the U.S. Army. She was commissioned a first lieutenant and served as a reserve medical officer in the U.S. Army. Up until this time, women physicians had served in the Women's Army Corps.

Sources: Kane, *Famous First Facts,* p. 36; Read and Witlieb, *The Book of Women's Firsts,* p. 7.

1968 • Elizabeth Matthew Lewis (b. 1916), a librarian at the U.S. Military Academy at West Point, began teaching the course EN 392: Introduction to Fine Arts. In doing so, she became the first female instructor at West Point.

Sources: Kane, *Famous First Facts,* p. 37.

1969 • Lieutenant Colonel Frances V. Chaffin and Lieutenant Colonel Shirley Rowell Heinze, both of the Women's Army Corps (WAC) became the first two women to graduate from the U.S. Army War College at Carlisle, Pennsylvania, in ceremonies on June 16. The Army War College was created in 1901 to provide army officers with instruction in advanced military tactics and strategies.

Sources: Kane, *Famous First Facts,* p. 38.

Elizabeth Matthew Lewis

1970 • Anna Mae Hays (b. 1920) and Elizabeth P. Hoisington (b. 1918) shared the honor of being the first women to become U.S. Army generals. Hays was promoted to the rank of brigadier general in the Army Nurse Corps; on the same date, Hoisington was promoted to the same rank in the Women's Army Corps.

Sources: Holm, *Women in the Military: An Unfinished Revolution,* p. 203; Sanders, *The First of Everything,* p. 158.

1978 • Mary Clarke (b. 1924) was the last commander of the Women's Army Corps (WAC). When the WAC was dissolved in 1978, Clarke was promoted to Major General, becoming the first woman to hold this office in the United States Army. She was the top-ranking female soldier when she retired after 36 years of service.

Sources: Holm, *Women in the Military: An Unfinished Revolution,* p. 401; Read and Witlieb, *The Book of Women's Firsts,* pp. 92–93.

1980 • On May 28, the U.S. Military Academy at West Point graduated its first class to include women. The top, or "distinguished," cadets graduate in order of overall performance. Andrea Hollen, a distinguished cadet, was the first woman cadet in the class of 1980 to receive her diploma. On March 9, 1976, 119 women became the first women accepted for admission to West Point, becoming members of the class of 1980; they became the first women enrolled on July 7, 1976. Of that group, 62 female cadets completed the course of study and training to graduate, 61 of whom participated in the May 28 ceremony. The 62nd cadet, along with a dozen male cadets, graduated on June 26, 1980. All received commissions as second lieutenants in the U.S. Army upon graduation from the academy.

Andrea Hollen

Sources: Kane, *Famous First Facts,* p. 37; Read and Witlieb, *The Book of Women's Firsts,* p. 459; U.S. Military Academy at West Point, Office of Public Information, correspondence, 1996.

1996 • Sgt. Heather Johnson (b. 1973) became the first woman to stand watch at the Tomb of the Unknowns in Arlington National Cemetery in Washington, D.C. on March 22, 1996.

Sources: Dongan, "New Military Culture," *CQ Researcher* (26 April 1996), pp. 361–83; "Changing of the Guard," *The New York Times* (23 March 1996), p. A10.

United States–Coast Guard

1979 • On April 16, Beverly Gwinn Kelley (b. 1952) took command of a U.S. Coast Guard vessel at sea, becoming the first woman to do so. From April 1979 through July 1981, Kelley commanded a Coast Guard patrol boat off the coast of Hawaii.

Sources: Kane, *Famous First Facts,* p. 177; Read and Witlieb, *The Book of Women's Firsts,* p. 238.

United States–Marines

1812 • Lucy Brewer concealed her female identity and enlisted in the marines as George Baker in 1812. She served aboard the U.S.S. *Constitution* in its winning battle during the War of 1812 on August 19 of that year.

Beverly Gwinn Kelley

Sources: Holm, *Women in the Military: An Unifinished Revolution,* p. 5; Kane, *Famous First Facts,* p. 3673; Read and Witlieb, *The Book of Women's Firsts,* p. 67.

FIRST WOMEN TO GRADUATE FROM THE U.S. MILITARY ACADEMY AT WEST POINT, 1980

Alesch, Donna S.	Albuquerque, New Mexico	Lewis, Debra M.	Dover, New Jersey
Ashworth, Ann S.	Greensboro, North Carolina	Maller, Danna	Cockeysville, Maryland
Barkalow, Carol A.	Laurel, Maryland	Martin, Vicki L.	Fenton, Michigan
Bemya, Brigit	Fremont, California	McCarthy, Debra L.	Grass Valley, California
Blyth, Rebecca A.	York, Pennsylvania	McEntee, Jane	New Braunfels, Texas
Bracey, Diane	Wood-Ridge, New Jersey	Moran, Sylvia T.	Homewood, Illinois
Calhoon, Janis M.	Cheektowaga, New York	Muir, Amy J.	Greenwich, Connecticut
Cicchini, Karen A.	Santa Maria, California	Nikituk, Sonya E.	South Saint Paul, Minnesota
Colister, Rught A.	College Park, Maryland	Null, Rita A.	Arbyrd, Missouri
Dallas, Joy S.	Fairborn, Ohio	Nyberg, Marene	Halifax, Massachusetts
Dawson, Denise I.	Woodbridge, Virginia	O'Connor, Erin M.	Bordentown, New Jersey
Fennessy, Robin R.	Elk Point, South Dakota	Perkins, Jane H.	Ridgewood, New Jersey
Fiedler, Bobbi L.	Vienna, Virginia	Pfluke, Lillian A.	Palo Alto, California
Fields, Anne W.	South Orleans, Massachusetts	Reichelt, S.P.	Panama City, Florida
Flynn, Mary E.	North Caldwell, New Jersey	Rosinski, Mary G.	St. Joseph, Michigan
Fulton, Brenda S.	Jensen Beach, Florida	Sheets, Grynnen G.	Edmond, Oklahoma
Gerard, Kathleen M.	Carlisle Barracks, Pennsylvania	Silvia, Kathleen	North Reading, Massachusetts
Goodland, K.	Ames, Iowa	Smith, Joan M.	Tenafly, New Jersey
Gridley, Mary E.	Dixon, Illinois	Stevens, Christi L.	Jacksonville Beach, Florida
Griffin, Eleanor R.	Ft. Sill, Oklahoma	Stoddard, Dianne L.	South Kent, Connecticut
Gucwa, Nancy L.	Staten Island, New York	Tepper, Terry J.	Elmsford, New York
Harrington, J. J.	Moore, Oklahoma	Todd, Regina C.	Peekskill, New York
Hinsey, Karen J.	Parker, Colorado	Trehapne, B. L.	Livonia, Michigan
Hollen, Andrea	Altoona, Pennsylvania	Turner, Doris A.	Lyndhurst, Ohio
Hughes, Ann M.	Garden City, Pennsylvania	Walker, P. M.	Detroit, Michigan
Johnson, Debra	Poughkeepsie, New York	Wheless, K. A.	Clearwater, Florida
Kaseman, Tamara C.	Fargo, North Dakota	Wildey, Kathryn A.	Spokane, Washington
Kellett, Susan P.	Kaneohe, Hawaii	Wright, Donna H.	Merrick, New York
Kelly, Karen L.	Naperville, Illinois	Young, Carol A.	Fairport, New York
Kinzler, Karen M.	Aiea, Hawaii	Zachgo, Kelly L.	San Antonio, Texas
Kirby, Clare	West Point, New York	Zech, Joan M.	Enumclaw, Washington

1918 • On August 13, Opha May Johnson became the first female member of the U.S. Marine Corps Reserve, when she was hired at the rank of private to serve as a clerk in the Washington, D.C. headquarters.

Sources: Kane, *Famous First Facts,* p. 364; Read and Witlieb, *The Book of Women's Firsts,* p. 230.

1943 • "Molly Marine" was the first statue of a woman in uniformed service in the U.S. armed services. Unveiled on November 10, 1943, in New Orleans, Louisiana, this monument was dedicated to the U.S. Marine Corps Women's Reserve.

Sources: O'Neill, *The Women's Book of World Records and Achievements,* pp. 537–38.

1953 • Barbara Olive Barnwell, a staff sergeant in the U.S. Marine Reserve, was the first woman to receive the U.S. Navy-Marine Corps medal for heroism. She was decorated by General Lemuel Cornick Shepherd, Jr., Commandant of the U.S. Marine Corps, in Washington, D.C. Barnwell was reward-

Brigadier General Margaret A. Brewer

ed for her courage in saving a soldier, Pfc. Frederick G Romann, from drowning in 1952 at Camp Lejeune, North Carolina.

Sources: Kane, *Famous First Facts,* p. 373; Read and Witlieb, *Women's Firsts,* p. 39.

1978 • Margaret A. Brewer (b. 1930) became the first female brigadier general in the U.S. Marine Corps. She served as director of information at marine headquarters in Washington, D.C. The Marine Corps was the last of the armed services in the United States to promote a woman to the rank of general.

Sources: Holm, *Women in the Military: An Unfinished Revolution,* p. 203; Kane, *Famous First Facts,* p. 363; Read and Witlieb, *The Book of Women's Firsts,* p. 67.

1985 • Gail M. Reals (b. 1937) was the first woman promoted to the rank of brigadier general in direct competition with men. Reals enjoyed a distinguished career in the U.S. Marine Corps between 1956 and her retirement in 1990.

Sources: Time (1 June 1990), p. 85; Read and Witlieb, *The Book of Women's Firsts,* p. 361.

United States–Navy

1917 • Loretta Walsh (b. 1898) was the first woman to enlist in the U.S. Navy. The navy was short-staffed during the first months after the United States entered World War I and permitted women to serve in stateside capacities. Walsh became a yeoman in charge of recruiting for the Naval Coastal Defense Reserve.

Brigadier General Gail M. Reals

Sources: Kane, *Famous First Facts,* p. 420; Read and Witlieb, *The Book of Women's Firsts,* pp. 467–68.

WOMEN'S FIRSTS

317

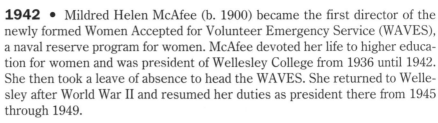

1942 • Mildred Helen McAfee (b. 1900) became the first director of the newly formed Women Accepted for Volunteer Emergency Service (WAVES), a naval reserve program for women. McAfee devoted her life to higher education for women and was president of Wellesley College from 1936 until 1942. She then took a leave of absence to head the WAVES. She returned to Wellesley after World War II and resumed her duties as president there from 1945 through 1949.

Sources: Beard, *Woman as Force in History,* p. 39; Howes, *American Women 1935–1940: A Composite Biographical Dictionary,* p. 579; Kane, *Famous First Facts,* p. 421; Read and Witlieb, *The Book of Women's Firsts,* pp. 275–76.

Mildred McAfee was the first director of the WAVES.

1948 • Frances L. Willoughby (1906–1984) was the first female physician to hold a regular U.S. Navy commission. She served in the naval reserve during World War II, but as a result of the Women's Armed Services Act of 1948, which mandated that there were to be no separate women's branches in the U.S. armed forces, she was in that year commissioned in the regular Navy.

Sources: Kane, *Famous First Facts,* p. 420; Read and Witlieb, *The Book of Women's Firsts,* pp. 484–85.

1950 • Bernice Rosenthal Walters was the first female physician assigned to U.S. navy shipboard duty. Walters, a lieutenant commander in the medical corps of the U.S. Naval Reserve, joined the reserves in 1943. Walters joined the crew of ten medical officers on board the Navy hospital ship, the U.S.S. *Consolation.*

Sources: Kane, *Famous First Facts,* p. 421; Read and Witlieb, *The Book of Women's Firsts,* p. 469.

1966 • Gale Ann Gordon (b. 1943) was the first woman to fly solo as a U.S. Navy pilot. In March, she took off and landed at Pensacola, Florida, where she served as a member of the Medical Service Corps.

Sources: Kane, *Famous First Facts,* p. 86; Read and Witlieb, *The Book of Women's Firsts,* p. 181.

1972 • Alene B. Duerk (b. 1920) was the first woman to be appointed a rear admiral in the U.S. Navy. She became head of the Navy Nurse Corps in 1970 and in 1972 was promoted from captain to rear admiral. She was the first woman to achieve the rank of admiral in any of the world's navies.

Sources: Holm, *Women in the Military: An Unfinished Revolution,* p. 203; Read and Witlieb, *The Book of Women's Firsts,* pp. 126–27.

1973 • Sister Elizabeth M. Edmonds (b. 1941) was the first nun to serve as a U.S. Navy officer. She was commissioned a first lieutenant on her graduation from the University of Pennsylvania Medical School in Philadelphia in 1973.

Sources: Read and Witlieb, *The Book of Women's Firsts,* p. 139.

1974 • Barbara Rainey (1948–1982) became the first woman to serve as a pilot in the U.S. Navy. She had a promising career as a naval pilot until her sudden death from unspecified causes while on active duty.

Barbara Rainey was the first woman pilot in the U.S. Navy.

Sources: Read and Witlieb, *The Book of Women's Firsts,* pp. 356–57.

1991 • Juliane Gallina (b. 1970) became the first woman to be named brigade commander at the U.S. Naval Academy in Annapolis, Maryland. In this capacity, Gallina leads the 4,300 members of the brigade, presides at ceremonies, and acts as a liaison between students and academy officers.

Sources: Read and Witlieb, *The Book of Women's Firsts.*

1992 • Darlene Iskra (b. 1952) became the U.S. Navy's first female skipper when she took command of the salvage vessel USS *Opportune.* Women at the time were prohibited from serving aboard combat ships by the U.S. Congress. As a result, in 1992, less than one of every six women in the U.S. Navy served at sea.

Source: Thompson, "Navy Ship's Skipper Is a Woman, A First," *Journal of Commerce and Commercial* (3 November 1992), vol. 394, no. 27847, p. B1.

1994 • Lieutenant Shannon Workman became the first woman to qualify as a combat-ready naval pilot. She completed her final requirements by landing on the ship U.S.S. *Eisenhower* off the Virginia coast.

Sources: Schmitt, "Navy Women Bringing New Era on Carriers," *The New York Times* (21 February 1994), p. A1.

Zimbabwe

1976 • Joice Nhongo (b. 1955), a Zimbabwe guerilla fighter, was the first woman to be appointed Camp Commander of Chimoio, the largest guerrilla and refugee camp in Mozambique. She soon became the most famous fighter in Robert Mugabe's forces. After the creation of Zimbabwe, she served in the new government as Minister of Community Development and Women's Affairs.

Sources: Uglow, *The Continuum Dictionary of Women's Biography,* pp. 400–1.

Organization and Group Firsts

Clubs and Organizations

1855 • The Young Women's Christian Association (YWCA) was the first social service organization serving Christian women. In England in 1855, two groups are founded—the English Prayer Union and the General Female Training Institute (a home for nurses returning from the Crimean War), forming the foundation of the Young Women's Christian Association. The two organizations expand their activities and merge in 1877 as the Young Women's Christian Association.

In the United States, the first group to meet in what would become the YWCA network was the Ladies' Christian Association of New York City, founded in 1858. In 1866, the first association to bear the name Young Women's Christian Association was formed in Boston. The YWCA required that its member organizations be affiliated with an evangelical Christian church until 1928, when a pledge to uphold the goals of the organization was substituted. YWCAs send missionaries to other parts of the world—including India, China, Japan, Korea, parts of Latin America, and (less often) Africa.

Sources: Read and Witlieb, *The Book of Women's Firsts,* p. 484.

1987 • The U.S. Supreme Court ruled on May 4, 1987, that Rotary Clubs (national service organizations) must admit women. Founded in 1907, the Rotary was so named because members—all businessmen—met in rotation at their places of business. The organization is dedicated to promoting the welfare of the community where its members do business.

Source: Time (18 May 1987), p. 61.

Organization Founders

1868 • Jane Cunningham Croly (1829–1901), a journalist who wrote under the pen name of Jenny June, was the organizer of the pioneering women's club Sorosis, in New York City in 1868. The club, the first professional club for women in the United States, was founded in response to women's exclusion from the New York Press Club's reception of Charles Dickens. Croly served as the president of Sorosis in 1870 and again between 1875 and 1886. Croly is also remembered as the author of the *History of the Women's Club Movement in America* (1898).

Sources: James, *Notable American Women,* vol. 1, pp. 409–11; June, *Memories of Jane Cunningham Croly;* Read and Witlieb, *The Book of Women's Firsts,* pp. 414–15.

1871 • Harriet Jemima Winifred Clisby (1830–1931) was the founder of the Women's Educational and Industrial Union, in Boston, Massachusetts, in 1871. A feminist physician, Clisby was born in England, grew up in Australia, trained as a nurse in London, received her medical degree in New York (in 1865), and finally retired to Geneva, Switzerland, where she founded L'Union des Femmes.

Sources: Uglow, *The Continuum Dictionary of Women's Biography,* p. 129.

Elizabeth Dmitrieva (1851–1910), a Russian socialist, was the organizer of the Women's Union for the Defense of Paris, a branch of the Socialist International, in 1871. A friend of Karl Marx, she escaped from Paris and returned to Russia after the defeat of the communards.

Sources: Uglow, *The Continuum Dictionary of Women's Biography,* pp. 170–71.

1886 • Julia Richman (1855–1912) served as the first president of the Young Women's Hebrew Association, from 1886 to 1890. The Young Women's Hebrew Association, founded in New York City in 1886, was the first national social service organization designed to meet the needs of Jewish women and girls. She was active in the field of education in New York City throughout her life.

Sources: James, *Notable American Women,* vol. 3, pp. 150–52; Read and Witlieb, *The Book of Women's Firsts,* pp. 368, 501.

Mary Smith Lockwood

1891 • Mary Smith Lockwood (b. 1831), Ellen Hardin Walworth (1832–1915), and Eugenia Washington founded the Daughters of the American Revolution (DAR) on October 11, 1890, in Washington, D.C. Lockwood was a leading member of the Woman's Suffrage Club of the District of Columbia and was an author of historical works. Notable among her works was *Historic Homes of Washington.*

The DAR was the first women's patriotic group based on heredity. To become a member, a woman must be over age 18 and able to prove that she descends directly from persons who aided in establishing independence of the United States from England. The DAR was chartered by the U.S. Congress in 1896 and must report to Congress annually. The DAR encourages the study of American history.

Sources: James, *Notable American Women,* vol. 3, pp. 150–52; *National Cyclopedia of American Biography,* vol. 3, p. 266; Read and Witlieb, *The Book of Women's Firsts,* pp. 368, 501.

1893 • Ida Bell Wells-Barnett (1862–1931), an American journalist, lecturer, and clubwoman, was the founder and first president of the Ida B. Wells Club, in Chicago, Illinois, in 1893. This organization devoted its energies to a variety of projects in the city's black community. Often called the first black female journalist, Wells-Barnett was also the founder of the first black women's suffrage organization, the Alpha Suffrage Club of Chicago.

Sources: James, *Notable American Women,* vol. 3, pp. 565–67; Uglow, *The Continuum Dictionary of Women's Biography,* p. 575.

1894 • Cornelia Foster Bradford (1847–1935) was the first person to establish a settlement house in New Jersey. In May of 1894, she opened Whitier House in Jersey City. The settlement organized a full program of educational, recreational, and social activities and by 1900 had helped to establish the city's first kindergarten, district nursing service, dental dispensary, and public playground.

Sources: James, *Notable American Women,* vol. 1, pp. 218–19; Scannell, *New Jersey's First Citizens,* vol. 1, pp. 56–58.

1895 • Octavia Hill (1838–1912), an English woman with a strong sense of social duty, was the cofounder of her country's National Trust for Places of Historic Interest or Natural Beauty. Commonly referred to by the abbreviated National Trust, it is an important conservation organization that began by preserving land in the Lake District. Hill also devoted her energies to housing and penal reform. Beginning in 1864, John Ruskin, Hill's art tutor, provided the financial resources Hill needed to purchase dilapidated housing for improvement in slum neighborhoods. In 1869, she cofounded the Charity Organization Society with Frederick Denison. Hill's published works on housing and conservation are *Homes of the London Poor* (1875) and *Our Common Land* (1878).

Sources: Bell, *Octavia Hill*; Magnusson, *Larousse Biographical Dictionary,* p. 711; Uglow, *The Continuum Dictionary of Women's Biography,* p. 260.

1896 • Margaret Murray Washington (1865–1925), who worked with her husband, Booker T. Washington, at Tuskegee Institute, was the founder of the National Association of Colored Women, in 1896 in Washington, D.C.

Sources: Chicago, *The Dinner Party,* p. 183.

Maud Ballington Booth (1865–1948) was the cofounder, with her husband Ballington Booth, of the Volunteers of America, in New York City in 1896. This organization, which followed the structure and purposes of the Salvation Army in many ways, was exclusively American and more democratic. Maud and Ballington Booth left the Salvation Army, in which both had worked ardently for many years in both Australia and the United States. They left over a dispute over the arbitrary and authoritative rule of its founder, General William Booth, Ballington Booth's father. After her husband's death in 1940, Maud Booth was elected as general and commander-in-chief of the Volunteers of America, thus becoming the first woman to hold this position.

Sources: James, *Notable American Women,* vol. 1, pp. 208–10; Welty, *Look Up and Hope!*

Early twentieth century • Josephine St. Pierre Ruffin (1842–1924), an African-American leader, was the founder of the Boston branch of the National Association for the Advancement of Colored People (NAACP). An active worker for civil rights throughout her life, Ruffin helped to found a number of orga-

Charlotte Vetter Gulick

nizations supported by abolitionist feminists such as Lucy Stone and Julia Ward Howe.

Sources: Uglow, *The Continuum Dictionary of Women's Biography,* p. 468.

1910 • Mary Hawes Wilmarth (1837–1919), a prominent leader in civic and reform causes and a close friend of Jane Addams, was the first president of the Women's City Club of Chicago, an organization that she helped to found in 1910.

Sources: James, *Notable American Women,* vol. 2, p. 251.

Charlotte Vetter Gulick (1866–1928), with her husband, Luther Halsey Gulick, and William Chauncey Langdon, founded the Camp Fire Girls in South

Casco, Maine, in 1910. Her husband and Langdon had recently helped establish the Boy Scouts, and she worked with them to establish a similar group for girls. The organization—the first non-sectarian, interracial group of its kind for girls—stresses character development and good mental and physical health.

Sources: O'Neill, *The Women's Book of World Records and Achievements,* pp. 112–13; Read and Witlieb, *The Book of Women's Firsts,* pp. 186–87.

Juliette Gordon Low founded the Girl Scouts in America with this group of Georgia girls.

1912 • Juliette Gordon Low (1860–1927) was the founder of the Girl Scouts of America. She organized the first American group of Girl Guides in Savannah, Georgia, on March 12, 1912. In 1915, the group's name was changed to the Girl Scouts. Low served as its first president until 1920. The niece of Juliette Gordon Low, Margaret "Daisy" Gordon, became the first American Girl Scout in 1912 when she joined the organization in Savannah, Georgia. Technically, Daisy Gordon was a "Girl Guide," as female Scouts were called in England, until Low changed the American organization's name in 1915.

Sources: James, *Notable American Women,* vol. 2, pp. 432–34; McCullough, *First of All: Significant Firsts by American Women,* p. 141; Read and Witlieb, *The Book of Women's Firsts,* pp. 181, 261–62.

1913 • Winifred Holt (1870–1945), with her sister Edith, founded the Lighthouses for the Blind (later The Lighthouse) in New York City in 1913.

The organization was devoted both to the prevention of blindness and to helping the blind become self-supporting.

Sources: Read and Witlieb, *The Book of Women's Firsts,* p. 214.

1916 • Lady Olave Baden-Powell (1889–1977) and Agnes Baden-Powell (1858–1945) were the cofounders of the English Girl Guides. In Sussex, during the first years of World War I, they began their work on founding this counterpart to Robert Baden-Powell's Boy Scouts. (Lady Olave was his wife, and Agnes was his sister.) In 1916, the organization was formalized, and Lady Baden-Powell took as its first director the title of Chief Commissioner.

Sources: Baden-Powell, *Window on my Heart*; Magnusson, *Larousse Biographical Dictionary,* p. 89; Uglow, *The Continuum Dictionary of Women's Biography,* p. 41.

1926 • In 1926 Gertrude Bonnin (1876–1938) founded the National Council of American Indians. She served as its first president until her death. The council was a reform group and the successor to the Society of American Indians.

Sources: Read and Witlieb, *The Book of Women's Firsts,* p. 61.

Dorothy Eustis

1930 • Dorothy Harrison Wood Eustis (1886–1946) was the first president of The Seeing Eye, an organization that trains dogs to serve as guides for the blind. She founded the organization in 1930, basing her school on a similar one in Potsdam, Germany, which trained guide dogs for World War I veterans.

Sources: James, *Notable American Women,* vol. 1, pp. 585–86; Read and Witlieb, *The Book of Women's Firsts,* pp. 146–47.

1935 • Mary McLeod Bethune (1875–1955) was the first president of the National Council of Negro Women, an organization she founded in 1935. Bethune devoted her life to the needs of to African Americans, especially to the needs of black girls and women. She began her career as a teacher, starting a school in 1904, which in 1929 became Bethune-Cookman College. In 1936 she became the first black woman to serve as a presidential advisor.

Sources: Read and Witlieb, *The Book of Women's Firsts,* pp. 50–51; Uglow, *The Continuum Dictionary of Women's Biography,* p. 65.

Margaret Isabel Cole (1893–1980), an ardent English socialist, was the cofounder, with her husband G. D. H. Cole, of the New Fabian Research Bureau, in London in 1935. This organization collected much of the data for the post-World War II Labour government's reforms.

Sources: Uglow, *The Continuum Dictionary of Women's Biography,* p. 131.

1957 • Eirlys Roberts (b. 1911) was the founder of the British Consumers' Association, in London in 1957. She served this organization as the first Head of the Research and Editorial Division between 1958 through 1973 and as editor of its influential magazine *Which?* between 1961 and 1977. She campaigned for safety standards and public accountability. Roberts has also been involved on behalf of consumers through various offices in the governance of the European Economic Community.

Sources: Uglow, *The Continuum Dictionary of Women's Biography,* pp. 460–61.

Jacqueline Bernard (b. 1921), an American journalist, was the cofounder, with Jim Egleson, of Parents Without Partners, in New York City in 1957. This self-help group was one of the earliest such organizations and now has a nationwide membership.

Sources: O'Neill, *The Women's Book of World Records and Achievements,* pp. 722–23.

1958 • Ethel Andrus (1884–1967) was the first president of the American Association of Retired Persons (AARP), an organization she founded in 1958. Andrus was also the founder in 1947 and first president of the National Retired Teachers Association (NRTA), work that led her to founding the larger association eleven years later.

Sources: Read and Witlieb, *The Book of Women's Firsts,* pp. 20–21.

1967 • Alicia Escalante, a Chicana activist from El Paso, Texas, was the founder of the first Chicano welfare rights group, the East Los Angeles Welfare Rights Organization, in Los Angeles, California, in 1967.

Sources: O'Neill, *The Women's Book of World Records and Achievements,* p. 716.

Ethel Andrus

1970 • Margaret E. Kuhn (b. 1905), a community activist throughout her life, was the founder of the Gray Panthers, in June 1970. This organization, the first of its kind in the United States, devoted its energies to fighting ageism and to bringing attention to the needs of the elderly in America.

Sources: O'Neill, *The Women's Book of World Records and Achievements,* p. 722.

1976 • Joyce Koupal (b. 1932), who with her husband cofounded People's Lobby in Los Angeles, California, in 1968, became its first female director in 1976. This organization worked for political reform and environmental issues.

Sources: O'Neill, *The Women's Book of World Records and Achievements,* p. 730.

Organization Leadership

Late 1850s • Carolina Maria Seymour Severance (1820–1914), a pioneering U.S. clubwoman, was the first woman to speak at the popular Parker Fraternity Lecture Course in Boston, Massachusetts, in the late 1850s. Active on behalf on women's rights and pacifism, she is remembered for her friendships with important leaders in the transcendentalist movement of her youth and with such suffragists as Julia Ward Howe.

Sources: Gibson, *Caroline M. Severance, Pioneer*; James, *Notable American Women,* vol. 3, pp. 265–67; Ruddy, *The Mother of Clubs: Caroline M. Severance;* Willard and Livermore, *A Woman of the Century.*

1890 • Caroline Scott Harrison (1832–1892) was elected first president-general of the Daughters of the American Revolution (the DAR) when the or-

Caroline Scott Harrison

ganization was founded on October 11, 1890. Active throughout her life in charity and social work, Harrison was also the wife of U.S. President Benjamin Harrison.

Flora Darling (1840–1910) was the first vice-president of the Daughters of the American Revolution (DAR), a position she assumed when the organization was founded. She resigned after a disagreement over power within the organization (she claimed to be the founder), then went on to found Daughters of the Revolution and U.S. Daughters of 1812.

Sources: Harper's Encyclopedia of United States History, vol. 3, p. 15; James, *Notable American Women,* vol. 2, pp. 145–46; *National Cyclopedia of American Biography,* vol. 1, pp. 135–36; Read and Witlieb, *The Book of Women's Firsts,* p. 197; Uglow, *The Continuum Dictionary of Women's Biography,* pp. 147–48.

1891 • Harriet Maxwell Converse (1836–1903) was the first white woman to become a Native American chief. In recognition of her successful work against a New York State bill to break up reservations, Converse was named honorary chief of the Six Nations (the Cayuga, Mohawk, Onondaga, Oneida, Seneca, and Tuscarora) at Tonawanda, New York, on September 18, 1891.

Sources: Read and Witlieb, *The Book of Women's Firsts,* pp. 100–1.

1892 • Victoria Earle Matthews (1861–1907), an American social worker, clubwoman, and author who was born into slavery at the time of the Civil War, was the first president of a club for black women, the Women's Loyal Union of New York and Brooklyn, founded in New York City in 1892.

Sources: Brown, *Homespun Heroines and Other Women of Distinction*; Davis, *Lifting as They Climb*; James, *Notable American Women,* vol. 2, pp. 510–11.

1896 • Mary Church Terrell (1863–1954) was the first president of the National Association of Colored Women. She served three terms in this capacity, from 1896 until 1901. Terrell was an influential leader in the suffrage and civil rights movements. From 1895 to 1901 and from 1906 to 1911, she served on the District of Columbia school board, the first black woman to do so.

Sources: Chicago, *The Dinner Party,* p. 185; Sicherman and Green, *Notable American Women: The Modern Period,* pp. 678–80.

Early twentieth century • Josephine Woempner Clifford McCrackin (1838–1920), an American writer and ardent conservationist, was the first female member of the California Game and Fish Protective Association. Her books, influenced by Bret Harte, convey her love of the rural southwest and women's struggles to settle this frontier. She published *Overland Tales* in 1877 and *The Woman Who Lost Him* in 1913.

Sources: James, *Notable American Women,* vol. 2, pp. 455–56.

1908 • Janie Barrett Porter (1865–1948), a black social welfare leader, was the first president of the Virginia State Federation of Colored Women's Clubs, in Richmond, Virginia, in 1908. She was also the founder, in October of 1890, of the Locust Street Social Settlement, the first settlement house in Virginia.

Sources: Daniel, *Women Builders;* James, *Notable American Women,* vol. 1, pp. 96–97; Ovington, *Portraits in Color,* pp. 181–93; Sickels, *Twelve Daughters of Democracy,* pp. 191–208.

1917 • Edith Elmer Wood (1871–1945) became the first woman to chair a national committee on housing in the United States when she was named head of the national committee on housing of the American Association of University Women in 1917. She served in this capacity until 1929. Wood went on to serve as a consultant to the housing division of the Public Works Administration (1933–1937) and to the U.S. Housing Authority (1938–1942).

Sources: Read and Witlieb, *The Book of Women's Firsts,* p. 492.

1918 • Mary Sheepshanks (1872–1958), an English feminist and pacifist, was the first secretary of the Fight the Famine Committee, a position which she assumed in London in December of 1918. This association later became the Save the Children Fund. Sheepshanks went on to become international secretary of this organization and, based in Geneva, organized in its name the first international scientific conference on Modern Methods of Warfare and the Protection of Civilians, in 1929.

Sources: Oldfield, *Spinsters of This Parish: The Life and Times of F.M. Mayor and Mary Sheepshanks;* Uglow, *The Continuum Dictionary of Women's Biography,* pp. 495–96.

1933 • Ray Strachey (1887–1940), an English feminist and an associate of the Bloomsbury Group through her brother-in-law, Lytton Strachey, was the first person to chair the Save the Children Fund Nursery Schools Committee, in London in 1933. She held this position until 1936. She is remembered also for her writings, including biographies of the women's rights leaders Frances Willard and Millicent Fawcett.

Sources: Strachey, *The Cause: A Brief History of the Women's Movement;* Uglow, *The Continuum Dictionary of Women's Biography,* pp. 521–22.

1971 • In 1971, Patricia McGowan Wald (b. 1928) and Dorothy Nepper-Marshall (1913–1986) became the first two women to serve as trustees of the Ford Foundation. Wald was a lawyer who was appointed a judge in the Washington, D.C. circuit of the U.S. Court of Appeals in 1979 and as chief judge in 1986.

Sources: Read and Witlieb, *The Book of Women's Firsts,* pp. 466–67.

1975 • Gloria D. Scott (b. 1938) of Houston, Texas, became the first black president of the Girl Scouts in October 1975. She had become active in scouting as a child. After receiving her Ph.D. in higher education, she joined the Girls Scouts' national board in 1969.

Sources: McCullough, *First of All: Significant Firsts by American Women,* p. 142.

1985 • Wilma P. Mankiller (b. 1945), who revitalized the Cherokee Nation, was the first woman to serve as its tribal chief when she was appointed in 1985. Between 1985 and her retirement in 1994, Mankiller increased the tribe's

Wilma Mankiller

membership from 55,000 to 156,000 and added three health centers and nine children's programs to the facilities on Cherokee land.

Sources: Read and Witlieb, *The Book of Women's Firsts,* p. 266.

1991 • Sarah Williamson (b. 1974) was the first girl to serve as mayor of Boys Town. She was elected May 2, 1991. Her office requires her to preside at various ceremonies, to serve as student council president at Boys Town High School, and to act as a role model for Boys Town's underprivileged and troubled boys and girls.

Sources: Read and Witlieb, *The Book of Women's Firsts,* p. 484.

Judith Daniels was the first woman president of the American Kennel Club, the nation's oldest dog care and dog registry organization based in New York City. Daniels is a California breeder, owner, and handler of Staffordshire bull terriers. As the organization's 18th—and first woman—president, Daniels said she did not view her appointment as a "woman's issue," but she called it an "opportunity to impact real and important change in a century-old, previously male-dominated organization."

Source: The New York Times (31 March 1995), p. B4.

Professions

Architecture

1869 • Harriet Morrison Irwin (1828–1897), a self-trained architect, was the first U.S. woman to patent an architectural innovation. On August 24, 1869, she applied for and received a patent for her design for a hexagonal house in Charlotte, North Carolina.

Sources: Vare and Ptacek, *Mothers of Invention,* pp. 165–66.

1880 • Margaret Hicks (1858–1883) was the first woman to receive a degree in architecture. She graduated from Cornell University in Ithaca, New York, in 1880. In 1878, prior to her graduation, she became the first U.S. woman to achieve architectural publication when her student project, "The Workman's Cottage," was published. Her career was cut short by her early death at the age of 25.

Sources: O'Neill, *The Women's Book of World Records and Achievements,* p. 608; Sanders, *The First of Everything,* p. 157.

1890s • Julia Morgan (1872–1957), with a degree in civil engineering from the University of California, was the first woman to study architecture at the École des Beaux Arts in Paris, in the 1890s. She went on to become the first licensed architect in California, in 1904. Her designs include the Mills College Library (1906); the Fairmont Hotel, San Francisco; and San Simeon, the home of publisher William Randolph Hearst (1919).

Sources: Chicago, *The Dinner Party,* p. 215; O'Neill, *The Women's Book of World Records and Achievements,* p. 609.

1890 • Louise Blanchard Bethune (1856–1913) was the first woman to become a professional architect in the United States. She opened an independent office in Buffalo, New York, in 1881, and on September 15, 1890, she became the first woman elected to full membership in the American Institute of Architects. Her work included schools in New York state and factories, housing projects, and banks.

Sources: James, *Notable American Women,* vol. 1, pp. 140–41; Kane, *Famous First Facts,* p. 27; Read and Witlieb, *The Book of Women's Firsts,* p. 49.

Sophia Hayden (1869–1953) was the first woman to graduate in architecture from the Massachusetts Institute of Technology in Cambridge, Massachusetts, in 1890. She won the competition to design the Women's Building at the

World's Columbian Exposition in Chicago in 1892–93 commemorating the 400th anniversary of Christopher Columbus's discovery of America. Hayden's design was for an Italian Renaissance exhibit hall with skylights. Devastated by the pressure of supervising such a large construction project and negative critical response to her work, Hayden never designed another building.

Sources: Chicago, *The Dinner Party,* p. 214; O'Neill, *The Women's Book of World Records and Achievements,* pp. xii, 608; Sicherman and Green, *Notable American Women: The Modern Period,* pp. 322–24.

1907 • Louise Caldwell Murdock (1858–1915), an interior designer in Wichita, Kansas, was the first woman to design and build a fireproof office building. Educated at the New York School of Fine and Applied Art, she is re-membered for a distinguished professional career during which she stressed interior simplicity and proportion as well as functionalism and harmony of house and landscape.

Sources: James, *Notable American Women,* vol. 2, pp. 601–2.

1920s • Lilia Skala (c.1900–1994), a stage and screen actress best known for her role as the feisty mother superior in the 1963 film *Lilies of the Field,* was the first woman to become a member of the Austrian Association of Engineers and Architects. Trained in architecture at the University of Dresden, Germa-ny, she helped design several buildings in Vienna, Austria, before leaving this profession for an acting career.

Sources: The (Cleveland) Plain Dealer (21 December 1994), p. 9-B.

1928 • Elizabeth Whitworth Scott (1898–1972), an English architect, was the first woman to design a theater for Shakespearean performances. Scott's design for the Shakespeare Memorial Theater at Stratford-upon-Avon was chosen from those of 22 other architects. She built the theater in partnership with Maurice Chesterton.

Sources: Uglow, *The Continuum Dictionary of Women's Biography,* p. 488.

1954 • Norma Merrick Sklarek (b. 1928) was the first African-American woman to be registered as an architect, in New York state in 1954. She went on to become the first African-American female fellow of the American Insti-tute of Architects in 1980.

Sources: Smith, *Black Firsts,* p. 1.

1960s • Eva Vescei (b. 1930), a Canadian architect, was the first woman to serve as project designer for a huge commercial complex, in Montreal in the 1960s. Place Bonaventure, called the largest building in the world, was com-pleted in 1967. In recognition of her work on this and other enormous projects, she was given the *Canadian Architect* award of excellence.

Sources: Uglow, *The Continuum Dictionary of Women's Biography,* p. 557.

1965 • Suzana Maria Antonakakis (b. 1935) , a Greek architect, was the co-founder, with her husband, of "Atelier 66," in 1965. "Atelier 66" is one of the leading partnerships in Greece and specializes both in new buildings and in restoration.

Sources: Uglow, *The Continuum Dictionary of Women's Biography,* p. 23.

1976 • Eileen Gray (1879–1976), a professional architect and designer, was the first Irish female designer to be the subject of a retrospective exhibition at the Victoria and Albert Museum, in London in 1976. She worked from the 1920s in a modern style with then innovative materials: steel, glass, and plastics.

Sources: Uglow, *The Continuum Dictionary of Women's Biography,* p. 235.

1980s • Gaetana Aulenti (b. 1927), an architect of international reputation, was the first woman to redesign a railway station as a museum. She spent six years during the 1980s transforming the Gare d'Orsay in Paris into the Musée d'Orsay, which houses a wide range of art created between 1789 and 1914.

Sources: Uglow, *The Continuum Dictionary of Women's Biography,* p. 35.

Demographics

1953 • Irene Barnes Taeuber (1906–1974), by profession a demographer, became the first female president of the Population Association of America. Affiliated with Princeton University throughout her professional life, Taeuber was an advocate of birth control.

Sources: Read and Witlieb, *The Book of Women's Firsts,* pp. 434–35.

Economics

1971 • Barbara Ward (1914–1981), an English economist and writer educated at Oxford, was the first woman to address the Vatican Council, in Rome in 1971. She was appointed to the Vatican Commission for Justice and Peace in 1967. She is also remembered for her publication of 16 books on economics and politics.

Sources: The Concise Dictionary of National Biography, p. 3124; Uglow, *The Continuum Dictionary of Women's Biography,* pp. 567–68.

Engineering

Seventeenth century • Baroness de Beausaleil, known for her work on the relationship between her country's power and independence and its use of natural resources, was the first female mining engineer in France. In *La Restitution de Reuton,* she recorded the location of mines and ore deposits throughout her country.

Sources: Chicago, *The Dinner Party,* p. 174.

Late nineteenth century • Nora Blatch, the daughter of Harriet Stanton Blatch and the granddaughter of Elizabeth Cady Stanton, was the first U.S. woman to earn a university degree in civil engineering.

Sources: Uglow, *The Continuum Dictionary of Women's Biography,* p. 71.

Harriet W. R. Strong (1844–1929) was the first president of the Business League of America. She was also the first woman elected to the Los Angeles Chamber of Commerce, having made a career as a water control engineer.

Sources: James, *Notable American Women,* vol. 3, pp. 405–6; Vare and Ptacek, *Mothers of Invention,* pp. 170–72.

1910s • Mary Engle Pennington (1872–1952), a specialist in the field of refrigeration, became the first chief of the U.S. Food Research Laboratory, a division of the U.S. Department of Agriculture, in about 1910.

Sources: Vare and Ptacek, *Mothers of Invention,* pp. 190–92.

1920s • E. G. McGill (b. 1903) was the first woman to qualify as an aeronautical engineer in Canada, in the 1920s. The daughter of Helen McGill (1871–1947), a pioneering feminist lawyer, E. G. McGill grew up in Vancouver and wrote a book about her mother's career in 1955.

Sources: Uglow, *The Continuum Dictionary of Women's Biography,* p. 345.

1927 • Elsie Eaves (1898–1983) was the first woman to be admitted to full membership in the American Society of Civil Engineers, in 1927. She worked on Colorado roads and railways until turning to a career in professional publications. Eaves was also a charter member of the Society of Women Engineers.

Sources: Read and Witlieb, *The Book of Women's Firsts,* pp. 134–35.

1948 • Edith Clarke (1883–1959) was the first woman to be elected a fellow of the American Institute of Electrical Engineers, and was also the first member of the Society of Women Engineers. Clarke was the first woman to earn a master's degree from the Massachusetts Institute of Technology (MIT). She taught engineering in Turkey at the Woman's College for one year after receiving her master's degree and then returned to the United States to become an engineer with General Electric.

Sources: Bailey, *The Remarkable Lives of 100 Women Healers and Scientists,* pp. 46–47; Read and Witlieb, *The Book of Women's Firsts,* pp. 91–92.

1952 • Marie Gertrude Rand (1886–1970) was the first woman to be named a fellow of the Illuminating Engineering Society of North America, in 1952. Trained as a psychologist, Rand had a distinguished career in the study of color perception and the workings of the eye.

Sources: Read and Witlieb, *The Book of Women's Firsts,* pp. 358–59.

1977 • Elizabeth Bailey (b. 1938) became the first woman to serve on the Civil Aeronautics Board (CAB) in 1977. Bailey, an economist, served until

1983 when she went on to become dean of the Graduate School of Industrial Administration at Carnegie Mellon University.

Sources: Read and Witlieb, *The Book of Women's Firsts,* p. 33.

Exploration

1519 • Marina (1501–1550), a Native Mexican princess, served as a guide to the explorer Hernando Cortéz during the Spanish conquest of Mexico. She became his mistress in 1519, and her work as an interpreter and scout are considered to have been crucial to his expedition.

Sources: Uglow, *The Continuum Dictionary of Women's Biography,* p. 358.

1890s • The first two people to discover the "Lewis Codex" were twin sisters known as the Lewis Gibsons. The recently widowed Agnes Lewis and her twin, Margaret Gibson, set out from Cambridge, England, in the 1890s on an expedition to Sinai, a region in what is now Israel. At St. Catherine's Monastery, the two women discovered some parchment the monks were using as a butter dish. Written on it was a previously unknown Syriac text of the Gospels, called now the "Lewis Codex."

Sources: Times Literary Supplement (21 October 1994), pp. 7–8.

1895 • Octavie Coudreau (1870–1910) was the first French woman to explore the Amazon River in Brazil. She and her husband set out together in 1895, but Coudreau worked on alone after his death in 1899. She was employed by the Para and Amazon states until 1906. Both with her husband and on her own, Coudreau wrote books about her experiences.

Sources: Uglow, *The Continuum Dictionary of Women's Biography,* pp. 138–39.

1909 • Agnes Deans Cameron (1863–1912) was a Canadian teacher before she decided to become an explorer and the first woman to travel from Chicago, Illinois, to the Arctic Ocean. In the same year she wrote a book about her trip, *The New North.*

Sources: Uglow, *The Continuum Dictionary of Women's Biography,* p. 104.

Flight Attendants

1930 • Ellen Church (b. 1905) became the first woman to serve as an airline stewardess. A registered nurse, Church suggested the name and idea of this new profession to her superiors at Boeing Air Transport, and on May 15, 1930, on a flight between Cheyenne, Wyoming, and Oakland, California, she became the first person to serve in this capacity. Church set a precedent, and for the next 12 years all stewardesses were required to be registered nurses.

Sources: Read and Witlieb, *The Book of Women's Firsts,* p. 90.

Floristry

1930s • Constance Spry (1886–1960), an English flower arranger and cook, was the first woman to open a school of floristry, in London in the 1930s. She began professional flower arranging in the 1920s, was instrumental in the founding of the Cordon Bleu Cooking School in London after World War II, and published 13 books on flowers and cooking.

Sources: The Concise Dictionary of National Biography, vol. III, p. 2817; Uglow, *The Continuum Dictionary of Women's Biography,* p. 511; *Who Was Who,* vol. V, pp. 1032–1033.

Geography

Nineteenth century • Isabella Bishop (c.1832–1904) was the first woman elected a member of the Royal Geographical Society in England. One of the first female world explorers, she wrote travelogues about her experiences in Asia.

Sources: Chicago, *The Dinner Party,* p. 180; *The Concise Dictionary of National Biography,* vol. III, p. 249–50; Ogilvie, *Women in Science,* pp. 38–39; *Who Was Who,* vol. I, pp. 65–66.

1921 • Ellen Semple (1863–1932) was the first female president of the Association of American Geographers. A teacher at the secondary and university level, Semple was elected to head this organization in 1921.

Sources: Read and Witlieb, *The Book of Women's Firsts,* pp. 400–1.

1925 • Harriet Chalmers Adams (1875–1937) was the organizer and the first president of the Society of Women Geographers, which she founded in 1925. The organization supported the aims and careers of professional female geographers by providing a forum for the exchange of information and news of job opportunities.

Sources: James, *Notable American Women,* pp. 11–12; Read and Witlieb, *The Book of Women's Firsts,* p. 8.

Landscape Architecture

1929 • Brenda Colvin (1897–1981), a pioneering landscape architect, was the cofounder of the Institute of Landscape Architects, in 1929. She served this British organization as secretary, vice president, and finally president from 1951 until 1953.

Sources: Uglow, *The Continuum Dictionary of Women's Biography,* pp. 133–34.

1948 • Sylvia Crowe (b. 1901) was a cofounder of the International Federation of Landscape Architects in England in 1948. She served as its secretary until 1958 and then as vice-president until 1970. She is known for designing new town landscapes.

Sources: Uglow, *The Continuum Dictionary of Women's Biography,* p. 141.

Law

c.1351 B.C. • Deborah (fl. 1351 B.C.) is the first and only female judge mentioned in the Scriptures. The only woman of her time to possess political power through popular consent, she was also a prophet, the only judge to perform prophetic functions before Samuel.

Sources: Chicago, *The Dinner Party,* p. 118; *The Old Testament*; Uglow, *The Continuum Dictionary of Women's Biography,* p. 154.

1869 • Arabella Aurelia Babb Mansfield (1846–1911) was the first female lawyer to be admitted to the bar, in 1869. She and her brother, who was three years her junior, attended Iowa Wesleyan University and received their degrees in three years in a graduation class of three. Arabella, known as "Belle," was valedictorian and her brother salutatorian. Belle and her husband, John Mansfield, took the Iowa bar exam together in 1866. Belle Mansfield was not immediately admitted to the bar, although her husband was, because the Iowa Code stated only that "any white male person" could be admitted. Later the same day, Belle Mansfield argued her own case before Judge Francis Springer, who made an interpretation of the statute's language to mean that "the affirmative declaration [for males] is not a denial of the right of females." It would be another three years before the statute was officially amended to specifically allow women to be admitted to the bar.

Sources: James, *Notable American Women,* vol. 2, pp. 492–93; McCullough, *First of All: Significant "Firsts" by American Women,* pp. 92–93; Read and Witlieb, *The Book of Women's Firsts,* pp. 267–68; Sanders, *The First of Everything,* p. 157.

1872 • Charlotte E. Ray (1850–1911) graduated from Howard University's School of Law in 1872 and became the first African-American woman lawyer. She was admitted to the bar in Washington, D.C. on April 23, becoming the first African-American woman to be admitted to the bar in the United States, and the first woman admitted to the bar in the District of Columbia.

Sources: James, *Notable American Women,* vol. 3, pp. 121–22; McCullough, *First of All: Significant "Firsts" by American Women,* p. 93; Smith, *Black Firsts,* p. 153.

1878 • Clara Shortridge Foltz (1849–1934) was the first woman to practice law in California. On September 5, 1878, she was admitted to practice in the Twentieth District Court in San Jose. In 1879 Foltz became the first woman appointed as clerk of the judiciary committee of the state legislature, a position she held until 1880. Foltz had a successful career in law and in 1910 became the first woman named to the State Board of Charities and Corrections, on which she served until 1912.

Sources: James, *Notable American Women,* vol. 1, pp. 642–43; Willard and Livermore, *A Woman of the Century.*

1879 • Belva Ann Bennett McNall Lockwood (1830–1917) became the first woman admitted to practice before the U.S. Supreme Court when she succeeded in lobbying for a bill that permitted women to argue cases before the nation's highest court. President Rutherford B. Hayes signed the bill on February 15, 1879, and in March Lockwood was admitted to practice.

Sources: Chicago, The Dinner Party, p. 192; McCullough, First of All: Significant "Firsts" by American Women, pp. 93–94; Read and Witlieb, The Book of Women's Firsts, pp. 257–58.

Belva Ann Bennett Lockwood was born in Royalton, New York, and educated at Genesee College. After being refused admission to two different law schools, Lockwood, in her 40s, gained acceptance to the national University Law School in Washington, D.C. She graduated in 1883 and was admitted to the bar. In both 1884 and 1888, she was nominated for president of the United States by the National Equal Rights Party, winning over four thousand votes. Lockwood was an ardent pacifist and served as a member of the nominating committee for the Nobel Peace Prize. She worked until age 76, successfully arguing a claim for the Eastern Cherokee Indians, which brought them an award of $5 million.

BELVA ANN LOCKWOOD

1883 • Carrie Burnham Kilgore (1838–1909), a U.S. lawyer and women's rights advocate, was the first woman to graduate from the University of Pennsylvania Law School, in Philadelphia in 1883. In 1887, she was appointed the first female master in chancery in the state of Pennsylvania.

Sources: Chicago Law Times (November 1886); Green Bag (1890), vol. 2, pp. 28–29; James, Notable American Women, vol. 2, pp. 329–30.

1885 • Belle Case La Follette (1859–1931), a leader in the Wisconsin progressive movement with her husband, Robert M. La Follette, was the first woman to receive a degree from the University of Wisconsin Law School, in Madison, Wisconsin, in 1885.

Sources: Doane, The La Follettes and the Wisconsin Idea; James, Notable American Women, vol. 2, pp. 356–58.

1888 • Marie Popelin (1846–1913) was the first woman to earn a degree as professor of law in Belgium, in 1888. Denied admission to the bar because she was female, Popelin became a leader in the women's rights movement in her native Belgium.

Sources: Chicago, The Dinner Party, p. 193.

1894 • Sophonisba Preston Breckinridge (1866–1948), an ardent feminist and worker for social causes, was the first woman to pass the bar exam in the state of Kentucky, in Lexington in 1894. She went on to become the first U.S. woman to receive a doctoral degree in political science, from the University of Chicago in 1901. Breckinridge then taught for many years at the University of Chicago's Graduate School of Social Service Administration. Her achievements in the field of social work were recognized by President Franklin D.

Roosevelt in 1933 when he chose her as a delegate to the Pan American Conference in Montevideo, the first woman to serve in this capacity.

Sources: James, *Notable American Women,* vol. 1, pp. 233–36.

1896 • Ellen Spencer Mussey (1850–1936) was a U.S. lawyer who struggled to practice her profession. She passed the bar examination without having earned a law degree, by oral examination in 1893. In 1896, Mussey founded the Washington College of Law in Washington, D.C. She opened her school to enable women—who were regularly refused admission to law schools in the 1890s—to study for and receive law degrees. Mussey became an expert in commercial and international law, and she was the first woman to serve as counsel for the Norwegian and Swedish legations, a position she held for 25 years beginning in 1893.

Sources: *Maryland Historical Magazine*; Uglow, *The Continuum Dictionary of Women's Biography,* p. 394.

1898 • Grace Raymond Hebard (1861–1936) was the first woman admitted to the bar in Wyoming, in Laramie in 1898. She did not practice law. However, since she had earned a doctoral degree in political economy by correspondence from Illinois Wesleyan University in 1893, she taught at the University of Wyoming. Hebard also served as librarian for the University of Wyoming and as a member of its board of trustees for nearly three decades, beginning in 1891.

Sources: James, *Notable American Women,* vol. 2, pp. 173–74; Wilson, *A History of the University of Wyoming.*

Early twentieth century • Marianne Beth (b. 1890) was the first Austrian woman to receive a doctorate in law. She specialized in international law and gained a reputation for her liberal and feminist views.

Sources: Chicago, *The Dinner Party,* p. 191.

Cornelia Sorabji (1866–1954) was the first woman in India to practice law. Educated at Decca College in Poona (where she was the first female student), at Gujarat College at Ahmadebad, and at Sommerville College, Oxford, she was the first woman allowed, by special Congregational Decree, to sit for the advanced examination, the Bachelor of Civil Law, in Oxford in 1893, 30 years before women were admitted to the English Bar. Sorabji returned to India and began to practice law. By 1904, she was appointed as legal advisor on behalf of women in purdah in Bihar, Orissa, and Assam. In 1923, she settled in Calcutta to practice as a barrister.

Sources: Sorabji, *The Memoirs of Cornelia Sorabji;* Uglow, *The Continuum Dictionary of Women's Biography,* p. 508.

1910 • Hortense Sparks Malsch Ward (1872–1944), a U.S. lawyer, was the first woman to pass the bar exam in Texas. She was admitted to the bar on August 30, 1910, in Galveston, Texas. She was also the first Texas woman admitted to practice before the United States Supreme Court, in Washington, D.C., on February 24, 1915.

Sources: James, *Notable American Women,* vol. 3, pp. 540–41.

c.1916 • Josepha Abiertas (1894–1929) was the first woman to graduate with a degree in law from the Philippine Law School at Capiz. She campaigned throughout her life for the needs of the poor and for votes for women. She was also the first woman to serve as president of The Woman's Christian Temperance Union in Manila.

Sources: Noble, *Contemporary Women Scientists of America,* p. 2; O'Neill, *The Women's Book of World Records and Achievements,* p. 719.

1916 • Emily Gowan Murphy (1868–1933), a Canadian lawyer, was the first female magistrate in the British Empire. In 1916 she was appointed to the juvenile court where she served until her retirement in 1931. Murphy worked to establish a special court to hear "difficult cases" (such as sexual assault) and was instrumental in bringing into being the Women's Court, also in 1916.

Sources: Saunders, *Emily Murphy, Crusader*; Uglow, *The Continuum Dictionary of Women's Biography,* pp. 392–93.

1918 • Kathryn Sellers (1871–1939) was the first woman to serve as head judge of a juvenile court. She was nominated by President Woodrow Wilson to head the juvenile court in Washington, D.C., in 1918, and held this position until her retirement in 1934.

Sources: Read and Witlieb, *The Book of Women's Firsts,* p. 400.

1919 • Helena Florence Normanton (1883–1957), a pioneering lawyer, was the first woman to be accepted by the Inns of Court, in London in 1919. She was also the first woman elected to the General Council of the Bar and one of the first to be made a King's Counsel in England, both in 1949. Normanton had a distinguished career in law and worked for women's legal rights.

Sources: Uglow, *The Continuum Dictionary of Women's Biography,* pp. 405–6; *Who Was Who,* vol. V, p. 822.

1920 • Florence Ellinwood Allen (1884–1966) was the first woman to serve as a judge in the United States. A graduate of New York University Law School, Ellinwood was elected common pleas court judge in Cleveland, Ohio, in 1920. In 1922, she became the first woman elected to the Ohio Supreme Court and in 1934 she became the first woman appointed to serve on the U.S. Court of Appeals.

Sources: Read and Witlieb, *The Book of Women's Firsts,* pp. 15–16.

1930s • Angie Elizabeth Brooks-Randolph (b. 1928) was the first woman to practice law in Liberia. She had also been the first woman to be accepted as a legal apprentice in that country. Educated in the United States and England, Brooks earned her law degree in London and is remembered as the second woman to serve as president of the United Nations General Assembly, a position she assumed in 1969. She was also the first woman in her country to hold a cabinet post. She has an international reputation as an activist and a humanitarian.

Sources: O'Neill, *The Women's Book of World Records and Achievements,* pp. 64–65; Uglow, *The Continuum Dictionary of Women's Biography,* pp. 90–91.

1949 • Bernita S. Matthews (1894–1988) was the first woman to serve as a U.S. federal district judge. She was appointed to the federal District Court for the District of Columbia by President Harry S Truman in 1949.

Sources: Read and Witlieb, *The Book of Women's Firsts,* p. 273.

1956 • Rose Heilbron (b. 1914), an English lawyer, was the first woman in the United Kingdom to hold the official position of recorder, in Burnley in 1956. She held this post until 1974. She has had a distinguished career in law and has served both as Queen's Counsel and a High Court judge.

Sources: Uglow, *The Continuum Dictionary of Women's Biography,* p. 253.

1965 • Elizabeth Lane (1905–1988), an English lawyer, was the first female judge in England. In 1965 she was named to the High Court in the Family Division, a post she held until her retirement in 1979.

Sources: Lane, *Hear the Other Side;* Uglow, *The Continuum Dictionary of Women's Biography,* p. 311.

1970 • Graciela Olivarez, who has devoted her life to the cause of economic opportunity for poor people, was the first woman to graduate from Notre Dame University's Law School in South Bend, Indiana, in 1970. She went on in the early 1970s to become the first woman to serve as chair of the board of the Mexican-American Legal Defense Educational Fund.

Sources: O'Neill, *The Women's Book of World Records and Achievements,* p. 716.

1971 • Helga Pederson (b. 1911), a distinguished Danish lawyer and politician, was the first female judge at the European Court of Human Rights, in 1971. Her particular interests have been prison reform and the rights of women.

Sources: Uglow, *The Continuum Dictionary of Women's Biography,* p. 428.

Gisèle Halimi (b. 1927), a French lawyer, was the founder of the feminist group Choisir, in Paris in 1971. This association was a reformist organization and greatly influenced the passage of liberal French laws concerning contraception and abortion in 1974.

Sources: Uglow, *The Continuum Dictionary of Women's Biography,* p. 244.

1979 • On June 27, 1979, Amalya L. Kearse became the first woman to be sworn in as judge in the U.S. Court of Appeals for the Second Circuit. At 42, Kearse was also one of the youngest persons to sit on the Second Circuit.

Sources: McCullough, *First of All: Significant "Firsts" by American Women,* pp. 89–90.

1987 • Dame Elizabeth Butler-Sloss (b. 1923), trained as an English lawyer, became the first female judge to sit in the Court of Appeal, in 1987. She thus holds the masculine title of "Lord Justice" as well as the feminine title "Dame," which she was given in 1979.

Sources: Uglow, *The Continuum Dictionary of Women's Biography,* p. 99.

Jill Wine-Banks

Jill Wine-Banks (b. 1943) was the first woman to serve as executive director of the American Bar Association. She was appointed in 1987 and served until 1990 as head of an association considered a conservative male bastion.
Sources: Read and Witlieb, *The Book of Women's Firsts,* p. 486.

1995 • Roberta Cooper Ramo (b. 1942), an attorney from Albuquerque, New Mexico, became the first woman to hold the office of president of the American Bar Association. Ramo assumed the leadership post in the 117-year-old ABA at its annual meeting in Chicago on August 9, 1995. Ramo graduated from the University of Chicago Law School in 1967. At a news conference, Ramo stated that, as president of the ABA, she hoped to promote education of school children about the Constitution, to continue financial support for the Legal Services Corporation, which provides legal advice and services for the poor, and to combat domestic violence.
Sources: *The New York Times* (11 August 1995), p. A13.

Roberta Cooper Ramo

Law Enforcement

1910 • Alice Stebbins Wells (b. 1873) took the civil service exam and, on the basis of her results, became the first woman to receive a regular appointment as a police officer, in Los Angeles, California, on September 2, 1910. She retired in 1940.
Sources: Read and Witlieb, *The Book of Women's Firsts,* pp. 474–75.

1972 • Joanne E. Pierce (b. 1941) and Susan Lynn Roley (b. 1947) were the first two women to serve as special agents of the Federal Bureau of Investigation. They passed a rigorous course at Quantico, Virginia, in 1972. The predecessor of the FBI, the Bureau of Investigation, hired its first female agent in 1911, but J. Edgar Hoover, who headed the FBI for 48 years, forbade the hiring of female agents. Since his death in 1972, women have regularly served in this capacity.
Sources: Read and Witlieb, *The Book of Women's Firsts,* pp. 347–48.

1985 • Penny Harrington (b. 1943) became the first woman to serve as police chief of a major U.S. city when she was appointed to this position in Portland, Oregon, in 1985. She resigned over a hiring controversy the following year.
Source: Read and Witlieb, *The Book of Women's Firsts,* pp. 194–95.

Library Science

1895 • Alice Sarah Tyler (1859–1944) was the first professionally trained woman to work at the Cleveland Public Library. With a certificate from the library school at the Armour Institute in Chicago, Tyler went to Cleveland as head cataloguer in 1895. In 1900, Tyler became the first person to serve as secretary of the Iowa State Library Commission. She devoted much of her energy to developing libraries throughout Iowa before returning to Cleveland in 1913 to become the first female director of the library school at Western Reserve University. In 1922, she founded and served as first president of the Cleveland Library Club. In 1925, she became the first woman to hold the title of dean and professor of library science at Western Reserve University.

Sources: Danton, *Pioneering Leaders in Librarianship*; James, *Notable American Women,* vol. 3, pp. 493–94.

1911 • Theresa West Elmendorf (1855–1932) was the first female president of the American Library Association. After a distinguished career in library service in Wisconsin and New York, she was elected to this position in 1911.

Sources: Read and Witlieb, *The Book of Women's Firsts,* p. 144.

1918 • Cofounder of the Ohio Library Association (1895) and its first female president (1903), Linda A. Eastman was the first woman to head a metropolitan library system. She was elected director of the Cleveland Public Library in 1918.

Sources: Read and Witlieb, *The Book of Women's Firsts,* p. 133.

1924 • Fanny Barrier Williams (1855–1944), an American lecturer, writer, and clubwoman, was the first woman and the first black person to serve on the Chicago Library Board, in 1924. She served until her retirement in 1926.

Sources: Davis, *Lifting as They Climb,* pp. 266–67; James, *Notable American Women,* vol. 3, pp. 620–22; Sewall, *The World's Congress of Representative Women,* vol. 2, pp. 696–711; Smith, *Black Firsts,* p. 198.

1930 • Sarah Byrd Askew (1877–1942), a leader in the county library movement who worked throughout her life for the New Jersey Public Library Commission, was the first person to receive an honorary degree from the New Jersey College for Women (later Douglass College) of Rutgers University, in 1930. She was honored for her scheme to bring books to military camps and troopships during World War I and for her later efforts to bring books to people in rural areas.

Sources: Danton, *Pioneer Leaders in Librarianship*; James, *Notable American Women,* vol. 1, pp. 61–62.

Miscellaneous

Fifth century B.C. • Artemisia of Halicarnassus was the first female sea captain. After the death of her husband during the fifth century B.C., she assumed command of his fleet and fought on the side of Xerxes in his second war against the Greeks.

Sources: Uglow, *The Continuum Dictionary of Women's Biography,* p. 29.

Twelfth century • Fibors, a twelfth-century French woman, was the first female troubadour. Little is known about her except that her brother was also a famous troubadour.

Sources: Chicago, *The Dinner Party,* p. 141.

Late seventeenth century • Dinah Nuthead was the first female printer in North America. She took over her husband's business at the time of his death in the late seventeenth century in Annapolis, Maryland.

Sources: James, *Notable American Women,* vol. 1, p. 662.

c.1718 • Anne Bonney (fl. 1720) and Mary Read (1690–1720) were the first female pirates on record. Bonney was born in Ireland and became the mistress of the pirate known as Captain "Calico Jack" Rackham. Mary Read, daughter of an English sailor, enlisted as a boy in the French infantry then, continuing to dress in male attire, served on board a Dutch ship. The two women worked together as pirates and were tried and convicted as criminals in Jamaica in 1720. Both were reprieved, however, when they (falsely) pleaded that they were pregnant.

Sources: Gartner, *Anne Bonney*; Strong, *Mary Read: The Pirate Wench*; Uglow, *The Continuum Dictionary of Women's Biography,* pp. 77–78, 451.

1810 • Sophie Blanchard (d. 1819) of France was the first woman to earn her living as a professional balloonist. In 1810, she became the Chief of Air Services to Napoleon and performed at royal functions.

Sources: Chicago, *The Dinner Party,* p. 191.

1856 • Mary Ann Patten (1837–1861) was the first woman to navigate a clipper ship. At the age of 19, Patten took over navigation of the ship, which had left New York City on July 1, 1856, because its captain, her husband, became seriously ill with tuberculosis. Pregnant with their first child, Patten arrived safely in San Francisco on November 15, 1856. Her husband died shortly after the birth of their son, and Patten herself died of tuberculosis four years later.

Sources: Read and Witlieb, *The Book of Women's Firsts,* pp. 331–32.

1878 • Emma M. Nutt (1849–1926) was the first female telephone operator in the United States. She worked in this capacity for the Telephone Dispatch Company in Boston, Massachusetts, from September 1, 1878, until her retirement in 1911.

Sources: Read and Witlieb, *The Book of Women's Firsts,* pp. 320–21.

1886 • Minnie Hill of Portland, Oregon, became the first woman steamboat captain west of the Mississippi River in 1886. She piloted the *Governor Newell* on the Columbia River for many years.

Sources: McCullough, *First of All: Significant Firsts by American Women,* p. 157.

1893 • Florence Kelley (1859–1932), an ardent social reformer, was the first female factory inspector for the state of Illinois. In recognition of her campaign against child labor and for the improvement of working conditions, especially for women, the governor appointed her chief factory inspector, a position she held from 1893 until 1897. Kelley also worked at Hull House in Chicago and, after 1899, at the Henry Street Settlement in New York City.

Sources: Blumberg, *Florence Kelley: The Making of a Social Pioneer*; Goldmark, *Impatient Crusader*; James, *Notable American Women,* pp. 316–19; Uglow, *The Continuum Dictionary of Women's Biography,* pp. 295–96.

1894 • Mary Becker Greene (1869–1949) became the first woman steamboat captain on the Mississippi River in 1894. Married to a riverboat captain, she took command of the company they founded after her husband died. Their *Delta Queen* steamboat is still in operation today.

Sources: McCullough, *First of All: Significant Firsts by American Women,* p. 155.

1902 • Fannie Merritt Farmer (1857–1915), the cookbook writer associated with the Boston Cooking School where she received her training, was also the founder of Miss Farmer's School of Cookery, in Boston in 1902.

Sources: Uglow, *The Continuum Dictionary of Women's Biography,* p. 196.

c.1910 • Jessie Kenney, suffragette Annie Kenney's younger sister, was the first woman to qualify as a radio officer. Jessie Kenney worked with Christabel Pankhurst in Paris in 1912 and toured the United States with Emmeline Pankhurst between 1914 and 1918. When she returned to England, she joined the Rosicrucian Order and rose to the level of master of the London chapter.

Sources: Kenney, *Memories of a Militant*; Uglow, *The Continuum Dictionary of Women's Biography,* p. 297.

1946 • Emily Post (1873–1960), a U.S. writer who made her reputation as an authority on etiquette, was the founder of the Emily Post Institute for the Study of Gracious Living, in 1946. She is best known for her book *Etiquette: The Blue Book of Social Usage,* first published in 1922, but she also hosted a radio program (in 1931) and wrote a syndicated column.

Sources: Post, *Truly Emily Post*; Uglow, *The Continuum Dictionary of Women's Biography,* p. 438.

Mid-twentieth century • Corrie Ten Boom (1892–1983), a survivor of Ravensbrook concentration camp and a spiritual leader in her native Holland during the Nazi occupation, was the first woman in the Netherlands to become a licensed watchmaker.

Sources: Ten Boom, *Autobiography*.

1956 • Dorothy Eady (1904–1981) was the first English woman to become Keeper of the Temple of Isis in Egypt. An expert on hieroglyphics, she believed that she was a reincarnated minor priestess.

Sources: Uglow, *The Continuum Dictionary of Women's Biography,* p. 181.

1960s • Laura Mountney Ashley (1925–1985), an English designer and businesswoman, was the first woman to establish a large worldwide corporation based on her own fashion designs. In 1953, she designed silk-screened scarves at home under her own name; by the 1960s, she and her husband had formed a design corporation and opened a shop in London under the name Ashley Mountney Ltd., which became Laura Ashley Ltd. in 1968. At the time of her death, the business included eleven factories and 225 shops and employed over four thousand staff.

Sources: A Concise Dictionary of National Biography, vol. I, p. 81; Magnusson, *Larousse Biographical Dictionary,* p. 70.

1973 • Angela Hernandez (b. 1949) was the first Spanish woman to challenge the 1908 law prohibiting women from becoming bullfighters. Her lawsuit failed in a Madrid court in 1973.

Sources: Uglow, *The Continuum Dictionary of Women's Biography,* p. 256.

1978 • Jane Cahill Pfeiffer (b. 1932) was the first woman to serve as chair of the board of the National Broadcasting Corporation (NBC), a position she held from 1978 until 1980. Pfeiffer has been active throughout her life in business and public service. (*See also* **Government: United States, 1966.**)

Sources: Read and Witlieb, *The Book of Women's Firsts,* pp. 343–44.

Organization Leadership

See also **Organization and Group Firsts**

1857 • Isa Craig Knox (1831–1903), a Scottish poet and feminist, was the first woman to serve as assistant secretary to the Social Science Association, in London in 1857. She is remembered as an author of verse and fiction for adults and children.

Sources: The Concise Dictionary of National Biography, vol. II, p. 1694; Uglow, *The Continuum Dictionary of Women's Biography,* pp. 139–40.

1884 • Charlotte Scott (1858–1931) was the first woman to be elected to the council of the American Mathematical Society. She was honored in 1894 while in the United States to set up the undergraduate and graduate programs in mathematics at the newly established Bryn Mawr College.

Sources: James, *Notable American Women,* vol. 3, pp. 259–60; Read and Witlieb, *The Book of Women's Firsts,* pp. 397–98; Uglow, *The Continuum Dictionary of Women's Biography,* p. 488.

1885 • Matilda Evans Stevenson (1849–1915) was the founder and first president of the Women's Anthropological Society of America, in 1885. Stevenson, an ethnologist, was particularly interested in the ceremonies and beliefs of the Zuni Indians.

Sources: Read and Witlieb, *The Book of Women's Firsts,* p. 423.

(*See* **Professions: Law, 1987.**)
(*See* **Professions: Law, 1995.**)

Scholarship

Tenth century • Gormlaith, a tenth-century writer, was the first female historian in Ireland. She wrote in both prose and verse in order to preserve Irish traditions.

Sources: Chicago, *The Dinner Party,* p. 137.

Twelfth century • Anna Commena (1083–1148) was the first woman to write an extensive work of historical scholarship. Her 15-volume history, *The Alexiad,* recounted the events of her father's reign in Byzantium and the first crusade.

Sources: Chicago, *The Dinner Party,* p. 132; Schmidt, *400 Outstanding Women of the World,* pp. 215–16; Uglow, *The Continuum Dictionary of Women's Biography,* p. 135.

Sixteenth century • Maria Bartola, a sixteenth-century Aztec woman named by the Spanish who destroyed her nation, was the first female historian from Mexico. She recounted the Spanish conquest from the point of view of an Aztec witness.

Sources: Chicago, *The Dinner Party,* p. 171.

1827 • Deborah Norris Logan (1761–1839), a collector of historical records also remembered for her charming and useful account of her husband's life, *Memoir of Dr. George Logan of Stenton* (1899), was the first female member of the Historical Society of Pennsylvania. She was elected to honorary membership in Philadelphia in 1827.

Sources: James, *Notable American Women,* vol. 2, pp. 418–19; Tolles, *George Logan of Philadelphia;* Wister and Irwin, *Worthy Women of Our First Century,* pp. 297–328.

1849 • Frances Manwaring Caulkins (1795–1869), a Connecticut historian, was the first woman elected to membership in the Massachusetts Historical Society, the oldest such organization in the United States, in Boston on April 26, 1849. For over a hundred years, Caulkins was the only female member of this society. She is remembered for her *History of Norwich* (1845) and her *History of New London* (1852).

Sources: James, *Notable American Women,* vol. 1, pp. 313–14.

Second half of the nineteenth century • Russian-born Sofia Kovalevskaya (1850–1891) was the first woman outside of Italy to hold a university chair. She earned her doctorate in math in Germany, then received a chair at the University of Stockholm in Sweden. There are several spelling variations of her name in publications outside of her native Russia.

Sources: Chicago, *The Dinner Party,* p. 192; Schmidt, *400 Outstanding Women of the World,* p. 346; Uglow, *The Continuum Dictionary of Women's Biography,* pp. 304–5.

(*See* **Professions: Organization Leadership, 1884.**)
(*See* **Professions: Organization Leadership, 1885.**)
(*See* **Professions: Law, 1894.**)

1922 • Eileen (Postan) Power (1889–1940) was the first English woman to establish her reputation as a historian of medieval women. Her first book, *Medieval English Nunneries,* was published in 1922; her last, *Medieval Women,* appeared posthumously in 1975.

Sources: The Concise Dictionary of National Biography, vol. III, p. 2427; Uglow, *The Continuum Dictionary of Women's Biography,* p. 439; *Who Was Who,* vol. III, p. 1097.

1927 • Edith Abbott (1876–1957), with the assistance of her friend Sophonisba Breckinridge, was the founder of the influential journal the *Social Science Review,* in 1927. A U.S. feminist and social reformer, Abbott was dean of the School of Social Studies Administration at the University of Chicago until her retirement in 1942.

Sources: Uglow, *The Continuum Dictionary of Women's Biography,* p. 2.

1930s • Zora Neale Hurston (1901–1960) was the first woman successfully to combine careers as a cultural anthropologist and an accomplished writer of fiction. She graduated from Barnard College in New York City in 1928 and went on to do important research into African-American folklore in the American South as well as in Haiti and Jamaica. She also established her reputation during the 1930s with fiction based on her knowledge of African-American experience. She is best known for her novel *Their Eyes Were Watching God,* published in 1937. She died in poverty after having worked for several years as a domestic servant. Her achievements were rediscovered in the 1980s. In February 1995 she became the first African-American woman to have her complete works published by the Library of America.

Sources: Newsweek (13 February 1995), p. 81; Uglow, *The Continuum Dictionary of Women's Biography,* p. 270; Walker, *In Search of Our Mothers' Gardens*.

1930 • Louise Phelps Kellogg (1862–1942), a professional historian, was the first woman to be elected president of the Mississippi Valley Historical Association, in Madison, Wisconsin, in 1930. This organization later became the prestigious Organization of American Historians. Kellogg worked throughout her life in research and administration at the Wisconsin State Historical Society in Madison, beginning in 1901.

Sources: Hopkins, *The Kelloggs in the Old World and the New*; James, *Notable American Women,* vol. 2, pp. 321–22.

1942 • Margaret Leech (1893–1974) was the first woman to receive the Pulitzer Prize for history. She was recognized in 1942 for *Reveille in Washington,* a study of life in the nation's capital during the Civil War.

Sources: Read and Witlieb, *The Book of Women's Firsts,* p. 250.

1943 • Nellie Neilson (1873–1947) was the first woman to serve as president of the American Historical Association. She was elected in 1943 because of her dedication to scholarship and teaching in the field of history. She was chair of the history department at Mount Holyoke College in South Hadley, Massachusetts, from 1903 until her retirement in 1939.

Sources: James, *Notable American Women*, vol. 2. pp. 613–14; Read and Witlieb, *The Book of Women's Firsts*, pp. 307–8.

1949 • Winifred Goldring (1888–1971) was the first woman to be elected president of the Paleontological Society, in 1949. She devoted her life to science and to teaching and received an honorary doctorate from Smith College in honor of her work in 1957.

Sources: Read and Witlieb, *The Book of Women's Firsts*, p. 180.

1950s • Hannah Arendt (1906–1975) was the first woman appointed a full professor at Princeton University. She was honored for her stature as a major political theoretician and more general philosopher.

Sources: Bruehl, *Hannah Arendt*; Chicago, *The Dinner Party*, p. 210; Uglow, *The Continuum Dictionary of Women's Biography*, p. 26.

1955 • Evelyne Annie Henriette Sullerot (b. 1924), a French feminist writer, was the founder and first secretary of the French movement for family planning, in Paris in 1955. She held the post of secretary until 1958. Trained as a sociologist, she made her career primarily as a journalist and the author of studies of female experience.

Sources: Sullerot, *Demain les Femmes*; Sullerot, *La Femme dans le Monde Moderne*; Sullerot, *La Vie des Femmes*; Uglow, *The Continuum Dictionary of Women's Biography*, p. 524.

c.1960s • Elizabeth Anscombe (b. 1919), the most distinguished female philosopher in twentieth-century Britain, was the first woman to translate and edit the posthumous works of the philosopher Wittgenstein. She has held research fellowships at both Oxford and Cambridge Universities and is known as a leading linguistic philosopher.

Sources: Uglow, *The Continuum Dictionary of Women's Biography*, p. 22.

Religion

In many religions, the first Being, the Creator of All, is feminine. The Mother-Goddess goes by many different names. A few examples are: Tiamat, She Who Gave Birth To All, in Babylon; Sedna, the Creator and Protector of the Inuit; Gaea, or Mother Earth, in Greece; Kali, who gives birth to all beings in India; Nut and her daughter Isis in Egypt; Inanna and Erishkegal, the Syrian Great Mother; and Nerthus, the Germanic Mother Earth.

Nearly all cultures look to a woman as the creative force, the source of all life. Even the Judaeo-Christian system of belief, which tried to suppress or even eliminate the Feminine, has Eve, the first woman and mother of all who follow; Sophia, Goddess of Wisdom, who declares, "I was there when he set the heavens in place...I was the craftsman at his side" (Proverbs 8: 27 and 30, NIV); and Mary, Mother of God, Queen of Heaven, Notre Dame. Mary shares many of the significant attributes of the Mother Goddess in her other characteristics: virgin birth, God as consort, death and resurrection of her son.

A quick survey of world religions will show the Mother Goddess, the First Woman, appearing consistently, though in different forms, all across the globe.

Source: Barker, *The NIV Study Bible: New International Version,* p. 1217.

Awards and Ceremonies

353 A.D. • Marcellina was the first nun to be recognized by the Christian Church in a religious ceremony, in Rome in 353 A.D. St. Ambrose, her brother, wrote his tract, *De Virginibus,* for her. In this work he delineated the rules by which nuns were to live.

Sources: Chicago, *The Dinner Party,* p. 130.

604 A.D. • Khadijah (564–619), a successful businesswoman in the Meccan tribe of Quraish, was the first woman to marry the prophet Muhammed in 604 A.D. Muhammed went on to have eleven more wives, but he and Khadijah had six children together and he remained faithful to her during her lifetime. She supported him after his first vision (in 610 A.D.) and enthusiastically encouraged him in his mission. According to the Koran, she is one of the "four perfect women."

Sources: Uglow, *The Continuum Dictionary of Women's Biography,* p. 298.

1897 • Maud Nathan (1862–1946), a leader in the women's suffrage movement, was the first woman to play a major role in an American Jewish worship service. In 1897, she was invited to read a paper at New York City's Temple Beth-El in place of the sermon. Nathan is also remembered for serving as the first vice-president of the Equal Suffrage League of New York in the 1890s.

Sources: James, *Notable American Women,* vol. 2, pp. 608–9; Nathan, *Once Upon a Time and Today;* Nathan, *Story of an Epoch-Making Movement.*

1973 • Mother Teresa (b. 1910), the Catholic nun who has devoted her life to serving others in need, was the first person to win the Templeton Foundation Prize for Progress in Religion. The foundation awarded her this honor in Englewood, New Jersey, in April of 1973, in recognition of her work in ministering to the ailing and poor in the slums of Calcutta, India. In 1979, Mother Theresa won the Nobel Prize for Peace.

Sources: Delaney, *Saints Are Now,* pp. 155–84; Wallechinsky and Wallace, *The People's Almanac,* p. 1130.

1995 • Sister Maatje, a Swiss nun, was the first woman to carry the symbolic cross during the Pope's Good Friday procession, in Rome, Italy, on April 14, 1995. She was accompanied by Pope John Paul II, who had decided to make this feminist gesture.

Sources: *The Willoughby (Ohio) News Herald* (14 April 1995), p. A5.

Beatifications and Canonizations

c.500 A.D. • St. Brigid (453–523), or Bridget, one of the patron saints of Ireland, is alleged to have founded at Kildare the first convent in Ireland, in the latter part of the fifth century A.D. She is believed to have lived from 453 to 523. However, whether she actually existed as a person or was rather a Christianization of the Celtic moon goddess Bridgit is debatable. Kildare was the site of shrine to the goddess Bridgit who was feasted with fire on February 1. St. Brigid's feast day is also February 1, which is also celebrated by lighting fires, and the nuns at the convent are said to have tended a sacred fire (which no man was allowed to approach) for many generations. St. Brigid and the goddess Bridgit corresponded in many other ways, too many to be mere coincidence. Regardless of the actual historical existence of a woman named Brigid who founded a convent at Kildare, the cult of St. Brigid is clearly a continuation of the ancient worship of Bridgit, the triune moon goddess.

Sources: Attwater, *The Avenel Dictionary of Saints,* p. 75; Greenspan, *Timetables of Women's History,* p. 65; Rees, *Christian Symbols, Ancient Roots,* p. 85; Walker, *Women's Encyclopedia of Myths and Secrets,* pp. 116–18.

1235 • Olga (892–971) was the first person to become a saint in the Russian Orthodox Church. Wife of prince Igor of Kiev, Olga was his co-regent from 945 to 964 while her son was a minor. She became a Christian in 957 and was baptized at Constantinople. When she returned to Russia, her influence encouraged the spread of Christianity throughout Russia.

Sources: Magnusson, *Larousse Biographical Dictionary,* p. 1102; Schmidt, 400 Outstanding Women of the World, p. 343.

1946 • Frances Xavier Cabrini (1850–1917) was the first United States citizen to be named a saint in the Roman Catholic Church. She was born in Italy and in 1880 founded a new religious order, the Missionary Sisters of the Sacred Heart. Pope Leo XIII sent Mother Cabrini to the United States in 1889 to work with Italian immigrants; she became known as Mother Cabrini for her charitable work, founding more than 67 shelters in the United States; Buenos Aires, Argentina; Paris, France; and Madrid, Spain. She was canonized on July 7, 1946, as the first American saint. Her feast day is November 13.

Sources: James, *Notable American Women,* vol. 1, pp. 274–76; Magnusson, *Larousse Biographical Dictionary,* p. 243; Read and Witlieb, *The Book of Women's Firsts,* p. 79.

1970 • In 1970, Catherine of Siena (1347–1380), patron saint of Italy, was one of the first two women to be declared a Doctor of the Church. The other was Teresa of Avila. Catherine was a mystical visionary who also worked tirelessly and fiercely as a reformer of the Church during a turbulent time in its history. She was a strong, vocal advocate for Pope Urban VI when he was opposed by a rival pope in 1378. She traveled widely with a group of followers, ministering to the poor and winning converts. Despite all Catherine's vigorous and successful efforts in the political realm, however, it was not for this she was canonized in 1461 but for her personal faith, charity, and holiness.

Sources: Anderson and Zinsser, *A History of Their Own,* pp. 220–21; Attwater, *The Avenel Dictionary of Saints,* pp. 211–12.

1975 • Elizabeth Ann Bayley Seton (1774–1821) was the first person—man or woman—born in the United States to be canonized as a saint in the Roman Catholic Church. She was beatified in 1963 and declared a saint in 1975. She was also the founder of the first Catholic order in the United States, the Sisters of Charity of St. Joseph, which she established in 1809. (*See also* **Religion: Founders, 1809.**)

Sources: James, *Notable American Women,* vol. 3, pp. 263–65; Read and Witlieb, *The Book of Women's Firsts,* pp. 401–2; Wallechinsky and Wallace, *The People's Almanac,* pp. 1301–2.

1987 • Edith Stein (1891–1942) was the first Jewish woman officially canonized in the Roman Catholic Church, in Cologne, Germany, in 1987. A German nun, Stein was born a Jew but was baptized a Catholic in 1922. In 1934, when she could no longer teach because of the Nazis' anti-Semitic laws, Stein entered a Carmelite convent, taking the name of Theresa Benedicta of the Cross. Considered a Jew by the Nazis, Stein was taken by train, along with approximately 1,200 other Catholic Jews, to the Auschwitz concentration camp during World War II. She was killed there in 1942.

Sources: Delaney, *Saints Are Now,* pp. 118–35; Uglow, *The Continuum Dictionary of Women's Biography,* pp. 515–16.

1995 • Mother Mary MacKillop (1842–1909), a pioneer teacher and the founder of the Sisters of St. Joseph of the Sacred Heart, became Australia's first blessed at a papal ceremony in Sydney, Australia, on January 19, 1995. Pope John Paul II honored this nineteenth-century nun for her miraculous curing of a woman from leukemia. The case for beatification of Mother Mary, the first step toward canonization, was made in 1925, and in 1975 the Vatican formally initiated the procedure. MacKillop has become a rallying symbol for feminist Australian Catholics.

Sources: Magnusson, *Larousse Biographical Dictionary,* p. 943; Montalbano, "Pope Beatifies Maverick Nun," *The Willoughby (Ohio) News-Herald* (20 January 1995), p. 1.

Converts

First century A.D. • Lydia, a successful businesswoman in Philippi during the first century A.D., is mentioned in the New Testament as an early convert to Christianity, probably the first convert in Europe. She sheltered Paul and his followers when they were in Macedonia.

Sources: Chicago, *The Dinner Party,* p. 130.

Third century A.D. • Flavia Julia Helena (c.255 A.D.–c.330 A.D.) was the first Roman empress to declare herself Christian. An influential supporter of the early Church, she was the mother of Constantine, the first Christian emperor of Rome.

Sources: Attwater, *The Avenel Dictionary of Saints,* p. 166; Chicago, *The Dinner Party,* p. 130; Parbury, *Women of Grace,* p. 54.

Seventh century • Hind al Hunnud, an Arabian leader, was the first woman of the Quraish tribe to convert to Islam. She initially opposed Muhammed and led her people into battle against him in 624 A.D. at Badr near Mecca. She later became a follower of Muhammed, however, and led her people in support of his political and religious causes.

Sources: Uglow, *The Continuum Dictionary of Women's Biography,* p. 260.

(See **Religion: Beatifications and Canonizations, 1235.)**

(See **Religion: Beatifications and Canonizations, 1987.)**

Elections and Appointments

Eighth century • Lioba (d. 782), an Anglo-Saxon woman born in Wessex and sent to Germany as a missionary with 30 nuns, was the first Abbess of the Convent of Tauberbischofsheim near Mainz. Encouraged by St. Boniface, she made her convent into one of the great centers of Christianity of her time. She is buried near Boniface's tomb at Fulda. She was subsequently herself made a saint.

Sources: Parbury, *Women of Grace,* pp. 62–63; Uglow, *The Continuum Dictionary of Women's Biography,* pp. 327–28.

1602 • Angélique Arnauld (1591–1661) was the first woman to become an abbess at the age of eleven. Her wealthy Jansenist family procured for her the abbacy of Port-Royal-les-Champs near Versailles in 1602. Arnauld headed the

POPE JOAN

A medieval legend tells of a woman who, in the mid-800s, disguised herself as a man and rose quickly within the Catholic order. She was soon made a cardinal by Pope Leo IV. At his death in 858 A.D., she was elected pope but was discovered to be a woman when she died giving birth during the inaugural ceremonies. Thus ends the tale of Pope Joan, first female pope.

Some believe the story has a factual basis; others, including some feminists, believe it is wholly fictitious. Bonnie Anderson and Judith Zinsser in *A History of Their Own* attribute the legend to a thirteenth-century French Dominican, Steven of Bourbon, who created the story to show the dangers and impossibility of a woman ever leading the Church. As Anderson and Zinsser see it:

> *Not only did the Church restrict and confine women, but the facts of their past achievements and authority were ridiculed. The woman remembered for exceptional learning, piety, and power was not Lioga, Saint Hilda, Herrad of Landsberg, or Hildegard of Bingen. [Instead, it was the fictitious Pope Joan, whose] woman's nature betrayed her. In Rome, she lusted for a young man, fornicated, and met a fitting end ... death in the gutters of Rome like a common whore.*

Most scholars believe that the story of Pope Joan is pure legend, and therefore, not a herald of women's achievement but rather a sensational fable. It overshadowed the memory of lives and writings of great female religious scholars and leaders.

Sources: Pardoe, *The Female Pope: The Mystery of Pope Joan;* Uglow, *The Continuum Dictionary of Women's Biography,* pp. 284–85.

abbey until 1630, when her sister took it over, returning to her post from 1642 until 1655. During her rule she introduced significant conservative reforms.

Sources: Parbury, *Women of Grace,* p. 38; Uglow, *The Continuum Dictionary of Women's Biography,* pp. 28–29.

(See **Religion: Founders, 1794.***)*

(See **Religion: Founders, 1813.***)*

1860 • Sister Julia McGroarty (1827–1901), a Roman Catholic nun and teacher, was the first American woman to rise to the rank of Mother Superior with the Sisters of Notre Dame de Namur, in Philadelphia, Pennsylvania, in 1860. She was also founder of Trinity College in Washington, D.C. (*See also* **Religion: Founders, 1900.**)

Sources: James, *Notable American Women,* vol. 2, pp. 466–68; Sister Helen Louise, *Sister Julia.*

1865 • Harriet Starr Cannon (1823–1896) was the first Mother Superior of the Episcopal Community of St. Mary. She and four other women, who elected Cannon their head, became the initial members in a service at St. Michael's Church in New York City in 1865. The community worked to feed and shelter the poor and in 1870 established St. Mary's Free Hospital for Poor Children. They opened St. Mary's School in New York City in 1868 and several others followed in New York State, Tennessee, and Wisconsin. At the time of Cannon's death, the community included 104 sisters.

Sources: James, *Notable American Women,* vol. 1, pp. 283–84; Sister Mary Hilary, *Ten Decades of Praise.*

1887 • Angela Thurston Kilgore Newman (1837–1910), an active church worker and reformer, was the first woman chosen to serve as a delegate to the Methodist General Conference, in Salt Lake City in September of 1887. In May of 1888, the assembly refused to seat her and four other women on the grounds of their sex. Women were not accepted as delegates until 1904.

Sources: James, *Notable American Women,* vol. 2, pp. 620–22.

1901 • Alma Bridwell White (1862–1946) was the first female bishop of any Christian church. In 1901 in Denver, Colorado, she founded the fundamentalist Methodist sect that became known after 1917 as the Pillar of Fire Church. As head of this religion, she held the title of bishop. A tireless traveler and preacher both in America and Europe, White was also the founder of seven schools, among them the Alma White College in New Jersey in 1921. In 1932 she took up painting, producing over three hundred mountain landscapes in a primitive folk style. White was also a prolific author, writing a five-volume autobiography, two radio dramas, several volumes of poetry, and over two hundred hymns.

Sources: James, *Notable American Women,* vol. 3, pp. 581–83; White, *Looking Back from Beulah;* White, *Some White Family History;* White, *The Story of My Life.*

1921 • Eva Carey was the first woman to hold an administrative office in the Protestant Episcopal Church in the United States. At the annual Diocesan Convention in Boston, Massachusetts, in 1921, Carey was elected a member of the Bishop's council.

Sources: Read and Witlieb, *The Book of Women's Firsts,* p. 84.

1922 • Belle Harris Bennett (1852–1922), a lay leader in the Southern Methodist Church, was the first female delegate from the Kentucky Annual Methodist Conference to the Southern Methodist General Conference. She was elected in Richmond, Kentucky, in 1922. An activist within her church, Bennett argued for full lay rights for women, eventually granted in 1919.

Sources: James, *Notable American Women,* vol. 1, pp. 132–34.

1940 • Aurelia Henry Reinhardt (1877–1948) became the first female moderator of the American Unitarian Association in 1940. In this capacity, she represented the Unitarian churches on official occasions. She enjoyed a distinguished career in education, serving as president of Mills College from 1916 until 1943 and as president of the American Association of University Women from 1923 until 1927.

Sources: Read and Witlieb, *The Book of Women's Firsts,* p. 364.

1967 • Ruth Stafford Peale (b. 1906) was the first woman president of the National Board of North American Missions, serving from 1967 through 1969.

With her husband, Norman Vincent Peale, she devoted her life to interfaith activities.

Sources: Read and Witlieb, *The Book of Women's Firsts,* p. 336.

1974 • In 1974, Claire Randall (b. 1919) became the first woman to serve as secretary (that is, director) of the National Council of Churches of Christ. Randall worked towards ecumenism, especially between Protestants and Roman Catholics.

Sources: Read and Witlieb, *The Book of Women's Firsts,* p. 359.

1975 • Barbara Herman (b. 1952) became the first female cantor in American Reform Judaism when she was chosen to serve in this capacity at Shalom Temple of Clifton-Passaic, New Jersey, in 1975.

Sources: Read and Witlieb, *The Book of Women's Firsts,* p. 202.

1977 • Beverly Messenger-Harris (b. 1947) was the first woman to serve as a rector of an Episcopal church. She assumed this position in June 1977, at Gethsemane Episcopal Church in Sherrill, New York.

Sources: Read and Witlieb, *The Book of Women's Firsts,* pp. 288–89.

Mary Michael Simpson (b. 1926) was the first woman to become a canon (a priest who assists the dean) in the Episcopal Church. She served in this capacity at the Cathedral of St. John the Divine in New York City from 1977 through 1987.

Sources: Read and Witlieb, *The Book of Women's Firsts,* pp. 408–9.

1982 • Cynthia L. Hale (b. 1952) was elected to head the Disciples of Christ in August 1982 at the National Convocation of the Christian Church. She was the first woman to be elected to this post.

Sources: Jet (30 August 1982), p. 24.

1989 • In February 1989 in Boston, Barbara Clementine Harris (b. 1931) became the first Episcopal woman bishop, causing a tremendous stir in the Anglican community throughout England and North America. Some male Episcopal clergy claimed they would not recognize her as bishop nor accept the priests she ordained. But Bishop Harris, as a black woman in America, had a long history of standing up to opposition and succeeding. Though told when hired as a teenager by the firm of Joseph V. Baker Associates that she was probably not worth her wages, she went on to become president of the firm. She picketed with the National Association for the Advancement of Colored People (NAACP), marched with Martin Luther King, Jr., registered voters in rural Mississippi, and worked as a prison chaplain. With no formal seminary education, Harris scored higher than seminary graduates on ordination exams and was ordained in 1980. As a priest, she supported homosexuals and criticized the Episcopal denomination as a "male-dominated racist church." Bishop Harris looked to Harriet Tubman as her "guiding spirit."

Sources: Ebony (May 1989), p. 40.

1992 • April Ulring Larson was the first woman to be appointed a Lutheran bishop in North America. She was installed in November 1992 as the head of the LaCrosse, Wisconsin, Synod, consisting of 40,000 Lutherans, 80 churches, and 97 clergy.

Sources: National Catholic Reporter (30 October 1992), p. 7.

Founders

Eighth century B.C. • Carmenta, an Etrurian poet, prophet, and queen, was the first person to build a temple at the site of what later became Rome. She led her people into the area and established her son as king, then organized the building of the first temple.

Sources: Chicago, *The Dinner Party,* p. 121.

Fourth century A.D. • Macrina (327–379) and her mother, St. Emmelia, founded the first women's community in Asia Minor. An active member of the early Christian Church, Macrina and her brothers, Bishops Gregory and Basil, were later declared saints.

Sources: Attwater, *The Avenel Dictionary of Saints,* p. 225; Chicago, *The Dinner Party,* p. 130; Greenspan, *Timetables of Women's History,* p. 61.

Fifth century • The first women's convents in Bethlehem were founded in the fifth century by St. Jerome with the significant help of two women, St. Paula and her daughter Eustochium (d. 419), who accompanied him to the Holy Land for this purpose.

Sources: Chicago, *The Dinner Party,* p. 130.

Sixth century • Ethelberga (d. 616) was the founder of the first Benedictine nunnery in England, in the sixth century. There she taught medicine to women and tended the sick.

Sources: Chicago, *The Dinner Party,* p. 136.

Queen Radegund (518–587), a German woman married against her will to the King of the Franks, was the first woman to establish a convent in France. She fled from her husband's court and founded a religious house and hospital at Poitiers.

Sources: Chicago, *The Dinner Party,* p. 134; Uglow, *The Continuum Dictionary of Women's Biography,* pp. 444–45.

c.600 • Brunhilda (d. 613), a Frankish queen, was the founder of the Abbey of Autun in France. Wife of Sigebert I, Brunhilda ruled during a turbulent period. Lothair II of Burgundy tortured her to death, and her ashes are buried in the abbey she founded.

Sources: Uglow, *The Continuum Dictionary of Women's Biography,* p. 93.

Bertha (d. 612), a French woman who married the King of Kent in England, was the founder of the first Christian church at Canterbury. Her marriage contract stipulated her right to practice her religion.

Sources: Chicago, *The Dinner Party,* p. 134; Greenspan, *Timetables of Women's History,* p. 69.

c.630 • Eanswitha (fl. 630), daughter of Eadbald of Kent, founded the first religious settlement for women in Anglo-Saxon England on land given to her by her father.

Sources: Chicago, *The Dinner Party,* p. 135; Parbury, *Women of Grace,* p. 36.

657 • Balthildis (c. 630–680), a Frankish queen, was the founder of both the Abbey of Corbie (in 657–661) and the Convent of Chelles (in 664–665), both in Neustria, the western Frankish kingdom where she ruled with Clovis II until 657 when she became regent for her son Lothair III.

Sources: Parbury, *Women of Grace,* pp. 22–23; Uglow, *The Continuum Dictionary of Women's Biography,* pp. 45–46.

659 • Hilda of Whitby (616–680) was the founder of an important monastery at Whitby, England, in 659. The institution housed both women and men in adjoining quarters, and Hilda became the first abbess. Among her subjects were St. John of Beverley and Caedmon, the first English religious poet. Five of the monks at Whitby during her tenure as abbess went on to become bishops. She was a strong and influential leader and was later made a saint.

Sources: Bede, *The Ecclesiastical History of the English Nation,* p. 731; Parbury, *Women of Grace,* pp. 55–58.

Late tenth century • Adelaide (931–999), a French noblewoman who became an Italian queen and empress, was the founder of the Cluniac monastery at Selz in Alsace, France. She was influential during the rules of her husbands, Lothair of Italy and, after Lothair's death, Otto I of Germany, and of her sons, Otto II and Otto III. Adelaide is also known for her influence on monastic development. She was made a saint in 1097.

Sources: Uglow, *The Continuum Dictionary of Women's Biography,* p. 6.

Twelfth century • Hildegard of Bingen (1098–1178), was founder and first abbess of the convent at Bingen in Germany. She also was the first woman to compose hymns for the mass. A learned woman, she wrote treatises on natural history and medicine and was an accomplished artist and musician. She was also a visionary whose revelations began in 1130.

Sources: Schmidt, *400 Outstanding Women of the World,* p. 389; Uglow, *The Continuum Dictionary of Women's Biography,* pp. 259–60.

Mélisande (1105–1160), Queen of Jerusalem, was the founder of the huge abbey at Bethany in Palestine in the 1130s. She ruled Jerusalem jointly with her husband, Fulk V of Anjou, beginning in 1131.

Sources: Uglow, *The Continuum Dictionary of Women's Biography,* p. 372.

Early thirteenth century • Clare of Assisi (1194–1253) was the founder and first woman to serve as abbess of the Clare Order, the female counterpart to the Franciscan Order. Known as the "Poor Clares," this order was set up by St. Francis at Assisi so that Clare and her female followers could live in the simple Franciscan way they desired.

Sources: Uglow, *The Continuum Dictionary of Women's Biography,* p. 126.

Thirteenth century • Isabel of France was the founder of the Abbey of Longchamps. Daughter of Louis VIII and Blanche of Castile (the thirteenth-century woman who ruled France as regent from 1226 until 1234 and again from 1248 until 1252), Isabel consciously chose a religious life rather than an arranged royal marriage and the world of powerful strife occupied by her mother.

Sources: Uglow, *The Continuum Dictionary of Women's Biography,* p. 70.

Early fourteenth century • Elizabeth of Portugal (1271–1336), a Portuguese queen born in France, was the founder of the Convent of the Poor Clares at Coimbra in Portugal, to which she retired after the death of her husband in 1325. She was canonized in 1625 for her work on behalf of the poor and the sick.

Sources: Uglow, *The Continuum Dictionary of Women's Biography,* p. 189.

1370 • Bridget Godmarsson (1303–1373) was the founder of the Order of the Holy Savior or the Bridgetines. Commanded in a revelation to found a new order, this Swedish noblewoman received papal permission in 1370 and began her austere order in Rome. Bridget was canonized in 1391 and became the patron saint of Sweden.

Sources: Uglow, *The Continuum Dictionary of Women's Biography,* p. 87.

1494 • In 1494 Angela Merici (1474–1540) founded the first women's teaching order in the Catholic Church. She went on to found the Ursuline Order in 1535, whose purpose was to educate girls and to give them individual attention. The Church did not officially approve the Order until 1565. Rome eventually canonized Angela Merici in 1807.

Sources: Chicago, *The Dinner Party,* p. 151.

1562 • Teresa of Avila (1515–1582), a Spanish saint, was the founder of St. Joseph's Convent at Avila in 1562. She went on to found 17 other Carmelite convents in her country. She combined a life of contemplation with practical activity and became, along with St. Catherine of Siena, one of the first two women to be officially declared a doctor of the Church, in 1970.

Sources: Attwater, *The Avenel Dictionary of Saints,* pp. 318–19; Sackville-West, *The Eagle and the Dove,* p. 3; Uglow, *The Continuum Dictionary of Women's Biography,* p. 535.

1603 • Barbe Jeanne Avrillot Acarie (1566–1618) was the first person to introduce the Carmelite order into France, in 1603. After the death of her hus-

Teresa of Avila

band in 1613, she entered the Carmel at Amiens and took the name Marie de l'Incarnation. She was beatified in 1794.

Sources: Uglow, *The Continuum Dictionary of Women's Biography,* p. 3.

1610s • Mary Joan Ward (1585–1645), an English Roman Catholic, was the founder of the lay pastoral group the "English Ladies" in England in the 1610s. Its members worked in the community and paid particular attention to women's needs. In 1621, English Catholic leaders appealed to the Pope to order the dissolution of the group, arguing that women were unsuited to pastoral work. In 1629, Ward's order was finally suppressed. She is also remembered as a founder of schools for girls and for the poor in France, Italy, Germany, Austria, and Hungary.

Sources: Chambers, *Life of Mary Ward;* Uglow, *The Continuum Dictionary of Women's Biography,* p. 569.

1633 • Louise de Marillac (1591–1660), a French aristocrat, was the founder of the order of the Daughters of Charity, in 1633. She was canonized in 1934 and named the patron saint of social workers by Pope John XXIII.

Sources: Uglow, *The Continuum Dictionary of Women's Biography,* p. 158.

1676 • Jeanne Marie Guyon (1648–1717), a French religious mystic, founded her own heretical version of Quietism, teaching complete indifference, even to eternal salvation. She traveled throughout Europe, advocating her position, and was arrested and condemned on several occasions for her beliefs.

Sources: Knox, *Enthusiasm,* pp. 319–20; Uglow, *The Continuum Dictionary of Women's Biography,* pp. 240–41.

1727 • Mother Superior Marie Tranchepain (d. 1733) arrived from France in 1727 with a dozen other Ursuline nuns to establish the first permanent convent in what would become the United States, in New Orleans, Louisiana. The original convent consisted of a small, two-story wooden building in the French Quarter of New Orleans, from which the sisters also ran their school for girls. The convent and gardens, rebuilt in 1750, still stand, but the sisters and their school—the Ursuline Academy—moved to larger quarters a few blocks north of the original site.

Sources: McCullough, *First of All,* pp. 106–7.

1766 • Barbara Ruckie Heck (1734–1804) was the cofounder, with her cousin, Phillip Embury, of the Methodist Church in the United States. In 1766, they set up the first Methodist Society in New York City.

Sources: Read and Witlieb, *The Book of Women's Firsts,* p. 199.

1790 • Ann Teresa Matthews (1732–1800) was the cofounder, with Frances Dickinson, of the first Roman Catholic convent in the newly established United States. She established the Carmel convent in Port Tobacco, Maryland, on October 15, 1790.

Sources: James, *Notable American Women,* vol. 2, pp. 509–10; Read and Witlieb, *The Book of Women's Firsts,* pp. 272–73.

1794 • Jemima Wilkinson (1752–1819), an American religious leader, was the founder of Jerusalem Township, a community near Keuka Lake, New York, in 1794. After having visions in her youth, Wilkinson named herself "The Public Universal Friend." With a number of followers eager to establish a utopian community, she funded exploration of Genesee County, New York, in the 1780s and continued to encourage western settlement throughout her life.

Sources: James, *Notable American Women*, vol. 3, pp. 609–10; Wisbey, Jr., *Pioneer Prophetess: Jemima Wilkinson, the Public Universal Friend.*

1809 • Elizabeth Ann Bayley Seton (1774–1821) was the founder of the first Catholic order in the United States, the Sisters of Charity of St. Joseph, which she established on September 14, 1809. She was later declared a saint. (*See also* **Religion: Beatifications and Canonizations, 1975.**)

Sources: James, *Notable American Women*, vol. 3, pp. 263–65; Read and Witlieb, *The Book of Women's Firsts*, pp. 401–2; Wallechinsky and Wallace, *The People's Almanac*, pp. 1301–2.

1812 • Mary Rhodes (1782–1853), a U.S. Roman Catholic nun, was the founder of the Sisters of Loretto, at Hardin's Creek, Kentucky, on April 25, 1812. Initially called the Friends of St. Mary at the Foot of the Cross, the small group of women was committed to simplicity and poverty. When its first head died soon after its foundation, in December of 1812, Rhodes was elected mother superior, and under her direction the order developed over the next decade, taking the name of the Sisters of Loretto. The order was approved formally in 1817, with Rhodes as its first head.

Sources: James, *Notable American Women*, vol. 3, pp. 140–41; Minogue, *Loretto Annals of the Century*; Spalding, *Sketches of the Early Catholic Missions of Kentucky.*

1813 • Catherine Spalding (1793–1858) was the first mother superior of the Sisters of Charity of Nazareth. She helped to found the sisterhood near Bardstown, Kentucky, and served as mother superior beginning in 1813.

Sources: Read and Witlieb, *The Book of Women's Firsts*, pp. 415–16.

1818 • Rose Philippine Duchesne (1769–1862), a French nun brought up and educated in Grenoble, was the founder of the American convents of the Sacred Heart. Duchesne was canonized a saint in 1988. She opened the first convent in St. Charles, Missouri, in 1818, but it did not prosper, nor did the convent opened the following year in Florissant. The first successful convent was at Grand Coteau, Louisiana, in 1821.

Sources: Foy and Avato, *1995 Catholic Almanac*, p. 391; James, *Notable American Women*, vol. 1, pp. 524–26.

1838 • Rebecca Gratz (1781–1869) founded the first Hebrew Sunday School Society in 1838 in Philadelphia, Pennsylvania. She devoted her life to charity work and religion, emphasizing the needs of women and children.

Sources: James, *Notable American Women*, vol. 2, pp. 75–76; Read and Witlieb, *The Book of Women's Firsts*, p. 184.

1840s • Catherine Mumford Booth (1829–1890) was the cofounder, with her husband William Booth, of the Salvation Army. Their work preaching on London street corners in the 1840s lead to their rejection of conventional Wesleyan Methodism and the development of the new evangelical and communitarian organization. Their militant Christian organization became known as the Salvation Army in 1865. Their daughter, Evangeline, would carry on her parents' work in the United States in the early 1900s. (*See* **Religion: Leaders, 1904.**)

Sources: Uglow, *The Continuum Dictionary of Women's Biography,* p. 78.

(See **Religion: Ordinations and Consecrations, 1845.***)*

1847 • Cornelia Augusta Connelly (1809–1879), a Roman Catholic nun who grew up in Philadelphia, was the founder and first head of the Society of the Holy Child Jesus, in Derby, England, in December of 1847. Connelly lead a dramatic life, moving from a marriage with children to a life of chastity dedicated to the education of the poor. Led by her mercurial husband into the Catholic faith and then into holy orders, she became dedicated to spiritual causes. Her husband, then a Catholic priest, removed her children from her care, sought to take over control of her new society, then renounced his vows and sought to restore his conjugal rights by court action. The court ruled in his favor in May of 1849, but was overturned on appeal in 1851 in a much publicized case. Cornelia Connelly's personal and spiritual struggles, however, confirmed her faith and her mission.

Sources: Connelly, *God Alone: An Anthology of the Spiritual Writings of Cornelia Connelly;* James, *Notable American Women,* vol. 1, pp. 373–75; Mother Marie Thérèse, *Cornelia Connelly: A Study in Fidelity.*

1852 • Mother Benedicta Riepp (1825–1862), a Roman Catholic nun born and educated in Germany, was the founder of the Sisters of Saint Benedict in the United States. She left Europe in 1852 and began the order with three sisters at the German colony of St. Mary's in Elk County, Pennsylvania, in July of that year. The Sisters of Saint Benedict has prospered in America and is dedicated to teaching and to maintaining orphanages, hospitals, and nursing homes for the ill and aged.

Sources: James, *Notable American Women,* vol. 3, pp. 160–61; Sister Grace McDonald, *With Lamps Burning;* Sister Mary Regina Baska, *The Benedictine Congregation of Saint Scholastica.*

1855 • Mother Angela Gillespie (1824–1887), a Roman Catholic nun born in Pennsylvania, was the founder of the Sisters of the Holy Cross in the United States. A small community of French sisters existed at Notre Dame University and at St. Mary's Academy in Bertrand, Michigan, but it was Gillespie, after a novitiate in France, who moved St. Mary's to South Bend, Indiana, in 1855 and developed the order. The school soon became St. Mary's College under her leadership. Nearly forty other schools had been established under her auspices by the time of her death.

Sources: James, *Notable American Women,* vol. 2, pp. 34–35; McAllister, *Flame in the Wilderness: Life and Letters of Mother Angela.*

1860 • Ellen Gould Harmon White (1827–1915) was the cofounder of the Seventh-Day Adventist Church, with her husband, James Springer White, in Battle Creek, Michigan, in 1860. White, an itinerant preacher and mystic visionary from her youth, and her husband traveled, spoke, and wrote of their beliefs in the 1840s and 1850s, but did not name or otherwise formalize their religion until 1860. White devoted her life to her religion and related causes, such as the abolition of slavery and higher education, particularly in Biblical study.

Sources: James, *Notable American Women,* vol. 3, pp. 585–88; White, *Ellen G. White: Messenger to the Remnant.*

(See **Religion: Elections and Appointments, 1865.**)

1871 • Caroline White Soule (1824–1903) served as the first president of the Woman's Centenary Association from 1871 until 1880. The purpose of this group, the first national organization of church women in the United States, was to assist preachers and their families and to help to educate female students in the ministry and to encourage them in missionary work.

Sources: Read and Witlieb, *The Book of Women's Firsts,* p. 415.

1875 • Helena Petrovna Blavatsky (1831–1891) was the founder of modern theosophy, a system of belief founded on a tradition of spiritualism and the occult. Born in Russia, Blavatsky arrived at her beliefs through travels in Turkey, Greece, India, and Tibet. In 1875 she founded the Theosophical Society in the United States.

Sources: James, *Notable American Women,* vol. 1, pp. 174–77; Ryan, *Helena Petrovna Blavatsky and the Theosophical Movement;* Uglow, *The Continuum Dictionary of Women's Biography,* p. 71.

1876 and 1879 • Mary Baker Eddy (1821–1910) was the founder of the Christian Science Association in 1876 and the Church of Christ, Scientist, in 1879 in Boston, Massachusetts. In 1883 she founded the *Christian Science Journal* and in 1908 the Christian Science Church's daily paper, *The Christian Science Monitor.* Eddy preached that disease was a false belief and that its cure lay in mental prescriptions.

Sources: *National Cyclopedia of American Biography,* vol. III, p. 80; Read and Witlieb, *The Book of Women's Firsts,* pp. 135–36.

Mary Baker Eddy

1880 • Frances Xavier Cabrini (1859–1917) founded a new religious order, the Missionary Sisters of the Sacred Heart, in Italy. *(See also* **Religion: Beatifications and Canonizations, 1946.**)

Sources: James, *Notable American Women,* vol. 1, pp. 274–76; Read and Witlieb, *The Book of Women's Firsts,* p. 79.

(See **Religion: Leaders, 1887.**)

1893 • Hannah Greenebaum Solomon (1858–1942) was the organizer of the first assembly of Jewish women in the United States. At the request of the producers of the World Columbian Exposition in Chicago, Illinois, in 1893 Solomon organized a group of Jewish women in an assembly that became the National Council of Jewish Women.

Sources: Read and Witlieb, *The Book of Women's Firsts,* p. 413.

1897 • Ursula Newell Gestefeld (1845–1921), who developed her own religious system of thinking after splitting with Mary Baker Eddy's Christian Science, was the founder and first president of the Exodus Club, in Chicago in 1897. From this group Gestefeld developed the Church of the New Thought in 1904 and the College of the Science of Being. Emphasizing logic and reasoning rather than any individual or church authority, she espoused her ideas in a monthly magazine, *Exodus,* of which she was the first and only editor, between 1896 and 1904.

Sources: Bates and Dittemore, *Mary Baker Eddy,* pp. 260, 291–93; James, *Notable American Women,* vol. 2, pp. 27–28.

1900 • Mother Mary Alphonsa Lathrop (1851–1926), the daughter of Nathaniel and Sophia Peabody Hawthorne, was the founder of the Dominican Congregation of St. Rose of Lima, in New York City on December 8, 1900. With her friend, Sister Mary Rose Huber, Lathrop directed the community in caring for terminally ill cancer patients.

Sources: James, *Notable American Women,* vol. 2, pp. 372–73.

Sister Julia McGroarty (1827–1901), a Roman Catholic nun and teacher, founded Trinity College in Washington, D.C., with the support of several other nuns in 1900. This school, located near Catholic University, was designed for women who wanted a Catholic education but were denied admission to Catholic University because of their gender. She was also the first American woman to rise to the rank of Mother Superior. (*See also* **Religion: Elections and Appointments, 1860.**)

Sources: James, *Notable American Women,* vol. 2, pp. 466–68; Sister Helen Louise, *Sister Julia;* Sister Mary Patricia Butler, *An Historical Sketch of Trinity College.*

(*See* **Religion: Elections and Appointments, 1901.**)

1920 • Mother Mary Joseph Rogers (1882–1955) founded the Maryknoll Sisters of St. Dominic in 1920 in Ossining, New York. Devoted to foreign missions, the group's name was originally The Foreign Mission Sisters of St. Dominic. Mother Mary Joseph Rogers served as its president from 1925 until her retirement in 1947.

Sources: Read and Witlieb, *The Book of Women's Firsts,* pp. 376–77.

1923 • Aimée Semple McPherson (1890–1944), a Canadian evangelist, founded the International Church of the Foursquare Gospel, in Los Angeles, California, in 1923. McPherson was initially active in the Salvation Army, then served as a missionary in Asia after her marriage to Robert Semple, a Pentecostal evangelist, in 1908. After his death in 1910, she began an evangelical crusade across the United States. Her church's theology emphasized Jesus' four roles as savior, baptizer, healer, and coming king. Faith healing also played a major role in the church. McPherson had a large following during the 1920s and 1930s and led a dramatic life; she died of an overdose of sleeping pills.

Sources: McPherson, *The Story of My Life;* McPherson, *This Is That;* Thomas, *Storming Heaven;* Uglow, *The Continuum Dictionary of Women's Biography,* p. 348.

1930 • In 1930, Gladys Aylward (1903–1970), an English missionary, founded with the help of a Scotswoman, Miss Dawson, "The Inn of the Sixth Happiness," a hotel in China at which local travelers were taught the gospel, in 1930. Aylward became a Chinese citizen in 1931, not returning to England until 1948. She returned to Taiwan in 1953 to work with refugees and orphans. A film based on her experiences (*The Inn of the Sixth Happiness,* starring Ingrid Bergman) was made in 1958.

Sources: Aylward and Hunter, *Gladys Aylward;* Uglow, *The Continuum Dictionary of Women's Biography,* p. 38.

(*See* **Religion: Beatifications and Canonizations, 1995.**)

Leaders

Eighth century B.C. • Sammuramat, an Assyrian queen of the eighth century B.C., was the first woman to develop the cult of the god Nabu. She ruled for 42 years and is the subject of more stories than any other figure in Assyrian history.

Sources: Uglow, *The Continuum Dictionary of Women's Biography,* p. 476.

First century A.D. • Thecla, according to legend, was the first woman to preach and to baptize converts to Christianity. She was one of Paul's followers and was responsible for converting many women to Christianity during the first century.

Sources: Chicago, *The Dinner Party,* p. 132.

(*See* **Religion: Converts, Seventh century.**)

631 • Bint Abi Bakr Aishah (613–678) was the first woman to become a Muslim leader. She was the favorite wife of Muhammed, the prophet and founder of Islam. After his death in 631, Aishah emerged as a powerful religious leader in the ensuing political turmoil. Her teachings contributed to the emergence of the Sunni Muslims.

Sources: Uglow, *The Continuum Dictionary of Women's Biography,* p. 11.

Eleventh century • Eleanor of Aquitaine (1122–1204), during her first marriage to Louis VII of France, became the first woman to lead a Crusade to the Holy Land. She organized 300 women, known as the Queen's Amazons, and prepared them for an ill-fated journey to the east. The failure of this Crusade ultimately led to Eleanor's divorce from Louis and remarriage to Henry of England, whom she helped attain the crown.

Sources: Chicago, *The Dinner Party,* pp. 74–75; Schmidt, *400 Outstanding Women of the World,* p. 171–72; Uglow, *The Continuum Dictionary of Women's Biography,* pp. 184–85.

Early thirteenth century • Hadewijch was the first woman to lead the Beguines, a group of laywomen who joined together as a religious community in Brabant in the Netherlands in the early thirteenth century. Hadewijch was also a teacher, a mystic, and a writer known for her courtly verse and prose letters.

Sources: Uglow, *The Continuum Dictionary of Women's Biography,* p. 243.

Late thirteenth century • Gertrude von Helfta (1256–1302), a German nun, was the initiator, with her friend Mechtilde von Hackeborn, of the cult of the adoration of the Sacred Heart. Gertrud was also a mystic who recorded her visions in two books.

Sources: Uglow, *The Continuum Dictionary of Women's Biography,* p. 223.

1635 • Anne Hutchinson (1591–1643) was the first woman to dissent against New England Puritan orthodoxy. She met with Puritans in her home in Boston, Massachusetts, to discuss both secular and theological issues and questioned what she saw as the Puritan emphasis on salvation through works. Hutchinson argued for salvation through grace and for a direct relation with God. She was tried, excommunicated, and banished from the colony in 1638.

Sources: Read and Witlieb, *The Book of Women's Firsts,* pp. 222–23; Uglow, *The Continuum Dictionary of Women's Biography,* pp. 270–71.

1774 • Ann Lee (1736–84) was the leader of the first Shaker group to come from England to the United States, in 1774. She emigrated with a group of Shakers—officially the United Society of Believers in Christ's Second Appearing—and settled in New York State. She believed Jesus would return as a woman and advocated equal rights for women and pacifism.

Sources: James, *Notable American Women,* vol. 2, pp. 385–87; Read and Witlieb, *The Book of Women's Firsts,* pp. 249–50.

1870 • Augusta Chapin (1836–1905) was the first woman to serve on the council of the Universalist Church. An ordained pastor, she was appointed to the council in 1870 in recognition of her work in theology and of her commitment to women's advancement. She was also the first woman in the United States to receive an honorary Doctor of Divinity from Lombard University in 1893.

Sources: James, *Notable American Women,* vol. 1, pp. 320–21; Read and Witlieb, *The Book of Women's Firsts,* pp. 87–88.

1887 • Lucy Jane Rider Meyer (1849–1922) was the first American to become a successful advocate of the deaconess movement, which encouraged the use of organized groups of lay women for social service as "deaconesses." A 1872 graduate of Oberlin College, Meyer organized the first American deacon-

ess home, in Chicago in the autumn of 1887. Her followers adopted a distinctive costume and in May of 1888 were recognized by the Methodist Episcopal Church.

Sources: Golder, *A History of the Deaconess Movement in the Christian Church;* James, *Notable American Women,* vol. 2, pp. 534–36; Meyer, *Deaconesses.*

1904 • Evangeline Booth (1865–1950), commander of the U.S. Salvation Army from 1904 to 1934 was the first woman to hold that post. She was the daughter of Catherine Booth and General William Booth, co-founders of the Salvation Army in England in 1865. (*See* **Religion: Founders, 1895.**) The Salvation Army has always treated women equitably within its organization; if a marriage occurs between two Salvation Army officers, the one with the lower rank is always promoted to the higher rank, so that the partners work together at the same level.

Sources: James, *Notable American Women,* vol. 1, pp. 204–6; O'Neill, *The Women's Book of World Records and Achievements,* p. 395; Read and Witlieb, *The Book of Women's Firsts,* pp. 61–62.

1960 • Fayvelle Mermey (1916–1977) was the first woman to serve as president of a synagogue. She headed the Larchmont Temple in suburban New York City for two terms, 1960–62 and 1972–74. Her election in 1960 was widely noted as evidence of the equality of women with men in temple administration in Reform Judaism.

Sources: O'Neill, *The Women's Book of World Records and Achievements,* p. 395.

Evangeline Booth

Missionaries

(*See* **Religion: Elections and Appointments, Eighth century.**)

1812 • Ann Hasseltine Judson (1789–1826) was the first U.S. woman to become a foreign missionary. She set out with her husband from Salem, Massachusetts, in February of 1812, and arrived in Rangoon, Burma, in July of 1813. Except for a few trips west for her health, she remained there until her death, working to convert the local people to Christianity and living through tumultuous circumstances brought on by British colonialism in the area.

Sources: James, *Notable American Women,* vol. 2, pp. 295–97; Knowles, *Memoir of Mrs. Ann H. Hudson, Late Missionary to Burma.*

Harriet Atwood Newell (1793–1812), a pioneering American missionary, was the first American to die in the foreign mission service, on November 30, 1812, in Port Louis, Isle of France, Mauritius. She died in all probability of tuberculosis complicated by a difficult pregnancy and a premature childbirth. Newell was on her way with her husband to a mission in Ceylon.

Sources: James, *Notable American Women,* vol. 2, pp. 619–20.

1827 • Cynthia Farrar (1795–1862) was the first unmarried U.S. woman to be sent overseas as a missionary. Sponsored by the American Board of Commissioners for Foreign Missions, she left Boston, Massachusetts, on June 5,

Ann Hasseltine Judson

1827, and on December 29, 1827, arrived in Bombay, India, where she began 34 years of service to the Marathi Mission.

Sources: Beaver, *All Loves Excelling: American Protestant Women in World Mission,* pp. 68–70; James, *Notable American Women,* vol. 1, pp. 600–1.

1923 • Alice Mildred Cable (1878–1952) and her friends Evangeline French (1869–1960) and Francesca French (1871–1960) were the first women to be granted permission from the Chinese government to preach to the nomadic tribes in the Gobi Desert, in 1923. These women devoted their lives to missionary work in the Far East and to careful observations of geography during their travels.

Sources: Platt, *Three Women;* Uglow, *The Continuum Dictionary of Women's Biography,* p. 101.

(*See* **Religion: Founders, 1930.**)

Ordinations and Consecrations

1752 • On January 29, 1752, Mary Terpin took her vows to become the first U.S.-born nun. Born in Illinois in 1731 of Canadian and Indian parents, Mary went to live and study with the Ursuline sisters at New Orleans, Louisiana, when she was 17. A year later she became a postulant. Upon taking her final vows in 1752, she became Sister St. Martha and spent the rest of her brief life at the convent. She died of tuberculosis in 1761, at the age of 30. (*See also* **Religion: Founders, 1727.**)

Sources: McCullough, *First of All,* p. 106.

1845 • Anne Ayres (1816–1896) became in 1845 the first woman to be consecrated as an Episcopal sister. She went on to found the Sisterhood of the Holy Communion in New York City.

Sources: James, *Notable American Women,* vol. 1, pp. 74–75; Read and Witlieb, *The Book of Women's Firsts,* p. 30.

1853 • Antoinette-Louisa Brown (1825–1921), who graduated from Oberlin College in 1850, became the first woman in the United States to be ordained a minister. The ordination took place at the First Congregational Church in Butler, New York, on September 15, 1853.

Sources: Ogilvie, *Women in Science,* p. 39; Read and Witlieb, *The Book of Women's Firsts,* p. 70; Sanders, *The First of Everything,* p. 158.

1863 • Olympia Brown (1835–1926) became the first woman to be ordained as a Universalist minister in 1863. A member of the Protestant Northern Universalists, she was ordained in Malone, New York. A graduate of Antioch College and of the theological school of St. Lawrence University, Brown became a charter member of the American Equal Rights Association in 1866. She resigned her pastorate in Racine, Wisconsin, to devote herself to the cause of women's suffrage in 1887.

Sources: James, *Notable American Women,* vol. 1, pp. 256–58; Read and Witlieb, *The Book of Women's Firsts,* p. 72.

Olympia Brown

1869 • Margaret Van Cott (1830–1914) became the first woman licensed to preach in the Methodist Episcopal Church, in 1869. She preached at revival meetings throughout the United States for over 30 years.

Sources: James, *Notable American Women,* vol. 3, pp. 506–7; Read and Witlieb, *The Book of Women's Firsts,* p. 462.

1871 • In 1871 Celia C. Burleigh (1827–1875) became the first woman to be ordained a minister in the Unitarian Church. She served at a parish in Brooklyn, Connecticut. She was a woman's suffrage advocate throughout her life.

Sources: Read and Witlieb, *The Book of Women's Firsts,* p. 76.

1880 • Anna Shaw (1847–1919) was the first woman to be ordained a minister in the Methodist Protestant Church, in 1880. She graduated from Boston University Divinity School in 1878, but then decided upon medicine as a career and graduated from Boston University Medical School in 1886. A lifelong advocate of women's rights, Shaw was president of the National American Woman Suffrage Association from 1904 until 1915.

Sources: Read and Witlieb, *The Book of Women's Firsts,* pp. 404–5; Uglow, *The Continuum Dictionary of Women's Biography,* pp. 494–97.

1965 • Rachel Henderlite (b. 1905) was the first woman to be ordained an American Presbyterian minister, in Richmond, Virginia, in 1965. She continued to be active in church service and administration throughout her life.

Sources: Read and Witlieb, *The Book of Women's Firsts,* p. 200.

1970 • Barbara Andrews (1934–1978) was the first woman to be ordained as a minister in the American Lutheran Church. She began her ministry in 1970 in Minneapolis, Minnesota, and at the time of her death was acting pastor of Resurrection Lutheran Church in Detroit, Michigan.

Sources: Read and Witlieb, *The Book of Women's Firsts,* p. 20.

1972 • Judith Hird (b. 1946) was the first woman to serve as a parish pastor in the Lutheran Church in America. She was named to this position at the Holy Cross Lutheran Church in Toms River, New Jersey, in 1972.

Sources: Read and Witlieb, *The Book of Women's Firsts,* p. 207.

Sally Priesand (b. 1946) was the first American woman ordained a rabbi in Reform Judaism, in 1972 in Cincinnati, Ohio. She has made her career by serving as rabbi in various congregations in New York and New Jersey.

Sources: Priesand, *Judaism and the New Woman;* Read and Witlieb, *The Book of Women's Firsts,* p. 350.

1974 • Jacqueline Means (b. 1937) became the first female Episcopal priest when, with 14 other women, she was ordained in 1974 in defiance of church law in Indianapolis, Indiana. When the Episcopal Church opened its priesthood to women, in 1976, it ruled that Means and the others ordained with her would be officially accepted into the Episcopal priesthood. The ordination became official on January 1, 1977.

Sources: O'Neill, *The Women's Book of World Records and Achievements,* p. 382; Read and Witlieb, *The Book of Women's Firsts,* pp. 285–86.

1980 • Marjorie Swank Matthews (1916–1986) was chosen to become the first woman bishop in the United Methodist Church, in August 1980.

Sources: The Christian Century (13 August 1980), p. 24.

1982 • Yvonne Reed Chappelle (b. 1938) was the first black woman to be ordained in the Unitarian-Universalist Church, in 1982. Chappelle graduated from the Howard School of Divinity.

Sources: Jet (11 February 1982), p. 32; Smith, *Black Firsts,* p. 339.

1985 • Amy Eilberg (b. 1954) was the first woman to be a Conservative Jewish rabbi. In February 1985, the Rabbinical Assembly of the Conservative movement amended its constitution to allow female rabbis. In May of the same year Eilberg was ordained.

Sources: Read and Witlieb, *The Book of Women's Firsts,* pp. 140–41.

Scholars and Artists

c.100 A.D. • Beruriah (c.100 A.D.), an ancient Hebrew scholar and legal expert, is the first and only woman mentioned in the Talmud. She wrote commentaries on the law, and when her husband tried to discredit her intellectual achievements by challenging her sexual fidelity, she killed herself.

Sources: Chicago, *The Dinner Party,* p. 118; Greenspan, *The Timetables of Women's History,* p. 51.

Eighth century • Rabi'ah al-'Adawiyyah (712–801), an Arab mystic, was the first woman to become a Sufi Muslim scholar. Brought up a Sunni Muslim from the al-Atik tribe, she lived in a hut in Basra in present-day Iraq and devoted her life to God.

Sources: Uglow, *The Continuum Dictionary of Women's Biography,* p. 444 .

1842 • Grace Aguilar (1816–1847), a writer of fiction and religious books, was the first Jewish woman to attempt to educate the English public about her religion. She wrote the first of several books about Jewish history and belief in 1842, emphasizing her concern about the position of women in Judaism.

Sources: Uglow, *The Continuum Dictionary of Women's Biography,* p. 9.

Witchcraft Trials

1275 • Angèle de la Barthe (d. 1275) was the first woman in France to be executed as a witch. She was accused of copulating with the devil, found guilty by Christian judges, and executed.

Sources: Chicago, *The Dinner Party,* p. 148.

1590 • Scottish lay-healer Geillis Duncan (d. 1590) was the first woman to be executed for witchcraft in the North Berwick trials. Her forced confession, during which she was compelled to name accomplices, brought about a persecution of witches that was officially sanctioned by the king.

Sources: Chicago, *The Dinner Party,* p. 148; Greenspan, *Timetables of Women's History,* p. 156.

1650 • Margaret Jones (d. 1650) was the first woman in America to be executed as a witch. A lay healer, Jones was accused of witchcraft by professionally trained male physicians who were jealous of her art, and she was subsequently tried and convicted in Massachusetts Bay Colony.

Sources: Chicago, *The Dinner Party,* p. 149; Levin, *Women and Medicine,* p. 194.

1669 • Gertrude Svenson (d. 1669) was the first of seventy victims of the worst mass witch hunt in Swedish history. Accused of kidnapping children in order to hand them over to the devil, Svenson was executed despite a lack of evidence.

Sources: Chicago, *The Dinner Party,* p. 150.

1692 • Bridget Bishop (d. 1692) was the first woman to be tried for witchcraft in Salem, Massachusetts. A special Court of Oyer and Terminer was convened in May of 1692 to examine cases of supposed possession and witchcraft. Bishop was condemned to death and hanged on June 10 of that year.

Sources: James, *Notable American Women,* vol. 2, p. 639.

Science

Anthropologists

1869 • Clemence Augustine Royer (1830–1902), an outstanding scholar, was the first person to translate the work of Charles Darwin into French. In 1869 she published her translation of his important book, *On the Origin of Species by Means of Natural Selection.* Trained in anthropology and archaeology, Royer later published her own book on the theory of evolution.
Sources: Chicago, *The Dinner Party,* p. 193; Uglow, *The Continuum Dictionary of Women's Biography,* p. 467.

1902 • Alice Fletcher (1838–1923) founded the American Anthropological Association. She was a serious student of Native North American tribes, working on their behalf in Washington and recording their life and rituals in the field. She was also active in the women's movement. In 1904, she published *The Hako: A Pawnee Ceremony.*
Sources: Read and Witlieb, *The Book of Women's Firsts,* p. 160; Uglow, *The Continuum Dictionary of Women's Biography,* p. 207.

c.1930 • Ruth Fulton Benedict (1887–1948) was the first American woman to become the preeminent leader of a learned profession. She was an outstanding anthropologist who, with a degree from Vassar College, went on to study under Franz Boas at Columbia University, from which she received her doctorate in 1923. She first specialized in the study of Native Americans, then in Egyptian and Japanese cultures. As she began to teach at Columbia University in the 1920s, she fostered the careers of Margaret Mead and, later, Zora Neale Hurston. Benedict became an assistant professor at Columbia in 1931 and published her famous introductory text, *Patterns of Culture* in 1934. She served as president of the American Anthropological Association from 1947 until 1948, and in 1948 Columbia University finally made her a full professor.
Sources: James, *Notable American Women,* vol. 1, pp. 128–31; Mead, *An Anthropologist at Work: Writings of Ruth Benedict.*

1976 • Margaret Mead (1901–1978), an American anthropologist, was the first woman to have a chair named after her at the American Museum of Natural History in New York City. This honor was announced in a full-page advertisement in the *New York Times* on December 16, 1976—Mead's seventy-fifth birthday.

Margaret Mead was born in Philadelphia, the oldest of five children, and was

Margaret Mead

educated at Barnard College. She was influenced by Columbia University anthropologist Ruth Benedict to pursue a career in anthropology. While a student at Barnard, Mead received her first grant to study in Samoa. In 1926, she was appointed assistant curator of ethnology at the American Museum of Natural History. As her career in anthropology progressed, she undertook expeditions to Samoa and New Guinea. Mead wrote about her observations in these two countries in *Coming of Age in Samoa* (1928) and *Growing up in New Guinea* (1930). She later theorized about the ways culture influenced the development of personality in such works as *Male and Female* (1949) and *Growth and Culture* (1941).

At age 38, with six books and nearly 100 publications to her credit, she became a mother. Her daughter, Mary Catherine Bateson, was fathered by Mead's third husband, English anthropologist Gregory Bateson, who left Mead shortly after their daughter's birth. Mary Catherine Bateson, who became an anthropologist herself, published a memoir about her parents entitled *With a Daugher's Eye: A Memoir of Margaret Mead and Gregory Bateson.*

Sources: Howard, *Margaret Mead*; Magnusson, *Larousse Biographical Dictionary,* p. 996; Mead, *Blackberry Winter*; *Smithsonian* 15 (September 1983), p. 188.

Archaeologists

c.1890 • Margaret Murray (1863–1963) was the first woman to conduct her own archeological digs. A professor and author from England, Murray specialized in Egyptology and later wrote extensively about witchcraft in Europe.

Sources: Chicago, *The Dinner Party,* p. 192; Uglow, *The Continuum Dictionary of Women's Biography,* p. 393.

1895 • The first all-female team to excavate the Temple of the Goddess Mut at Karnac in Egypt was led by Margaret Benson (daughter of the then Archbishop of Canterbury) and Helen Gourlay. Working as amateur archaeologists, the two English women and their team spent two years at the site, both digging and entertaining the European aristocracy who came to visit the famous temple.

Sources: *The (London) Times Literary Supplement* (21 October 1994), pp. 7–8.

c.1900 • Esther Boise Van Deman (1862–1937), an American scholar, was the first female Roman field archeologist. Educated at Bryn Mawr College in Pennsylvania and at the University of Chicago, from which she received her doctorate in 1898, she won a fellowship to the American School of Classical Studies in Rome, Italy, in 1901. After 1906, she lived and worked in Rome. Associated with the American Academy there, she made her career as a field researcher, a teacher, and a writer.

Sources: James, *Notable American Women,* vol. 3, pp. 507–8; Van Deman, *The Atrium Vestae*; Van Deman, *The Building of the Roman Aqueducts*.

1901 • Harriet Boyd Howes (1871–1945), an American archaelogist, was the first person to discover the site of the ancient Minoan town of Gournia, on the island of Crete, in 1901. She spent three years excavating the area, then published her findings in a report still used today.

Sources: James, *Notable American Women,* vol. 2, pp. 160–61; *The (London) Times Literary Supplement* (21 October 1994), pp. 7–8.

1902 • Zelia Maria Magdalena Nuttall (1857–1933), a pioneering American archaeologist specializing in Mexico, was the first person to establish the historical authenticity of two Mexican codices. To the first of these she gave her name, the *Codex Nuttall,* when it was published with her commentary in 1902. She held the position of special honorary assistant in Mexican archeology at Harvard's Peabody Museum in Cambridge, Massachusetts, from 1886 until her death. She was the only woman in a group of pioneering archaelogists working in America at the turn of the century.

Sources: James, *Notable American Women,* vol. 2, pp. 640–42.

1932 • Mary Swindler (1884–1967) was the first female editor in chief of the *American Journal of Archaeology,* a position she held from 1932 until 1946. She studied Greek archaeology at Bryn Mawr College in Pennsylvania, where she was a professor of classical archaeology from 1931 until 1949.

Sources: Read and Witlieb, *The Book of Women's Firsts,* p. 432.

c.1950 • Dame Kathleen Mary Kenyon (1906–1978), a professional archaelogist, was the first person successfully to excavate the site of Jericho. Kenyon also excavated at sites in Jerusalem, where she was director of the British School of Archaeology from 1951 to 1966. One of the founders of the Institute of Archeology in London, England, Kenyon's publications include *Digging Up Jericho* (1957), *Archaeology in the Holy Land* (1956), and *Digging Up Jerusalem* (1974).

Sources: Magnusson, *Larousse Biographical Dictionary,* p. 821; *The (London) Times Literary Supplement* (21 October 1994), pp. 7–8.

1959 • Mary Douglas Leakey (b. 1913), an English archaelogist working with her husband, the anthropologist Louis Leakey, discovered the skull in the Olduvai Gorge in Tanganyika (now part of Tanzania) that became known as the famous "missing link" in human evolution. This discovery suggested that people had evolved in different branches and approximately a million years earlier than had previously been supposed. After her husband's death in 1972, she took over as Director of the Olduvai Gorge excavations, becoming the first woman to hold this position. Through her work she became the leading authority on prehistoric technology and culture.

Sources: Leakey, *Disclosing the Past*; Uglow, *The Continuum Dictionary of Women's Biography,* p. 316.

Astronauts and Cosmonauts

1960 • Geraldyn (Jerrie) Cobb (b. 1931) was the first woman to qualify as a U.S. astronaut. She passed the 75 required exams in February of 1960, but as a woman was denied the opportunity to go into space. In 1962, she urged President Lyndon Baines Johnson to appoint her as the first female astronaut; in 1963, she was one of three women recommended for astronaut service. The National Aeronautics and Space Administration (NASA) was not yet ready to accept women in this capacity, however, and rejected all three female candidates.

Source: Read and Witlieb, *The Book of Women's Firsts,* pp. 94–95.

1963 • Valentina Tereshkova (b. 1937), a Russian cosmonaut, was the first woman in space, and only the tenth human being to orbit the earth. Before joining the cosmonaut program in 1962, Tereshkova was an amateur parachutist.

Valentina Tereshkova

She was the solo pilot of the spaceship, Vostok VI, which was launched on June 16, 1963. Tereshkova orbited the earth 48 times, traveling over 1.2 million miles before returning to earth three days later. Tereshkova went on to a distinguished career as a representative of her country for diplomatic purposes.

Sources: Magnusson, *Larousse Biographical Dictionary,* p. 1442; Uglow, *The Continuum Dictionary of Women's Biography,* pp. 353–54.

1978 • Sally Ride (b. 1951) was one of the first six women selected by NASA for the U.S. Space Shuttle program in 1978. She went on to a distinguished career in physics, but continues to serve as a spokesperson for space exploration.

Sources: Read and Witlieb, *The Book of Women's Firsts,* pp. 370–71; Uglow, *The Continuum Dictionary of Women's Biography,* p. 458.

1979 • Margaret Rhea Seddon (b. 1947) was the first U.S. woman to achieve the full rank of astronaut, after completing her training and evaluation period in August 1979. She flew her first space mission aboard the *Discovery* on April 12, 1985.

Sources: Read and Witlieb, *The Book of Women's Firsts*, pp. 399–400.

1982 • Svetlanta Saviskaya, a female cosmonaut from Russia, was the first woman to walk in space, in August 1982. She went up in a Soyuz T-5 capsule and performed this feat while docking with the Salyut 7 space station.

Sources: Levin, *Women and Medicine*, p. 31.

1984 • Kathryn D. Sullivan (b. 1951) became the first U.S. woman to participate in extra-vehicular activity in space during a mission in October 1984. Her activity demonstrated the possibility of in-flight satellite refueling.

Sources: Read and Witlieb, *The Book of Women's Firsts*, p. 429.

Astronomers

c.1000 B.C. • Aglaonike, a Greek woman born in Thessaly probably about 1000 B.C., was the first female astronomer. Mentioned by Plutarch, she was familiar with celestial phenomena and knowledgeable in the prediction of lunar eclipses.

Sources: Ogilvie, *Women in Science*, pp. 25–26.

Seventeenth century • Maria Cunitz (1610–1664) was the first female astronomer in Europe. A German scientist, Cunitz's simplification of the Rudolphine Tables was acclaimed throughout seventeenth-century Europe.

Sources: Chicago, *The Dinner Party*, p. 175; Uglow, *The Continuum Dictionary of Women's Biography*, p. 142.

c.1680 • Jeanne Dumée, a French astronomer, was the first woman to write a book in defense of the theories of Polish astronomer Nicolas Copernicus (1473–1543). She prefaced her work with an apology, defending women's capacity for serious thought.

Sources: Uglow, *The Continuum Dictionary of Women's Biography*, p. 177.

1798 • Caroline Herschel (1750–1848) was the first woman to discover a comet. A gifted musician as well as an astronomer, Herschel followed her brother from Germany, where she was born, to England, where she assisted him in his scientific work and looked after his household. She later discovered seven additional comets. In 1835, she and Mary Somerville, became the first two women to be elected as honorary members of the Royal Astronomical Society.

Sources: Chicago, *The Dinner Party*, pp. 85–86; Lubbock, *The Herschel Chronicle*; Ogilvie, *Women in Science*, pp. 96–99.

1835 • Mary Fairfax Greig Somerville (1780–1872) and Caroline Herschel (1750–1848) were the first two women to become honorary members of the Royal Astronomical Society, in 1835. Herschel was honored for her work in astronomy and her discovery of comets. Somerville was honored for her writing on a range of scientific subjects. Somerville also gave her name to one of the first two women's colleges at Oxford University.

Sources: Ogilvie, *Women in Science,* pp. 161–66; Uglow, *The Continuum Dictionary of Women's Biography,* p. 506.

1847 • Maria Mitchell (1818–1889) became the first U.S. woman to discover a new comet, on October 1, 1847. The comet was later named for her. Regarded as one of the first women astronomers, she made her discovery at Nantucket, Massachusetts. She gained worldwide fame and was awarded a gold medal by King Frederick IV of Denmark. Mitchell was also the first (and until 1943 the only) woman elected to the American Academy of Arts and Sciences, on May 30, 1848. The Academy honored her for her discovery of the comet. In 1873 she was the founder of the Association of the Advancement of Women, as well as vice-president of the American Social Science Association.

Maria Mitchell was born August 1, 1818, to Quaker parents on Nantucket, Massachusetts. Her father, William Mitchell, was the master of a school and owned an excellent telescope that he used to conduct independent investigations. Maria Mitchell was her father's enthusiastic pupil, becoming his assistant at age 11. Maria helped her father make thousands of observations of meridian altitudes of stars, for the determination of time and latitude, and of moon culmination's and occultation's for longitude. Among the instruments they used in their observations were an altitude and azimuth circle, a four-inch equatorial telescope, and a two-inch Dolland telescope. Some of her later accomplishments include being appointed one of the original computers for the new *American Ephemeris and Nautical Almanac* in 1849 and being elected to the American Association for the Advancement of Science in 1850.

MARIA MITCHELL

In 1865, Maria was offered a teaching position by Matthew Vassar who had founded a women's college to rival the best men's colleges in America. She accepted and he built her an observatory with a twelve-inch telescope, the third largest in the country. When she learned that her salary was less that those earned by men with less reputation in their fields, she launched a successful protest that she be granted a salary equal with other professors. She resigned from the Vassar College faculty in 1888, but the Vassar trustees elected to place her on indefinite leave of absence with full salary. She died at Lynn, Massachusetts, on June 28, 1889. After her death, the alumnae of Vassar College established an endowed chair of astronomy as a memorial to her.

*Sources:*McCullough, *First of All: Significant Firsts by American Women,* pp. 113–14; Ogilvie, *Women in Science,* pp. 133–39; Read and Witlieb, *The Book of Women's Firsts,* pp. 294–95.

Late nineteenth century • Dorothea Klumpke (1861–1942), an American astronomer, was the first woman elected to the Astronomical Society in

France, in the late nineteenth century. Klumpke was educated in her native San Francisco and with her sisters (among them Augusta, who became a physician) in Paris. She was recognized for a distinguished career in her field in which she achieved a number of firsts: she was the first woman allowed to work at the Paris Observatoire and the first woman to earn a doctorate in mathematics there.

Sources: Uglow, *The Continuum Dictionary of Women's Biography,* p. 301.

1889 • Antonia Maury (1866–1952) was the first woman to discover two double stars. A double star is known as a binary; it is a pair of stars revolving around a common center of gravity. She determined the period of the spectral lines of the stars Mizar and Beta Aurigae while doing research at the Harvard Observatory.

Sources: Uglow, *The Continuum Dictionary of Women's Biography,* p. 366.

c.1900 • American Henrietta Swan Leavitt (1868–1921) was the first person to discover 2,400 variable stars, half of those known at the time. After graduating from Radcliffe College where she developed an interest in astronomy, she became a volunteer at the Harvard College Observatory in Cambridge, Massachusetts. She joined the staff there in 1902 and quickly became the first female head of the photographic photometry. By 1912, she successfully demonstrated that there was a relationship between the brightness of stars and the period of their light variation. While studying the constellation Cepheid, Leavitt observed that the apparent magnitude of a star's light and its relative distance from the earth could be calculated according to a mathematical formula. This discovery was significant in making it possible to calculate the distances of stars and led to further investigations of the Milky Way galaxy.

Sources: Magnusson, *Larousse Biographical Dictionary,* p. 872; Uglow, *The Continuum Dictionary of Women's Biography,* pp. 316–17.

1910 • Williamina Stevens Fleming (1857–1911) was the first person to discover "white dwarfs," hot, extremely dense and compact stars in their final evolutionary stage. She published her discovery in 1910. Fleming was also the first woman to be appointed to the Royal Astronomical Society in Greenwich, England, in 1906, and the first woman to serve as curator of astronomical photographs at Harvard University (beginning in 1898). She was also the first American woman to be selected to the Royal Astronomical Society in 1906.

Sources: James, *Notable American Women,* vol. 1, pp. 628–30; Read and Witlieb, *The Book of Women's Firsts,* p. 159.

1938 • Annie Jump Cannon (1863–1941) was the first woman to hold the post of William Cranch Bond Astronomer at Harvard University. She was honored for her work in simplifying the existing system of astronomical classification and for her work in cataloguing stars.

Sources: Bailey, *The Remarkable Lives of 100 Women Healers and Scientists,* pp. 36–37; James, *Notable American Women,* vol. 1, pp. 281–83; Ogilvie, *Women in Science,* pp. 51–52.

1960s • Alla Genrikhovna Massevitch (b. 1918), one of Russia's most distinguished astronomers, was the first Russian woman to be put in charge of tracking space vehicles. A professor of astrophysics at the Moscow University since 1948, she has specialized since the 1960s in tracking space vehicles through the use of visual, photographic, and laser techniques.

Sources: Uglow, *The Continuum Dictionary of Women's Biography,* p. 365.

1972 • Margaret Eleanor Burbidge (b. 1920) was the first female director of the Royal Greenwich Observatory in Greenwich, England. However, during her tenure in 1972–73, she was denied the traditional title of Astronomer Royal because of her gender. Burbidge went on to become the first female president of the American Astronomical Society (1976–1978) and of the American Association for the Advancement of Science (1981).

Sources: Uglow, *The Continuum Dictionary of Women's Biography,* pp. 95–96.

Biochemists

1947 • Born and educated in Prague in the present Czech Republic, Gerty Radnitz Cori (1896–1957) became the first U.S. woman to win the Nobel Prize for physiology or medicine. She shared this honor with her husband, Carl Cori, and with Bernardo Houssay of Argentina. The Coris were the third husband and wife team to win a Nobel Prize. (The first two were the Curies in 1903 and the Joliet-Curies in 1935.) Gerty Cori and her husband were both on the faculty of the Medical School at Washington University in St. Louis. The Coris were recognized for several discoveries, including the synthesis of glycogen in a test tube.

Sources: Haber, *Women Pioneers of Science,* p. xiv; McGrayne, *Nobel Prize Women in Science,* pp. 93–116; Read and Witlieb, *The Book of Women's Firsts,* pp. 102–3.

Biologists

Twentieth century • Rebecca Lancefield (1895–1981) was the first person to categorize the organism responsible for rheumatic fever.

Sources: Vare and Ptacek, *Mothers of Invention,* p. 118.

1903 • Nettie Maria Stevens (1861–1912) was the first woman to demonstrate that sex is determined by a particular chromosome. Edmund Beecher Wilson made the same discovery in the same year, but each was working separately. Stevens worked at Bryn Mawr College in Pennsylvania, where she was a professor of biology from 1903 until her death.

Sources: Ogilvie, *Women in Science,* pp. 167–69; Read and Witlieb, *The Book of Women's Firsts,* p. 422.

1920s • Lady Mary Bruce was the first honorary female member of the Royal Microscopical Society. She was honored for her work in 1887 with her husband, Sir David Bruce, in culturing the *Brucella* bacterium that caused un-

dulant fever. Also known as Malta or Mediterranean fever, undulant fever is
passed from infected cows or goats to humans through milk and is characterized by a recurrent fever and swollen joints.

Sources: Vare and Ptacek, *Mothers of Invention*, p. 117.

1925 • Florence Rena Sabin (1871–1953) was the first female member of
the National Academy of Sciences. She was honored for her medical research
in the field of histology (microscopic study of tissues), during which she determined the origin of red corpuscles. Sabin was associated with Johns Hopkins
University for twenty-five years. She became the school's first female faculty
member in 1902, and in 1917 became Johns Hopkins' first female full professor. In 1924–1926, Sabin served as the first female president of the American

Association of Anatomists. She was also the first woman elected to the New York Academy of Sciences and the first female member of the Rockefeller Institute.

Sources: Haber, *Women Pioneers of Science,* pp. 30–40; Ogilvie, *Women in Science,* pp. 153–56; Read and Witlieb, *The Book of Women's Firsts,* pp. 386–87.

1928 • Alice Evans (1881–1975) became the first female president of the Society of American Bacteriologists. This organization, now the American Society for Microbiology, promotes education in microbiology and encourages professional and ethical standards.

Sources: Read and Witlieb, *The Book of Women's Firsts,* pp. 147–48; Vare and Ptacek, *Mothers of Invention,* pp. 128–30.

Mid-twentieth century • Charlotte Friend (1921–1987), a U.S. microbiologist who devoted her career to cancer research, was the first person to discover that a virus can cause leukemia in mammals. She did most of her research at the Sloan-Kettering Institute for Cancer Research and at the Experimental Cell Biology Center at Mt. Sinai School of Medicine in New York City.

Sources: Uglow, *The Continuum Dictionary of Women's Biography,* pp. 64–78.

1972 • Cornelia Mitchell Downs (1892–1987) was the first woman to hold the position of Sommerfield Distinguished Professor of Bacteriology at the University of Kansas in Lawrence. She was honored for her life's work on tularemia, or "rabbit fever."

Sources: Bailey, *The Remarkable Lives of 100 Women Healers and Scientists,* pp. 58–59.

Botanists

1744 • Eliza Lucas Pinckney (1723–1793), an American agricultural pioneer, was the first woman to cultivate indigo in South Carolina, on her plantation near Charleston. Pinckney was perhaps the first woman planter in colonial America. Carefully researching various crops, especially those that flourished in the West Indies, she also experimented with flax, hemp, and silk, establishing a successful plantation and lucrative trade with England. A dress made from her silk was given to the Princess of Wales in England.

Sources: Ravenel, *Eliza Pinckney*; Uglow, *The Continuum Dictionary of Women's Biography,* p. 433.

1886 • Emily Gregory (1840–1897), a U.S. botanist who received her doctorate from the University of Zürich, was the first woman to be elected to the American Society of Naturalists.

Sources: Ogilvie, *Women in Science,* p. 182.

c.1890 • Mary Katharine Layne Brandegee (1844–1920), a U.S. physician who devoted her life to the study of botany, cofounded (with her husband, an amateur naturalist) *Zoe,* a botanical journal. Brandegee published her observations between 1890 and 1908.

Sources: Ogilvie, *Women in Science,* p. 46.

The first half of the twentieth century • Alice Eastwood (1859–1953) was the first woman to be starred for distinction in every volume of *American Men of Science* published during her lifetime. She was also the founder and first director of the California Botanical Club. With little formal training, Eastwood became one of the most knowledgeable systematic botanists of the period, specializing in the flowering plants of the Rocky Mountains and the California coast.

Sources: Bailey, *The Remarkable Lives of 100 Women Healers and Scientists,* pp. 64–65; Ogilvie, *Women in Science,* pp. 79–80; Sicherman and Green, *Notable American Women: The Modern Period,* pp. 216–17.

1913 • Ethel Sargant (1863–1918), an English botanist, was the first woman to serve on the council of the Linnaean Society. She was especially interested in the cytology (structure and function of cells) and morphology (form and structure) of plants and in the evolution of plant species.

Sources: Ogilvie, *Women in Science,* pp. 156–57.

1929 • Margaret Clay Ferguson (1863–1951) became the first female president of the Botanical Society of America. She made her career in teaching, research, and administration at Wellesley College.

Sources: Ogilvie, *Women in Science,* pp. 84–85.

c.1948 • Agnes Robertson Arber (1879–1960) was the first female botanist to be made a Fellow of the Royal Society in England. She was honored for her extensive and authoritative work with herbs, water plants, and plant morphology.

Sources: Uglow, *The Continuum Dictionary of Women's Biography,* p. 25.

1950s • Frances Perry (b. 1908) was the first woman to become a council member of the Royal Horticultural Society. She established her career during the 1950s and is known for her articles and books on horticulture, among them *Flowers of the World* (1973).

Sources: O'Neill, *The Women's Book of World Record and Achievements,* p. 6.

1950 • E. Lucy Braun (1889–1971) became the first female president of the Ecological Society of America. She was also the first president of the Ohio Academy of Science (1933–1934). In 1952, Braun was awarded the Mary Soper Pope Medal for her achievements in the field of botany.

Sources: Read and Witlieb, *The Book of Women's Firsts,* pp. 64–65.

Chemists

First century • Maria the Jewess, a first-century Alexandrian alchemist, is known as one of the founders of the science of chemistry and the first woman to work as a modern chemist. She invented apparatus that remained in use for centuries, including the double boiler to maintain substances at a constant temperature, a device still known today as a "bain-marie."
Sources: Uglow, *The Continuum Dictionary of Women's Biography,* p. 356.

1777 • Marie Lavoisier (1758–1836), with her husband Antoine Lavoisier, who is known as "the founder of modern chemistry," was the first woman to coin the word "oxygen" (oxygène), in his Paris laboratory. She assisted him in his experiments with combustion and respiration. They developed together the law of conservation of matter in chemical changes and established the basis of chemical nomenclature.
Sources: Uglow, *The Continuum Dictionary of Women's Biography,* p. 315.

1805 • Jane Marcet (1769–1858) was the first English writer to direct her work on scientific subjects specifically to women. In 1805 she published her very popular *Conversations on Chemistry: Intended More Specifically for the Female Sex,* which went through 16 British and 15 American editions. Michael Faraday was introduced to electrochemistry when, as an apprentice, he bound an edition of the book in 1810.
Sources: Uglow, *The Continuum Dictionary of Women's Biography,* p. 354.

Twentieth century • American scientist Dorothy Martin Simon (b. 1919) was the first person to isolate an isotope of calcium, an important scientific achievement useful in the field of nuclear research.
Sources: Vare and Ptacek, *Mothers of Invention,* p. 143.

Early twentieth century • Charlotte Auerbach (b. 1899), a German-born scientist educated in both Germany and Scotland, was the first person to discover mustard gas as a deadly weapon of chemical warfare.
Sources: Uglow, *The Continuum Dictionary of Women's Biography,* pp. 34–35.

1930s • Gladys Anderson Emerson (1903–1984) was the first person to isolate vitamin E. She performed experiments in Berkeley, California, in the 1930s and isolated this vitamin in its pure crystalline form from wheat germ oil.
Sources: Uglow, *The Continuum Dictionary of Women's Biography,* p. 191.

Early 1940s • Dorothy Crowfoot Hodgkin (b. 1910) was the first person to use a computer to analyze a biochemical problem. During World War II, Hodgkin used this computer technology to study the structure of penicillin and of vitamin B12. A noted scientist, in 1964 she became the third woman to receive the Nobel Prize for chemistry. In 1965, she received the Order of Merit, the first woman so honored since Florence Nightingale. She was also the first Wolfson Research Professor of the Royal Society, a post she held from 1960 until 1977. In 1968, she was the first woman to be elected a Fellow of the Australian Academy of Science. She was honored for her work as a chemist in the field of crystallography.

Sources: Haber, *Women Pioneers of Science,* pp. 105–16; Uglow, *The Continuum Dictionary of Women's Biography,* p. 261.

1945 • Dame Kathleen Yardley Lonsdale (1903–1971), an Irish scientist specializing in physical chemistry, especially the study of crystals, became the first female Fellow of the Royal Society, in London, England. She was honored for research that led to the development of X-ray crystallography. The youngest of ten children and the daughter of an Irish postmaster, she was the first scientist to use Fourier analysis to study molecular structures. When the Royal Society agreed to elect woman fellows, Lonsdale was the first female elected.

Sources: Magnusson, *Larousse Biographical Dictionary,* p. 912; Uglow, *The Continuum Dictionary of Women's Biography,* p. 332.

1948 • Elizabeth Sullivan, an authority on the chemistry of wheat proteins and on the chemistry and biochemistry of baking, was the first woman to receive the Osborne Medal, the highest honor of the American Association of Cereal Chemistry. Sullivan has made her scientific career in industry.

Sources: O'Neill, *The Women's Book of World Records and Achievements,* pp. 30–31.

c.1950 • Ruth Patrick (b. 1907), a U.S. scientist, was the first female research director at the Du Pont Company. She was also the first woman to chair the board of the Academy of Natural Sciences.

Sources: Vare and Ptacek, *Mothers of Invention,* pp. 179–80.

1951 • Rosalind Franklin (1920–1958), an English microchemist, was the first person to deduce the helical structure of DNA, the basic unit of genetic identity. Slighted by her colleagues, she was the fourth team member responsible for the discovery of the "double helix." She was no longer living when Maurice Wilkins, James Watson, and Francis Crick, the other scientists working with her, received a Nobel Prize for their joint achievement in 1962. The work of this team of scientists is considered to be the beginning of the discipline of molecular biology.

Sources: Sayre, *Rosalind Franklin and DNA;* Uglow, *The Continuum Dictionary of Women's Biography,* p. 213; Vare and Ptacek, *Mothers of Invention,* pp. 214–16.

1953 • Allene R. Jeanes was the first woman to receive the U.S. Department of Agriculture's Distinguished Service Award, in Washington, D.C. She was recognized with the highest honor this department gives for her research on dextrans and development of a blood-volume expander for these biopolymers. She received this award again in 1955, and in 1962 she became the first woman in the USDA to receive the Federal Woman's Award for her pioneering chemical research on starches and microbial polysaccharides.

Sources: O'Neill, *The Women's Book of World Records and Achievements,* p. 31.

1975 • Rachel Fuller Brown (1898–1980) became the first woman to receive the Pioneer Chemist Award from the American Institute of Chemists. She was honored for her discovery of a pneumonia vaccine in the 1920s and for her work with Elizabeth Hazer to isolate the first antifungal antibiotic in 1950.

Sources: Haber, *Women Pioneers of Science,* pp. 63–72; Read and Witlieb, *The Book of Women's Firsts,* pp. 72–73.

1976 • Stephanie L. Kwolek (b. 1923), a U.S. chemist working for E. I. Du Pont, was the first person to spin a polyamide macromolecule from low-temperature liquid crystal solutions.

Sources: Vare and Ptacek, *Mothers of Invention,* pp. 192–93.

Computer Scientists

1945 • Grace Brewster Murray Hopper (1906–1992) was the first person to develop operating programs for the first digital computer, in 1945, as a result of her work for the U.S. Navy during World War II. She went on to a distinguished career in computer science. Hopper was the first person to develop the concept of automatic programming from which the first English-language compiler system was incorporated into the widely used Common Business Oriented Language (COBOL). After her retirement from the Navy in 1966, she continued to work in her field, and in 1973 she became the first person in the Naval Reserve to be promoted (to the rank of Captain in her case) while on the retired list.

Sources: Read and Witlieb, *The Book of Women's Firsts,* pp. 214–15; Uglow, *The Continuum Dictionary of Women's Biography,* p. 265.

Earth Scientists

Second century • Hestiaea, a Homeric scholar, was the first woman to attempt a scientific exploration of the places named in the *Iliad,* in the second century in Alexandria, Egypt. She was also the first person to call into question the generally accepted theory that New Ilium was the site of ancient Troy.

Sources: Chicago, *The Dinner Party,* p. 127.

Twelfth century • Alpis de Cudot, a twelfth-century French thinker, was the first woman to argue that the earth was round. She theorized that the earth was a solid mass in the form of a globe and that the sun was larger than the earth.

Sources: Chicago, *The Dinner Party,* p. 145.

1885 • Erminnie A. Platt Smith (1836–1886) was the first woman to serve as an officer for the American Association for the Advancement of Science. Her special interests were crystallography and mineralogy.

Sources: Read and Witlieb, *The Book of Women's Firsts,* p. 410.

Entomologists

1900 • Eleanor Anne Ormerod (1828–1901) was the first woman to be awarded an honorary LL.D. from the University of Edinburgh, in 1900. She was recognized for her work in entomology and for her commitment to imparting information about insects to the agricultural community.

Sources: Ogilvie, *Women in Science,* pp. 142–43.

1930 • Edith Marion Patch (1876–1954) became the first female president of the Entomological Association of America. She specialized in economic and ecological entomology. At the beginning of her academic career in 1903, she organized the Department of Entomology at the University of Maine at Orono, and in 1904 she became its first head.

Sources: Ogilvie, *Women in Science,* pp. 143–44.

Geneticists

1931 • Barbara McClintock (1902–1992) was the first female doctoral student at the California Institute of Technology. She went on to become the first female president of the Genetics Society of America, in 1944. McClintock won the Nobel Prize for medicine and physiology on October 10, 1983, receiving recognition for her achievement in discovering the genetic nature of cross fertilization in corn. Her work has far-reaching implications for the study of genetics not only in other plants but in animals.

Sources: Levin, *Women and Medicine,* pp. 177–80; McGrayne, *Nobel Prize Women in Science,* pp. 144–74.

1939 • Kate Sessions (1857–1940) was the first woman to receive the Meyer Medal from the American Genetic Association. She was honored for her work in introducing foreign plants into the United States.

Sources: O'Neill, *The Women's Book of World Records and Achievements,* p. 34; Read and Witlieb, *The Book of Women's Firsts,* p. 401.

Geologists

1894 • Florence Bascom (1862–1945) became the first woman to be elected a fellow of the Geological Society of America and subsequently the first woman to serve as its vice-president. She was also the first woman to receive an appointment to the U.S. Geological Survey. In addition to her firsts in the field of geology, in 1893 Bascom had become the first woman to earn a doctorate from Johns Hopkins University in Baltimore, Maryland. She taught geology at Bryn Mawr College in Pennsylvania for most of her career.

Sources: Bailey, *The Remarkable Live of 100 Women Healers and Scientists,* pp. 14–15; James, *Notable American Women,* pp. 108–10; Ogilvie, *Women in Science,* pp. 36–37.

1981 • Doris Malkin Curtis (1914–1991) was the first woman to serve as president of the American Geological Institute. In 1990, she became the first female president of the Geological Society of America, a position she held until her death.

Sources: Read and Witlieb, *The Book of Women's Firsts,* pp. 110–11.

Ichthyologists

1880 • Rosa Smith Eigenmann (1858–1947), a U.S. ichthyologist, was the first female member of the San Diego Society of Natural History. She had a distinguished career in science, specializing in the study of fishes of North and South America.

Sources: James, *Notable American Women,* vol. 1, pp. 565–66; Ogilvie, *Women in Science,* p. 81.

Immunologists

1940s • Pearl Luella Kendrick (1890–1980), a U.S. scientist in the Michigan Department of Health, was the first person to develop the standard DPT (diphtheria, pertussis, and tetanus) vaccine. Working with her colleague Grace Eldening, she developed a vaccine for pertussis (whooping cough) in 1939, then went on to develop the combined immunization that has virtually eradicated these childhood diseases from the Western world.

Sources: Uglow, *The Continuum Dictionary of Women's Biography,* p. 297.

1950 • Gertrude B. Elion (b. 1918) was the first person to develop a drug that attacks viruses while working at the Burroughs Wellcome Company laboratory in Tuckahoe, New York. Her discovery was important for the treatment of cancer and AIDS (Acquired Immune Deficiency Syndrome). In 1988, Elion and her colleague, George Hitchings, shared the Nobel Prize for physiology or medicine. In 1991, Elion was the first woman to be inducted into the National Inventors Hall of Fame in Akron, Ohio. She was honored for her many achievements in the field of drug research.

Sources: Cobblestone: The History Magazine for Young People, (June 1994), pp. 32–33; McGrayne, *Nobel Prize Women in Science,* pp. 280–303.

Marine Biologists

1962 • Rachel Louise Carson (1907–1964) was the first woman to focus public attention on the danger of pesticides. Trained as a marine biologist, Carson became best-known as a naturalist with the publication in 1951 of *The Sea Around Us,* and in 1962 of her powerful work, *Silent Spring,* which exposed the consequences of America's use of environmental pollutants. Carson testified before the U.S. Senate on the effects of marine pollution on the ocean's food chain. Largely on the strength of her testimony, controls were placed on pollution. Carson was one of the scientists who helped launch the ecology movement.

Sources: Bailey, *The Remarkable Lives of 100 Women Healers and Scientists,* pp. 40–41; Chicago, *The Dinner Party,* p. 200; Haber, *Women Pioneers of Science,* p. 9.

1970 • Sylvia Earle Mead (b. 1935), an American marine biologist, was the first woman to become a mission leader on the Tektite II Project. This group of scientists studied human behavior in isolated and confined quarters and were required to live underwater for two weeks on the floor of Great Lameshur Bay off the coast of St. John in the Virgin Islands.

Sources: Uglow, *The Continuum Dictionary of Women's Biography,* pp. 141–54.

1973 • Dixie Lee Ray (b. 1914), a marine biologist, became the first woman to head the Atomic Energy Commission in Washington, D.C., in February 1973. She went on to a career in politics, becoming the first female governor of the state of Washington in 1976.

Sources: Uglow, *The Continuum Dictionary of Women's Biography,* pp. 92–106.

Mathematicians

Sixth century B.C. • Theano (fl. 540–510 B.C.), an ancient Greek mathematician, was the first person to write of the idea of the "golden mean," a major contribution to early social philosophy.

Sources: Chicago, *The Dinner Party,* p. 123; Uglow, *The Continuum Dictionary of Women's Biography,* p. 538.

Fifth century • Hypatia (370–415), a Greek philosopher, mathematician, and scientist, was the first woman to invent an astrolabe, an instrument that calculated the position of celestial bodies, and a hydroscope, a device for measuring the specific gravity of liquids. Educated in Athens, she taught at the University of Alexandria in Egypt. Hypatia was a pagan, and was misunderstood by Christians. A fanatical mob of Christian zealots attacked and killed her during a conflict in a church,

Sources: Magnusson, *Larousse Biographical Dictionary,* p. 753; Schmidt, *400 Outstanding Women of the World,* p. 211.

Eighteenth century • Emilie du Châtelet (1706–1749), a mathematician, astronomer, philosopher, and scientific writer, was the first person to translate Newton's *Principia* into French. Her translation was published after her death.

Sources: Chicago, *The Dinner Party,* p. 175; Uglow, *The Continuum Dictionary of Women's Biography,* p. 175.

Late eighteenth century • Maria Gaetana Agnesi (1718–1799) was the first woman admitted to the Bologna Academy of Sciences. She was honored for her achievements in mathematics, science, and philosophy, for which she drew on her prodigious knowledge of several languages.

Sources: Ogilvie, *Women in Science,* pp. 26–28; Uglow, *The Continuum Dictionary of Women's Biography,* pp. 7–8.

1976 • Julia B. Robinson (1920–1985) was the first woman mathematician elected to the National Academy of Sciences. She was honored in 1976 for her work on solving logic problems by using number theories.

Sources: Read and Witlieb, *The Book of Women's Firsts,* p. 375.

1977 • Ada Byron, Countess of Lovelace (1815–1852), was the first woman to have a computer programming language (ADA) named after her. In 1976 the U. S. Department of Defense began to develop this high-level universal language in Washington, D.C., and chose its name to honor the daughter of Lord Byron. During her lifetime she was reputed to have been a pioneering mathematician, although recent research has suggested that she had difficulty understanding basic scientific concepts.

Sources: Stein, *Ada: A Life and a Legacy*; Uglow, *The Continuum Dictionary of Women's Biography,* pp. 335–36.

Naturalists

1909 • Annie Montague Alexander (1867–1949) established the first natural history museum on the west coast of the United States, in Berkeley, California. Naturalist Joseph Grinnell was her collaborator and served as the museum's first director. Alexander also established the University of California at Berkeley's Department of Paleontology in the same year. She devoted her life to this field and to the sciences of botany, ornithology, and mammology.

Sources: Bailey, *The Remarkable Lives of 100 Women Healers and Scientists,* pp. 4–5.

1930 • Caroline Dormon (1888–1971) was one of the first three women to be elected to associate membership in the Society of American Foresters. Dormon made her career as a naturalist and conservationist in her native Louisiana.

Sources: Bailey, *The Remarkable Lives of 100 Women Healers and Scientists,* pp. 54–55.

1962 • Joy Gessner Adamson (1910–1980), a professional conservationist, was the founder of the World Wildlife Fund, in the United States in 1962. Born in Austria to British parents, Adamson married British game warden George Adamson, and the two lived and worked for many years in Kenya. Joy Adamson is best known for her experiences with the lioness Elsa, a tame lion cub whom she taught to return to the wild. Adamson wrote about her experiences with Elsa in *Born Free* (1960), which became the basis for a feature film; *Elsa* (1961); *Forever Free* (1962); and *Elsa and Her Cubs* (1965). Adamson was murdered in her home in Kenya in 1980.

Sources: Magnusson, *Larousse Biographical Dictionary,* p. 11; Uglow, *The Continuum Dictionary of Women's Biography,* pp. 4–5.

Paleontologists

1820 • Mary Anne Mantell was the first person to discover a dinosaur. She found a strange tooth in Cuckfield Quarry in Sussex, England, which lead to the identification of the first dinosaur.

Sources: Uglow, *The Continuum Dictionary of Women's Biography,* p. 22.

1824 • Mary Anning (1799–1847) was the first person to discover a plesiosaurus. She found an almost perfect fossil of this creature in Dorset, England. Her first major discovery had been made in 1811 when she discovered the fossil skeleton of an ichthyosaurus, which was later displayed in the British Museum of Natural History. In 1828, she discovered in the same area the first associated skeleton of a pterodactyl of the small dimorphoden family. Anning, who was born in Lyme Regis, England, was not formally trained as a paleontologist. After the death in 1810 of her father, a carpenter and vendor of scientific specimens, she was forced to pursue a career to support herself.

Sources: Ogilvie, *Women in Science,* p. 31; Uglow, *The Continuum Dictionary of Women's Biography,* p. 22.

Physicists

1690 • Anne Finch Conway (1631–1679), an English scientific theorist, was the first woman to challenge the theories of both René Descartes and Isaac Newton. Her book, *The Principles of the Most Ancient and Modern Philosophy,* first published in 1690, developed her idea that nature was an integrated material and spiritual organism.

Sources: Alic, *Hypatia's Heritage*; Uglow, *The Continuum Dictionary Of Women's Biography,* p. 137.

1895 • Margaret Eliza Maltby (1860–1944), a physicist who made her career as a professor at Barnard College in New York City, was the first U.S. woman to receive a doctoral degree from the University of Göttingen in Germany.

Sources: Haber, *Women Pioneers of Science,* pp. 9–10; James, *Notable American Women,* vol. 2, pp. 587–88; Ogilvie, *Women in Science,* pp. 124–25.

1903 • Marie Curie (1867–1934) became the first woman to win a Nobel Prize when she won the award in physics, an honor she shared with her husband Pierre and Antoine Henri Becquerel, a colleague at the Sorbonne in Paris. The prize was awarded for their discovery of radioactivity. When Pierre Curie died in 1906, Marie was appointed to fill his chair as professor of physics at the Sorbonne, becoming the first woman in France to receive professorial rank. Marie Curie was also the first person to win two Nobel Prizes when she was awarded the prize for chemistry in 1911, an honor she earned for the isolation of pure radium.

Sources: McGrayne, *Nobel Prize Women in Science,* pp. 11–36; Ogilvie, *Women in Science,* pp. 64–72; Sanders, *The First of Everything,* p. 166.

Marie Curie with U.S. President Herbert Hoover.

1906 • Hertha Marks Ayrton (1854–1923), an English physicist, won the Hughes Medal, becoming the first woman to be awarded a medal by the Royal Society in England. She was honored for her work on the motion of waves and formation of sand ripples. Earlier, in 1898, she became the first woman elected to the Institution of Electrical Engineers, and in 1904 she became the first woman to read a paper before the Royal Society. Ayrton was also the inventor of a sphygmograph, an instrument used to measure the pulse. During World War I, Ayrton invented the Ayrton Fan for dispersing poisonous gases. Her husband was William Edward Ayrton, an engineer and inventor.

Sources: Ogilvie, *Women in Science,* pp. 32–34; Uglow, *The Continuum Dictionary of Women's Biography,* p. 38; Vare and Ptacek, *Mothers of Invention,* p. 159.

1926 • Katherine Burr Blodgett (1898–1979) was the first woman to earn a doctorate in physics from Cambridge University in England. She went on to a distinguished career in her field, inventing nonreflective glass in 1938.

Sources: Bailey, *The Remarkable Lives of 100 Women Healers and Scientists,* pp. 22–23.

1930s • Lise Meitner (1878–1968) was the first person to use the term "nuclear fission," referring to the splitting of the atom. This term grew out of her work in nuclear physics with Dr. Otto Hahn at the University of Berlin where she was a research assistant. Meitner and Hahn continued to collaborate for over 30 years in laboratories in Germany, Austria, Denmark, and Sweden. She worked on her own in both the United States and England. In 1966, when the U.S. Atomic Energy Commission gave its Enrico Fermi Award to the team of researchers with whom Meitner had collaborated, she became the first woman to receive this award.

Sources: Haber, *Women Pioneers of Science,* pp. 41–51; Levin, *Women and Medicine,* pp. 45–48; McGrayne, *Nobel Prize Women in Science,* pp. 37–63.

1934 • Ida Eva Noddack (b. 1896), a German chemist, was the first woman to suggest the possibility of nuclear fission in the bombardment of radium when Enrico Fermi first reported his experiments in 1934. Her idea was initially ignored, but credited five years later. Noddack (working with her husband Walter Karl Friedrich Noddack) was also the first woman to discover the missing elements technetium (formerly known as masurium) and rhenium, numbers 43 and 75 on the periodic table, respectively. The latter was named rhenium after the Rhine River near which she was born.

Sources: Uglow, *The Continuum Dictionary of Women's Biography,* p. 404.

1935 • Irène Joliot Curie (1897–1956), the daughter of Marie and Pierre Curie, was the codiscoverer of the neutron, an important subatomic particle. With her husband, she was honored for this achievement with the Nobel Prize for chemistry in 1935.

Sources: Chicago, *The Dinner Party,* p. 192; Uglow, *The Continuum Dictionary of Women's Biography,* p. 286.

1949 • Elda Emma Anderson (1899–1961) was the first person to serve as chief of education and training in the Health Physics Division of the Oak Ridge National Laboratory in Oak Ridge, Tennessee, in 1949. Anderson, a physicist with the Manhattan Project, which developed the atom bomb in 1945, worked throughout her life to protect people and the environment from the harmful effects of radiation.

Sources: Bailey, *The Remarkable Lives of 100 Women Healers and Scientists,* pp. 8–9.

1958 • Chien Shiung Wu (b. 1912), a nuclear physicist who was born in China but emigrated to the United States in 1936, was the first woman to receive an honorary doctorate in science from Princeton University, in 1958. In 1941, she became the first woman to teach at Princeton. She was also the first woman to win the Comstock Prize from the National Academy of Sciences in the

Chien Shiung Wu

late 1950s, the first woman to receive the Wolf Prize from Israel, and the first female president of the American Physical Society. Additionally, in 1972 Wu became the first person to hold the Pupin Professorship in Physics at Columbia University.

Sources: McGrayne, *Nobel Prize Women in Science,* pp. 255–79; Vare and Ptacek, *Mothers of Invention,* pp. 153–57.

1962 • Marguerite Perey (1909–1975), a French physicist who worked in Marie Curie's laboratory beginning in 1929, became the first female member of the French Academy of Science.

Sources: Uglow, *The Continuum Dictionary of Women's Biography,* p. 429; Vare and Ptacek, *Mothers of Invention,* p. 148.

1963 • Maria Goeppert-Mayer (1906–1972) was the first U.S. woman to win the Nobel Prize for physics. Sharing the honor with two men (Eugene Paul Wigner and Hans Jensen), she was awarded the prize on December 10, 1963, for her work on the theory of the stability of atomic nuclei.

Sources: Haber, *Women Pioneers of Science,* pp. 83–96; Uglow, *The Continuum Dictionary of Women's Biography,* pp. 228–29.

1977 • Xide Xie (b. 1921), a Chinese physicist of international reputation, founded the Modern Physics Institute in Shanghai, China. With a doctorate in her field from the Massachusetts Institute of Technology (MIT), she made her career at Fudan University and at the Institute of Technical Physics, both in Shanghai.

Sources: Uglow, *The Continuum Dictionary of Women's Biography,* p. 594.

Physiologists

1896 • Ida Henrietta Hyde (1857–1945), a U.S. physiologist, was the first woman to receive a doctoral degree from the University of Heidelberg in Germany. During an illustrious career in marine biology, Hyde became the first woman to do research at Harvard Medical School (while holding an Irwin Research Fellowship at Radcliffe College in 1896–1897) and the first woman elected to membership in the American Physiological Society, in 1902.

Sources: James, *Notable American Women,* vol. 2, pp. 247–49; Ogilvie, *Women in Science,* pp. 103–4.

Early 1970s • Estelle Ramey (b. 1917), a U.S. physiologist and endocrinologist, was the founder of the Educational Forum of the Association for Women in Science. As president of this association in the early 1970s, Ramey worked for positions of greater power for women in her field.

Sources: Noble, *Contemporary Women Scientists of America,* pp. 49–63.

c.1990 • Rita Levi-Montalcini (b. 1909) was the first woman admitted to the Pontifical Academy of Sciences in Rome, Italy. She was recognized for her work in neuroembryology for which she also received the Nobel Prize in medicine and physiology in 1986. In addition, she was the first woman to be included in the Alfred P. Sloan Foundation series of autobiographies of scientists.

Sources: McGrayne, *Nobel Prize Women in Science,* pp. 201–24; Uglow, *The Continuum Dictionary of Women's Biography,* p. 325.

Psychologists

1905 • Mary Whiton Calkins (1863–1930) was the first woman to serve as president of the American Psychological Association. Having trained with William James at Harvard, she became a professor of psychology and philosophy at Wellesley College. (*See also* **Education: Organizations and Associations, 1918.**)

Sources: James, *Notable American Women,* vol. 1, pp. 278–80; Ogilvie, *Women in Science,* p. 51.

1916 • Leta Stetter Hollingworth (1886–1939), a U.S. educational psychologist, was the first person to submit theories of male superiority to scientific investigation. She completed her doctoral thesis on this subject at Columbia University in New York City in 1916. She went on to a distinguished career in her field and wrote several now classic books on the development of children and adolescents. Hollingworth was also the first civil service psychologist in the state of New York. When she reported for duty at Bellevue Hospital in New York City in 1914, she identified herself as a psychologist and the head of the Psychopathic Service needed an explanation of her new profession.

Sources: Haber, *Women Pioneers of Science,* pp. 52–62; James, *Notable American Women,* vol. 2, pp. 209–10.

Margaret Floy Washburn

1929 • June Etta Downey (1875–1932) and Margaret Floy Washburn (1871–1931) were the first two women to be elected to membership in the Society of Experimental Psychologists. Both women made their careers as university professors, Downey at the University of Wisconsin and Washburn at Vassar College. Downey began her teaching career at the University of Wyoming, and in 1907 she was made head of the Department of Psychology and Philosophy, the first woman to head such a department at a state university.

Sources: Bailey, *The Remarkable Lives of 100 Women Healers and Scientists,* pp. 56–57; James, *Notable American Women,* vol. 1, pp. 514–15; Ogilvie, *Women in Science,* pp. 74–75.

Science Professors

1731 • Laura Maria Caterina Bassi (1711–1778) was the first female professor of physics at any university. In 1731, after receiving a doctoral degree, she was appointed chair of physics at the University of Bologna in Italy.

Sources: Uglow, *The Continuum Dictionary of Women's Biography,* p. 51.

1899 • Anna Bostford Comstock (1854–1930) was the first female professor at Cornell University in Ithaca, New York. She was appointed an assistant professor of nature study in 1899, but because of protest from the board of trustees, she was demoted to the rank of lecturer the following year.

Sources: Bailey, *The Remarkable Lives of 100 Women Healers and Scientists,* pp. 48–49; Comstock, *The Comstocks of Cornell;* Ogilvie, *Women in Science,* pp. 61–62.

Scientific Artists

1675 • Maria Sibylla Merian (1647–1717) was the first German woman to become a scientific illustrator. She published her first volume of botanical and entomological illustrations (*The New Book of Flowers*) in Nuremberg, Germany. She went on to travel widely in Europe and in the East and West Indies. Although she published several more books detailing flowers and insects, she died in poverty.

Sources: Uglow, *The Continuum Dictionary Of Women's Biography,* pp. 374–75.

1750s • Anne Manzolini (1716–1774) was the first woman to become famous throughout Europe for her anatomical models. Not formally trained, Manzolini learned anatomy and wax modeling from her husband, who was a professor of anatomy at the University of Bologna. She was appointed as a university lecturer at his death and in 1760 became professor of anatomy with the additional title of "modellatrice." She was elected a member of the Russian Royal Scientific Association and the British Royal Society.

Sources: Uglow, *The Continuum Dictionary of Women's Biography,* p. 353.

1841 • Lucy Sistare Say (1801–1885), a scientific artist who learned her skills in large measure to illustrate her husband's entomological work, became the first female member of the Academy of Natural Sciences of Philadelphia in 1841.

Sources: Ogilvie, *Women in Science,* p. 158.

1883 • Marianne North (1830–1890), an English botanist, traveler, and painter, was the first woman to give her name to a previously unclassified capucin tree. At the age of 40, she began traveling to tropical and exotic locations to paint flowers. While in the Seychelles in 1883, she discovered a tree that was later named *Northia seychellana* in her honor. Her artwork was given to Kew Gardens in London, where a gallery named for her to display her work was opened in 1882.

Sources: Uglow, *The Continuum Dictionary of Women's Biography,* p. 406.

1929 • Malvina Hoffman (1887–1966), a U.S. artist who studied in Paris with Auguste Rodin and learned anatomy at a local medical school, was the first person commissioned to sculpt different racial types. In order to complete her work, the Field Museum of Natural History in Chicago sent her to travel around the world for two years.

Sources: Hoffman, *Heads and Tales,* 1936; Hoffman, *Yesterday Is Tomorrow: A Personal History;* Uglow, *The Continuum Dictionary of Women's Biography,* p. 262.

Zoologists

Late nineteenth century • Emilie Snethlage (1868–1929) was the first female director of the Zoological Museum and Gardens at Porto Belho in Brazil. A zoologist, ornithologist, and ethnologist, Snethlage traveled extensively under primitive conditions in rural Brazil.

Sources: Chicago, *The Dinner Party,* p. 193.

Twentieth century • Geraldine Thiele was the first person to invent an injectable drug to cure shin splints in horses. This product saved the lives of valuable race horses. She also invented a mouthwash for horses that helps to prevent tooth decay and a horse feed that keeps manure from smelling offensively.

Sources: Vare and Ptacek, *Mothers of Invention,* p. 117.

1920s • Sidnie Milana Manton (1902–1979), an English zoologist, was the first woman to do pioneering work on invertebrates, in Cambridge, England, in the 1920s. She studied how wormlike animals with legs (centipedes and millipedes) walk and how the embryos of crustaceans (lobsters, shrimp, etc.) develop. In 1929, she undertook an expedition to the Great Barrier Reef off the coast of Australia and continued her research there. She continued her research and writing at Cambridge and London Universities and was awarded the Linnaean Gold Medal in recognition of her work in 1963.

Sources: Uglow, *The Continuum Dictionary of Women's Biography,* p. 353; *Who Was Who,* vol. VII, p. 19.

1929 • Florence Merriam Bailey (1863–1948) became the first woman to be a fellow of the American Ornithologists' Union (AOU). She was honored for her lifelong interest in birds. In 1885 she was the first woman to become an associate member of the AOU and won its prestigious Bruster Medal in 1931, the first woman to receive this award. She was honored for her book *Birds of New Mexico* (1928).

Sources: James, *Notable American Women,* vol. 1, pp. 82–83; Ogilvie, *Women in Science,* pp. 34–35; Read and Witlieb, *The Book of Women's Firsts,* pp. 33–34.

Mid-twentieth century • Miriam Louisa Rothschild (b. 1908), an English zoologist who specialized in parasitology, was the first person to analyze the jumping mechanism of the flea. She was also the first person to host the International Flea Conference, at her country home in Northamptonshire in 1977. Educated at home because her father did not believe in sending girls to school, she catalogued his ten thousand species of fleas in five illustrated volumes. She went on to a distinguished career in science and was awarded several honorary degrees. In 1968 she was appointed chair of the biology department at London University.

Sources: Uglow, *The Continuum Dictionary of Women's Biography,* pp. 465–66.

1960 • Jane Goodall (b. 1934), an English zoologist, was the first woman to undertake a long-term study of chimpanzees in their natural habitat. She began her work on the shores of Lake Tanganyika in Tanzania in 1960 and completed her study six years later. She has since published work on wild dogs, jackals, and hyenas.

Sources: Goodall, *In the Shadow of Man*; Uglow, *The Continuum Dictionary of Women's Biography,* p. 231.

1967 • Dian Fossey (1932–1985) was the first female primatologist to work successfully with gorillas in the African wild and devoted her life to their study. She began her study under the sponsorship of archaeologist Louis Leakey and moved to Rwanda to pursue her research in 1967. There she founded in the same year the Karisoke Research Center. Her interests shifted from observation of gorillas to their preservation, as recorded in her book *Gorillas in the Mist* (1983), which became the basis for a feature film. She was found dead at her camp under mysterious circumstances in 1985.

Sources: Brockman, *An African Biographical Dictionary,* p. 119; Uglow, *The Continuum Dictionary of Women's Biography,* p. 210.

Sports

Adventure and Travel

1811 • Marie Dorion (1790–1850), a Native American woman who with her husband Pierre helped to explore and settle the far western United States, was the first woman to go on an overland expedition to Astoria in Oregon. She set out with her family from St. Louis, Missouri, in March 1811. The group was led by Wilson Price Hunt, with Marie and Pierre Dorion serving as interpreters. They arrived at Astoria, Oregon, at the mouth of the Columbia River, on February 15, 1812. Marie Dorion gave birth to a child along the way and is remembered for her courage and perseverance while struggling to make a home in this uncharted territory.

Sources: James, *Notable American Women,* vol. 1, pp. 502–3.

1876 • Maria Spelterina was the first woman to cross the Niagara Rapids by walking on a cable that spanned the Niagara River in 1876. The rapids are in the Niagara River just above Niagara Falls on the border between New York and Ontario, Canada.

Sources: Woolum, *Outstanding Women Athletes: Who They Are and How They Influenced Sports in America,* p. 25.

1890 • Nellie Bly (pseudonym of Elizabeth Cochrane Seaman, 1865–1922), a U.S. journalist, was the first woman to beat the 80-day around-the-world record set by the fictional Phineas Fogg in Jules Verne's *Around the World in Eighty Days.* Her newspaper, *The World,* in New York, sent her on the mission, which she accomplished, traveling by train, handcar, ship, and burro. She sailed from Hoboken, New Jersey, on November 14, 1889, and arrived 72 days later by train in New York City on January 25, 1890.

Sources: Read and Witlieb, *The Book of Women's Firsts,* pp. 57–58; Uglow, *The Continuum Dictionary of Women's Biography,* pp. 490–91.

1901 • Anna Edson Taylor (1858–1921) was the first woman to succeed in going over Niagara Falls on the border between New York and Ontario, Canada. On October 24, 1901, she went over Horseshoe Falls, on the Canadian side of Niagara Falls, in a padded barrel. She completed this feat for a cash award, which she used to pay off a loan on a ranch in Texas.

Sources: Read and Witlieb, *The Book of Women's Firsts,* p. 438.

1909 • Alice Huyler Ramsay (1887–1983) was the first woman to drive across a continent in a car. On June 6, 1909, she set out from New York City with three female passengers. They completed the trip 41 days later when they arrived in San Francisco, California, on August 8.

Sources: Read and Witlieb, *The Book of Women's Firsts,* p. 357.

1910 • Neysa McMein (1888–1949), a U.S. illustrator for popular journals and a well-known socialite of her age, was, with her friend, the publicist Beulah Livingstone, the first woman to make a flight on Count Zeppelin's dirigible.

Sources: Baragwanath, *A Good Time Was Had;* James, *Notable American Women,* vol. 2, pp. 476–77.

1916 • Adeline and Augusta Van Buren, sisters from New York, were the first two women to cross the continental United States on motorcycles. The purpose of their trip was to convince the U.S. government that women were capable of serving in the armed forces should the United States enter World War I. When Adeline Van Buren volunteered for the army in 1917, however, she was rejected because of her sex.

Sources: Read and Witlieb, *The Book of Women's Firsts,* pp. 460–61.

1921 • Eleanor Medill Patterson (1881–1948) was the first woman to make a boat trip through Idaho's Salmon River Rapids in 1921. (*See also* **Media: Newspapers, 1934.**)

Sources: James, *Notable American Women,* vol. 3, pp. 26–29; Read and Witlieb, *The Book of Women's Firsts,* p. 322.

1924 • Alexandra David-Neel (1869–1968), a French explorer of Central Asia, was the first European woman to enter the holy city of Lhasa in Tibet. She entered disguised as an old Tibetan woman. David-Neel went on to write several books about her experiences, including *My Journey to Lhasa* (1927).

Sources: Magnusson, *Larousse Biographical Dictionary,* p. 389; Uglow, *The Continuum Dictionary of Women's Biography,* p. 149.

1927 • Violet Cordery was the first woman to drive around the world, traveling 10,266 miles across five continents at an average speed of just over 24 miles per hour.

Sources: Woolum, *Outstanding Women Athletes: Who They Are and How They Influenced Sports in America,* p. 26.

1947 • Edith Ronne (b. 1919), wife of Finn Ronne who lead the expedition, was one of the first women to land on Antarctica. With the scientist Jenny Darlington, she landed at Marguerite Bay, Antarctica, on March 12, 1947.

Sources: Read and Witlieb, *Women's Firsts,* pp. 377–78.

1985 • Libby Riddles (b. 1956) became the first woman to win the Iditarod Trail Sled Dog Race on March 20, 1985. The annual race is a 1,100-mile (1,827-kilometer) marathon from Anchorage to Nome, Alaska.

Sources: Woolum, *Outstanding Women Athletes: Who They Are and How They Influenced Sports in America,* p. 30.

1986 • Ann Bancroft (b. 1955) was the first woman to walk to the North Pole when she and her five male companions reached the North Pole by dogsled on May 1, 1986. A physical education teacher, Bancroft endured 12-hour days and numerous hardships as she and her team and 21 dogs completed the expedition.

Sources: Read and Witlieb, *The Book of Women's Firsts,* p. 35; Woolum, *Outstanding Women Athletes: Who They Are and How They Influenced Sports in America,* p. 30.

1994 • Liv Arnesen (b. 1954) was the first woman to ski unaccompanied from the edge of the Antarctic continent to the South Pole. She completed her 50-day, 750-mile trip on December 24, 1994. She pulled a 200-pound sledge loaded with food and equipment and endured temperatures as low as 40° below zero.

Sources: The (Cleveland) Plain Dealer (6 January 1995), pp. 1A, 18A.

Archery

1880 • The Pearl Archery Club was organized by women in New Orleans, Louisiana. It was one of the first sports organizations for women in the southern United States.

Sources: Woolum, *Outstanding Women Athletes: Who They Are and How They Influenced Sports in America,* p. 25.

1922 • Alice Blanche Legh (1855–1948) was the first woman to achieve the record of 23 British archery championships. She attained this record over a career of 41 years, between 1881 and 1922. She held two record runs of seven and eight consecutive titles, ending in 1892 and 1909 respectively. Archery was the first sport to be taken up successfully by women.

Sources: Uglow, *The Continuum Dictionary of Women's Biography,* p. 319.

1972 • Doreen Wilber (b. 1930) was the first woman to win the Olympic individual archery championship in Munich, West Germany, in 1972, the first year the event was held. A housewife from Jefferson, Iowa, Wilber set a world record of 2,424 points.

Sources: Read and Witlieb, *The Book of Women's Firsts,* pp. 481–82.

1973 • Linda Meyers, who began shooting at the age of 12, was the first U.S. woman to win the World Championship of Archery in 1973. She competed in her first World Championship in 1970.

Sources: O'Neill, *The Women's Book of World Records and Achievements,* p. 558.

Drag racer Shirley
Muldowney

Auto Racing

1909 • The first all-female auto race was held on January 12, 1909. Sponsored by the Woman's Motoring Club, all 12 entrants raced from New York City to Philadelphia, returning to New York several days later.

Sources: Read and Witlieb, *The Book of Women's Firsts,* p. 301.

1964 • Donna Mae Mins became the first woman to win a Sports Car Club of America championship in 1964, beating out 31 men in the Class II production category for imported two-seaters.

Sources: Woolum, *Outstanding Women Athletes: Who They Are and How They Influenced Sports in America,* p. 28.

1965 • Margaret Laneive "Lee" Breedlove set a women's land speed record at 308.65 miles per hour on the Bonneville Salt Flats, Utah, on November 4, 1965.

Sources: Woolum, *Outstanding Women Athletes: Who They Are and How They Influenced Sports in America,* p. 28.

1975 • Shirley Muldowney (b. 1942) became the first woman licensed in the United States to drive top fuel dragsters in 1975. Muldowney, known in drag racing as "Cha Cha," was also the first woman to qualify for the top competition in hot rod racing when she qualified to compete for the supercharged, nitro-burning, unlimited AA-fuel dragster category.

Sources: O'Neill, *The Women's Book of World Records and Achievements,* p. 589; Woolum, *Outstanding Women Athletes: Who They Are and How They Influenced Sports in America,* p. 29.

Janet Guthrie

1976 • Mary McGee, a U.S. driver of cars, trucks, and motorcycles, was the first woman to race in the Baja 1000 off-road competition in California. She was also the first woman to compete in the Mexico Wild Desert Peninsula Race, the first to race in the International Motocross Series and the first to drive in Grand Prix motorcycle tournaments.

Sources: O'Neill, *The Women's Book of World Records and Achievements*, p. 590.

Janet Guthrie (b. 1938) became the first woman to compete in a major stock car race when she competed in the World 600 in Charlotte, North Carolina, on May 30, 1976. She finished in 15th place among 40 drivers, winning $3,555. Janet Guthrie became the first woman to drive in the Indianapolis 500 auto race when she qualified to enter in May 1976. She failed to finish the race because her car broke down, but on May 29, 1978, she tried again and became the first woman to complete this race, finishing eighth among the 33 other drivers.

Sources: The Los Angeles Times (31 May 1976), p. 6; O'Neill, *The Women's Book of World Records and Achievements,* p. 589; Read and Witlieb, *The Book of Women's Firsts,* pp. 187–88.

Aviation

1910 • Bessica Raiche (1874–1932) was the first U.S. woman to fly an airplane solo, in September 1910. She accomplished this in Mineola, New York. Her flight was not made with spectators from the general public. An advocate of women's rights, Raiche later became a physician and practiced medicine in California.

Sources: Read and Witlieb, *The Book of Women's Firsts,* p. 356.

1917 • Katherine Stinson (1891–1977) was the first woman to pilot her own plane on a tour of Japan and China, in 1917. Until her marriage in 1928, Stinson devoted her life to flying both professionally and as a sport.

Sources: Read and Witlieb, *The Book of Women's Firsts,* pp. 424–25.

1920s • Sophia Heath (1890–1934) was the first airline pilot for the Royal Dutch Airlines in the 1920s. Heath was an advocate of women's athletics and founded the Women's Amateur Athletic Association, in England in 1922. As a result of her work on behalf of women in sports, women competed in track and field medal events at the Olympics for the first time in 1928. In 1928, she became the first woman to fly solo from South Africa to England. She soon after became the first person to land at 50 different airfields and 17 unofficial landing fields, achieving a record of 67 landings in England in a single day.

Sources: Chicago, *The Dinner Party,* p. 193; Uglow, *The Continuum Dictionary of Women's Biography,* pp. 252–53.

1921 • Bessie Coleman (1893–1926) was the first black female pilot. She was also the first woman from the United States to earn an international pilot's license, in 1921. Coleman gave stunt shows worldwide and died while rehearsing for an exhibition for the Jacksonville, Florida, Negro Welfare League.

Sources: Gaymon, *215 African American Women You Should Know About,* p. 16; Smith, *Black Firsts,* p. 255.

1924 • Ruth Nichols (1901–1960) was the first woman to receive an international hydroplane license, in 1924, the year she graduated from Wellesley College. She devoted her life to amateur and professional flying and was the first woman to work as a commercial pilot (in 1932) as well as the first woman to pilot a twin-engine jet (in 1955).

Sources: Read and Witlieb, *The Book of Women's Firsts,* pp. 311–13.

1927 • Lady Mary Bailey (1890–1960) was the first woman to fly across the Irish Sea, in 1927, the year she received her pilot's license. In 1928, she flew with her five children as the sole pilot from Croyden, England, to Cape Town,

South Africa, and back to demonstrate female independence and her faith in light aircrafts.

Sources: Uglow, *The Continuum Dictionary of Women's Biography,* p. 42.

Phoebe Fairgrave Omlie (1902–1975) was the first woman to be granted a transport pilot's license by the U.S. Department of Commerce, in 1927. Omlie devoted her life to flying both as a sport and a profession.

Sources: Read and Witlieb, *The Book of Women's Firsts,* pp. 324–25.

1930 • Laura Ingalls was the first woman to complete a transcontinental flight. She left Roosevelt Field, New York, in a Moth bi-plane on October 5, 1930, and landed in Glendale, California, on October 9. The trip required nine stops and took 30 hours and 27 minutes.

Sources: Kane, *Famous First Facts,* p. 80–81; Read and Witlieb, *The Book of Women's Firsts,* pp. 225–26.

Amy Johnson Mollison (1903–1941) was the first woman to fly solo from London to Australia, in May 1930. She was also the first woman to pass the test for the British Ground Engineers' License and the first woman to fly across the Atlantic Ocean from east to west. She and her husband, James Allen Mollison, took off from Pendine, Wales, on July 22, 1933, and crash landed 38-½ hours later at Stratford, Connecticut. Amy Johnson Mollison died while flying for the Women's Auxiliary Air Force during World War II.

Sources: Kane, *Famous First Facts,* p. 87; Uglow, *The Continuum Dictionary of Women's Biography,* pp. 285–86.

1932 • Marian Cummings (1892–1984) became the first woman to receive a commercial pilot's license, in 1932. She was a corporate pilot for her husband's New York law firm and during World War II was a captain in the Civil Air Patrol and a ferry pilot in the Army Air Corps.

Sources: Read and Witlieb, *The Book of Women's Firsts,* p. 109.

Amelia Earhart (1898–1937) achieved many firsts as an aviator. She was the first woman to complete a solo transatlantic flight. On May 20, 1932, she left Harbor Grace, Newfoundland, and landed on May 21 in Londonderry, Ireland. Earhart's flight covered 2,026 miles in 14 hours and 56 minutes.

Earhart was also the first woman to complete a transcontinental flight without stopping. She left New York on August 24, 1932, and landed in Los Angeles 19 hours and five minutes later. The trip covered 2,600 miles. A few years later, on January 11–12, 1935, she completed the first solo flight from California to Hawaii. Attempting a flight around the world in 1937, Earhart lost contact with the Coast Guard near Howland Island in the Pacific, where she is presumed to have died.

Sources: James, *Notable American Women,* vol. 1, pp. 538–41; Kane, *Famous First Facts,* p. 81; Read and Witlieb, *The Book of Women's Firsts,* pp. 130–32; Sanders, *The First of Everything,* p. 97.

1934 • Helen Richey (1910–1947) was the first woman to fly airmail transport. She made her first flight on December 31, 1934, from Washington, D.C., to Detroit, Michigan, via Pittsburgh, Pennsylvania, and Cleveland, Ohio.

Sources: Read and Witlieb, *The Book of Women's Firsts,* p. 368.

Anne Spencer Morrow Lindbergh (b. 1906) was the first woman to receive the National Geographic Society Hubbard Gold Medal. She was honored for her work as copilot and radio operator on flights with her husband, Charles A. Lindbergh, over five continents to survey transoceanic air routes. The results of their work became known as the Charles A. Lindbergh Aerial Survey. The medal was presented on March 31, 1934, in Washington, D.C. by Dr. Gilbert Grosvenor, president of the National Geographic Society.

Sources: Kane, *Famous First Facts,* p. 373; Read and Witlieb, *The Book of Women's Firsts,* pp. 254–55.

1935 • Jean Gardner Batten (1909–1982), the New Zealand aviator, became the first woman to fly over the south Atlantic from England to Brazil in 1935, establishing a record speed for the flight.

Sources: Uglow, *The Continuum Dictionary of Women's Biography,* p. 52.

1936 • Beryl Markham (1902–1986) was honored as the first woman to fly solo across the Atlantic Ocean from east to west in 1936. After crash-landing in Nova Scotia, she was given a ticker-tape parade in New York City. However, in 1933, Amy Johnson Mollison had flown from Wales to Connecticut, thus preceding Markham by three years. While living in California she wrote her well-known autobiography *West with the Night,* which describes her experience in Africa as well as her love of flying. (*See also* **Sports: Horse Racing, 1920.**)

Sources: Markham, *West with the Night;* Uglow, *The Continuum Dictionary of Women's Biography,* p. 358.

1941 • Alma Heflin (b. 1910) became the first female test pilot in Lock Haven, Pennsylvania, on November 12, 1941. She tested standard production aircrafts for the Piper Aircraft Corporation.

Sources: Kane, *Famous First Facts,* pp. 87–88.

1947 • Ann Shaw Carter (b. 1922) was the first woman to get a helicopter rating, which she received at the Westchester County Airport in Westchester, New York, on June 9, 1947. Carter also earned a commercial airplane license and a seaplane rating.

Sources: Read and Witlieb, *The Book of Women's Firsts,* p. 85.

1948 • Jacqueline Cochran (1910–1980), the first female jet pilot, became the first woman to achieve Mach 1, the speed of sound, on May 18, 1948. She achieved this record in an F-86 jet. Cochran started flying in 1932 and was the first woman to enter the Trans-American Bendix Race, in 1935. She was the first woman to break the sound barrier, in a Sabre jet in 1953.Cochran was also

Jacqueline Cochran

the first living woman to be inducted into the American Aviation Hall of Fame, in 1971.

Sources: Cochran and Brinley, *Jackie Cochran*; Read and Witlieb, *The Book of Women's Firsts*, pp. 95–96; Sanders, *The First of Everything*, p. 99; Uglow, *The Continuum Dictionary of Women's Biography*, pp. 130–31.

1955 • The Whirly Girls became the first U.S. association of female helicopter pilots in 1955. At that time, there were only 13 licensed female helicopter pilots in the world.

Sources: Read and Witlieb, *The Book of Women's Firsts*, p. 478.

1956 • Maria Atanassova was the first female pilot to work for a commercial airline. She was made a full pilot for the Soviet airline Aeroflot in 1956. She caused a sensation when she landed at Heathrow Airport in England in 1966: it was the first time a woman had piloted a large jet aircraft at an airport outside of Russia.

Sources: Sanders, *The First of Everything,* p. 100.

1964 • Geraldine (Jerrie) Mock (b. 1925) became the first woman to fly solo around the world when she completed her flight in a single-engine plane. She took off from Port Columbus, Ohio, on March 19, 1964, made 21 stops, and logged 22,858.8 miles before returning home on April 17.

Sources: Read and Witlieb, *The Book of Women's Firsts,* pp. 295–96; Woolum, *Outstanding Women Athletes: Who They Are and How They Influenced Sports in America,* p. 28.

1966 • Anne Burns, an English flyer, was the first woman to win the British Glider Championships, held in England in 1966. She has an international reputation in this sport and has been twice honored with the Queen's Commendation for valuable service in the air, in 1955 and 1963.

Sources: O'Neill, *The Women's Book of World Records and Achievements,* p. 591.

1971 • Sheila Christine Scott (1927–1988), an English aviator, was the first person to make a solo light aircraft flight around the world. She flew equator to equator over the North Pole in 1971. Scott was also the founder and first governor of the British section of the Ninety Nines and founder of the British Balloon and Airships Club.

Sources: Scott, *Barefoot in the Sky;* Uglow, *The Continuum Dictionary of Women's Biography,* p. 489.

1973 • Bonnie Tiburzi (b. 1948) became the first female jet pilot to be hired by a major airline in the United States when she was selected to serve as the third officer on an American Airlines Boeing 727 in 1973.

Sources: Read and Witlieb, *The Book of Women's Firsts,* p. 446.

Emily Howell (b. 1939) was the first woman to become a commercial airline pilot in the United States. She was hired by Frontier Airlines in January 1973.

Sources: Sanders, *The First of Everything,* p. 100.

1986 • Jeana Yaeger (b. 1952) was the first woman to fly nonstop around the world without refueling. She began her trip at Edwards Air Force Base in the Mojave Desert of California on December 14, 1986, and returned on December 23. With copilot Dick Rutan, Yaeger flew a lightweight craft, the "Voyager," designed by Dick's brother Burt.

Sources: Read and Witlieb, *The Book of Women's Firsts,* p. 499; Uglow, *The Continuum Dictionary of Women's Biography,* pp. 595–96.

Baseball

1867 • The first women's baseball team was organized in 1867 in Philadelphia, Pennsylvania. Called the Dolly Vardens, they shocked their audiences by appearing in red dresses that were immodestly short—well above than ankle. Their ball was made of yarn.

Sources: McCullough, *First of All: Significant Firsts by American Women*, p. 131.

1868 • Nannie Miller became the first woman to serve as captain of a baseball team in 1868 in Peterboro, New Hampshire. She was also the catcher of the team, a squad of 50 women who wore blue and white tunics reaching to their knees, white stockings and straw hats.

Sources: Kane, *Famous First Facts*, p. 7.

1883 • The New York Gothams baseball team held the first "Ladies' Day" on June 17, 1883, allowing women into baseball parks either at a reduced rate or free of charge, signaling the acceptance of women spectators at public sporting events.

Sources: Woolum, *Outstanding Women Athletes: Who They Are and How They Influenced Sports in America*, p. 24.

1931 • Verne Beatrice Mitchell, professionally known as "Miss Jack Mitchell," became the first woman to play in major league baseball. She was signed to pitch by the Chattanooga (Tennessee) Lookouts on April 1, 1931, when she was only 17 years old. In her first trip to the mound, in an exhibition game with the New York Yankees on April 3, 1931, she struck out both Babe Ruth and Lou Gehrig.

Sources: McCullough, *First of All: Significant Firsts by American Women*, p. 130; Woolum, *Outstanding Women Athletes: Who They Are and How They Influenced Sports in America*, p. 26.

1943 • The first professional women's baseball leagues were formed in the early 1940s when the major league team players went off to World War II. In 1943, Philip Wrigley formed the All American Girls Baseball League in Chicago, consisting of four teams of women softball players. They played high-caliber games that drew many fans, but after the war, the women returned to amateur softball.

Sources: McCullough, *First of All: Significant Firsts by American Women*, p. 131.

1963 • Nancy Lotsey (b. 1955) was the first girl to play in organized baseball competition with boys. She was the pitcher on the local team of the New Jersey Small-Fry League in 1963.

Sources: Read and Witlieb, *The Book of Women's Firsts*, pp. 259–60.

1972 • Berenice Gera became the first woman umpire in professional baseball in January 1972 with the Class A New York-Penn (minor) League. In June, she took the field in a game between two minor league teams, the Auburn Phillies and the Geneva Rangers. This would be the only game she called, however, due to severe criticism both before and during her debut. She quit and took her baseball career on to the New York Mets front office.

Sources: McCullough, *First of All: Significant Firsts by American Women*, p. 161; Woolum, *Outstanding Women Athletes: Who They Are and How They Influenced Sports in America*, p. 29.

1973 • The first lawsuit challenging Little League Baseball's "no girls" rule was filed on behalf of Carolyn King in Detroit, Michigan, on June 28, 1973. The Detroit courts dismissed the case, but after a newspaper story appeared all over the country, many similar lawsuits followed. On June 12, Little League baseball announced that its teams would be open to girls, and on September 7, the national organization signed an order agreeing to ban sex discrimination.

Sources: McCullough, *First of All: Significant Firsts by American Women,* p. 129; Woolum, *Outstanding Women Athletes: Who They Are and How They Influenced Sports in America,* p. 29.

1974 • Bunny Taylor (b. 1963) was the first girl to pitch a no-hit game in Little League, in 1974, the first year that girls were allowed to play officially in Little League on teams of their own.

Sources: O'Neill, *The Women's Book of World Records and Achievements,* p. 567.

Lonny Moss was the first woman to serve as general manager of a minor league baseball team. She managed the Portland, Oregon, Mavericks during the 1974 season.

Sources: O'Neill, *The Women's Book of World Records and Achievements,* p. 567.

Girls were permitted for the first time to play in Little League baseball when President Gerald Ford signed the legislation to open the organization officially to children of both sexes on December 26, 1974.

Sources: Read and Witlieb, *The Book of Women's Firsts,* p. 256.

1978 • Linda Williams of Houston, Texas, became the first woman to play on a high school varsity baseball team. She had been practicing with the Wheatley High School Wildcats during the preseason, but the University Interscholastic League forced her to stop because of her sex. On March 25, 1978, a Houston judge reinstated her.

Sources: McCullough, *First of All: Significant Firsts by American Women,* p. 129.

1980 • Crystal Fields (b. 1969) of Cumberland, Maryland, became the first girl to win the Pitch, Hit, and Run championship on July 18, 1980. She defeated seven boys to win the national baseball skills competition held in Seattle, Washington.

Sources: Read and Witlieb, *The Book of Women's Firsts,* p. 155.

1988 • Julie Croteau took the field for NCAA Division III St. Mary's College of Maryland in 1988 as the first woman to play on a men's collegiate baseball team.

Sources: Woolum, *Outstanding Women Athletes: Who They Are and How They Influenced Sports in America,* p. 30.

1994 • Ila Borders was the first woman to pitch in a college baseball game when she pitched for Southern California College in a 12-1 victory against Claremont Mudd-Scripps in Costa Mesa, California, on February 22, 1994.

Sources: *The New York Times* (23 February 1994), p. B10.

Basketball

1892 • The Director of Physical Education at Smith College in Northampton, Massachusetts, Senda Berenson (1868–1954) was the first woman to introduce basketball at a woman's college. She organized the team and arranged to play several intercollegiate games.

Sources: Kane, *Famous First Facts,* p. 107; Read and Witlieb, *The Book of Women's Firsts,* pp. 41–42.

1896 • The first women's intercollegiate basketball game took place at the Armory Hall in San Francisco between Stanford and the University of California at Berkeley on April 4, 1896. Stanford won the contest, 2-1.

Sources: Woolum, *Outstanding Women Athletes: Who They Are and How They Influenced Sports in America,* p. 25.

1972 • The Association for Intercollegiate Athletics for Women (AIAW) held its first women's collegiate basketball championship on March 19, 1972. Immaculata College defeated West Chester State, 52-48.

Sources: Woolum, *Outstanding Women Athletes: Who They Are and How They Influenced Sports in America,* p. 29.

1975 • The Immaculata College basketball team was the first women's team to win in a game at Madison Square Garden in New York City. During the first women's game played in this famous arena, Immaculata College won against Queen's College, in 1975.

Sources: O'Neill, *The Women's Book of World Records and Achievements,* p. 567.

1976 • The Soviet basketball team, captained by Uliana Semenova, was the first team to win an Olympic gold medal in basketball, in Montreal, Canada, in 1976, the first year that this sport became an official event. This virtually unchallenged team went on to win the Women's World Championship for the sixth consecutive time in 1976.

Sources: O'Neill, *The Women's Book of World Records and Achievements,* p. 567.

The first Olympic women's basketball team from the United States competed in Montreal, Canada, in July 1976, the first year in which this event was open to female competitors. The team won the silver medal.

Sources: McCullough, *First of All: Significant Firsts by American Women,* p. 134.

1977 • The first women's basketball league, the Women's Basketball Association, was formed in New York City. The first WBA game was played the following year.

Sources: McCullough, *First of All: Significant Firsts by American Women,* p. 133.

The first all-America girls' high school basketball squad was chosen by *Parade* magazine in 1977. The squad, made up of 40 girls from 26 states, represented the best competitors regardless of position.

Sources: O'Neill, *The Women's Book of World Records and Achievements,* p. 568.

1978 • Carol "Blaze" Blazejowski (b. 1957) was the first person to win the Margaret Wade Trophy for the best woman collegiate basketball player in the United States. After graduation from Montclair State College, she went on to a career in the Women's American Basketball Association.

Sources: Read and Witlieb, *The Book of Women's Firsts,* p. 55.

The first game of the Women's Professional Basketball League took place between the Chicago Hustle and the Milwaukee Does on December 9, 1978.

Sources: Woolum, *Outstanding Women Athletes: Who They Are and How They Influenced Sports in America,* p. 30.

1979 • Ann Meyers was the first woman to sign a contract to play in the National Basketball Association. On August 30, 1979, she signed a one-year contract with the Indiana Pacers.

Sources: Woolum, *Outstanding Women Athletes: Who They Are and How They Influenced Sports in America,* p. 30.

1982 • Louisiana Tech defeated Cheney State 76-62 to win the first women's basketball championship sponsored by the National Collegiate Athletic Association (NCAA) on March 28, 1982.

Sources: Woolum, *Outstanding Women Athletes: Who They Are and How They Influenced Sports in America,* p. 30.

1985 • Former University of Kansas basketball star Lynette Woodard (b. 1959) became the first female player for the Harlem Globetrotters on October 7, 1985. She played in her first game in Seattle, Washington, on November 13, 1985.

Sources: Read and Witlieb, *The Book of Women's Firsts,* p. 493; Woolum, *Outstanding Women Athletes: Who They Are and How They Influenced Sports in America,* p. 30.

1986 • Nancy Lieberman (b. 1958) became the first woman to play on a men's professional basketball team when she played for the Springfield Fame, a Massachusetts team of the United States Basketball League, in June 1986. The team takes its name for the fact that Springfield is home to the the Basketball Hall of Fame. The ball from this historic game was placed in the Boston Museum of Science. Lieberman, who was a three-time All-American basketball player at Old Dominion University from 1978 to 1980, went on to a career as a sportscaster for ESPN and Prime Network, covering the Continental Basketball Association's women's basketball games.

Sources: Read and Witlieb, *The Book of Women's Firsts,* pp. 252–53; *Sports Illustrated* (23 June 1986), p. 64.

1990 • Bernadette Locke became the first woman to coach a major college men's sport when she accepted the position of assistant coach on the University of Kentucky men's basketball team in June 1990.

Sources: Woolum, *Outstanding Women Athletes: Who They Are and How They Influenced Sports in America,* p. 31.

Lynette Woodard

1991 • Sandra Ortiz-Del Valle (b. 1951) officiated the United States Basketball League (USBL) game between the New Haven Skyhawks and the Philadelphia Spirit on July 15, 1991, making her the first woman to officiate a men's professional basketball game.

Sources: Woolum, *Outstanding Women Athletes: Who They Are and How They Influenced Sports in America,* p. 31.

Bicycling

1895 • Annie Loundonberry was the first woman to make a bicycle trip around the world. She began on June 26, 1894, at the State House in Boston,

Massachusetts, and finished on September 12, 1895 in Chicago, Illinois. For this she collected a $10,000 bet for completing the trip within 15 months.

Sources: Kane, *Famous First Facts.*

1896 • The first women's bicycle race began in Madison Square Garden in New York City on January 6, 1896, much to the distaste of the League of American Wheelmen. By the end of the race at midnight on January 12, all 13 of the original starters had finished. The winner was Frankie Nelson, who rode over 418 miles.

Sources: McCullough, *First of All: Significant Firsts by American Women,* p. 134; Woolum, *Outstanding Women Athletes: Who They Are and How They Influenced Sports in America,* p. 25.

1937 • The National Amateur Bicycling Association held its first U.S. women's bicycling championship in Buffalo, New York, on September 4, 1937. Doris Kopsky of Belleville, New Jersey, won the one-mile race in 4 minutes, 22.4 seconds.

Sources: Woolum, *Outstanding Women Athletes: Who They Are and How They Influenced Sports in America,* p. 26.

1950s and 1960s • Beryl Burton (b. 1937) was the first and only woman to beat male bicyclists in open events. Since 1959, she has held the British woman's "Best All-Rounder" title for cycling.

Sources: Uglow, *The Continuum Dictionary of Women's Biography,* p. 97.

1969 • Cyclist Audrey McElmury won the women's world road racing championship in Bruno, Czechoslovakia, in 1969. With her victory, McElmury became the first American—man or woman—to win a world road racing title.

Sources: Woolum, *Outstanding Women Athletes: Who They Are and How They Influenced Sports in America,* p. 28.

1973 • Sheila Butz (b. 1950) of Detroit, Michigan, was the first U.S. woman to win a world cycling title. She achieved this honor by winning a European race that concluded in San Sebastian, Spain.

Sources: Wallechinsky and Wallace, *The People's Almanac,* p. 1215.

Boating

1875 • The first women's crew team was introduced at Wellesley College in Massachusetts. The boats at that time were large enough to accommodate ten women in full skirts. By the 1940s, women's crew had grown into a serious sport at many women's colleges.

Sources: McCullough, *First of All: Significant Firsts by American Women,* p. 136.

1936 • Sally Stearns, the first woman coxswain of a men's college varsity crew, led Rollins College's shell in a race against Marietta College on May 27, 1936.

Sources: Woolum, *Outstanding Women Athletes: Who They Are and How They Influenced Sports in America,* p. 26.

1948 • Karen Koff, a Danish athlete, was the first woman to win an Olympic gold medal in canoeing, in London, England, in 1948, the first year this sport was admitted to Olympic competition.

Sources: O'Neill, *The Women's Book of World Records and Achievements,* p. 572.

1969 • Sharon Sites Adams (b. 1930) of the United States became the first woman to sail a boat alone across the Pacific Ocean in 1969. Adams left Yokohama, Japan, on May 12 and arrived in San Diego, California, on July 25, covering approximately 5,620 miles in 74 days, 17 hours, and 15 minutes.

Sources: Read and Witlieb, *The Book of Women's Firsts,* p. 8; Woolum, *Outstanding Women Athletes: Who They Are and How They Influenced Sports in America,* p. 28.

1974 • Rebecca Johnson, a student at the University of Iowa, was the first woman to make a solo canoe trip down the Mississippi River. The 2,400-mile trip from Lake Itasca, Minnesota, ended 96 days later in New Orleans, Louisiana.

Sources: McCullough, *First of All: Significant Firsts by American Women,* p. 136.

1976 • Christine Scheiblich, an athlete representing East Germany, was the first woman to win an Olympic gold medal in single sculls rowing competition, in Montreal, Canada, in 1976, the first time that this event was open to women.

Sources: O'Neill, *The Women's Book of World Records and Achievements,* p. 572.

The Bulgarian women's double sculls rowing team was the first to win an Olympic gold medal in this event, at the Montreal, Canada, games in 1976, the first time this event was open to female competitors.

Sources: O'Neill, *The Women's Book of World Records and Achievements,* p. 572.

The East German women's coxed fours rowing team was the first such team to win an Olympic gold medal, in Montreal, Canada, in 1976, the first year in which this event was open to women.

Sources: O'Neill, *The Women's Book of World Records and Achievements,* p. 572.

The Bulgarian women's team of coxswainless pairs was the first such team to win an Olympic gold medal in this rowing event, in Montreal, Canada, in 1976, the first year in which this event was open to women.

Sources: O'Neill, *The Women's Book of World Records and Achievements,* p. 572.

The East German women's eights rowing team was the first such team to win an Olympic gold medal in this event, in Montreal, Canada, in 1976, the first time that this event was open to female competitors.

Sources: O'Neill, *The Women's Book of World Records and Achievements,* p. 572.

The East German women's coxed quad sculls team was the first such team to win an Olympic gold medal in this rowing event, in Montreal, Canada, in 1976, the first year in which this event was open to women.

Sources: O'Neill, *The Women's Book of World Records and Achievements,* p. 572.

Joan Lind, an international sculling competitor since 1972, was the first U.S. woman to win an Olympic medal in rowing. She achieved this distinction in Montreal, Canada, in 1976, when she won the silver medal in the single scull event.

Sources: O'Neill, *The Women's Book of World Records and Achievements,* p. 584.

Cadet Susan K. Donner, of the U.S. Coast Guard Academy's first class to admit women, became the first woman to win a varsity letter there in November 1976 for her skill as a skipper and crew member in intercollegiate sailing competition. The U.S. Coast Guard Academy was the first military service academy to admit women.

Source: Women in the Coast Guard: Moments in History, p. 1.

1977 • At age 50, Betty Cook (b. 1927) became the first woman to win a major offshore motorboat race when she won the Bushmills Grand Prix off Newport Beach, California, on March 27, 1977.

Sources: Woolum, *Outstanding Women Athletes: Who They Are and How They Influenced Sports in America,* p. 29.

Clare Mary Francis (b. 1946), an English sailor who has written both nonfictional and fictional books based on her experiences as a woman at sea, was the first female skipper in the Whitbread Round the World Event, in 1977–1978. She and her crew came in fifth. In 1976, she was the first and only woman to finish the Royal Western Singlehanded Transatlantic Race, from Falmouth, England, to Newport, Rhode Island.

Sources: Francis, *Come Hell or High Water*; Uglow, *The Continuum Dictionary of Women's Biography,* p. 211.

1978 • Krystyna Chojnowska-Liskiewicz (b. 1936) was the first woman to sail alone around the world. She set out in March 1976 and completed her trip two years later in March 1978.

Sources: Uglow, *The Continuum Dictionary of Women's Biography,* p. 123; Woolum, *Outstanding Women Athletes: Who They Are and How They Influenced Sports in America,* p. 29.

1981 • Sue Brown from Oxford University became the first woman to cox against Cambridge University in the 152-year history of the Oxford-Cambridge race on April 4, 1981. Brown coxed the Oxford crew to an eight-length victory over Cambridge.

Sources: Woolum, *Outstanding Women Athletes: Who They Are and How They Influenced Sports in America,* p. 30.

1991 • Nance Frank became the first female skipper to enter an ocean sailboat race with an all-female crew when she and her crew of 12 raced from Annapolis, Maryland, to Newport, Rhode Island, in June 1991. She finished eighth in a fleet of nine boats.

Sources: Read and Witlieb, *The Book of Women's Firsts,* p. 165.

1995 • In 1995, yacht racer and financier Bill Koch entered the first all-women's crew in the America's Cup race. The initial 22 crew members, selected from 650 applicants, included five Olympic medalists and six experienced yacht racers. Among them were: J. J. Isler, two-time Rolex Yachtswoman of the Year and the first woman captain of the sailing team at Yale University; Shelly Beattie, better known as Siren on the television program *American Gladiators;* and Susie Nairn, an aerospace engineer at NASA's microgravity division

Sources: Motor Boat and Sailing (July 1994), p. 13; *People Weekly* (20 February 1995), p. 84.

Bowling

1916 • Forty women organized the Woman's National Bowling Association (now the Women's International Bowling Congress) on November 29, 1916, in St. Louis, Missouri. It is the largest sports organization for women in the world. Founders included Ellen Kelly, Gertrude Dornblasser, and Catherine Menne.

Sources: Read and Witlieb, *The Book of Women's Firsts,* p. 63; Woolum, *Outstanding Women Athletes: Who They Are and How They Influenced Sports in America,* p. 26.

1917 • The first official women's bowling tournament was sponsored by the Woman's National Bowling Association, now the Women's International Bowling Congress (WIBC). The Progress team of St. Louis, Missouri, won the first team championship, and Mrs. A. J. Koester, also of St. Louis, won the all-events title.

Sources: Read and Witlieb, *The Book of Women's Firsts,* p. 63; Woolum, *Outstanding Women Athletes: Who They Are and How They Influenced Sports in America,* p. 26.

1930 • Jennie Kelleher of Madison, Wisconsin, was the first woman to bowl a perfect 300 game on February 12, 1930.

Sources: Woolum, *Outstanding Women Athletes: Who They Are and How They Influenced Sports in America,* p. 26.

1977 • Lucy Giovinco was the first U.S. woman to win the Women's Bowling World Cup Competition. In 1977, she averaged 178 points per game and bowled a remarkable 620 in a three-game round to beat her opponent by 116 points.

Sources: O'Neill, *The Women's Book of World Records and Achievements,* p. 558.

Boxing

1876 • Nell Saunders defeated Rose Harland in the first women's boxing match in the United States on March 16, 1876.

Sources: Woolum, *Outstanding Women Athletes: Who They Are and How They Influenced Sports in America,* p. 25.

1940 • On May 2, 1940, Belle Martell of Van Nuys, California, became the first woman boxing referee. She officiated her first card of eight bouts in San Bernardino, California.

Sources: Woolum, *Outstanding Women Athletes: Who They Are and How They Influenced Sports in America,* p. 26.

1974 • Carol Polls was the first U.S. woman to become an official boxing judge. She received her license in 1974 and worked primarily in New York.

Sources: O'Neill, *The Women's Book of World Records and Achievements,* p. 559.

1975 • Marion Bermudez (b. 1952) was the first woman to compete successfully in the previously all-male Golden Gloves Boxing Tournament, held in 1975 in Mexico City, Mexico. She won her first match against a man after only seven practice rounds the week before. Bermudez was also a national karate champion and competed against men in that sport as well.

Sources: O'Neill, *The Women's Book of World Records and Achievements,* p. 559.

1977 • Eva Shain (b. 1929) was the first woman to judge a world heavyweight boxing match. She judged in the Muhammad Ali-Ernie Shavers fight at Madison Square Garden in New York City on September 29, 1977.

Sources: Read and Witlieb, *The Book of Women's Firsts,* p. 404.

1991 • Cora Masters Wilds became the first woman named to the Washington, D.C. Wrestling and Boxing Commission.

Sources: Jet (29 January 1991), p. 52.

Bridge

1974 • Rika Marcus, a British competitor in international play since 1935, was the first woman to attain the rank of World Bridge Federation "Grandmaster," in 1974. At that time she had won 12 international championships, a record for a woman.

Sources: O'Neill, *The Women's Book of World Records and Achievements,* p. 592.

Bullfighting

1949 • Conchita Verrill Cintròn (b. 1922) was born in Chile and grew up in Brazil, where it was popular for young women to fight bulls. She made her first appearance in the bull ring in Mexico at the age of 15. In 1949, she defied the law and became the first woman to fight a bull in a ring in Spain.

Sources: Cintròn, *Goddess of the Bullring*; Read and Witlieb, *The Book of Women's Firsts,* pp. 90–91; Uglow, *The Continuum Dictionary of Women's Biography,* p. 125.

1957 • In Cuidad Juarez, Mexico, Patricia McCormick entered the arena as the first U.S. woman bullfighter on January 25, 1957.

Sources: Woolum, *Outstanding Women Athletes: Who They Are and How They Influenced Sports in America,* p. 27.

Chariot Racing

Third century B.C. • Cynisca, the daughter of the King of Sparta, was the first female athlete to enter the Olympic games, as a chariot driver, during the third century B.C. in ancient Greece. She was also the first female horse-breeder in recorded history.

Sources: Chicago, *The Dinner Party,* p. 123.

Euryleon was the first woman to win a victory in the two-horse chariot race during the Olympic games, in the third century B.C. A statue was erected in her honor in Sparta to celebrate her triumph.

Sources: Chicago, *The Dinner Party,* p. 123.

Checkers

1939 • Gertrude Huntley, a U.S. schoolteacher, was the first woman to become a champion checkers player. She won a national tournament in 1939 and as of that time has been listed as the unofficial U.S. Women's Champion.

Sources: O'Neill, *The Women's Book of World Records and Achievements,* p. 592.

Croquet

1936 • Dorothy Dyne Steel (1884–1965), England's best croquet player, was the first woman to win the Open Croquet Championship four times: in 1925, 1933, 1935, and 1936. Only two other women to date have ever won this event. She was the first player to win the Women's Championship 15 times (between 1919 and 1939) and the first person to win 31 croquet titles in a lifetime of play.

Sources: Uglow, *The Continuum Dictionary of Women's Biography,* p. 515.

Curling

1947 • The U. S. Women's Curling Association was founded in Milwaukee, Wisconsin, on October 23, 1947.

Sources: Woolum, *Outstanding Women Athletes: Who They Are and How They Influenced Sports in America,* p. 27.

1952 • The St. Andrew Golf Club hosted the first bonspiel for women curlers in the New York area on January 15, 1952.

Sources: Woolum, *Outstanding Women Athletes: Who They Are and How They Influenced Sports in America,* p. 27.

Diving

1912 • Greta Johansson, a Swedish athlete, was the first woman to win an Olympic gold medal in platform diving, in Stockholm, Sweden, in 1912, the first year this event was open to women.

Sources: O'Neill, *The Women's Book of World Records and Achievements,* p. 572.

1920 • Aileen Riggin (b. 1906), a U.S. athlete, was the first woman to win an Olympic springboard diving event during the first Olympics that the event was held, in 1920, in Antwerp, Belgium. In 1924, she became the first athlete to win Olympic medals in both swimming and diving events.

Sources: O'Neill, *The Women's Book of World Records and Achievements,* p. 572; Read and Witlieb, *The Book of Women's Firsts,* pp. 371–72.

1948 • At the summer Olympics in London, England, in 1948, Vicki Manolo Draves became the first woman to win a gold medal in both diving events in the same Olympics.

Sources: Mallon, *Quest for Gold: The Encyclopedia of American Olympics,* p. 83.

Aileen Riggin

Fencing

1912 • The Amateur Fencers League of America sponsored the first women's national fencing championship. A. Baylis of the Fencers Club won the foils competition.

Sources: Woolum, *Outstanding Women Athletes: Who They Are and How They Influenced Sports in America,* p. 25.

1924 • Ellen Osiier, a Danish competitor, was the first woman to win an Olympic gold medal in individual foil fencing, in Paris, France, in 1924, the first year that this event was open to women.

Sources: O'Neill, *The Women's Book of World Records and Achievements,* p. 572.

1960 • The Soviet women's fencing team was the first to win an Olympic gold medal in team foil fencing, in Rome, Italy, in 1960, the first time that this event was officially open to women.

Sources: O'Neill, *The Women's Book of World Records and Achievements,* p. 572.

Field Hockey

1901 • Constance Applebee (1883–1981) was the first person to introduce the sport of field hockey in the United States. While studying at Harvard University in 1901, she suggested that field hockey be made part of the track and field sport course. The first game was played with ice hockey sticks on a concrete yard outside the Harvard gym.

Constance Applebee

Sources: Uglow, *The Continuum Dictionary of Women's Biography,* p. 24.

1922 • The U.S. Field Hockey Association, founded in 1922, was the first organization to establish standards for women field hockey players in the United States. When the U.S. sent its first field hockey team to the Olympics in 1984, these female players won a bronze medal.

Sources: Read and Witlieb, *The Book of Women's Firsts,* p. 209.

Fishing

1496 • The fifteenth-century English prioress Dame Juliana Berners (b. 1388) is the first female fly fisher on record. She is the author of *The Book of St. Albans,* a compendium of essays on field sports first published in 1496, which includes her "Treatyse of Fysshynge Wyth an Angle."

Sources: Chicago, *The Dinner Party,* p. 152; *The New York Times* (18 August 1994), p. A14.

1932 • The first women's fly fishing club was founded in the United States in 1932. Its "patron saint" is Dame Juliana Berners (b. 1388), whose treatise on fly fishing was first published in 1496. The original organization included approximately 90 members, most of who had been fishing in Catskill streams at the turn of the twentieth century.

Sources: *The New York Times* (18 August 1994), p. A14.

1991 • Vojai Reed became the first woman to compete in a Bass Anglers Sportsman Society tournament in 1991. The Missouri Invitational at Truman Lake was run by the U.S. Army Corps of Engineers, who threatened to cancel the tournament if women were not allowed to participate.

Sources: *Sports Illustrated* (13 May 1991), p. 100.

Football

1970 • Pat Palinkas, who had signed a contract with the Orlando, Florida, Panthers in the Atlantic Coast Professional Football League, held the ball for the point-after-touchdown kicks. She was the first woman to play in a professional football game on August 15, 1970.

Sources: Woolum, *Outstanding Women Athletes: Who They Are and How They Influenced Sports in America,* p. 28.

1974 • The first women's professional football league was founded in the United States in 1974. The league included 10 teams, all coached by men, and played 10 games each year. Every player earned $25 per game.

Sources: Read and Witlieb, *The Book of Women's Firsts,* p. 161.

Golf

1542 • Mary Queen of Scots was the first known female golfer. She openly advocated this game, which originated in Scotland, during her reign (1542–1587).
Sources: Sanders, *The First of Everything,* p. 218.

1893 • Margaret Scott (b. 1875) was the first woman to become British Ladies' Golf Champion, in 1893, the year of the formation of the Ladies' Golf Union, which sponsored competition in this sport. Scott held the title three times, after which she retired from competitive golf.
Sources: Uglow, *The Continuum Dictionary of Women's Biography,* pp. 488–89.

1895 • Mrs. Charles B. Brown won the first, though unofficial, national women's golf tournament, held at Meadowbrook Hunt Club near Hempstead, Long Island, New York, in November 1895. Brown scored 132 for 18 holes.
Sources: Read and Witlieb, *The Book of Women's Firsts,* pp. 70–71; Woolum, *Outstanding Women Athletes: Who They Are and How They Influenced Sports in America,* p. 24.

1900 • Margaret Abbott was the first person to win an Olympic gold medal in golf. She won this honor at the Olympics in Paris, France, in 1900.
Sources: O'Neill, *The Women's Book of World Records and Achievements,* p. 561; Read and Witlieb, *The Book of Women's Firsts,* p. 4.

1924 • Joyce Wethered (b. 1901), a famous English amateur golfer, was the first woman to win the English Ladies' Golf Championship during five successive years, 1920 through 1924. Wethered wrote at length about her sport and was known for her intense concentration while playing the game.
Sources: Uglow, *The Continuum Dictionary of Women's Biography,* pp. 577–78; Wallechinsky and Wallace, *The People's Almanac,* p. 1186.

1941 • Eleanor Dudley won the first women's National Intercollegiate Golf Championship sponsored by Ohio State University on July 3, 1941.
Sources: Woolum, *Outstanding Women Athletes: Who They Are and How They Influenced Sports in America,* p. 26.

1944 • Hope Seignious, Betty Hicks, and Ellen Griffin founded and incorporated the Women's Professional Golf Association (WPGA) in 1944.
Sources: Woolum, *Outstanding Women Athletes: Who They Are and How They Influenced Sports in America,* p. 27.

1946 • Patty Berg defeated Betty Jameson in the final round to win the first U.S. Women's Open golf tournament on September 1, 1946.
Sources: Woolum, *Outstanding Women Athletes: Who They Are and How They Influenced Sports in America,* p. 27.

Mildred Didrikson Zaharias (1914–1956), nicknamed "Babe," was the first three-time winner of the Associated Press poll for Woman Athlete of the Year, in 1932, 1945, and 1946. Zaharias, known especially for her achievements in golf, won over a 40-year career more medals and tournaments and set more sports records than any other twentieth-century athlete, male or female. In 1947, she was the first U.S. woman to win the British Ladies Golf Championship in Edinburgh, Scotland.

Sources: Peper, *Golf in America: the First One Hundred Years*; Read and Witlieb, *The Book of Women's Firsts,* pp. 502–3; Woolum, *Outstanding Women Athletes: Who They Are and How They Influenced Sports in America,* p. 27; Zaharias, *This Life I've Led.*

1949 • Patty Berg (b. 1918) became the first president of the Ladies Professional Golf Association (LPGA) in 1949. One of the United States' pioneer professional female golfers, Berg was also one of the founders of this athletic organization.

Sources: Peper, *Golf in America: the First One Hundred Years*; Wallechinsky and Wallace, *The People's Almanac,* p. 1182.

Wilson Sporting Goods agreed to sponsor the formation of the Ladies Professional Golf Association (LPGA) on May 29, 1949. The group became an officially chartered organization in 1950.

Sources: Woolum, *Outstanding Women Athletes: Who They Are and How They Influenced Sports in America,* p. 27.

1976 • Judy Rankin was the first professional female golfer to win more than $100,000 in a single season.

Sources: Woolum, *Outstanding Women Athletes: Who They Are and How They Influenced Sports in America,* p. 29.

Sally Little, a South African athlete, was the first woman to win the Women's International Golf Tournament, offered for the first time in 1976. This victory was her first in six years of professional competition.

Sources: O'Neill, *The Women's Book of World Records and Achievements,* p. 561.

1978 • Nancy Lopez (b. 1957) became the first woman to win five straight Ladies Professional Golf Association (LPGA) tournaments when she won her fifth tournament in 1978. She won the LPGA tournament again in 1985 and 1989. In 1985 she set a record for prize money, becoming the first woman to earn over $416,000.

Sources: Read and Witlieb, *The Book of Women's Firsts,* pp. 258–59; Uglow, *The Continuum Dictionary of Women's Biography,* p. 333.

1980 • For the first time, the Professional Golf Association (PGA) allowed female caddies in the U.S. Open at the Baltusrol Golf Club in Springfield, New Jersey, in June 1980. Pamela Shuttleworth of Santa Monica, California, caddied for PGA player Jim Dent.

Sources: Woolum, *Outstanding Women Athletes: Who They Are and How They Influenced Sports in America,* p. 30.

Elizabeth Rawls (b. 1928) was the first female rules official for a U.S. Open men's golf championship, in 1980. After a distinguished career in women's amateur and professional golf, Rawls formally retired in 1975.

Sources: Read and Witlieb, *The Book of Women's Firsts,* pp. 360–61.

1986 • Ayako Okamoto (b. 1951), an outstanding Japanese professional golfer, was the first woman to score 17 under par at the U.S. golf tournament, the Elizabeth Arden Classic, in 1986.

Sources: Uglow, *The Continuum Dictionary of Women's Biography,* p. 410.

1990 • Juli Inkster (b. 1960) of Los Altos, California, became the first woman to win the only professional golf tournament in the world in which women and men compete head-to-head in December 1990. Juli parred the eighteenth hole of the Spalding Invitational Pro-Am at Pebble Beach, California, for a one-stroke victory over Professional Golf Association (PGA) tour member Mark Brooks.

Sources: Woolum, *Outstanding Women Athletes: Who They Are and How They Influenced Sports in America,* p. 31.

Gymnastics

Late nineteenth century • Elin Kallio (1859–1927) was the founder of the first athletic association for women in northern Europe. She helped to popularize gymnastics in Finland and devoted her life to teaching athletics and to writing books about sports.

Sources: Chicago, *The Dinner Party,* p. 193.

1928 • The Dutch women's gymnastics team was the first team to win an Olympic gold medal for all-around competition, in Amsterdam, the Netherlands, in 1928, the first time that this event was open to women.

Sources: O'Neill, *The Women's Book of World Records and Achievements,* p. 572.

1952 • Maria Gorokhovskaya, a Soviet competitor, was the first woman to win an Olympic gold medal in gymnastics for her individual performance. She achieved this record at the games in Helsinki, Finland, in 1952, the first time that this event was open to women.

Sources: O'Neill, *The Women's Book of World Records and Achievements,* p. 572.

Yekaterina Kalintschuk, a Soviet competitor, was the first woman to win an Olympic gold medal in vault gymnastics, in Helsinki, Finland, in 1952, the first year in which this event was open to women.

Sources: O'Neill, *The Women's Book of World Records and Achievements,* p. 572.

Margit Korondi, an Hungarian athlete, was the first woman to win an Olympic gold medal in the uneven parallel bars gymnastics event, in Helsinki, Finland, in 1952, the first year this event was open to women.

Sources: O'Neill, *The Women's Book of World Records and Achievements,* p. 572.

Nina Botscharova, a Soviet athlete, was the first woman to win an Olympic gold medal in the balance beam gymnastics event, in Helsinki, Finland, in 1952, the first time that this event was open to women.

Sources: O'Neill, *The Women's Book of World Records and Achievements,* p. 572.

Agnes Keleti, an Hungarian athlete, was the first woman to win an Olympic gold medal in the free exercise gymnastics event, in Helsinki, Finland, in 1952, the first year in which this event was open to women.

Sources: O'Neill, *The Women's Book of World Records and Achievements,* p. 572.

1964 • Larissa Latynina (b. 1935), a Russian gymnast, was the first person to win 18 medals during the course of three Olympic Games. In the games played in 1956, 1960, and 1964, she won more Olympic medals than anyone else in any sport: six individual golds, three golds as a team member, five silver, and three bronze medals.

Sources: Uglow, *The Continuum Dictionary of Women's Biography,* p. 313.

1968 • Vera Caslavska-Oklozil (b. 1942), a Czech athlete, was the first woman to win seven individual gold Olympic medals in gymnastics. She won three at the 1964 Olympic games and four more at the games in 1968.

Sources: O'Neill, *The Women's Book of World Records and Achievements,* p. 562.

1970 • Cathy Rigby (b. 1952) was the first U.S. athlete to win a medal at the World Gymnastics Championships. In 1970, she won a silver medal for her performance on the balance beam.

Sources: O'Neill, *The Women's Book of World Records and Achievements,* p. 562.

1972 • Olga Korbut (b. 1955), a Russian gymnast, was the first person to demonstrate in competition a backwards somersault on uneven parallel bars, during the Olympic Games in Munich, Germany, in 1972. She was the first and only female to do a back flip on the balance beam during these games, at which she won three gold medals.

Sources: O'Neill, *The Women's Book of World Records and Achievements,* pp. 561–62; Smith, *Olga Korbut;* Uglow, *The Continuum Dictionary of Women's Biography,* p. 304.

1975 • Ludmilla Tourisheva, a Russian athlete, was the first female gymnast to hold all the gold medals in both European and world championships at one time, in 1976.

Sources: O'Neill, *The Women's Book of World Records and Achievements,* p. 562.

1977 • Stephanie Willim, a U.S. athlete, was the first woman to win the All-Around title as well as every individual event at the Elite Gymnastics Championships, the first such sweep in American Athletic Union (AAU) history, in 1977.

Sources: O'Neill, *The Women's Book of World Records and Achievements,* p. 562.

1984 • Mary Lou Retton (b. 1968) was the first U.S. female gymnast to win a gold medal at the Olympics, in Los Angeles, California, in July 1984. She was the most decorated U.S. athlete at these games and went on to a career in commercials and small parts in films. She soon became the first woman to appear on the front of a "Wheaties" box, a traditional showcase for male athletes.

Sources: The (Cleveland) Plain Dealer (31 July 1994), p. 17D.

Handball

1976 • The Soviet women's handball team was the first handball team to win an Olympic gold medal, in Montreal, Canada, in 1976, the first time this sport was officially offered as an event and the first year in which this event was open to female competitors.

Sources: O'Neill, *The Women's Book of World Records and Achievements,* pp. 568, 572.

Horse Racing

1804 • Alicia Meynell, an English woman, was the first female jockey. She rode against Captain William Flint in a four-mile race in York, England, on August 25, 1804.

Sources: Woolum, *Outstanding Women Athletes: Who They Are and How They Influenced Sports in America,* p. 24.

1907 • Dorothy Tyler (b. 1893) was the first female jockey to ride in the United States. Riding her own horse, Blackman, Tyler won a quarter-mile race in her hometown of Joplin, Missouri.

Sources: Read and Witlieb, *The Book of Women's Firsts,* p. 454.

1920 • Beryl Markham (1902–1986) was the first woman in Africa to be granted a racehorse trainer's license, in Kenya in 1920. In the 1950s she became the first woman to have six Kenyan Derby winners and the first to win the top trainer's award five times. (*See also* **Sports: Aviation, 1936.**)

Sources: Markham, *West with the Night*; Uglow, *The Continuum Dictionary of Women's Biography,* p. 358.

1935 • The Jockey Club of the United States licensed Mary Hirsch in 1935, making her the first woman trainer of thoroughbred race horses. In 1937, Hirsch became the first woman trainer of a horse that ran in the Kentucky Derby.

Sources: Read and Witlieb, *The Book of Women's Firsts,* p. 207; Woolum, *Outstanding Women Athletes: Who They Are and How They Influenced Sports in America,* p. 26.

1943 • An English woman, Judy Johnson, rode Lone Gallant to a tenth place finish in a field of 11 horses in a steeplechase event at the Pimlico Racetrack at Baltimore, Maryland, on April 27, 1943. She was the first woman steeplechase jockey to race at a major American racetrack.

Sources: Woolum, *Outstanding Women Athletes: Who They Are and How They Influenced Sports in America,* p. 26.

1968 • On October 30, 1968, Kathy Kusner (b. 1940) became the first woman to receive a jockey's license when she was granted one from the Maryland Racing Commission. The license permitted her to race thoroughbred horses at major tracks.

Sources: Read and Witlieb, *The Book of Women's Firsts,* p. 245; Woolum, *Outstanding Women Athletes: Who They Are and How They Influenced Sports in America,* p. 28.

1969 • Barbara Jo Rubin (b. 1949) was the first female jockey to win a regular parimutuel thoroughbred race. She won at Hobby Horse Hall racetrack in Nassau, the Bahamas, on January 28, 1969, riding Fly Away. On February 22, Rubin rode Cohesion to victory at Charles Town, West Virginia, to become the first woman jockey to win a race at a U.S. thoroughbred track.

Sources: Read and Witlieb, *The Book of Women's Firsts,* pp. 383–84; Woolum, *Outstanding Women Athletes: Who They Are and How They Influenced Sports in America,* p. 28.

1970 • Diane Crump (b. 1949) was the first female jockey to ride in the Kentucky Derby, in Louisville, Kentucky. She rode Fathom in the Churchill Downs classic, coming in 15th in a field of 17. Crump was also the first U.S. woman jockey to ride at a parimutuel track; she rode her first mount to a tenth-place finish at a Hialeah, Florida, race track on February 7, 1969. She went on to a lucrative career as a jockey and a horse trainer.

Sources: Read and Witlieb, *The Book of Women's Firsts,* pp. 108–9; Woolum, *Outstanding Women Athletes: Who They Are and How They Influenced Sports in America,* p. 28.

1971 • Mary Bacon was the first woman jockey to ride one hundred winners, posting her one hundredth victory on June 30, 1971, at the Thistledown Race Track in Cleveland, Ohio, aboard California Lassie.

Sources: Woolum, *Outstanding Women Athletes: Who They Are and How They Influenced Sports in America,* p. 28.

1973 • Robyn Smith became the first woman jockey to win a stakes race when she rode North Sea to victory in the $27,450 Paumanauk Handicap at Aqueduct Raceway, Queens, New York, on March 1, 1973.

Sources: Woolum, *Outstanding Women Athletes: Who They Are and How They Influenced Sports in America,* p. 29.

1985 • Patricia Cooksey, the second woman to ride in the Kentucky Derby (in 1984) was the first female jockey to ride in the Preakness, at Pimlico racetrack in Baltimore, Maryland, in 1985. She rode on a horse named Tajawa and finished sixth.

Sources: Read and Witlieb, *The Book of Women's Firsts,* p. 108.

1993 • Julie Krone (b. 1964), a U.S. jockey, was the first woman to win a Triple Crown event. She came in first, riding Colonial Affair, at New York's Belmont Stakes in 1993. Two years earlier, she was the first woman to ride at Belmont. Her performances have been plagued with injuries, but she is a determined and strong rider who has had a stellar career in her field.

Sources: The New York Times (14 January 1995), p. 38; Woolum, *Outstanding Women Athletes: Who They Are and How They Influenced Sports in America,* p. 31.

Horseback Riding

1902 • Mrs. Adolph Ladenburg of Saratoga, New York, introduced an innovative horse show riding outfit on August 31, 1902, wearing a split skirt rather than the traditional ankle-length attire. She also rode her horse astride rather than sidesaddle, one of the first women to do so in public.

Sources: Woolum, *Outstanding Women Athletes: Who They Are and How They Influenced Sports in America,* p. 25.

1911 • Nan Jane Aspinall was the first woman to ride on horseback across the United States alone. She began her journey in San Francisco, California, on September 1, 1910, and concluded it in New York City on July 8, 1911. She spent 108 days in actual travel and covered over 4,500 miles.

Sources: Read and Witlieb, *The Book of Women's Firsts,* p. 26.

1962 • Pat Smythe (b. 1928), an English equestrienne, was the first woman to win the British Show Jumping Association championships eight times, in 1962. Her first win was in 1952. She was also the first woman invited to join the British show jumping team under Harry Llewellyn for their first tour abroad, in the 1940s.

Sources: Smythe, *Jump for Joy*; Uglow, *The Continuum Dictionary of Women's Biography,* p. 504.

Ice Hockey

1992 • Manon Rheaume became the first woman to play in the National Hockey League (NHL). Rheaume, a hockey goaltender since the age of five and the first girl to play in Canada's Major Junior Hockey League, joined the Tampa Bay (Florida) Lightning and played her first exhibition game in the NHL in October 1992.

Sources: *People Weekly* (28 September 1992); *Time* (5 October 1992), p. 24.

Luge and Bobsled

1967 • Otrum Enderlein, a German athlete, was the first woman to hold four luge titles. She earned her first at the 1964 Winter Olympics in Innsbruck, Austria, and the others between that date and 1967. When she won the Olympic gold medal, she became the first woman to do so, for 1964 was the first year in which this Olympic event was open to female competitors.

Sources: O'Neill, *The Women's Book of World Records and Achievements,* pp. 564–65.

Marathon Running

1966 • The first woman to compete unofficially in the Boston Marathon was Roberta Gibb (Bingay) (b. 1942). On April 19, 1966, she hid in the bushes near the starting line and leapt into the pack of male runners just after the official start. She wore a hooded sweatshirt to disguise her appearance because women were not allowed to run in the race. She finished ahead of 415 men—

over half of those who raced—but officials denied that a woman had run that day.

Sources: McCullough, *First of All: Significant Firsts by American Women*, p. 145; *Women's Sports and Fitness* (April 1994), p. 48; Woolum, *Outstanding Women Athletes: Who They Are and How They Influenced Sports in America*, p. 28.

1967 • Katherine Switzer became the first woman to register to run in the Boston Marathon in 1967. Since the race was closed to women, she registered unofficially as "K. Switzer." Published photographs of an official trying to remove her number created an outcry of public opinion. Switzer competed officially in this race when it was finally opened to women in 1972.

Sources: O'Neill, *The Women's Book of World Records and Achievements*, p. 576; Read and Witlieb, *The Book of Women's Firsts*, pp. 432–33; Sanders, *The First of Everything*, p. 158; Woolum, *Outstanding Women Athletes: Who They Are and How They Influenced Sports in America*, p. 28.

1972 • Nina Kuscik from Huntington, Long Island, was the first official woman finisher in the 76th Boston Marathon. On April 17, 1972, the first year that women were allowed to enter the race, Kuscik and eight other women took to the Boston Streets as official registrants, even though women had been running unofficially since 1966. Kuscik finished with a time of 3 hours, 8 minutes, 58 seconds, ahead of at least two-thirds of the men.

Sources: McCullough, *First of All: Significant Firsts by American Women*, p. 147; Woolum, *Outstanding Women Athletes: Who They Are and How They Influenced Sports in America*, p. 29.

1975 • Marion May was the first woman marathon runner to win in an open competition against men. The first time she had ever competed in an official marathon, she defeated 53 men in the Fairbanks, Alaska, Midnight Sun Marathon on June 14, 1975.

Sources: McCullough, *First of All: Significant Firsts by American Women*, p. 145.

Miscellaneous

1877 • The new Ladies Club for Outdoor Sports held its first meeting at New Brighton, Staten Island, New York, on June 13, 1877. Club members played archery, lawn tennis, and croquet.

Sources: Woolum, *Outstanding Women Athletes: Who They Are and How They Influenced Sports in America*, p. 24.

Early twentieth century • Madame A. Milliat was the founder of the Federation Sportive Feminine International, in Paris. An advocate for women's athletics, Milliat organized an Olympic games for women when women were denied the right to participate in the Olympic Games in 1922.

Sources: Chicago, *The Dinner Party*, p. 193.

1920 • Marjorie Voorhies won the first national tournament for women horseshoe pitchers.

Source: Woolum, *Outstanding Women Athletes: Who They Are and How They Influenced Sports in America*, p. 26.

1923 • In 1923, Lou Henry Hoover (1875–1944), wife of Herbert Hoover, who later became president of the United States, organized the first women's division of the National Amateur Athletic Federation. She strove to encourage American girls to participate in a wide range of sports.

Sources: Read and Witlieb, *The Book of Women's Firsts,* p. 306.

1928 • Women competed in the Olympics for the first time in 1928, in Amsterdam, the Netherlands. Due to the international efforts of women's rights groups on behalf of female athletes, the Olympic Committee met in Prague in 1925 to debate the issue of women's participation and finally decided to admit women to Olympic competition.

Sources: Chicago, *The Dinner Party,* p. 193.

1968 • Enriqueta Basilio became the first woman to light the Olympic flame at the opening ceremonies of the games in 1968 in Mexico City, Mexico.

Sources: Woolum, *Outstanding Women Athletes: Who They Are and How They Influenced Sports in America,* p. 28.

Janice Lee York Romary (b. 1928) of San Mateo, California, was the first woman to carry the U.S. flag at the Olympic Games. She carried the U.S. flag in the opening ceremonies of the summer Olympics at Mexico City, Mexico. She participated in her first Olympics twenty years earlier and had an established reputation as a fencer.

Sources: Read and Witlieb, *The Book of Women's Firsts,* p. 377; Woolum, *Outstanding Women Athletes: Who They Are and How They Influenced Sports in America,* p. 28.

1971 • A New York State Education Department law went into effect on May 27, 1971, that permitted girls to compete as members of boys' teams in noncontact sports.

Sources: Woolum, *Outstanding Women Athletes: Who They Are and How They Influenced Sports in America,* p. 28.

1973 • Dacie Schileru was the first woman to compete in a National Collegiate Athletic Association (NCAA) event, in 1973, the first year women were declared eligible for competition sponsored by this association. She qualified for diving competition in the swimming championships.

Sources: Read and Witlieb, *The Book of Women's Firsts,* p. 394.

1974 • Laura Cross (b. 1962), a U.S. 12-year-old, was the first girl to win the Detroit Soap Box Derby, in Detroit, Michigan, in 1974. One of only five girls in the 33-car field, she dedicated her victory to "womanhood."

Sources: O'Neill, *The Women's Book of World Records and Achievements,* p. 589.

1975 • Karren Stead (b. 1964) became the first girl to win the National Soap Box Derby on August 3, 1975, in Akron, Ohio. In addition to the title, she won a $3,000 scholarship.

Sources: McCullough, *First of All: Significant Firsts by American Women,* p. 154.

In a suit brought by *Sports Illustrated* reporter Melissa Ludtke, U.S. District Court Judge Constance Baker Motley ruled on September 25, 1975, that major league baseball cannot legally bar a woman sportswriter from the locker room after a game.

Sources: Woolum, *Outstanding Women Athletes: Who They Are and How They Influenced Sports in America*, p. 30.

1986 • Harriet Hamilton of Fisk University was the first black female athletic director in the Southern Intercollegiate Athletic Conference, in 1986.

Sources: Smith, *Black Firsts*, p. 363.

1987 • The first National Women in Sports Day was celebrated in Washington, D.C., on February 4, 1987.

Sources: Woolum, *Outstanding Women Athletes: Who They Are and How They Influenced Sports in America*, p. 31.

1988 • On August 1, Phyllis Holmes began her term as president of the National Association of Intercollegiate Athletics (NAIA), the first woman to serve as president of any national coed sports organization.

Sources: Woolum, *Outstanding Women Athletes: Who They Are and How They Influenced Sports in America*, p. 31.

1991 • Elizabeth Primrose-Smith (b. 1948) was the first woman to run the U.S. Olympic Festival, the nation's largest multisport competition. She became head of the festival in 1991 when it was held in Los Angeles, California.

Sources: Read and Witlieb, *The Book of Women's Firsts*, pp. 350–51.

The National Collegiate Athletic Association (NCAA) elected Judy Sweet as its first female president in January 1991.

Sources: Woolum, *Outstanding Women Athletes: Who They Are and How They Influenced Sports in America*, p. 31.

Barbara Hedges was named athletic director for the University of Washington in May 1991. She was the first female athletic director of a National Collegiate Athletic Assocition (NCAA) Division I school that includes football.

Sources: Woolum, *Outstanding Women Athletes: Who They Are and How They Influenced Sports in America*, p. 31.

1992 • Terry Taylor became the first woman sports editor at the Associated Press wire service in October 1992. In 1994, she was director of worldwide sports coverage for the AP at their New York City office.

Sources: *Editor & Publisher* (26 February 1994), p. 15.

Mountain Climbing

1838 • Henriette d'Angeville (1795–1871) was the first woman to organize and undertake her own ascent of France's Mont Blanc. Other women had previously made it to the top by being hauled up, but in September 1838, d'Angeville reached the summit on her own after a three-day climb.

Sources: Uglow, *The Continuum Dictionary of Women's Biography,* p. 146.

c.1850 • Harriet Hosmer (1830–1908), a U.S. sculptor of international reputation, was the first woman to climb Mount Hosmer in Missouri, a mountain subsequently named after her. Her father encouraged a rigorous program of athletic activity after the early deaths of Hosmer's mother, sister, and brother. Hosmer went on to a distinguished career as an artist, studying in Boston and Rome, where she settled for most of her life. The most successful female sculptor of her day, she wore men's attire while working and established a studio that employed several stonecutters.

Sources: National Cyclopedia of American Biography, vol. I, p. 381. Uglow, *The Continuum Dictionary of Women's Biography,* p. 267.

1871 • Lucy Walker (1836–1916), an English mountaineer, was the first woman to climb the Matterhorn, in Switzerland. She reached the summit on July 20, 1871. Earlier, she had been the first woman to climb two other Swiss peaks: the Weisshorn and the Lyskamm. She was one of the first members of the Ladies' Alpine Club (the first society for female mountaineers, founded in London in 1907) and served as its second president, beginning in 1912.

Sources: Uglow, *The Continuum Dictionary of Women's Biography,* p. 565.

1888 • Katy Richardson (1864–1927), an English mountaineer, was the first person to climb the Aiguille de Bionnassay and to traverse the eastern ridge of the Dôme de Gouter, a route previously thought impossible, in the French Alps in 1888. Her remarkable athletic career between 1882 and 1893 included six pioneer first ascents and fourteen first ascents by a woman.

Sources: Uglow, *The Continuum Dictionary of Women's Biography,* p. 457.

1890 • On August 10, 1890, 20-year-old Fay Fuller reached the summit of Mount Rainier in Washington, the first woman to do so. Her only equipment was a blanket roll and a walking stick she made from a shovel handle.

Sources: McCullough, *First of All: Significant Firsts by American Women,* p. 149.

1900 • Mary Morris Vaux Walcott (1860–1940), a self-trained artist and naturalist and ardent athlete, was the first woman to climb Mount Stephen in British Columbia, Canada, in 1900. She is remembered for her definitive work, a result of her lifelong interest in nature, *North American Wild Flowers,* published by the Smithsonian Institute in 1925.

Sources: James, *Notable American Women,*, vol. 3, pp. 525–26; Walcott, *North American Wild Flowers*.

1907 • Elizabeth Le Blond (1861–1934) was the first president of the Ladies' Alpine Club, in London in 1907. This organization, the female counterpart of the all-male Alpine Club, encouraged mountaineering and scientific discovery. Le Blond achieved a number of firsts: she was the first woman to lead climbing parties without local guides (in the 1890s), and she was the first woman, with her friend Lady Evelyn McDonnel, to climb with ropes (during their ascent of Piz Palu in Italy in 1900).

Sources: Uglow, *The Continuum Dictionary of Women's Biography,* pp. 317.

1908 • Annie Smith Peck (1850–1935), a teacher by training and profession, was the first person to climb the north peak of Mount Huascaran in Peru, in 1908. At an altitude of 21,812 feet, this was at the time the highest altitude reached by any climber in the Western Hemisphere.

Sources: James, *Notable American Women,*, vol. 3, pp. 40–42; Read and Witlieb, *The Book of Women's Firsts,* pp. 337–38; Uglow, *The Continuum Dictionary of Women's Biography,* p. 427.

1932 • Miriam Underhill (b. 1900), a U.S. mountaineer, was the first woman to lead a group composed only of women on a successful ascent of the Matterhorn in Switzerland, reaching the summit on August 12, 1932. She was also the first woman to pioneer a route to the Torre Grande in the Italian Dolomites, a route now called the Via Miriam, in 1927. In 1928, she made the first traverse of the Grépon to be led by a woman and in the same year became the first person to complete a traverse of the Aiguille du Diable, both in the Alps.

Sources: Uglow, *The Continuum Dictionary of Women's Biography,* p. 552; Underhill, *Give Me the Hills.*

1954 • Claude Kogan (1919–1959), a French mountaineer, had a distinguished career in her active life that included a number of firsts. She was the first European woman to climb Cho Oyo, a peak in the Himalayas and reached the height of 25,000 feet, the highest point ever reached by a European woman, in 1954. Earlier, she was the first woman to reach the top of Sakantay in Peru's Cordillera Vilcabamba, in 1952, and the first person to climb Nun in the Punjab, in 1953. In 1955, she was the first person to ascend Ganesh Himal in the Himalayan range. She was also the first person to address a joint meeting of the Ladies' Alpine Club and the Alpine Club, in London in the mid-1950s. She died while leading an all-female party on an ascent of Cho Oyo.

Sources: Uglow, *The Continuum Dictionary of Women's Biography,* p. 302.

1975 • Junko Tabei (b. 1939), a Japanese mountaineer, was the first woman to reach the summit of Mount Everest. As deputy leader of an all-female Japanese expedition, she reached the top on May 16, 1975.

Sources: *The (Cleveland) Plain Dealer* (19 May 1996), p. 3-A.

1978 • Headed by American Arlene Blum, the first all-female expedition to climb Annapurna, the world's tenth-highest mountain, in the Himalayan mountains in Nepal, succeeded in reaching the summit in 1978. Two women died in the attempt.

Sources: Read and Witlieb, *The Book of Women's Firsts,* p. 206; Uglow, *The Continuum Dictionary of Women's Biography,* p. 73.

Beverly Johnson of Wyoming became the first woman to scale El Capitan in Yosemite National Park on October 2, 1978.

Sources: Woolum, *Outstanding Women Athletes: Who They Are and How They Influenced Sports in America,* p. 30.

Parachuting

1913 • Georgia "Tiny" Broadwick (1895–1978) was the first woman to free-fall parachute from an airplane. On June 21, 1913, Broadwick jumped from a plane flying at 1,000 feet near Los Angeles, California, and landed safely in a barley field.

Sources: Read and Witlieb, *The Book of Women's Firsts,* p. 69.

1977 • Mary Ledbetter was the first woman to win the World Accuracy Title in parachuting. She achieved this record at the twelfth annual Parachuting Championship in Rome, Italy, in 1977. In eight jumps from 2,500 feet, her total accumulated distance from the target was less than four feet.

Sources: O'Neill, *The Women's Book of World Records and Achievements,* p. 591.

Polo

1910 • Eleonora Sears (1881–1968) was the first woman to play against men in a polo match. The game took place at Narragansett Pier, Rhode Island, on August 13, 1910. She played for two periods riding sidesaddle and two periods astride.

Sources: Read and Witlieb, *The Book of Women's Firsts,* p. 398.

Rodeo

1956 • The College Rodeo Nationals featured a women's event for the first time; the barrel race was won by Kathleen Younger of Colorado A&M.

Sources: Woolum, *Outstanding Women Athletes: Who They Are and How They Influenced Sports in America,* p. 27

Shooting

1952 • Sponsored by the National Rifle Association, the first match was held for the Randle Women's International Team Trophy in 1952, which goes to the winning 10-woman team in a small-bore rifle match. The U.S. women's team won for the first 13 years before the British triumphed in 1965.

Sources: Woolum, *Outstanding Women Athletes: Who They Are and How They Influenced Sports in America,* p. 27.

1975 • Margaret Murdock, a U.S. athlete competing against men, was the first woman to win a gold medal in the overall shooting events at the Pan American Games. She achieved this record in 1975.

Sources: O'Neill, *The Women's Book of World Records and Achievements,* p. 565.

Skating, Figure

1908 • Madge Sayers, an English figure skater, was the first woman to win an Olympic gold medal in individual competition, in London, England, in 1908, the first year in which this event was open to female competitors.

Sources: O'Neill, *The Women's Book of World Records and Achievements,* p. 574.

1952 • Jeannette Altwegg (b. 1930) was the first English skater to be awarded an Order of the British Empire medal, in 1952. She was honored for her achievements in figure skating in world championships and at the 1952 Olympics at Oslo, Norway, where she won a gold medal.

Sources: Uglow, *The Continuum Dictionary of Women's Biography,* p. 14.

1953 • Tenley Albright (b. 1935) was the first U.S. woman to win the World Figure Skating Championship on February 15, 1953. Three years later, on February 2, 1956, Albright won the gold medal in figure skating at the winter Olympic Games in Cortina, Italy, the first American woman to do so. At the time, Albright was a premedical student; she eventually became a successful physician.

Sources: Woolum, *Outstanding Women Athletes: Who They Are and How They Influenced Sports in America,* p. 27.

Skating, Ice

1820s • Henriette Gertrud Walpurgis Sontag (1806–1854), a German soprano of international fame, was the first woman to skate on the Spree River that runs through Berlin, in the 1820s. Idolized throughout Europe, she died of cholera while touring in Mexico.

Sources: Uglow, *The Continuum Dictionary of Women's Biography,* pp. 506–7.

Skating, Ice Dancing

1976 • Ludmilla Pakhomova, a Russian athlete, with her partner Alexander Gorshkov, was the first woman to win a gold medal in Olympic ice dancing. She achieved this distinction the first time this event was offered in Olympic competition, in Innsbruck, Austria, in 1976.

Sources: O'Neill, *The Women's Book of World Records and Achievements,* p. 563.

Tenley Albright

Skating, Roller

1976 • Natalie Dunn (b. 1956) was the first U.S. athlete to win the world title in figure roller skating, in Rome, Italy, in 1976. She successfully defended her crown the following year in Montreal, Canada. Dunn won her first event at the age of seven and in 1972 took the national women's singles title.

Sources: O'Neill, *The Women's Book of World Records and Achievements,* p. 565; Read and Witlieb, *The Book of Women's Firsts,* p. 127.

Skating, Speed

1960 • Helga Haase, a German athlete, was the first woman to win an Olympic gold medal in the 500-meter speed skating event, in Squaw Valley, California, in 1960, the first time this event was open to female competitors.

Sources: O'Neill, *The Women's Book of World Records and Achievements,* p. 574.

Klara Guseva, representing the Soviet Union, was the first woman to win an Olympic gold medal in the 1,000-meter speed skating event, in Squaw Valley, California, in 1960, the first year in which this event was open to women.

Sources: O'Neill, *The Women's Book of World Records and Achievements,* p. 574.

1964 • A schoolteacher from Siberia, USSR, Lydia Skoblikova (b. 1939), was the first athlete (male or female) to win four gold medals in a single winter Olympics. She achieved this triumph in 1964 during the games held at Innsbruck, Austria. Her gold medals were won in four speed skating events: 500-meters, 1,000 meters, 1,500 meters, and 3,000 meters. She had won the gold medal in both the 1,500 and 3,000 meters speed skating events at the 1960 Winter Olympics in Squaw Valley, California.

Sources: O'Neill, *The Women's Book of World Records and Achievements,* p. 574; Wallechinsky and Wallace, *The People's Almanac,* p. 1211.

1994 • On February 23, 1994, Bonnie Blair (b. 1964) became the first U.S. woman to win five gold medals at a winter Olympics when she won the 1,000 meter speed skating race in Hamar, Norway. Winning an additional bronze medal during this Olympiad, Blair became the United States' most successful winter Olympian.

Sources: The New York Times (24 February 1994), p. A1.

Skiing

1941 • Joy Piles Lucas (b. 1917) was the first woman to be certified as a professional ski instructor. She passed her certification exam in April 1941, and has made a career teaching skiing.

Sources: Read and Witlieb, *The Book of Women's Firsts,* p. 263.

1948 • Hedy Schlunegger, a Swiss athlete, was the first woman to win an Olympic gold medal in downhill skiing, in St. Moritz, Switzerland, in 1948, the first year in which this event was open to women.

Sources: O'Neill, *The Women's Book of World Records and Achievements,* p. 574.

Gretchen Fraser (b. 1919) became the first U.S. woman to win a medal in skiing when she won a silver medal in the women's alpine combined event at the Winter Olympics held in St. Moritz, Switzerland, on February 4, 1948. The next day she earned the first gold medal in skiing awarded to a U.S. skier when she won the special slalom event.

Sources: O'Neill, *The Women's Book of World Records and Achievements*, p. 574; Read and Witlieb, *The Book of Women's Firsts*, p. 166.

1952 • Andrea Mead Lawrence (b. 1932), a U.S. skier, was the first woman to win an Olympic gold medal in the giant slalom, in Oslo, Norway, in 1952, the first year in which this event was open to female competitors.

Sources: O'Neill, *The Women's Book of World Records and Achievements*, p. 574.

Lydia Wideman, a Finnish athlete, was the first woman to win an Olympic gold medal in the 10-kilometer cross-country skiing event. She achieved this record in Oslo, Norway, in 1952, the first year in which this event was open to female competitors.

Sources: O'Neill, *The Women's Book of World Records and Achievements*, p. 574.

1956 • The Finnish women's ski team was the first women's team to win an Olympic gold medal in the 4x5-kilometer relay. This team achieved its record at the winter games in Cortina d'Ampezzo, Italy, in 1956, the first year in which this cross country event was open to female competitors.

Sources: O'Neill, *The Women's Book of World Records and Achievements*, p. 574.

1964 • Klaudia Boyerskikh, a Soviet athlete, was the first woman to win an Olympic gold medal in the 5-kilometer cross-country skiing event. She achieved this record in Innsbruck, Austria, in 1964, the first year in which this event, also called Nordic skiing, was open to women.

Sources: O'Neill, *The Women's Book of World Records and Achievements*, p. 574.

1974 • Marion Lee Post (b. 1955) was the first athlete to win the Women's Ballet and Freestyle Ski Competition, in 1974, the first time it was held. She became champion when she skied a nearly perfect run in the 60-second routine.

Sources: O'Neill, *The Women's Book of World Records and Achievements*, p. 566.

Julie Meissner, a ski instructor and racing coach from Idaho, was the first woman to win the all-around Freestyle event at the Women's International Ballet and Freestyle Ski Competition. She achieved this distinction the first time this event was held, in 1974.

Sources: O'Neill, *The Women's Book of World Records and Achievements*, p. 566.

Soccer

1981 • Betty Ellis (b. 1941) was hired by the North American Soccer League as a referee. Ellis became the first woman to officiate at a professional soccer game when she served as a referee at a match between the San José Earthquakes and the Edmonton Drillers on May 10, 1981.

Sources: Read and Witlieb, *The Book of Women's Firsts,* p. 144; Woolum, *Outstanding Women Athletes: Who They Are and How They Influenced Sports in America,* p. 30.

1991 • The United States was the first team to win the Women's World Soccer Championship. The U.S. team defeated Norway in final playoffs on November 30, 1991, in Guangzhov, China.

Sources: Read and Witlieb, *The Book of Women's Firsts,* p. 413; Woolum, *Outstanding Women Athletes: Who They Are and How They Influenced Sports in America,* p. 31.

Softball

1976 • The Connecticut Falcons were the first women's softball team to win the women's World Series championship title. This team beat the San Jose Sunbirds during the first women's World Series, held in 1976.

Sources: O'Neill, *The Women's Book of World Records and Achievements,* p. 569.

Squash

1928 • Eleanora Sears (1881–1968) won the first U.S. women's squash racquets singles championship at the Round Hill Club in Greenwich, Connecticut.

Sources: Woolum, *Outstanding Women Athletes: Who They Are and How They Influenced Sports in America,* p. 26.

Surfing

1975 • Margo Oberg (b. 1955), who won her first surfing title at the Menehune Competition at La Jolla, California, at the age of 12, was the first woman to win the Hang Ten International Surfing Competition, held in Malibu, California, in 1975. This was the first professional surfing contest held for women.

Sources: O'Neill, *The Women's Book of World Records and Achievements,* p. 585.

Swimming

1907 • Australian swimmer and actress Annette Kellerman (1888–1975) appeared on Revere Beach in Boston, Massachusetts, in a one-piece bathing suit, one of the first women to appear in public in such attire.

Sources: Woolum, *Outstanding Women Athletes: Who They Are and How They Influenced Sports in America,* p. 25.

1912 • The British women's relay swimming team was the first women's team to win an Olympic gold medal in the 4x100-meter freestyle relay event,

Annette Kellerman

in Stockholm, Sweden, in 1912, the first year in which this event was open to women.

Sources: O'Neill, *The Women's Book of World Records and Achievements,* p. 573.

Fanny Durack (1894–1960), an Australian athlete, was the first woman to win a swimming event at an Olympic Games. She won the 100-meter freestyle event, the only one then open to women, in Stockholm, Sweden, in 1912.

Sources: O'Neill, *The Women's Book of World Records and Achievements,* p. 572; Uglow, *The Continuum Dictionary of Women's Biography,* p. 178.

1914 • The Amateur Athletic Union (AAU) permitted the registration of women swimmers in 1914. The next year, the AAU began considering and establishing women's swimming records.

Source: Woolum, *Outstanding Women Athletes: Who They Are and How They Influenced Sports in America,* p. 25.

1916 • The Amateur Athletic Union held its first national championships in women's swimming, both indoors and outdoors, with four events including races of 440 and 880 yards and one mile, plus one diving contest.

Source: Woolum, *Outstanding Women Athletes: Who They Are and How They Influenced Sports in America,* p. 26.

1924 • Martha Norelius (1908–1955), a U.S. athlete, was the first woman to win an Olympic gold medal in the 400-meter freestyle swimming event, in Paris, France, in 1924, the first year that this event was open to women.

Sources: O'Neill, *The Women's Book of World Records and Achievements,* p. 572.

Sybil Bauer, a swimmer representing the United States, was the first woman to win an Olympic gold medal in the 100-meter backstroke event, in Paris, France, in 1924, the first year in which this event was open to female competitors. When she won this race, Bauer became the first woman to break an existing men's world swimming record, with a time for the 100-meter backstroke of 1.232 minutes.

Sources: O'Neill, *The Women's Book of World Records and Achievements,* p. 572; Woolum, *Outstanding Women Athletes: Who They Are and How They Influenced Sports in America,* p. 26.

Lucy Morton, a swimmer from Great Britain, was the first woman to win an Olympic gold medal in the 200-meter breaststroke event, in Paris, France, in 1924, the first year in which this event was open to women.

Sources: O'Neill, *The Women's Book of World Records and Achievements,* p. 573.

Sybil Bauer

1926 • U.S. swimmer Gertrude Ederle (b. 1906) was the first woman to swim the English Channel. She left Cap Gris-Nez, France, on August 6, 1926, and reached Dover, England, 14 hours and 31 minutes later, breaking the previous men's record by one hour and 59 minutes.

Sources: Read and Witlieb, *The Book of Women's Firsts,* pp. 137–38; Uglow, *The Continuum Dictionary of Women's Biography,* p. 183.

1932 • Helene Madison of Seattle, Washington, became the first woman ever to swim one hundred yards in less than one minute.

Sources: Woolum, *Outstanding Women Athletes: Who They Are and How They Influenced Sports in America,* p. 26.

1944 • Swimmer Ann Curtis (b. 1926) became the first woman to win the James E. Sullivan Award of the Amateur Athletic Union (AAU) in 1944. The award is given to the amateur athlete who best advances the cause of sportsmanship during that year.

Sources: McCullough, *First of All: Significant Firsts by American Women,* p. 158; Woolum, *Outstanding Women Athletes: Who They Are and How They Influenced Sports in America,* p. 27.

Ann Curtis

1950 • Florence Chadwick (1919–1995) was the first woman to swim both ways across the English Channel. She swam from France to England in 1950, setting a new record of 13 hours and 20 minutes; and the next year, she swam the more difficult route from England to France. (*See* **Sports: Swimming, 1951.**) Over her lifetime, Chadwick swam the English Channel four times and the Catalina Channel between California and Catalina Island three times.

Sources: *The New York Times* (19 March 1995), p. A47; Uglow, *The Continuum Dictionary of Women's Biography*, p. 117; Woolum, *Outstanding Women Athletes: Who They Are and How They Influenced Sports in America*, p. 27.

1951 • In September 1951, Florence Chadwick (1919–1995) was the first woman to swim the English Channel using the more difficult route from England to France. Her time was 16 hours and 22 minutes, and she was the first woman to complete a round trip: 12 women, including Chadwick herself (*See* **Sports: Swimming, 1950**), had previously swum the English Channel from France to England (a somewhat easier feat). Chadwick went on to become the first woman to swim the 21-mile channel between Catalina Island and Los Angeles, California, in 1952.

Sources: *The New York Times* (19 March 1995), p. A47; Uglow, *The Continuum Dictionary of Women's Biography*, p. 117.

1956 • Shelley Mann, a swimmer from the United States, was the first woman to win an Olympic gold medal in the 100-meter butterfly event, in Melbourne, Australia, in 1956, the first year in which this event was open to female competitors.

Sources: O'Neill, *The Women's Book of World Records and Achievements*, p. 573.

Dawn Fraser

Late 1950s • Dawn Fraser (b. 1937), an Australian athlete, was the first woman to swim 100 meters and 110 yards in under a minute. She was also the first competitor to win the 100-meter freestyle gold medal at the Olympic games in three successive games: in 1956, 1960, and 1964.

Sources: Uglow, *The Continuum Dictionary of Women's Biography*, p. 213.

1960 • The U.S. women's relay swimming team was the first women's team to win an Olympic gold medal in the 4x100-meter medley relay event, in Rome, Italy, in 1960, the first year in which this event was open to female competitors.

Sources: O'Neill, *The Women's Book of World Records and Achievements*, p. 573.

1964 • Donna de Varona (b. 1947), a U.S. swimmer, was the first woman to win an Olympic gold medal in the 400-meter individual medley event, in Tokyo, Japan, in 1964, the first year in which this event was open to women.

Sources: O'Neill, *The Women's Book of World Records and Achievements*, p. 573.

1968 • Djurdjica Bjedov, a Yugoslavian swimmer, was the first woman to win an Olympic gold medal in the 100-meter breaststroke, in Mexico City, Mexico, in 1968, the first year in which this event was open to women.

Sources: O'Neill, *The Women's Book of World Records and Achievements*, p. 572.

Donna de Varona

Ada Kok, a swimmer from the Netherlands, was the first woman to win an Olympic gold medal in the 200-meter butterfly event, in Mexico City, Mexico, in 1968, the first year in which this event was open to women.

Sources: O'Neill, *The Women's Book of World Records and Achievements,* p. 573.

Deborah Meyers (b. 1952) became the first woman to win three individual Olympic gold medals at one competition when, at the 1968 Olympics in Mexico City, Mexico, she won the 200-, 400-, and 800-meter freestyle events. She was the first woman to win both the 200- and 800-meter events.

Sources: O'Neill, *The Women's Book of World Records and Achievements,* p. 572; Read and Witlieb, *The Book of Women's Firsts,* p. 289.

Lillian Debra Watson (b. 1950) was the first woman to win the Olympic 200-meter backstroke event. She achieved this feat in 1968 at the Mexico City, Mexico games, the first year this event was held.

Sources: O'Neill, *The Women's Book of World Records and Achievements,* p. 572; Read and Witlieb, *The Book of Women's Firsts,* pp. 473–74.

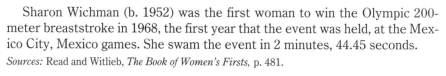

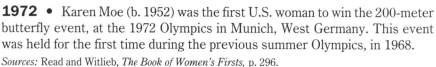

Sharon Wichman (b. 1952) was the first woman to win the Olympic 200-meter breaststroke in 1968, the first year that the event was held, at the Mexico City, Mexico games. She swam the event in 2 minutes, 44.45 seconds.

Sources: Read and Witlieb, *The Book of Women's Firsts,* p. 481.

1972 • Karen Moe (b. 1952) was the first U.S. woman to win the 200-meter butterfly event, at the 1972 Olympics in Munich, West Germany. This event was held for the first time during the previous summer Olympics, in 1968.

Sources: Read and Witlieb, *The Book of Women's Firsts,* p. 296.

1973 • The first Women's World Invitational Swim Meet was held at East Los Angeles College, California, in February 1973.

Sources: Woolum, *Outstanding Women Athletes: Who They Are and How They Influenced Sports in America,* p. 29.

Karen Moe

1975 • Diana Nyad (b. 1949), a U.S. athlete, was the first person to swim across Lake Ontario. The 32-mile non-stop journey took this marathon swimmer 20 hours. Also this year, Nyad swam around Manhattan Island in 7 hours, 57 minutes, breaking a record set by Bryan Somers almost 50 years before.

Sources: O'Neill, *The Women's Book of World Records and Achievements,* p. 586; Woolum, *Outstanding Women Athletes: Who They Are and How They Influenced Sports in America,* p. 29.

1976 • The first East German women's team to win a gold medal in swimming at the Olympic Games was led by Kornelia Ender (b. 1958) in Montreal, Canada, in 1976. During these games the East Germans took 11 of the 13 gold medals awarded.

Sources: O'Neill, *The Women's Book of World Records and Achievements,* p. 586.

1984 • Tracie Ruiz (b. 1963) was the first athlete to win the synchronized swimming event at an Olympic games. The event was approved for competition three months before Ruiz won it at the Olympic games in 1984 in Los Angeles, California.

Sources: Read and Witlieb, *The Book of Women's Firsts,* p. 385.

Tracie Ruiz

Tennis

1887 • Lottie Dod (1871–1960), known at the age of 12 as "the little wonder," was the first female tennis prodigy. In 1887, two months short of her sixteenth birthday, she became the first teenager ever to win the women's singles at Wimbledon.

Sources: Uglow, *The Continuum Dictionary of Women's Biography,* p. 171.

1896 • The first national women's tennis championships in the United States were held at the Philadelphia, Pennsylvania, Country Club in 1896. The singles championship was won by Ellen Hansell Allardice.
Sources: Read and Witlieb, *The Book of Women's Firsts,* p. 440.

1905 • May Sutton Bundy (1887–1975) was the first woman to win the women's singles title at the Wimbledon Lawn Tennis Championships, in 1905, defeating Doris K. Douglas of Great Britain. She won the title again in 1907. A competitor until 1928, Sutton was inducted into the International Tennis Hall of Fame in 1956.
Sources: Read and Witlieb, *The Book of Women's Firsts,* pp. 431–32; Woolum, *Outstanding Women Athletes: Who They Are and How They Influenced Sports in America,* p. 25.

1914 • Dorothea Douglass (1878–1960), an avid tennis player throughout her life, was the first woman to win seven Wimbledon singles titles. She won in 1903, 1904, 1906, 1910, 1911, 1913, and 1914. She might well have increased this number had Wimbledon not closed for five years during World War I.
Sources: Uglow, *The Continuum Dictionary of Women's Biography,* pp. 172–73.

1917 • Lucy Diggs Slowe (1885–1937) became the first black woman to be a U.S. national champion in any sport when in August 1917 she won the women's singles event at the all-black American Tennis Association championships, held in Druid Hill Park in Baltimore, Maryland.
Sources: Smith, *Black Firsts,* p. 404.

1919 • French tennis champion Suzanne Lenglen (1899–1938) revolutionized women's tennis dress by appearing for a match in a short-sleeved, one-piece pleated dress, without a petticoat.
Sources: Woolum, *Outstanding Women Athletes: Who They Are and How They Influenced Sports in America,* p. 26.

1920s • Suzanne Lenglen (1899–1938), an outstanding French athlete despite her poor background and persistent health problems, is the woman ranked first in all-time ratings of female tennis players. She dominated the game in her own country from 1914, when she won the international Clay Court Championship at St. Cloud, and was the world's best-known amateur tennis star from her first Wimbledon title in 1919 until she turned professional in 1926. She won the French championship seven times (although she missed the event in 1924 because of jaundice). She died of pernicious anemia on the eve of Wimbledon in 1938 and was awarded a posthumous Cross of the Légion d'Honneur in France.
Sources: Magnusson, *Larousse Biographical Dictionary,* p. 882; Uglow, *The Continuum Dictionary of Women's Biography,* pp. 321–22.

1923 • The first international women's tennis competition was the Wightman Cup, established by Hazel Hotchkiss Wightman (1886–1974). Hotchkiss Wightman donated a silver vase, in honor of her husband George Wightman, to the U.S. Lawn Tennis Association as a prize in international women's team

tennis. The first match, between the United States and Great Britain, took place in Forest Hills, New York, and was won by Hotchkiss and her partner, Eleanor Goss, for the United States.

Sources: Read and Witlieb, *The Book of Women's Firsts,* p. 481; Uglow, *The Continuum Dictionary of Women's Biography,* p. 580; Woolum, *Outstanding Women Athletes: Who They Are and How They Influenced Sports in America,* p. 26.

1924 • Hazel Hotchkiss Wightman (1886–1974) became the first woman to win an Olympic gold medal in mixed doubles tennis, in 1924 in Paris, France. With Helen Wills (later Moody), Hotchkiss Wightman was a member of the first U.S. women's doubles team to win a gold medal, also at the 1924 Olympics.

Sources: Read and Witlieb, *The Book of Women's Firsts,* p. 217.

Helen Wills (b. 1905) (later Moody) was the first U.S. woman to win gold medals in both women's singles and doubles tennis at the same Olympic games, in 1924 in Paris, France. She and Hazel Hotchkiss Wightman defeated Great Britain in the doubles match.

Sources: Read and Witlieb, *The Book of Women's Firsts,* p. 485.

1931 • On June 23, 1931, Lili de Alvarez appeared on center court at Wimbledon wearing shorts, the first woman to don such radical attire in the prestigious tennis event.

Sources: Woolum, *Outstanding Women Athletes: Who They Are and How They Influenced Sports in America,* p. 26.

1935 • Helen Wills Moody (b. 1905), a U.S. tennis player known for her expressionless concentration, was the first person to win the singles at Wimbledon eight times, in 1935. She was also the first woman to win 31 titles in the combined tournaments at Wimbledon, Forest Hills, and Paris, between 1926 and 1938, when she retired.

Sources: Uglow, *The Continuum Dictionary of Women's Biography,* pp. 386–87.

Ora Mae Washington (1898–1971) was the first black woman to win seven consecutive titles in the American Tennis Association, in 1935. This all-black organization held its tournaments at Druid Hill Park in Baltimore, Maryland, beginning in 1917.

Sources: O'Neill, *The Women's Book of World Records and Achievements,* p. 583; Smith, *Black Firsts,* p. 404.

1950 • Althea Gibson (b. 1927), a black woman, broke the color barrier in tennis playing at the U.S. National Tennis Championship at Forest Hills, New York. (*See also* **Sports: Tennis, 1957.**)

Sources: Woolum, *Outstanding Women Athletes: Who They Are and How They Influenced Sports in America,* p. 27.

1953 • Maureen Connolly (1934–1969) became the first woman to win the grand slam of tennis in 1953. After winning the Wimbledon Championship in England in 1952, she went on to win the Australian, French, and U.S. tennis

Opposite page: French tennis champion Suzanne Lenglen.

Helen Wills Moody

championships, thus achieving the four triumphs that comprise the "grand slam" in this sport.

Sources: Read and Witlieb, *The Book of Women's Firsts,* pp. 99–100; Uglow, *The Continuum Dictionary of Women's Biography,* pp. 135–36; Wallechinsky and Wallace, *The People's Almanac,* p. 1188; Woolum, *Outstanding Women Athletes: Who They Are and How They Influenced Sports in America,* p. 27.

1957 • Althea Gibson (b. 1927) was the first black woman player to win a Wimbledon tennis title in the women's singles on July 6, 1957. Later that month, on July 21, Gibson won the first national clay court singles championship, the first black woman to win a major U.S. tennis title.

Sources: Woolum, *Outstanding Women Athletes: Who They Are and How They Influenced Sports in America,* p. 27.

1968 • Althea Gibson (b. 1927), a U.S. tennis player, was the first black person inducted into the International Tennis Hall of Fame, in 1968. Her career in sports includes a number of firsts: she was the first black invited to play in the American Lawn Tennis Association championships, in 1950; she was the first black to win at Wimbledon, in 1957; and she was the first black athlete to win a major U.S. national championship when she played at Forest Hills, New York, also in 1957. In 1991 she became the first black woman to receive the Theodore Roosevelt Award of the NCAA.

Sources: Chicago, *The Dinner Party*, p. 193; Gibson and Curtis, *So Much to Live For*; Smith, *Black Firsts*, p. 405; Uglow, *The Continuum Dictionary of Women's Biography*, pp. 223–24.

1970 • Billie Jean King (b. 1943); Gladys Heldman, publisher of *World Tennis* magazine; and eight other players organized the Virginia Slims Tennis Tournament in Houston, Texas, in 1973. It was the first tournament for women professional tennis players held separate from male players.

Sources: Woolum, *Outstanding Women Athletes: Who They Are and How They Influenced Sports in America*, p. 28.

Tennis star Billie Jean King (b. 1943) was the first female athlete in any sport to earn more than $100,000 in a single season, in 1970.

Sources: Woolum, *Outstanding Women Athletes: Who They Are and How They Influenced Sports in America*, p. 28.

Billie Jean King

1971 • Phyllis Graber was the first woman to become a member of a previously all-male New York City high school varsity tennis team. She achieved this distinction in 1971 when, supported by the New York Civil Liberties Union and the Human Rights Commission, she became a member of the boys' varsity tennis team at Jamaica High School in Queens. As a result of her determination, it was ruled that girls can compete with boys in non-contact sports in New York.

Sources: O'Neill, *The Women's Book of World Records and Achievements*, p. 583.

1973 • The United States Tennis Association (USTA) announced that the U.S. Open tennis championships would award equal prize money to women and men on July 19, 1973.

Sources: Woolum, *Outstanding Women Athletes: Who They Are and How They Influenced Sports in America*, p. 29.

1974 • Kazuko Sawamatsu (b. 1951) became the first female tennis player in Japan to turn professional when she won a title at the prestigious Wimbledon Championships in 1974. In her own country she had won 192 consecutive tournaments, a world record.

Sources: O'Neill, *The Women's Book of World Records and Achievements*, p. 583.

1980s • Martina Navratilova (b. 1957), a tennis player who was born in Czechoslovakia but defected to the United States while competing at the U.S. Open in New York in 1975, is the first athlete to win over nine million dollars in prize money. She is known internationally as a tennis star but also for her outspoken and courageous views on lesbian issues and for the Martina Foundation. This organization, which she founded in 1983 with a large portion of her prize money, is devoted to helping underprivileged children throughout the world.

Sources: Uglow, *The Continuum Dictionary of Women's Biography,* p. 397.

Track and Field

1923 • The Amateur Athletic Union (AAU) sponsored the first major outdoor track and field meet for women at Newark, New Jersey, in 1923. Winners were 100-meter dash: Frances Rupert (12 seconds); 80-meter hurdles: Hazel Kirk (9.6 seconds); 400-meter relay: the Meadowbrook Club team of Philadelphia (52.4 seconds); high jump: Catherine Wright (4 feet, 7 1/2 inches); long jump: Helen Dinnehey (15 feet, 4 inches); eight pound shot put: Bertha Christophel (30 feet, 10 1/2 inches); discus throw: Babe Wolbert (71 feet, 9 1/2 inches); javelin: Roberta Ranck (59 feet, 7 3/4 inches); softball throw: Elinor Churchill (284 feet, 5 3/4 inches).

Sources: Woolum, *Outstanding Women Athletes: Who They Are and How They Influenced Sports in America,* p. 26.

1925 • The first woman to clear the five-foot barrier in the high jump was Phyllis Green of Great Britain on July 11, 1925.

Source: Woolum, *Outstanding Women Athletes: Who They Are and How They Influenced Sports in America,* p. 26.

1928 • Lina Radke, a German runner, was the first woman to win an Olympic gold medal in the 800-meter track and field event, in Amsterdam, the Netherlands, in 1928, the first year in which this event was open to women. It was subsequently discontinued and not open again to female competitors until 1960, when a Soviet woman, Lyudmila Schevtsova, won this grueling event.

Sources: O'Neill, *The Women's Book of World Records and Achievements,* p. 573.

Ethel Catherwood, a Canadian athlete, was the first woman to win an Olympic gold medal in the high jump, in Amsterdam, the Netherlands, in 1928, the first year in which this track and field event was open to female competitors.

Sources: O'Neill, *The Women's Book of World Records and Achievements,* p. 573.

Halina Konopacka (b. 1900), a Polish athlete, was the first woman to win an Olympic gold medal in the discus, in Amsterdam, the Netherlands, in 1928, the first year in which this track and field event was open to women.

Sources: O'Neill, *The Women's Book of World Records and Achievements,* p. 573.

The Canadian women's track and field team was the first team to win an Olympic gold medal in the 4x100-meter relay, in Amsterdam, the Netherlands, in 1928, the first time that this event was open to female competitors.

Sources: O'Neill, *The Women's Book of World Records and Achievements,* p. 573.

Elizabeth Robinson (b. 1912) was the first woman to win the 100-meter dash at the Olympics in 1928 in Amsterdam, the Netherlands, the first time the event was held. She went on to a career in sports, specializing in shooting as well as running.

Sources: O'Neill, *The Women's Book of World Records and Achievements,* p. 573; Read and Witlieb, *The Book of Women's Firsts,* pp. 374–75.

1932 • Jean Shiley (b. 1911) was the first U.S. woman to win the high jump event at an Olympic games, in 1932 in Los Angeles, California. From 1929 until 1932, she was the American Athletic Union (AAU) high jump champion.

Sources: Read and Witlieb, *The Book of Women's Firsts,* p. 406.

1948 • Olga Gyarmati, an Hungarian athlete, was the first woman to win an Olympic gold medal in the long jump, in London, England, in 1948, the first year in which this track and field event was open to women.

Sources: O'Neill, *The Women's Book of World Records and Achievements,* p. 573.

Micheline Ostermyer, a French athlete, was the first woman to win an Olympic gold medal in the shot put, in London, England, in 1948, the first year in which this track and field event was open to female competitors.

Sources: O'Neill, *The Women's Book of World Records and Achievements,* p. 573.

Fanny Blankers-Koen (b. 1918) was the first woman to win four Olympic gold medals in track events. She achieved this honor at the Olympic games in London, England, in 1948, coming in first in the 100 meters, 200 meters, 80-meter hurdles and the 4x100 meters relay.

Sources: O'Neill, *The Women's Book of World Records and Achievements,* p. 573; Uglow, *The Continuum Dictionary of Women's Biography,* p. 70.

1958 • The first woman to clear six feet in the high jump was Romanian Iolanda Balas (b. 1936) on October 18, 1958. (*See also* **Sports: Track and Field, 1964.**)

Source: Woolum, *Outstanding Women Athletes: Who They Are and How They Influenced Sports in America,* p. 27.

1960 • Wilma Rudolph (1940–1994) was the first female runner to win three gold medals at a single Olympic games. In 1960 in Rome, Italy, she won the 100-meter and the 200-meter events and was on the winning team for the 400-meter relay. In 1980, Rudolph was named to the Women's Sports Hall of Fame.

Sources: Altman, *Wilma Rudolph: Run for Glory;* Read and Witlieb, *The Book of Women's Firsts,* pp. 384–85; Uglow, *The Continuum Dictionary of Women's Biography,* p. 468.

1964 • Mary Denise Rand (b. 1940) was the first English woman to win an Olympic gold medal. She won this honor for the long jump at the 1964 Tokyo, Japan, Olympics, where she became the first woman to jump a distance of 22'2".

Sources: Uglow, *The Continuum Dictionary of Women's Biography,* pp. 447–48.

Iolanda Balas

Betty Cuthbert (b. 1938), an Australian runner, was the first woman to win an Olympic gold medal in the 400-meter track and field event, in Tokyo, Japan, in 1964, the first year in which this event was open to women.

Sources: O'Neill, *The Women's Book of World Records and Achievements,* p. 573.

Irena Press, a Soviet athlete, was the first woman to win an Olympic gold medal in the pentathlon, in Tokyo, Japan, in 1964, the first year in which this track and field event was open to women.

Sources: O'Neill, *The Women's Book of World Records and Achievements,* p. 573.

Iolanda Balas (b. 1936) was the first athlete to win two Olympic gold medals in the high jump event. She won gold medals in both the 1960 and the 1964

Wilma Rudolph

Olympics in Rome, Italy and Tokyo, Japan respectively, breaking the Olympic record each time. (*See also* **Sports: Track and Field, 1958**.)

Sources: Uglow, *The Continuum Dictionary of Women's Biography,* p. 44.

1970 • Chi Cheng (b. 1944) of Taiwan was the first woman to run one hundred yards in 10 seconds in an official competition on June 13, 1970.

Sources: Woolum, *Outstanding Women Athletes: Who They Are and How They Influenced Sports in America,* p. 28.

1972 • The East German women's track and field team was the first to win an Olympic gold medal in the 4x400-meter relay, in Munich, West Germany, in 1972, the first time that this event was open to female athletes.

Sources: O'Neill, *The Women's Book of World Records and Achievements,* p. 573.

Lyudmila Bragina (b. 1943) became the first woman to win the Olympic 1,500-meter track event the first time this event was introduced, at the 1972 Olympics in Munich, West Germany. She set a world record for both women and men of 4 minutes, 1.4 seconds.

Sources: O'Neill, *The Women's Book of World Records and Achievements,* p. 573; Uglow, *The Continuum Dictionary of Women's Biography,* p. 85.

1975 • The U.S. women's lacrosse team, led by co-captains Meryl Werley and Connie Lanzel, beat the British team for the first time, in England.

Sources: O'Neill, *The Women's Book of World Records and Achievements,* p. 569.

1976 • Ivanka Khristova was the first Bulgarian woman to win an Olympic gold medal in a track and field event. At the summer Olympic games in Montreal, Canada, in 1976, Khristova came in first in the shot put and simultaneously set a world record.

Sources: O'Neill, *The Women's Book of World Records and Achievements,* p. 579.

Late 1970s • Marita Koch (b. 1957), a German track star, was the first woman to break the record of 49 seconds for 400 meters and 22 seconds for 200 meters. She has been voted the best female athlete in the world three times: in 1978, 1979, and 1982. During her career she set 16 world records outdoors and 14 world bests indoors.

Sources: Uglow, *The Continuum Dictionary of Women's Biography,* p. 302.

1984 • Joan Benoit (later Samuelson) (b. 1957), a U.S. athlete, won a gold medal for the women's marathon (26 miles, 385 yards) the first time it was held as an Olympic event in Los Angeles, California. Her running time was 2 hours, 24 minutes, and 52 seconds.

Sources: Read and Witlieb, *The Book of Women's Firsts,* pp. 46–47; Uglow, *The Continuum Dictionary of Women's Biography,* pp. 563–64.

1985 • Ingrid Kristiansen (b. 1956), a Norwegian athlete known for her achievements in cross-country skiing and especially in running, was the first person to set world records at 5,000 meters (in 1981 and 1984), at 10,000 meters (in 1985), and in the marathon (in 1985). She was undefeated in 1986, her best year.

Sources: Uglow, *The Continuum Dictionary of Women's Biography,* p. 306.

1989 • Lori Norwood became the first U.S. woman to win the individual title at the World Modern Pentathlon Championships.

Sources: Woolum, *Outstanding Women Athletes: Who They Are and How They Influenced Sports in America,* p. 31.

1990 • The first "women only" triathlon was held in Long Beach, California, in June 1990. More than 2,000 women competed in the three events: an ocean swim, a bicycle race, and a marathon run.

Sources: Read and Witlieb, *The Book of Women's Firsts,* p. 449.

Trapshooting

1913 • Harriet D. Hammond organized the first trapshooting club for women in Wilmington, Delaware, in July 1913.

Sources: Woolum, *Outstanding Women Athletes: Who They Are and How They Influenced Sports in America,* p. 25.

Volleyball

1968 • The Soviet women's volleyball team was the first team to win an Olympic gold medal in this event, in Mexico City, Mexico, the first year in which Olympic volleyball competition was open to female athletes.

Sources: Wallechinsky, *The Complete Book of the Olympics,* p. 504.

1975 • Mary Jo Peppler (b. 1944) was the first woman to win the volleyball Superstars competition the first year this event was held. She was voted outstanding volleyball player in the world at the 1970 International Games in Bulgaria and served as a member of the U.S. Olympic team in 1968.

Sources: O'Neill, *The Women's Book of World Records and Achievements,* p. 570.

1976 • Inna Ryskal (b. 1944), a Russian athlete, was the first woman to win four Olympic medals in volleyball. She won a silver medal at the 1964 Summer Olympic Games in Tokyo, Japan, and gold medals in 1968 (at Mexico City, Mexico), 1972 (at Munich, West Germany), and 1976 (Montreal, Canada).

Sources: O'Neill, *The Women's Book of World Records and Achievements,* p. 570.

The Soviet women's volleyball team was the first women's volleyball team to win three consecutive Olympic gold medals. They achieved this record at the 1976 Olympic Games in Montreal, Canada after having won in 1972 at Munich, West Germany and in 1968 at Mexico City, Mexico. This team was also the first to win a total of six championship titles—in 1952, 1956, 1960, 1968, 1970, and 1973.

Sources: O'Neill, *The Women's Book of World Records and Achievements,* p. 570; Wallechinsky, *The Complete Book of the Olympics,* pp. 504–5.

Weightlifting

1977 • Jan Todd bench pressed 176-¼ pounds, deadlifted 441 pounds, and lifted 424-¼ pounds from a squat to become the first woman ever to lift more than one thousand pounds in three power lifts.

Sources: Woolum, *Outstanding Women Athletes: Who They Are and How They Influenced Sports in America,* p. 29.

Bibliography

A

Acker, Ally. *Reel Women: Pioneers of the Cinema, 1896 to the Present*. New York: Continuum, 1991.

Adams, Brian. *La Stupenda: A Biography of Joan Sutherland*. Melborne: Hutchinson of Australia, 1980.

Alic, Margaret. *Hypatia's Heritage: A History of Women in Science from Antiquity through the Nineteenth Century*. Boston: Beacon Press, 1986.

Allen, A. J., Miss. *Ten Years in Oregon: Travels and Adventures of Dr. E. White and Lady, West of the Rocky Mountains*. Ithaca, New York: Mack, Andrus, and Co., Printers, 1848.

Altman, Linda Jacobs. *Wilma Rudolph: Run for Glory*. St. Paul, Minnesota: EMC Corp., 1975.

Ardoin, John. *The Callas Legacy: A Biography of a Career*. New York: Scribner, 1982.

Arnold, John, and Deidre Morris. *Monash Biographical Dictionary of 20th Century Australia*. Port Melbourne, Australia: Reed Reference Publishing, 1994.

Auriol, Jacqueline. *I Live to Fly*. New York: Dutton, 1970.

B

Bacon, Margaret Hope. *Valiant Friend: The Life of Lucretia Mott*. New York: Walker, 1980.

Bailey, Brooke. *The Remarkable Lives of 100 Woman Healers and Scientists*. Holbrook, Massachusetts: Bob Adams, 1994.

Banner, Lois W. *Elizabeth Cady Stanton: A Radical for Woman's Rights*. Boston: Little, Brown, 1980.

Baragwanath, John. *A Good Time Was Had*. New York: Appleton-Century-Crofts, 1962.

Baron, Beth. *The Women's Awakening in Egypt: Culture, Society, and the Press*. New Haven/London: Yale University Press, 1994.

Benedict, Ruth. *An Anthropologist at Work: Writings of Ruth Benedict, by Margaret Mead*. Boston: Houghton Mifflin, 1959.

Birks, Tony. *Lucie Rie*. Radnor: Chilton Trade Book Pub., 1987.

Blum, Arlene. *Annapurna: A Woman's Place*. San Francisco: Sierra Club Books, 1980.

Bosworth, Patricia. *Diane Arbus: A Biography*. New York: Knopf, 1984.

Briggs, Asa. *A Dictionary of Twentieth-Century World Biography*. Oxford: Oxford University Press, 1992.

Brockman, Norbert C. *An African Biographical Dictionary*. Santa Barbara: ABC-Clio, 1994.

Bruno, Giuliana. *Streetwalking on a Ruined Map: Cultural Theory and the City Films of Elvira Notari*. Princeton: Princeton University Press, 1993.

Buckley, Gail Lumet. *The Hornes: An American Family*. Boston: G. K. Hall, 1987.

Bulman, Joan. *Jenny Lind: A Biography*. London: J. Barrie, 1956.

Burnett, James. *Billie Holiday*. New York: Hippocrene Books, 1984.

C

Canadian Who's Who, Vol. 92. Toronto: University of Toronto Press, 1994.

Carter, Morris. *Isabella Stewart Gardner and Fenway Court.* Boston: Houghton Mifflin Company, 1925.

Charles-Roux, Edmonde. *Chanel and Her World.* New York: Vendome Press, 1981.

Chicago, Judy. *The Dinner Party.* New York: Anchor, 1979.

Cintròn, Lola Verrill. *Goddess of the Bullring; the Story Of Cinchita Cintròn, the World's Greatest Matadora.* London: F. Muller, 1961.

Clare, Sheridan. *To the Four Winds.* London: Deutsch, 1957.

Cobblestone: The History Magazine for Young People. June 1994.

Cochran, Jacqueline, with Maryann Bucknum Brinley. *Jackie Cochran.* New York: Bantam Books, 1987.

Cohen, Aaron I. *International Encyclopedia of Women Composers.* New York: Books & Music USA, Inc., 1987.

Collis, Louise. *Impetuous Heart: The Story of Ethel Smyth.* London: W. Kimber, 1984.

Comstock, Anna Botsford. *The Comstocks of Cornell: John Henry Comstock and Anna Botsford Comstock.* New York: Comstock Publishing Associates, 1953.

Cox, Ross. *Adventures on the Columbia River. 1831.* Sutro Branch, California State Library, Occasional Papers. Reprint Series No. 26. San Francisco: 1941.

Curie, Eve. *Madame Curie: A Biography.* New York: Da Capo Press, 1937.

D

Damon, Ethel Moseley. *Koamalu: A Story of Pioneers on Kauai.* Honolulu: Honolulu Star-Bulletin Press, 1931.

Davis, Allen Freeman. *Spearheads for Reform: The Social Settlements and the Progressive Movement, 1890-1914.* New York: Oxford University Press, 1979.

Davis, Burke. *Amelia Earhart.* New York: Putnam, 1972.

Day, Dorothy. *The Long Loneliness.* New York: Harper, 1952.

Delaney, John J., ed. *Saints Are Now.* Garden City, New York: Doubleday, 1981.

Delaunay, Sonia. *Sonia Delaunay: Rhythms and Colours.* Greenwich: New York Graphic Society, 1972.

DeValois, Ninette. *Come Dance with Me.* Cleveland: World Publishing Company, 1957.

———. *Invitation to the Ballet.* London: John Lane, 1937.

Dunbar, Janet. *Laura Knight.* London: Collins, 1975.

Duncan, Isadora. *My Life.* Tel-Aviv: Ketuvim, 1929.

———. *"Your Isadora": The Love Story of Isadora Duncan & Gordon Craig.* New York: Random House, 1974.

E

Edwards, George Thornton. *Music and Musicians of Maine.* Portland: The Southworth Press, 1928.

Erens, Patricia. *Sexual Stratagems: The World of Women in Film.* New York: Horizon Press, 1979.

F

Ferrin, Mary Upton. *Woman's Defence.* Peabody: C.D. Howard, 1869.

FitzLyon, April. *Maria Malibran: Diva of the Romantic Age.* London: Souvenir Press, 1987.

———. *The Price of Genius: A Life of Pauline Viardot.* London: John Calder, 1964.

Flannery, James W. *Miss Annie F. Horniman and the Abbey Theatre.* Dublin: Dolmen Press, 1970.

Flexner, Eleanor. *Century of Struggle: The Woman's Rights Movement in the United States.* Cambridge: Belknap Press of Harvard University Press, 1959.

Fonteyn, Dame Margot. *A Dancer's World: An Introduction.* London: Star Book, 1978.

———. *Margot Fonteyn*. New York: Knopf, 1976.

Fowler, Gene. *Father Goose*. New York: Blue Ribbon Books Inc, 1934.

Francis, Clare. *Come Hell or High Water*. Lancashire, England: Magna Print Books, 1979.

Freeland, Michael. *Jane Fonda: A Biography*. New York: St. Martin's Press, 1988.

Fuller, Loie. *Fifteen Years of a Dancer's Life*. London: H. Jenkins Ltd., 1913.

G

Gall, Susan, and Irene Natividad. *The Asian-American Almanac: A Reference Work on Asians in the United States*. Detroit: Gale Research, 1995.

Garden, Mary, and Louis Biancolli. *Mary Garden's Story*. New York: Simon and Schuster, 1951.

Gaume, Matilda. *Ruther Crawford Seeger: Memoirs, Memories, Music*. Metuchen: Scarecrow Press, 1986.

Gibson, Althea, with Richard Curtis. *So Much to Live For*. New York: Putnam, 1968.

Gipson, Richard McCandless. *The Life of Emma Thursby*. New York: The New York Historical Society, 1940.

Glackens, Ira. *William Glackens and the Ashcan Group*. New York: Crown Publishers, 1957.

Gompers, Samuel. *Seventy Years of Life and Labor: An Autobiography*. New York: E.P. Dutton & Company, 1925.

Goodall, Jane. *In the Shadow of Man*. Boston: Houghton Mifflin, 1971.

Gowing, Sir Lawrence. *A Biographical Dictionary of Artists*. Oxfordshire: Andromeda Oxford Ltd., 1995.

Grey, Beryl. *Red Curtain Up*. New York: Dodd, Mead, 1958.

———. *Through the Bamboo Curtain*. New York: Reynal, 1965.

Guest, Barbara. *Herself Defined: The Poet H.D. and Her World*. Garden City: Doubleday, 1984.

Guest, Ivor Forbes. *Adeline Genee: A Lifetime of Ballet Under Six Reigns*. London: A. and C. Black, 1958.

———. *The Romantic Ballet in Paris*. Middletown: Wesleyan University Press, 1966.

Guggenheim, Peggy. *Out of this Century: Confessions of an Art Addict*. London: Deutsch, 1980.

H

Haber, Louis. *Women Pioneers of Science*. New York: Harcourt Brace Jovanovich, 1979.

Hafkin, Nancy J., and Edna G. Bay, eds. *Women in Africa: Studies in Social and Economic Change*. Stanford, California: Stanford University Press, 1976.

Halliwell, Leslie. *The Filmgoer's Companion*. New York: Hill and Wang, 1970.

Hamel, Frank. *The Lady of Beauty*. London: Chapman and Hall, 1912.

Harding, Bertita. *Concerto: The Story of Clara Schumann*. London: G.C. Harrap, 1961.

Havemeyer, Louisine W. *Sixteen to Sixty: Memoirs of a Collector*. New York: Ursus Press, 1961.

Hay, Margaret Jean, and Sharon Stichter, eds. *African Women South of the Sahara*. London/New York: Longman, 1984.

Hayes, Harold. *The Dark Romance of Dian Fossey*. New York: Simon and Schuster, 1988.

Hayne, Donald. *The Autobiography of Cecil B. DeMille*. New York: Garland Pub., 1959.

Head, Edith, and Paddy Calistro. *Edith Head's Hollywood*. New York: Dutton, 1983.

Henry, Alice. *Women and the Labor Movement*. New York: George H. Doran Company, 1923.

Hinton, David B. *The Films of Leni Riefenstahl*. Metuchen: Scarecrow Press, 1978.

Hoffman, Malvina. *Heads and Tales*. New York: C. Scribner's Sons, 1936.

Hoffman, Malvina. *Yesterday Is Tomorrow: A Personal History*. New York: Crown Publishers, 1965.

Hoge, Alice Albright. *Cissy Patterson*. New York: Random House, 1966.

Holiday, Billie, and William Dufty. *Lady Sings the Blues*. New York: Doubleday, 1956.

Hopkins, Timothy. *The Kelloggs in the Old World and the New*. San Francisco: Sunset Press and Photo Engraving Co., 1903.

Howard, Jane. *Margaret Mead, a Life*. New York: Simon and Schuster, 1984.

Hoxie, Richard Leveridge. *Vinnie Ream*. San Francisco: A. Roman, 1871.

I

Iwai, Seiicho. *Biographical Dictionary of Japanese History*. Tokyo and San Francisco: Kodansho International Ltd., 1978.

J

James, Edward T., *et al.*, eds., *Notable American Women: A Biographical Dictionary*. Cambridge: Harvard University Press, 1971.

Johnston. *The Work of Dorothy Arzner: Towards a Feminist Cinema*. London: British Film Institute, 1975.

Jones, Enid Huws. *Margery Fry: The Essential Amateur*. London: Oxford University Press, 1966.

Jones, F. O. *A Handbook of American Music and Musicians*. Buffalo: C.W. Moulton, 1886.

Josephson, Hanna Geffen. *The Golden Threads: New England's Mill Girls and Magnates*. New York: Duell, Sloan and Pearce, 1949.

K

Kane, Nathan Joseph. *Famous First Facts*. New York: H.W. Wilson, 1981.

Katz, Ephraim. *The Film Encyclopedia*. New York: Crowell, 1979.

Kearns, Martha. *Kathe Kollwitz: Woman and Artist*. Old Westbury: Feminist Press, 1976.

Kerensky, Oleg. *Anna Pavlova*. New York: Dutton, 1973.

Keynes, Milo. *Lydia Lopokova*. London: Weidenfeld and Nicolson, 1983.

Knight, Dame Laura. *The Magic of a Line: The Autobiography of Laura Knight*. London: W. Kimber, 1965.

Kshessinska, Matilda Feliksovna. *Dancing Petersburg: The Memoirs of Kshessinska*. New York: Da Capo Press, 1960.

Kuhn, Walt. *The Story of the Armory Show*. New York: The Author, 1938.

L

Larue, C. Steven. *International Dictionary of Opera*. Detroit: St. James Press, 1993.

Leach, Joseph. *Bright Particular Star: The Life & Times of Charlotte Chushman*. New Haven: Yale University Press, 1970.

Leakey, Mary D. *Disclosing the Past*. Garden City, New York: Doubleday, 1984.

Lehmann, Lilli. *My Path through Life*. New York: G.P. Putman's Sons, 1914.

Levi-Montalcini, Rita. *In Praise of Imperfection: My Life and Work*. New York: Basic Books, 1988.

Levin, Beatrice. *Women and Medicine: Pioneers Meeting the Challenge!* Lincoln, Nebraska: Media Publishing, 1988.

Lieb, Sandra R. *Mother of the Blues: A Study of Ma Rainey*. Amherst: University of Massachusetts Press, 1981.

Loesser, Arthur. *Men, Women and Pianos: A Social History*. New York: Simon and Schuster, 1954.

Lubbock, Constance Ann Herschel, Lady, ed. *The Herschel Chronicle; The Life-Story of William Herschel and His Sister, Caroline Herschel*. New York: The MacMillan Company; Cambridge, England: The University Press, 1933.

Lutyens, Elisabeth. *A Goldfish Bowl*. London: Cassell, 1972.

Lutz, Alma. *Crusade for Freedom: Women of the Antislavery Movement*. Boston: Beacon Press, 1968.

———. *Created Equal: A Biography of Elizabeth Cady Stanton, 1815-1902.* New York: The John Day Company, 1940.

M

Macpherson, Don. *Leading Ladies.* New York: St. Martin's, 1986.

Magnusson, Magnus. *Larousse Biographical Dictionary.* Edinburgh: Larousse Kingfisher Chambers, Inc., 1994.

Magriel, Paul David. *Chronicles of the American Dance.* New York: Holt, 1948.

Maitland, Sara. *Vesta Tilley.* London: Virago, 1986.

Makeba, Miriam. *Makeba: My Story.* New York: New American Library, 1988.

Marion, Frances. *How to Write and Sell Film Stories.* New York: Garland Pub., 1937.

Markham, Beryl Clutterbuck. *West with the Night.* Boston: Houghton Mifflin, 1942.

Markova, Dame Alicia. *Giselle and I.* New York: Vanguard Press, 1961.

———. *Markova Remembers.* Boston: Little, Brown, 1986.

Masson, Georgina. *Courtesans of the Italian Renaissance.* New York: St. Martin's Press, 1975.

Matthews, Peter, ed. *The Guinness Book of World Records, 1994.* New York: Facts on File, Inc., 1993.

Matthews, W.S.B. *A Hundred Years of Music in America: An Account of Musical Effort in America.* Chicago: G.L. Howe, 1889.

McCullough, Joan. *First of All: Significant "Firsts" by American Women.* New York: Holt, Rinehart and Winston, 1980.

McGrayne, Sharon Bertsch. *Nobel Prize Women in Science: Their Lives, Struggles and Momentous Discoveries.* New York: Birch Lane Press, 1993.

McKenna, Marian Cecilia. *Myra Hess: A Portrait.* London: Hamilton, 1976.

Mead, Margaret. *Blackberry Winter; My Earlier Years.* New York: Simon and Schuster, 1972.

———. *Letters from the Field.* New York: Harper and Row, 1977.

Miller, William D. *Dorothy Day: A Biography.* San Francisco: Harper & Row, 1982.

N

Nash, Mary. *The Provok'd Wife: The Life and Times of Susannah Cibber.* Boston: Little, Brown, 1977.

Negri, Pola. *Memoirs of a Star.* Garden City: Doubleday, 1970.

Newman, Edgar Leon. *Historical Dictionary of France from the 1814 Restoration to the Second Empire.* Westport, Connecticut: Greenwood, 1987.

Nijinksa, Bronislava. *Bronislava Nijinksa: Early Memoirs.* Durham: Duke University Press, 1992.

Noble, Iris. *Contemporary Women Scientists of America.* New York: Julian Messner, 1979.

O

Ogilvie, Marilyn Bailey. *Women in Science: Antiquity through the Nineteenth Century.* Cambridge, Massachusetts: M.I.T. Press, 1986.

Ogundipe-Leslie, Molara. *Re-Creating Ourselves: African Women & Critical Transformations.* Trenton, New Jersey: Africa World Press, Inc., 1994.

Olsen, Kirstin. *Chronology of Women's History.* Westport: Greenwood Press, 1994.

O'Neill, Lois Decker, ed. *The Women's Book of World Records and Achievements.* Garden City, New York: Doubleday, 1979.

P

Parsons, Louella O. *The Gay Illiterate.* Garden City: Doubleday, Doran and Co., 1944.

Peck, Mary Gray. *Carrie Chapman Catt.* New York: The H.W. Wilson Company, 1944.

Pena, Israel. *Teresa Careno.* Caracas: Fudacion Eugenio Mendoze, 1953.

Peper, George, ed. with Robin McMillan and James A. Frank. *Golf in America: The First One Hundred Years.* New York: Harry N. Abrams, Inc., 1988.

Petteys, Chris. *Dictionary of Women Artists.* Boston: G.K. Hall & Co., 1985.

Ponder, Winifred. *Clara Butt: Her Life-Story.* New York: Da Capo Press, 1978.

Popp, Adelheid. *The Autobiography of a Working Woman.* Chicago: F.G. Browne, 1913.

Q

Quant, Mary. *Quant by Quant.* London: Cassell, 1966.

R

Rambert, Marie. *Quicksilver: The Autobiography of Marie Rambert.* London: Macmillan, 1972.

Raven, Susan, and Alison Weir. *Women of Achievement: Thirty-Five Centuries of History.* New York: Harmony Books, 1981.

Ravenel, Harriott Horry Rutledge. *Eliza Pinckney.* New York: C. Scribner's Sons, 1896.

Read, Phyllis, and Bernard L. Witlieb. *The Book of Women's Firsts.* New York: Random House, 1992.

Ricker, Marilla M. *I Am Not Afraid, Are You?* East Aurora: Roycrofters, 1917.

Rolka, Gail Meyer. *100 Women Who Shaped World History.* San Francisco: Bluewood Books, 1994.

Romero, Patricia W., ed. *Life Histories of African Women.* London: The Ashfield Press, 1988.

Rosen, Marjorie. *Popcorn Venus.* New York: Avon, 1974.

Rosenstiel, Leonie. *Nadia Boulanger: A Life in Music.* New York: W.W. Norton, 1982.

Ross, Alexander. *Adventures of the First Settlers on the Oregon or Columbia River.* Chicago: R. R. Donnelley & Sons Company, 1923.

Russo, Vito. *The Celluloid Closet: Homosexuality in the Movies.* New York: Harper & Row, 1987.

S

Sadie, Stanley. *The New Grove Dictionary of Opera.* London: Macmillan Press Ltd., 1992.

Sanders, Dennis. *The First of Everything.* New York: Delacorte Press, 1981.

Sayre, Anne. *Rosalind Franklin and DNA.* New York: Norton, 1975.

Scarborough, Elizabeth, and Laurel Furumoto. *Untold Lives: The First Generation of American Women Psychologists.* New York: Columbia University Press, 1987.

Schiaparelli, Elsa. *Shocking Life.* New York: Dutton, 1954.

Schneider, Joyce Anne. *Flora Tristan: Feminist, Socialist, and Free Spirit.* New York: Morrow, 1980.

Schneiderman, Rose, and Lucy Goldthwaite. *All For One.* New York: P.S. Eriksson, 1967.

Scott, Sheila. *Barefoot in the Sky; An Autobiography.* New York: Macmillan, 1974.

Shelton, Suzanne. *Divine Dancer: A Biography of Ruth St. Denis.* Garden City: Doubleday, 1981.

Shipman, Nell. *The Silent Screen & My Talking Heart: An Autobiography.* Boise: Boise State University, 1987.

Sills, Beverly. *Bubbles: An Encore.* New York: Grosset & Dunlap, 1981.

Skelton, Geoffrey. *Richard and Cosima Wanger: Biography of a Marriage.* London: Gollancz, 1982.

Slide, Anthony. *Early Women Directors.* South Brunswick: A. S. Barnes, 1977.

Slonimsky, Nicolas. *Baker's Biographical Dictionary of Musicians, Sixth Edition.* New York: Schirmer Books, 1978.

———. *Baker's Biographical Dictionary of Musicians, Eighth Edition.* New York: Schirmer Books, 1992.

Smith, Jay H. *Olga Korbut.* Mankato, Minnesota: Creative Education, 1974.

Smith, Jessie Carney. *Black Firsts: 2,000 Year of Extraordinary Achievement.* Detroit: Gale Research, 1994.

———. *Notable Black American Women.* Detroit: Gale Research, 1992.

Smith, John M., and Tim Cawkwell. *The World Encyclopedia of Film.* New York: World Publishing, 1972.

Smyth, Ethel. *Impressions that Remained.* London: Longmans, Green, and Co., 1919.

Smythe, Colin. *Seventy Years: Being the Autobiography of Lady Gregory.* Gerrards Cross: Smythe, 1974.

Smythe, Pat. *Jump for Joy.* New York: Dutton, 1955.

Spada, James. *Grace: The Secret Lives of a Princess.* New York: Dell, 1987.

———. *Streisand: The Woman and the Legend.* New York: Pocket Books, 1983.

Stanton, Elizabeth Cady. *History of Woman Suffrage.* Vol. 1, 1881.

———. *Eighty Years and More.* New York: European Publishing Company, 1898.

Stanton, Elizabeth Cady, and Harriot Stanton Blatch. *Elizabeth Cady Stanton as Revealed in Her Letters, Diary and Reminiscences.* New York: Harper & Brothers, 1922.

Stassinopoulos, Arianna Huffington. *Maria Callas: The Woman Behind the Legend.* New York: Simon and Schuster, 1981.

St. Denis, Ruth. *Ruth St. Denis: An Unfinished Life.* Brooklyn: Dance Horizons, 1939.

Stein, Dorothy. *Ada: A Life and a Legacy.* Cambridge, Massachusetts : MIT Press, 1985.

Sterling, Philip. *Sea and Earth: The Life of Rachel Carson.* New York: Crowell, 1970.

Stern, Madeleine B. *We the Women: Career Firsts of Nineteenth-Century America.* New York: Schulte Publishing, 1962.

Stewart, William Rhinelander. *The Philanthropic Work of Josephine Shaw Lowell.* New York: The Macmillan Company, 1911.

Stodelle, Ernestine. *Deep Song: The Dance Story of Martha Graham.* New York: Schirmer Books, 1984.

Stokowski, Olga Samaroff. *An American Musician's Story.* New York: W.W. Norton, 1939.

Swartout, Annie Fern. *Missie: An Historical Biography of Annie Oakley.* Blanchester: Brown Publishing Company, 1947.

T

Tharp, Louise Hall. *Mrs. Jack.* Boston: Little, Brown, 1965.

Thompson, Wayne C., Susan L. Thompson, and Juliet S. Thompson. *Historical Dictionary of Germany.* Metuchen, New Jersey: Scarecrow Press, 1994.

Tierney, Helen. *Women's Studies Encyclopedia,* vol. 2. New York: Greenwood Press, 1990.

U

Uglow, Jennifer S., ed. *The Continuum Dictionary of Women's Biography.* New York: Continuum, 1989.

Underhill, Miriam. *Give Me the Hills.* Riverside, Connecticut: Chatham Press in Association with the *Appalachian Mountain Club.* Distributed by Viking Press, 1971.

Upton, George P. *Theodore Thomas: A Musical Biography.* Chicago: A. C. McClurg, 1905.

V

Vaganova, Agrippina Iakovlevna. *Basic Principles of Classical Ballet.* New York: Dover Publications, 1969.

Van Deman, Esther Boise. *The Atrium Vestae.* Publication No. 108. Washington, D.C.: Carnegie Institution of Washington, 1909.

———. *The Building of the Roman Aqueducts.* Publication No. 423. Washington, D.C.: Carnegie Institution of Washington, 1934.

Vanderbilt, Gloria. *Once Upon a Time: A True Story.* New York: Knopf, 1985.

Vare, Ethlie Ann, and Greg Ptacek. *Mothers of Invention: From the Bra to the Bomb, Forgotten Women and Their Unforgettable Ideas.* New York: William Morrow, 1988.

W

Wallechinsky, David. *The Complete Book of the Olympics.* New York: Penguin Books, 1984.

———. *The Complete Book of the Olympics.* Boston: Little, Brown, 1996.

Wallechinsky, David, and Irving Wallace. *The People's Almanac.* Garden City: Doubleday, 1975.

Weiser, Marjorie P.K., and Jean S. Arbeiter. *Womanlist.* New York: Atheneum, 1981.

Wemyss, Francis Courtney. *Twenty-six Years of the Life of an Actor and Manager.* New York: Burgess, Stringer, 1847.

West, Mae. *Goodness Had Nothing to Do with It.* New York: Avon, 1959.

White, Maude Valerie. *Friends and Memories.* London: E. Arnold, 1914.

Who Was Who, 1897–1915, vol. I. London: A & C Black, 1920.

Who Was Who, 1916–1928, vol. II. London: A & C Black, 1929.

Who Was Who, 1929–1940, vol. III. London: A & C Black, 1941.

Who Was Who, 1941–1950, vol. IV. London: A & C Black, 1952.

Who Was Who, 1951–1960, vol. V. London: A & C Black, 1961.

Who Was Who, 1961–1970, vol. VI. London: A & C Black, 1971.

Who Was Who, 1971–1980, vol. VII. London: A & C Black, 1981.

Who Was Who in America, 1607–1896, historical volume. Chicago: Marquis Who's Who Inc., 1963.

Who Was Who in America, 1897–1942, vol. 1. Chicago: Marquis Who's Who Inc., 1981.

Who's Who of American Women, 18th ed. Chicago: Marquis Who's Who, 1993.

Wigman, Mary. *The Language of Dance.* Middletown: Wesleyan University Press, 1966.

Willard, Frances Elizabeth, and Mary A. Livermore. *Glimpses of Fifty Years: The Autobiography of an American Woman.* New York: Source Book Press, 1889.

———. *A Woman of the Century.* Buffalo: Moulton, 1893.

Williams, Michael W. *The African American Encyclopedia.* New York: Marshall Cavendish, 1993.

Williams, S. W. *Queenly Women, Crowned and Uncrowned.* Cincinnati: Cranston and Stowe, 1885.

Williams, Shirley. *A Job to Live: The Impact of Tomorrow's Technology on Work and Society.* New York: Penguin Books, 1985.

———. *Politics is for People.* Cambridge: Harvard University Press, 1981.

Williamson, George C. *Lady Anne Clifford.* Kendal: Wilson, 1922.

Winnemucca, Sarah. *Life Among the Piutes: Their Wrongs and Claims.* New York: G.P. Putnam, 1883.

Wistrich, Robert S. *Who's Who in Nazi Germany.* London: Routledge, 1982.

The World Book Encyclopedia. Chicago: World Book, Inc., 1987.

Z

Zaharias, Babe Didrikson. *This Life I've Led; My Autobiography as told to Harry Paxton.* New York: Barnes, 1955.

Zophy, Angela Howard. *Handbook of American Women's History.* Garland Reference Library of the Humanities, 1990.

Zukor, Adolph. *The Public is Never Wrong: The Autobiography of Adolph Zukor.* New York: Putnam, 1953.

Calendar of Firsts

January

March

April

May

June

July

August

September

October

Index by Year

The first women's convents in Bethlehem 359

The founder of the University at Constantinople 133

Late 5th century

Founder of the first convent in Ireland, according to legend 352

6th century

Founder of the first Benedictine nunnery in England 359

The first woman to establish a convent in France 359

527

The first actress to become an empress 176

7th century

Founder of the first Christian church at Canterbury 360

Founder of the first religious settlement for women in Anglo-Saxon England 360

The first Quraish woman to convert to Islam 355

c.600

Founder of the Abbey of Autun 359

604

The first woman to marry the prophet Muhammed 351

631

The first woman to become a Muslim leader 367

657

Founder of the Abbey of Corbie 360

659

Founder and first head of the monastery at Whitby 360

664

Founder of the Convent of Chelles 360

8th century

The first abbess of the Convent of Tauberbischofsheim 355

The first woman to become a Sufi Moslem scholar 373

797

The first woman to rule the Byzantine Empire alone 176

Late 8th century

The director of the first major convent scriptorium 267

The first Englishwoman to have her portrait reproduced 72

The first queen consort allowed to issue coins in her own name 72

The first Russian Orthodox saint 353

10th century

The first female historian in Ireland 347

The first playwright in medieval Europe 267

The first woman to paint an extensive cycle of miniatures 63

900–918

The first woman to attempt to unify England under one ruler 165

941

Founder of the Association for the Advancement of Psychoanalysis 228

Late 10th century

Founder of the Cluniac monastery at Selz in Alsace 360

11th century

The first person to introduce support for the perineum during labor 230

The first person to stitch a perineum after childbirth 230

The first physician to give written advice on the care of newborn children 230

The first woman to lead a Crusade 367

Early 11th century

The first known novelist 270

c.1030

The first Saxon woman to rule Norway 185

c.1060

The first woman to ride naked through the streets of Coventry 37

12th century

Founder and first abbess of the convent at Bingen, Germany 360

Founder of the convent of Bethany 360

The first female troubadour 344

The first woman in the West whose self-portrait has survived 63

The first woman poet to write in German 254

The first woman to argue that the earth was round 389

The first woman to be a professional writer in France 264

The first woman to write an extensive work of historical scholarship 347

Early 12th century

Founder of the city of Jiblah, Yemen 216

c.1120

The first German woman to practice medicine 227

13th century

Founder of the Abbey of Longchamps 361

The first French actress whose achievements were recorded in her own name 94

Early 17th century

The first Dutch woman to paint still lifes 64

The first person to introduce and popularize the maxim 264

c.1600

The first person to treat anemia with iron 226

1602

The first woman to become an abbess at the age of eleven 355

1603

The first person to introduce the Carmelite order into France 361

1607

The first Native American woman to save the life of an Englishman 116

1610s

Founder of the lay pastoral group the "English Ladies" 362

1611

The first woman to be arrested for wearing men's clothes 111

The first woman to organize and host a great French salon 264

c.1615

The first female ruler of India to issue coins in her own name 177

1620s

The first female opera composer 73

1620

The first woman aboard the Mayflower to give birth in North America 233

1630s

The first woman to attend the University of Utrecht in the Netherlands 156

1631

The first female Dutch artist to portray sexual harassment 64

1633

Founder of the order of the Daughters of Charity 362

1635

The first woman to dissent against New England Puritan orthodoxy 368

1639

The first person to form an Ursuline convent and school in Quebec, Canada 133

1644

The first woman to be crowned king 192

1645

The first woman to receive an American colonial land grant 112

1647

The first woman in America to demand suffrage 30

Mid-17th century

Founder of the Society of Friendship 256

The first woman to introduce the idea of a literary salon in Greece 268

1650s

The first person to invent and sell the "medicine" called "Mana of St. Nicholas of Bari" 112

1650

The first U.S. woman to become a published poet 275

The first woman in America to be executed as a witch 373

1655

The first woman in America to vote 30

1656

The first woman to perform on the English stage 94

1669

The first victim of the worst mass witch-hunt in Sweden 374

1670

The first woman to play the title role of Bérénice in French playwright Jean Racine's famous play 94

1671

The first Englishwoman to write a textbook on midwifery, *The Midwife's Book* 221

1675

The first German woman to become a scientific illustrator 399

1676

Founder of a mystical and heretical version of Quietism 362

1678

The first woman to receive the degree of Doctor of Philosophy 130

1763

The first woman to write an authoritative history of England 257

1766

Cofounder of the Methodist Church in the United States 362

1768

The founder of Trevecca College in Brecknockshire, England 134

1769

Cofounder of the Royal Academy, London 64

The first Canadian novelist 254

1770s

The first person to introduce the novelist Fanny Burney to literary society 257

1775

The first female postmaster 194

1776

The first colony or state to allow women the right to vote 194

1777

The first woman to coin the word "oxygen" 387

1778

The first woman to lead a revolt against the Spanish in Ecuador 303

1779

The first woman to receive a U.S. Army pension 311

1780

Cofounder of the first relief organization of the American Revolutionary War 122

The first woman to lead a rebellion against the Spanish in Peru 307

The first woman to organize a revolt against the Spanish government in Colombia 303

1783

The first president of the Russian Academy 273

The first woman to serve as Director of the Academy of Arts and Sciences in Russia 273

1789

The first woman at the head of the Women's March during the French Revolution 2

The first woman to storm the Bastille at the outset of the French Revolution 2

1790s

The first woman to make her name as a wax-modeller and operator of wax museums 108

c.1790

The organizer of the maternity and children's hospital at Port Royal 226

1790

Cofounder of the first Roman Catholic convent in the United States 362

Founding of the Club des Tricoteuses 2

1791

The first Dutch woman to speak out for the rights of women during the French Revolution 2

The first woman to sing the role of the Queen of the Night in Mozart's opera *The Magic Flute* 74

1792

The first Englishwoman to challenge Rousseau's notions of female inferiority 257

1793

Founder of the Republican Revolutionary Society 2

1794

Founder of Jerusalem township in western New York 363

1795

The first woman to obtain an apartment in the Louvre 65

The first woman whose work led to the founding of the Religious Tracts Society 258

1798

The first woman to discover a comet 380

Late 18th century

The first major female novelist 257

The first person to introduce picture books for preschool children 143

The first woman admitted to the Bologna Academy of Sciences 392

19th century

The first black female sculptor to exhibit in the United States 92

The first woman elected a member of the Royal Geographical Society 336

c.1800

The first female choreographer in the United States 39

1800

The first First Lady to live in the White House 121

The first French salon hostess to be painted by David 65

c.1802

The first German woman to write a book advocating the education of women 267

1802

The first woman on record to enlist in the U.S. Army 311

1803

The only woman on the Lewis and Clark Expedition 116

1804

The first female jockey 430

The first woman to be exiled from France by Napoleon 264

The first woman to work as a pharmacist 233

1805

The first English writer to direct her work on scientific subjects specifically to women 387

1808

The first U.S. woman to print an edition of the Bible 275

1809

The first Bolivian woman to lead a revolt against Spanish rule in her country 303

The first woman to receive a U.S. patent 110

The founder of the first Catholic order in the United States 363

1811

The first woman to go on an overland expedition to Astoria, Oregon 403

1812

Founder of the Sisters of Loretto 363

The first U.S. woman to become a foreign missionary 369

The first woman to enlist in the U.S. Marines 315

1813

The first mother superior of the Sisters of Charity of Nazareth 363

1814

The founder of the Middlebury Female Seminary in Middlebury, Vermont 134

The organizer of the first institution for the higher education of women 134

c.1815

The first English-speaking woman to receive a degree from an established university 223

1815

The first woman to receive a doctorate in obstetrics from a German university 228

1816

The first woman to lead the Sunday School Movement in the United States 143

1818

Founder of the first American convents of the Sacred Heart 363

c.1820

The first female hero to be painted by the famous Spanish painter, Goya 308

1820s

The first woman to receive the title lieutenant-general for her military leadership of the Greeks in their struggle for independence against the Turks 306

1820s and 1830s

The first woman to inspire operas by three of the great composers of her day 74

c.1820

The first French woman to invent a pelvimeter and a vaginal speculum 227

1820

The first person to discover a dinosaur 394

1821

The first woman in England to suggest that prisons should be a place for rehabilitation 30

The founder of the Troy Female Seminary, Troy, New York 134

1822

The first woman to be granted a military pension from a state government 311

1824

The first person to discover a plesiosaurus 394

The first person to involve the deaf Beethoven in the performances of his own work 74

The first woman's labor organization 15

1825

The first female manager in the American iron industry 111

1827

The first female member of the Historical Society of Pennsylvania 347

The first unmarried U.S. woman to be sent overseas as a missionary 369

The first U.S. woman to discover a new comet 381

1848

First woman to wear bloomers 112

Founder of the Club for Emancipation of Women in France 172

The first person to design bloomers 3

The first U.S. writer to emphasize the role of women in the development of the United States 276

The first woman elected to the American Academy of Arts and Sciences 381

The first woman in Massachusetts to petition the legislature for "the redress of grievances of her sex" 3

The first Women's Rights Convention 3

The founder of the Philadelphia School of Design (industrial art) 135

1849

The first American actress to play the part of Hamlet in Shakespeare's play 95

The first American woman to receive a medical degree 234

The first woman elected to membership in the Massachusetts Historical Society 347

The first woman enrolled as a recognized physician in the Medical Registered of the United Kingdom 234

The first woman to run for election to the French National Assembly 172

Late 1840s

The first female student to enroll at Ohio Wesleyan University in Delaware, Ohio 157

1850s

Founder of the Fredrika Bremer League 4

The first person to use open lectures as a means of education 145

The first woman to be seriously considered for the position of Poet Laureate 259

c.1850

Founder of the Women's Museum Association 135

The first female doctor to engage extensively in major surgery 234

The first woman to climb Mount Hosmer 436

1850

Founder of the newspaper *Italia* 270

The first African American woman to graduate from college 130

The first national convention in the United States to advocate women's rights 5

1851

The first sorority (Adelphian Society/Alpha Delta Phi) 150

The first woman to hold a chair at a legally authorized school 234

The first woman to serve as a faculty member in an American medical school 235

The first woman to serve as a hospital intern in the United States 236

1852

Founder of the feminist periodical *O Jornal das Senhoras* 286

Founder of the Sisters of Saint Benedict in the United States 364

The first British woman to manage an ironworks 104

The first woman to advance the American abolitionist cause through a popular novel 276

1853

The first principal of Milwaukee Female College in Milwaukee, Wisconsin 152

The first woman to attend the Munich Art Academy in Germany 66

The first woman to be ordained a minister in the United States 371

The founder of Lindenwood College in St. Charles, Missouri 135

1854

The first successful female novelist in Australia 253

The first woman to lay the foundation for the system of modern nursing 223

c.1855

Founder of the New York Infirmary for Women and Children 234

1855

Founder of the Sisters of the Holy Cross in America 364

Founding of English Prayer Union, later Young Women's Christian Association 321

Founding of the General Female Training Institute, later the Young Women's Christian Association 321

The first woman on record to keep her own name after marriage 5

1856

Founder of the first women's patriotic society in the United States 116

The first black woman to teach white children 145

The first feminist writer in Sweden 274

The first woman to navigate a clipper ship 344

1857

The first person to operate a private kindergarten in America 145

The first woman to serve as assistant secretary to the Social Science Association 346

1858

The first person to introduce the idea of medical records 236

The first woman to establish a steam bakery in the American South 108

1859

The first accredited physician to practice in Great Britain 234

The first editor of *Mrs. Beeton's Book of Household Management* 259

The first woman to establish a system for the education of women in Eastern Europe 145

1860s

The first two Russian women to receive medical degrees 232

c.1860

Cofoounders of the American Women's Educational Association 152

1860

Cofounder of the Seventh-Day Adventist Church 365

Founder of the Institute of Hygiene 6

Founding of the Society for Promoting the Employment of Women 6

The first American woman to rise to the rank of superior within the Sisters of Notre Dame de Namur 356

The first person to put into practice the idea of accurate tissue-paper dress patterns 108

The first textbook for nurses, *Notes on Nursing,* is published 223

The first woman to take and pass the French baccalaureat exam 130

1861

Cofounders of the radical journal *The Interpreter* 6

The first head the U.S. Army Nursing Corps 236

The first journal to be produced by women in Australia 253

The first woman to be pictured on Confederate currency 102

The first woman to beome a commissioned officer in the Confederate Army 311

The first woman to help other women emigrate to Australia 6

The first woman to receive an M.A. degree in the American South 130

The first woman to serve on the surgical staff of a modern army in wartime 236

1862

The first woman to earn the title of Printer and Publisher in Ordinary to the Queen 16

The founder of the Penn School on the island of St. Helena 135

1863

Founder of the New York Medical College and Hospital for Women 236

The first black woman to attain the rank of principal in the New York City public school system 152

The first black woman to serve as a nurse in the U.S. armed services 312

The first major female photographer 91

The first woman to be admitted to the New York College of Pharmacy 238

The first woman to be ordained as a Universalist minister 371

The first woman to perform major surgery 237

The first woman to serve as principal of a normal school 152

1864

The first American woman to sing in a work by German opera composer Richard Wagner 75

The first black female physician in the United States 237

The first woman to practice dentistry independently 237

c.1865

The first English female physician 223

1865

The first female instructor at the Pennsylvania Academy of the Fine Arts 146

The first Mother Superior of the Episcopal Community of St. Mary 356

The first president of the Association for Women's Education in Germany 150

The first woman to be awarded the Congressional Medal of Honor in the U.S. 312

The first woman to serve as "Lady Principal" of Vassar College in New York 152

1866

Founder of the London School of Hospital for Women 223

The first dean of the first women's medical college in the United States 125

The first organization in the United States to advocate national women's suffrage 31

The first president of the American Equal Rights Association 30

The first woman to graduate from an U.S. dental school 237

The first woman to receive a federal U.S. commission for sculpture 92

The first woman to register for courses at the Women's Medical College of the New York Infirmary 232

The founder and first secretary of the London Schoolmistresses' Association 136

1867

Founder and first editor of *Argosy* 259

The first organized women's baseball team 412

The first person to organize a publicly funded kindergarten in the United States 145

The first woman in Missouri to take a public stand for women's suffrage 31

The first woman to serve as editor of *Harper's Bazaar* 286

1868

Founding of the Association International des Femmes (International Association of Women) 6

Founding of the women's club, Sorosis 321

The first editor of the *Chicago Legal News* 291

The first English woman to speak publicly on women's suffrage 31

The first woman to captain a baseball team 413

The first woman to work for the U.S. State Department 194

1869

Cofounder of the National Women's Suffrage Association 7

Founder of the radical Republican paper *Les Mouches et L'Araignée* 291

The first black woman to hold a position of independent trust in an educational institution (the Institute for Colored Youth in Philadelphia) 153

The first female lawyer to be admitted to the bar 337

The first national labor organization for women 16

The first principal of a day school for the deaf (the Boston School for Deaf-Mutes) 153

The first two women's suffrage associations in the United States 31

The first U.S. woman to patent an architectural innovation 331

The first woman admitted to the Ecole de Médécine in Paris, France 238

The first woman licensed to preach in the Methodist Episcopal Church 371

The first woman superintendent of a public school system (Wilmington, North Carolina) 153

The first woman to host interracial receptions in Damascus, Syria 120

The first women's suffrage law in the United States 195

The founder and first editor of *The Agitator* 6

The founder of her own college at Benslow House, Hitchin 136

c.1870

The first woman to found and endow a women's college (Smith College, Northampton, Massachusetts) 136

1870

First woman to serve on the council of the Universalist Church 368

The first professor of hygiene at the Woman's Medical College, Chicago 237

The first state university to open its medical school to female students 143

The first to win the Hope Scholarship at the University of Edinburgh, Scotland 229

The first U.S. woman to serve as a justice of the peace 195

The first widow of a U.S. president to receive a pension 195

The first woman to be awarded the Chemistry Prize at the University of Edinburgh, Scotland 229

The first woman to represent the United States as a trained medical missionary in Asia 238

1871

Founding of the Women's Educational and Industrial Union 322

The first female college president (Evanston College for Ladies in Illinois) 125

The first president of the Woman's Centenary Association 365

The first woman member of the American Institute of Homeopathy 238

The first woman ordained as a Unitarian minister 371

The first woman to climb the Matterhorn 436

1872

Founder of the Association for the Advancement of Medical Education of Women 238

The first African-American woman lawyer in the United States 337

The first person to perform an ovariotomy 238

The first woman admitted to the bar in the District of Columbia 337

The first woman to receive a degree under the auspices of the Women's Medical Courses in St. Petersburg 232

The first woman to run for president of the United States 195

The founder of the Society for Promoting Women's Education 145

1873

Founder of the Association of the Advancement of Women 381

Founder of the first American women's temperance league 37

The first editor of the children's magazine *St. Nicholas* 277

The first female member of the British Medical Association 223

The first person to receive an American diploma in nursing 238

The first president of the Association for the Advancement of Women 7

The first woman to open and teach in a United States public kindergarten 146

The founder and first editor of the *Kindergarten Messenger* 145

1874

Founder of the Brazilian feminist journal *O Domingo* 286

Founder of the London School of Medicine for Women 232

Founder of the Women's Provident and Protective League 16

Founding of the first labor organization for women in England, the Women's League 16

Founding of the Women's Christian Temperance Union 37

The first woman to practice as a doctor in Victoria, Australia 219, 219

c.1880

The first African American newspaperwoman in North America 292

The first Secretary for Health, Education and Welfare for Jewish Palestine 157

1880

Cofounder of the Union of Russian Workers of the South 16

Founder of the Missionary Sisters of the Sacred Heart 365

One of the first sports organizations for women 405

The first female member of the San Diego Society of Natural History 391

The first female minister in the Methodist Protestant Church 372

The first person to introduce "applied physics" at Wellesley 147

The first person to open an art pottery in Cincinnati, Ohio 66

The first woman to be elected to the New York Academy of Medicine 238

The first woman to earn a doctorate from the University of Pennsylvania 131

The first woman to receive a degree in architecture 331

The founder and first president of Newnham College of Cambridge University 137

1881

Founder and first president of the American Red Cross 240

The first female delegate to the Greenback Party's state convention in Michigan 196

The first female vice-president of the Chicago Medical Society 237

The first woman to serve as a notary public in the District of Columbia 196

The first woman to stand for municipal election in France 172

The founder of Spelman College, Atlanta, Georgia 137

1882

Founding of Sharada Sadan, a home for Indian widows 8

The co-founder of the Federation Française des Sociétés Feministes 155

The first active president of Wellesley College 125

The first Presbyterian woman to serve as a medical missionary in China 240

The first president of the Women's National Press Association 292

The first woman to earn a doctoral degree from the University of Zurich, Switzerland 125

The world's first birth control clinic, Amsterdam, the Netherlands 231

1883

Founder of the Voluntary Relief Society for the Sick and Poor 240

The first "Ladies' Day" allowing women into baseball parks 413

The first female pharmacist 240

The first two female physicians to practice in Hawaii 240

The first woman appointed to the U.S. Civil Service 196

The first woman to graduate from the University of Pennsylvania Law School 338

The founder of the Western Association of Collegiate Alumnae, Evanston, Illinois 158

1884

Cofounder of the Fabian Society 261

The first person to write a guide to literature for Peruvian women 272

The first president of the first Women's Suffrage Society in Victoria, Australia 8

The first South African novelist to write about the oppression of women in her country 273

The first state college for women in the United States 143

The first woman to be elected to the council of the American Mathematical Society 346

1885

Founder and first president of the Women's Anthropological Society of America 346

Founder of the Women's Hospital in Edinburgh 232

The first department of women's work in an American labor union 16

The first female college faculty member to become a dean 125

The first Japanese woman licensed to practice Western medicine 230

The first woman in Sweden to have a national women's organization named after her 274

The first woman to become an associate member of the American Ornithologists' Union (AOU) 400

The first woman to receive a degree from the University of Wisconsin Law School 338

The first woman to serve as an officer for the American Association for the Advancement of Science 389

1886

First woman to be pictured on U.S. currency 102

Founding of the Battersea branch of the Women's Co-operative Guild 112

Founding of the Danish Women's Progress Association 8

The first Hindu woman to earn a medical degree 229

The first person to set up a training school for nurses in Japan 239

The first United States nursing school for black women 143

The first woman steamboat captain west of the Mississippi River 344

The first woman to be elected to the American Society of Naturalists 385

The first woman to be married to a president in the White House 121

The founder, among others, of the Training College for Women Teachers, Cambridge, England 150

1887

Founder of the weekly *El Peru Illustrado* 272

The first American to become a successful advocate of the deaconess movement 368

The first female mayor 196

The first female member of the Board of Public Education in Philadelphia, Pennsylvania 155

The first female tennis prodigy 448

The first woman chosen to serve as a lay delegate to the Methodist General Conference 357

The first woman to be admitted to the Ecole Pratiques des Hautes Etudes of the University of Paris 157

The first woman to serve as a U.S. marshal 196

1888

Author of the first petition for women's suffrage submitted to the New Zealand House of Representatives 32

Founder of the Brazilian feminist journal *A Familia* 286

Founding in Australia of the Dawn Club, a feminist discussion group 8

The first black woman to sing opera and art songs in the United States 77

The first person to climb the Aiguille de Bionnassay and to traverse the eastern ridge of the Dôme de Gouter 436

The first woman to earn a degree as professor of law in Belgium 338

The first woman to obtain a first-class honours degree in history at a British University 131

1889

Founder of the first women's union in New Zealand 17

The first person to formulate a socialist theory of women's emancipation 8

The first president of Mount Holyoke College 126

The first vice president of the International Council of Women 19

The first woman to discover two binaries or double stars 382

The founder of Barnard College of Columbia University, New York 138

The founder of the first night school at which immigrants could learn English and American history 157

The founder of the German Women's Teachers' Association, Berlin 137

1890s

Founder of the first feminist association in Greece 268

The first female leader in the Phillipines' stuggle for independence 188

The first person to establish nursing as a profession in Greece 228

The first person to found a progessive kindergarten in Germany, in Hamburg 138

The first two people to discover the "Lewis Codex" 335

The first woman to own a London investment company 111

The first woman to perform in the Buffalo Bill Wild West Show 73

The first woman to study architecture at the École des Beaux Arts in Paris 331

The founder of a school to train women as apprentices and clerks 138

The founder of home economics classes at the YMCA at Hamilton 139

c.1890

Cofounder of *Zoe,* a botanical journal 385

Founder of the Pechey-Phipson Sanitarium near Nasik, India 229

Organizer of the first consumers' organization in America, the National Consumers' League 238

The first female psychotherapist in France 227

1890

The cofounder and first coeditor of *Critica Sociale* 286

The first English woman to receive a medal from the Russian Red Cross 223

The first female employee in the executive office of the United States government 196

The first female president of the Montgomery County Medical Society in Pennsylvania 131

The first president of Mills College, the oldest women's college on the U.S. West Coast 126

The first president of the American College for Girls, Turkey 127

The first president of the Consumer Council 122

The first woman elected to full membership in the American Institute of Architects 331

The first woman to beat the 80-day around-the-world record set by the fictional Phineas Fogg in Jules Verne's *Around the World in Eighty Days* 403

The first woman to become a professional architect in the United States 331

The first woman to design a state seal 197

The first woman to graduate in architecture from the Massachusetts Institute of Technology 331

The first woman to scale Mount Rainier 436

The first woman to write a novel at the age of nine 261

The first Texas woman admitted to practice before the United States Supreme Court 339

The first U.S. correspondent to report from the front during World War I 287

The first woman to be a general manager of a Hollywood film studio 104

The first woman to head a department at Stanford University 147

The first woman to write a modernist "stream-of-consciousness" novel 261

c.1916

The first woman to graduate with a degree in law from the Philippine Law School at Capiz 340

1916

Cofounders of English Girl Guides 326

Founder of the American Folk Dance Society 42

The first Amateur Athletic Union (AAU) national championships in women's swimming 445

The first civil service psychologist in the state of New York 398

The first female magistrate in the British Empire 340

The first movie star to form and own a film company 52

The first non-Indian member of the Indian Women's University at Poona 148

The first official women's bowling organization 421

The first person to direct a feature-length wildlife adventure film 51

The first person to submit theories of male superiority to scientific investigation 398

The first two women to cross the continental United States on motorcycles 404

The first woman elected to U.S. House of Representatives 198

The first woman to organize a secret news correspondence service during the German occupation of Belgium 289

The first women to win the Pulitzer Prize for biography 279

1917

A founder of the Indian Women's Association 148

Cofounder of the Hogarth Press 262

Founder of Lois Weber Productions 50

Founder of the Lithuanian Women's Freedom Association 13

The first woman employed by the U.S. Army as a teacher 148

The cofounder of the Judge Baker Foundation 245

The first and only female member of Les Six, a group of innovative French musicians 80

The first black woman to be a U.S. national champion in any sport 449

The first female full professor at Johns Hopkins University 384

The first female member of any legislative body in the British Empire 162

The first official women's bowling tournament 421

The first president of the Mandarin Film Company 52

The first three women to sit in the U.S. Electoral College 199

The first woman professor at the Columbia University Medical School 243

The first woman to chair a meeting in India at which a labor strike was called 20

The first woman to conduct orchestral concerts in France 80

The first woman to earn a Doctorate of Public Health 243

The first woman to enlist in the U.S. Navy 317

The first woman to organize female fighting troops during World War I 307

The first woman to pilot her own plane on a tour of Japan and China 408

The first woman to serve full time as an organizer for the Amalgamated Clothing Workers of America 20

1918

Founder of French newspaper *L'Europe Nouvelle* 293

Founder of La Société des Films Musidora 51

Founder of the Communist Party in Germany 173

The first female member of the U.S. Marine Corps Reserve 316

The first female recording artist to sell a million copies of a record 80

The first female reporter for *The Plain Dealer* 293

The first person to sing the role of Leonora in *La Forza del Destino* 81

The first president of the American Philosophical Association 151

The first woman to be elected a minister of Parliament in the United Kingdom 167

The first woman to head a metropolitan library system 343

The first woman to run for the U.S. Senate 200

The first woman to serve as a member of the Landsting in Denmark's Parliament 164

The first woman to serve as a political commissar in the Red Army 308

The first woman to serve as head judge of a juvenile court 340

The first woman to serve as manager of a major symphony orchestra 81

The first woman to serve in the first Bolshevik government 190

The founder and first dean of the New Jersey College for Women in New Brunswick, New Jersey 140

The founder of the feminist periodical Die Frau im Staat 138

The world's first female ambassador 177

1919

First woman bank president to employ an all-female staff 103

Founder of the Save the Children Fund 115

Founder of the Women's International League for Peace and Freedom 29

The first director of the mental hygiene clinic of the YWCA 248

The first female lawyer to be accepted by the Inns of Court 340

The first female president of the Association of American Geographers 336

The first female professor and the first head of the department of nutrition at the College of Medicine 148

The first person to inaugurate professional training for dietitians at the College of Medicine at the State University of Iowa at Ames 148

The first president of the American Association of University Women 151

The first U.S. woman to earn an international pilot's license 408

The first woman in the British Empire to achieve cabinet rank 163

The first woman to hold an administrative office in the Protestant Episcopal Church in the United States 357

The first woman to preside over the U.S. House of Representatives 201

The first woman to receive the Pulitzer Prize for fiction 280

The first woman to serve as director of a major opera company 81

The first woman to serve as head of any large Christian organizational body (the Northern Baptist Convention) 155

The first woman to win the Miss America Beauty Pageant 73

The first woman to win the Pulitzer Prize for drama 280

1922

Founder of the Women's Amateur Athletic Association 408

Organizer and first president of the Brazilian Association for the Advancement of Women 12

The first director of the Communist Party Women's Department in China 163

The first English woman to establish her reputation as a historian of medieval women 348

The first European film star to be invited to Hollywood 54

The first female delegate from the Kentucky Annual Methodist Conference to the Southern Methodist General Conference 357

The first female Democratic nominee (unsuccessful) for U.S. senate from Wisconsin 36

The first female film critic in England 294

The first female president of the Co-operative Congress 12

The first organization to establish standards for women field hockey players 425

The first person to write a series of film scripts starring a dog 54

The first woman federal labor mediator 21

The first woman to achieve the record of 23 British archery championships 405

The first woman to serve (unofficially) as a U.S. delegate to the League of Nations 201

The first woman to serve in the U.S. Foreign Service 202

The first woman to serve in the U.S. Senate 202

The founder of the Merrill-Palmer Institute of Human Development and Family Life, Detroit, Michigan 141

The first woman elected to the Ohio Supreme Court 340

1923

British delegate to the first International Labor Organization Conference 22

Founder of the International Church of the Foursquare Gospel 366

Organizer of the first American conference on birth control 244

The author of the original draft of the Equal Rights Amendment to the U.S. Constitution 12

The first female director of the U.S. Bureau of Home Economics 202

The first international women's tennis competition 449

The first major outdoor track and field meet for women 454

The first woman elected to the U.S. Congress 202

The first woman Federal Bureau of Investigation (FBI) agent 202

The first woman to be chosen as a grand officer in the Legion of Honor 280

The first woman to find the bacteria that causes scarlet fever 246

The first woman to receive an honorary degree from Yale University 281

The first woman to receive the Pulitzer Prize in poetry 281

The first women's division of the National Amateur Athletic Federation 434

1924

Cowriter of the first book of crossword puzzles 282

Founder of *Egyptian Woman* 11

Founder of the Women's Suffrage League in Japan 182

Founder of the Women's Union, Egypt 11

Founder of the Workers' Birth Control Group, England 12

Member of the first U.S. women's doubles tennis team to win an Olympic gold medal 451

The first athlete to win Olympic medals in both swimming and diving events 424

The first dean at Western Reserve University School of Nursing 243

The first European woman to enter the holy city of Lhasa in Tibet 404

The first female president of the American Association of Anatomists 384

The first female president of the American Federation of Teachers 151

The first professional women barbers admitted to a barber's union 22

The first U.S. woman to head a news service in Berlin, Germany 294

The first U.S. woman to win gold medals in both women's singles and doubles tennis at the same Olympic games 451

The first woman in the American South to serve in a state senate 202

The first woman to be elected governor of a U.S. state 202

The first woman to design a theater for Shakespearean performances 332

The first woman to fly solo from South Africa to England 408

The first woman to head a major division of the U.S. Department of State 203

The first woman to win an Academy Award 55

The first woman to win an Olympic gold medal in the 800-meter track and field event 454

The first woman to win an Olympic gold medal in the discus event 454

The first woman to win an Olympic gold medal in the high jump 454

The first woman to win the 100-meter dash at the Olympic games 455

The first woman whose fictional life was chronicled as both male and female 262

The first women's gymnastics team to win an Olympic gold medal 428

The first women's track and field team to win an Olympic gold medal in the 4x100-meter relay 454

Winner of the first U.S. women's squash racquets singles championship 443

World Party for Equal Rights for Women was founded 13

1929

Cofounder of the Institute of Landscape Architects 336

Cofounder of the radical Society of the Devotees of the Artistic Film 55

Founder and first president of the Council of Lithuanian Women 13

The first female cabinet minister in England 169

The first female president of the Botanical Society of America 386

The first person commissioned to sculpt different racial types 399

The first two women to be elected to membership in the Society of Experimental Psychologists 398

The first woman elected to the board of directors of the American Grocery Manufacturers' Association 104

The first woman to be a fellow of the American Ornithologists' Union (AOU) 400

The first woman to be a stunt pilot in motion pictures 93

The first woman to direct a sound film 55

The first woman to serve as head of the Newark Public Library 198

1930s

The first ballerina of international stature to be trained in England 45

The first person to develop the concept of bibliotherapy 246

The first person to isolate vitamin E 387

The first person to use the term "nuclear fission" 396

The first woman to open a school of floristry 336

The first woman to pass the test for the British Ground Engineers' License 409

The first woman to practice law in Liberia 340

1930

Founder of "The Inn of the Sixth Happiness" 367

One of the first three women to be elected to associate membership in the Society of American Foresters 393

The first airline stewardess 335

The first American female composer to receive a Guggenheim Fellowship 82

The first director of the Whitney Museum 70

The first female member of the American Pediatric Society 246

The first female president of the Entomological Association of America 390

The first person to receive an honorary degree from the New Jersey College for Women 343

The first woman professor of psychiatry at Columbia University 249

The first woman to be elected president of the Mississippi Valley Historical Association 348

The first woman to bowl a perfect 300 game 421

The first woman to chair the National Birth Control Council 225

The first woman to complete a transcontinental flight 409

The first woman to earn her doctorate in mathematics from the Massachusetts Institute of Technology 133

The first woman to fly solo from London to Australia 409

The first woman to head the board of directors of a U.S. railroad 105

The first woman to receive the honorary degree of Doctor of Hebrew Letters from the Jewish Institute of Religion 157

1931

Cofounders of the Macnaghten-Lemare Concerts, an ongoing series of performances of contemporary music 82

Founder of Sadler's Wells theatre company in London 97

Founder of the literary periodical *Sur* 253

The first female doctoral student at the California Institute of Technology (Caltech) 390

The first Japanese film actress to star in a "talkie" 57

The first person to make a German film produced cooperatively 57

The first woman admitted to the Prussian Academy of Literature 267

The first woman to play in major league baseball 413

The first woman to serve as president of the Irish Trades Union Congress 22

The first woman to wear shorts at Wimbledon 451

The first woman to win an Academy Award for writing 55

The first woman to win the American Ornithologists' Union's Bruster Medal 400

The founder and first director of the Royal Ballet, London 44

1932

Cofounded the Group Theatre 97

Co-inventor of the "pinboard" animation technique 57

The first and only woman whose sculpture is featured at a German war memorial 92

The first U.S. woman to win the high jump event at an Olympic games 455

The first woman elected to the U.S. Senate 203

The first woman ever to swim one hundred yards in less than one minute 445

The first woman to complete a non-stop transcontinental flight 409

The first woman to complete a solo transatlantic flight 409

The first woman to head a U.S. state political party organization 203

The first woman to lead a group composed only of women on a successful ascent of the Matterhorn 437

The first woman to receive a commercial pilot's license 409

The first woman to work as a commercial pilot 408

The first women's fly fishing club 425

1933

The first First Lady to hold a press conference 121

The first person to use muscle therapy in the treatment of poliomyelitis 219

The first woman elected a member of the General Medical Council of Great Britain 225

The first woman to be appointed a cabinet member in a presidential administration 204

The first woman to be elected as speaker in a state house of representatives 204

The first woman to fly across the Atlantic Ocean from east to west 409

The first woman to serve as a U.S. foreign minister 204

The first woman to serve as U.S. delegate to the Pan American Conference 339

The first woman to serve in the National Recovery Administration 21

1934

Founder and first president of the Opera Artists Association 22

Founder of the Agrupacion de Mujeres Antifacistas 191

Founder of the Guggenheim-Jeune Art Gallery 70

The first female editor-in-chief of the *American Journal of Archeology* 378

The first woman to be given the title "National Women's Leader" in Germany 173

The first woman to fly airmail transport 410

The first woman to publish a large metropolitan daily newspaper 294

The first woman to receive the National Geographic Society Hubbard Gold Medal 410

The first woman to serve on the U.S. Court of Appeals 340

The first woman to suggest the possibility of nuclear fission 396

1935

Codiscoverer of the subatomic particle the neutron 396

Founder of the Markova-Dolin Ballet 44

Founder and first president of the National Council of Negro Women 326

Organizer and first director of the Federal Theatre Project 97

The first black woman to win seven consecutive titles in the American Tennis Association 451

The first person to win the singles tennis title at Wimbledon eight times 451

The first woman to be made an honorary life president of the National Education Association 154

The first woman to become a member of a commodity exchange 110

The first woman to complete a solo flight from California to Hawaii 409

The first woman to fly over the south Atlantic from England to Brazil 410

The first woman to win a Nobel Prize for literature 281

The first woman trainer of thoroughbred race horses 430

1936

The first female speaker of the Finnish Parliament 171

The first woman coxswain of a men's college varsity crew 418

The first woman to receive the Mary Mahoney Medal 246

The first woman to serve as minister of health in the Spanish Popular Front government 192

The first woman to win the Open Croquet Championship four times 423

1937

Founder of clinics for the treatment of poliomyelitis in Britain 219

The first person to demonstrate that sulfa drugs successfully inhibited the activity of meningococcal bacteria 247

The first U.S. women's bicycling championship 418

The first woman to conduct a symphony orchestra in London 82

The first woman to receive the Academy Award for best supporting actress 57

The first woman to receive the Pulitzer Prize for distinguished correspondence 295

The first woman to win an Adacemy Award for songwriting 83

The first woman trainer of a horse that ran in the Kentucky Derby 430

1938

Founding of Pepperidge Farm 105

The first author of a comprehensive chronicle of women in medicine 247

The first woman to conduct regular subscription concerts with the Boston Symphony Orchestra 82

The first woman to hold the post of Chief Designer at Paramount Studio 48

The first woman to hold the post of William Cranch Bond Astronomer at Harvard University 382

The first woman to lead the All-India Muslim Women's Committee 186

The first woman to write an "anti-novel" 265

1939

The first British woman to use serialism in her musical compositions 83

The first female network news analyst and diplomatic correspondent in American radio 299

The first female page in the U.S. House of Representatives 204

The first female professor at Cambridge University 149

The first woman to become a champion checkers player 423

The first woman to conduct regular subscription concerts with the New York Philharmonic Orchestra 82

The first woman to receive the Meyer Medal from the American Genetic Association 390

The first woman to serve as president of the British section of PEN 263

The first woman to synthesize glycogen in a test tube 247

1940s

Cofounder of the International Music Fund 84

Founder of Bint-E-Nil, the Daughters of the Nile 13

The first black woman to become a regular member of an opera company 85

The first female modern jazz musician to achieve international acclaim 84

The first person to develop the standard DPT (diphtheria, pertussis, and tetanus) vaccine 391

The first woman to be named "Mother of Berlin" 173

The first woman to earn a master's degree from the Massachusetts Institute of Technology (MIT) 334

The first woman to make her career as an actor, director, producer, and writer of American films 58

The first woman to play a leading role in the Greek resistance movement during World War II 176

The first woman to serve Mahatma Gandhi as medical attendant 229

The first woman to succeed as an independent filmmaker 57

c.1940

The first woman president of the American Pediatrics Society 247

The first woman to discover an antiserum for influenza meningitis 247

1940

Cofounder of Les Trois Arts, a ballet company 84

The first female artist to have her first solo exhibition at the age of eighty 70

The first female moderator of the American Unitarian Association 357

The first woman boxing referee 422

The first woman to publish a syndicated comic strip 295

The first woman to receive an Academy Award for film editing 58

The first woman to serve as Head of Pathology in the Neurological Department of the Nuffield Military Hospital 225

The first woman to study and perform African dance as a scholarly subject 44

1941

Founder of the American Institute of Psychoanalysis 228

The first female test pilot 410

The first woman to be certified as a professional ski instructor 441

The first woman to become a full professor at an Episcopal or Anglican seminary 149

The first woman to serve as head of the Academy of Motion Picture Arts and Sciences 58

Winner of the first women's National Intercollegiate Golf Championship 426

1942

First female members of the boilermakers union 22

The first black artist to be given a long-term contract with MGM film studio 84

The first director of the Women Accepted for Volunteer Emergency Service (WAVES) 318

The first director of the Women's Army Auxiliary Corps 313

The first editor of the *New York Times* crossword puzzle 282

The first woman to be awarded the order of the Purple Heart 308

The first woman to receive the Pulitzer Prize for history 348

The founder of the Dar al Hanam boys' school in Saudi Arabia 141

1943

The first female president of the American Historical Association 348

The first statue of a woman in uniformed service in the U.S. Armed services 316

The first woman steeplechase jockey to race at a major American racetrack 430

The first woman to serve as president of the General Council of the Trades Union Congress 23

The first woman to win an Olympic gold medal in canoeing 419

The first woman to win an Olympic gold medal in downhill skiing 441

The first woman to win an Olympic gold medal in the long jump 455

The first woman to win an Olympic gold medal in the shot put 455

The first woman to win four Olympic gold medals in track events 455

The founder and first director of the Opera School in London 85

1949

The first female president of the Paleontological Society 349

The first person to give a solo trumpet recital at Carnegie Hall in New York 85

The first president of the Ladies Professional Golf Association (LPGA) 427

The first Swedish woman to serve as principal director of the Department of Social Sciences at UNESCO 192

The first woman ambassador to represent her country in the United States 178

The first woman elected to the General Council of the Bar 340

The first woman to become a bullfighter in Spain 422

The first woman to serve as a federal district judge in the United States 341

The first woman to serve as a U.S. ambassador 206

The first woman to serve as treasurer of the United States 206

The first woman to win an Emmy award 300

The formation of the Ladies Professional Golf Association (LPGA) 427

Mid-20th century

The first black actress to be acclaimed as a star in American cinema 58

The first black American woman to achieve international acclaim in opera 85

The first person to discover that a virus can cause leukemia in mammals 385

1950s

The first female council member of the Royal Horticultural Society 386

The first U.S. woman to establish her reputation as a serious film critic 288

The first woman appointed a full professor at Princeton University 349

The first woman to be incarcerated in the maximum security prison of Sing Sing 207

The first woman to become a conductor in China 86

c.1950

Cofounder of L'École des Trois Gourmandes 113

The first African American woman to be elected a Fellow of the American College of Surgeons 248

The first black female surgeon in the American South 248

The first female chief staff veterinarian in the USDA 248

The first female delegate to the American Veterinary Medical Association House of Delegates 248

The first female inspector in charge of the USDA Federal Meat Inspection Division 248

The first female research director at Du Pont 388

The first female supervisor in the U.S. Department of Agriculture Federal Meat Inspection Division 248

The first full professor of anesthesiology 247

The first person successfully to excavate the site of Jericho 378

The first woman to chair the board of the Academy of Natural Sciences 388

The first woman to operate on the heart 248

The first woman to publish the Greek newspapers *Kathimerini* and *Messinvrine* 295

1950

Broke the color barrier in tennis 451

Founder of the London Festival Ballet 44

The first African American woman to win the Pulitzer Prize for poetry 282

The first black invited to play in the American Lawn Tennis Association championships 453

The first female director of the American Public Welfare Association 207

The first female graduate of the University of Georgia College of Veterinary Medicine 248

The first female physician assigned to U.S. Navy shipboard duty 318

The first female president of the Ecological Society of America 386

The first person to develop a drug that attacks viruses 391

The first person to lead an anti-American demonstration in Viet Nam 216

The first woman elected to the Association of American Physicians 248

The first woman to receive the U.S. Department of Agriculture (USDA) distinguished service gold medal 206

The first woman to serve in a cabinet-level position in Nicaragua 185

The first woman to swim both ways across the English Channel 446

The first woman to teach at Chicago Law School 152

1951

Founding and first managing director of Marimekko 105

The first person to deduce the helical structure of DNA 388

The first woman to head a United Nations Committee of the General Assembly 194

The first women's ski team to win an Olympic gold medal in the 4x5-kilometer relay 442

1957

Cofounder of Parents Without Partners 327

Founder of the British Consumers' Association 326–27

Founder of the Opera Company of Boston 90

The Equal Pay and Opportunity Council is formed in New Zealand 24

The first black woman player to win a Wimbledon tennis title 452

The first black woman to win a major U.S. tennis title 452

The first female U.S. Air Force Academy officer 310

The first U.S. woman bullfighter 422

The first woman to have a ballet school in St. Petersburg, Russia renamed after her 45

The first woman to serve as a presidential spokesperson 290

1958

First woman stock exchange director 110

Founder and first president of the American Association of Retired Person (AARP) 327

Founder of The Artists' Company 84

The first black woman from South Africa to gain an international reputation as a singer 87

The first person to serve as director of the Norwegian State Opera in Oslo 87

The first woman to head a permanent delegation to the United Nations 192

The first woman to receive an honorary doctorate in science from Princeton University 396

1959

The first African American woman to have her play produced on Broadway 282

The first female to become a full professor at Johns Hopkins University 250

The first person to discover the famous "missing link" in human evolution 378

The first production by a black writer to receive the New York Drama Critics Circle Award 282

The first woman to chair the Composers Guild of Great Britain 87

The first woman to receive the American Institute of Graphic Arts' gold medal 70

1960s

The first Colombian woman to be elected to the Senate 164

The first female designer to popularize the miniskirt 49

The first Russian woman in charge of tracking space vehicles 383

The first woman to create an international reputation by playing mystery writer Agatha Christie's Miss Marple 59

The first woman to establish a large international corporation based on her own fashion designs 345

The first woman to serve as minister of social affairs in Egypt 165

The first woman to serve as project designer for a huge commercial complex 332

1960

First head of the Federation of Cuban Women 13

The first election for U.S. Senate in which both candidates were women 208

The first female assistant director general of the International Labour Organization 194

The first female runner to win three gold medals at a single Olympic games 455

The first Inuit woman to chronicle the life of her people in her art 70

The first Wolfson Research professor of the Royal Society 387

The first woman Assistant Director-General of the International Labor Organization (ILO) 24

The first woman president of a synagogue 369

The first woman to anchor radio coverage of a political party's national convention 299

The first woman to be elected to the American Antiquarian Society 282

The first woman to conduct an orchestra on Broadway 88

The first woman to qualify as a U.S. astronaut 378

The first woman to receive an award from the American Academy of Arts and Letters 282

The first woman to study chimpanzees 400

The first woman to win an Olympic gold medal in the 1,000-meter speed skating event 441

The first woman to win an Olympic gold medal in the 500-meter speed skating event 441

The first women's team to win an Olympic gold medal in team foil fencing 424

The first women's team to win an Olympic gold medal in the 4x100-meter medley relay swimming event 446

The world's first female prime minister 192

1961

Founder of Woman Strike for Peace 13

The first woman to chair the national committee of the American Communist Party 208

The first woman to serve as a U.S. president's personal physician 249

1962

Founder of the World Wildlife Fund 393

The first English woman named to serve as an ambassador 170

The first female member of the French Academy of Science 397

The first woman ambassador to represent the United States in a Communist nation 208

The first woman to serve as ambassador from Colombia 164

The first woman to win the British Glider Championships 412

1967

Founder of the College of Education in Saudi Arabia 141

Founder and first director of the Opera Orchestra of New York 89

The first African American woman to be appointed associate dean and professor at the New York Medical College 250

The first female primatologist to work successfully with gorillas in the wild 401

The first film editor to receive a solo credit among the screen titles 60

The first woman allowed to attend the annual members' banquet of the Royal Academy 71

The first woman president of the National Board of North American Missions 357

The first woman to hold four luge titles 432

The first woman to own a seat on the New York Stock Exchange 111

The first woman to play the organ in Westminster Cathedral and Westminster Abbey 88

The first woman to register to run in the Boston Marathon 433

1968

The first black congressman elected to the U.S. House of Representatives from New York 210

The first black person inducted into the International Tennis Hall of Fame 453

The first female instructor at the U.S. Military Academy at West Point 314

The first female member of the Pacific Stock Exchange 111

The first woman swimmer to win three individual Olympic gold medals at one competition 447

The first woman to be elected a Fellow of the Australian Academy of Science 387

The first woman to carry the U.S. flag at the Olympic Games 434

The first woman to hold the Slade Professorship at Cambridge University 263

The first woman to light the Olympic flame at the opening ceremonies 434

The first woman to receive a jockey's license 430

The first woman to win an Olympic gold medal in the 100-meter breaststroke swimming event 446

The first woman to win an Olympic gold medal in the 200-meter butterfly swimming event 447

The first woman to win both the 200- and 800-meter freestyle swimming events 447

The first woman to win seven individual gold Olympic medals in gymnastics 429

The first woman to win the Olympic 200-meter backstroke swimming event 448

The first woman to win the Olympic 200-meter breaststroke swimming event 448

The first women's volleyball team to win an Olympic gold medal 459

1969

Cofounder and first editor of the feminist journals *Redstockings* and *Notes from the Second Year* 14

Cofounder of the literary periodical *Poétique* 265

The first American to win a world road bicycle racing title 418

The first female jockey to win a regular parimutuel thoroughbred race 431

The first female journalists admitted into membership in Sigma Delta Chi 290

The first German woman to serve as ambassador to the Council of European States 174

The first Jordanian woman to serve as an ambassador 183

The first two women to graduate from the U.S. Army War College 314

The first U.S. woman jockey to ride at a parimutuel track 431

The first woman jockey to win a race at a U.S. thoroughbred track 431

The first woman to head an independent federal administrative agency 210

The first woman to sail a boat alone across the Pacific Ocean 419

The first woman to serve as prime minister of Israel 180

1970s

The first "coloured" South African writer to establish an international reputation 273

The first Asian American woman to achieve a successful career in documentary filmmaking 60

The first black person to attain the rank of Professor at a South African university 150

The first female dairy editor of the *Farm Journal* 288

The first female writer from Ghana to achieve an international reputation 268

The first filmmaker to work with an all-female staff of technicians 60

The first girl to serve as a national officer of the Future Farmers of America 101

The first woman to achieve ministerial rank in Fiji 171

The first woman to become a division director in the U.S. Foreign Agricultural Service 210

The first woman to preside over the United Nations Security Council 177

1970

Founder of Feministes Révolutionaires 15

Founder of the Gray Panthers 327

Founder of first union of Native American dance performers 25

One of the first two women declared a Doctor of the Church 354

The first American feminist film director 61

The first female athlete in any sport to earn more than $100,000 in a single season 453

The first female jockey to ride in the Kentucky Derby 431

The first tournament for women professional tennis players held separate from male players 453

The first U.S. athlete to win a medal at the World Gymnastics Championships 429

The first woman named international vice president of the United Auto Workers union 24

The first woman to be ordained as a minister in the American Lutheran Church 372

The first woman to chair the International Press Institute 290

The first woman to graduate from Notre Dame University's Law School 341

The first woman to hold a cabinet-level post in Portugal 188

The first woman to lead the Red Army Faction 174

The first woman to moderate a debate between U.S. presidential candidates 300

The first woman to play in a professional football game 425

The first women to become U.S. Army generals 314

The first women to serve in the White House Police Force 210

1971

Cofounder of *Ms.* magazine 289

Cofounder of the National Women's Political Caucus 13

Founder of the Chiswick Women's Aid Society 15

New York state law allowing girls to compete on boys' teams for the first time 434

The first female U.S. Air Force general 310

The first female ambassador from Australia 160

The first female judge at the European Court of Human Rights 341

The first female president of a state medical society 250

The first female U.S. Secret Service agents 211

The first female trustees of the Ford Foundation 329

The first living woman to be inducted into the American Aviation Hall of Fame 411

The first person to make a solo light aircraft flight around the world 412

The first two women appointed inspectors for the U.S. Postal Service 211

The first woman elected to the National Press Club 297

The first woman jockey to ride one hundred winners 431

The first woman to address the Vatican Council 333

The first woman to be elected to the Songwriters' Hall of Fame 83

The first woman to conduct at Philharmonic Hall in New York 88

The first woman to head an overseas television news bureau 301

The first woman to receive the Pulitzer Prize for national reporting 296

The first woman to serve as an industrial civil engineer in the U.S. Air Force 310

The first woman to win a fellowship for directing from the Director's Guild of America 61

1972

Founder of the Pink Panthers movement in Japan 182

Founder of first prostitutes' union (COYOTE) 25

The first American woman ordained a rabbi in Reform Judaism 372

The first Conservative woman to serve as a whip in the House of Lords 170

The first female director of the New York Stock Exchange 214

The first female director of the Royal Greenwich Observatory 383

The first female member of the U.S. Air Force Band 310

The first female president of the National Student Association 151

The first female special agents of the modern Federal Bureau of Investigation 342

The first person to demonstrate in competition a backwards somersault on uneven parallel bars 429

The first U.S. woman to chair a national political party 211

The first U.S. woman to win the 200-meter butterfly swimming event 448

The first woman elected to the board of the National Endowment for the Arts 47

The first woman to be appointed a rear admiral in the U.S. Navy 318

The first woman to become head of daytime programming at a major television network 301

The first woman to deliver the keynote address at a major U.S. political party's national convention 211

The first woman to finish the Boston Marathon officially 433

The first woman to head a copy desk at the *New York Times* 297

The first woman to serve as a parish pastor in the Lutheran Church in America 372

The first woman to win the Olympic 1,500 meter track event 458

The first woman to win the Olympic individual archery championship 405

The first woman umpire in professional baseball 413

The first women's collegiate basketball championship 415

The first women's track and field team to win an Olympic gold medal in the 4x400 -meter relay 458

1973

Cofounder of the Black Feminist Organization 214

Founder of the Civil Rights Party in Israel 181

The first African American female mayor in the United States 211

The first female U.S. Air Force chaplain 310

The first female jet pilot to be hired by a major U.S. airline 412

The first female pilot for a commercial airline in the U.S. 412

The first female vice president of Duke University 214

The first lawsuit challenging Little League Baseball's "no girls" rule 414

The first nun to serve as a U.S. Navy officer 318

The first person to win the Templeton Foundation Prize 352

The first Spanish woman to challenge the law prohibiting women from becoming bullfighters 346

The first U.S. woman to win a world cycling title 418

The first U.S. woman to win the World Championship of Archery 405

The first woman jockey to win a stakes race 431

The first woman to command a North Atlantic Treaty Organization (NATO) military unit 307

The first woman to compete in a National Collegiate Athletic Association (NCAA) event 434

The first woman to direct at the Lincoln Center playhouse in New York 98

The first woman to head the Atomic Energy Commission 392

The first woman to head the Greek Committee of Amnesty International 27

The first woman to receive the John Peter Zenger Award 290

The first woman to serve as president of Zero Population Growth 250

The first woman to serve in the cabinet of the Malaysian government 183

The first Women's World Invitational Swim Meet 448

The national Little League Baseball organization signed an order agreeing to ban sex discrimination 414

1974

The first Agri-Women Coordinator 102

The first athlete to win the first international Women's Ballet and Freestyle Ski Competition 442

The first Australian woman to serve as a career diplomat 161

The first female secretary of the National Council of the Churches of Christ 358

The first female tennis player in Japan to turn professional 453

The first girl to pitch a no-hit game in Little League 414

The first girl to win the Detroit Soap Box Derby 434

The first girls admitted to Little League baseball 414

The first secretary of state for women's affairs in France 172

The first U.S. woman to become an official boxing judge 422

The first woman to achieve the rank of minister in France 173

The first woman to attain the rank of World Bridge Federation "Grandmaster" 422

The first woman to be ordained an Episcopal priest 372

The first woman to chair the Republican National Committee 212

The first woman to conduct at a major European opera house (Barcelona, Spain) 88

The first woman to earn her reputation as a male travel writer 263

The first woman to head the education division of the U.S. Department of Health, Education and Welfare 212

The first woman to head the news staff of a major U.S. daily newspaper 297

The first woman to head the White House bureau of a major news service 297

The first woman to make a solo canoe trip down the Mississippi River 419

The first woman to manage a minor league baseball team 414

The first woman to serve as a college president in Canada 128

The first woman to serve as a pilot in the U.S. Navy 318

The first woman to serve as mayor of a large U.S. city 212

The first woman to serve as speaker of the Canadian Senate 163

The first woman to win an Academy Award as a producer 61

The first woman to win the all-around Freestyle event at the first Women's International Ballet and Freestyle Ski Competition 442

The first women's professional football league 425

The founder of the Noor Al-Hussein Foundation 133

The world's first female president 159

1975

First woman officer of the Federal Reserve System 103

First woman to serve as coordinator of women's activities for the AFL-CIO 25

The cofounder of the Susan Smith McKinney Stewart Society 250

The first female ambassador to the Vatican 193

The first female cantor in American Reform Judaism 358

The first female gymnast to hold all the gold medals in both European and world championships at one time 429

The first female president of Smith College 128

The first girl to win the National Soap Box Derby 434

The first native-born American to be canonized as a saint 354

The first person to swim across Lake Ontario 448

The first prime minister of the Central African Republic 163

The first woman appointed secretary of housing and urban development (HUD) in a U.S. cabinet 212

The first woman both to serve on and to chair the executive committee of the National Labor Relations 25

The first woman licensed in the United States to drive top fuel dragsters 406

The first woman reporter allowed in a major league baseball locker room 435

The first woman to achieve cabinet rank in Mauritania 183

The first woman to be elected president of the Screen Actors Guild 25

The first woman to compete successfully in the Golden Gloves Boxing Tournament 422

The first woman to head a major labor union in North America 25

The first woman to head the Black Panther Party 212

The first woman to lead a political party in Britain 171

The first woman to qualify for the top competition in hot rod racing 406

The first woman to reach the summit of Mount Everest 437

The first woman to receive a Pulitzer Prize for commentary 297

The first woman to receive the Pioneer Chemist Award from the American Institute of Chemists 389

The first woman to serve as a sportswriter on the staff of the *New York Times* 297

The first woman to serve as governor of a state whose husband had not previously held the same office 212

The first woman to serve as president of the Screen Actors' Guild 61

The first woman to serve as secretary of state for consumer protection in Portugal 189

The first woman to serve as U.S. chief of protocol 212

The first woman to win a gold medal in the overall shooting events at the Pan American Games 439

The first woman to win a regulation marathon competing against men 433

The first woman to win the Hang Ten International Surfing Competition 443

The first woman to win the International Jerusalem Prize 270

The first women's basketball team to win in Madison Square Garden 415

1976

First female president of the Harvard Law Review 112

First Irish women to receive Nobel Peace Prize 30

Founder of the feminist journal *Sorcières* 266

Founder of the Northern Ireland Peace Movement 29

The first and only woman sailor to finish the Royal Western Singlehanded Transatlantic Race 420

The first female co-anchor of a daily evening news program 301

The first Japanese woman to serve as a diplomat with ministerial rank 182

The first military service academy, the U.S. Coast Guard Academy, admits women 420

The first person to serve as minister of education in a unified Viet Nam 216

The first person to spin a polyamide macromolecule from low-temperature liquid crystal solutions 389

The first U.S. athlete to win the world title in figure roller skating 440

The first U.S. woman to win an Olympic medal in rowing 420

The first U.S. women's basketball team to compete in the Olympics 415

The first woman mathematician elected to the National Academy of Sciences 393

The first woman to anchor a network television evening newscast 301

The first woman to chair the national convention of a major U.S. political party 213

The first woman to compete in a major stock car race 407

The first woman to conduct the Metropolitan Opera 90

The first woman to drive in the Indianapolis 500 auto race 407

The first woman to have a chair named after her at the American Museum of Natural History 375

The first woman to race in the Baja 1000 off-road competition 407

The first woman to receive an Albert Lasker Basic Medical Research Award 251

The first woman to receive Billboard's FM (radio) Personality of the Year 299

The first woman to win a gold medal in Olympic ice dancing 439

The first woman to win a varsity letter at the U.S. Coast Guard Academy 420

The first woman to win an Olympic gold medal in single sculls rowing competition 419

The first woman to win four Olympic medals in volleyball 459

The first woman to win the Women's International Golf Tournament 427

The first women to be admitted to the U.S. Air Force Academy 310

The first women's basketball team to win an Olympic gold medal 415

The first women's coxed fours rowing team to win an Olympic gold medal 419

The first women's coxed quad sculls team to win an Olympic gold medal 419

The first women's handball team to win an Olympic gold medal 430

The first women's softball team to win the women's World Series championship title 443

The first women's team of coxswainless pairs to win an Olympic gold medal 419

The first women's team of eights to win an Olympic gold medal in the rowing event 419

The first women's team to win an Olympic gold medal in double sculls rowing 419

The first women's volleyball team to win three consecutive Olympic gold medals 459

1977

The first all-America girls' high school basketball squad 415

The first American-born woman to receive a Nobel Prize in science 251

The first black woman to serve officially in a president's cabinet 213

The first female president of a local union of the United Mine Workers of America 26

The first time that women had been selected as Rhodes Scholars 158

The first U.S. woman to win the Women's Bowling World Cup Competition 421

The first woman (and first black person) to serve as assistant secretary for administration in the U.S. Department of Agriculture 213

The first woman ever to lift more than one thousand pounds in three power lifts 460

The first woman president of the University of Chicago 128

The first woman to be appointed U.S. secretary of commerce 214

The first woman to be named "Star Farmer of Kansas" 102

The first woman to become a canon in the Episcopal Church 358

The first woman to chair the Equal Employment Opportunities Commission 214

The first woman to have a computer programming language named after her 393

The first woman to hold the top legal post, solicitor, in the U.S. Department of Labor 25

The first woman to judge a world heavyweight boxing match 422

The first woman to receive the American Film Institute's Life Achievement Award 58

The first woman to serve as president of the National Council of Switzerland 193

The first woman to serve as rector of an Episcopal church 358

The first woman to serve on the Civil Aeronautics Board (CAB) 334

The first woman to sweep the American Athletic Union (AAU) Elite Gymnastics Championships 429

The first woman to win a major offshore motorboat race 420

The first woman to win an award from the Directors Guild of America 62

The first woman to win the World Accuracy Title in parachuting 438

The first women's professional basketball league 415

1978

One of the first women selected for the U.S. Space Shuttle program 379

The first all-female expedition to climb Annapurna in the Himalayas 437

The first female brigadier general in the U.S. Marine Corps 317

The first female chair of the board of the National Broadcasting Corporation (NBC) 346

The first game of the Women's Professional Basketball League 416

The first winner of the Margaret Wade Trophy for the best woman collegiate basketball player 416

The first woman president of the University of Chicago 128

The first woman to become a member of the Chinese Central Committee 164

The first woman to complete the Indianapolis 500 auto race 408

The first woman to hold the rank of major general in the U.S. Army

The first women to join the White House Honor Guard 308

The first woman to play on a high school varsity baseball team 414

The first woman to sail alone around the world 420

The first woman to scale El Capitan in Yosemite National Park 438

The first woman to win five straight Ladies Professional Golf Association (LPGA) tournaments 427

1979

First woman pictured on a U.S. coin 103

The first female judge in the U.S. Court of Appeals for the Second Circuit 341

The first female opera singer to be appointed director of the New York City Opera 90

The first female president of the American Academy and Institute of Arts and Letters 283

The first secretary of the U.S. Office of Education 215

The first U.S. woman to achieve the full rank of astronaut 380

The first woman to serve as prime minister of Britain 171

The first woman to sign a contract to play in the National Basketball Association 416

The first woman to take command of a U.S. Coast Guard vessel at sea 315

World record for a high fall for a stunt woman 93

1980

The first African American female fellow of the American Institute of Architects 332

The first female caddy in the U.S. Open golf championship 427

The first female member of the Académie Française 266

The first female rules official for a U.S. Open men's golf championship 427

The first girl to win the Pitch, Hit, and Run championship 414

The first graduating class of the U.S. Military Academy at West Point to include women 315

The first woman chosen to become a bishop in the United Methodist Church 372

The first woman prime minister of a Caribbean country 165

The first woman prime minister of Dominica 165

The first woman to be elected to the AFL-CIO executive council 26

The first woman to be put in charge of production at a major film studio 107

The first woman to receive a diploma in the first graduating class of the U.S. Military Academy at West Point that included women 315

The first women's orchestra to consist entirely of women and to perform only works composed by women 90

The world's first female head of state to be democratically elected 177

1981

Founder and first president of the National Museum of Women in the Arts 72

The first actress to win the Academy Award for best actress four times 60

The first female associate justice of the U.S. Supreme Court 215

The first female prime minister of Norway 186

The first woman to officiate at a professional soccer game 442

The first woman to serve as president of the American Geological Institute 391

1982

Founder of the Pan-Arab Women's Organization 255

The first American to direct an independent film shown in competition at the Cannes Film Festival in France 62

The first black woman ordained in the Unitarian-Universalist Church 372

The first female president of *The Harvard Lampoon* 289

The first female prime minister of a Communist country 217

The first woman elected to head the Disciples of Christ 358

The first woman president of the Republic of Malta 183

The first woman to walk in space 380

The first women's basketball championship sponsored by the National Collegiate Athletic Association (NCAA) 416

1983

Founder of Women's Action for Nuclear Disarmament 30

The first female governor general of Canada 163

The first novel by a black woman to win both the American Book Award and the Pulitzer Prize 283

The first person to use the term *womanist* 283

The first woman to head the largest textile industry in the world 164

The first woman to produce, direct, co-author, star in, and sing in a major motion picture 62

The first woman director of United British Artists 99

The first woman to win a Pulitzer Prize for music 90

1984

The first athlete to win an Olympic synchronized swimming event 448

The first U.S. female gymnast to win a gold medal at the Olympics 429

The first U.S. woman to participate in extra-vehicular activity in space 380

The first woman to appear on the front of a "Wheaties" box 429

The first woman to be nominated by a major political party as a candidate for vice president of the United States 216

The first woman to become head of a large trade union 27

The first woman to win an Olympic gold medal for the women's marathon event 458

1985

The first female chief of the Cherokee Nation 329–30

The first female player for the Harlem Globetrotters 416

The first female president of the Philippines 188

The first Japanese Equal Employment Opportunity Law 182

The first novel by a black woman to be made into a major motion picture 283

The first runner to set world records at 5,000 meters, 10,000 meters, and the marathon 458

The first woman promoted to the rank of brigadier general in the U.S. Marine Corps in direct competition with men 317

The first woman to become a Conservative Jewish rabbi 373

The first woman to serve as police chief of a major U.S. city 342

The first woman to win a civil suit as a battered wife 27

The first woman to win the Iditarod Trail Sled Dog Race 404

1986

The first black female athletic director in the Southern Intercollegiate Athletic Conference 435

The first citizen passenger to fly with astronauts on a space mission 118

The first female president of Lincoln University 128

The first woman to become the leader of a major political party in Japan 182

The first woman to direct an American television mini-series 301

The first woman to fly nonstop around the world without refueling 412

The first woman to play on a men's professional basketball team 416

The first woman to walk to the North Pole 405

1987

The first female executive director of the American Bar Association 342

The first female judge to sit in the Court of Appeal 341

The first Jewish woman canonized in the Roman Catholic Church 354

The first National Women in Sports Day 435

The first woman to do play-by-play coverage of a National Football League game 301

The first woman to head a motion picture corporation 107

The U.S. Supreme Court rules that Rotary Clubs must admit women 321

1988

The first woman to become prime minister of Pakistan 186

The first woman to play on a men's collegiate baseball team 414

The first woman to serve as president of any national coed sports organization 435

1989

The first black woman to direct a feature-length Hollywood film 63

The first Episcopal woman bishop 358

The first U.S. woman to win the individual title at the World Modern Pentathlon Championships 458

1990

The first "women only" triathlon 459

The first African American woman to direct, write, produce, and sing in a 35 millimeter film 63

The first female Navaho Indian to become a surgeon 251

The first female president of the Geological Society of America 391

The first woman appointed Surgeon General of the U. S. Public Health Service 251

The first woman president at a Big Ten university 129

The first woman president of Ireland 179

The first woman to coach a major college men's sport 416

The first woman to receive a Lifetime Achievement Award from the American Cinema Editors 63

The first woman to win the only professional golf tournament in the world in which women and men compete head-to-head 428

1991

The first black woman to receive the Theodore Roosevelt Award of the NCAA 453

The first female president of the American Kennel Club 330

The first female skipper to enter an ocean sailboat race with an all-female crew 420

The first girl to become mayor of Boys Town 330

The first woman appointed composer-in-residence by a major U.S. orchestra 91

The first woman named to the Washington, D.C. Wrestling and Boxing Commission 422

The first woman president of the National Collegiate Athletic Association (NCAA) 435

The first woman to be inducted into the National Inventors Hall of Fame 391

The first woman to be named brigade commander at the U.S. Naval Academy 319

The first woman to compete in a Bass Anglers Sportsman Society tournament 425

The first woman to officiate a men's professional basketball game 417

The first woman to ride in the Belmont Stakes 431

The first woman to run the U.S. Olympic Festival 435

1992

The first female skipper in the U.S. Navy 319

The first woman Lutheran bishop in North America 359

The first woman sports editor at the Associated Press wire service 435

The first woman to be White House press secretary 290

The first woman to play in the National Hockey League (NHL) 432

1993

The first African American to be named Poet Laureate of the United States 283

The first African American woman to win the Nobel Prize in literature 283

The first female jockey to win a Triple Crown event 431

The first female president of Texas Southern University 129

The first woman defence minister in Canada 163

The first woman poet to read from her work at a presidential inauguration 283

The first woman prime minister of Turkey 193

The first woman to be elected speaker of Parliament in Japan 182

The first woman to head a national television network 301

The first woman to head an Ivy League school (University of Pennsylvania) 129

1994

The first female cadet at The Citadel college in Charleston, South Carolina 158

The first female fighter pilot in the U.S. Air Force 310

The first U.S. woman to win five gold medals at a winter Olympics 441

The first woman to pitch in a college baseball game 414

The first woman to qualify as a combat-ready pilot in the U.S. Navy 319

The first woman to ski unaccompanied from the edge of the Antarctic continent to the South Pole 405

1995

The first African American woman to have her complete works published by the Library of America 348

The first all-women's crew for the America's Cup race 420

The first Australian to be beatified 354

The first woman president of the highest court in Germany 174

The first woman to carry the cross during the Pope's Good Friday procession 352

The first woman to serve as president of the American Bar Association 342

1996

The first woman to stand watch at the Tomb of the Unknowns in Arlington National Cemetery 315

Index

Novello, Antionia C. 251
NOW. *See* National Organization for Women
Noyes, Clara Dutton 243
Nur, Jahan 177
Nuremberg trials 175
Nureyev, Rudolph 45
Nursing 219, 223, 224, 225, 230, 236, 237, 238, 239, 241, 242, 246, 247, 321
Nuthead, Dinah 344
Nuttall, Zelia Maria Magdalena 377
Nutt, Emma M. 344
Nutting, Mary Adelaide 242
Nuytten, Bruno 72
Nwapa, Flora 272
Nyad, Diana 448
Nyembe, Dorothy 118, 191
Nzinga, Mbande 159

O

Oakley, Annie 73
Oberg, Margo 443
Oberlin College 5, 92, 130, 153, 371
O'Connor, Sandra Day 215, 251
Occupational Safety and Health Administration (OSHA) 25
Ocobock, Susanne M. 310
Offa II, King of Mercia 72
Ogata, Sakado 182
O'Grady, Jane 24
Ohio 157, 241, 293, 386, 412
  Akron 391, 434
  Cincinnati 66, 78, 156, 237, 372
  Cleveland 37, 243, 293, 299, 340, 342, 343, 431
  Oberlin 5, 130
Ohio College of Dental Surgery 237
Ohio Wesleyan University 157
O'Neill, Kitty 93
O'Neill, Rose 110
Okamoto, Ayako 428
O'Keeffe, Georgia 69
Oklahoma 197, 211
Olga 353
Olivarez, Graciela 341
Oliver, Ruby 63
Olowo, Bernadette 193
Olympic Games 408, 415, 419, 419–20,

423, 424, 426, 428–29, 432, 433, 434, 439, 441–42, 443–48, 454–58, 459
Omlie, Phoebe Fairgrave 409
Ontario, Canada 220, 303, 403
"On the Pulse of Morning" 283
Open Door Council 34
Opera 73, 74, 75, 77, 78, 79, 80, 81, 97
Opera School in London 85
Opera Workshop Department at Boston University 90
Oregon 28, 248, 403
  Portland 153, 342, 414
Organizations 321–30
Orinda. *See* Philips, Katherine
Ormerod, Eleanor Anne 390
Ortiz-Del Valle, Sandra 417
OSHA. *See* Occupational Health and Safety Administration
Osiier, Ellen 424
Ostermyer, Micheline 455
O'Sullivan, Mary Kenney 17
Otto-Peters, Luise 150
Overseas Chinese Affairs Commission 11
Owen, Ruth Bryan 204
Oxford University 33, 131, 132, 133, 138, 158, 349, 381, 420

P

Pabst, George Wilhelm 82
Pacifism 6, 10, 12, 19, 28, 30, 34, 36, 198
Pacini 74
Packard, Sophia B. 137
Paderewski, Jan 78
Pakhomova, Ludmilla 439
Pakistan 186, 187
Pakistani
  Bhutto, Benazir 186
  Jinnah, Fatima 186
  Khan, Liaquat Ali 186
Palcy, Euzhan 63
Paleontologists 349, 394
Palestine 28, 360
  See also Israel
Palinkas, Pat 425
Palm, Etta Aelders 2
Palmer, Alice Elvira Freeman 125
Palmer, Frances Flora Bond 65

Palmer, Lizzie Pitts Merrill 141
Palmer, Sophia 242
Pan-American Association for the Advancement of Women 12
Pan American Games 439
Panayotatou, Angelique G. 229
Pandit, Vijaya Lakshmi 178
Pankhurst, Christabel Harriette 32, 33, 36
Pankhurst, Emmeline Goulden 7, 32, 36
Pankhurst, Estelle Sylvia 36
Pankhurst, Richard Marsden 7
Papua New Guinea 269
Parachuting 438
Paraguay 187
Paraguayan
  Vallejo, Isabel Arrua 187
Pardo-Barzán, Emilia 274
Parent-Teacher Association 150
Paris Conservatory 76, 78, 80, 81, 88
Paris Opera 43
Park, Maud Wood 36
Parker, Claire 57
Parren, Kallirhoe 9
Parrish, Celestia Savannah 150
Parsons, Louella Oettinger 293
Pasta, Giuditta Maria Costanza 74
Patch, Edith Marion 390
Paterson, Emma 16
Patrick, Mary Mills 127
Patrick, Ruth 388
Patten, Mary Ann 344
Patterson, Eleanor Medill 294, 404
Patti, Adelina 75
Paul, Alice 12, 13, 34
Paula, Saint 359
Pavlova, Anna 42, 50
Payne, Sylvia May 224
Peabody, Elizabeth Palmer 145
Peace Corps 129
Peach Melba 78
Peale, Norman Vincent 358
Peale, Ruth Stafford 357
Pearce, Louise 246
Pearl Archery Club 405
Pechey-Phipson, Edith 229
Peck, Annie Smith 437
Pederson, Helga 341
Peeters, Clara 64